Contents

Acknowledgements

Text and diagrams reproduced by kind permission of:
Guinness Book of Records; New Scientist, IPC Magazines; Oliver and Boyd; The Highway Code, The Road Traffic Act, The Department of Transport, The Casualty Report 1986, Drive, (all under crown copyright) HMSO; Pergamon; Open University; Oxford University Press; Hobsons Publishing; General Motors; Fiat; Sonotek, FFR Ultrasonics, Queensbury; Heinemann; Hilger, Institute of Physics Publishing; J Murray and Sons; Simon and Schuster; Edward Arnold Publishing; Dover Publishing; Hotpoint, Peterborough; McGraw Hill Publishing; Littlewoods.

Every effort has been made to contact the holders of copyright material, but if any have been inadvertently overlooked the publishers will be pleased to make the necessary arrangements at the first opportunity.

Photographs
The publishers would like to thank the following for permission to reproduce photographs:
(T = top, B = bottom, C = centre, L =left, R = right)
AEA Technology 162B, 164, 168B, 170; Professor J F Allen 216BR; Allsport/David Cannon 6; Allsport/Tony Duffy 7, 8, 14; Allsport/Vandystadt 11, 20 CR, 49R; Allsport/Bob Martin 10, 13, 15B, 45B; Allsport/Mike Powell 16; Allsport/Pascal Roundeau 33; Allsport/Sylvain Cazenave/Vandystadt 23CR; Allsport/Jon Nicholson 23T; Alton Towers 39TR; Associated Press Ltd 102CR, 162TL; Mark Wagner/Aviation Images 39CL; BT Pictures 110B; Barnaby's Picture Library 21TC; John Birdsall Photography 61TL, 68, 77, 89, 93, 101, 105, 122T, 126TL, 195, 197, 214L, 217; Blackpool Pleasure Beach 47; Chris Bonington Picture Library 50; The Biblioteca Ambrosiana, Milan/Bridgeman Art Library, London 127; Neill Bruce 30; Peter Roberts Collection/Neill Bruce 62, 76; J Allan Cash Photolibrary 134BR; Andrew J Purcell/Bruce Coleman Ltd 49L; Alison Cooley 54T; EEV Ltd 145B; Fiat Auto UK 63C&B; Vivien Fifield 203, 221B; Ford Motor Company Ltd 27T; Peter Gould 84, 107, 126CR; Ronald Grant Archive 134TL; Hewlett Packard Ltd 80, 82; JET Joint Undertaking 173B, 174T; Mark Jordan 47B, 100, 210; Andrew Lambert 57BL, 113, 225, 229; School of Materials, University of Leeds 57BR, 58L; Dr M R Lindsay 15C; John Millar Photography 189T; Mirror Syndication International 31CR; NASA 28, 184, 188; Stephen Dalton/NHPA 60; ANT/NHPA 230; Northern Picture Library 46; Adam Opel AG 63T; Oxford University, SPM Unit 160T; Betty Press/Panos Pictures 51; Pictures Colour Library Ltd 17; Polaroid AG 120; RAF School of Aviation Medicine 39BR, 43; RAPRA Technology Ltd 52; Redferns 102B; Rex Features Ltd 216 TL; Science Photo Library 1, 19, 37, 58CR, 61CL, 71, 81, 86L, 87, 119, 121, 126B, 128, 129, 132, 133, 134TR, 135, 140, 141, 144, 145TL&CR, 147, 158, 159, 160B, 167, 168T, 172, 173, 175, 177, 180, 181, 183, 189CR, 190, 191, 193, 216TR. 228B; Shout 222; Giboux/Liaison/FSP 61TR; Novosti/Gamma/FSP 166; Tony Stone Images 23CR, 36, 42, 45T, 54C, 59, 86R, 110T, 221CL, 228T; Telegraph Colour Library 21TL; C & S Thompson 111, 214R; Universal Pictures/Amblin Entertainment 146; Volvo Car UK Ltd 27C, 29, 31BL; Zefa Pictures Ltd 20, 24, 202, 207.
Cover Photograph: Science Photo Library

Collins Advanced Modular Sciences

Physics Core

Frank Ciccotti and Dave Kelly

Series Editor: Mike Coles

Collins Educational
An Imprint of HarperCollins*Publishers*

Published by Collins Educational
An imprint of HarperCollins*Publishers*
77–85 Fulham Palace Road
Hammersmith
London
W6 8JB

First published 1995

ISBN 0 00 322380 9

Typographic design by Ewing Paddock at PearTree Design
Design by Ann Miller

Edited by Mark Jordan and Alan Trewartha

Picture research by Caroline Thompson

Illustrations by Barking Dog Art, Tom Cross, Jerry Fowler, Mainline Design, TTP International

Printed and bound by Rotolito Lombarda

Reprinted 1996

To the student

This book aims to make your study of advanced science successful and interesting. The authors have made sure that the ideas you need to understand are covered in a clear and straightforward way. The book is designed to be a study of scientific ideas as well as a reference text when needed. Science is constantly evolving and, wherever possible, modern issues and problems have been used to make your study interesting and to encourage you to continue studying science after your current course is complete.

Working on your own

Studying on your own is often difficult and sometimes textbooks give you the impression that you have to be an expert in the subject before you can read the book. I hope you find that this book is not like that. The authors have carefully built up ideas, so that when you are working on your own there is less chance of you becoming lost in the text and frustrated with the subject.

Don't try to achieve too much in one reading session. Science is complex and some demanding ideas need to be supported with a lot of facts. Trying to take in too much at one time can make you lose sight of the most important ideas – all you see is a mass of information. Use the learning objectives to select one idea to study in a particular session.

Chapter design

Each chapter starts by showing how the science you will learn is applied somewhere in the world. Next come learning objectives which tell you exactly what you should learn as you read the chapter. These are written in a way which spells out what you will be able to do with your new knowledge, rather like a checklist – they could be very helpful when you revise your work. At certain points in the chapters you will find key ideas listed. These are checks for you to use, to make sure that you have grasped these ideas. Words written in **bold type** appear in the glossary at the end of the book. If you don't know the meaning of one of these words check it out immediately – don't persevere, hoping all will become clear.

The questions in the text are there for you to check you have understood what is being explained. These are all short – longer questions are included in a support pack which goes with this book. The questions are straightforward in style – there are no trick questions. Don't be tempted to pass over these questions, they will give you new insights into the work which you may not have seen. Answers to questions are given in the back of the book.

Good luck with your studies. I hope you find the book an interesting read.

Mike Coles, Series Editor
University of London Institute of Education, June 1995

1 Olympic dynamics

'Citius, Altius, Fortius' is the motto of the Olympic games. It means 'Swifter, Higher, Stronger', a challenge which athletes have tried to meet since the modern Olympic games began in 1896.

In the last 10 years, world records have been set for all the major athletic disciplines. What has given modern athletes the edge over their predecessors?

One answer is the increasing impact of science. Teams of scientists advise modern athletes. Physiologists design training routines, nutritionists plan special diets and psychologists work on an athlete's state of mind. Electronic measurements of heart-rate, temperature and even brain activity, are used to monitor performance.

Fig. 1 World pole-vaulting records

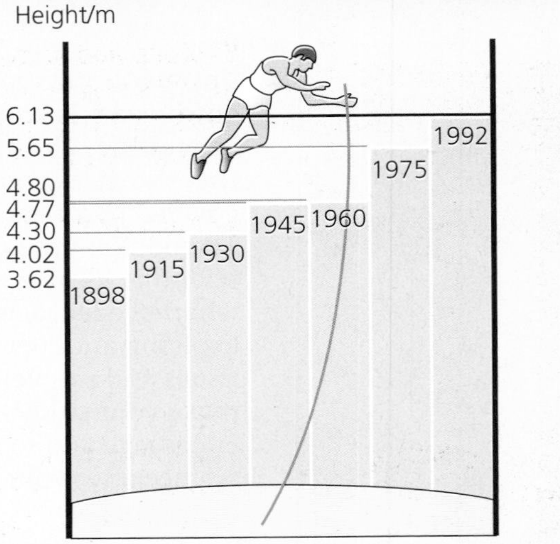
Height/m
6.13
5.65
4.80
4.77
4.30
4.02
3.62
1898
1915
1930
1945
1960
1975
1992

The improvement in pole-vault heights owes more to material science than athletic coaching. The poles have progressed from bamboo, through metal, to glass-fibre reinforced plastic.

Chris Boardman used the psychological technique of 'visualisation' – the mental action-replay of a good performance – to help him win a gold medal. His racing was also helped by the engineers who designed his bike, his clothes and his helmet.

The influence of biochemistry has been more controversial. The first evidence of systematic drug use came during the 1950s when athletes began using anabolic steroids to build muscle. This has had most impact in disciplines which rely on strength, such as sprinting, weightlifting or the throwing events.

Science has also played a part in the measurement of achievement. Electronic timing now allows records to be broken by one-hundredth of a second. Wind speed is measured using an ultrasonic device, and displayed alongside the winning times. Any records that are set with a strong wind in the athletes' favour will not stand. Research in biomechanics now uses computer simulation to analyse athletic performance. These computer models use the laws of motion, and accurate data about the athlete, to suggest slight changes in style which could make that vital millisecond of difference.

1.1 Learning objectives

After working through this chapter, you should be able to:

- **explain** the difference between vector and scalar quantities;
- **add** and subtract vector quantities;
- **resolve** vectors into perpendicular components;
- **define** displacement, speed, velocity and acceleration;
- **interpret** velocity–time and displacement–time graphs;
- **recall** and use the equations of uniformly accelerated, linear motion;
- **apply** the linear motion equations to motion in two dimensions;
- **describe** the motion of an object in free-fall, including the idea of terminal velocity.

1.2 Setting the pace

Marita Koch broke the women's world record for 400 m in 1985.

Vectors and scalars

In 1985 Marita Koch ran 400 m in a record-breaking time of 47.60 s. Her average speed during the race was:

$$\text{average speed (m s}^{-1}) = \frac{\text{distance moved (m)}}{\text{time taken (s)}} = \frac{400 \text{ m}}{47.6 \text{ s}} = 8.40 \text{ m s}^{-1}$$

The 400 m is run over one complete lap of a running track. At the end of the race, the runner in the inside lane will be back where she started. We say that her **displacement** is zero. Displacement describes the *effect* of a journey, rather than distance travelled. Displacement and distance have the same units, but displacement, *s*, is defined as the distance covered *in a certain direction*. (Do not confuse with seconds, s.) Displacement is a **vector** quantity. It has a magnitude (size) and a direction. A vector needs two numbers to describe it (Fig. 2).

Distance is a **scalar** quantity. It has magnitude only, so it can be described by just one number. **Velocity** is speed in a given direction, so it is a vector quantity.

$$\text{velocity (m s}^{-1}) = \frac{\text{displacement (m)}}{\text{time (s)}}$$

Fig. 2 Describing vectors

A 20 km cycle race may cause a displacement of 10 km in a direction 30° north of east. This displacement is the vector ***a***.

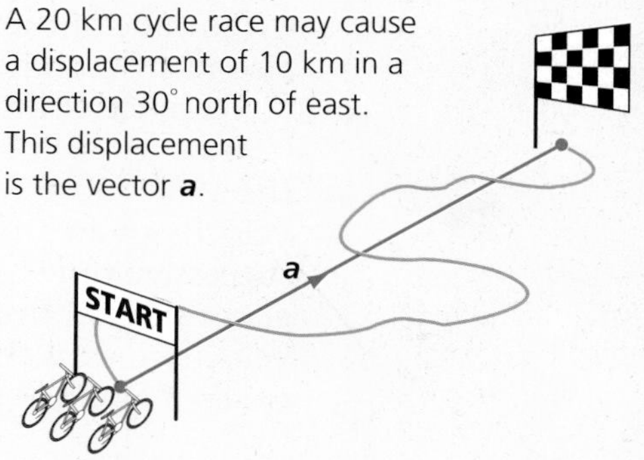
START
a

Speed is a scalar quantity. For motion in a straight line (linear motion), velocity and speed have the same magnitude. For non-linear motion, velocity can change even if the speed stays the same.

1 Athletes in a 1500 m race can run a lap at a steady speed, but their velocity changes. Why?

2 In 1986, Ingrid Kristiansen of Norway won a women's 10 000 m race (25 laps of a 400 m track) in a record time of 30 minutes 13.74 s.
a What was her average speed during the race?
b What was her average velocity?

Fig. 3 Instantaneous velocity

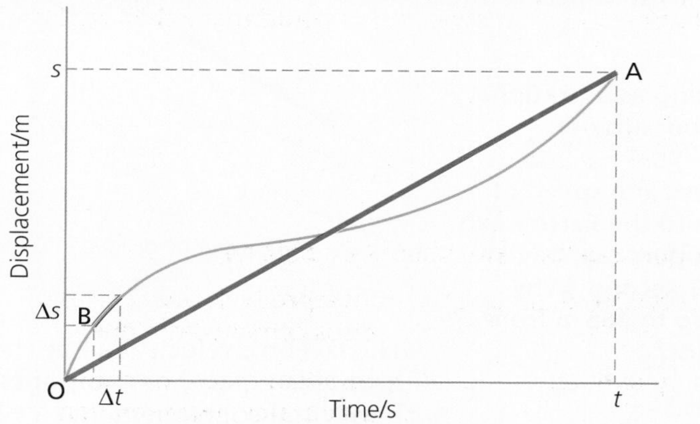
s
A
Displacement/m
Δs
B
O
Δt
Time/s
t

The average velocity between O and A is s/t. The average velocity around B is $\Delta s/\Delta t$. If Δt is small we can regard this as the instantaneous velocity at B.

Average and instantaneous values

A 100 m race is run in a straight line, so the speed and the magnitude of the velocity are the same. In the Barcelona Olympics in 1992, Linford Christie ran this distance in 9.96 s. His average velocity for the race was:

$$v = \frac{s}{t} = \frac{100.0 \text{ m}}{9.96 \text{ s}} = 10.04 \text{ m s}^{-1}$$

Linford ran the first 10 m in 1.87 seconds, a velocity of just over 5 m s^{-1}. He ran the last 10 m at a velocity of 11.36 m s^{-1}.

In reality, velocity is measured as an average. It is a measurement of displacement over a certain time. If that time interval is very small, we are close to measuring the **instantaneous velocity** (Fig. 3). The delta symbol, Δ, represents a change in a quantity.

If the time interval Δt is very small, any motion will be approximately linear so the magnitude of the instantaneous velocity is also its instantaneous speed.

Florence Griffith-Joyner was timed at 0.91 s over each 10 m from 60 m to 90 m in the 1988 100 m final. If the instantaneous velocity of an athlete is the same in successive time intervals they are running at constant or uniform velocity. Uniform velocity means that equal distances are covered in equal times, in a straight line.

3 Does the highest average speed or the highest instantaneous speed win races? Explain your answer.

4 Is it the average speed or the instantaneous speed which is more important in a long jumper's run up? Explain your answer.

Key ideas

- Velocity and displacement are vectors. They have a magnitude and a direction.
- Distance and speed are scalars. They only have a magnitude.
- Average velocity is found by considering the total displacement in a certain time.
- The instantaneous velocity is found by considering very small time intervals.

1.3 Components of velocity

Relative motion

Velocity is always measured relative to an observer. Two athletes running together at uniform velocity appear stationary *relative* to one another, while the track appears to move backwards. Every measurement of velocity depends on the relative motion, or the frame of reference, of the observer. Each time you record a velocity, you should specify the frame of reference. In practice, we rarely do this because most measurements are made with respect to the surface of the Earth.

5 Is there such a thing as a 'stationary' object? Explain your answer.

6 The equator moves at a speed of 465 m s^{-1} relative to the Earth's axis. Olympic high jumpers can stay in the air for up to 1 second. Why don't they land up to 465 m from their take-off point?

Resolving vectors

In 1986, Fatima Whitbread broke the UK women's javelin record when she threw the javelin a distance of 77.44 m. The release speed for the javelin was about 27 m s^{-1}. Its *horizontal* speed was only about 23 m s^{-1}. This is because the javelin is thrown at an angle of about 30° to the ground.

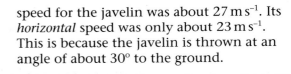

Fig. 4 Resolving velocity

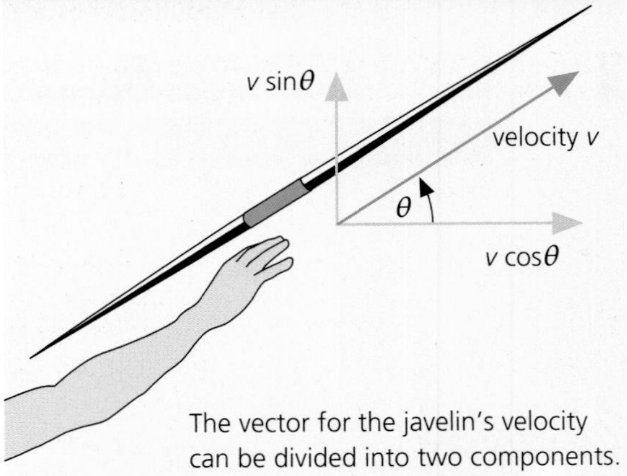
v sinθ
velocity v
θ
v cosθ

The vector for the javelin's velocity can be divided into two components.

The javelin's velocity can be thought of as having two parts, or **components**; a horizontal component and a vertical component (Fig. 4). All vectors can be divided up into two components by a process called resolving.

Vector addition is more complicated than scalar addition. Adding together two *distances* of 3 m will always produce the answer 6 m. Adding together two *displacements* of 3 m could give a result from 0 to 6 m. This is because we have to take the direction of the displacements into account.

Fig. 5 Adding vectors by scale drawing

The resultant, ***a+b***, of adding two vectors, ***a*** and ***b***, can be found by:

placing them 'nose to tail', so that the arrows follow on. The resultant is the straight line that connects the start of ***a*** to the end of ***b***;

or

by drawing ***a*** and ***b*** from the same point and constructing a parallelogram. The diagonal of the parallelogram is the resultant.

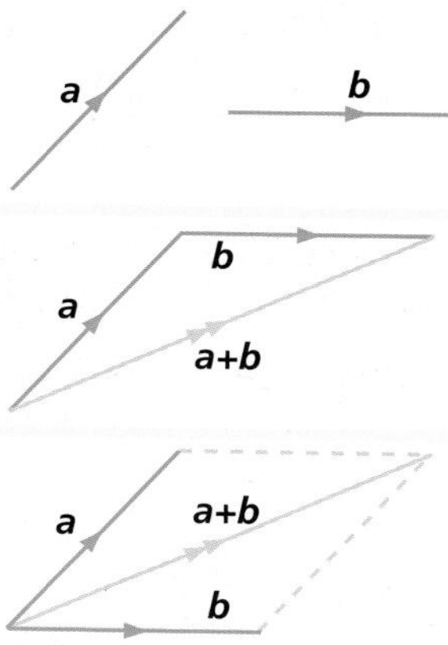
a
b
a
b
a+b
a
a+b
b

You can add vectors by drawing a scale diagram and measuring the length and direction of the **resultant** (Fig. 5). The resultant is the sum of any number of vectors. Vector additions can also be solved using trigonometry (Fig. 6).

Fig. 6 Adding vectors using trigonometry

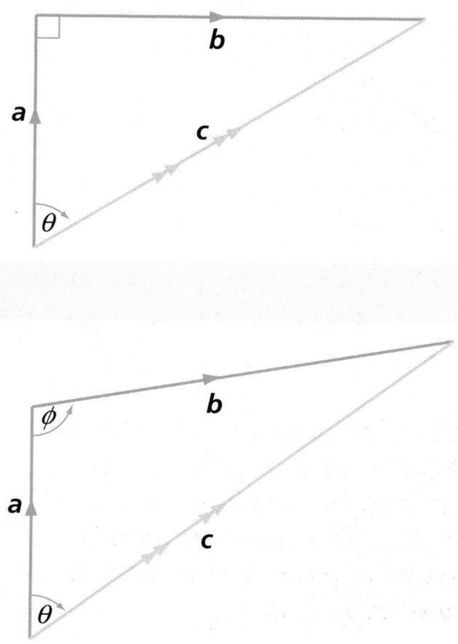
b
a
c
θ
φ
b
a
c
θ

Vectors at right angles

Find the magnitude of *c* with Pythagoras' theorem:

$c^2 = a^2 + b^2$, so $c = \sqrt{(a^2 + b^2)}$.

Find the angle θ from

$\tan\theta = b/a$, so $\theta = \tan^{-1} b/a$.

For two vectors at angle ϕ

Find the magnitude of *c* with the cosine rule: $c^2 = a^2 + b^2 - 2ab\cos\phi$

Find the angle θ from the sine rule:

$$\frac{\sin\theta}{b} = \frac{\sin\phi}{c}$$

Fig. 7 Worked example of resolving

Records in events such as the javelin are not recognised if a wind speed greater than 2 m s^{-1} is blowing in the competitor's favour. If the wind is blowing at an angle to the event we can calculate how much it helps the athlete.

A wind blows at 5 m s^{-1} at an angle of 30° to the throwing direction. The component in the direction of the throw is 5 cos 30° = 4.33 m s^{-1}.

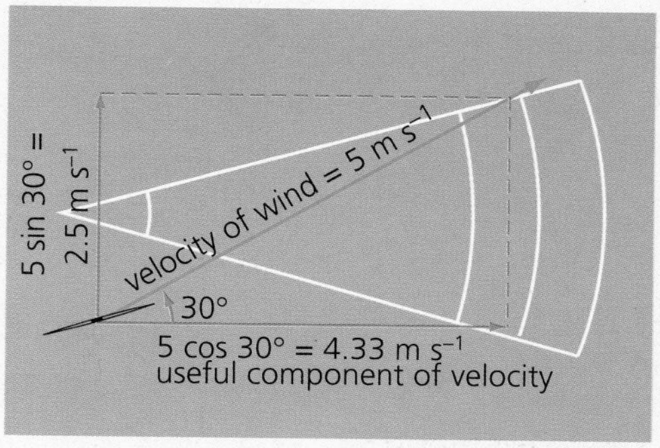
5 sin 30° =
2.5 m s⁻¹
velocity of wind = 5 m s⁻¹
30°
5 cos 30° = 4.33 m s⁻¹
useful component of velocity

7 **A shot-putter releases the shot at a velocity of 12.5 m s^{-1} at an angle of 41° to the horizontal. What is the horizontal velocity of the shot?**

Acceleration

In a 100 m race it is vital to get a good start. A sprinter needs to increase her velocity as quickly as possible. The rate at which velocity increases is called acceleration:

$$\text{acceleration} = \frac{\text{change in velocity}}{\text{time taken for change}}$$

Since velocity is measured in m s^{-1} and time is in seconds, acceleration has units of m s^{-1}/s, written as m s^{-2}. Acceleration takes place in a certain direction and is therefore a vector quantity.

Any change in velocity, a change in speed *or* just a change in direction, constitutes an acceleration. If the acceleration is in the opposite direction to the velocity, it will act to reduce the velocity. This is often referred to as a deceleration or retardation.

Fig. 8 Velocity–time graph

A velocity–time graph can be used to find the acceleration at a given time. The instantaneous acceleration at any time is given by the slope of the tangent at that point. The tangent at a point can be approximated by taking a small change in the velocity, Δv, over a small time interval, Δt. The average acceleration is then given by $\Delta v/\Delta t$. As Δt gets smaller $\Delta v/\Delta t$ gets closer to the instantaneous acceleration.

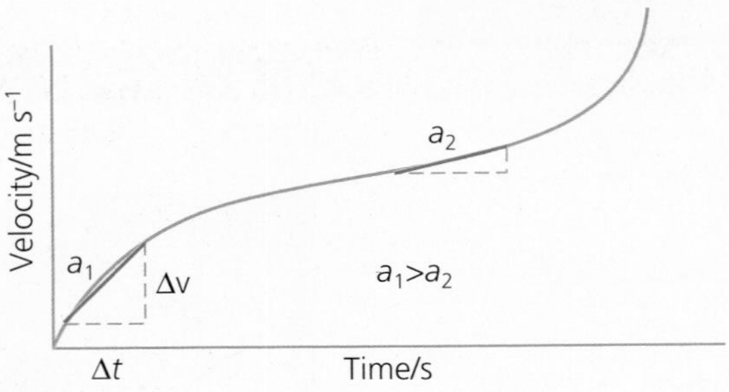

Velocity/m s⁻¹
a₂
a₁
Δv
a₁>a₂
Δt
Time/s

Two seconds into a 100 m race a top sprinter reaches a speed of $10\,\text{m}\,\text{s}^{-1}$. The average acceleration is $5\,\text{m}\,\text{s}^{-2}$. A sprinter achieves a much higher acceleration at the instant she leaves the starting blocks. The acceleration at a particular moment is defined in a similar way to instantaneous velocity (Fig. 8). If we consider the change in velocity, Δv, in a very small interval of time, Δt, then:

$$\text{instantaneous acceleration} = \frac{\Delta v}{\Delta t}$$

8 A tennis ball is dropped and bounces up again. Sketch the ball
a as it falls,
b as it bounces up.
Mark in the direction of the velocity and the acceleration in each case.

Key ideas

- A single vector may be resolved into two components.
- Vectors can be added and subtracted by scale drawing or by trigonometry.
- Acceleration is a vector quantity. It is the rate of change of velocity.

Air resistance has little effect on compact objects that are moving slowing. Divers are effectively in free fall.

Free fall and terminal velocity

An object is said to be in free fall if the only force acting on it is gravity. Experiments show that on Earth the acceleration due to gravity, g, is about $9.8\,\text{m}\,\text{s}^{-2}$, though the exact value varies from place to place.

The acceleration due to gravity at a particular place is the same for all objects. The mass of a free-falling diver has no effect on her acceleration. Heavy or light, she would reach the water in the same time.

However, an object falling on Earth is never quite in free fall. The atmosphere always exerts a drag force on a moving object. The effect of this air resistance is negligible for sprinters, jumpers or even divers, but in some sports, such as cycling or skiing, it is a dominant factor. This is because the drag force due to **air resistance** increases with speed. For a sky diver, the resistive force due to air resistance increases as the diver accelerates until it is equal to the downward force of gravity.

When this happens, the sky diver stops accelerating and falls at a constant speed. We say the diver has reached **terminal velocity** (Fig. 9). For a sky diver in a head-down position the terminal velocity is about $82\,m\,s^{-1}$ (185 mph). In the upper atmosphere, where the air is less dense, speeds of up to $280\,m\,s^{-1}$ (625 mph) have been reached.

Air resistance also depends on the area and the mass of the object. In general, a dense object with a small surface area will experience a low air resistance, and have a higher terminal velocity.

Fig. 9 Terminal velocity

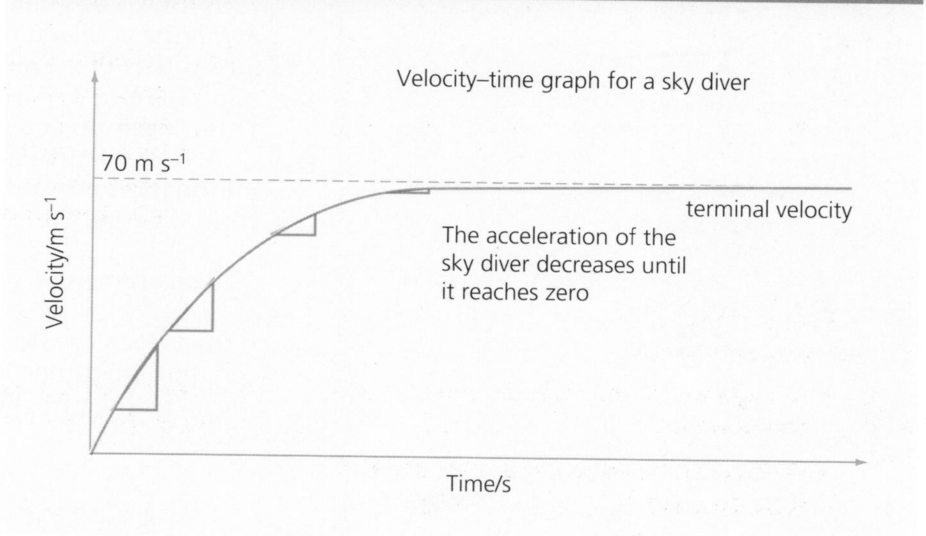
Velocity–time graph for a sky diver
70 m s⁻¹
Velocity/m s⁻¹
terminal velocity
The acceleration of the sky diver decreases until it reaches zero
Time/s

Sky divers reach their terminal velocity when the downward force of gravity is equal to the force of air resistance.

High-speed skiing is one of the fastest sports. Speed skiers wear streamlined clothes and adopt a crouching position to reduce air resistance. The record speed is over $230\,km\,h^{-1}$ ($65\,m\,s^{-1}$).

Key ideas

- All objects, whatever their mass, fall at the same acceleration due to gravity. On Earth, this acceleration is approximately $9.8\,m\,s^{-2}$.
- The force of air resistance acting on an accelerating falling body increases, until it balances the force due to its weight. At this point, the object falls at its terminal velocity.

Fig. 10 Representing motion graphically

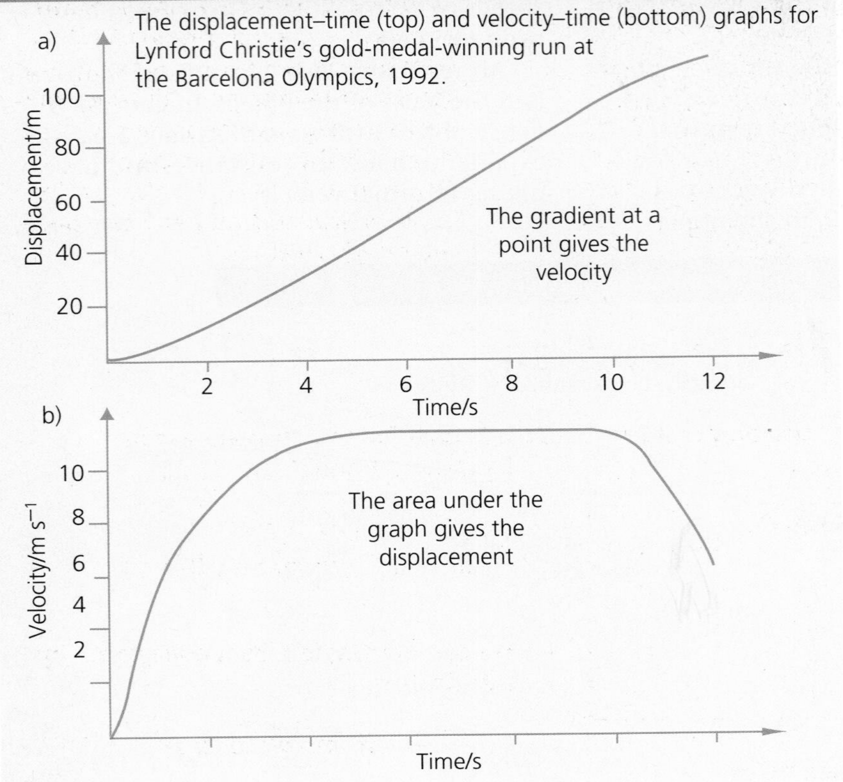

a)
Displacement/m
100
80
60
40
20
2
4
6
8
10
12
Time/s
The gradient at a point gives the velocity
b)
Velocity/m s⁻¹
10
8
6
4
2
Time/s
The area under the graph gives the displacement

The displacement–time (top) and velocity–time (bottom) graphs for Lynford Christie's gold-medal-winning run at the Barcelona Olympics, 1992.

Time and motion graphs

Graphs showing how the displacement, velocity and acceleration of an object vary with time are an excellent way of visualising motion. A displacement–time graph can provide us with information on velocity. The velocity at any given time is $\Delta s/\Delta t$. This is the same as the gradient of the graph in Fig. 10a.

Another way of looking at an athlete's motion is to show how their velocity varies with time. The gradient of this graph is $\Delta v/\Delta t$, the acceleration. A straight line means that the velocity is changing by the same amount over equal time intervals. This is uniform acceleration.

A velocity–time graph can also give information about the displacement. For constant velocity:

$$\text{displacement} = \text{velocity} \times \text{time}$$

If the velocity varies, the displacement at a certain time can be found by calculating the area under the line up to that point (Fig. 10b).

We can see how acceleration, velocity and displacement are linked by plotting graphs which show how the motion of an object varies with time. Think about a tennis ball, dropped from a height of 1m, which bounces three times before being caught again. Because we are dealing with vector quantities we need to decide on a **sign convention**. In this case we will take **down** as negative and treat ground-level as zero displacement.

Acceleration. The ball is always accelerating under gravity, $a = -10$ m s^{-2}, except for the very brief time that it is touching the ground, when the acceleration will be upwards. As soon as the ball loses contact with the ground, its acceleration will be -10 m s^{-2} once more. The ball will transfer some energy each time it hits the ground so each bounce will be lower than the previous one and the bounces will get closer together.

Velocity. The ball is dropped, so its initial velocity is zero. The gradient of the velocity–time graph is the instantaneous acceleration of the ball. The graph will be straight, with a gradient of -10 m s^{-2}, until the ball hits the ground. Then the ball rapidly slows to a halt and accelerates back up. After the ball has left the ground, the velocity will decrease as the ball rises, until it is zero again at the top of the bounce.

Displacement. The gradient of the displacement–time graph is the instantaneous velocity, so the slope starts at zero and becomes increasingly negative until the ball hits the ground. The displacement does not go negative because we have taken ground level to be zero.

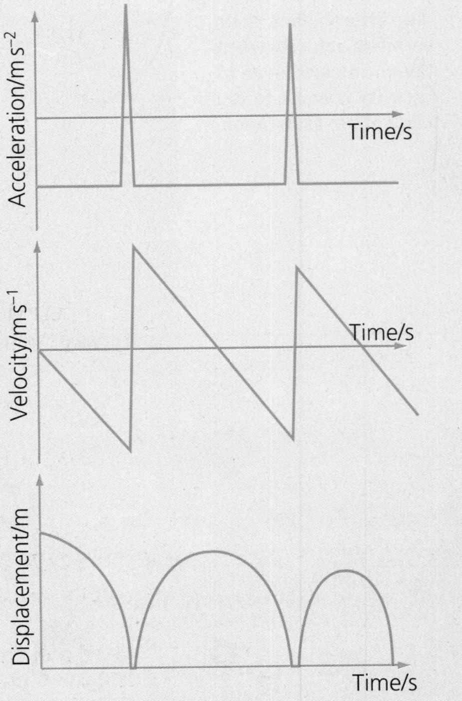

Acceleration/m s⁻²
Time/s
Velocity/m s⁻¹
Time/s
Displacement/m
Time/s

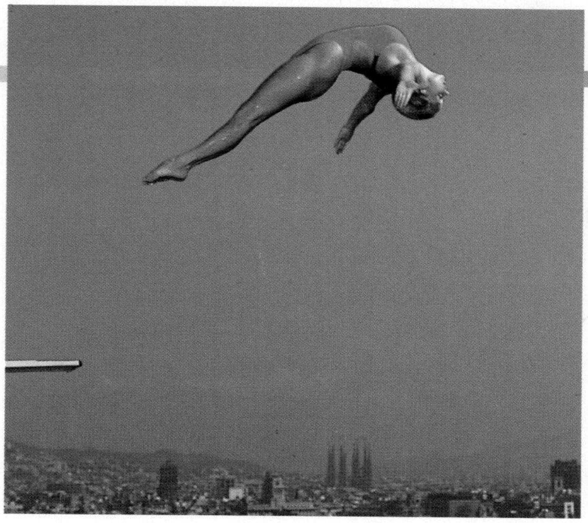

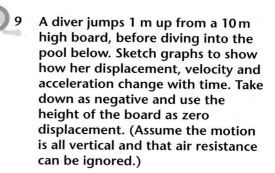

9 **A diver jumps 1 m up from a 10 m high board, before diving into the pool below. Sketch graphs to show how her displacement, velocity and acceleration change with time. Take down as negative and use the height of the board as zero displacement. (Assume the motion is all vertical and that air resistance can be ignored.)**

1.4 Equations of linear motion

There are five important variables that can be used to describe motion.

Quantity	Symbol
displacement	s
initial velocity	u
final velocity	v
acceleration	a
time	t

These quantities are linked by the equations of linear motion:

1 The definition of acceleration gives us the first equation:

$$\text{acceleration} = \frac{\text{change in velocity}}{\text{time taken}}$$

$$\text{or, } a = \frac{v-u}{t}$$

$$at = v - u$$

$$\text{So, } v = u + at \quad \text{(Equation 1)}$$

2 The definition of velocity leads to the second equation:

$$\text{velocity} = \frac{\text{displacement}}{\text{time}}$$

$$\text{or, displacement} = \text{velocity} \times \text{time}$$

When the velocity changes at a constant rate, we take the average velocity as half-way between the initial and final values.

$$\text{displacement} = \text{average velocity} \times t$$

$$s = \tfrac{1}{2}(u+v)t \quad \text{(Equation 2)}$$

3 It is possible to eliminate v from Equations 1 and 2 (Fig. 11):

$$s = \tfrac{1}{2}(u + u + at)t$$

$$s = ut + \tfrac{1}{2}at^2 \quad \text{(Equation 3)}$$

4 We can eliminate t from equation 3 by substituting

$$t = \frac{v-u}{a} \quad \text{(from Equation 1)}$$

$$\text{So, } s = u\left(\frac{v-u}{a}\right) + \tfrac{1}{2}a\left(\frac{v-u}{a}\right)^2$$

This simplifies to: $v^2 = u^2 + 2as$ (Equation 4)

Fig. 11 Derivation of Equation 3

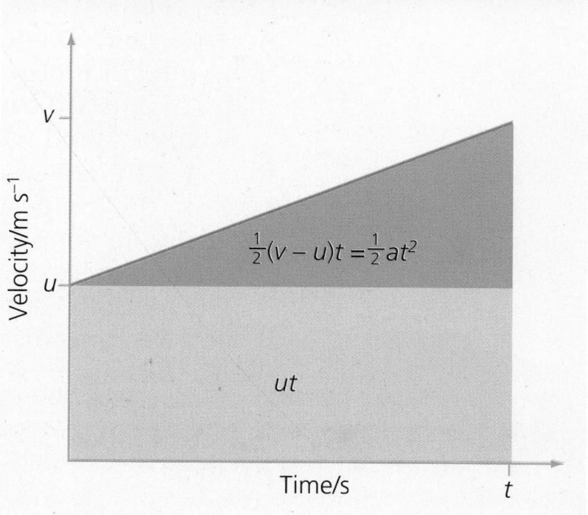

Velocity/m s^{-1}
v
u
$\frac{1}{2}(v-u)t = \frac{1}{2}at^2$
ut
Time/s
t

Each equation has one of the five variables missing. If you know any three of the five variables you should be able to calculate the other two. These equations only work for motion in a straight line, where the acceleration is constant.

If a 100 m sprinter initially accelerates at 2.0 $m\,s^{-2}$ and maintains this acceleration over the whole race, we can use the equations to calculate how fast he will cross the finishing line and how long he will take. To find the final velocity you could use:

$$v^2 = u^2 + 2as$$
$$= 0 + 2 \times 2.0 \times 100$$

The final velocity, $v = \sqrt{400} = 20\ m\,s^{-1}$

The time taken for the race would be:

$$t = \frac{v-u}{a}$$
$$= \frac{20.0\ m\,s^{-1} - 0}{2.0\ m\,s^{-2}}$$
$$= 10.0\ s$$

In reality, sprinters achieve a higher acceleration than this at the start of the race, though it cannot be maintained throughout the race (Fig. 10).

10 When a golfer hits a ball the club only touches the ball for about 0.0005 s, but the ball leaves the tee at a speed of 75 $m\,s^{-1}$. What is the average acceleration of the golf ball while it is in contact with the club?

Key ideas

- The equations of linear motion apply to a body that is moving in a straight line, with uniform acceleration:

$$v = u + at \qquad s = \tfrac{1}{2}(u+v)t \qquad s = ut + \tfrac{1}{2}at^2 \qquad v^2 = u^2 + 2as$$

1.5 For a few centimetres more

Motion in two dimensions

In the 1968 Olympic games in Mexico City, the American Bob Beamon almost cleared the long jump pit! His jump of 8.90 m was 70 cm further than anyone had ever jumped at that time.

To understand a long jumper's motion we need to deal with movement in two dimensions. After take-off, the jumper moves horizontally *and* vertically. To complicate things still further, the velocity changes direction throughout the jump.

The motion seems complex, but we can simplify it. First we concentrate on the motion of just one point, the **centre of mass**. In the air, no matter how the jumper moves his arms or legs, his centre of mass will follow a symmetrical path, known as a parabola.

We can simplify things further by treating the two-dimensional movement as a combination of horizontal and vertical motion (Fig. 12). Vertical motion is totally independent of horizontal motion.

USA
254

Fig. 12 Long jump trajectory

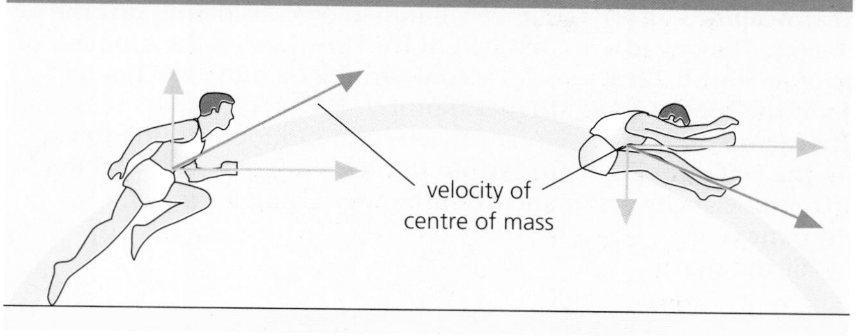
velocity of
centre of mass

A record-breaking long jumper has to combine top-class sprinting with a high jumper's spring into the air. A good sprinter achieves a top speed of about $12\,m\,s^{-1}$; a high jumper leaves the ground with a vertical velocity of about $4.5\,m\,s^{-1}$. If a long-jumper could combine these performances, how far would he be able to jump?

Strictly speaking, the equations of motion only apply to movement in a straight line, but we can use them to describe a long jump if we treat the vertical and horizontal velocities separately.

The **vertical** take-off velocity will determine the time of flight. We can use $v = u + at$ to find the time spent in the air:

$$t = \frac{v-u}{a}$$

$$= \frac{(-4.5\ m\,s^{-1}) - 4.5\ m\,s^{-1}}{-9.8\ m\,s^{-2}}$$

$$= 0.92\ s$$

The **horizontal** velocity can be used to find the length of the jump. We can use $s = ut + \frac{1}{2}at^2$, but since $a = 0$, this is just $s = ut$:

length of jump, $s = 12\ m\,s^{-1} \times 0.92\ s = 11\,m$

The world record for the long jump is about 2 m less than this theoretical result. There are a number of places where our simple model does not match the real event:

a A long jumper has to drop his horizontal speed so that he is in contact with the board long enough to gain some vertical speed;

b Air resistance can impose a horizontal retardation of up to $0.2\ m\ s^{-2}$ (it has little affect on the vertical motion);

c We have treated the jumper as if he was a single point and the distance we have calculated is that travelled by the centre of mass. The actual jump may be longer than this because a good long jumper will have his centre of mass over the board at take-off and behind his heels on landing, thereby increasing the time of flight.

This approach to athletics is typical of the way physics works. We try to understand a very complex system by identifying its essential features and creating a theoretical model. Experiments and measurements are used to check how closely our model reflects the real world.

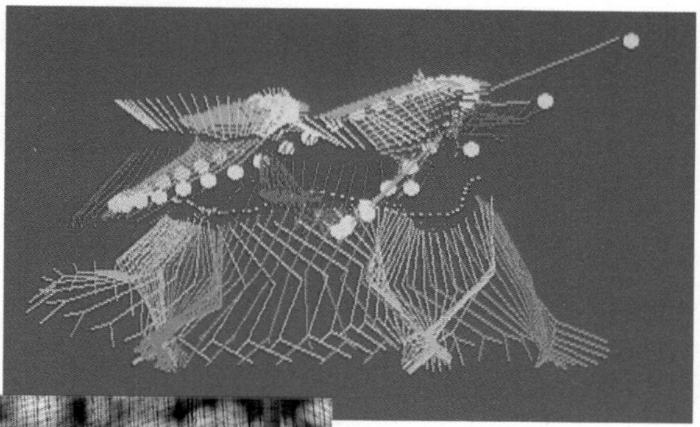

12

High-speed computers can be used to model athletes' performance and help improve their technique.

11 The best high jumpers achieve a vertical take-off velocity of about $4.8\,m\,s^{-1}$. A typical high jumper's 'centre of mass' is 0.95 m above the ground. Use the equations of motion to estimate the height that this jumper can reach.

12 The divers of La Quebrada leap from the cliffs near Acapulco into the sea, 26.7 m below. They need a horizontal range of at least 8.22 m to clear the rocks at the foot of the cliff. Assuming they jump horizontally from the cliff-edge

a Estimate the horizontal velocity needed to clear the rocks.

b How fast do they hit the sea?

Getting the right angle

Throwing the 'hammer' requires great strength. In 1986, the Russian Yuriy Sedykh set a world record with a throw of 86.74 m.

The 'hammer' is a small tungsten ball fastened to the end of a 1.22 m chain. It has a mass of 7.26 kg. The thrower whirls the hammer round three times before releasing it. The speed of release depends on how quickly the thrower can spin round in the 2 m circle, but the length of the throw also depends on the angle of release. A good thrower will release the hammer at a speed of about 26 m s^{-1}. We can use the equations of motion to find the best angle.

The distance thrown is determined by the horizontal speed and the time of flight. The time of flight depends on the vertical component of the velocity. The problem can be simplified by considering just the first half of the throw; from the moment of release to when the hammer reaches its highest point.

Fig. 13 Velocity of a 'hammer'

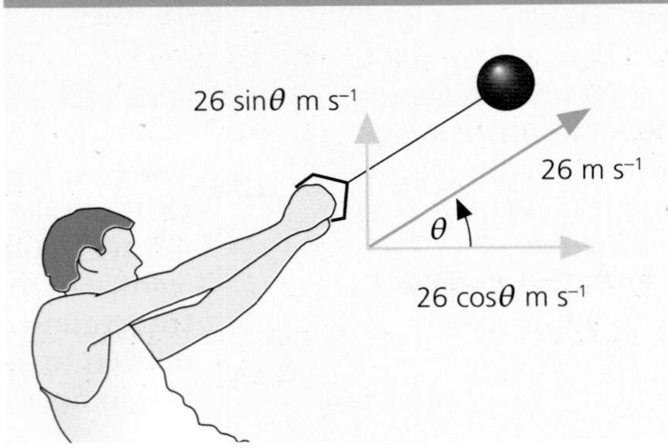

26 sinθ m s⁻¹
26 m s⁻¹
θ
26 cosθ m s⁻¹

For the vertical motion, s is unknown, $u = 26 \sin\theta$ m s^{-1}, $v = 0$ m s^{-1}, $a = -9.8$ m s^{-2} and t is unknown. Using $v = u + at$:

$$t = \frac{v-u}{a}$$

$$= \frac{0 - 26\sin\theta \text{ m s}^{-1}}{-9.8 \text{ m s}^{-2}}$$

$$= 2.65\sin\theta \text{ seconds}$$

The time for the whole flight is:
$2 \times 2.65 \sin\theta = 5.30 \sin\theta$

$$\text{distance} = \text{horizontal velocity} \times \text{time}$$

$$= 26\cos\theta \text{ m s}^{-1} \times 5.30\sin\theta \text{ s}$$

$$= 138\sin\theta\cos\theta \text{ metres}$$

But $\sin\theta\cos\theta = \frac{1}{2}\sin 2\theta$, so:
distance = $69 \sin 2\theta$ m

The greatest range will be achieved when $\sin 2\theta$ has its greatest value. The largest value of $\sin 2\theta$ is 1, so the hammer thrower has a maximum range of 69 m.

When $\sin 2\theta = 1$, $2\theta = 90°$ and $\theta = 45°$. Theoretically, the best angle at which to release the hammer is 45°, In fact, because the hammer is released from above ground level the best angle of release is slightly less than 45°.

13 Theoretically the optimum take-off angle for a projectile is 45°. Why don't long jumpers take off at this angle?

Key ideas

- Horizontal motion does not affect vertical motion.
- Problems of two-dimensional motion (projectiles) can be solved by resolving the initial velocity into *vertical* and *horizontal* components and applying the equations of linear motion to each component separately.

2 Balancing forces

Civil engineers have occasionally underestimated the destructive force of the wind with catastrophic consequences. In 1879, a tornado wrecked the Tay railway bridge in Scotland, killing 71 people. Even relatively low wind speeds can be destructive. In 1940, the Tacoma Narrows bridge in the USA was brought down by a wind of only 18 m s^{-1}.

In an attempt to avoid such disasters, engineers now subject their bridge designs to rigorous scrutiny. The new Tokyo Bay suspension bridge was tested with gigantic hammers which delivered 100-tonne blows to the middle of the 600 m long central span. A much longer bridge, connecting Honshu and Shikoku, is now being built. When it is completed in 1998, it will include the longest suspension bridge in the world. Wind tunnel tests on a 1:100 scale model suggest that the 2 km central span will be stable at wind speeds of up to 90 m s^{-1}.

Engineers and architects must identify the forces and moments that could act on each part of the bridge in a variety of conditions in order to design and build stable structures.

The islands of Honshu and Shikoku are connected by 10 km of suspension and cable-stayed bridges.

2.1 Learning objectives

After working through this chapter, you should be able to:

- **identify** the external forces acting on an object;
- **draw** free-body diagrams;
- **explain** what is meant by centre of mass;
- **resolve** forces into perpendicular components;
- **add** forces to find the resultant force;
- **calculate** the moment of a force;
- **recall** the conditions necessary for equilibrium;
- **apply** the principle of moments and the polygon of forces to objects in equilibrium.

2.2 Identifying the forces

Bridges are subject to a range of different forces:

- weight
- contact force
- friction
- tension

Weight

Weight is the force that acts on a mass due to the gravitational attraction of the Earth. An object's weight depends on its mass, m, and the **gravitational field strength**, g. This is the gravitational force that acts on each kilogram of mass. The gravitational field strength is measured in newtons per kilogram, N kg^{-1}. The value of g at the Earth's surface is approximately 9.8 N kg^{-1}. On Earth, a mass of 1 kg has a weight of 9.8 N.

weight (N) = mass (kg) × gravitational field strength (N kg^{-1})

$$W = mg$$

1 a An astronaut has a mass of 80 kg. What is their weight on Earth?

b The same astronaut would weigh 128 N on the Moon. Calculate the gravitational field strength on the Moon.

The gravitational attraction of the Earth acts on every particle in an object. Adding up all these forces gives the total weight of the object. This **resultant force** can be thought of as acting at a single point. This point is called the **centre of gravity** of the object (Fig. 1). Because weight always acts vertically down, towards the centre of the Earth, we can represent this force by a single vertical arrow from the centre of gravity.

Fig. 1 Centre of gravity

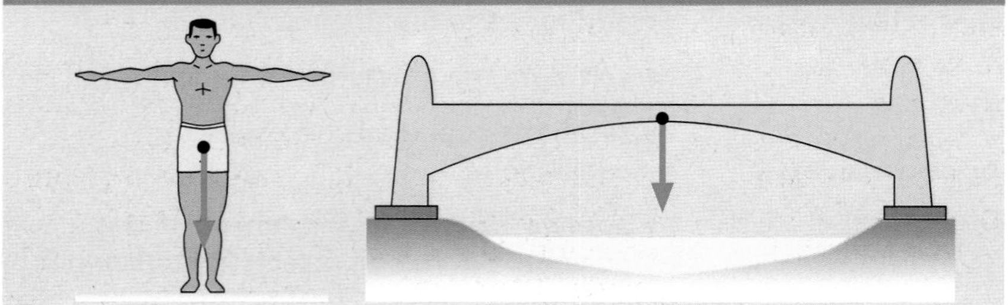

Fig. 2 Finding the centre of mass

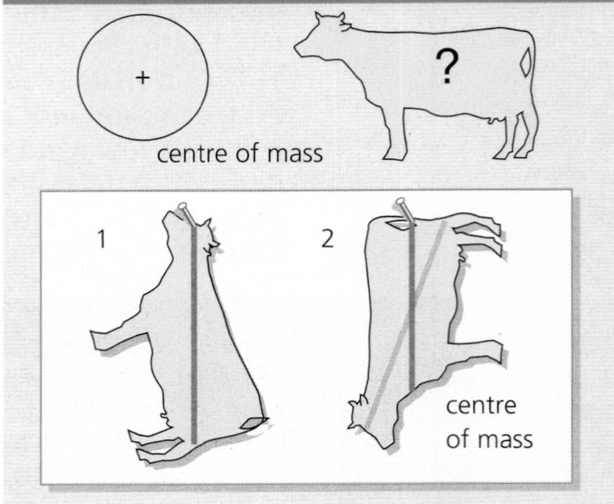
centre of mass
?
1
2
centre
of mass

The **centre of mass** (Fig. 2) of an object is not exactly the same thing as its centre of gravity, though near the Earth's surface (where the force of gravitational attraction is almost constant) they can be regarded as the same point. The position of the centre of mass determines what happens to an object when a force is applied to it. If the resultant force acting on an object passes through its centre of mass, it will accelerate *without* rotating. Imagine trying to push a car that is parked on some extremely slippery ice. If you push through the centre of mass, the car will move forward without spinning. If the line of action of your force does not pass through the centre of mass, the car will rotate, as well as moving forward (Fig. 3).

Fig. 3 Pushing and spinning

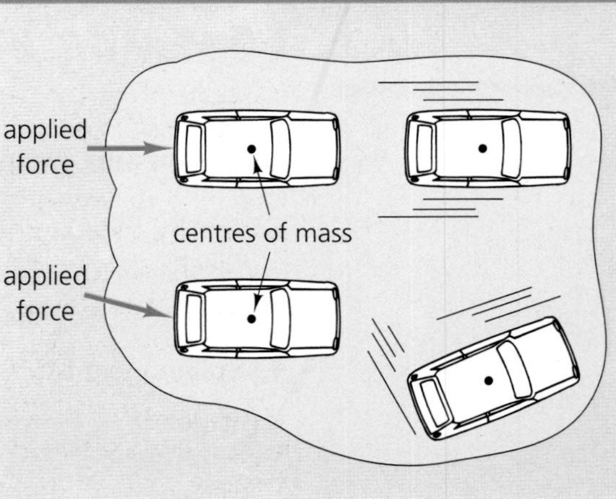
applied
force
centres of mass
applied
force

Key ideas

- The weight of a body = mass × gravitational field strength.
- The centre of gravity is the point at which all the weight appears to act.
- The centre of mass is the point through which an applied force causes no rotation.

Contact force

When two solid surfaces are touching, they exert a contact force on each other. This force is sometimes called the **reaction**. For example, it is the contact force between your feet and the ground that prevents the gravitational attraction of the Earth pulling you through the floor.

When two objects are pushed together, the atoms in each surface repel each other. Like compressed springs, the atoms exert a greater force as they are pushed closer together. The resultant force between the surfaces is the sum of all the inter-atomic repulsions. The component of this force which is at right angles to the surfaces is called the normal contact force, or the perpendicular reaction (Fig. 4).

Fig. 4 Resultant contact force

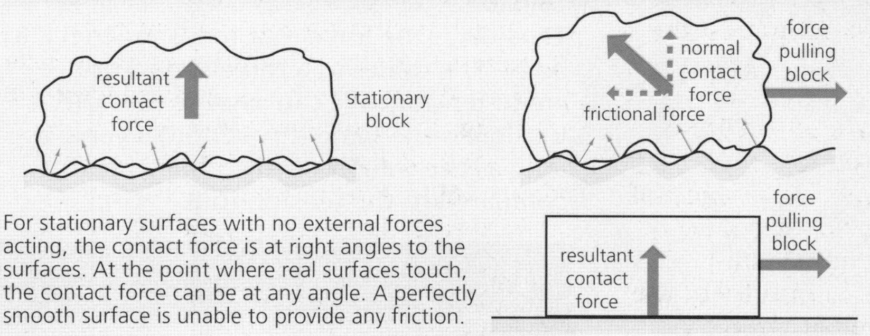
resultant
contact
force
stationary
block
normal
contact
force
force
pulling
block
frictional force
force
pulling
block
resultant
contact
force

For stationary surfaces with no external forces acting, the contact force is at right angles to the surfaces. At the point where real surfaces touch, the contact force can be at any angle. A perfectly smooth surface is unable to provide any friction.

If the surfaces are in relative motion, or if an external horizontal force is acting, the resultant contact force will not be at right angles to the surface. We can treat the resultant as the combination of two forces. The component at right angles to the surface is the normal contact force. The component parallel to the surface is called the frictional force. For perfectly smooth surfaces there would be no friction and the only force would be the normal contact force.

2 **Sketch the bridge shown in Fig. 5. Mark in the forces acting on the bridge.**

Fig. 5 Forces on a beam bridge

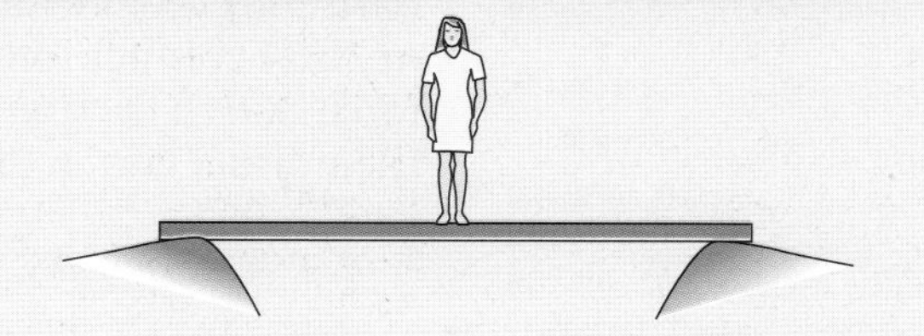

Friction

A frictional force acts between two solid surfaces in contact when they are in relative motion, or if a force is trying to slide them across each other. Friction acts to oppose the sliding.

A false-colour scanning electron micrograph of crystalline tungsten. Even the smoothest surfaces look like a mountain landscape at high magnifications.

The actual area of contact between two surfaces can be as little as 0.01% of the full surface area. Since pressure at a point is the force per unit area, the pressure at these points is extremely high. The high pressure tends to join the two surfaces, actually 'welding' them together at these small points of contact.

Surfaces will not slide across each other unless an applied force breaks these 'welds'. At the point when the surfaces start to slide, the applied force is just sufficient to overcome the **limiting friction**. When the surfaces are moving, a frictional force acts against the relative motion. The size of this **dynamic friction** is usually less than the limiting friction. The relative speed of the two surfaces does not have very much effect on dynamic friction.

The area of the surfaces has no influence on the friction. The frictional force between two surfaces just depends on how hard they are pressed together, i.e. the **normal** contact force between them. The force due to friction, F, is proportional to the normal contact force, N.

$$F \propto N, \text{ or } F = \mu N$$

The constant of proportionality, μ, is known as the coefficient of friction. Its size depends on the nature of the surfaces. Rough surfaces, such as sandpaper, exert a large frictional force; the coefficient of friction between sandpaper and wood is high (Fig. 6).

Fig. 6 Forces acting on a block

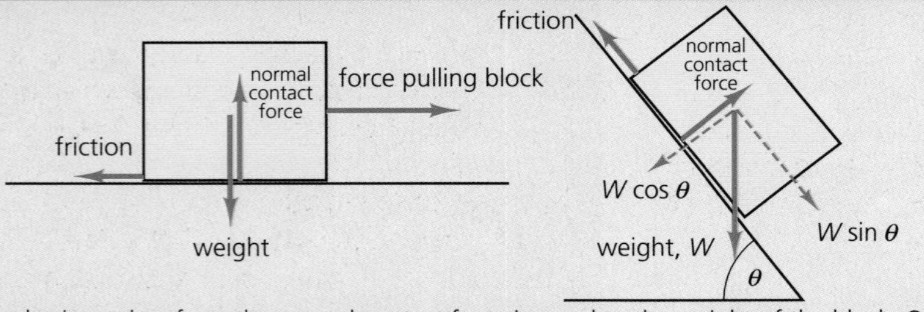

normal contact force
force pulling block
friction
weight
friction
normal contact force
W cos θ
W sin θ
weight, W
θ

On a horizontal surface, the normal contact force is equal to the weight of the block. On an inclined surface, only a component of the block's weight, $W \cos \theta$, pulls it onto the surface. The normal contact force is therefore less than the weight of the block.

Although frictional forces tend to prevent surfaces sliding over each other, they do not act to prevent all motion: imagine trying to cycle when the bicycle tyre has no grip on the road at all. Even when you walk it is the frictional force acting between the road and your shoe that allows you to move forward.

3 'On icy roads a car is more likely to skid if it is fully loaded.' Do you agree with this statement? Explain your answer.

4 Estimate the pressure at the points of contact for a 2 cm steel cube resting on a steel surface. (Density of steel ≈ 8000 kg m^{-3})

5 The coefficient of friction between snow and skis is about 0.02.

a What limiting frictional force acts on a skier of mass 50 kg on horizontal ground?

b Why is the frictional force less than this when the skier is on a steep slope?

Tension

Tension is the force that tends to stretch a body. The cables in a cable-stayed bridge are in tension. We can assume that the tension is the same throughout a cable as long as the weight of the cable is small compared to the tension in it.

The cables exert a force on the bridge that acts in the same direction as the cable, along its length, pulling on the roadway and the pylon that it is attached to.

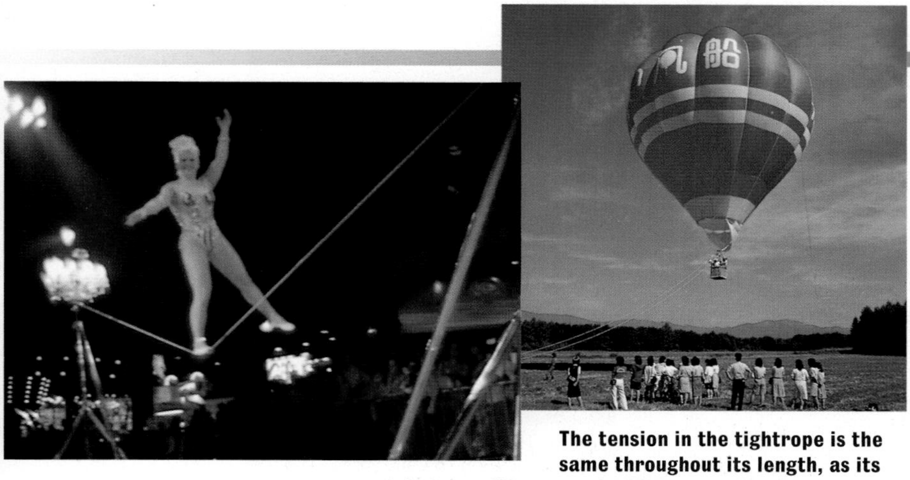

The tension in the tightrope is the same throughout its length, as its weight is small compared with the weight of the acrobat. The tension in the balloon cable changes along its length.

A solid object, like a metal rod, can act in tension, pulling on the objects that it is connected to. A rod may also act in compression, pushing outwards on the objects that are squashing it.

The force exerted by the rod is caused by the forces between its molecules. Like the force in a spring, these intermolecular forces vary, depending on whether the rod is being stretched or compressed. When the rod is being stretched, the molecules are slightly further apart and an attractive force between the molecules tries to restore their original separation. When the molecules are pushed closer together, because the rod is being squashed, a repulsive force acts in a direction that would restore the equilibrium separation.

Fig. 7 Tension and compression

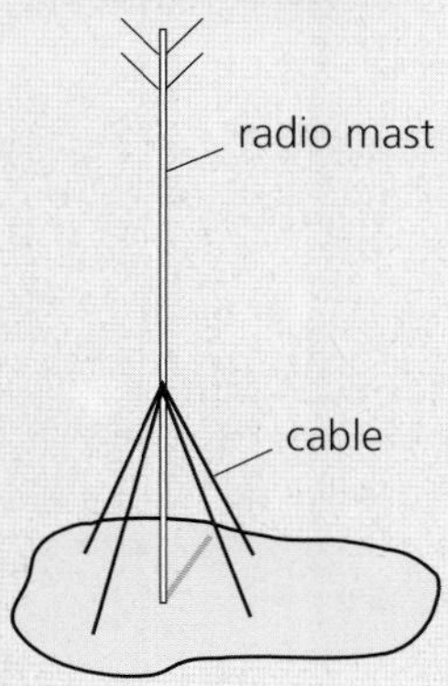

radio mast
cable

6 What are the forces acting on the radio mast (Fig. 7)? Which parts of the structure are in tension? Which are in compression?

Free-body diagrams

The forces acting on a real object, such as the central span of a bridge, are often complex. We can try to understand the situation by drawing a simplified picture of the situation, known as a free-body diagram (Fig. 8). There are several assumptions that engineers make when drawing a free-body diagram:

- Forces are vector quantities – they have a size and a direction. We represent forces on a diagram using arrows, pointing in the direction of the force and labelled with the magnitude. The examples in this chapter are restricted to systems of coplanar forces (2-dimensional problems).
- All the forces which do not act directly on an object are ignored; e.g. the reaction of the ground on the supports does not act directly on the central span of a bridge.
- We are not concerned with the set of balanced forces that are internal to the system; we can ignore any tension or compression in the span itself.
- We can sometimes combine several forces into one; although a vehicle on a bridge touches the road at several points, we need only consider a single contact force acting through the centre of mass of the vehicle.

Fig. 8 Simple free-body diagram

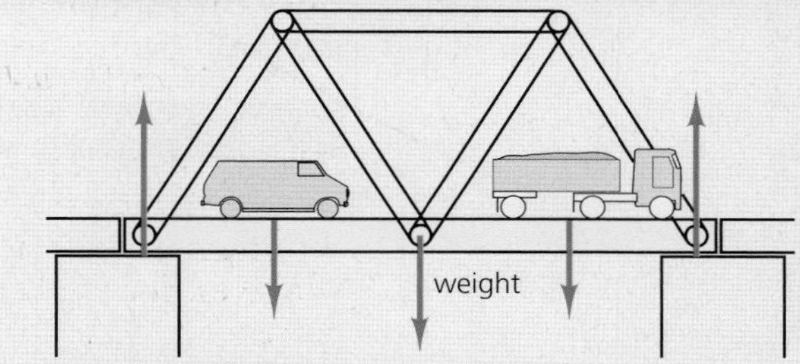

weight

Ignoring friction, the forces that act directly on the central span of the bridge are: its own weight, contact forces from the vehicles and contact forces from the supports.

7 Draw a free-body diagram for a child sliding down a playground slide. Label each of the forces.

The resultant force

Once we have identified all the forces which act on a structure, we can simplify the picture even further by combining them to form a single force. We add the vectors representing the individual forces to give the **resultant** force (Fig. 9).

Fig. 9 Polygon of forces

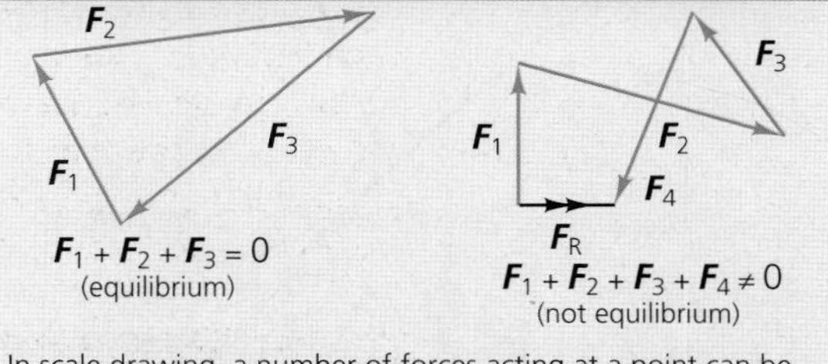

F_2
F_1
F_3
$F_1 + F_2 + F_3 = 0$
(equilibrium)
F_3
F_1
F_2
F_4
F_R
$F_1 + F_2 + F_3 + F_4 \neq 0$
(not equilibrium)

In scale drawing, a number of forces acting at a point can be added together by placing them 'nose to tail'. If the resulting polygon is closed,this means that the resultant force is zero and the point is in equilibrium.

An object is in **equilibrium** if it is stationary or if it moves at constant velocity. For equilibrium, the resultant force must be zero. This condition for equilibrium applies to the separate parts of a bridge, as well as to the whole structure.

8 The bridge in Fig 8. is in equilibrium. Draw its 'polygon of forces'.

Suppose that an engineer suspects that a certain joint in the bridge may fail if the weight of traffic increases any further. When the bridge is not loaded with traffic, the joint is in equilibrium under the action of three forces. There is a contact force from the support, a tension in girder A and a compression from girder B.

Fig. 10 Joint examination

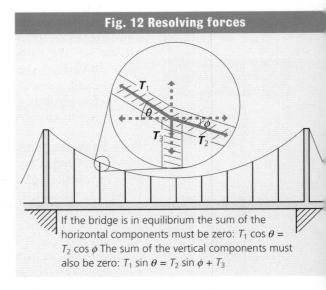

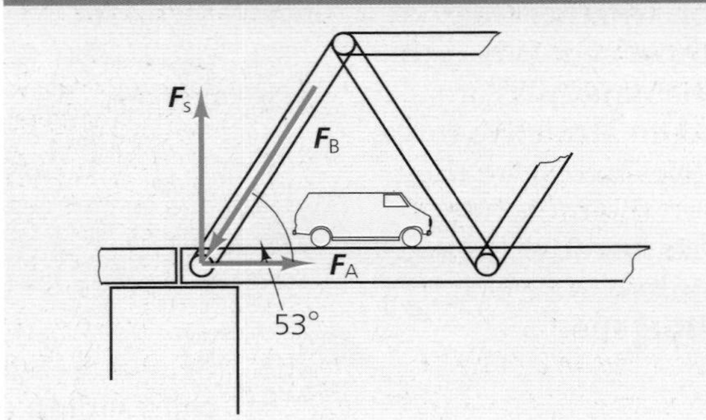

F_S
F_B
F_A
53°

9 Study Fig. 10. Given that F_A is 3000 N and F_B is 5000 N, what is the magnitude of F_s?

In reality, friction will act at the joint, so $\boldsymbol{F}_s$ will not be vertical. Suppose that, with the bridge under load, $\boldsymbol{F}_B$ increases to 8000 N and $\boldsymbol{F}_A$ = 3500 N. In order to find the contact force required to maintain equilibrium, we can use a scale drawing or the cosine rule (Fig. 11). More complex problems can be simplified by resolving forces into horizontal and vertical components (see Chapter 1). At equilibrium, the sum of all the horizontal components must be zero, and the sum of all the vertical components must be zero (Fig. 12).

Fig. 11 Scale drawing vectors

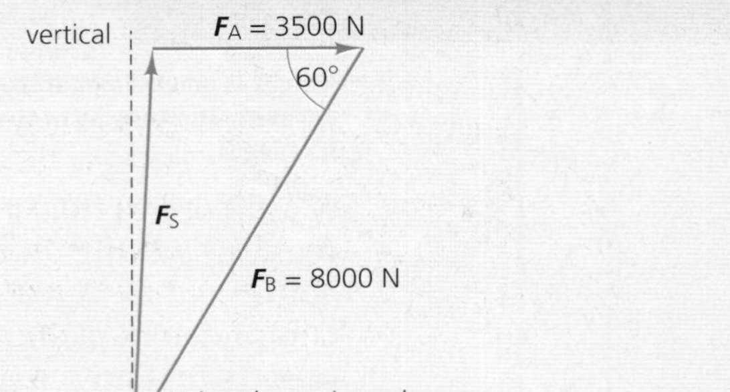

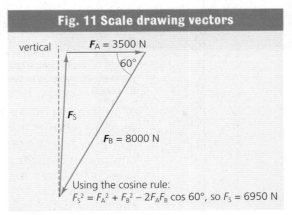

vertical
F_A = 3500 N
60°
F_S
F_B = 8000 N

Using the cosine rule:
$F_S^2 = F_A^2 + F_B^2 - 2F_AF_B \cos 60°$, so F_S = 6950 N

10 A car of mass 1000 kg is parked on a ramp inclined at 15° to the horizontal. If the car is in equilibrium, find the normal contact force and the frictional force between the car and the road.

Fig. 12 Resolving forces

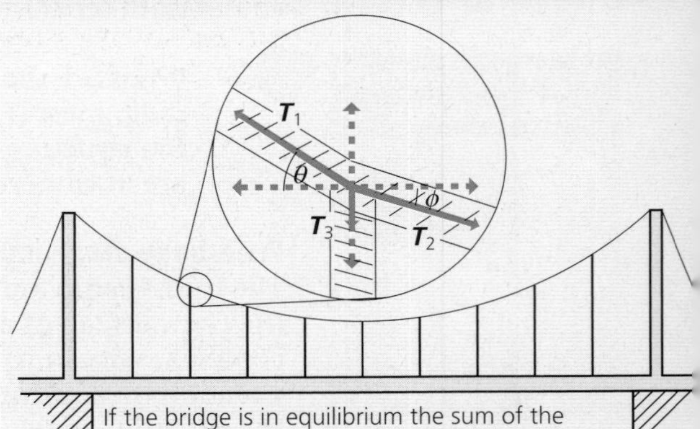

T_1
θ
ϕ
T_3
T_2

If the bridge is in equilibrium the sum of the horizontal components must be zero: $T_1 \cos\theta = T_2 \cos\phi$ The sum of the vertical components must also be zero: $T_1 \sin\theta = T_2 \sin\phi + T_3$

Key ideas

- The resultant force on an object is found by the vector addition of all the forces acting on it.
- An object which is stationary, or moving at constant velocity, is in equilibrium.
- At equilibrium, there is no resultant force acting on the object and the sum of both the horizontal and vertical components must be zero.

2.3 Forces in balance

Sailboarding can be exhilarating. There is no rudder so you have to steer by tilting the sail. In very light winds you can stand upright, but when the wind gets stronger you have to lean into it. Then the sail tries to lift you and the board out of the water. This reduces the drag and the board gets faster. Speeds of up to 45 km h^{-1} are possible. Staying upright is a considerable challenge at first. You have to balance all the forces that are acting on you.

Buoyancy

When a sailboard rests on the beach, its weight is opposed by the normal contact force from the sand. Once on the water, a buoyancy force, the **upthrust**, acts on the sailboard. All objects that are partly, or wholly, submerged in a fluid experience this force. Upthrust is caused by the pressure that the fluid exerts on the object. Pressure is the average force per unit area. It is a **scalar** rather than a vector quantity. At a given depth it acts equally in all directions. The force acts at right angles to the surface of any object that is submerged in the fluid (Fig. 13).

Fig. 13 Origin of upthrust

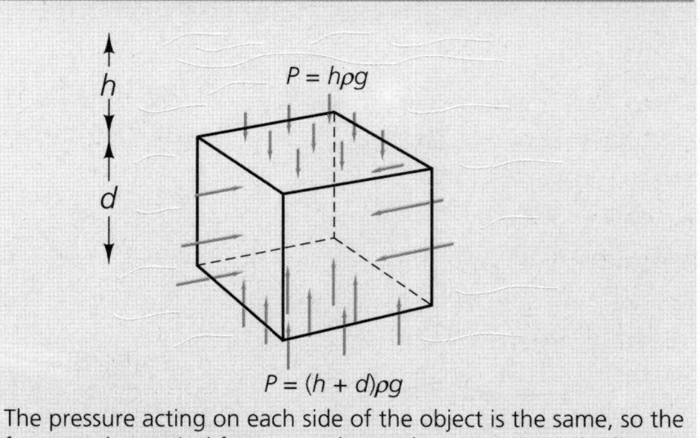

h
d
P = hρg
P = (h + d)ρg

The pressure acting on each side of the object is the same, so the force on the vertical faces cancel out. The pressure on the lower face is greater than that on the upper face.

Upthrust is due to the difference in fluid pressure between the top and bottom of an object. The fluid pressure at a depth of h metres in a fluid of density ρ kg m^{-3} is $h\rho g$.

If the object has a depth d, the extra pressure, P, on the lower surface, area A, is:

$$P = (h + d)\rho g - h\rho g = d\rho g$$

As force = pressure × area, the upthrust, U, is given by:

$$U = P \times A$$
$$U = d\rho g \times A$$
$$U = dA\rho \times g$$
$$U = V\rho g$$

The upthrust, which acts vertically upwards, is equal to the weight of the volume of fluid displaced by the object. If it is large enough, it will balance the weight of the object and the object will float (Fig. 14). A sailboard floats when it has displaced its own weight of water.

Some high performance sailboards cannot displace enough water to float under the weight of a person. They can only 'float' when the board is moving, so they rely on a component of the wind's force to stop them from sinking.

Fig. 14 Keeping afloat

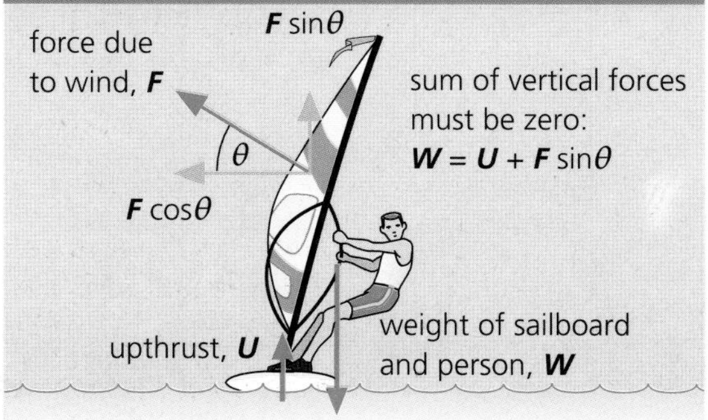

force due to wind, F
F sinθ
θ
F cosθ
sum of vertical forces must be zero: W = U + F sinθ
upthrust, U
weight of sailboard and person, W

Drag

Dead-running is sailing with the wind directly behind you. The force exerted by the wind depends on the density of the air and the area of the sail. The size of the force is also approximately proportional to the wind's velocity squared. The velocity is measured relative to the sailboard, so the faster the sailboard travels on a dead-run, the less force the wind exerts (Fig. 15).

The same principles apply to objects moving through still air. As a bicycle and cyclist move through the atmosphere they have to push the air out of the way. This produces a force known as drag, or in this case, air resistance. The size of the drag is proportional to the square of the relative velocity between bike and air.

Air resistance always acts to reduce the relative motion between the object and the air. The air will exert the same drag force on you whether you are cycling at 10 m s^{-1} on a still day, or if you are stationary in a 10 m s^{-1} wind. Air resistance is only zero when there is no relative motion between the object and the air.

Fig. 15 Apparent wind

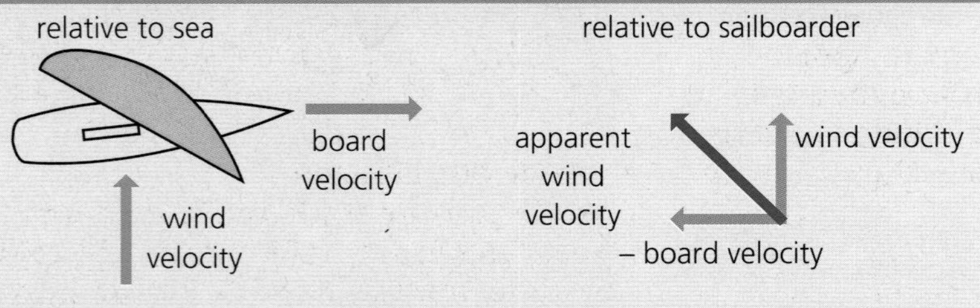
relative to sea
relative to sailboarder
board velocity
wind velocity
apparent wind velocity
wind velocity
– board velocity

When the sailboard moves, the force due to air resistance is a combination of its movement through the air and the wind direction.

Aerodynamic forces

A force caused by the air flow across the sail means that a sailboard can also move into the wind.

As a fluid flows over a surface it exerts a pressure on it. The pressure depends on the speed of the flow. The quicker the flow, the lower the pressure – this phenomenon is called the Bernoulli Effect. Because a curved surface has a faster flow on one side than the other, the Bernoulli effect causes a force at right angles to the flow (Fig. 16). This force allows sailboards to move into the wind. The same effect is used to give aircraft lift and to make wind turbines rotate.

Fig. 16 Aerodynamic lift

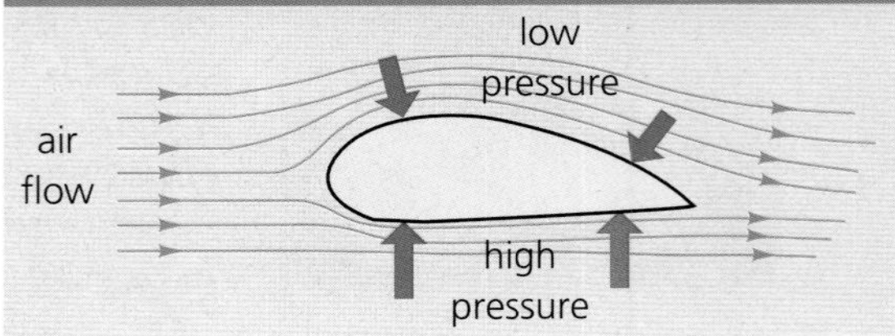
low pressure
air flow
high pressure

Fig. 17 Tacking into the wind

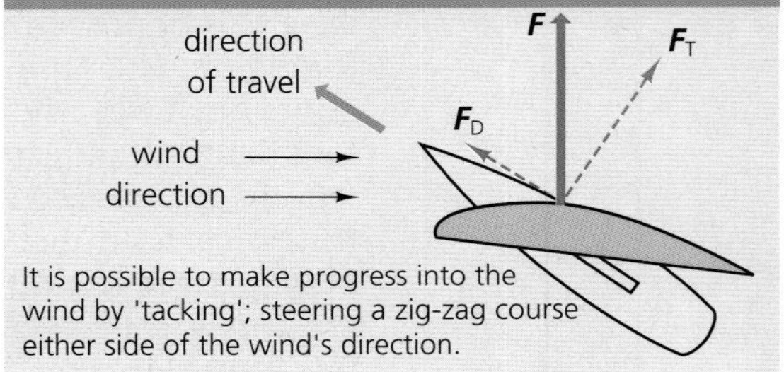
direction of travel
F
F_T
F_D
wind direction

It is possible to make progress into the wind by 'tacking'; steering a zig-zag course either side of the wind's direction.

For a sailboard, the wind blowing over the curved surface of the sail creates a lower pressure on the convex side. The perpendicular force on the sail can be split into two components; a transverse force, $\boldsymbol{F}_T$, and a driving force, $\boldsymbol{F}_D$ (Fig. 17).

11 Explain how a horizontal wind can lift the roof off a house.

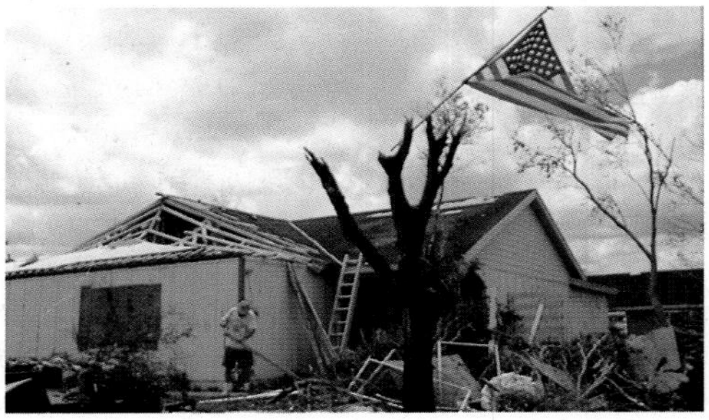

Key ideas

- Fluids exert an upthrust on any submerged objects. The upthrust is equal to the weight of fluid displaced.
- Air resistance acts to oppose the motion of an object relative to the air.
- Increasing the speed of flow of a fluid across a surface reduces the pressure exerted on that surface.

The moment of a force

The transverse force acting on the sail (Fig. 17) tends to tip the sail and mast sideways. This turning effect of a force is called its **moment**. The moment of a force about a given point depends on the size of the force and the perpendicular distance between the point and the line of action of the force:

moment (N m) = force (N) × perpendicular distance of point from line of action of force (m)

Fig. 18 Staying upright

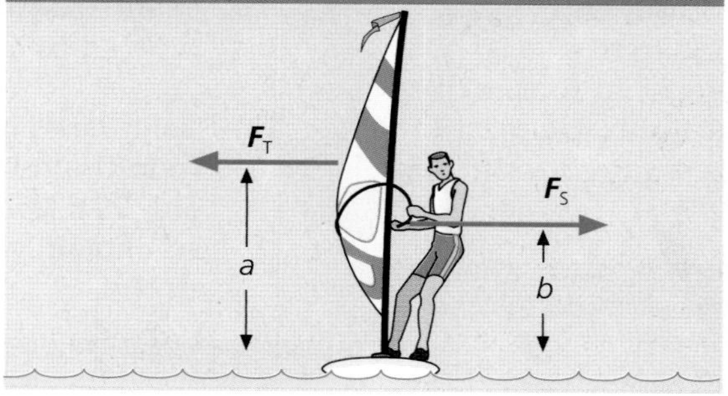

F_T
a
F_S
b

The transverse force of the wind, F_T, tends to tip the sailboard in an anticlockwise direction (Fig. 18). If the sailboard is to stay upright, the windsurfer has to apply a force, F_S, that has a clockwise moment. The mast pivots freely where it joins the board. The moments acting about that point are:

anticlockwise moment, $= F_T \times a$
clockwise moment, $= F_S \times b$

For equilibrium, the moments must balance, so $F_T \times a = F_S \times b$.

There may be several forces causing turning effects. If an object is to be in equilibrium, all the clockwise moments must be balanced by the anticlockwise moments. This is known as the principle of moments:

For an object to be in equilibrium, the sum of the clockwise moments about any point must be equal to the sum of the anticlockwise moments about that point.

It is important to remember that the moment depends on the *perpendicular* distance from the force to the pivot. As the wind speed increases, the boardsailor needs to lean at an increasingly large angle into the wind. We can see why this is if we treat the board and the sailor as one object. The important external forces acting are the weight of the sailor, W_s, and the force of the wind on the sail, F_s.

As F_s gets larger, the anti-clockwise turning moment increases (Fig. 19). To maintain balance, the boardsailor has to increase the clockwise turning moment by increasing the perpendicular distance, a, between the line of action of his weight and the pivot by leaning out as far as possible.

Fig. 19 Using your weight

F_s
b
a
W_s

Torque and couples

The flexible joint where the mast joins the board is unlikely to be completely free of friction. The effect of this friction is to oppose rotation. It is known as a frictional torque. A torque may also cause rotation. When you grip a screwdriver to tighten a screw you are exerting a frictional torque on it. A torque produces or opposes rotation but does not cause any linear acceleration.

Two equal forces that act in opposite directions do not cause any linear acceleration. However, if they do not pass through the same point they will cause rotation. A pair of forces like this are known as a couple. The torque produced by a couple is equal to the magnitude of the force multiplied by the distance between them (Fig. 20, page 26). An important example of a couple is the turning effect produced in an electric motor.

Fig. 20 Turning effect of a couple

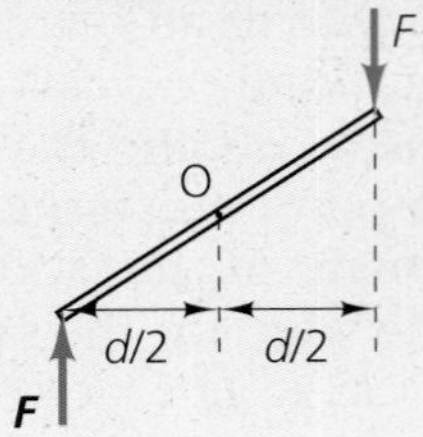
F
O
d/2
d/2
F

The moment of each force about O is $\boldsymbol{F} \times d/2$. The total turning effort, or torque = $2 \times \boldsymbol{F} \times d/2 = \boldsymbol{F} \times d$.

Worked example

The mass of the rig on a sailboard is 20 kg and its centre of gravity is 2 m from the bottom end. The rig is pulled into position using a rope which is connected to the mast, 1.5 m from the bottom end, and is initially at an angle of 25° to the horizontal. There is a frictional torque of 50 N m in the joint that holds the mast to the board. What force is required to lift the rig from the horizontal?

Fig. 21 Example of turning forces

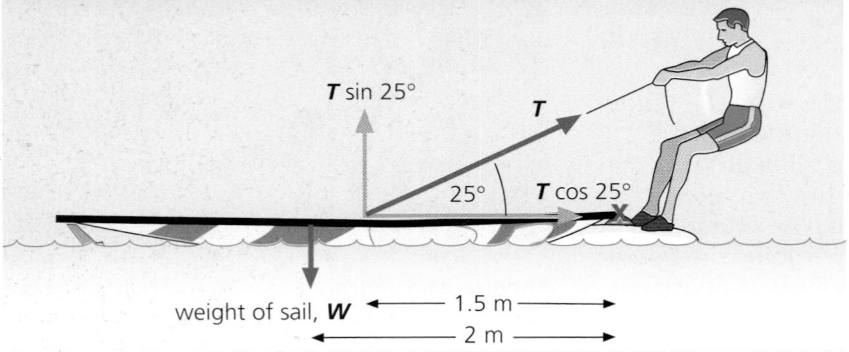
T sin 25°
T
25°
T cos 25°
weight of sail, W
1.5 m
2 m

The first step in all mechanics problems is to draw a diagram (Fig. 21) showing all the relevant forces. The next step is to simplify the forces. In this case, the tension, T, can be resolved into horizontal and vertical components. (The horizontal component of the tension, $T \cos 25°$, has no moment since it passes through X.) We calculate the moments of the forces about the joint, X. The sum of the anticlockwise moments is:

$$200 \text{ N} \times 2 \text{ m} + \text{frictional torque} = 450 \text{ N m}$$

The sum of the clockwise moments is:

$$T \sin 25° \text{ N} \times 1.5 \text{ m} = 0.634\ T \text{ N m}$$

These moments balance when $0.634\ T = 450$. The rig can be lifted when $T > 710$ N.

12 **Explain why the tension in a sailboard rope decreases as the sail is lifted to a vertical position.**

13 **Sailboards use a daggerboard to help them to remain stable (see Fig. 22). Use the idea of moments to explain why the daggerboard is useful.**

Fig. 22 Anatomy of a sailboard

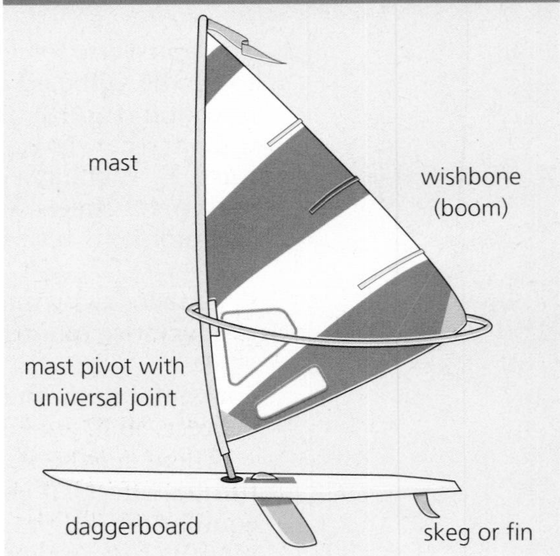
mast
wishbone
(boom)
mast pivot with
universal joint
daggerboard
skeg or fin

Key ideas

- The moment, or turning effect, of a force about a point is equal to the force multiplied by the perpendicular distance from the point to the line of action of the force.
- For an object to be in equilibrium the sum of the moments about a point must be zero; i.e. the sum of the clockwise moments must balance the sum of the anticlockwise moments.

Driving forces

In a car crash, your life could be saved by a small, gas-filled balloon. Most modern cars are equipped with an 'air bag', fitted in the centre of the steering wheel, which inflates during a collision to protect the driver's head. The air bag has to be electronically triggered, and then chemically inflated, in less than 50 milliseconds (ms). It takes you 200 ms to blink an eye.

Design features such as the air bag help to explain why UK roads are at their safest level since records began in 1926 (Fig. 1). Despite an enormous increase in traffic, the number of annual road fatalities has actually decreased. This rate has been kept down by developments in two areas of road safety.

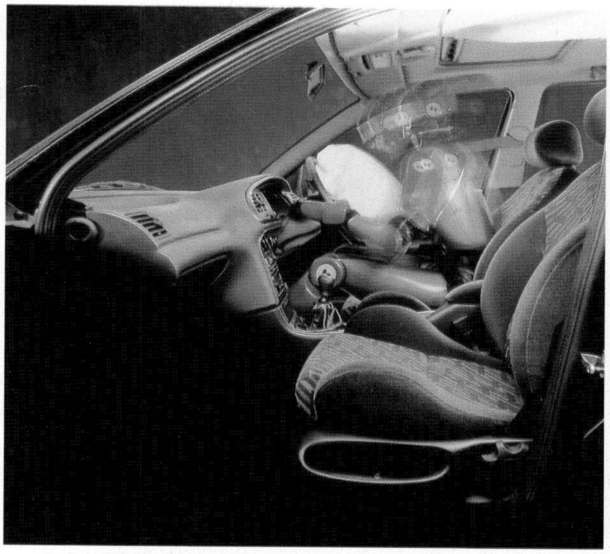

An air bag is tested using one of Ford's dummies.

Fig. 1 Trends in UK road deaths

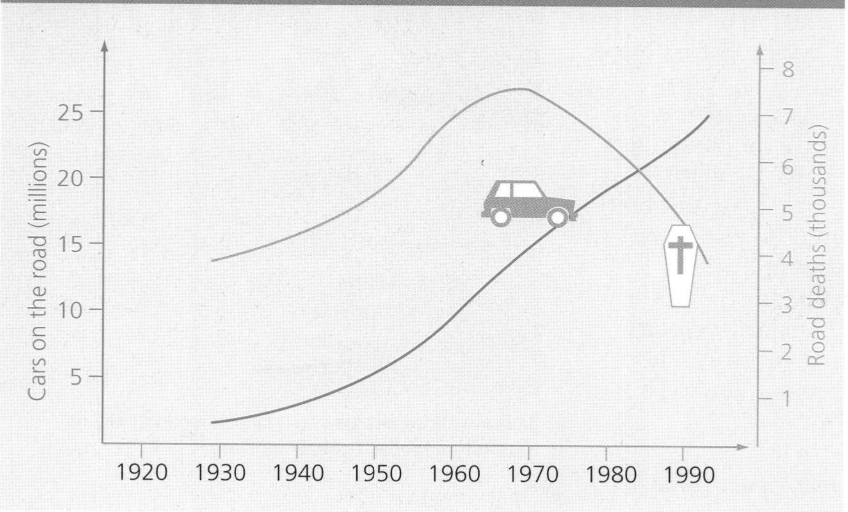
Cars on the road (millions)
25
20
15
10
5
Road deaths (thousands)
8
7
6
5
4
3
2
1
1920
1930
1940
1950
1960
1970
1980
1990

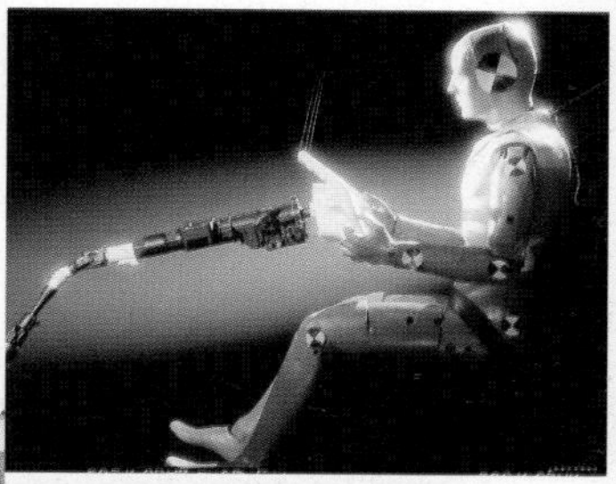

The roll bar (1966), the collapsible steering column (1973) and antilock braking (1984) have all helped improve secondary safety.

Primary safety measures aim to stop accidents happening. Cars are now equipped with better brakes, steering and suspension systems, while driver visibility has been improved through the development of modern headlights, window washers and demisters. Probably the most significant advance in primary safety is the improvement of road design, with better layout, surfaces and street lighting.

Secondary safety features are intended to reduce the injuries of those involved in an accident. In a crash, it is important that the **kinetic energy** of the vehicle is absorbed mainly in the bonnet and boot, while the passenger compartment stays rigid. Seat belts and air bags are designed to restrain passengers and make their deceleration as controlled as possible, avoiding excessive forces on the head or abdomen.

In an effort to improve safety, accident research teams from manufacturers such as Volvo have analysed thousands of crashes using high-speed video photography and computers. The results of these tests can be interpreted using Newton's laws of motion.

3.1 Learning objectives

After working through this chapter, you should be able to:

- **recall** Newton's laws of motion;
- **explain** the motion of real objects in terms of Newton's laws;
- **use** Newton's second law to calculate the forces needed to accelerate objects;
- **use** the principle of momentum conservation;
- **apply** the principle of conservation of energy to problems of motion;
- **calculate** the mechanical work done by a force, and the power developed;
- **define** the newton and the joule.

3.2 Staying alive

Newton's first law

Head-on collisions are the most common cause of severe and fatal injuries in car accidents. A front-end crash into a stationary object at only 30 km h^{-1} (19 mph) can cause serious injury. Modern cars have a range of 'occupant restraint systems' designed to decelerate passengers in a controlled way. Without them, passengers would carry on at their original velocity, until the steering wheel or the windscreen decelerated them! It would be wrong to say that the passengers are being hurled forward by the force of the crash. Passengers continue at constant velocity until a force changes their motion. The people in the car are obeying Newton's first law:

An object will remain at rest, or continue to move with uniform velocity, unless acted upon by an external, resultant force.

At first sight, many objects do not appear to obey Newton's first law. If you remove the driving force from a car, it will not keep moving at constant velocity; turn off the engine and the car will quickly come to a stop. This is because a combination of air-resistance and frictional forces make up the 'external force'. On Earth it is difficult to avoid these forces, but in space, where there is negligible resistance to motion, Newton's first law can be observed more clearly.

Space-walking astronauts experience virtually no restrictive forces to their motion.

1 In a campaign to encourage people to wear rear-seat safety belts, the Department of Transport claimed that, in an accident, 'An adult passenger sitting in the back of a car will be thrown forward with a force of $3\frac{1}{2}$ tonnes. That's the weight of an elephant.'
Rewrite this safety warning using Newton's first law.

2 Head-restraints are designed to prevent neck injuries. Why are they especially helpful in rear-impact accidents?

Momentum

A quarter of all accidents involve collisions from the side. Many cars now have reinforced bars in the doors to try to maintain a survival space after a collision. The effectiveness of the bars depends on how large the forces are. A greater force is needed to stop a 100 km h^{-1} juggernaut than a 15 km h^{-1} bicycle! Clearly, the size of the forces in a crash will depend on the mass and the velocity of the vehicles. The product of mass and velocity is called **momentum**:

$$\text{momentum} = \text{mass} \times \text{velocity}$$
$$p = mv$$

Momentum is measured in kg m s^{-1}.

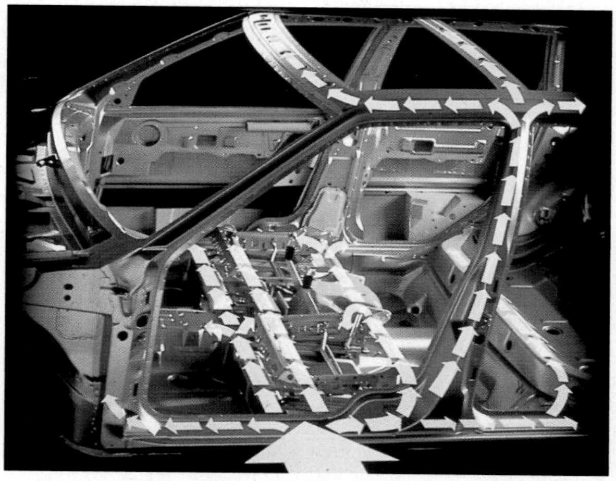

In a side-on crash there is only about 20 cm between the point of impact and the occupant. Volvo's Side Impact Protection System (SIPS) transmits the force of an impact around the roof and floor of the car.

Newton's second law

The more momentum an object has, the harder it is to stop it. If the object has to lose all of its momentum quickly, as in a crash, the force needed will be even greater. Newton's second law puts this formally:

The rate of change of momentum of a body is directly proportional to the external, resultant force acting upon it. The change of momentum takes place in the direction of that force.

Fig. 2 Force and acceleration

A car accelerating due to a force F. It starts with velocity u and after a time t it has a velocity v.

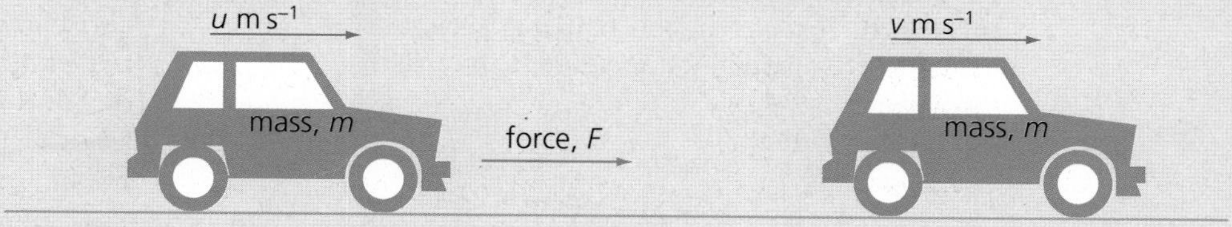

u m s⁻¹
mass, m
force, F
v m s⁻¹
mass, m

Newton's second law says that force is proportional to the rate of change of momentum.

We can express Newton's second law in symbols: ▶ $F \propto \dfrac{\Delta p}{\Delta t}$

The change in momentum is: ▶ $\Delta p = m_2 v - m_1 u$

So, for a steady change over a time interval, t: ▶ $F \propto \dfrac{m_2 v - m_1 u}{t}$

If the mass of the object does not change we can substitute m for m_1 and m_2: ▶ $F \propto \dfrac{m(v-u)}{t}$

Acceleration, $a = \dfrac{v-u}{t}$, so: ▶ $F \propto ma$

Putting in a constant, k, we get: ▶ $F = kma$

One newton is defined as the force that will cause an acceleration of 1 m s^{-2} when it is applied to a mass of 1 kg. This means k is always equal to 1, so: ▶ $F = ma$

If the mass of the object changes, as in the case of a rocket using up fuel, you need to use the full statement of Newton's second law. The mass of a car does not change significantly as it drives along, so Newton's second law simplifies to $F = ma$.

M1 CAW

A Lamborghini Diablo has a mass of 1449 kg and can accelerate from 0 to 60 mph (26.8 m s⁻¹) in 3.9 s.

We can use $F = ma$ to calculate the average resultant force required by a Lamborghini Diablo to achieve its acceleration. In S.I. units:

$$a = \frac{v - u}{t} = \frac{26.8\ \text{m s}^{-1} - 0\ \text{m s}^{-1}}{3.9\ \text{s}} = 6.88\ \text{m s}^{-2}$$

Therefore, the average resultant force on the car has to be:

$$F = ma = 1449\ \text{kg} \times 6.88\ \text{m s}^{-2} = 9970\ \text{N}$$

The forces that act on a car and its occupants during an accident can be much larger than this. If the Lamborghini is involved in a crash, its speed could drop from 60 mph (26.8 m s^{-1}) to zero in less than one tenth of a second. This is an acceleration of:

$$a = \frac{v - u}{t} = \frac{0 - 26.8\ \text{m s}^{-1}}{0.1\ \text{s}} = -268\ \text{m s}^{-2}$$

The avarage force on the car is given by:

$$F = ma = 1449\ \text{kg} \times -268\ \text{m s}^{-2} = -390\ 000\ \text{N}$$

The negative sign shows that the force acts in the opposite direction to the velocity; it is a 'retarding' force.

In a head-on collision, even at moderate speed, the deceleration can be as high as 200 m s^{-2}. This is 20 times the acceleration due to the Earth's gravity, g. The force on a passenger will be roughly 20 times their weight.

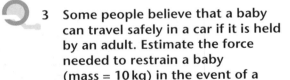

3 **Some people believe that a baby can travel safely in a car if it is held by an adult. Estimate the force needed to restrain a baby (mass = 10 kg) in the event of a crash.**

4 ***The Highway Code*** **claims that you need 23 m to come to rest if you make an emergency stop at a speed of 30 mph (48.3 km h^{-1}). Nine metres of this is 'thinking distance', before you apply the brakes. What average breaking force is needed if the mass of the car is 1500 kg? (Hint: you will need to find the average deceleration of the car.)**

Resistive forces

In reality, the Lamborghini Diablo must provide a larger driving force than 9970 N because it must also overcome forces holding the car back. When a vehicle is being driven on a flat, straight road, there are two forces opposing its motion (Fig. 3):

- **Air resistance**: This 'drag' force depends on the size and shape of the vehicle and is roughly proportional to the squared speed of the car;
- **Frictional force**: This 'rolling resistance' is roughly proportional to speed.

Fig. 3 Horizontal forces acting on a moving vehicle

resultant force, F
air resistance, A
rolling friction, R
driving force, D

The resultant force on the car, $F = D - A - R$. When a car is travelling at constant velocity, F must be zero, so $D = A + R$.

Reducing the force

We can use Newton's second law to calculate the force on a passenger in a car crash. During the crash the force will vary, but the average force will be

$$F = \frac{\text{final momentum} - \text{initial momentum}}{\text{time taken to decelerate}}$$

$$= \frac{\Delta(mv)}{\Delta t}$$

The initial momentum depends on the velocity of the car; the final momentum is zero. Therefore all that we can do to reduce the force is to increase the time over which the collision occurs. Design features such as crumple zones, collapsible steering columns and air bags all increase the time taken for the passenger to come to a stop. Many people believe that modern cars are 'weak' and too easily damaged in a crash. In fact they are designed so that the bonnet and boot deform relatively easily. It is this 'weakness' that saves lives.

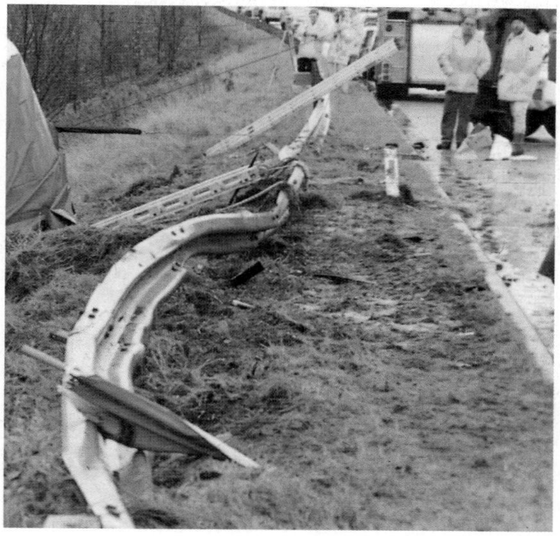

5 Motorway crash barriers are designed to deform as a vehicle hits them (as above). Use Newton's second law to explain why this is safer than a rigid safety barrier.

TP630
30MPH

Newton's third law

When a car hits a stationary object, the front of the car stops almost instantly. The passenger compartment takes longer to stop; its deceleration changes as the front of the car crumples. For a car travelling at 60 km h^{-1} (less than 40 mph) the deceleration may peak at 60g but it is likely to average about 20g over the duration of the crash (around 100 ms).

Crumple zones reduce the deceleration of the passenger compartment.

Fig. 4 Deceleration of the passenger compartment during a crash

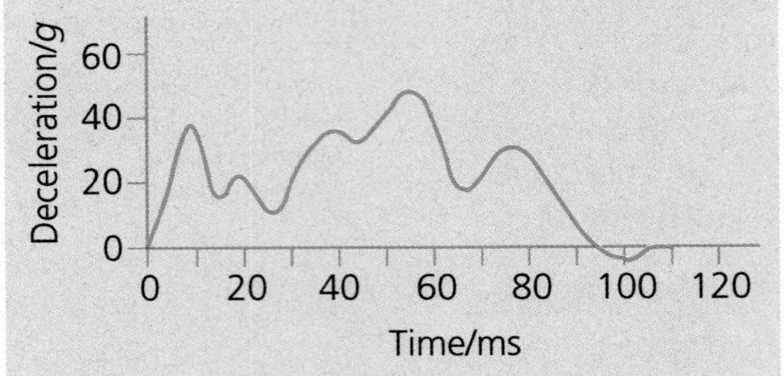

Deceleration/g
60
40
20
0
0
20
40
60
80
100
120
Time/ms

Fig. 5 Forces in a seat belt system

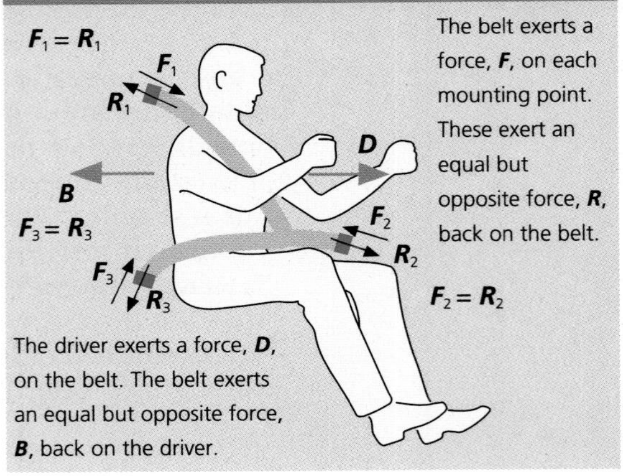

$F_1 = R_1$
F_1
R_1
D
B
$F_3 = R_3$
F_2
R_2
F_3
R_3
$F_2 = R_2$
The belt exerts a force, F, on each mounting point. These exert an equal but opposite force, R, back on the belt.
The driver exerts a force, D, on the belt. The belt exerts an equal but opposite force, B, back on the driver.

A seat belt can reduce the average deceleration on the driver to between $10g$ and $15g$. The belt achieves this because of its **elasticity**. It stretches slightly during the collision. The tension in the belt then restrains the driver. As the driver is exerting a force on the seat belt, the seat belt is exerting an equal but opposite force on the driver (Fig. 5).

The seat belt exerts a force on each of its three mounting points, which in turn pull back on the belt. These pairs of forces are examples of Newton's third law:

When body A exerts a force on body B, body B exerts an equal but opposite force on body A.

This law is often written as 'Every action has an equal and opposite reaction'. This can be misleading. It is important to realise that the two forces, the 'action' and the 'reaction', act on different objects. If the equal and opposite forces acted on the same object there would never be a resultant force and, by Newton's first law, nothing would ever accelerate. The law is not only relevant when two objects are in contact; it also applies when the interaction is at a distance, perhaps due to gravitational attraction.

6 Sketch a parked car and draw in arrows to show the forces acting on:
a the car;
b the Earth.
Carefully explain which pairs of forces are equal according to:
c Newton's first law;
d Newton's third law.

7 What force pushes a car forward as it accelerates?

Key ideas

- Newton's first law of motion states:
  An object will remain at rest, or continue to move with uniform velocity, unless acted upon by an external, resultant force.
- Newton's second law of motion states:
  The rate of change of momentum of a body is directly proportional to the external, resultant force acting upon it. The change of momentum takes place in the direction of that force.
- For constant mass, $F = ma$.

  A force of 1 N will accelerate a mass of 1 kg at a rate of 1 m s^{-2}.
- Newton's third law states:
  If body A exerts a force on body B, then body B exerts an equal but opposite force back on body A.

3.3 Stopping safely

Work

It is obviously better to stop a car safely, before a crash ever takes place. A reliable braking system is the most important safety mechanism in a car. The frictional forces need to be very large if the car is to stop in a very short distance.

We can calculate how much energy is transferred by using the concept of **work**. In physics the word 'work' has a particular meaning. Physicists say that work is done when a force moves through a distance. If you push a car along a road you have done some work against resistive forces. If you lift a mass you have done some work against the force of gravity.

work done = force × distance moved in the direction of the force

$$W = Fs$$

F is measured in newtons and s is in metres. The unit of work is the joule (1 J = 1 N m).

Although the force and the distance moved in a given direction are both vector quantities, work is a **scalar** quantity (see Chapter 1). If the directions of the force and the displacement are at an angle θ, the equation for work becomes:

$$W = Fs \cos\theta \quad \text{(Fig. 6)}$$

Fig. 6 Work done at an angle θ

There is no movement in the direction of the vertical component, $F \sin\theta$, so this part of the force does no work. The tractor moves a horizontal distance, s. The horizontal component of the force is $F \cos\theta$, so the work done = $F \cos\theta \times s$.

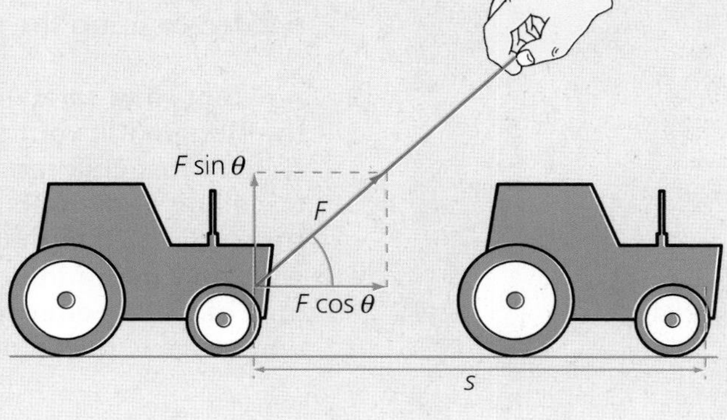
F sin θ
F
F cos θ
s

Brake pads (seen glowing above) can get extremely hot as the kinetic energy of the car is transferred to them.

When the road conditions are good, a car travelling at 70 mph (31 m s^{-1}) can usually be brought safely to a halt in 75 m. To calculate the work done we need to find the force required. The acceleration can be found using the equations of linear motion:

$$v^2 = u^2 + 2as$$

$$\text{or, } a = \frac{v^2 - u^2}{2s}$$

since $v = 0$, $u = 31$ m s^{-1} and $s = 75$ m:

$$a = -\frac{(31 \text{ m s}^{-1})^2}{2 \times 75 \text{ m}}$$
$$= -6.4 \text{ m s}^{-2}$$

For a car of mass 1000 kg the average braking force is given by:

$$F = ma$$
$$= 1000 \text{ kg} \times 6.4 \text{ m s}^{-2}$$
$$= 6400 \text{ N}$$

The work done is therefore:

$$W = Fs$$
$$= 6400 \text{ N} \times 75 \text{ m}$$
$$= 480 \text{ kJ}$$

Most forces vary with distance. To calculate the total work done by a changing force, we need to divide the total distance moved into short steps, each of length Δx (Fig. 7). If Δx is small enough, the force will not change significantly within each step. The work done in each step is just the force multiplied by Δx. But the force multiplied by Δx is also the area of the rectangle under the curve. To find the total work done we need to add together the work done in each step. This is the sum of the areas of all the rectangular strips. So, for a varying force, the work done is the area beneath the force–distance graph.

Fig. 7 Work done by a changing force

The work done in moving a distance Δx is $F\Delta x$. This is the area of the shaded rectangular strip. The total work done by the changing force in moving through distance s is the area of all such strips, i.e. the total area below the curve.

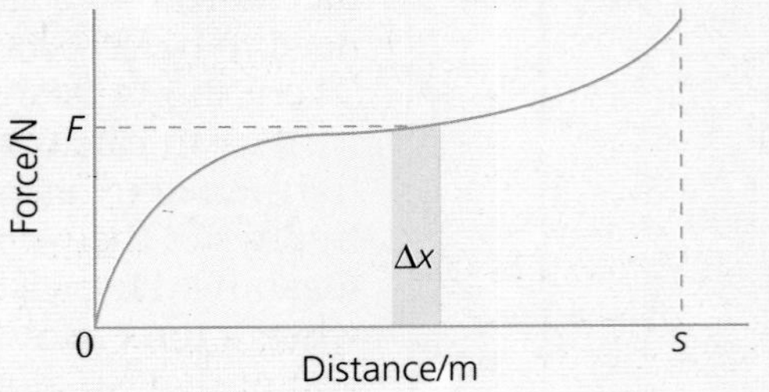

Force/N
F
Δx
0
s
Distance/m

Energy

In physics, an object is said to have **energy** if it can do work. A car may have energy because of its motion (**kinetic energy**), or because of its position (**potential energy**).

Petrol is a very concentrated store of energy, about 50 MJ per litre. This energy can be transferred to kinetic energy of the car by combustion of fuel in the engine. Whenever work is done, energy is transferred. When a car slows down, work is done by the brakes against friction and the car's kinetic energy is transferred to the brakes. The exchange is exact, so the rise in internal energy of the brakes, air and road is equal to the original kinetic energy of the car. This energy balance applies to all situations:

The principle of conservation of energy says that *the total amount of energy in any isolated system is constant.*

It is important to stress the word 'isolated' because energy can flow into, or out of, a system. We couldn't apply the principle just to the car alone, because not all of its kinetic energy transfers to the brakes; some will be transferred to the air and the road.

Fig. 8 An expression for kinetic energy

The amount of energy stored in a moving car depends on its mass and its velocity. Consider the work done against friction as the car slows to a halt:

Suppose a constant frictional force, F, is used to slow the car down over a distance, s. The work done is: ▶ $W = Fs$

In an isolated system, all of this energy must have come from the original kinetic energy of the car, so: ▶ $E_k = W = Fs$

We can replace F using $F = ma$: ▶ $E_k = mas$

and s by using $v^2 = u^2 + 2as$ or $s = \dfrac{v^2 - u^2}{2a}$ ▶ $E_k = ma\dfrac{(u^2 - v^2)}{2a}$

(a is negative: a deceleration) $= \frac{1}{2}mu^2 - \frac{1}{2}mv^2$

The final velocity of the car is zero, so the original kinetic energy of the car was: ▶ $E_k = \frac{1}{2}mu^2$

In general, the kinetic energy of an object of mass m and velocity v is given by: ▶ $E_k = \frac{1}{2}mv^2$

In this proof we assumed that the force was constant, though the final equation works even if the force varies.

8 The stopping distances for cars travelling at 50 mph is given as 38 m in the Highway Code.

a Find the kinetic energy of a van (mass = 2000 kg) moving at 50 mph (22.4 m s^{-1}).

b How much work needs to be done by braking forces to stop the van?

c Calculate the average braking force needed to bring the van to rest.

9 A recent road safety campaign had the slogan 'Kill your speed, not a child'. Most children hit by a car travelling at 40 mph are killed, while those hit at 20 mph usually escape with only minor injuries. Use the idea of kinetic energy to explain why there is such a major change.

Power

In an emergency stop, kinetic energy has to be transferred from the car as quickly as possible. The *rate* at which energy is transferred, or work is done, is known as the power of a system:

$$\text{power} = \frac{\text{work done}}{\text{time taken}}$$
$$= \text{energy transferred per second}$$

Power is measured in joules per second, or watts (W). Most cars can manage a deceleration of around 1*g* ($10\,\mathrm{m\,s^{-2}}$). For a 1000 kg car travelling at 70 mph ($31\,\mathrm{m\,s^{-1}}$), the braking power is considerable:

$$F = ma$$
$$= 1000\ \mathrm{kg} \times 10\ \mathrm{m\,s^{-2}}$$
$$= 10\,000\ \mathrm{N}$$

The stopping distance can be found from:

$$v^2 = u^2 + 2as$$

$$\text{or,}\quad s = \frac{v^2 - u^2}{2a}$$

Since $v = 0$, $u = 31\,\mathrm{m\,s^{-1}}$ and $a = -10\,\mathrm{m\,s^{-2}}$:

$$s = \frac{0 - (31\ \mathrm{m\,s^{-1}})^2}{-20}$$
$$= 48\ \mathrm{m}$$

The time taken to stop can be found from:

$$v = u + at$$

$$\text{or,}\ t = \frac{v - u}{a}$$

$$\text{so,}\ t = \frac{0 - 31\ \mathrm{m\,s^{-1}}}{-10\ \mathrm{m\,s^{-2}}}$$
$$= 3.1\ \mathrm{s}$$

$$\text{power} = \frac{\text{work done}}{\text{time taken}}$$
$$= \frac{10\,000\ \mathrm{N} \times 48\ \mathrm{m}}{3.1\ \mathrm{s}}$$
$$= 155\ \mathrm{kW}$$

In reality the situation is more complex. The safest way of stopping a car is not usually to apply the largest possible force to the brakes; the wheels may stop turning but the car can continue in a skid! Modern cars use an Antilock Braking System, or ABS (Fig. 9).

Fig. 9 Braking force and wheel speed

In an ABS system, sensors are used to calculate wheel speed and deceleration. An electronic unit uses this data to detect when the wheels are about to lock and instead begins releasing and re-applying the brake, up to 10 times per second.

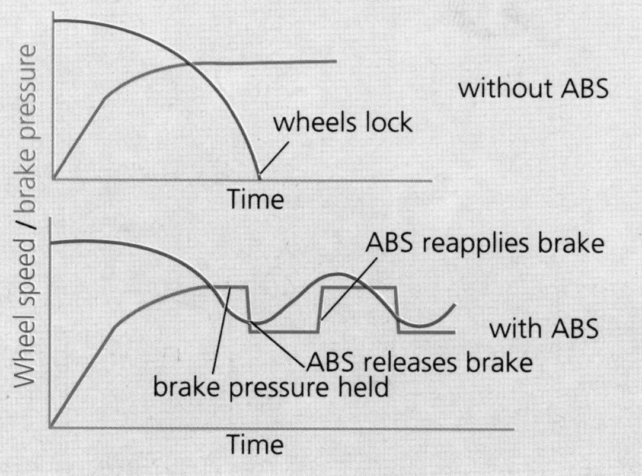

Wheel speed / brake pressure
without ABS
wheels lock
Time
ABS reapplies brake
with ABS
ABS releases brake
brake pressure held
Time

The power of a car engine affects the maximum speed of the car and the maximum force that it can exert on the road.

$$\text{Since power} = \frac{\text{work}}{\text{time}}$$
$$\text{and work} = \text{force} \times \text{distance}$$
$$\text{then power} = \frac{\text{force} \times \text{distance}}{\text{time}}$$
$$= \text{force} \times \text{velocity}$$
$$P = Fv$$

For a given power, an engine can exert a large force at a low speed, or a smaller force at higher speed. A car's gearbox allows you to control this balance.

10 A car has a mass of 1445 kg and its engine can deliver a maximum power of 112 kW.

a Estimate the maximum force that it can exert at 20 mph ($32\,\mathrm{km\,h^{-1}}$), and at 40 mph ($64\,\mathrm{km\,h^{-1}}$).

b What else would you need to know before you could estimate its maximum acceleration at these speeds?

Fig. 10 Working with forces, energy and power

Combined effect of resistive forces for a 38-tonne juggernaut

Road speed (km h^{-1})	Total resistive force (N)
80	4265
88	4740
96	5250
105	5805
113	6395

For a vehicle to accelerate, the force supplied by the engine has to increase. The power output of the engine also has to increase at higher road speeds.

Suppose the vehicle is travelling at a steady 80 km h^{-1} when the driver applies the accelerator pedal.

If the tractive force (i.e. the driving force of the road on the wheels) increases to 5250 N, what would the instantaneous acceleration of the lorry be?

The resultant horizontal force on the lorry is:

5250 N – 4265 N = 985 N

From Newton's second law:

$$a = \frac{F}{m} = \frac{985\ \text{N}}{38 \times 10^3\ \text{kg}} = 0.026\ \text{m s}^{-2}$$

The table above shows how the resistive force increases as the lorry accelerates. As the resultant force gets less, so does the acceleration. Eventually the tractive force and the resistance will be equal again and the lorry will move at a steady speed.

What is the output power of the engine at (a) 80 km h^{-1} (b) 113 km h^{-1}?

The power can be calculated from power = force × velocity

(a) $$v = \frac{80\ \text{km h}^{-1} \times 1000\ \text{m}}{3600\ \text{s}} = 22.2\ \text{m s}^{-1}$$

$$\text{power} = 4265\ \text{N} \times 22.2\ \text{m s}^{-1} = 94.8\ \text{kW}$$

(b) At 113 km h^{-1}, using the same method, power = 201 kW, over twice the output power at 80 km h^{-1}!

The lorry is travelling at 113 km h^{-1} when the engine cuts out suddenly. How much work will the lorry do against the resistive forces as it slows to 80 km h^{-1}?

Since the force varies as the vehicle slows down, it is not possible to use the equation, work = force x distance, directly. An easier approach is to say that the energy to do the work comes from the kinetic energy of the lorry.

Work done against resistance forces = E_k transferred from lorry

$$E_k = \tfrac{1}{2} m(u^2 - v^2) = \tfrac{1}{2} \times 38 \times 10^3\ \text{kg} \times (31.1^2 - 22.2^2)\ \text{m}^2\,\text{s}^{-2} = 9 \times 10^6\ \text{J}$$

Key ideas

- Work is done when a force is moved through a distance in the direction of the force. The work done by a changing force is equivalent to the area under a force vs. distance graph.
- Energy is the capacity to do work.
- The principle of conservation of energy says: 'The total amount of energy in any isolated system is constant'.
- Power is the rate at which work is done.

3.4 Concerning collisions

Fig. 11 Conservation of momentum in a crash

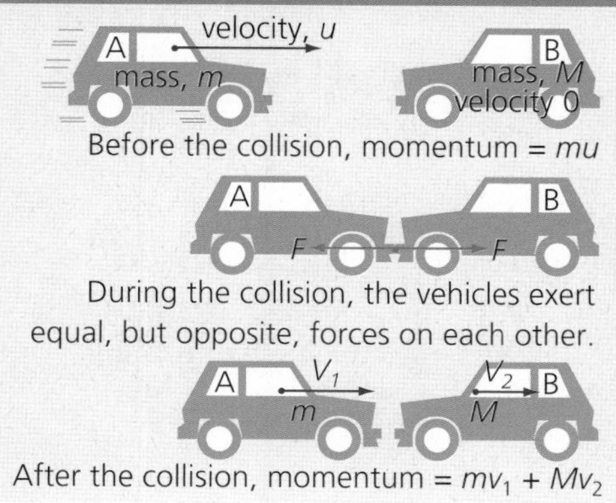

velocity, u
A
mass, m
B
mass, M
velocity 0
Before the collision, momentum = mu
A
B
F
F
During the collision, the vehicles exert equal, but opposite, forces on each other.
A
V_1
m
V_2
B
M
After the collision, momentum = $mv_1 + Mv_2$

The force that acts between the vehicles during the collision causes A to lose momentum and B to gain momentum. The total momentum of the vehicles does not change; $mu = mv_1 + Mv_2$.

Conservation of momentum

When a car travelling at high speed crashes into a stationary car, Newton's second law can be applied to both vehicles:

For Car A
change in momentum = force × time

For Car B
change in momentum = – force × time

Newton's third law says that both vehicles are subject to the same size force. The minus sign shows that they act in opposite directions (momentum is a vector quantity). The time of impact is also the same for both vehicles. Hence, the change in momentum has to be the same size for each car. This means that any momentum lost by the first car will be gained by the second car. Therefore, the total momentum before the crash will be the same as the total momentum after the crash. Of course, external forces such as friction will slow the cars down. If there were *no* external forces, the total momentum in the system would be the same before and after the collision. This fundamental principle is known as the *conservation of momentum*;

The total momentum of a system does not change, provided that no net external force is acting.

It is not always obvious that this law is being obeyed. When a car's brakes are applied and it comes to rest, where has the momentum of the system gone? The answer depends on what you regard as the system. If you are treating the car as the system, then its momentum has not been conserved. If you regard the car *and* the road as the system, there are no significant external forces, since the friction between the two is now an 'internal' force acting between different parts of the same system.

The conservation law suggests that any momentum lost by a car slowing down will be gained by the Earth. Hitting the car brakes must speed up the Earth a little! Of course the reverse is also true; every time a car accelerates away from the traffic lights it pushes the Earth back the other way.

11 During a television advert designed to demonstrate the safety of their cars, a Volvo is driven off a tall building and falls to the ground. How does the conservation of momentum apply here?

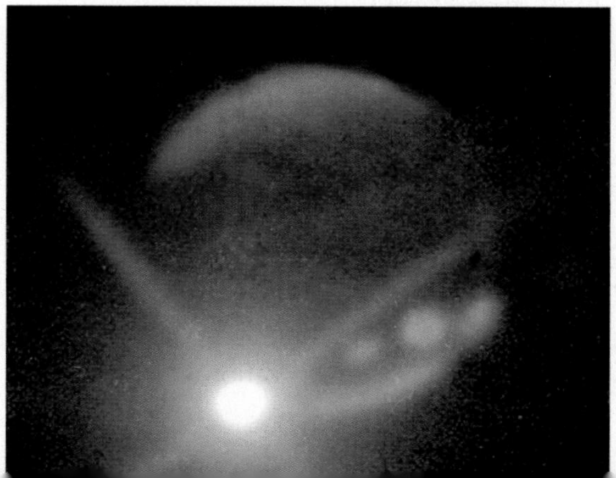

Energy in collisions

The study of collisions is very important in physics, quite apart from its relevance to car crashes. On a microscopic level, collisions between constantly moving gas molecules help us to understand the behaviour of gases. At the other end of the scale, astronomers have learned much by studying the collision of comet Shoemaker-Levy with Jupiter.

Fragment K of Shoemaker-Levy hits Jupiter

Collisions are described as either elastic or inelastic. In an **elastic collision**, no kinetic energy is lost. Collisions between molecules in a gas can be treated as being perfectly elastic. Some collisions between sub-atomic particles are also elastic, such as those that take place between neutrons and carbon atoms in the moderator of a nuclear reactor.

In an **inelastic collision**, kinetic energy is transferred to other forms (Fig. 12). Collisions between everyday objects tend to generate sound and heat and are therefore inelastic. Car crashes fall into this category. Safety features, like crumple zones and air bags, are designed to transfer kinetic energy. As the crumple zones progressively collapse, the kinetic energy of the car does work against the interatomic forces in the metal and is finally transferred as internal energy in the car body. As the driver hits the air bag, the gas escapes and the energy of the driver is transferred to the kinetic energy of the gas molecules.

The conservation of momentum applies to both types of collision. Suppose that in poor visibility on a motorway a car runs into the back of a stationary van. The car is moving at 50 mph (22.2 m s^{-1}) immediately before the impact and has a mass of 1050 kg. The van has a mass of 1200 kg. After the collision the two vehicles are locked together. We can use the conservation of momentum to calculate the speed at which the two vehicles move immediately after the collision.

a The car's momentum before the collision = 1050 kg × 22.2 m s^{-1} = 2.33 × 10^4 kg m s^{-1}

The van is stationary before the collision so it has no momentum. The total momentum before the collision = 2.33 × 10^4 kg m s^{-1}

Conservation of momentum says that the total momentum after the collision must also be 2.33 × 10^4 kg m s^{-1}

Fig. 12 Momentum and energy in inelastic collisions

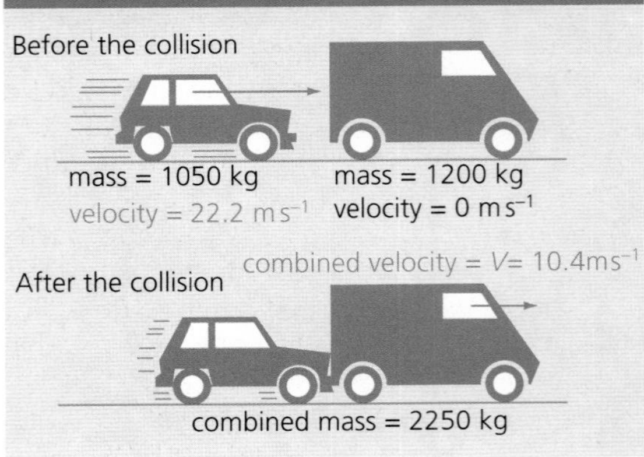
Before the collision
mass = 1050 kg
velocity = 22.2 m s^{-1}
mass = 1200 kg
velocity = 0 m s^{-1}
After the collision
combined velocity = V= 10.4ms^{-1}
combined mass = 2250 kg

b The vehicles are now locked together so that their combined mass is:

$$m = 1050\ \text{kg} + 1200\ \text{kg}$$
$$= 2250\ \text{kg}$$

Since velocity $= \dfrac{\text{momentum}}{\text{mass}}$

the velocity after the collision is:

$$v = \frac{2.33 \times 10^4\ \text{kg m s}^{-1}}{2250\ \text{kg}}$$
$$= 10.4\ \text{m s}^{-1}\ (23\ \text{mph})$$

The kinetic energy before the collision is entirely due to the car:

$$E_k = \tfrac{1}{2}mv^2$$
$$= \tfrac{1}{2} \times 1050\ \text{kg} \times (22.2\ \text{m s}^{-1})^2$$
$$= 2.59 \times 10^5\ \text{J}$$

After the collision:

$$E_k = \tfrac{1}{2} \times 2250\ \text{kg} \times (10.4\ \text{m s}^{-1})^2$$
$$= 1.22 \times 10^5\ \text{J}$$

137 kJ of kinetic energy has been dissipated during the collision; enough energy to throw you about 200 m up into the air.

Key ideas

- Conservation of momentum states: The total momentum of a system does not change, provided that there is no net external force.
- In an elastic collision, kinetic energy is conserved. In an inelastic collision, kinetic energy is transferred to other forms. The conservation of momentum applies to both types of collision.

4 In a spin

A group of psychologists helped to design the £10 million 'Nemesis' ride at Alton Towers. They recommended high accelerations (up to 4*g*) and near collisions to produce a thrilling experience.

The intense competition between theme parks for the most exciting, yet safe, 'white-knuckle ride' is pushing rides to the limits of human endurance. The physics of circular motion can have unpleasant effects on the human body. High accelerations caused by sudden changes in direction have already proved fatal to a number of jet fighter pilots.

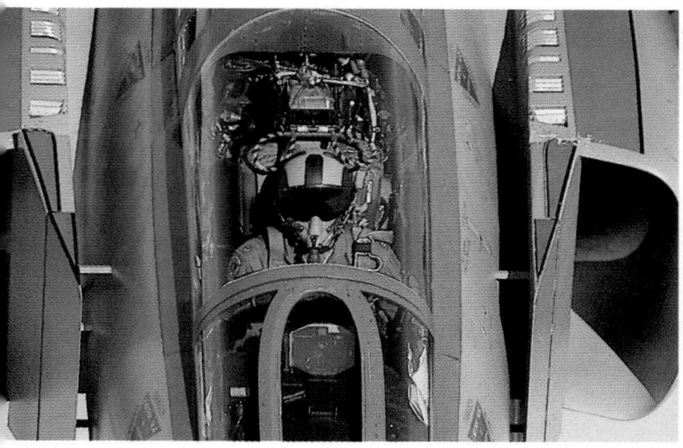

As you go into a high-speed turn in a modern jet fighter your legs and arms begin to feel heavier. It becomes difficult to hold your head up and you start to lose your colour vision. If you don't pull out of the turn, the edges of your field of view can go completely black. It's like looking down a tunnel; the circle of vision gets smaller and smaller until you are completely blind. You lose consciousness soon after that.

4.1 Learning objectives

After working through this chapter, you should be able to:

- **define** angular velocity;
- **apply** Newton's laws to circular motion;
- **explain** the idea of centripetal acceleration;
- **calculate** the forces on objects moving in circles.

4.2 Moving in circles

Angular frequency

RAF scientists at the Institute of Aviation Medicine at Farnborough are studying the effects of high accelerations on jet pilots. The pilots are strapped in a capsule at the end of a long rotor arm and are whirled round in the 'human centrifuge'.

'Spin-drying' the pilot. The size of the pilot's acceleration can be varied by changing the speed of rotation.

When the centrifuge rotates at a constant rate, the pilot moves at a steady speed. Even so, the pilot is still accelerating. Acceleration is the rate of change of velocity (see Chapter 1). Velocity is a vector quantity, so acceleration can arise from a change in either magnitude *or* direction. The direction of the pilot's motion is constantly changing, so the pilot is accelerating.

Fig. 1 Changing velocity

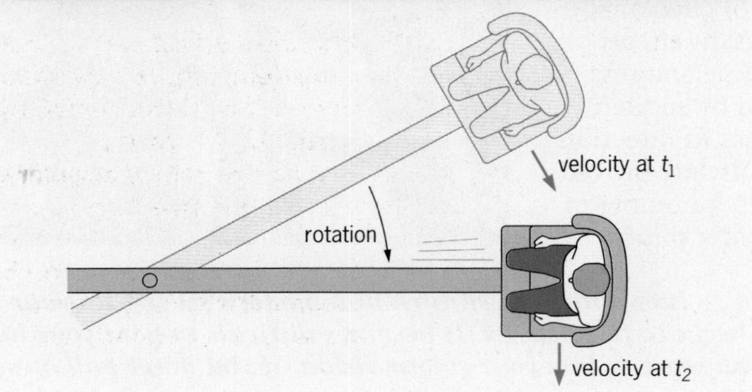
velocity at t_1
rotation
velocity at t_2

At any instant, the direction of the pilot's motion is along the tangent to the circle (Fig. 1). If the restraining straps broke, the pilot would move in a straight line along a tangent, in accordance with Newton's first law.

The size of a pilot's acceleration depends on how quickly the centrifuge spins. The time for one rotation is known as the **period**, T. The number of rotations in a given time is called the **angular frequency**, f ($f = 1/T$). In **S.I.** units, the angular frequency is measured in rotations per second, or Hz.

1 What is the angular frequency of the Earth as it rotates about its axis?

Angular velocity

The rate of turning in car engines or washing machines is measured in revolutions per minute (rpm). For example, the typical 'speed' of a spin drier is 1000 rpm. However, physicists use **angular velocity** to measure how quickly something rotates. Angular velocity is the angle turned through in one second. The angle turned through can be measured in degrees. An alternative unit, preferred by scientists, is the **radian** (Fig. 2).

Fig. 2 The radian

An arc of a circle that is the same length as the radius subtends an angle of one radian.

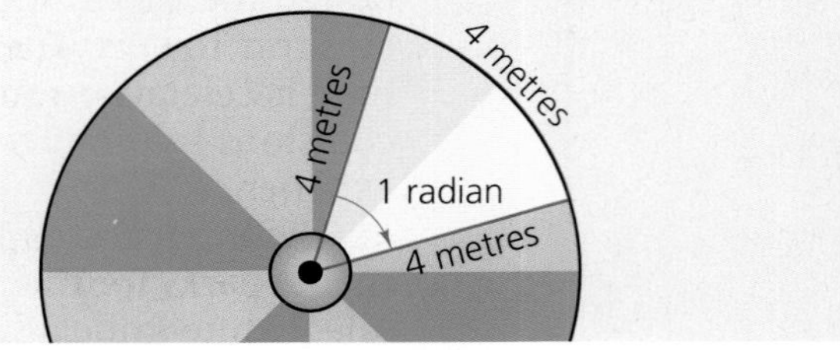
4 metres
4 metres
1 radian
4 metres

One radian is defined as the angle subtended at the centre of a circle by an arc whose length is equal to the radius.

If you ride on a fairground roundabout of radius 4 m, you turn through one radian each time you travel 4 m round the circumference of the circle.

We can find the size of an angle in radians using the ratio:

$$\text{angle (radians)} = \frac{\text{distance on circumference}}{\text{radius of circle}}$$

$$\theta = \frac{s}{r}$$

This can be rewritten to allow us to calculate the distance travelled round a circle, $s = r\theta$.

For one full rotation, the arc length is equal to the circumference, $s = 2\pi r$. The angle you have turned through is therefore:

$$\theta = \frac{2\pi r}{r} = 2\pi \text{ radians}$$

This is equivalent to 360°, so:

$$1 \text{ radian} = \frac{360°}{2\pi} = 57.3° \text{ (to 3 s.f.)}$$

The abbreviation for radian is rad.

$$\text{One degree} = \frac{2\pi}{360} = 0.017 \text{ rad}$$

The angular velocity, ω, is the angle turned through per second. It has units of radians per second. Since a full rotation is equivalent to 2π radians, the angular velocity is $2\pi \times$ the number of rotations per second.

$$\omega = 2\pi f \quad \text{or} \quad \omega = \frac{2\pi}{T}$$

2 **A pilot is in a centrifuge that spins at 10 rpm. What is the pilot's angular velocity in rad s^{-1}?**

3 **What is the angular velocity of the Earth due to its annual orbit of the Sun?**

Angular velocity and linear speed

An object moving at a steady angular velocity has a constant speed. The magnitude of the speed depends on the radius. The link between angular velocity and speed can be deduced from the definition of the radian:

angle turned through, $\theta = \frac{s}{r}$

If this takes t seconds:

$$\text{angular velocity, } \omega = \frac{\theta}{t} = \frac{s/r}{t}$$
$$= \frac{s}{tr} = \frac{\text{speed}}{r}$$

The symbol v is used for the *magnitude* of the linear velocity, i.e. the speed.

$$\omega = \frac{v}{r} \quad \text{or} \quad v = r\omega$$

4 **The United States Air Force uses a centrifuge with a 5 m radius to train their pilots. If the centrifuge has a period of 3 seconds;**
a **what is the pilot's angular velocity?**
b **what is his speed?**

5 **What is the Earth's speed in its orbit around the Sun? (Mean Earth–Sun distance = 14.9 × 10^{10} m)**

Key ideas

- An object moving at constant speed in a circle is accelerating. Its instantaneous velocity is along the tangent to the circle.
- Angular frequency = 1 / period.
- Angles can be measured in radians (2π rad = 360°).
- Angular velocity, $\omega = 2\pi f$ and is measured in radians per second.
- Speed depends on radius and angular velocity, $v = r\omega$.

4.3 Centripetal acceleration

The size of a jet-fighter's acceleration when cornering at high speed is crucial to the safety of the pilot. Above 4*g* (g = 9.8 m s^{-2}), the visual symptoms of grey-out and black-out begin to occur. Theme park rides usually keep the accelerations below 3*g*, though they sometimes touch 4*g* for short periods. The size of the acceleration depends on two factors:

- how sharp the turn is, i.e. the radius of curvature;
- how quickly the plane is travelling.

For an object moving in a circle the change of velocity, $\Delta\boldsymbol{v}$, is always towards the centre of the circle (Fig. 3, p42). Therefore, the acceleration is also towards the centre of the circle. For a small time interval, Δt, the acceleration is given by:

$$\boldsymbol{a} = \frac{\Delta \boldsymbol{v}}{\Delta t}$$

N.B. The symbol $\boldsymbol{v}$ represents the velocity vector. It is used when both the magnitude and the direction of velocity are important. The symbol v is just the magnitude of the velocity, i.e. the speed.

Fig. 3 Accelerating towards the centre

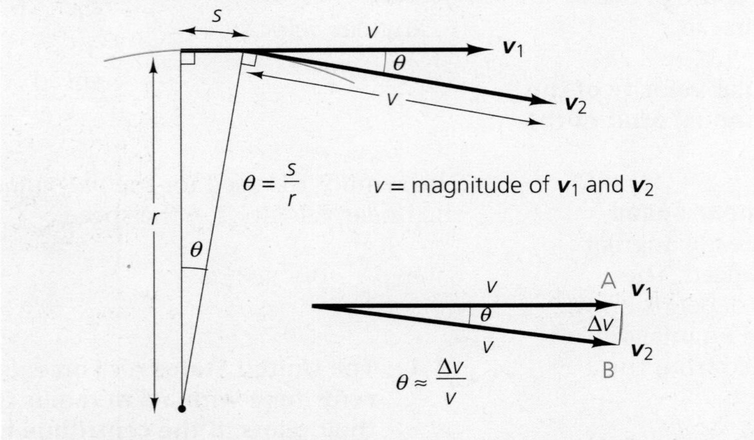
s
v
v1
θ
v
v2
r
θ = s/r
v = magnitude of v1 and v2
θ
v
A
v1
θ
Δv
v
v2
B
θ ≈ Δv/v

In a short time interval, Δt, the plane moves through a small angle, θ

Study the vector triangle in Fig. 3. If the time interval is very small, θ will be a small angle and the vector $\Delta \boldsymbol{v}$ will be almost the same length as the arc BC. Because the object is moving at constant speed, $\boldsymbol{v}_1$ and $\boldsymbol{v}_2$ have the same magnitude, which we write as v. The angle θ, in radians, is therefore given by:

$$\theta = \frac{\Delta v}{v}$$

giving $\Delta v = \theta \times v$

The magnitude of the acceleration is:

$$a = \frac{\Delta v}{\Delta t} = \frac{\theta \times v}{\Delta t}$$

If the object has an angular velocity ω:

$$\theta = \omega \times \Delta t$$

so $$a = \frac{\omega \times \Delta t \times v}{\Delta t} = \omega v$$

We can eliminate either the speed or the angular velocity from this equation using the expression $v = r\omega$:

$$a = r\omega^2 \quad \text{or} \quad a = \frac{v^2}{r}$$

This acceleration is always directed towards the centre of the circle and is known as **centripetal** acceleration.

6 On the 'Thunderlooper' at Alton Towers, passengers hurtle round a 23 m radius loop at speeds of up to 60 mph (26 m s^{-1}). What is their maximum centripetal acceleration?

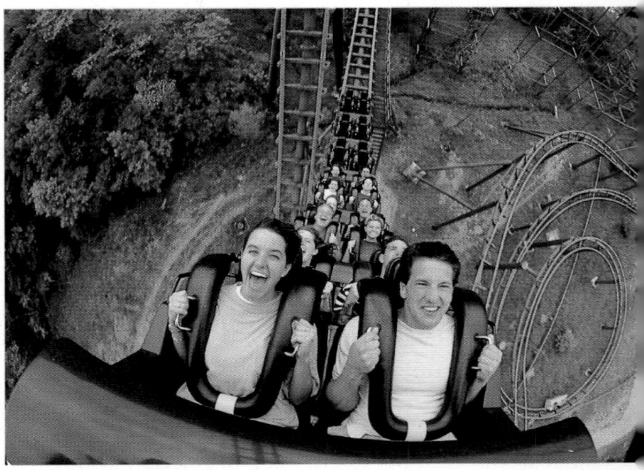

4.4 Surviving '*g*-forces'

Modern fighter planes can travel at speeds over 1500 km h^{-1} (400 m s^{-1}). If a pilot wants to turn at this speed, and keep the acceleration below 3*g*, the radius of the turn will have to be quite large:

$$r = \frac{v^2}{a}$$

$$= \frac{(400\ \text{m s}^{-1})^2}{30\ \text{m s}^{-2}} \approx 5\ \text{km}$$

Pilots need to manoeuvre through sharper turns than this. Modern aircraft are built to withstand accelerations of up to 12*g*, far higher than the human body can tolerate. How can pilots fly such planes?

The severe effects of high acceleration experienced by fighter pilots are caused by poor blood flow to the brain. When pilots turn their aircraft so that the cockpit is on the inside of the curve, blood drains from the head and accumulates in the lower body and legs. The brain becomes starved of oxygen.

At relatively low acceleration, the body can adapt. The heart rate can increase to raise the blood pressure. This ensures that the brain gets an adequate supply of oxygenated blood.

Fig. 4 Effects of sustained g-forces

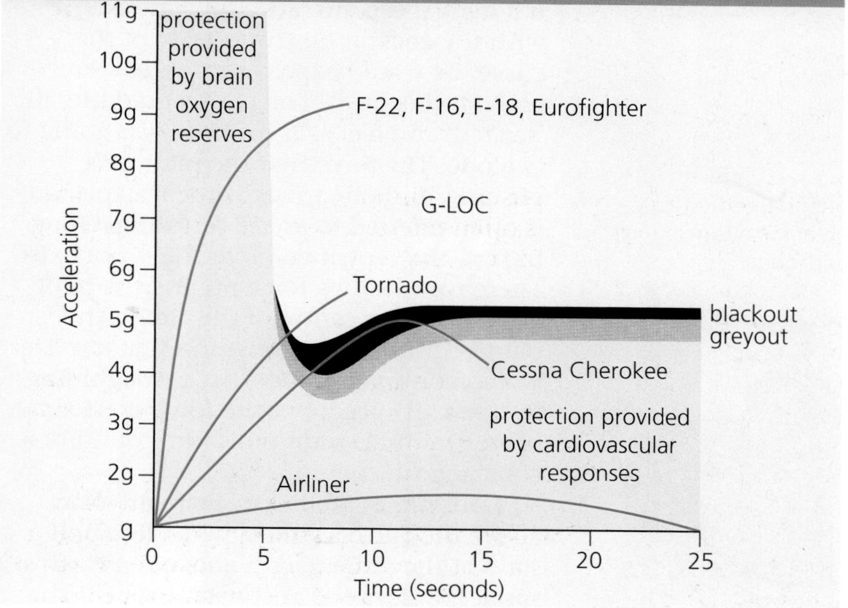
11g
10g
9g
8g
7g
6g
5g
4g
3g
2g
g
Acceleration
protection provided by brain oxygen reserves
F-22, F-16, F-18, Eurofighter
G-LOC
Tornado
blackout
greyout
Cessna Cherokee
protection provided by cardiovascular responses
Airliner
0
5
10
15
20
25
Time (seconds)

Fig. 5 Sources of centripetal forces

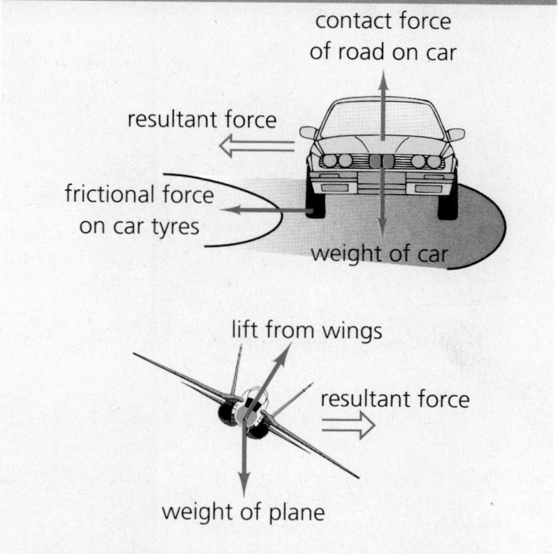
contact force of road on car
resultant force
frictional force on car tyres
weight of car
lift from wings
resultant force
weight of plane

A centrally directed (centripetal) force has to be supplied in order to move in a circle.

At high acceleration, the brain's oxygen reserves can last for periods of up to 5 seconds. Any longer, than this and the pilot is likely to experience visual blackout and then G-LOC (gravity-induced loss of consciousness). The centrifuge is used to train pilots to cope with these effects. A combination of anti-g straining manoeuvres and breathing techniques can raise the blood pressure in the upper body and brain.

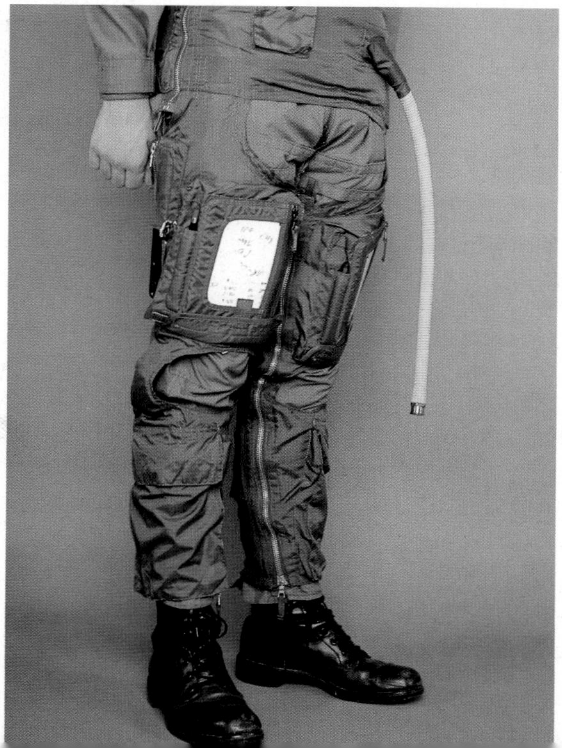

Pilots wear tight-fitting trousers that automatically inflate when high accelerations occur. These squeeze the blood out of the legs and abdomen, back towards the brain.

Forces in circular motion

Any object moving in a circular path accelerates towards the centre of the circle. Newton's second law says that a force is needed to cause this acceleration. This is sometimes referred to as the centripetal force. The centripetal force is not an extra force that arises due to the circular motion; it is the **resultant** of all the real forces acting on the body (Fig. 5).

For an object of constant mass, the force is given by $F = ma$. We know that for an object moving in a circle $a = v^2 / r$. The resultant force must be:

$$F = \frac{mv^2}{r} \quad \text{or} \quad F = mr\omega^2$$

When the Thunderlooper train (see Question 6) is fully loaded, it has a mass of about 7000 kg. The track has to exert a force of over 200 000 N to accelerate the train around the loop.

7 a What causes the force that enables a car to drive round a traffic roundabout?

b Estimate the size of this force for a car driving round a large traffic island.

Fig. 6 Points of view

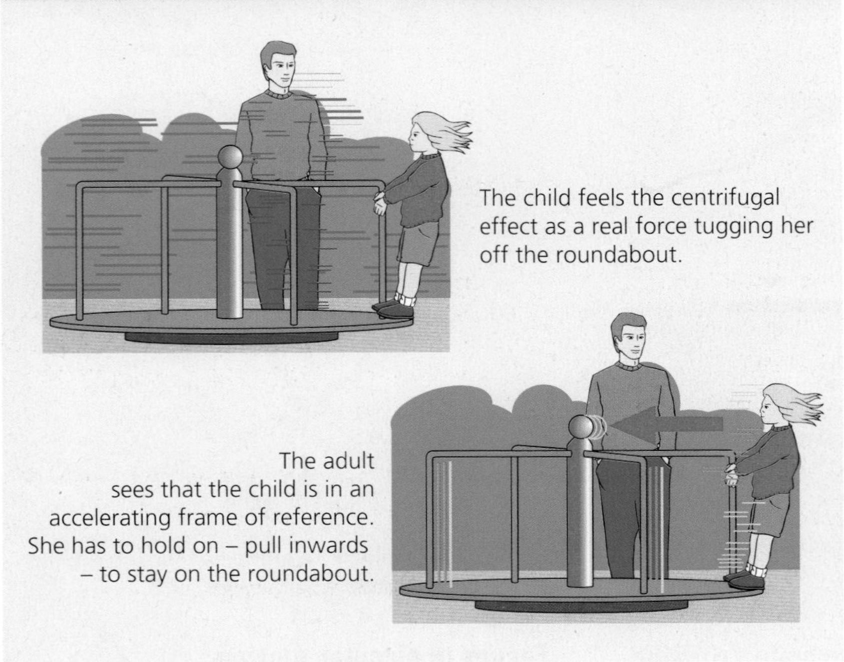
The child feels the centrifugal effect as a real force tugging her off the roundabout.
The adult sees that the child is in an accelerating frame of reference. She has to hold on – pull inwards – to stay on the roundabout.

Fig. 7 How a satellite really stays up

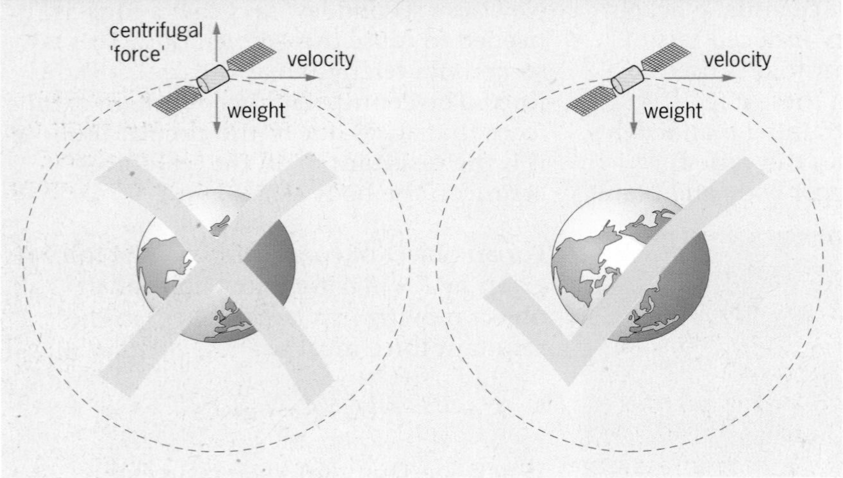
centrifugal 'force'
velocity
weight
velocity
weight

Centrifugal effect

If a high-speed aircraft pilot was to turn with the cockpit on the outside of the curve, he would experience a huge flow of blood to his head. The pilot would literally 'see red' and feel as if his head was going to explode. The force that the pilot *feels* pushing his body towards the cockpit roof is often referred to as the centrifugal force. In fact, the centrifugal force does not exist. There isn't really a force pulling the pilot away from the centre of the circle. The pilot is just obeying Newton's first law. He would continue to move in a straight line at constant speed, but the force exerted by his restraining straps pulls him round in a circular path.

Consider a satellite in a circular orbit above the Earth's atmosphere (Fig. 7). It stays at the same height above the Earth's surface and travels at constant speed. The only significant force acting on the satellite is the pull of the Earth's gravity, i.e. the satellite's weight.

Therefore there is a resultant force on the satellite. This force acts towards the centre of the Earth. It would be wrong to say that the satellite is in equilibrium; it is constantly accelerating towards the centre of the Earth.

8 'A hammer thrower whirls round in a circle, gaining speed until the centrifugal force is great enough to carry the hammer a long way.'
Rewrite this explanation correctly.

Key ideas

- An object moving in a circular path is not in equilibrium; it is accelerating towards the centre of the circle.
- The resultant force on the object acts towards the centre of the circle. This centripetal force is the resultant of the real forces acting on the object.
- The size of the centripetal force is $F = \frac{mv^2}{r} = mr\omega^2$.

Horizontal circles

The riders on the swinging chairs move in a large circle. As the ride speeds up, the chairs swing further out. At top-speed, the riders move in a horizontal circle, with the chains at a large angle from the vertical.

Fig. 8 Forces on a 'Chairoplane'

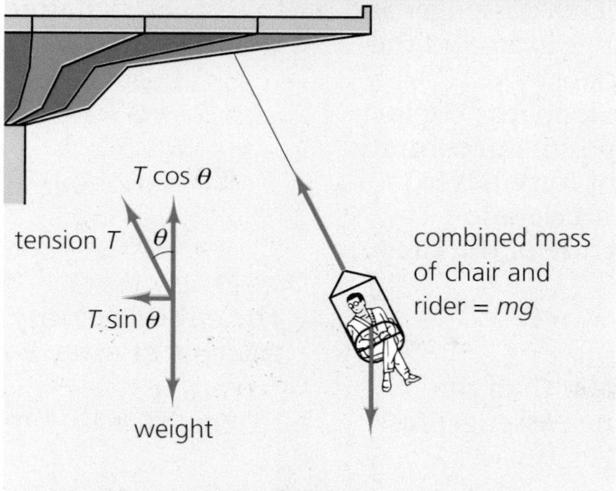
T cos θ
tension T
θ
T sin θ
weight
combined mass of chair and rider = mg

The resultant force, $T \sin\theta$, provides the centripetal force.

To build an exciting but safe ride, designers need to know the maximum centripetal acceleration that passengers will experience. We can draw a diagram to represent the forces acting on the chair and passenger (Fig. 8). The tension in the chain can be resolved into horizontal and vertical components.

Once the ride has reached a steady speed the chair moves horizontally. This means that the vertical forces must balance:

$$T\cos\theta = W = mg$$

Horizontally, the chair is not in equilibrium; there is a resultant centripetal force, $T \sin \theta$:

$$T\sin\theta = \frac{mv^2}{r}$$

If we divide these equations we get:

$$\frac{T\sin\theta}{T\cos\theta} = \frac{mv^2/r}{mg}$$

$$\text{so,}\quad \tan\theta = \frac{v^2}{gr}$$

where $\sin\theta / \cos\theta = \tan\theta$.

This equation tells us that the angle, θ, does not depend on the mass of the chair and rider. If the circle has a radius of 10 m and the riders hang at a maximum angle of 60° to the vertical, the top speed will be:

$$v^2 = gr\tan\theta$$
$$= 9.8\ \text{m s}^{-1} \times 10\ \text{m} \times \tan 60° = 170$$
$$v = \sqrt{170} = 13.0\ \text{m s}^{-1}$$

The centripetal acceleration,

$$a = \frac{v^2}{r}$$
$$= \frac{170\ \text{m}^2\,\text{s}^{-2}}{10\ \text{m}}$$
$$= 17.0\ \text{m s}^{-1}\ (\text{about } 1.7g)$$

9 **There is very little frictional force on the ice track of a bob-sleigh run. Explain, using a forces diagram, how a bob-sleigh is able to corner.**

10 **Suppose that the bob-sleigh is taking a corner with a radius of curvature of 20 m and the maximum angle of the track is 45° to the vertical. Calculate the highest speed at which the corner can be taken.**

Vertical circles

The 'Corkscrew' ride at Alton Towers takes its victims through two complete 360° vertical turns and reaches speeds of up to 65 km h^{-1} along its 750 m track.

The contact force between a passenger and the seat varies as the car goes around the Corkscrew's vertical circle.

At the bottom of the loop, the contact force, R_B, acts in the opposite direction to the weight. The resultant force has to provide the centripetal acceleration upwards, towards the centre of the circle.

$$R_B - W = \frac{mv^2}{r} \quad \text{or} \quad R_B = W + \frac{mv^2}{r}$$

The contact force is greater than the passenger's weight, so the passenger feels pushed into their seat (Fig. 9).

Fig. 9 Forces around the loop

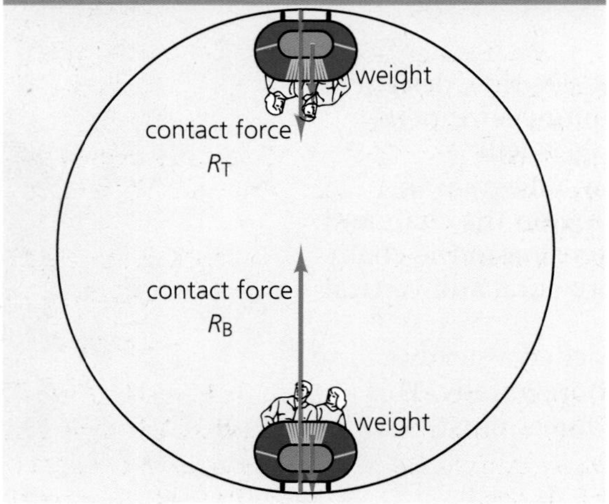
weight
contact force
R_T
contact force
R_B
weight

At the top of the loop, the contact force, R_T, is in the same direction as the weight. Together these forces provide the centripetal acceleration downwards, towards the centre of the circle.

$$R_T + W = \frac{mv^2}{r} \quad \text{or} \quad R_T = \frac{mv^2}{r} - W$$

The contact force depends on the speed. Suppose that the speed stays constant during the loop. For a passenger of mass 50 kg travelling at a velocity of 18 m s^{-1} around a loop with a radius of about 11 m:

$$R_T = \frac{50\ \text{kg} \times (18\ \text{m s}^{-1})^2}{11\ \text{m}} - 500\ \text{N}$$
$$= 970\ \text{N}$$

The passenger feels pushed upwards into the seat with a force equal to about twice her weight. If the speed was reduced, the contact force would decrease. There is a critical value of the speed at which the contact force drops to zero, and an unrestrained passenger would begin to fall out of the ride.

$$R_T = 0 = \frac{mv^2}{r} - W$$
$$\frac{mv^2}{r} = W = mg$$
$$v^2 = gr$$

The critical velocity is independent of the passenger's mass. For the example above:

$$v = \sqrt{gr} = 10.4\ \text{ms}^{-1}$$

11 Suppose that you whirl a 1 kg mass on the end of a spring balance at a steady speed in a vertical circle. If you spin it just quickly enough to prevent the mass falling on your head, explain how you would expect the balance reading to vary during one revolution.

12 If a stunt pilot flew in a vertical circle of radius 500 m, what is the minimum speed that she would need to maintain to keep her in her seat at the top of the loop?

13 If the pilot flew that same loop at 100 m s^{-1}, what would her acceleration be? If she had a mass of 60 kg what would the resultant force on her be;
a at the top of the loop?
b at the bottom of the loop?

Key ideas

- For an object moving in a horizontal circle, the vertical forces balance. The resultant horizontal force causes a centripetal acceleration.
- For an object moving in a vertical circle, the horizontal forces balance. At constant speed, the size of the centripetal force stays the same, but other forces, e.g. contact forces or tension, may vary in size.

4.5 Gathering speed

The Pepsi Max Big One at Blackpool pleasure beach is the World's tallest rollercoaster.

The rollercoaster is the biggest attraction at the theme park. We try to make the ride more thrilling than our competitors', and that means speed!

In order to achieve high speeds, most rollercoaster rides begin by pulling the 'train' to the top of a steep incline. The 'Pepsi-Max Big One' is the largest rollercoaster in the World. The top of the ride is 72 m above the ground. One way to calculate the maximum speed that the passengers will reach is to use the concept of gravitational potential energy.

The work done against gravity in pulling the train up to this height is:

$$\begin{aligned} \text{work} &= \text{force} \times \text{distance} \\ &= \text{weight} \times \text{height gained} \\ &= mg \times \Delta h \end{aligned}$$

This is just the work done against gravity. We have ignored work against the resistive forces of friction and air resistance. The work done against gravity is stored as gravitational potential energy, E_p, in the train. The change in potential energy is:

$$\Delta E_p = mg\Delta h$$

The gravitational field strength, g, changes very slightly as the train moves away from the ground. However, for small values of Δh, this change is so small that it can be neglected.

As the train begins to plummet down the first drop, the potential energy of the train due to its position transfers to kinetic energy, E_k, due to its motion. If we ignore any work done against friction by the train, the conservation of energy says that:

$$E_k \text{ gained} = E_p \text{ lost}$$
$$\tfrac{1}{2}mv^2 = mg\Delta h$$
$$v^2 = 2g\Delta h$$

At the bottom of the drop, its speed is:

$$v = \sqrt{2 \times 10 \times 72}$$
$$= 38 \text{ m s}^{-1}$$

Key ideas

- Gravitational potential energy, $E_p = mg\Delta h$
- In the absence of resistive forces, all of the gravitational potential energy will be transferred to kinetic energy when a mass falls through Δh.

14 A roller-coaster car is pulled up an incline and allowed to drop around a track with a 23 m radius loop (Fig. 10).

a What is the minimum speed at which the car can loop-the-loop, without passengers falling out?

b What is the minimum initial height needed by the car if it is to achieve this speed?

Fig. 10 Loop-the-loop

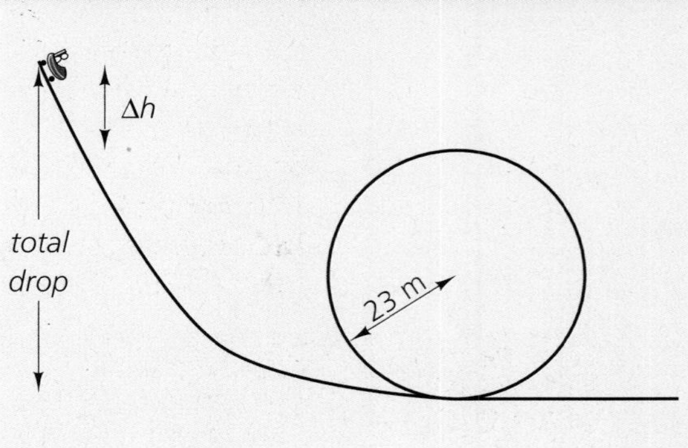

Δh
total drop
23 m

5 Natural strength

Some of the latest recruits to the US army have eight legs. Golden Orb spiders have been enlisted for their ability to manufacture silk with remarkable mechanical properties. Researchers 'silk' the spiders by taping them, on their backs, to a table. The silk is slowly withdrawn from their spinnerets by winding it around the spindle of a low-speed electric motor. In a day, each spider can produce a thread over 300 m long.

The spider's silk is at least twice as strong as ordinary steel, yet it can absorb enormous amounts of energy and stretch by more than 30% of its original length before breaking. Furthermore, it only becomes brittle at temperatures below –60 °C. For these reasons, the US army are investigating the feasibility of making light, bullet proof vests from the silk.

Research teams all over the world are currently attempting to unravel the silk's structure, so far without success. Molecular biologists are trying to isolate the genes that are responsible for the silk's production. The silk has an enormous range of potential uses, from the manufacture of parachutes to the soles of running shoes.

The Golden Orb spider produces seven different kinds of silk. The longest strands in the web are the strongest and can trap small birds.

Spider silk can cope with sudden loads, which makes it an ideal material to make stronger, lighter parachutes.

5.1 Learning objectives

After working through this chapter, you should be able to:

- **explain** what is meant by tensile stress and tensile strain;
- **calculate** the Young modulus for a material;
- **derive** and use the formula for the energy stored in an elastic material;
- **relate** the structure of a material to its mechanical properties.

5.2 Hanging by a thread

Mountain climbers need ropes that are strong and light. This requires a material of low density and high strength.

A spider can suspend itself on a thread that is only a few thousandths of a millimetre thick. A human abseiling down a cliff face needs something more substantial. The most important physical property of a climber's rope is its strength, the maximum load that it can support without breaking. Ropes for rock-climbing are usually designed to withstand a load 25 times the climber's weight. However, the rope mustn't be too bulky, or it would be difficult to carry.

Under stress

We can assess the strength of a material using the idea of tensile stress. The **tensile stress**, σ, applied to a material is the force per unit cross-sectional area (Fig. 1).

$$\text{tensile stress} = \frac{\text{force}}{\text{area}}$$

$$\sigma = \frac{F}{A}$$

Fig. 1 Tensile stress

These ropes are under the same tensile stress.

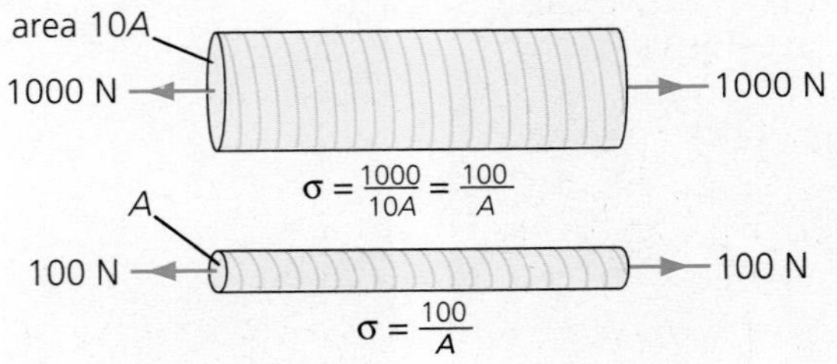

area 10A
1000 N
1000 N
σ = 1000/10A = 100/A
A
100 N
100 N
σ = 100/A

Tensile stress has units of N m^{-2}, or pascals (Pa). The largest tensile stress that can be applied to a material before it breaks is known as its **ultimate tensile stress** (UTS). This value is sometimes referred to as the material's breaking stress (Table 1).

Table 1 Materials with high tensile strength

Material	Density (kg m^{-3})	UTS (MPa)
Nylon	1130	85
Stainless steel	7930	600
Carbon fibre	1750	1900
Kevlar 49	1440	3100

Kevlar is a strong synthetic polymer. Cables made from Kevlar are so strong that they are used to tether oil rigs. We can use the equation for tensile stress to calculate how thick a Kevlar climbing rope would have to be to support a load of 15 000 N.

From Table 1, the ultimate tensile stress of Kevlar is 3100 MPa. The cross-sectional area of rope is:

$$A = \frac{F}{\sigma}$$

$$= \frac{15000\ \text{N}}{3100 \times 10^{6}\ \text{Pa}}$$

$$= 4.84 \times 10^{-6}\ \text{m}^2$$

As the cross-sectional area of the rope is πr^2, $r = 1.24 \times 10^{-3}$ m. The rope would need to have a diameter of only 2.5 mm. A 50 m length of this rope would have a mass of only 0.35 kg.

1 a What is the heaviest fish that could be lifted out of the water using a 2 mm diameter line made from nylon (UTS = 85 MPa)?

b If the fish struggles, the force on the line may increase to five times its weight. How thick will the nylon line need to be now?

Taking the strain

The most remarkable property of the Golden Orb spider's silk is the distance that it can stretch before it breaks. The increase in length of a material caused by a tensile force is called the extension. A rope's extension under a given load depends upon the original length of the rope. A long rope will stretch further than a short one if they are subjected to the same force, so the extension is usually given as a fraction of the original length. This ratio is known as the **tensile strain**.

$$\text{tensile strain} = \frac{\text{extension}}{\text{original length}}$$

Strain has no units, because the extension and original length are both measured in metres.

Steel wire can undergo a strain of 0.01 before it breaks and Kevlar can manage 0.04. The silk from a spider has a breaking strain of between 0.15 and 0.30. This enables it to absorb the kinetic energy of an insect, transferring it to internal energy in the web.

Spider's silk can deform without breaking, making it a useful material for the manufacture of bullet-proof vests.

Spider silk is highly **elastic**. After being stretched it will return to its original length. Many materials do not return to their original length after being subjected to a strain. When the tensile force is removed, the material remains deformed. This is called **plastic** behaviour. Putty behaves in this way.

We tend to classify materials as either elastic or plastic, but many materials show both types of behaviour depending on the stress applied. For small values of stress, polythene behaves elastically, returning to its original dimensions when the stress is removed. Above a critical value of stress, known as the yield stress, the polythene begins to be plastically deformed. We say that it has passed its **elastic limit**. Materials which have large plastic deformations are known as **ductile**. Glass fibres can be extremely strong but they show hardly any plastic deformation before they break. Materials like this are said to be **brittle** (Fig. 2).

Fig. 2 Stress–strain curves

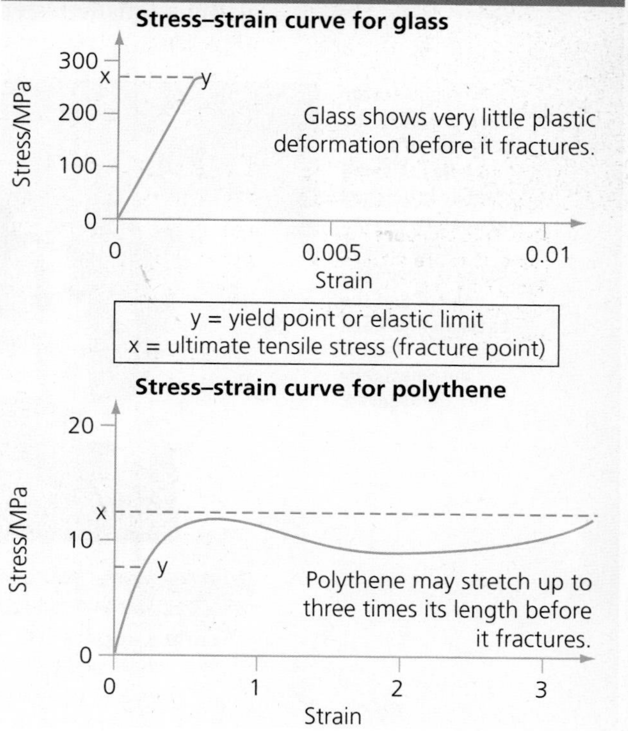
Stress–strain curve for glass
Stress/MPa
300
200
100
0
x
y
Glass shows very little plastic deformation before it fractures.
0
0.005
0.01
Strain
y = yield point or elastic limit
x = ultimate tensile stress (fracture point)
Stress–strain curve for polythene
Stress/MPa
20
10
0
x
y
Polythene may stretch up to three times its length before it fractures.
0
1
2
3
Strain

2 A 50 m nylon rope will stretch about 7.5 cm when supporting an 80 kg man. What is the size of the tensile strain?

Key ideas

- Tensile stress is the force per unit area acting on a material.
- Tensile strain is the extension of a material per unit length.
- Elastic materials regain their original shape when an applied stress is removed.
- Plastic materials are permanently deformed following the application of stress.
- Plastic deformation begins to occur at the elastic limit.
- Ductile materials show large plastic deformations.
- Brittle materials do not deform plastically.

5.3 Stiffness

Strength is not the only important property of climbing rope. It is important that the rope does not stretch too much when the mountaineer is suspended from it. The amount of strain caused by a given stress depends on the **stiffness** of a material.

In a school laboratory the stiffness of small samples of material can be measured using a tensile tester, or Searle's apparatus (Fig. 3).

A tensile tester can measure the stiffness of metal samples. A small bar is gripped between two jaws. A large tensile force is gradually applied and the extension at each load is automatically measured.

Fig. 3 Searle's apparatus

Searle's apparatus

1 Two identical wires are suspended from the same support.
2 Both wires are initially loaded with a small mass to remove any kinks.
3 One wire is loaded and its new length is compared to the control wire to find the extension. Changes in temperature do not affect the results. If temperature increases, both wires will expand by the same amount, since they are made of the same material.

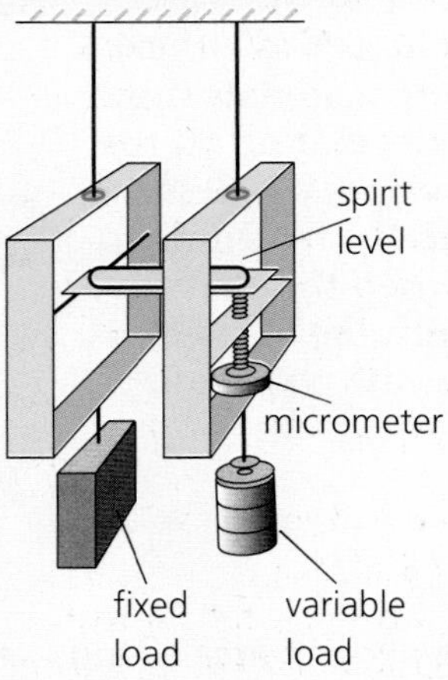
spirit level
micrometer
fixed load
variable load

For some materials, plotting a graph of tensile force against extension produces a straight line at low values of stress (Fig. 4). In this linear region, the material obeys Hooke's law. The load (F) is proportional to extension (e), or:

$$F = ke$$

Fig. 4 Hooke's law graph

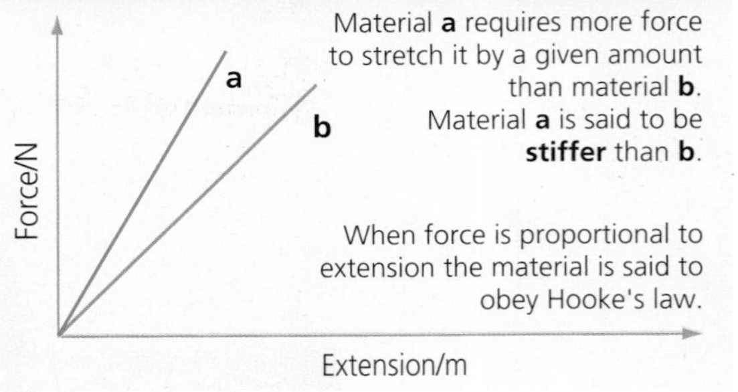
a
b
Force/N
Extension/m
Material **a** requires more force to stretch it by a given amount than material **b**. Material **a** is said to be **stiffer** than **b**.
When force is proportional to extension the material is said to obey Hooke's law.

The constant, k, is measured in N m^{-1} and is equal to the force needed to stretch the wire by 1 metre. A large value of k means that the material is difficult to stretch, and it is said to be stiff. For a wire which obeys Hooke's law:

$$F \propto e$$

Since A and l are both constants for a particular wire:

$$\frac{F}{A} \propto \frac{e}{l}$$

tensile stress $\propto$ tensile strain

tensile stress = constant $\times$ tensile strain

This constant is known as the **Young modulus** and is given the symbol E.

$$E = \frac{\text{tensile stress}}{\text{tensile strain}} = \frac{Fl}{eA}$$

Because stress is measured in pascals and strain has no units, the Young modulus has units of pascals, Pa.

The Young modulus is the gradient of the stress–strain graph and therefore measures the stiffness of a material. A high Young modulus means that a large stress is needed to produce even a small strain. The Young modulus takes into account the cross-sectional area and original length of the sample. This means it can be used to compare the stiffness of different materials, even if they have different dimensions (Table 2).

A rigid structure, such as a bridge, needs a material with a high Young modulus, like steel. Something that is designed to deform easily, such as a squash ball, relies on a material with a low Young modulus, like rubber.

Table 2 Stiffness of materials

Material	Young modulus (GPa)
Carbon fibre	270
Steel	210
Kevlar 49	124
Copper	117
Bone	28
Polystyrene	3.8
Nylon	3
Rubber	0.02

3 A climber's rope needs to be strong, but also light. The ratio UTS/ρ, where ρ is the density of the material, is a useful measure of strength per unit weight. Similarly, the ratio E/ρ gives a measure of a material's stiffness per unit weight. Use these criteria, and data in Tables 1 and 2, to find the most suitable material for a climber's rope.

For a metal, the Young modulus does not remain constant at higher values of stress. Beyond a point known as the limit of proportionality, stress is no longer proportional to strain. At a slightly higher stress, a material begins to be permanently deformed; this point is the elastic limit (Fig. 5).

Metals obey Hooke's law over most of the elastic region, so the limit of proportionality and the elastic limit almost coincide. Some polymers, like rubber or silk, may be elastic right up until they break, but they often don't obey Hooke's law at all.

Fig. 5 Stress–strain graphs for a metal and a polymer (rubber)

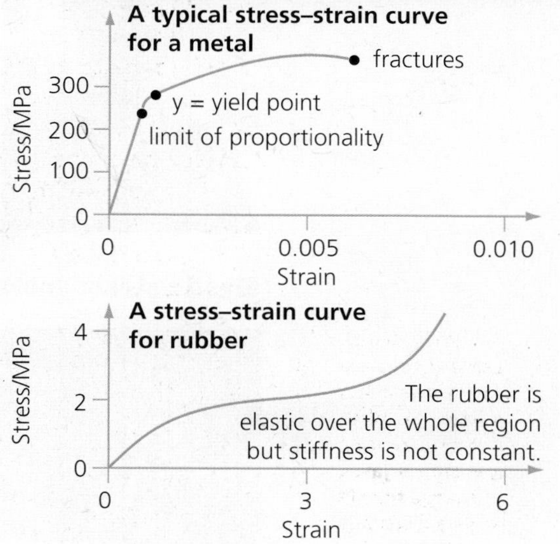

A typical stress–strain curve for a metal
fractures
y = yield point
limit of proportionality
Stress/MPa
300
200
100
0
0
0.005
0.010
Strain
A stress–strain curve for rubber
The rubber is elastic over the whole region but stiffness is not constant.
Stress/MPa
4
2
0
0
3
6
Strain

Fig. 6 Stress–strain curves

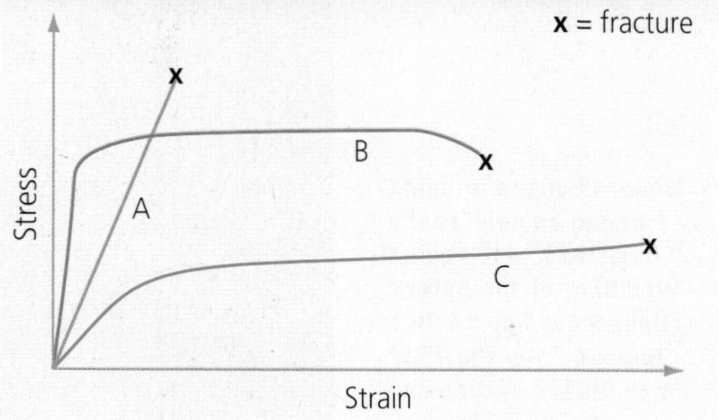

x = fracture
A
B
C
Stress
Strain

4 The graphs in Fig. 6 show the stress–strain curves for three different materials. Which material
a is the stiffest?
b is the strongest?
c is the most ductile?
d has the lowest yield stress?

Key ideas

- For materials which obey Hooke's law, force is proportional to extension (up to the limit of proportionality).
- The Young modulus, E, is a measure of the stiffness of a material. E = stress / strain.

5.4 Bouncing back

The first half of the jump, when the cable is slack, is horrifying. You free-fall for up to 30 m with the ground rushing up at you at an alarming rate. Then the cable begins to stretch and slow your descent. The cords get tighter, until you slow to a stop and begin to accelerate back up. You get quite close to your original height, before you start falling again.

Elastic strain energy

Modern bungee jumping began on April Fool's Day, 1979, when some members of the Oxford Dangerous Sports Club jumped from the 75 m high Clifton suspension bridge in Bristol.

As bungee cords stretch, the kinetic energy of the jumper is transferred to elastic strain energy in the cords. Work is done against the tension in the rubber cord and this is stored as elastic strain energy in the stretched cord. The work done by a constant force is given by:

work (J) = force (N) × distance moved (m)

But the force exerted by a bungee cord changes as the cord is stretched. The force varies from zero, for the unstretched cord, to a maximum force, F, when the cord reaches its full extension, e. If the cord obeys Hooke's law, the average force exerted is:

$$\frac{(0 + F)}{2} = \tfrac{1}{2}F$$

Therefore, the work done against the average force is:

$$W = \tfrac{1}{2}Fe$$
$$= \tfrac{1}{2}(ke)e = \tfrac{1}{2}ke^2$$

Fig. 7 Force–extension graph

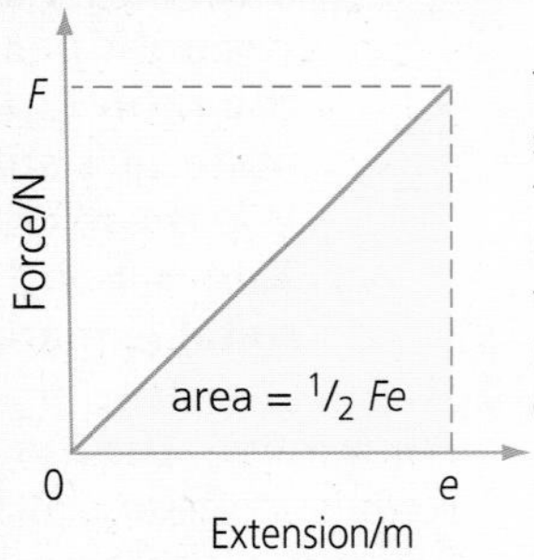

F
Force/N
area = 1/2 Fe
0
e
Extension/m

The work done in stretching a material that obeys Hooke's law is $^1/_2$ *Fe*. This is equivalent to a constant force of $^F/_2$ moving through the extension e.

The strain energy stored in a stretched cord is equal to $\tfrac{1}{2}Fe$. If the cord was originally l metres long and has a cross-sectional area of A m², then its volume, V, equals $A \times l$. The strain energy stored per unit volume of the cord is given by:

$$\frac{W}{V} = \frac{\tfrac{1}{2}Fe}{Al}$$
$$= \tfrac{1}{2}\frac{F}{A}\frac{e}{l}$$
$$= \tfrac{1}{2}\text{stress} \times \text{strain}$$

For some materials, such as metal wire, it is possible to recover all of this stored energy (provided that the material has not been extended beyond its elastic limit). This is not the case for a rubber cord. More work is done in stretching a rubber cord than is released when the cord is unloaded. This type of behaviour is known as hysteresis (Fig. 8). Each time the rubber is stretched and released, some energy is transferred as internal energy in the rubber.

Fig. 8 Hysteresis of rubber

Area A represents the energy transferred to internal energy in the rubber band in each loading and unloading cycle.

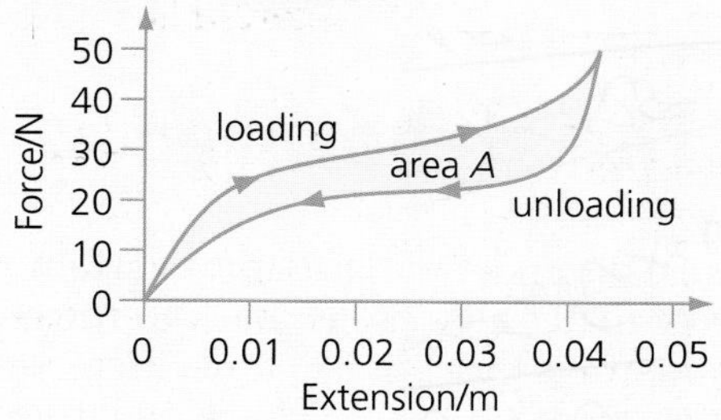

Force/N
50
40
30
20
10
0
loading
area A
unloading
0
0.01
0.02
0.03
0.04
0.05
Extension/m

Bungee cords can be made from a variety of natural or synthetic rubbers. Most types only obey Hooke's law over a limited range of extensions. Rubber tends to stretch easily at first and become much stiffer at high extensions; the expression for strain energy may only be approximately correct over part of the cord's extension.

If the rubber does not obey Hooke's law at all, then the expression $W = \frac{1}{2}Fe$ cannot be used to calculate the elastic strain energy. The work done in stretching the cord can be found by using a force vs. extension graph (Fig. 8). The elastic strain energy recovered is the area below the curve as the rubber is unloaded. The area between the two curves is the energy transferred to the rubber as internal energy. The larger the area of the 'hysteresis loop', the greater the rise in internal energy of the rubber, and the hotter the rubber will get. A rubber is called **resilient** if it has a hysteresis loop with a small area.

The number of bungee cords attached to a jumper depends on the person's mass. At least three cords are used for a jumper of mass 80 kg.

The cords will stretch until the jumper's potential energy, E_P, has been transferred as elastic strain energy in the bungee. For the type of bungee described in Fig. 9, this happens when the cords have stretched by about 12.75 m. The jumper will then have fallen a total distance of 27.75 m.

$$\Delta E_P = mg\Delta h$$
$$= 80 \text{ kg} \times 10 \text{ m s}^{-2} \times 27.75 \text{ m}$$
$$= 22\,200 \text{ J}$$

The elastic strain energy stored in each cord is therefore 22 200 J / 3 = 7400 J

Since $\frac{1}{2}Fe$ = 7400 J, the tensile force exerted by each cord must be:

$$\frac{2 \times 7400 \text{ J}}{12.75 \text{ m}} = 1160 \text{ N}$$

The stress in each cord will then be:

$$\frac{1160 \text{ N}}{2.0 \times 10^{-4} \text{ m}^2} = 5.8 \times 10^6 \text{ Pa},$$

well below the ultimate tensile stress of the rubber. The rebound height of the jumper depends on the type of rubber used for the bungee cord. Jumpers typically rebound to about 75% of their original height.

Fig. 9 Stress–strain curve for a bungee jump

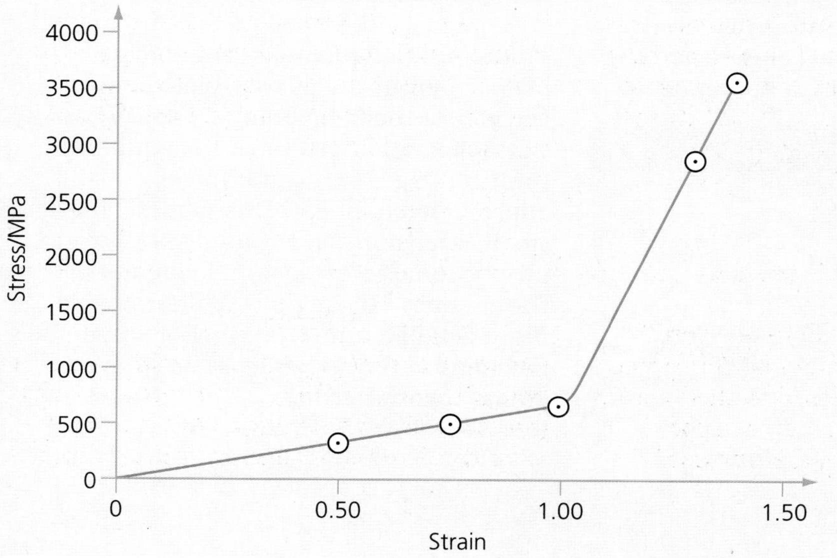

Stress/MPa
4000
3500
3000
2500
2000
1500
1000
500
0
0
0.50
1.00
1.50
Strain

5 Spider's silk is stiffer than rubber and has a much lower resilience. What would a bungee jump be like if silk was used instead of the usual rubber cords?

6 What difference would it make to a bungee jumper if more cords were used?

7 **'Sandbagging' is a variant on the bungee jump. A jumper holds onto a heavy sandbag, then drops it at the bottom of the jump. This has been banned in some countries as it puts spectators and the jumper in danger. Why is it dangerous to the jumper?**

Key ideas

- The energy stored in a stretched material is known as elastic strain energy. Elastic strain energy is the area below a force vs. extension graph. If the material obeys Hooke's law, strain energy $= \frac{1}{2} Fe$.
- For some materials, the work done in stretching them is greater than the energy transferred when they are unloaded. This is called hysteresis.

5.5 The secret's in the structure

As we have seen, there are huge differences in the mechanical properties of materials. These differences are due to the ways in which the atoms of each material are joined together.

Interatomic forces

Solid materials are held together by the forces between their atoms. These interatomic forces are due to the electrical forces between charged particles, i.e. electrons and positive ions. The force between two adjacent atoms depend on their separation (Fig. 10). Although the exact form of the interatomic force vs. distance curve depends on the type of material, some features are common to all solids.

- There is an equilibrium separation between two atoms, x_0, where the resultant force on the atoms is zero;
- If two atoms are pushed closer than the equilibrium separation, a net repulsive force acts on the atoms, pushing them back to the equilibrium position. This force increases rapidly as the atoms are pushed closer together;
- If atoms are pulled apart by a tensile force, a force of attraction between positive nuclei and negative electrons acts to restore them to their equilibrium position. For small separations, this attractive force increases as the atoms are pulled further apart. However, as the distance between the atoms becomes larger, the force becomes weaker. The force approaches zero when the atoms are a long way apart;
- Atoms in a solid are not stationary; they vibrate around their average equilibrium separation, x_0, alternately repelling and attracting their neighbour atoms.

Fig. 10 Interatomic forces

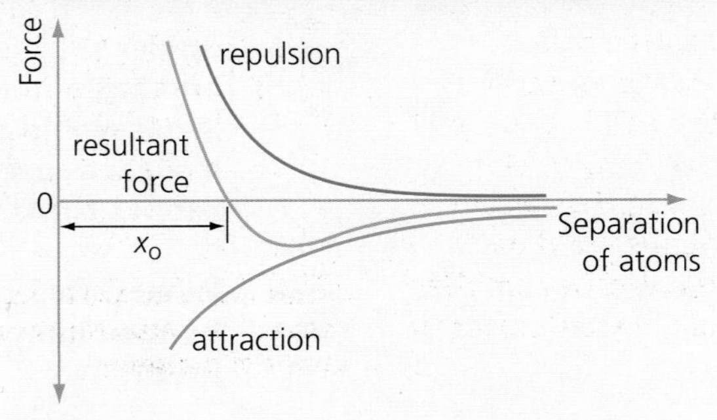

Force
repulsion
resultant
force
0
x_0
Separation
of atoms
attraction

This simplified picture of the forces between atoms helps to explain some features of the behaviour of a solid. For example, on either side of the equilibrium position (Fig. 10) the graph is approximately linear. This suggests that, for small extensions and compressions, force is proportional to extension, i.e. materials should obey Hooke's law. We can gain a more detailed understanding of a material's mechanical properties by seeing how its atoms are arranged.

Metals

Metals are crystalline materials. Atoms in a metal are arranged in an ordered way (Fig. 11). Metals can be pictured as a matrix of positive ions surrounded by a 'sea' of electrons.

Fig. 11 Arrangement of metal atoms

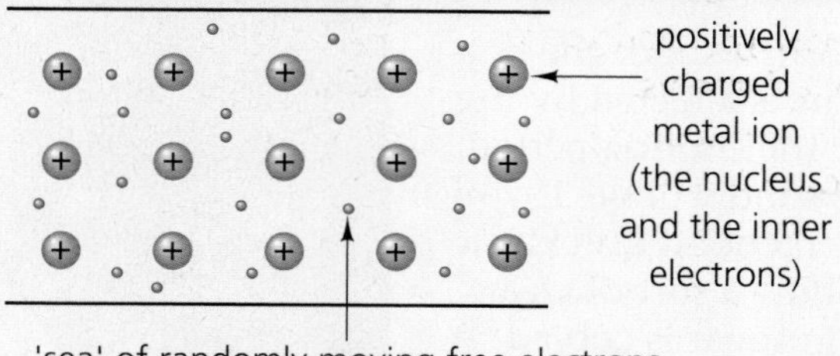
positively charged metal ion (the nucleus and the inner electrons)
'sea' of randomly moving free electrons

The forces that act on each ion are largely **isotropic**; the force is the same in all directions. Each positive ion pulls on the surrounding electrons in the same way. This tends to create a close-packed structure.

Fig. 12 FCC and HCP structures

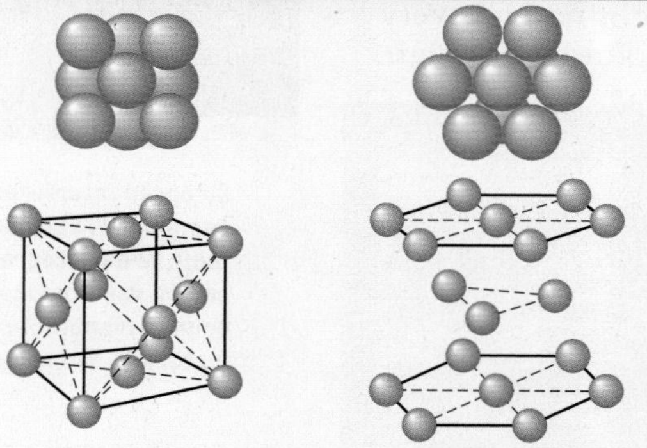
face-centred cubic (FCC)
hexagonal close-packed (HCP)

Some metals can deform plastically under tensile stress. For example, copper is highly ductile. When the tensile stress is high enough, entire planes of copper atoms slide over each other. To accomplish this 'yielding' many atoms have to be pulled further apart. Plastic deformation is helped by the presence of imperfections in the crystal called dislocations (Fig. 13). Because of these imperfections, metals yield at stresses that are thousands of times smaller than we would expect from the interatomic force curve.

Bubble rafts can be used to illustrate the types of defect that arise in crystal structures.

Fig. 13 Movement of a dislocation

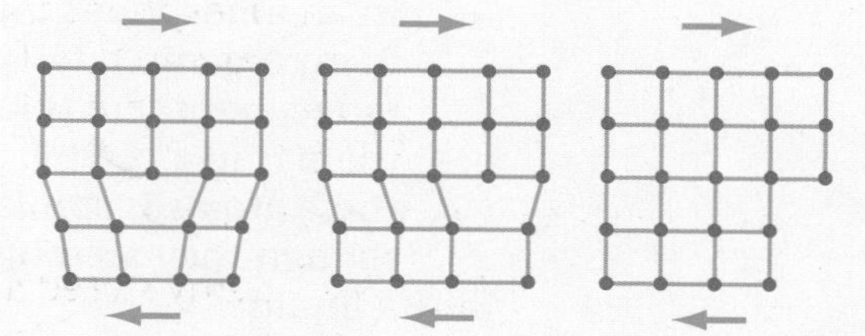

Other imperfections in the crystal structure can affect a metal's mechanical properties (Fig. 14).

Fig. 14 Substitutional and interstitial impurites

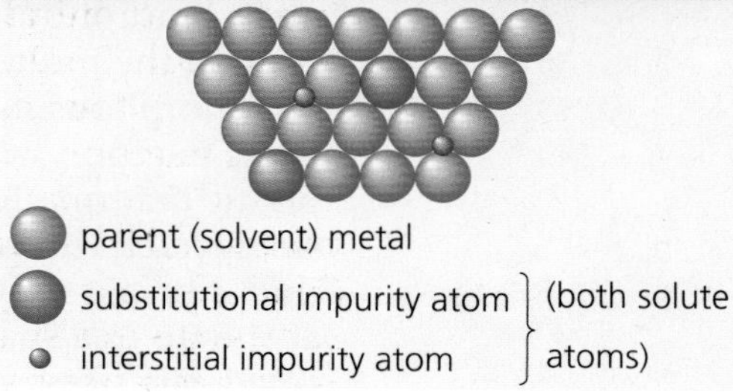
parent (solvent) metal
substitutional impurity atom
interstitial impurity atom
(both solute atoms)

A real sample of metal is not a single crystal, it is actually a **polycrystalline** material. A metal is composed of millions of crystals, or grains, all at different angles to each other. However, it is possible, under carefully controlled conditions, to grow individual metal crystals that have an almost flawless structure. These are known as whiskers.

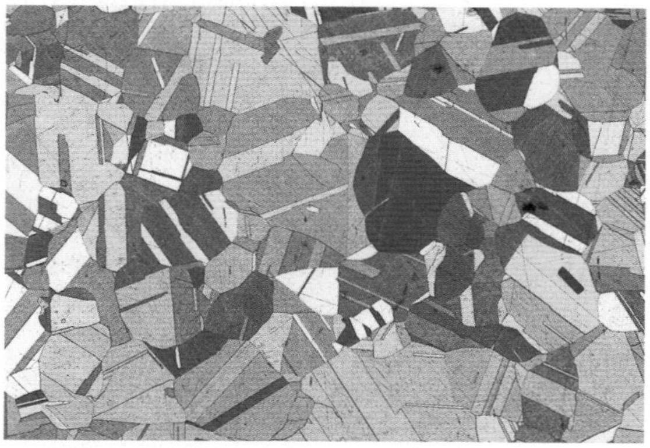

Metals can be etched to reveal their polycrystalline nature. This photograph shows the grain structure in a sample of copper.

Glasses

Glass is an **amorphous** material. The atoms in an amorphous material may be arranged in an organised fashion over a very short range, but there is no long-range order as there is in a crystal. The arrangement of these atoms is similar to that of a liquid, though they are not as mobile as atoms in a liquid.

As a liquid cools to form a solid, the arrangement of the atoms is affected by the cooling rate. The longer the cooling period, the more crystalline the solid will be. If you melt some sugar and then cool it quickly, it forms an amorphous solid – a sort of clear, brittle toffee. If the liquid sugar is cooled more slowly, a crystalline, cloudy, fudge-like material is produced. It is possible to make amorphous samples of metal by cooling the molten metal quickly.

Amorphous materials tend to be brittle. Glass fractures with very little, if any, plastic deformation. The presence of a small crack will weaken a piece of glass, so that it breaks very easily. Because the area at the tip of a sharp crack or notch is very small, the stress at that point is very high. In a ductile material, some plastic deformation can take place, increasing the area at the tip of the crack and reducing the stress. A brittle material can not undergo plastic deformation so the crack tends to propagate through the material, causing fracture.

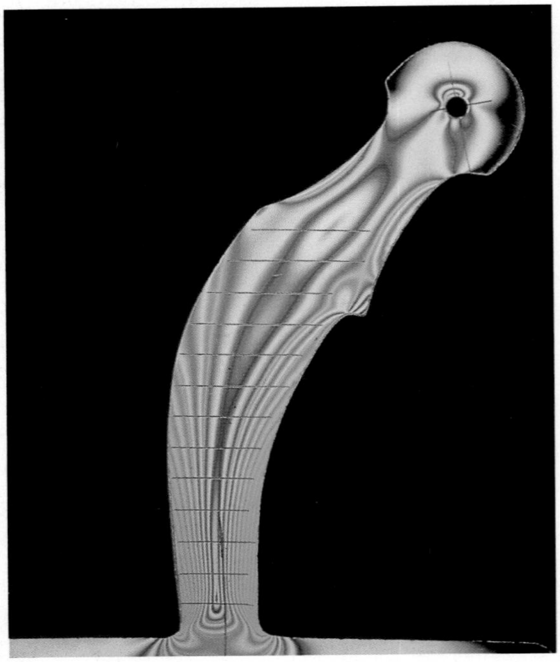

Coloured interference patterns are visible when a component, such as this model of an artificial hip joint, are photographed using polarised light. They can be used to locate regions of high stress, helping manufacturers to choose suitable materials and designs.

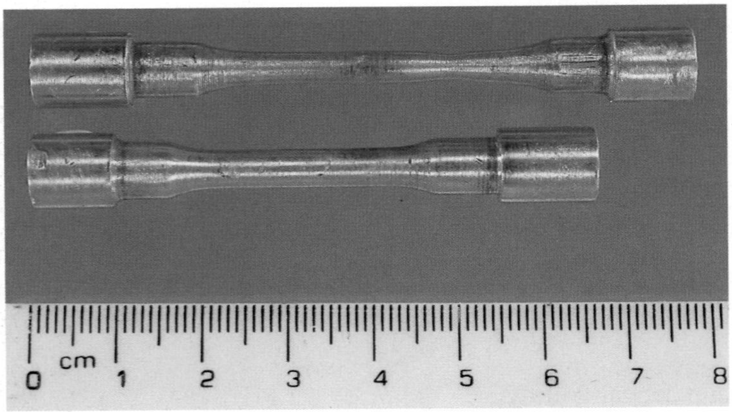
cm
0
1
2
3
4
5
6
7
8

A ductile material fractures slowly under tension. A copper wire becomes narrow, forming a 'waist' before it breaks. A brittle material such as cast iron fractures suddenly when a crack travels through it at high speed.

Key ideas

- Metals are polycrystalline materials. Their mechanical properties are affected by imperfections in their crystal structure.
- Amorphous materials, like glass, have no long-range order.
- Brittle materials tend to fracture suddenly, as cracks propagate through the material.
- Ductile materials yield, and form a 'waist' before they fracture.

Polymers

A polymer is a material made from giant chain-like molecules. Each molecule can contain thousands or millions of atoms. Rubber and silk are natural polymers. Perspex, polythene and Kevlar are all artificial polymers. Some polymers show plastic behaviour, while others are brittle.

Amorphous polymers

Some polymers have no long-range order – their molecules are arranged irregularly. The mechanical behaviour of these amorphous polymers depends on temperature. Each polymer has a glass transition temperature, T_G. Below this temperature, parts of the polymer chain cannot move because their thermal energy is too small to let them separate from neighbouring chains. The material is therefore stiff and brittle.

Above the glass transition temperature, the energy of the molecules is high enough to allow movement between adjacent molecular chains. The polymer in this phase behaves more like rubber than glass.

The rubber molecules in a bungee cord are initially tangled up and coiled in a random way. When the cord is put under tension the coiled molecules begin to unwind (Fig. 15). The long chains are prevented from slipping past each other by cross-links between the chains. When the stress is removed, these cross-links pull the molecules back into their original coiled shape and the bungee goes back to its original length. If more cross-links are added, the rubber becomes more difficult to stretch. A process known as vulcanisation adds cross-links, usually using sulphur atoms, to make the rubber stiffer, stronger and to improve its resistance to wear.

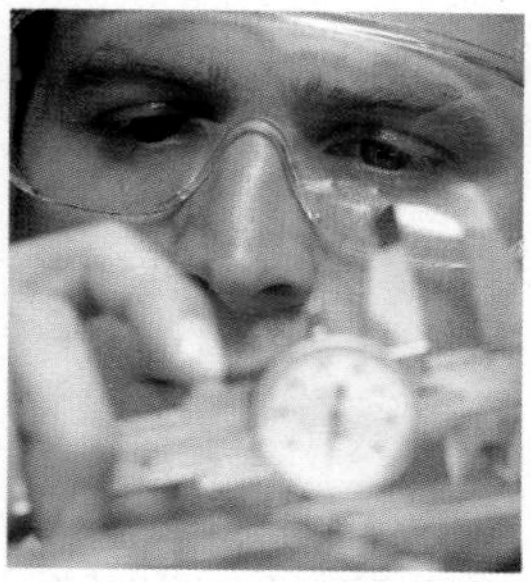

Perspex has a glass transition temperature of 120 °C, well above room temperature. Perspex safety glasses are brittle.

Fig. 15 Stretching polymer chains

tensile
stress

In an unstretched rubber band the polymer chain molecules are coiled in a random way.

Under stress the molecules untangle and become aligned.

Semi-crystalline polymers

Some polymers have well-ordered, crystalline regions. Long-chain molecules can fold to form parallel rows of atoms, known as lamella. At the ends of the folds are less ordered, amorphous regions (Fig. 16).

When a stress is applied to a semi-crystalline polymer the lamella begin to unfold. The molecules become realigned to form fibrils. At very high values of stress, the fibrils break down and the polymer chains become highly ordered. The material is now extremely strong. You can

Fig. 16 Polymer stretching

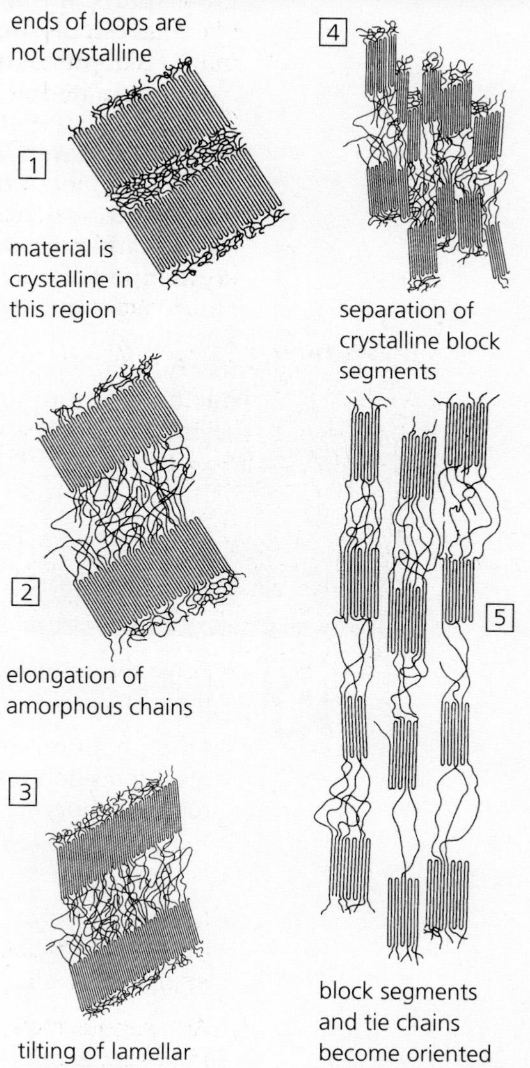
ends of loops are not crystalline
1
material is crystalline in this region
2
elongation of amorphous chains
3
tilting of lamellar chain folds
4
separation of crystalline block segments
5
block segments and tie chains become oriented with the tensile axis

demonstrate this process, known as 'cold-drawing', by stretching the polythene rings used to hold cans of drink together. The material has a small elastic region, but when you exert a higher stress the extension becomes permanent; the polythene flows into a neck that gradually increases in length. The polythene becomes very strong along its length, but weaker if you exert a force across its width. This is because the forces between atoms in the polymer chain are stronger than the forces between adjacent chains.

8 Fibre-glass is used in the construction of boats and aircraft parts. It is made from glass fibres set in plastic resin. What are the benefits of using this combination of materials?

The spider's web

The silk produced by a spider is still puzzling the scientists who are trying to analyse and reproduce it. It is a semi-crystalline polymer, with lines of up to ten amino acid molecules forming the lamella. The strength of such a polymer depends on its crystalline regions, and its elasticity is due to its amorphous regions. Spider silk seems to have less well-ordered crystalline regions than most polymers, but the amorphous regions are more orderly than normal. It takes about 20 different amino acids to build the chain, whereas most artificial polymers have only one or two basic building blocks. It may be that the secret of the spider's silk lies in the sheer complexity of its polymer chains.

Key ideas

- Polymers consist of long, chain-like molecules.
- Amorphous polymers are glassy below their glass transition temperature, T_G, and rubbery above it.
- Semi-crystalline polymers have crystalline and amorphous regions.
- Some polymers, like rubber, are capable of very large elongation.

6 The electric car

I suffer from asthma, and so do my children. Traffic in the town centre is heavy so I avoid going when it's busy in case car fumes trigger an attack. People die of asthma. It's about time we did something about vehicle exhaust emissions.

Air filtration masks are increasingly popular in smog-ridden cities such as Los Angeles.

PARKING
3rd ST 1100

Exhaust emissions from cars account for much of the airborne pollution of cities. About 90% of atmospheric carbon monoxide comes from car exhausts. The poisonous gas can kill red blood cells. Nitrogen oxides at levels of only two parts per million are enough to trigger an asthma attack. About half of the nitrogen oxides in the UK come from car exhausts. Unburnt hydrocarbons from vehicle exhausts are responsible for corrosive and irritant 'petrochemical smog' in cities throughout the world.

In an effort to reduce vehicle-related pollution, the state government of California has laid down strict requirements for car exhaust emissions. By the year 2003, 10% of cars sold in California must be 'zero-emission'. One way to meet these requirements is to develop electrically powered vehicles. The electrical manufacturer Siemens estimates that the world market for electric cars will be 500 000 per year by the year 2001. To make electric cars attractive to customers, designers must try to maximise the power output of the car, whilst keeping the bulk of the batteries to a minimum.

6.1 Learning objectives

After working through this chapter, you should be able to:

- **explain** what is meant by the terms current, potential difference and resistance;
- **define** power and efficiency;
- **derive** and use equations for electrical power;
- **explain** the relationship between e.m.f., internal resistance and terminal p.d.;
- **predict** how current and potential difference vary with resistance;
- **explain** the limitations of Ohm's law;
- **define** and use the concept of resistivity.

6.2 Power and energy

La Jamais Contente

Electric cars have been around since 1899, when an electrically powered car, 'La Jamais Contente', took the land speed record at 105 kilometres per hour. Electric vehicle technology then fell to the wayside as car designers found chemicals to be a more compact energy store than batteries; a litre of petrol has roughly the same energy content as 100 kg of lead–acid batteries.

One of the main problems with electric cars lies in making a big enough store of energy that can be transferred rapidly into kinetic energy.

Scientists use the word **power** to describe the rate of transfer of energy:

$$\text{power} = \frac{\text{energy transferred}}{\text{time}}$$

$$P = \frac{\Delta W}{\Delta t}$$

Energy is measured in joules (J); power is measured in watts (W). One watt is 1 joule per second.

Table 1 Power – orders of magnitude

light emitting diode dashboard warning light	~ milliwatts (mW)
car radio	~ watts
car head lamps	~ 100 watts
sports car petrol engine	~ 100 kW

An alternative unit of energy is the kilowatt hour. This is equivalent to a power of 1 kW transferring energy for 1 hour.
(1 kW h = 1000 W × 3600 s = 3.6 MJ)

Most motorists want cars with a reasonable top speed and adequate acceleration. These factors depend on the car's power.

Table 2 Typical vehicle specifications

	Electric car	Petrol car
top speed	80 km h^{-1}	140 km h^{-1}
acceleration to 50 km h^{-1}	10 s	5 s
carrying capacity	250 kg	400 kg
vehicle mass	1000 kg	900 kg

Electric cars tend to be heavier because of the mass of the batteries (Table 2).

An idea of the power needed by a vehicle to accelerate can be found by calculating the change in kinetic energy. For example, what power is needed to accelerate a 1000 kg car to 50 km h^{-1} in 10 seconds?

kinetic energy at 50 km h^{-1} = $\frac{1}{2}mv^2$

$$v = 50\ \text{km h}^{-1} = \frac{50\,000\ \text{m}}{3600\ \text{s}} = 13.9\ \text{m s}^{-1}$$

$$E_k = \tfrac{1}{2}mv^2 = \tfrac{1}{2} \times 1000\ \text{kg} \times (13.9\ \text{m s}^{-1})^2 = 96\,600\ \text{J}$$

$$P = \frac{\Delta W}{\Delta t} = \frac{96\,600\ \text{J}}{10\ \text{s}} = 9660\ \text{W, or } 9.7\ \text{kW}$$

This is actually an underestimate because the calculation ignores energy transferred because of friction and air resistance.

1 Work out the electric vehicle's kinetic energy at its top speed. How long would it take to reach top speed at a constant power of 9.7 kW? (Ignore work done against friction, etc.)

2 A sports car has the same mass as the electric vehicle but a more powerful engine. How will this affect:

a its acceleration?

b its kinetic energy at 50 km h^{-1}?

c its top speed?

6.3 Efficiency

The sleek body of the GM Impact is designed to improve the electric car's efficiency.

Efficiency is a measure of the amount of energy that is transferred into a useful form:

$$\text{efficiency} = \frac{\text{useful power output}}{\text{total power input}} = \frac{\text{useful energy output}}{\text{total energy input}}$$

A totally efficient machine would transfer all the input energy (or power) into useful output energy (or power).

Efficiency is often written as a percentage.

Fig. 1 Calculating the efficiency of an electric car

An electric car of mass 800 kg climbs a 10% gradient at 10 m s^{-1}. The input power to the motors is 12 kW.

In 1 second, the increase in potential energy is:

$mg\Delta h = 800\text{ kg} \times 10\text{ m}s^{-2} \times 1\text{ m} = 8000\text{ J}$

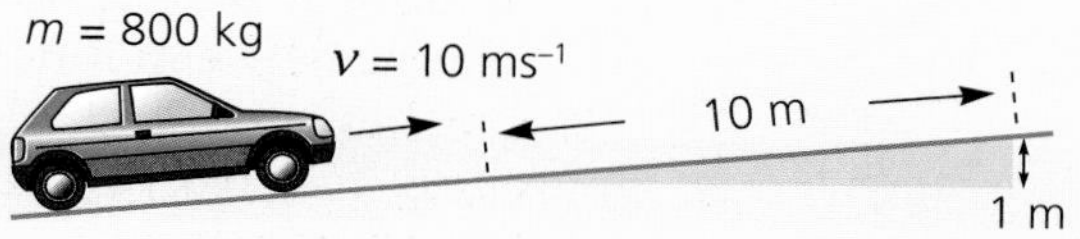

m = 800 kg
v = 10 ms⁻¹
10 m
1 m

$$P = \frac{\Delta W}{\Delta t} = \frac{mg\Delta h}{\Delta t}$$
$$= \frac{800\text{ kg} \times 10\text{ m}s^{-2} \times 1\text{ m}}{1\text{ s}}$$
$$= 8\text{ kW}$$

$$\text{efficiency} = \frac{\text{power output}}{\text{power input}}$$
$$= \frac{8\text{ kW}}{12\text{ kW}}$$
$$= 0.67,\text{ or } 67\%$$

Internal combustion engines are only about 30% to 40% efficient. Electric motors can also act in reverse – as electrical generators – when the car is going downhill or braking. An electric vehicle could therefore recharge its own batteries.

6.4 Battery technology

In 1994, a petrol-powered vehicle could deliver around 600 MJ of energy from a tank of fuel, compared with 25 MJ of useful energy from about half a tonne of lead–acid batteries. The electric car of the future needs a lightweight battery with a high energy capacity.

Batteries are chemical reactors which transfer energy as electricity. But what does that mean?

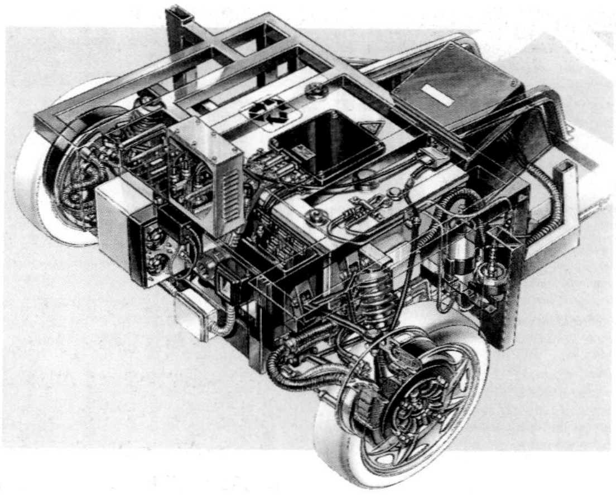

Under the bonnet of Fiat's 'Downtown'.

Charge

Electricity concerns the flow of **charge** in a circuit. Objects which feel electrical forces possess electrical charge. Charge is a fundamental property of matter, like mass. We know that particles can have different amounts of mass and that masses are affected by gravitational fields. In a similar way, particles can have different amounts of charge and can be affected by electric fields. Particles can have either positive or negative charge. Particles with the same sort of charge will repel each other and particles with opposite charges attract.

Atoms have negatively charged electrons which are held close to the positively charged nucleus of the atom. Atoms as a whole are electrically neutral; there is no net charge.

If an electron is added to an atom, a negative **ion** is formed. A positive ion is created by taking an electron away from a neutral atom (Fig. 2). Batteries transfer charge between ions in chemical reactions.

Fig. 2 The formation of ions by electron transfer

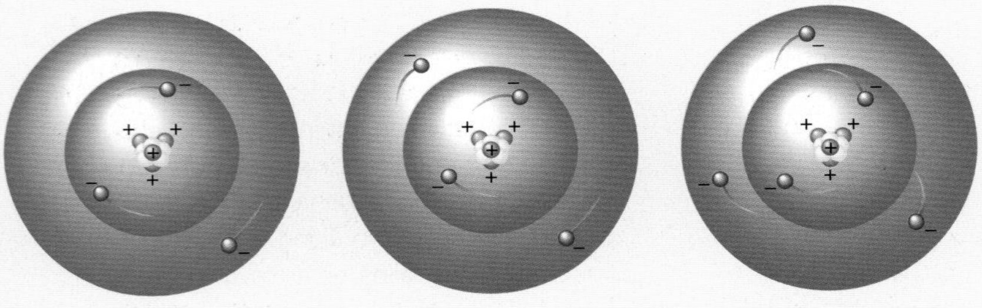
positive ion
neutral atom
negative ion

Adding electrons to a neutral atom gives a negative ion, removing electrons gives a positive ion.

Fig. 3 Charging a non-conductor using friction

Some non-conductors can be electrically charged by friction. When a balloon is rubbed with a dry cloth, some of the electrons on the surface of the balloon move to the cloth, leaving the ballon with a net positive charge. If the cloth was insulated, it would now be negatively charged. However, you are quite a good conductor, so this negative charge passes through your body to earth.

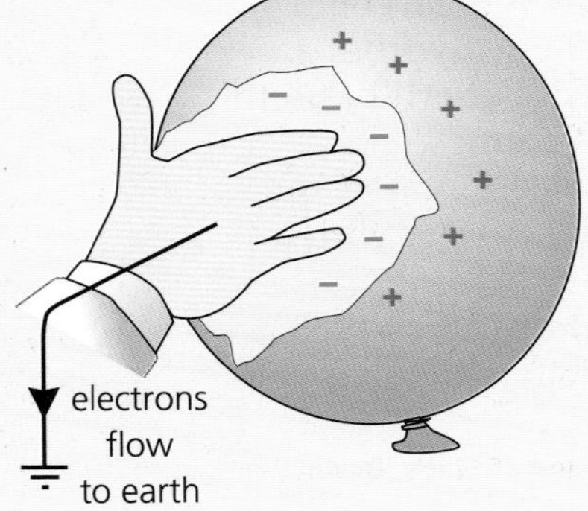
electrons flow to earth

In metals, some electrons are free to move around between the atoms. This enables metals to conduct electricity. If a conductor is placed near an electric charge, charges can be *induced* on the conductor (Fig. 4).

Fig. 4 Induced charge

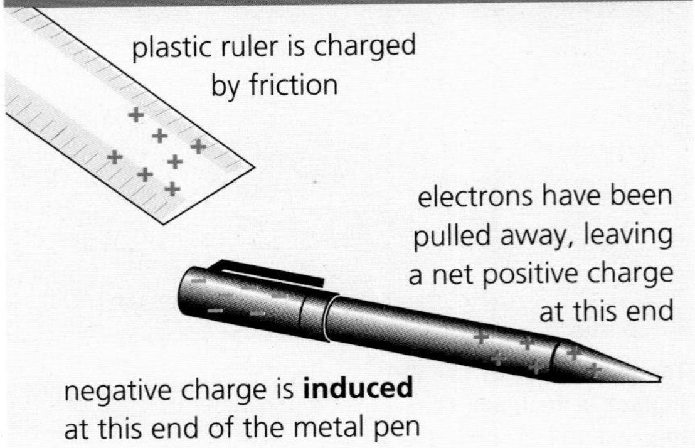
plastic ruler is charged by friction
electrons have been pulled away, leaving a net positive charge at this end
negative charge is **induced** at this end of the metal pen

We measure charge in coulombs (C). The charge of one electron is only 1.6×10^{-19} C.

3 How many electrons make up 1 coulomb?

Current

Current is a flow of charged particles of any sort. For example, positive and negative ions moving through a battery produce a current. Current is measured in amperes (A).

A current of 1 ampere means that 1 coulomb of charge passes a given point in a circuit every second. Current is the rate of flow of charge.

$$\text{current (A)} = \frac{\text{charge flowing (C)}}{\text{time taken (s)}}$$

In symbols: $I = \dfrac{Q}{t}$

Fig. 5 Conventional current

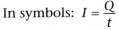

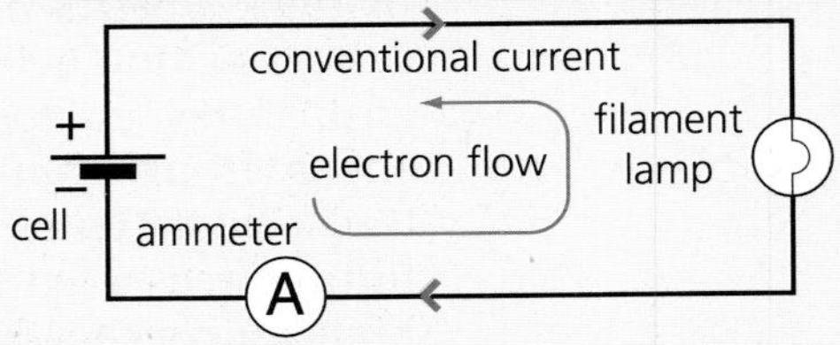
conventional current
filament lamp
electron flow
cell
ammeter
A

We traditionally show current moving in the direction that positive charges would move. This is known as conventional current. In a metal wire it is actually the negative charges (the electrons) that move the other way, but this has the same effect.

Any charge which flows into a component must also flow back out. Therefore, in a series circuit the current is the same all around the circuit. Where it splits into several branches, the total current must stay the same.

Fig. 6 Series and parallel arrangements of components

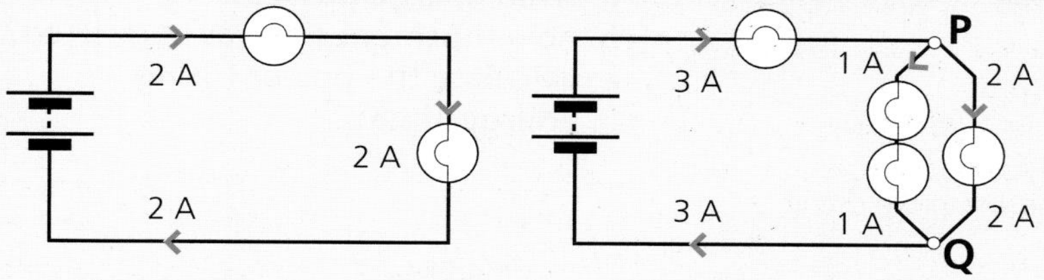
2 A
2 A
2 A
3 A
1 A
P
2 A
3 A
1 A
2 A
Q

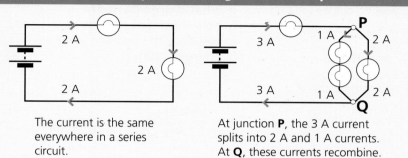

The current is the same everywhere in a series circuit.

At junction **P**, the 3 A current splits into 2 A and 1 A currents. At **Q**, these currents recombine.

4 **In 2 seconds, 5 coulombs of positive particles flow to the right and 5 coulombs of negative particles flow to the left (Fig. 5). Is there any current? If so, how much and in which direction is the conventional current flowing?**

5 **If 32 coulombs of charge flow into a motor in 0.2 seconds, what is the current?**

Capacity

One of the most useful things to know about a battery is its **capacity**. Capacity is measured in ampere-hours (A h). One ampere-hour means a current of 1 A can flow for 1 hour, or 0.5 A for 2 hours, etc. The capacity is a measure of the total amount of charge which the battery can push around a circuit.

The battery pack for the prototype Vauxhall 'Astra Impuls II' has a capacity of 42.5 A h. This battery therefore delivers the equivalent of 42.5 A of current for 1 hour. Using charge = current × time:

$$\text{charge} = 42.5\text{ A} \times 3600\text{ s} = 153\,000\text{ C}$$

When this battery is discharged, 153 000 coulombs could flow around the circuit.

Potential difference

In an electric car, energy from the battery is transferred into kinetic energy. The amount of energy that is transferred when unit charge moves between two points in a circuit is represented by the **potential difference**, or **p.d.** (sometimes called the **voltage**).

Electrical p.d. is similar to gravitational p.d. If you drop something, its gravitational potential energy changes to kinetic energy as it falls. The higher you lift the object, the greater its final velocity and the higher the energy with which it hits the ground. In the same way, a higher electrical p.d. tends to make charge move faster.

The unit of potential difference is the **volt** (V). When a charge of 1 coulomb passes through a potential difference of 1 volt, it does 1 joule of work. This is how physicists define the volt.

$$\text{potential difference (V)} = \frac{\text{work done (J)}}{\text{charge (C)}}$$

$$V = \frac{W}{Q}$$

Potential difference is measured using a voltmeter connected in parallel with the component. Since p.d. is a measure of the difference *across* a component, the probes are placed on either side of the component.

Fig. 7 Potential difference

Potential differences across series circuits simply add up.

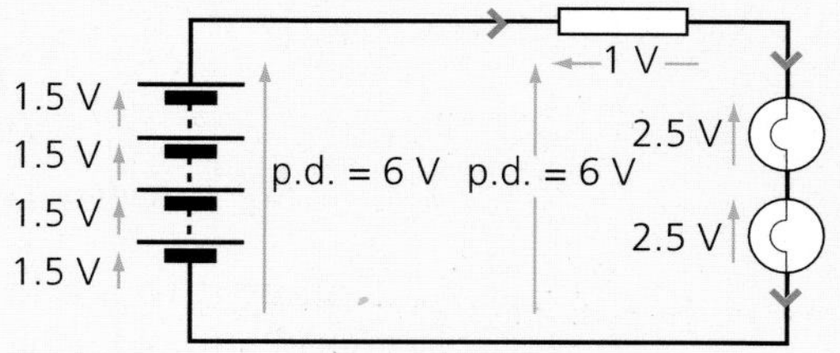
1 V
1.5 V
1.5 V
1.5 V
1.5 V
p.d. = 6 V
p.d. = 6 V
2.5 V
2.5 V

Potential differences across parallel components are equal.

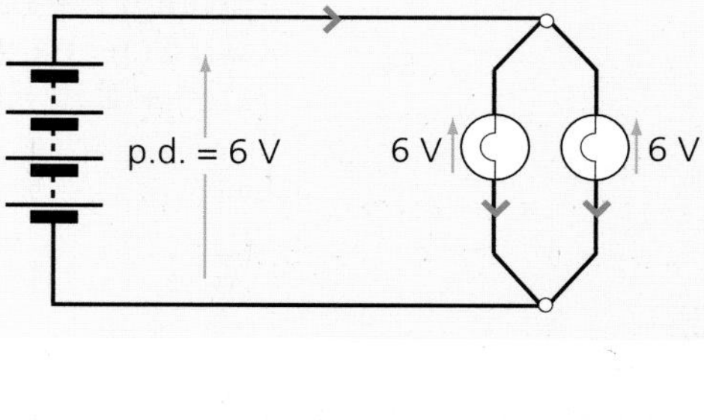
p.d. = 6 V
6 V
6 V

Fig. 8 Using ideas about voltage: energy storage of batteries

Fiat intend to use a sodium–sulphur battery in the 'Downtown' electric car. The battery has a rating of 108 V, 160 A h. How does the energy stored in this battery compare with the 25 MJ of energy stored in half a tonne of lead–acid batteries?

You can calculate the energy stored by this battery by first working out the total charge which the battery delivers:

160 A h means 160 A for 1 hour, giving $Q = 160\ \text{A} \times 3600\ \text{s} = 576\ 000\ \text{C}$

108 V means that each coulomb transfers 108 J from the battery to the circuit.

From $V = \frac{W}{Q}$, or $W = VQ$

available energy, $W = 108\ \text{V} \times 576000\ \text{C}$
$= 62.2\ \text{MJ}$

6 A charge of 2 C was moved through a p.d. of 160 V in an electric motor. How much energy was transferred?

7 In a battery charger, a current of 3 A flowed through a p.d. of 12 V for 5 seconds.

a what charge passed?

b how much energy was converted?

c calculate the power (using energy/time).

Power

The power delivered by a battery depends on the p.d. between the terminals and the amount of current flowing in the circuit. You can combine the definitions of current and p.d. to derive the equation for electrical power.

Suppose a current of I amperes flows through a p.d. of V volts for t seconds.

We can deduce an equation for power output.

From $P = \frac{W}{t}$, $V = \frac{W}{Q}$ and $I = \frac{Q}{t}$,

$$P = \frac{QV}{t} = \frac{ItV}{t} = IV$$

So, power = current × voltage

Follow through this worked example on the Fiat Panda Elettra. The car has a 72 V, 13.6 kW h battery and an electric motor rated at 9.2 kW. What current flows through the battery? How long would it take to recharge the battery with a charger rated at 220 V, 8 A?

First find the current that passes through the battery:

For the motor, $P = IV$

$$9.2\ \text{kW} = I \times 72\ \text{V}$$
$$I = \frac{9200\ \text{W}}{72\ \text{V}} = 128\ \text{A}$$

Find the power of the charger:

$$P = IV = 8\ \text{A} \times 220\ \text{V} = 1760\ \text{W}$$

Now find out how long it takes to deliver the energy needed:

For the battery, $P = \frac{W}{t}$

$$1760\ \text{W} = \frac{13.6\ \text{kW h}}{t}$$
$$t = \frac{13.6 \times 1000 \times 3600\ \text{J}}{1760\ \text{W}} = 27818\ \text{s (7.7 hours)}$$

With this powerful battery charger, an overnight charge would be just enough.

6.5 Resistance

Fig. 9 Free electrons in a metal

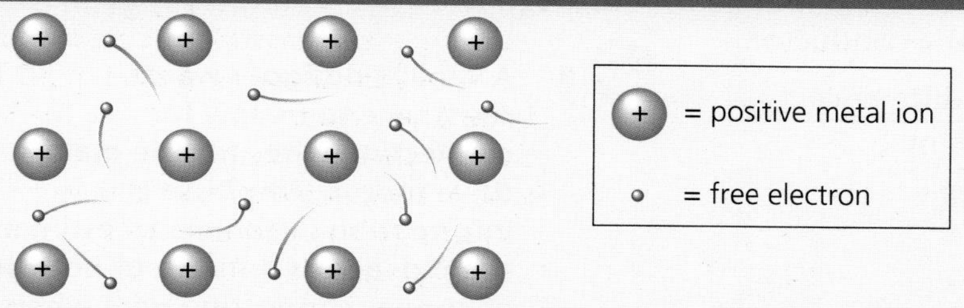

= positive metal ion
= free electron

Electrons break loose from their parent atoms, leaving a 'gas' of free electrons in between positive metal ions.

Resistance of metals

Metals are the most common conductors used in electrical circuits. They are good conductors of electricity because of the presence of free electrons which can move between the positively charged metal ions (Fig. 9).

A potential difference applied across the metal sets up an **electric field**. This makes the electrons accelerate until they collide with positive ions in the metal. The electrons then accelerate and collide again with other positive ions. All these collisions mean that the wire resists the flow of electrons. Therefore, a potential difference is needed across the conductor to keep the current flowing – i.e. to replace the energy lost by the electrons in collisions.

The energy lost by the electrons is transferred to the positive ions as vibrational energy so the wire gets hotter. More current would mean more collisions and so more heating.

A resistor converts electricity to heat energy. This can be exploited in vehicle design: e.g. in heating elements for a windscreen demister. However, resistive heating of wires is one of the main causes of inefficiency in electric motors.

Ohm's law

In 1827, Georg Simon Ohm showed that the current flowing through a metal conductor was proportional to the p.d. across the conductor (Fig. 10). This simple rule holds for metals and a few other substances, but only under limited conditions. The rule breaks down if temperature changes. Other physical conditions, such as light intensity, pressure, strain and magnetic fields, can affect the resistance of some materials. There are some things (water, electrolytes, semiconductor diodes, light bulbs) for which the rule does not work at all. These are called non-ohmic conductors.

Ohm's law must be stated very cautiously: 'Provided that temperature and other physical conditions remain constant, the current through a conductor is proportional to the potential difference across the conductor.'

Fig. 10 Ohmic and non-ohmic conduction

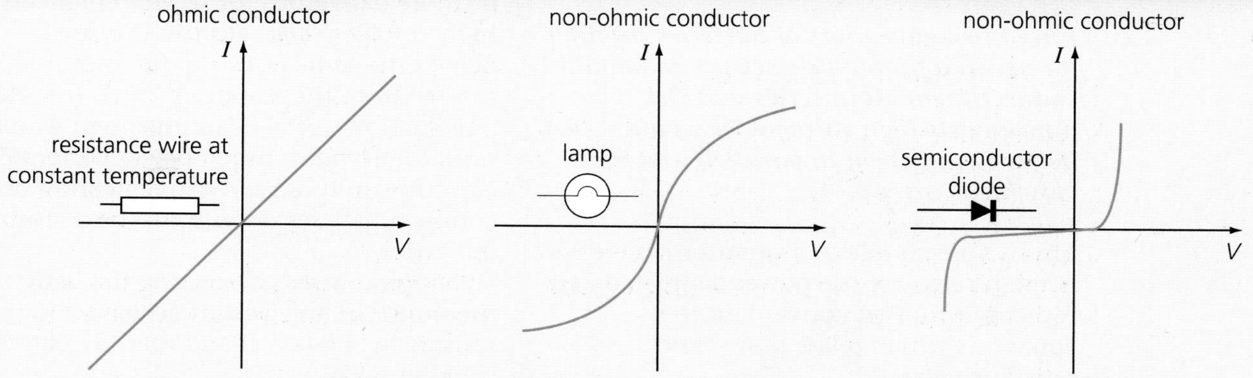

ohmic conductor
I
resistance wire at constant temperature
V
non-ohmic conductor
I
lamp
V
non-ohmic conductor
I
semiconductor diode
V

An ohmic conductor gives a straight line graph.

The lamp filament gets hot, so Ohm's law does not apply.

A diode conducts electricity in a more complicated way.

If a component is a good resistor, it needs a high p.d. to make a current flow. A good conductor only needs a small p.d. to make the same current flow. The ratio of p.d. to current is the resistance of a conductor.

$$\text{resistance} = \frac{\text{potential difference}}{\text{current}}$$

$$R = \frac{V}{I}, \; I = \frac{V}{R} \text{ or } V = IR$$

Resistance is measured in ohms (Ω). A resistance of 1 Ω would need a p.d. of 1 V to make a current of 1 A flow through it.

8 A vehicle designer wants resistance to be low for connecting wires for the main drive motor. Why? Use the information in Table 3 to estimate the p.d. across 1 metre of both sorts of copper connecting wire when the current is 100 A.

9 The p.d. across a heating element is 4 V when 6 A flows. What will the p.d. be when 9 A flows? What have you assumed?

Table 3 Orders of magnitude of resistance relating to electric vehicles

1 m copper connecting wire from battery to motor	~ 0.002 Ω
1 m copper connecting wire from battery to headlights	~ 0.1 Ω
PVC insulation between adjacent wires	~ 1 MΩ

6.6 Power and resistance

I need to connect lots of batteries together for use in a prototype electric car. Should I connect them all in series and risk a dangerously high voltage? Or would it be better to put them in parallel, and have very high currents?

This is an example of a situation where we need to calculate the power dissipated in a resistor. It is often convenient to use equations which relate power and resistance directly.

We know: $P = IV$ and $V = IR$

Eliminating V gives: $P = I \times IR$

$P = I^2R$

Eliminating I gives: $P = \frac{V}{R}V$

$P = V^2/R$

The battery modules in an electric vehicle could all be connected in series or in parallel. The total energy storage in either case would be the same, but the p.d. across the cells would be different. The series (high p.d. or 'voltage') arrangement would be more dangerous for service engineers: high voltages cause electric shocks. To deliver the same power to the motor, we can see from the equation $P = IV$ that the parallel (low voltage) arrangement would need to provide a much bigger current. This current would cause resistive heating of the connecting wires. Would this be a severe limitation?

Suppose wires connecting the battery to the motor in an electric van have a resistance of 0.005 Ω and that the battery supplies 6 kW.

Fig. 11 Ducato van battery arrangement

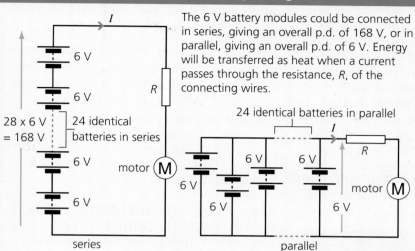

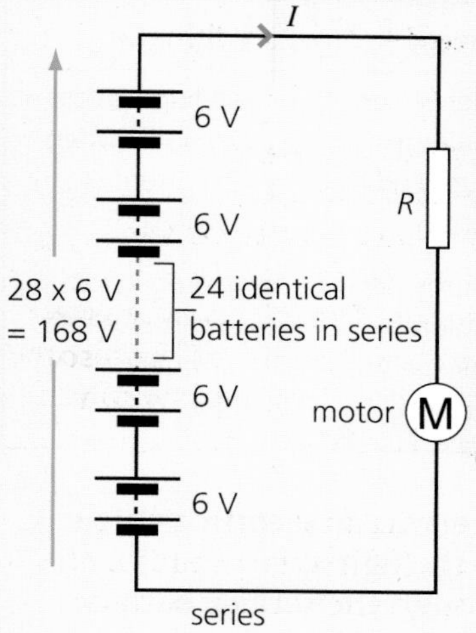

I
6 V
6 V
R
28 x 6 V
= 168 V
24 identical
batteries in series
6 V
motor
M
6 V
series

The 6 V battery modules could be connected in series, giving an overall p.d. of 168 V, or in parallel, giving an overall p.d. of 6 V. Energy will be transferred as heat when a current passes through the resistance, *R*, of the connecting wires.

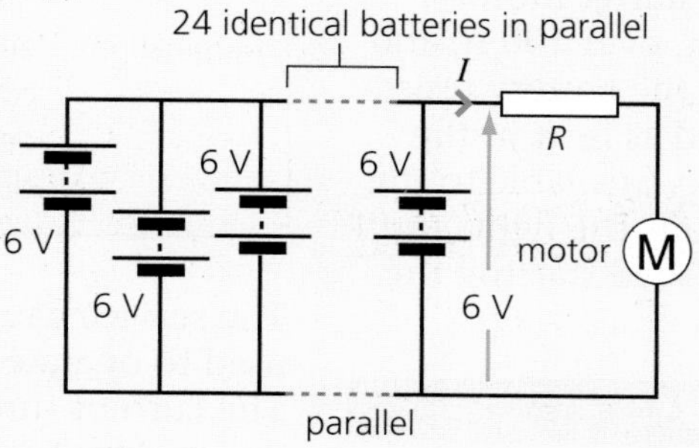

24 identical batteries in parallel
I
R
6 V
6 V
6 V
6 V
6 V
motor
M
parallel

In the series case, the battery p.d. is $28 \times 6\ \text{V} = 168\ \text{V}$.

To deliver 6 kW requires a current of:

$$I = \frac{P}{V}$$
$$= \frac{6000\ \text{W}}{168\ \text{V}} = 35.7\ \text{A}$$

Then power lost in wires is:

$$P = I^2R$$
$$= (35.7\ \text{A})^2 \times 0.005\ \Omega = 6.4\ \text{W}$$

The efficiency of energy transfer is:

$$\text{efficiency} = \frac{6000\ \text{W} - 6.4\ \text{W}}{6000\ \text{W}}$$
$$= 0.999 \text{ or } 99.9\%$$

In the parallel case, the battery p.d. is 6 V. To deliver 6 kW requires a current of:

$$I = \frac{P}{V}$$
$$= \frac{6000\ \text{W}}{6\ \text{V}} = 1000\ \text{A}$$

Then power lost in wires is:

$$P = I^2R$$
$$= (1000\ \text{A})^2 \times 0.005\ \Omega = 5000\ \text{W}$$

The efficiency of energy transfer is:

$$\text{efficiency} = \frac{6000\ \text{W} - 5000\ \text{W}}{6000\ \text{W}}$$
$$= 0.167 \text{ or } 16.7\%$$

It is clear that the series arrangement is preferable in electric cars despite the risk of electric shock. The dramatic difference of efficiency (16.7% compared with 99.9%) could be overcome by making the connecting wires thicker, but this would add weight and cost more.

10 An engineer suggests a compromise arrangement of batteries in series and parallel as shown below.

Each cell has a p.d. of 6 V

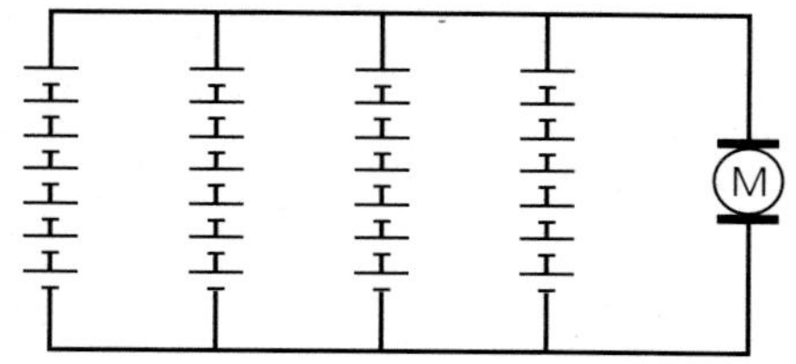

M

Calculate the efficiency of energy transfer for the same system using this arrangement of batteries. Comment on the safety and suitability of the proposal.

Key ideas

- Conventional current flows from + to –.
- Current, *I*, is the rate of flow of charge,

  $I = \frac{Q}{t}$

- Potential difference, *V*, is the energy per unit charge,

  $V = \frac{W}{Q}$

- Resistance, *R*, is a measure of a component's opposition to current,

  $R = \frac{V}{I}$

- Power, *P*, is the rate of conversion of energy,

  $P = \frac{E}{t} = IV = I^2R = \frac{V^2}{R}$

6.7 Internal resistance and e.m.f.

You may have noticed that the lights go dim and the car stereo dies when the starter motor of a petrol-engined car is switched on. The battery has an **internal resistance** which is only significant when large currents are needed. The starter motor draws a very large current, over 100 A, and the internal resistance of the battery resists this flow. Energy is wasted as heat in the battery, leaving less energy available to the rest of the circuit. This dims the lights until the starter motor has finished starting the engine.

Fig. 12 Internal resistance and e.m.f.

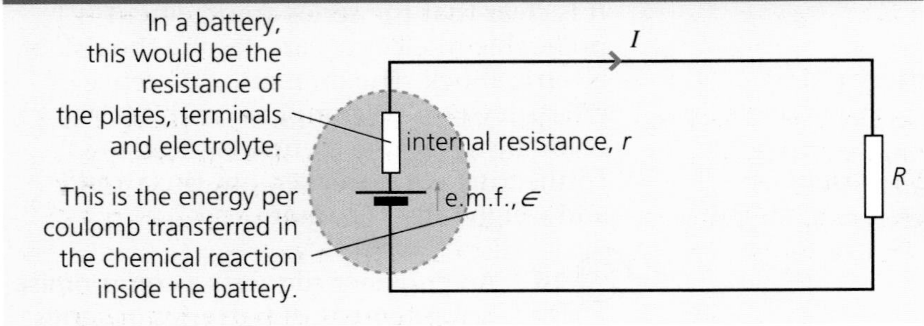

In a battery, this would be the resistance of the plates, terminals and electrolyte.
This is the energy per coulomb transferred in the chemical reaction inside the battery.
I
internal resistance, r
e.m.f., ∈
R

When a current flows in a circuit, work must be done by the battery to move the charge. We say that the battery produces an **electromotive force**, or **e.m.f.**, which gives each coulomb of charge the energy required to keep the current flowing.

$$\epsilon = \frac{E}{Q}$$

where ϵ = electromotive force
E = energy generated
Q = charge

However, a potential difference is needed to push current through the internal resistance of the battery. Energy is wasted by heating this resistance. When a current passes through the battery, the p.d. across its terminals (the **terminal p.d.**) is less than the e.m.f.

$$\text{p.d.}_{\text{terminal}} = \epsilon - \text{p.d.}_{\text{internal resistance}}$$

The terminal p.d. depends on the current flowing. The efficiency of energy transfer to a circuit therefore depends on current. The larger the current flowing, the larger the energy lost in the internal resistance.

	Energy	Voltmeter
e.m.f.	energy per coulomb produced by battery	reading across terminals when no current is flowing
terminal p.d.	energy per coulomb delivered to circuit	reading across terminals when current is flowing

The service battery in an electric vehicle is used to operate the lights, fans, radio, etc. The current through the service battery varies, depending on which devices are switched on. Suppose 4.5 A flows through a battery with internal resistance 0.2 Ω and e.m.f. of 12 V. How efficient is the battery at transferring energy to this current?

Fig. 13 Service battery circuit

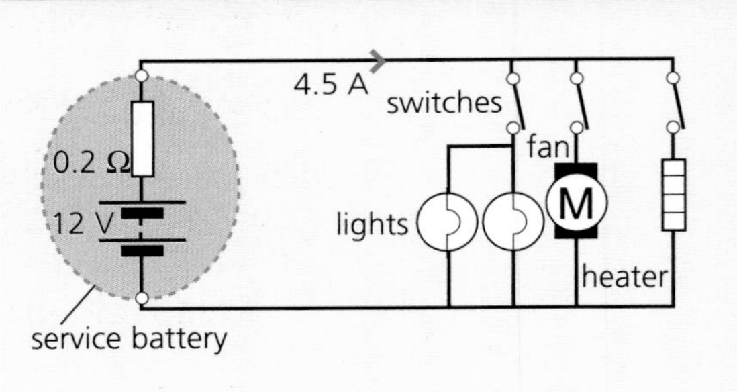

4.5 A
switches
fan
M
0.2 Ω
12 V
lights
heater
service battery

$$\begin{aligned}\text{p.d.}_{\text{internal resistance}} &= IR \\ &= 4.5\ \text{A} \times 0.2\ \Omega \\ &= 0.9\ \text{V}\end{aligned}$$

$$\begin{aligned}\text{p.d.}_{\text{terminal}} &= \epsilon - \text{p.d.}_{\text{internal resistance}} \\ &= 12\ \text{V} - 0.9\ \text{V} \\ &= 11.1\ \text{V}\end{aligned}$$

For every coulomb of charge which flows through it, the battery produces 12 J but only delivers 11.1 J. The efficiency is therefore:

$$\begin{aligned}\text{efficiency} &= \frac{11.1\ \text{J}}{12\ \text{J}} \\ &= 0.925 \text{ or } 92.5\%\end{aligned}$$

11 What is the efficiency when 30 A flows through the battery?

In an electric car the motor current is large, so the power wasted in the internal resistance of the car battery will also be large. It is therefore important that the internal resistance is kept as low as possible in the main storage batteries. Even so, the batteries may need a cooling system.

E.m.f. and terminal p.d. calculations can often be solved using formulae.

$$\epsilon = \text{p.d.}_{\text{terminal}} + \text{p.d.}_{\text{internal resistance}}$$
$$= V + Ir$$
$$= IR + Ir$$
$$\epsilon = I(R + r)$$

This is the statement of Ohm's law for the whole circuit.

Example: An electronic sensor (Fig. 14) acts as a source of e.m.f. The p.d. across the sensor is 5.0 V when 1.2 mA flows but drops to 1.8 V when 3.0 mA flows. What is the internal resistance of the sensor?

From, $\epsilon = V + Ir$

$$\epsilon = 5.0\ \text{V} + 0.0012\ \text{A} \times r$$
$$\epsilon = 1.8\ \text{V} + 0.0030\ \text{A} \times r$$

Eliminating ϵ,

$$5.0\ \text{V} + 0.0012\ \text{A} \times r = 1.8\ \text{V} + 0.0030\ \text{A} \times r$$
$$5.0\ \text{V} - 1.8\ \text{V} = 0.0030\ \text{A} \times r - 0.0012\ \text{A} \times r$$
$$3.2\ \text{V} = 0.0018\ \text{A} \times r$$
$$r = \frac{3.2\ \text{V}}{0.0018\ \text{A}}$$
$$= 1777\ \Omega \text{ or } 1.8\ \text{k}\Omega$$

Fig. 14 An electronic sensor

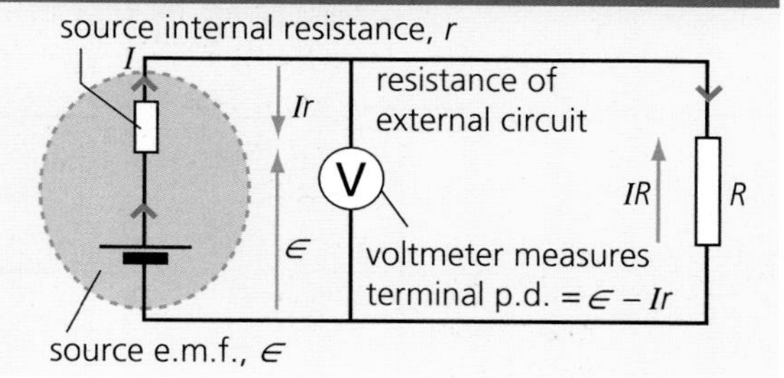

source internal resistance, r
I
Ir
resistance of external circuit
V
IR
R
ϵ
voltmeter measures terminal p.d. = ϵ – Ir
source e.m.f., ϵ

12 The current through an electric vehicle's main storage battery is 120 A, the terminal p.d. is 168 V and the internal resistance 0.1 Ω. What is the e.m.f.?

13 A car battery delivers 112 W of power to a 7 Ω resistor. The e.m.f. of the battery is 30 V. What is the internal resistance?

Key ideas

- E.m.f. is the energy per unit charge transferred by a source.
- Terminal p.d. is less than e.m.f. because of the voltage drop across the internal resistance of the cell:

  $\epsilon = V + Ir$
  $\epsilon = I(R + r)$

6.8 Wiring it up

If you look at any car wiring diagram, you are confronted by a huge mass of circuitry and wire. Electronic circuits in an electric car are even more complicated. They would be impossible to follow if they couldn't be simplified to a few basic arrangements.

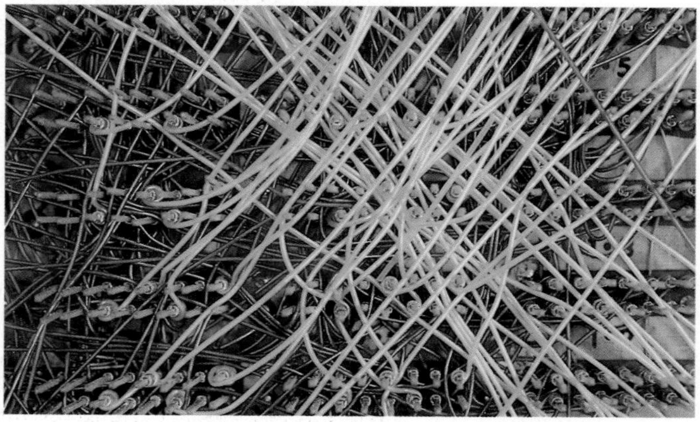

Resistors in series

The same current passes through all resistors in a series circuit. The p.d. across the whole series is the sum of the p.d.s across each resistor (Fig. 15).

Fig. 15 P.d. across resistors in series

The p.d. across the chain of resistors is the sum of the p.d.s across each of the resistors.

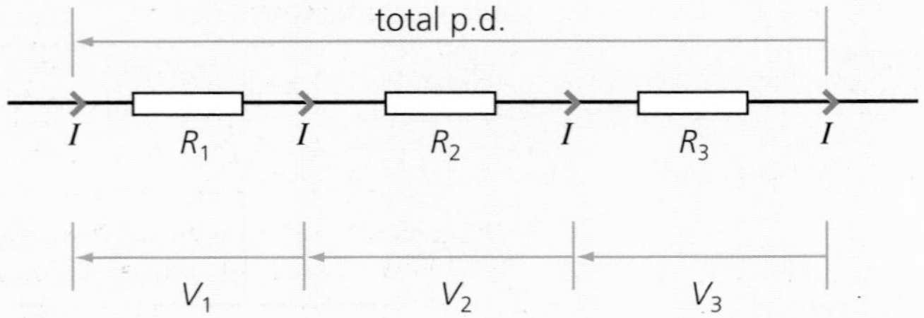

total p.d.
I
R1
I
R2
I
R3
I
V1
V2
V3

This arrangement could be replaced by a single resistor R_T which would pass the same current for the same total p.d.

$$R_T = \frac{\text{p.d.}_{\text{total}}}{\text{current}}$$
$$= \frac{V_1 + V_2 + V_3 + \cdots}{I}$$
$$= \frac{V_1}{I} + \frac{V_2}{I} + \frac{V_3}{I} + \cdots$$
$$R_T = R_1 + R_2 + R_3 + \cdots$$

Resistors in parallel

We can assume the connecting wires in circuit diagrams have no resistance. Therefore the p.d. across each parallel resistor is the same. The total current is the sum of the currents through each resistor (Fig. 16).

Fig. 16 P.d. across parallel resistors

Parallel resistors have the same p.d. across them. The total current I, is the sum of currents through each of the resistors.

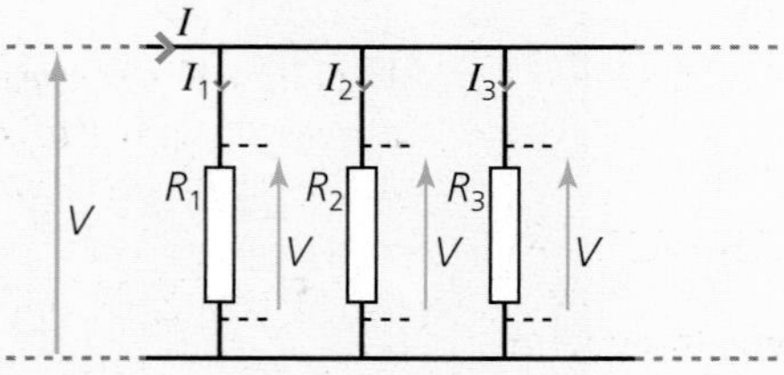

I
I1
I2
I3
R1
R2
R3
V
V
V
V

$$\text{total resistance } (R_T) = \frac{\text{p.d. } (V)}{\text{current } (I)}$$
$$I = \frac{V}{R_T}$$
$$\text{and } I = I_1 + I_2 + I_3 + \cdots$$
$$= \frac{V}{R_1} + \frac{V}{R_2} + \frac{V}{R_3} + \cdots$$
$$\text{so, } \frac{V}{R_T} = \frac{V}{R_1} + \frac{V}{R_2} + \frac{V}{R_3} + \cdots$$
$$\text{Divide by } V, \quad \frac{1}{R_T} = \frac{1}{R_1} + \frac{1}{R_2} + \frac{1}{R_3} + \cdots$$

For just two resistors, the formula

$$R_T = \frac{R_1 \times R_2}{R_1 + R_2}$$

is often easier to use, but it does not extend simply for more resistors.

Fig. 17 Power and resistor arrangements

A demister is to be made up of 3 Ω and 6 Ω heating elements operated from a 12 V service battery of negligible internal resistance. Different powers could be obtained by using just one element or by combining the two in series or parallel. What would be the power in each case?

	total resistance	power = V^2/R
single A	3 Ω	144/3 = 48 W
single B	6 Ω	144/6 = 24 W
in series	6 + 3 = 9 Ω	144/9 = 16 W
in parallel	$\frac{1}{R_T} = \frac{1}{6} + \frac{1}{3} = \frac{1}{2}$	
	$R_T = 2\ \Omega$	144/2 = 72 W

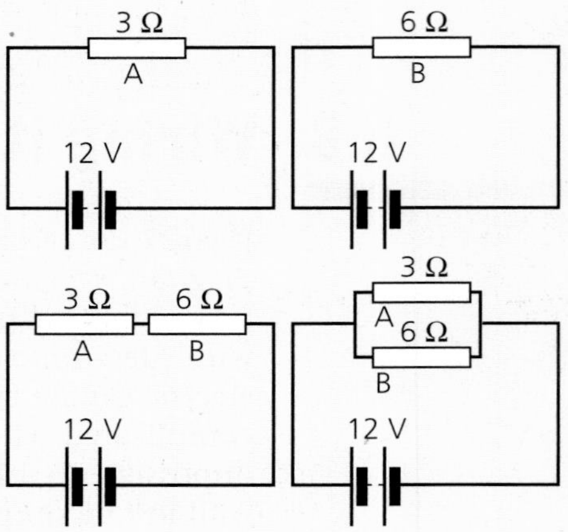

3 Ω
A
12 V
6 Ω
B
12 V
3 Ω
6 Ω
A
B
12 V
3 Ω
A
6 Ω
B
12 V

Combining series and parallel circuits

Real circuits can consist of a mixture of series and parallel elements. Suppose that the series arrangement of demister elements (Fig. 17) is connected in parallel with the rear-screen heating element which has a resistance of 1 Ω. How could you calculate what current flows?

Fig. 18 Combined series and parallel circuits

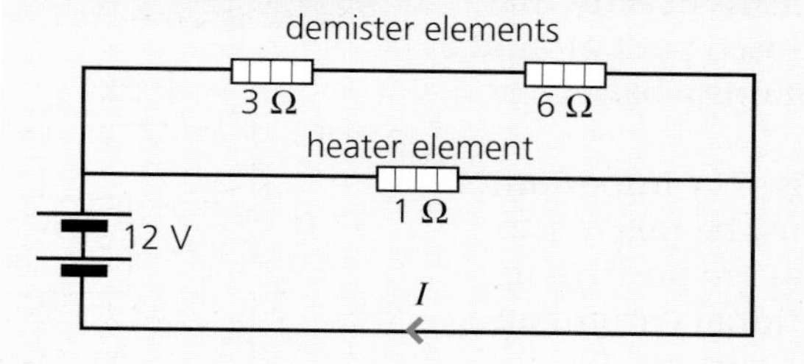

demister elements
3 Ω
6 Ω
heater element
1 Ω
12 V
I

First, tackle series elements: the resistance of the top branch is 9 Ω. The total resistance is given by:

$$\frac{1}{R_T} = \frac{1}{R_1} + \frac{1}{R_2} = \frac{1}{9\ \Omega} + \frac{1}{1\ \Omega}$$

$$R_T = \frac{9\ \Omega}{10} = 0.90\ \Omega$$

$$\text{So, } I = \frac{V}{R}$$

$$= \frac{12\ \text{V}}{0.90\ \Omega} = 13.3\ \text{A}$$

14 Find the current in each of the circuits in Fig. 19:

Fig. 19 Current problems

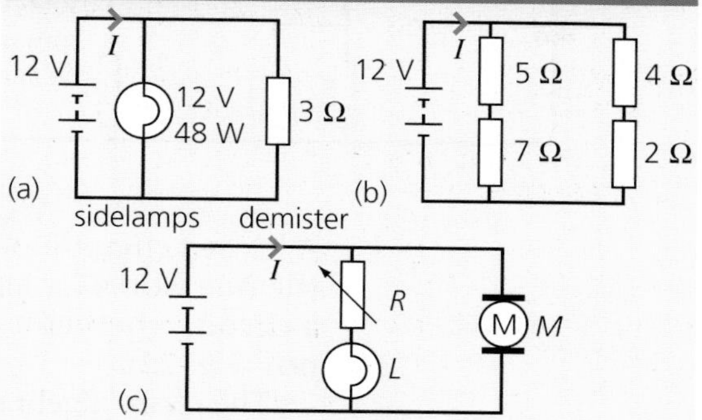

12 V
I
12 V
48 W
3 Ω
(a)
sidelamps
demister
12 V
I
5 Ω
4 Ω
7 Ω
2 Ω
(b)
12 V
I
R
M
L
(c)

R = dimmer resistor, currently set at 10 Ω
L = dashboard light, resistance 5 Ω at this setting
M = heater fan motor, resistance 30 Ω

15 Find the p.d. marked V in each of the circuits in Fig. 20:

Fig. 20 P.d. problems

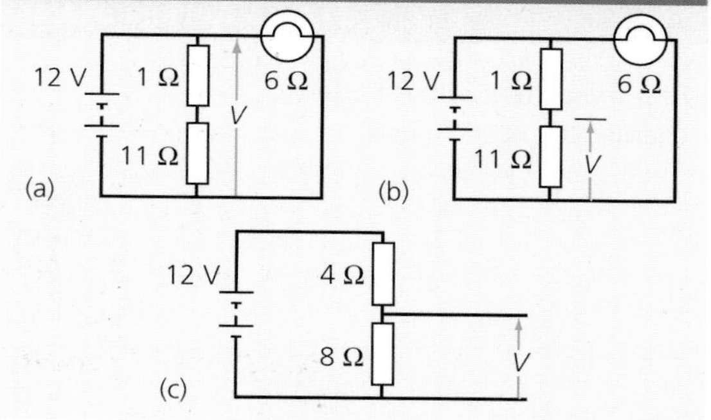

12 V
1 Ω
6 Ω
V
11 Ω
(a)
12 V
1 Ω
6 Ω
11 Ω
V
(b)
12 V
4 Ω
8 Ω
V
(c)

6.9 Complex circuits

It can take a long time to reduce complex circuits to simple series and parallel arrangements. **Kirchhoff's laws** offer a formal set of rules to follow in simplifying circuits (Fig. 21).

Fig. 21 Kirchhoff's laws

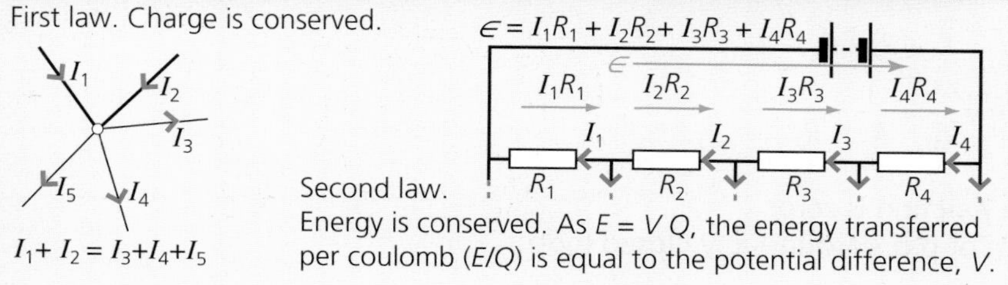

First law. Charge is conserved.
I1
I2
I3
I5
I4
I1+ I2 = I3+I4+I5
∈ = I1R1 + I2R2+ I3R3 + I4R4
I1R1
I2R2
I3R3
I4R4
I1
I2
I3
I4
R1
R2
R3
R4
Second law.
Energy is conserved. As E = V Q, the energy transferred per coulomb (E/Q) is equal to the potential difference, V.

Kirchhoff's first law: *The algebraic sum of currents at a junction is zero.*

$$\sum I = 0$$

Charge is conserved: the charge entering a junction is equal to the charge leaving.

Kirchhoff's second law: *Around a closed circuit loop, the algebraic sum of the e.m.f.s is equal to the algebraic sum of the p.d.s.*

$$\sum \epsilon = \sum IR \qquad \text{(for a resistive circuit)}$$

Energy is conserved.

Fig. 22 E.m.f.s in closed circuit loops

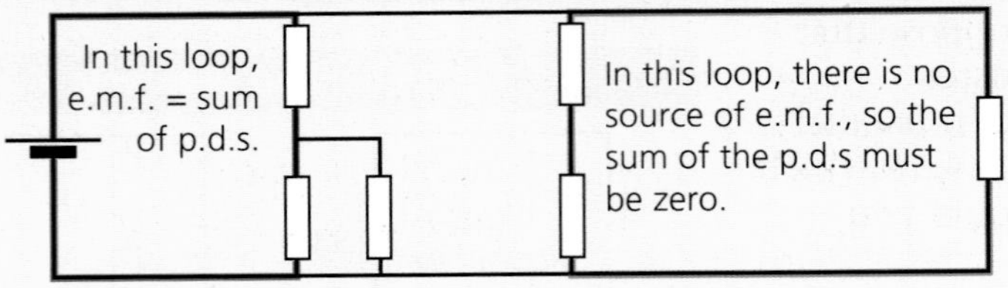
In this loop, e.m.f. = sum of p.d.s.
In this loop, there is no source of e.m.f., so the sum of the p.d.s must be zero.

A 'closed circuit loop' means exactly that; the rule works for any closed path around a circuit, whether it contains a battery or not (Fig. 22).

The term 'algebraic' is very important: it means that direction must be taken into consideration. Quantities are positive in the direction of conventional current and negative if opposing this current. For example, in a battery charger circuit, the e.m.f. of the charger 'opposes' the e.m.f. of the battery which you are charging.

Fig. 23 Worked example

Find the current in this battery charger circuit:

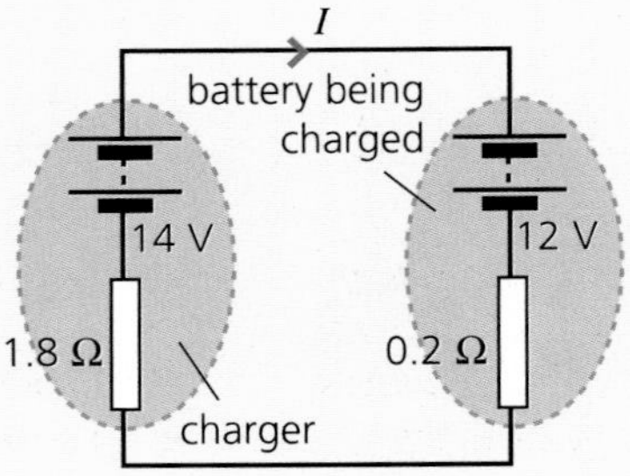
I
battery being charged
14 V
12 V
1.8 Ω
0.2 Ω
charger

sum of e.m.f.s is 14 V – 12 V = 2 V

sum of p.d.s is $I \times 0.2\ \Omega + I \times 1.8\ \Omega$

$= I \times 2\ \Omega$

Kirchhoff's 2nd law says sum of e.m.f.s = sum of p.d.s

so $2\ \text{V} = I \times 2\ \Omega$

$I = 1\ \text{A}$

16 **A voltage regulator for an instrument panel keeps a steady 9.0 V across the instruments. The service battery is nominally 12 V but can fluctuate between 11 and 14 V. The instrument panel needs a fairly constant 0.1 A. Find the maximum power dissipation in the 10 Ω resistor (Fig. 24).**

Fig. 24 Power problem

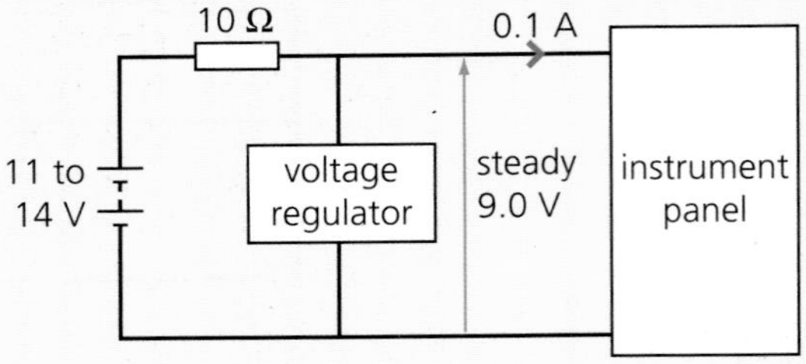
10 Ω
0.1 A
11 to 14 V
voltage regulator
steady 9.0 V
instrument panel

17 **Calculate the current *I* in each of the circuits in Fig. 25.**

Fig. 25 More current problems

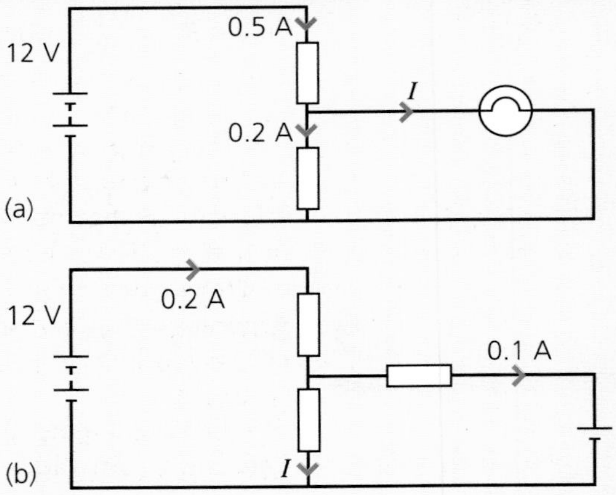
12 V
0.5 A
I
0.2 A
(a)
12 V
0.2 A
0.1 A
I
(b)

Key ideas

- Resistors in series: $R_T = R_1 + R_2 + R_3 + \cdots$
- Resistors in parallel: $\dfrac{1}{R_T} = \dfrac{1}{R_1} + \dfrac{1}{R_2} + \dfrac{1}{R_3} + \cdots$
- Kirchhoff's laws are:
  (1) sum of currents at a junction is zero;
  (2) sum of e.m.f.s = sum of p.d.s around any closed loop.

6.10 Meters and measurement

Electrical methods of measuring are very popular in science and technology. One of the main advantages is that the measuring instrument can be 'remote', so you do not need to be able to see the engine to know whether it is too hot or if the oil has fallen to a dangerously low level.

Potential dividers

Many sensors rely on a change of resistance to make their measurement. These sensors are often used in an arrangement of resistors called a **potential divider**. The accelerator in an electric vehicle could be a potential divider which uses a variable resistor (Fig. 26).

Fig. 26 An accelerator system using a variable resistor

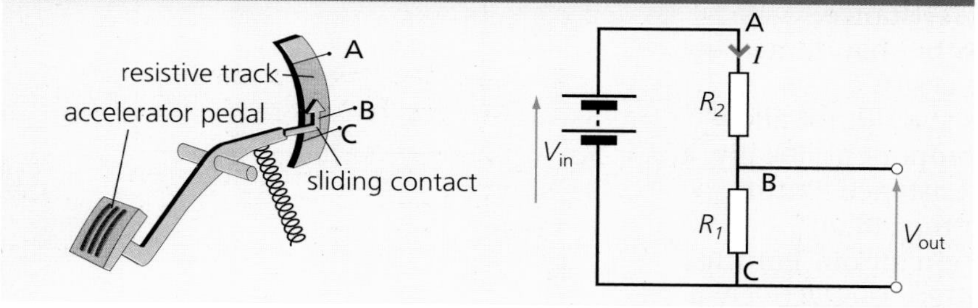

resistive track
accelerator pedal
A
B
C
sliding contact
A
I
R_2
V_{in}
B
R_1
C
V_{out}

As the pedal is depressed, it changes the point of contact on the resistive track, so changing the relative values of the two resistors. This alters the output voltage, information which the computer control unit uses to control the motor. How does the output voltage depend on the size of the resistors?

Assume that no current is drawn from the 'output' terminals. Then the same current, I, flows through both resistors:

$$I = \frac{V}{R} = \frac{V_{in}}{R_1 + R_2}$$

V_{out} is the p.d. across resistor R_1. Substituting I into the expression

$$V_{out} = IR$$

$$= \frac{V_{in}}{R_1 + R_2} \times R_1$$

$$V_{out} = V_{in} \times \frac{R_1}{R_1 + R_2}$$

The voltage is divided in the same ratio as the resistors, i.e.

$$\frac{V_{out}}{V_{in}} = \frac{\text{output resistance}}{\text{total resistance}}$$

To measure other quantities, a sensor resistor is used. For temperature, one of the resistors in the potential divider can be replaced by a thermistor (Fig. 27). The resistance of most thermistors goes down as temperature rises. By putting the thermistor at the top of the potential divider, the total resistance will fall as temperature rises, so the output voltage gets bigger.

Fig. 27 Effect of a thermistor

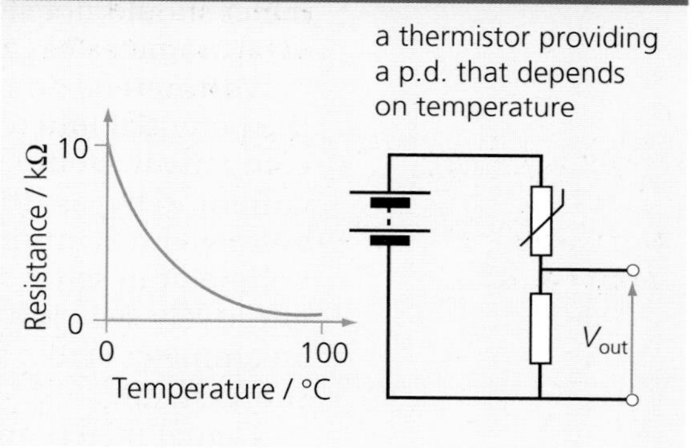

a thermistor providing a p.d. that depends on temperature
Resistance / kΩ
10
0
0
100
Temperature / °C
V_{out}

Despite the curved resistance–temperature graph, the thermistor can be quite a useful 'linear' sensor. Over a limited temperature range – when the resistance of the thermistor is around the same size as the resistor – the potential divider's output rises roughly linearly with increasing temperature.

18 Write down the output voltage of these potential dividers in Fig. 28:

Fig. 28 Potential dividers

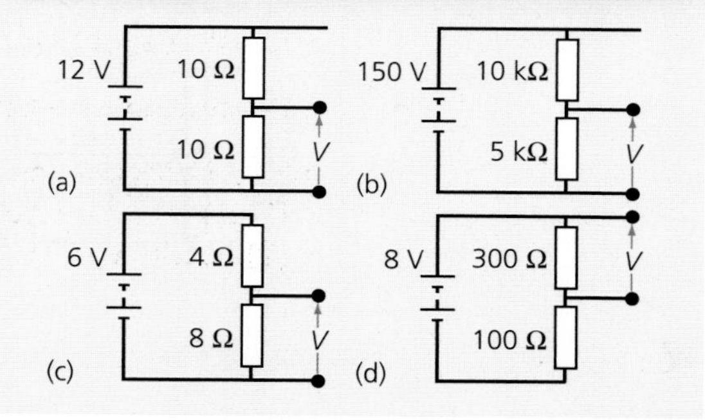

12 V
10 Ω
10 Ω
V
(a)
150 V
10 kΩ
5 kΩ
V
(b)
6 V
4 Ω
8 Ω
V
(c)
8 V
300 Ω
100 Ω
V
(d)

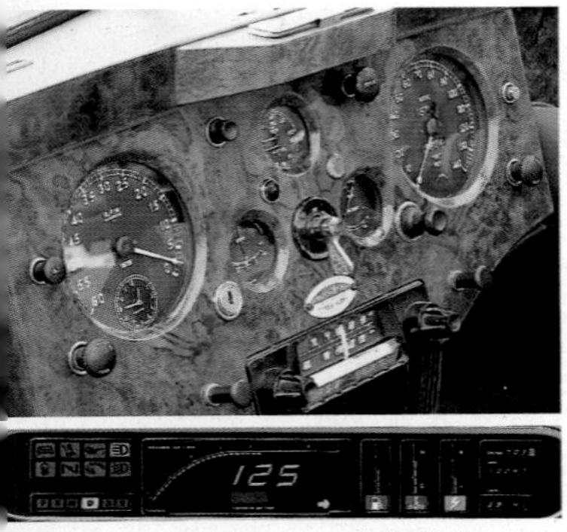
125

Analogue and digital displays.

Meter displays

Displaying results of electrical measurements is done in two ways: moving coil meters (analogue) or digital meters.

Digital meters have replaced moving coil meters in most scientific instruments because they are easier to read accurately and often give a more precise reading. However, car drivers are not as concerned with accuracy; they need to be able to take in the reading at a glance. The analogue display can give a better picture of the information, including red zones for danger!

Changing scales

Ammeters measure the current which flows through a circuit so the circuit needs to be broken to put an ammeter in. The meter should not stop the flow at all, so an ideal ammeter has zero resistance.

Voltmeters, on the other hand, measure the potential difference across a component. Voltmeters should not allow current to bypass the component: ideally, a voltmeter has infinite resistance. Putting a voltmeter in series with the circuit effectively switches the circuit off. Putting an ammeter across a battery is effectively a short circuit.

Digital meters are very high resistance voltmeters, typically reading up to 0.2 V with a resistance of well over 1 MΩ. P.d.s in electric cars may be up to 300 V. The range of the basic meter is extended using a potential divider. A voltmeter module cannot measure current directly: hardly any current could flow through its high resistance. Instead, current is allowed to pass through a low resistance, and the digital meter measures the voltage across the resistor (Fig. 29).

Fig. 29 Digital meters

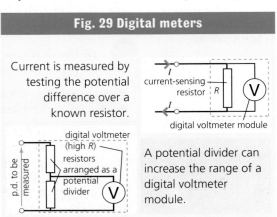

Current is measured by testing the potential difference over a known resistor.

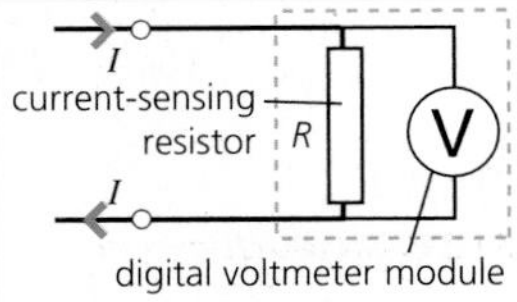
I
current-sensing resistor
R
V
I
digital voltmeter module

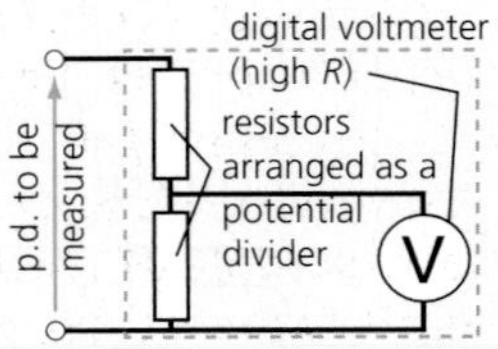
digital voltmeter (high R)
resistors arranged as a potential divider
p.d. to be measured
V

A potential divider can increase the range of a digital voltmeter module.

In moving coil meters, it is the current through the coil which makes the coil turn around. The current needed for full scale deflection (f.s.d.) varies between types of meter, but is usually between 100 μA and 10 A. To allow a sensitive meter to measure a bigger current, you have to make some of the current bypass the meter. This is done with a '**shunt**' resistor (Fig. 30).

Fig. 30 Using a 'shunt' resistor

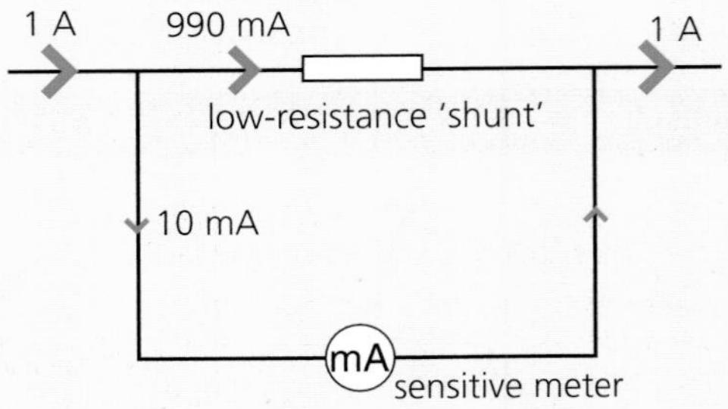
1 A
990 mA
1 A
low-resistance 'shunt'
10 mA
mA
sensitive meter

To convert a moving coil meter into a voltmeter, you put a resistor in series with it. This resistor is called a '**multiplier**' because it multiplies the range of the meter (Fig. 31). It cuts down the current entering the voltmeter at the higher voltage.

Fig. 31 Using a 'multiplier' resistor

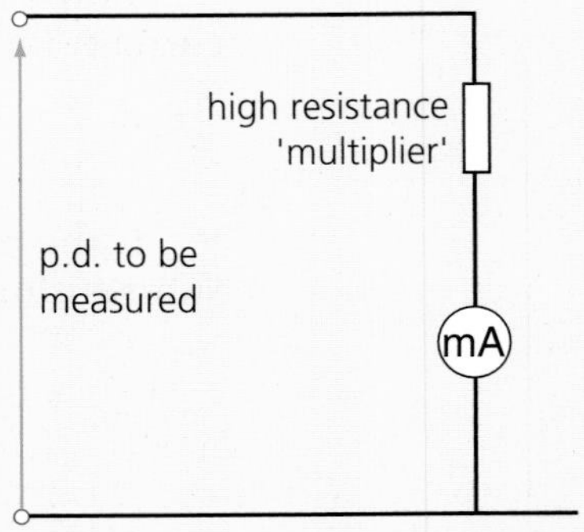
high resistance 'multiplier'
p.d. to be measured
mA

19 **The main motor current in an electric car is to be monitored by using the motor supply leads as the 'shunt' of an ammeter. Each supply lead has resistance 0.003 Ω. Draw the required circuit and suggest a suitable moving coil meter to allow 300 A to be measured. Why would a moving coil meter be better than a digital meter in this application?**

Key ideas

- Ideal ammeters have no resistance. Ideal voltmeters have infinite resistance.
- Digital meters use high resistance voltmeter modules. To make them into ammeters, they are connected in parallel with a current sensing 'shunt' resistance.
- Moving coil meters are current operated. They can measure a bigger current if connected to a shunt resistor. They can be made into voltmeters by connecting a series resistor.

6.11 Resistance of materials

If electric cars are to be successful, they need to be as light and efficient as possible. I need to avoid energy losses by choosing the right materials. Weight and cost are both important. How can I be sure that copper wire is the right material to use?

Resistivity

Copper is a good conductor but has a high density and is increasingly expensive. Development of electric vehicles is likely to put pressure on dwindling world reserves of copper. Aluminium is more abundant, less dense but not as good a conductor. How can we compare different materials and shapes of conductor to make this evaluation?

The length and cross-sectional area of a material affect its resistance (Fig. 32).

Fig. 32 Resistance and shape

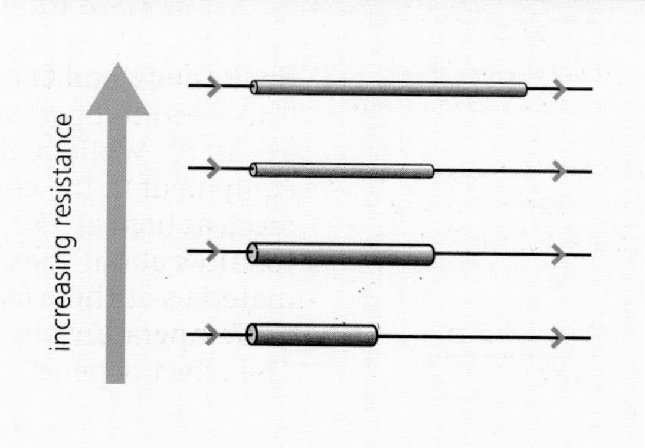
increasing resistance

Using the model of resistance arising from collisions between electrons and lattice ions, we can deduce that:

- Resistance is proportional to length, because doubling the length would double the chance of collision:

$$R \propto l$$

- Resistance is inversely proportional to cross-sectional area, because doubling the area would double the number of moving electrons, thereby doubling the current and halving the resistance:

$$R \propto \frac{1}{A}$$

Combining these relationships gives:

$$R \propto \frac{l}{A}$$

We write:

$$R \propto \frac{l}{A} \text{ or } R = \frac{\rho l}{A} \text{ or } \rho = \frac{RA}{l}$$

where ρ is a constant called **resistivity**. Resistivity has the unit Ω m.

If you set $l = 1$ m and $A = 1$ m^2, then the resistivity, ρ, is the resistance of a standard size sample of material of unit length and unit area of cross section.

Table 4 Typical resistivity values

Class of	Resistivity / Ω m
metals	~ 10^{-7}
semiconductors	~ 10^{2}
insulators	~ 10^{10}

Good resistors are bad conductors and vice versa. We often talk about conduction rather than resistance:

$$\text{conductivity} = \frac{1}{\text{resistivity}}$$

Conductivity is measured in siemens per metre (S m^{-1}).

Nichrome wire can be used in a heating element for a windscreen demister. A 100 cm length of wire of diameter 1.22 mm had a resistance of 0.50 Ω. What is the resistivity of Nichrome?

$$\begin{aligned} \text{Area} &= \pi r^2 \\ &= \pi \times (0.61 \times 10^{-3}\ \text{m})^2 \\ &= 1.17 \times 10^{-6}\ \text{m}^2 \end{aligned}$$

$$\begin{aligned} \text{So, } \rho &= \frac{RA}{l} \\ &= \frac{0.50\ \Omega \times 1.17 \times 10^{-6}\ \text{m}^2}{1.00\ \text{m}} \\ &= 5.8 \times 10^{-7}\ \Omega\,\text{m} \end{aligned}$$

We can use resistivity to evaluate alternative materials for connecting leads. Suppose the connecting lead from the storage battery to the motor in an electric van is 3.5 metres long and must have a resistance of less than 0.001 Ω. How would the diameters and masses of copper and aluminium wires (Table 2) compare?

Table 5 Resistivity data

Material	Resistivity / Ω m	Density / kg m^{-3}
copper	1.7×10^{-8}	8930
aluminium	2.7×10^{-8}	2710

$$\begin{aligned} \text{For copper, } \rho &= \frac{RA}{l} \\ A &= \frac{\rho l}{R} \\ &= \frac{1.7 \times 10^{-8}\ \Omega\,\text{m} \times 3.5\ \text{m}}{0.001\ \Omega} \\ &= 6.0 \times 10^{-5}\ \text{m}^2 \end{aligned}$$

$$\begin{aligned} \text{and A} &= \pi r^2 \\ r^2 &= \frac{6.0 \times 10^{-5}\ \text{m}^2}{\pi} \\ r &= 0.0044\ \text{m} \\ \text{diameter} &= 8.8\ \text{mm} \end{aligned}$$

$$\begin{aligned} \text{mass} &= \text{density} \times \text{volume} \\ &= 8930\ \text{kg m}^{-3} \times 6.0 \times 10^{-5}\ \text{m}^2 \times 3.5\ \text{m} \\ &= 1.9\ \text{kg} \end{aligned}$$

Similarly, for aluminium,

$$\begin{aligned} A &= \frac{\rho l}{R} \\ &= \frac{2.7 \times 10^{-8}\ \Omega\,\text{m} \times 3.5\ \text{m}}{0.001\ \Omega} \\ &= 9.5 \times 10^{-5}\ \text{m}^2 \end{aligned}$$

So radius = 0.0055 m, diameter = 11 mm and mass = 0.90 kg

The poorer conduction of aluminium can be compensated for by making the aluminium cable about 25% thicker than copper cable. The aluminium cable would still be lighter. Though this results in a weight saving of more than 50%, the manufacturer would need to take into account the cost of manufacture and other properties (ease of connecting, flexibility, corrosion resistance, etc.) of the materials before making a decision.

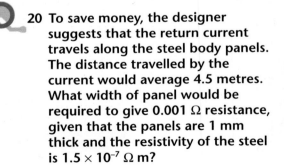

20 To save money, the designer suggests that the return current travels along the steel body panels. The distance travelled by the current would average 4.5 metres. What width of panel would be required to give 0.001 Ω resistance, given that the panels are 1 mm thick and the resistivity of the steel is 1.5 × 10^{-7} Ω m?

Resistance and temperature

Cars need to operate in temperatures as low as –40 °C, while temperatures of electrical equipment in the engine compartment could reach as high as 150 °C. It is clearly important to know about the electrical properties of materials at these extremes of temperature.

Temperature always affects conduction. The effect depends on the type of material.

Metals: There are free electrons in metals even at absolute zero. Increasing the temperature makes the random motion of the electrons faster and the positive ions vibrate more. This leads to more collisions between the drifting electrons and the ions, so that current is reduced. Resistance increases when temperature goes up.

The effect can be significant: both aluminium and copper show about an 80% increase in resistance over the range –40 to +150 °C.

Insulators: At absolute zero, all the electrons are tied to the atoms. There is no conduction at all. At room temperature this is still roughly true. At much higher temperatures, thermal energy may be enough to free some electrons, thereby allowing conduction. Resistance decreases with increased temperature.

At high temperatures, you would need to be careful about choosing insulators for use in the motors, near brakes or inside high-temperature sodium–sulphur batteries.

Table 6 Effect of increasing temperature on resistivity

Material	Change in resistivity	Reason
metal	increases	more vibration of ions
semiconductor	decreases (usually)	more ion vibration makes resistivity rise more charge carriers makes resistivity fall
insulator	decreases	thermal energy releases more charge carriers

Semiconductors: The energy needed to release charge carriers in semiconductors is much less than it is in insulators. Thermal energy is enough to release some electrons for conduction.

Pure semiconductors conduct a little at room temperature. Increasing the temperature increases ion vibrations, which tends to reduce current, as in metals. The increasing number of charge carriers at higher temperatures is dominant, however, so for most semiconductors the resistance decreases as temperature goes up.

Fig. 33 How resistance depends on temperature

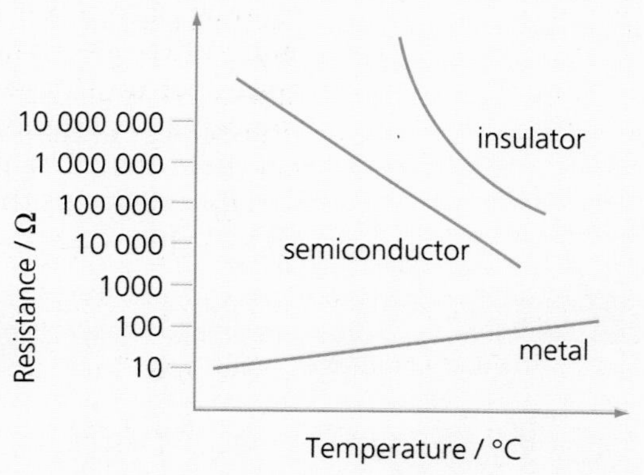
10 000 000
1 000 000
100 000
10 000
1000
100
10
Resistance / Ω
insulator
semiconductor
metal
Temperature / °C

21 What are the major problems that need to be overcome by electric vehicle designers?

Key ideas

- Resistivity, ρ, is the resistance of a 1 m^2 by 1 m specimen, $R = \frac{\rho l}{A}$
- Resistivity is measured in Ω m.

7 Defibrillators

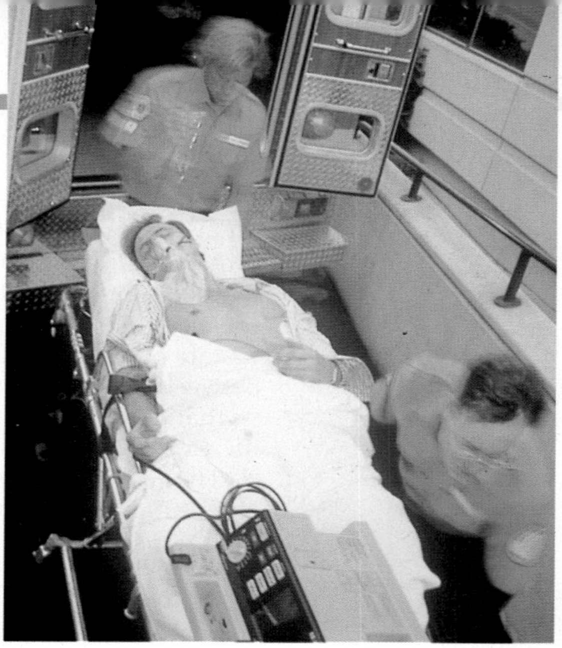

John collapsed at work on Monday morning. While he could still speak, he complained of severe chest pains. In the ambulance, his heart stopped and he lost consciousness. He was lucky: the paramedic in the ambulance had a defibrillator. John survived his heart attack. Heart attacks kill one in four people in industrialised, wealthy countries. Fatty foods, lack of exercise and smoking all contribute to death or illness related to the heart.

The heart is a tremendously reliable pump, operating at seventy or so beats per minute throughout your life (Fig. 1). It has its own pacemaker (the *sino-atrial node*) which fires electrical signals 60 to 100 times per minute. Most heart muscle cells are capable of generating electrical pulses on their own. The pulse from the sino-atrial node keeps them all beating in the right sequence.

Fig. 1 Sequence of actions in a heartbeat

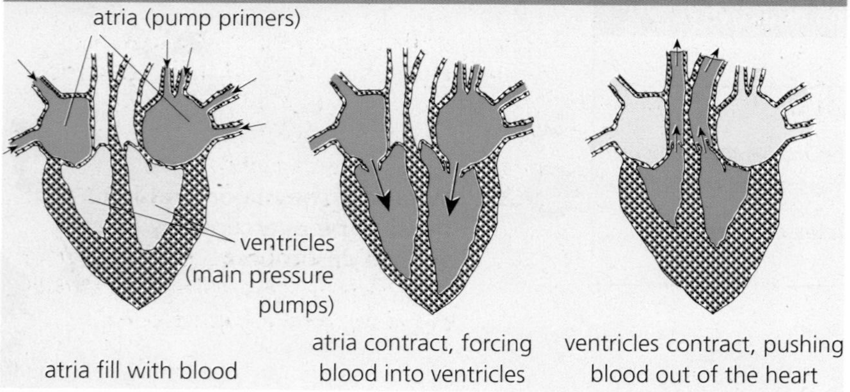
atria (pump primers)
ventricles
(main pressure
pumps)
atria fill with blood
atria contract, forcing
blood into ventricles
ventricles contract, pushing
blood out of the heart

Blocked coronary arteries, caused by the build-up of fatty deposits on the walls, can reduce the blood supply to the heart. This can result in the death of small regions of heart muscle. These dead areas make the heart prone to electrical disturbances which upset the normal pumping rhythm. In the worst case, *ventricular fibrillation* starts: the heart's muscles contract randomly and therefore don't squeeze the ventricles, stopping the flow of blood.

The **defibrillator** that saved John's life delivered a carefully controlled shock to his heart. This stopped the process of ventricular fibrillation and started his regular heart rhythm again. Though the machines have saved many lives, the use and availability of defibrillators has been hindered until recently by their lack of portability and cost. By understanding how a defibrillator works, we can see how designers are trying to make a less expensive model that is more compact and easier to use.

7.1 Learning objectives

After working through this chapter, you should be able to:

- **explain** what is meant by capacitance;
- **state** factors which affect the capacitance of a parallel plate capacitor;
- **derive** equations for series and parallel arrangements of capacitors;
- **describe** the structure of a cathode-ray tube (CRT);
- **explain** how a CRT is used to display wave forms.

7.2 Capacitance

A defibrillator needs to transfer a precise amount of energy to a patient. In making this transfer we need to strike a balance between the effectiveness of the applied shock and the safety of the patient. The best way to do this is to use a **capacitor** (Fig. 2).

Fig. 2 Capacitors

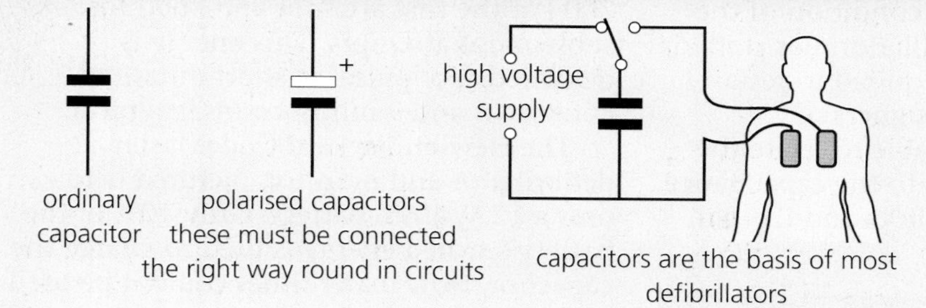

+
high voltage
supply
ordinary
capacitor
polarised capacitors
these must be connected
the right way round in circuits
capacitors are the basis of most
defibrillators

A capacitor is a component that is able to store electrical charge. It behaves a bit like a rechargeable battery, except that the energy is stored in electric fields instead of chemical reactions. The simplest capacitor consists of just two parallel plates (Fig. 3).

When charge is stored on the plates of a capacitor, the potential difference between the plates rises. The potential difference is proportional to the amount of charge stored. **Capacitance** (farads) is defined as the charge stored (coulombs) per volt:

$$C = \frac{Q}{V}$$

Fig. 3 Charging and discharging

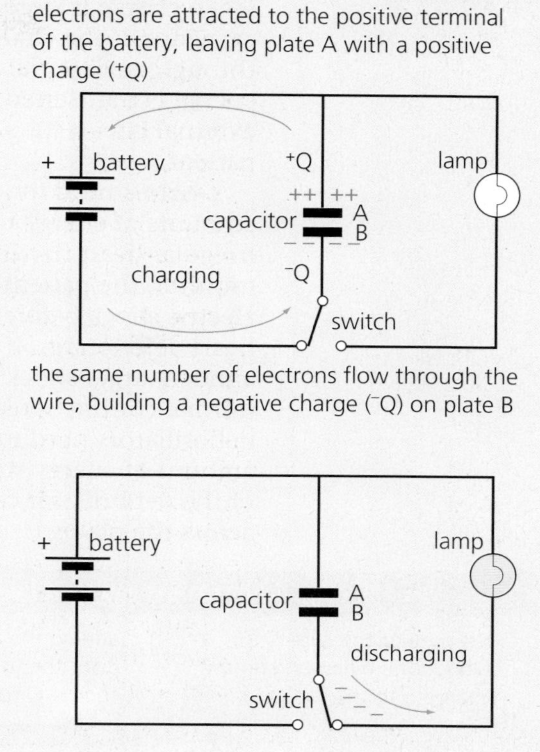

electrons are attracted to the positive terminal of the battery, leaving plate A with a positive charge (⁺Q)
+
battery
⁺Q
lamp
++ ++
capacitor
A
B
charging
⁻Q
switch
the same number of electrons flow through the wire, building a negative charge (⁻Q) on plate B
+
battery
lamp
capacitor
A
B
discharging
switch

It is difficult to manufacture capacitors with a large capacitance. Most capacitors have a capacitance of less than one hundredth of a farad. Many electrical circuits use capacitors that have capacitances between 10^{-12} F and 10^{-9} F.

Q 1 All insulators allow *some* current to flow. How do you think this affects the charge on a capacitor?

7.3 Energy storage

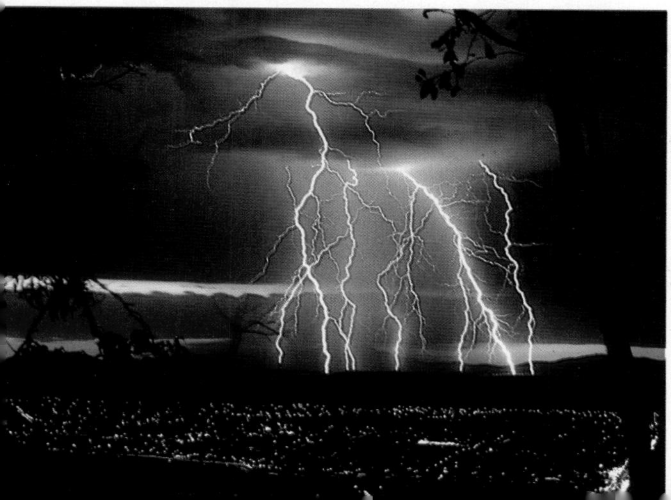

Electric fields

A strong **electric field** exists in the region between a capacitor's plates. The field is uniform between the plates and its strength is often expressed in terms of the potential difference per metre. In the same way that an object in a gravitational field will experience a force, any charged particle in the space between the plates will experience an electrostatic force.

Thunderclouds can generate potential differences of 100 MV or more, creating electric field strengths high enough to make air conduct.

Energy is needed to set up the electric field when charge is stored on the plates of a capacitor. If the charge is allowed to flow through an external circuit, the stored energy is transferred to the circuit. The external circuit for a defibrillator is the patient.

Doctors need to transfer different amounts of energy to patients. If an irregular heart rhythm is seen on the monitor, the patient can be given a small electric shock before the condition of the heart deteriorates. If fibrillation has started, a much larger shock is required to restart normal contractions. Designers of defibrillators need to be able to relate the amount of energy stored to the capacitance of the defibrillator capacitors and the p.d. across the plates.

Fig. 4 Energy stored by a capacitor

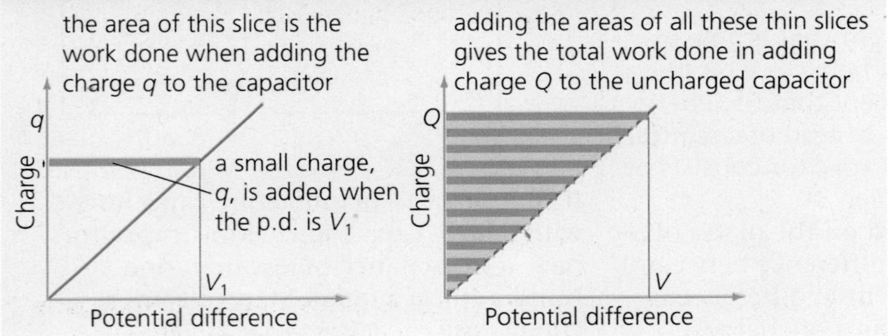
the area of this slice is the work done when adding the charge q to the capacitor
q
Charge
a small charge, q, is added when the p.d. is V_1
V_1
Potential difference
adding the areas of all these thin slices gives the total work done in adding charge Q to the uncharged capacitor
Q
Charge
V
Potential difference

The charge stored by a capacitor is proportional to p.d. ($Q = CV$). Suppose the p.d. across the capacitor is already V_1 when a small amount of charge, q, is added. Using the definition of p.d. = work done per unit charge (see Chapter 6), the work done is $W = qV_1$. This is the same as the area of a little slice in Fig. 4.

The total work done charging the capacitor is the combined area of all the little slices. These add up to the area of the triangle ($\frac{1}{2}$ base × height). Therefore:

$$\text{energy stored} = \text{total work done} = \tfrac{1}{2}QV$$

It is rare that the charge, Q, is measured directly, so it is more useful to substitute $Q = CV$ into the equation, giving:

$$\text{energy stored, } E = \tfrac{1}{2}CV^2$$

2 Human skin has quite a high resistance. Would it be better to build a defibrillator using a small capacitance charged to a large p.d. or a large capacitance charged to a small p.d.? Explain your answer.

Small irregularities in heart rhythm can be corrected by transferring around 10 J of energy to the patient. Stopping fibrillation needs much more energy: in adults, about 200 J at the first attempt and 360 J for subsequent attempts. This energy is delivered as a 'pulse' of short duration – between 3 and 9 milliseconds is typical.

The Hewlett Packard CodeMaster defibrillator and monitor, pictured below, uses a 12 V, 4 A h battery. Only 10% of the battery's stored energy is used to charge the capacitor. How many times could it be used at the 360 J setting?

The charge, Q, is given by:
$Q = It = 4\ \text{A h} = 4\ \text{A} \times 3600\ \text{s} = 14\,400\ \text{C}$

Energy supplied by the battery:
$QV = 14\,400\ \text{C} \times 12\ \text{V} = 172\,800\ \text{J}$

But only 10% is available for charging, so $E = 17\,280$ J. At 360 J per discharge, the maximum number available is:

$$\frac{17\,280\ \text{J}}{360\ \text{J}} = 48 \text{ discharges}$$

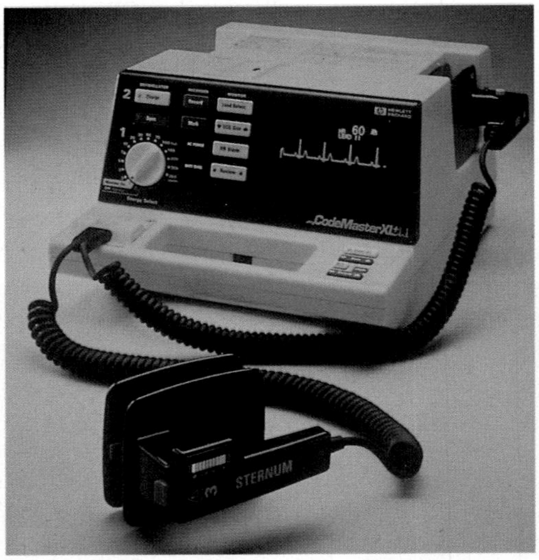
CodeMaster XL+
STERNUM

3 The manufacturing limit for portable high voltage capacitors is about 100 μF. What charging p.d. would be needed to store 360 J?

Voltages around 2700 V are difficult to achieve on portable equipment, particularly as the operator needs the capacitor to recharge rapidly for further shocks. Doctors need a recharge time of 5 seconds. What charging current is required?

At 2700 V, charge stored on a 100 μF capacitor is:

$$Q = CV$$
$$= 100 \times 10^{-6}\ \text{F} \times 2700\ \text{V}$$
$$= 0.27\ \text{C}$$

To deliver this in 5 seconds needs a mean charging current, *I*, of:

$$I = \frac{Q}{t} = \frac{0.27\ \text{C}}{5\ \text{s}} = 0.054\ \text{A}$$

This may seem small, but the mean charging power would be:

$$P = \frac{E}{t} = \frac{360\ \text{J}}{5\,\text{s}} = 72\ \text{W}$$

Most defibrillators use a small sealed lead–acid battery to meet this power requirement.

Key ideas

- Capacitors store charge.
- Charge in a capacitor creates an electric field. Energy is stored in the field between the plates of a capacitor: $E = \frac{1}{2}QV = \frac{1}{2}CV^2$
- Capacitance (C) is the charge stored (Q) per volt: $C = \frac{Q}{V}$

7.4 Capacitor construction

A defibrillator needs to use a capacitor with a maximum capacitance of 100 μF and must operate at several thousand volts. How easy is this to achieve in practice?

Capacitors store charge on plates, so doubling the area, *A*, would be like having two storage areas. The dimensions of a capacitor affect its capacitance:

$$\text{capacitance} \propto \text{area}$$

Fig. 5 Factors affecting capacitance

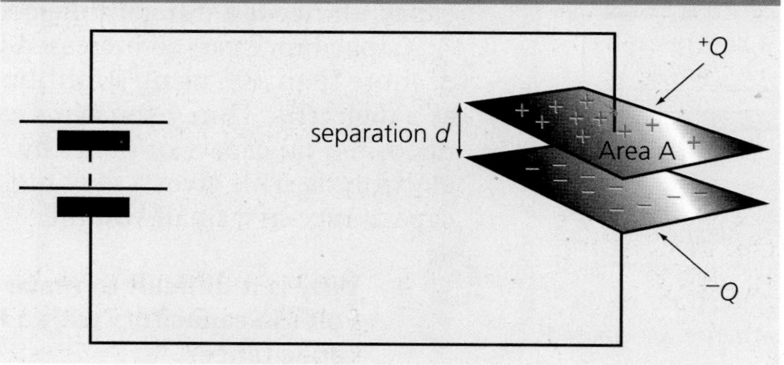

+Q
separation d
Area A
−Q

The distance, *d*, between the plates is also important. There are opposite charges on the plates. When the plates are closer, these opposite charges attract more. This makes it easier to charge the capacitor. Its capacitance rises. For parallel plates, capacitance is:

$$C \propto \frac{1}{\text{distance}}$$

$$\text{so, } C \propto \frac{\text{area}}{\text{distance}}$$

If the plates are separated by a vacuum, the constant of proportionality is ε_0 ('epsilon-nought').

$$C = \frac{\varepsilon_0 A}{d}$$

where A = area of one plate
d = distance between the plates
ε_0 is a constant called the 'permittivity of free space' $= 8.85 \times 10^{-12}\ \text{F m}^{-1}$

Ambulance crews need defibrillators that are small enough to be portable. Size restrictions mean that the maximum area for the capacitor plates is about 10 cm by 12 cm. Suppose the capacitor were made of two metal plates 1 mm apart. Would this give a big enough capacitance?

$$C = \frac{\varepsilon_0 A}{d}$$
$$= \frac{8.85\times10^{-12}\ \text{F m}^{-1}\times0.10\ \text{m}\times0.12\ \text{m}}{0.001\ \text{m}}$$
$$= 1.06\times10^{-10}\ \text{F}$$

This is much less than the 100 μF needed. Commercial capacitors use several methods for making capacitance bigger:

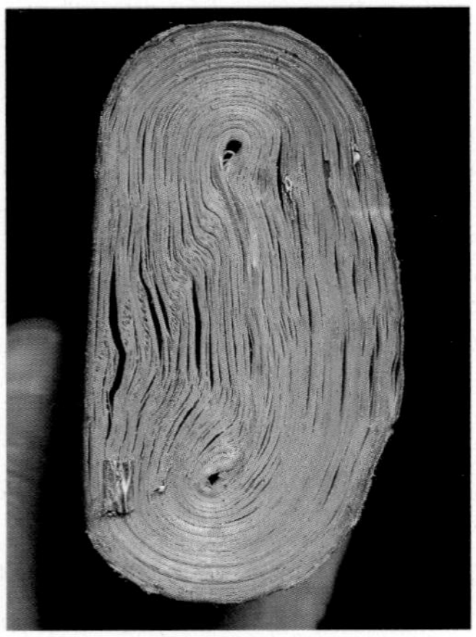

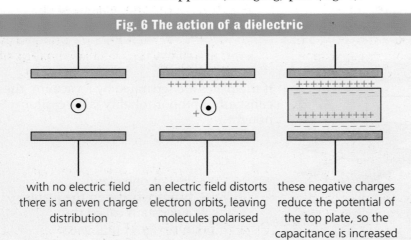

- Increase the area – many square metres of very thin metal foil can be wound into a capacitor body (left).
- Decrease the distance the two plates are held apart using a very thin film of insulating material.
- Use an insulator called a '**dielectric**'. The molecules of the dielectric are polarised in the electric field between the plates. This gives rise to an opposing electric field which lowers the potential difference across the capacitor. More charge is therefore required on the plates to match the applied (charging) p.d. (Fig. 6).

Fig. 6 The action of a dielectric

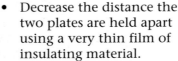

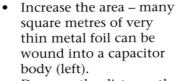

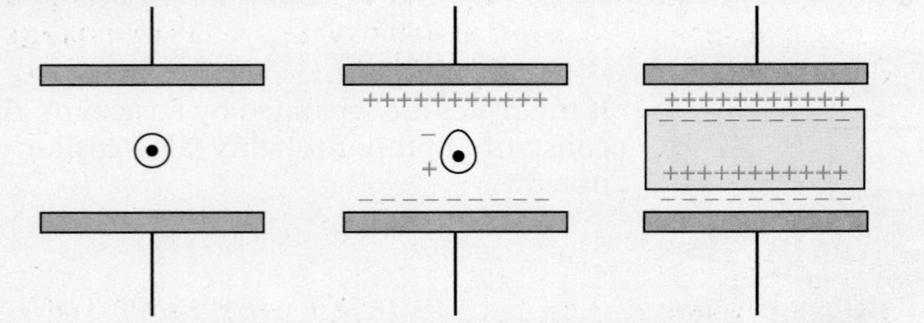
with no electric field there is an even charge distribution
an electric field distorts electron orbits, leaving molecules polarised
these negative charges reduce the potential of the top plate, so the capacitance is increased

The factor by which capacitance increases when using dielectrics is called '**relative permittivity**'. For example, mica has a relative permittivity of 5. Parallel plates separated by mica would have five times the capacitance of a vacuum-filled capacitor of the same size.

High voltages across a capacitor can cause electrical breakdown, where electrons are torn from the atoms in the dielectric. The dielectric then conducts. In air, about 3000 V mm^{-1} will cause conduction. Mica can withstand 150 000 V mm^{-1} before it starts to conduct.

A medical defibrillator needs a capacitor with a capacitance of about 100 μF which will withstand a p.d. of about 3000 V. The minimum thickness, *d*, of mica you would be able to use is:

$$\frac{3000\ \text{V}}{150000\ \text{V mm}^{-1}} = 0.02\ \text{mm}$$

Mica has a relative permittivity of 5, so its capacitance is:

$$C = \frac{5\varepsilon_0 A}{d}$$

The area of plates needed will therefore be:

$$A = \frac{Cd}{5\varepsilon_0}$$
$$= \frac{100\times10^{-6}\ \text{F}\times0.02\times10^{-3}\ \text{m}}{5\times8.85\times10^{-12}\ \text{F m}^{-1}}$$
$$= 45\ \text{m}^2$$

Unfortunately, this is too large for a single capacitor as mica is brittle and difficult to work with over such a large area. In addition, the total volume of insulator needed would be too large. Clearly the capacitor needs a different dielectric.

Capacitance can be increased by a factor of more than 300 using strontium titanate as a dielectric. Thin, even films can be deposited on capacitor plates by electrolysis. This gives a very high capacitance in a small volume.

Q4 Why is it difficult to make high voltage capacitors with a high capacitance?

7.5 Capacitor combinations

Another way of increasing capacitance at high voltages involves wiring smaller capacitors in series and parallel combinations. Instead of using one high-capacitance capacitor for a defibrillator, it is possible to use a combination of smaller capacitors to achieve the required capacitance.

Fig. 7 Capacitors in parallel

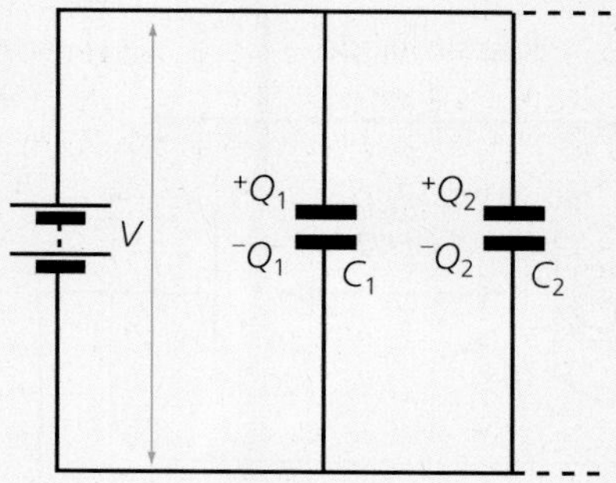

V
$^+Q_1$
$^-Q_1$
C_1
$^+Q_2$
$^-Q_2$
C_2

The p.d. across each capacitor is the same. The total charge stored is:

$Q = Q_1+Q_2+Q_3+...$

The combined capacitance is therefore:

$$C = \frac{Q}{V} = \frac{(Q_1+Q_2+Q_3+...)}{V}$$

$$= \frac{Q_1}{V} + \frac{Q_2}{V} + \frac{Q_3}{V} + ... = C_1+C_2+C_3+...$$

$C = C_1+C_2+C_3+...$

A capacitor with high capacitance can be made by wiring several smaller capacitors in parallel (Fig. 7). The p.d. across each capacitor will be the same, so each capacitor needs to be able to withstand the 'operating' voltage. This is several kilovolts in a defibrillator.

Fig. 8 Capacitors in series

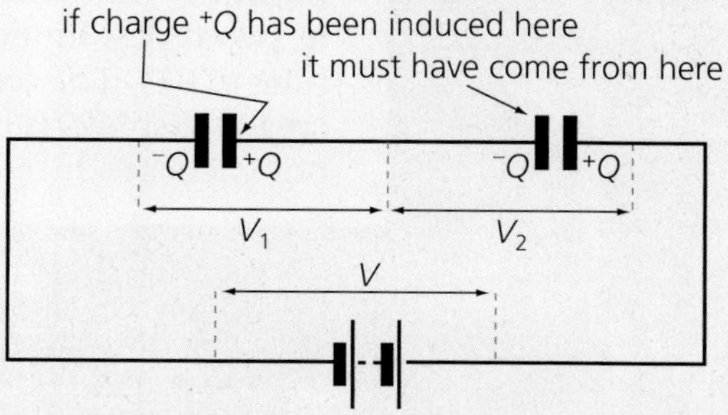

if charge ^+Q has been induced here
it must have come from here
^-Q
^+Q
^-Q
^+Q
V_1
V_2
V

Each capacitor holds the same charge ^+Q on its positive plate. The p.d. across the whole series is the sum of the p.d.s across each capacitor.

$V = V_1+V_2$

So, $\frac{Q}{C} = \frac{Q}{C_1} + \frac{Q}{C_2}$

Dividing by Q gives

$\frac{1}{C} = \frac{1}{C_1} + \frac{1}{C_2}$

The combined capacitance of two or more capacitors connected in series is *less* than the individual capacitors (Fig. 8). This seems to be a 'waste' of capacitance, but an advantage of this arrangement is that the p.d. across each capacitor is reduced. You could therefore build a capacitor with a high operating voltage using capacitors with lower operating voltages.

The equations for resistor and capacitor combinations are similar, except *series* and *parallel* are swapped; i.e. resistors in series add up, capacitors in parallel add up.

5 **Suppose you connected a 60 μF capacitor and a 40 μF capacitor in series across a 1000 V supply. What would be the combined capacitance and the p.d. across each capacitor?**

6 **How could you make a 100 μF capacitor with a working voltage of 3000 V for a defibrillator using 50 μF capacitors with a working voltage of 1000 V?**

Key ideas

- Commercial capacitors contain a 'dielectric'. The dielectric can increase the capacitance.
- The capacitance of a parallel plate capacitor depends on the size and separation of the plates.
- $C = \frac{\varepsilon_0 A}{d}$ for parallel plates in a vacuum.
- Capacitors in parallel: $C = C_1 + C_2 + C_3 + ...$
- Capacitors in series: $\frac{1}{C} = \frac{1}{C_1} + \frac{1}{C_2} + \frac{1}{C_3} + ...$

7.6 Displaying the heartbeat

Golden Goose
FREE COCKTAILS TO ALL PLAYERS

Most defibrillator machines have a monitor. The visual display is usually one of two types: liquid crystal or cathode-ray tube (CRT). The technology of liquid crystal displays is constantly improving, but CRTs produce better picture quality.

Rays from the cathode

Towards the end of the nineteenth century, one of the most interesting areas of scientific study was the discharge of electricity through gases at low pressures.

At very low pressures, the gas in the glass discharge tube started to glow in the region opposite the negative electrode (**cathode**). The glow seemed to be due to rays coming from the cathode. It was found that the 'cathode rays' could be moved around (deflected) by electric and magnetic fields. Deflection experiments in the 1890s showed that these rays from the cathode were negatively charged particles of very small mass. Their properties did not depend on the type of gas in the tube. We now call these particles 'electrons'. Electrons are emitted in larger quantities by heating the cathode. This gives the electrons enough energy to escape from the metal surface in a process called **thermionic emission** (Fig. 9). When the metal has lost electrons, it develops a net positive charge which pulls the electrons back. If another positive electrode (the **anode**) is fitted to the tube, electrons can be pulled away from the cathode. A high-voltage supply connected between cathode and anode will therefore set up a stream of electrons (a current) through the tube.

Fig. 9 A thermionic valve

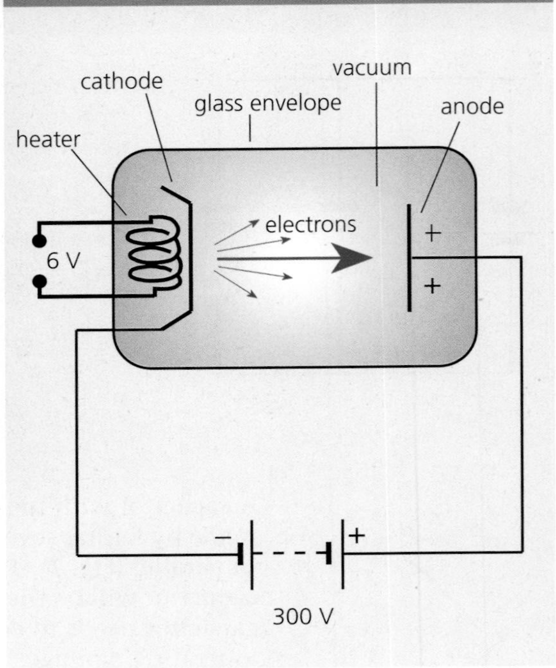
cathode
vacuum
glass envelope
anode
heater
electrons
6 V
+
+
−
+
300 V

The energy required to remove an electron from a material is known as the **work function**. In modern CRTs, the cathode is normally coated with a compound with a low work function. Even so, the operating temperature is usually above 1200 K.

7 **Explain why a higher cathode temperature is needed if the material of the cathode has a high work function.**

8 **The heater circuit needs a high-current supply at low voltage. The anode–cathode circuit needs a high voltage but little current. Why?**

The cathode-ray display tube

In the second half of the twentieth century, the cathode-ray display tube – in its guise as the television set – changed the nature of leisure time. The ability to display a moving picture has also been a great advantage to scientists and technologists. Physicists use cathode-ray tubes in oscilloscopes. Most computers still use cathode-ray tubes as monitors. The underlying mechanism is the same in all these applications (Fig. 10).

Fig. 10 A cathode-ray tube

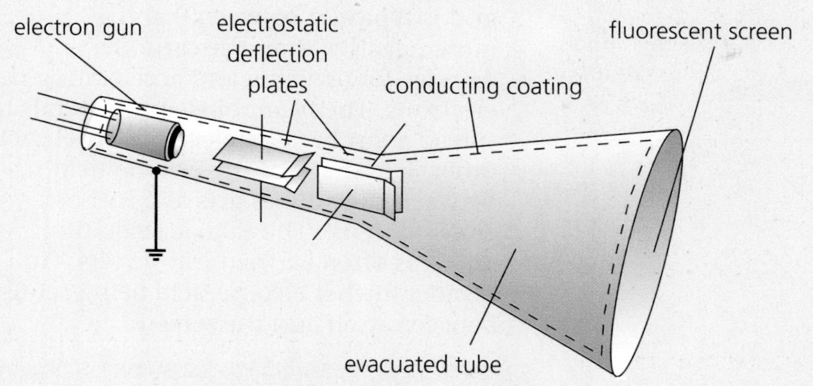

electron gun
electrostatic deflection plates
conducting coating
fluorescent screen
evacuated tube

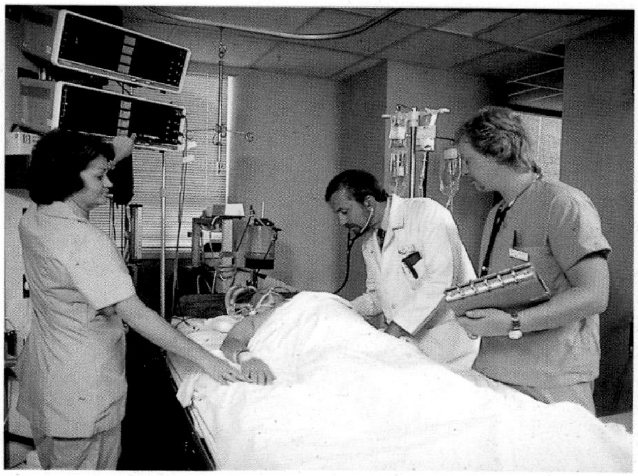

A patient's heartbeat can be displayed using a cathode-ray oscilloscope.

The deflection system

A cathode-ray tube would only produce a bright dot in the middle of the screen if it did not steer the electron beam. The trace on an ECG screen is produced by the electron beam scanning across the face of the tube. To do this, a deflection system is needed.

The deflection system can be of two types: electrostatic or magnetic. Electrostatic deflection is more commonly used in small or portable equipment like defibrillators.

The display screen

Some chemical compounds (e.g. zinc sulphide) accept energy from the high-speed electrons and emit the energy in the form of visible light. Chemicals which undergo this 'fluorescence' are usually called *phosphors*. Some screens have a glow which persists after the electron beam has passed – an effect called phosphorescence.

Electrons are continually hitting the screen. Eventually, the screen will build up a negative charge and start to repel electrons. To prevent this happening, electrons on the screen must be allowed to reach the anode. The inside of the tube is coated with a conductor (e.g. graphite) to allow this current to flow.

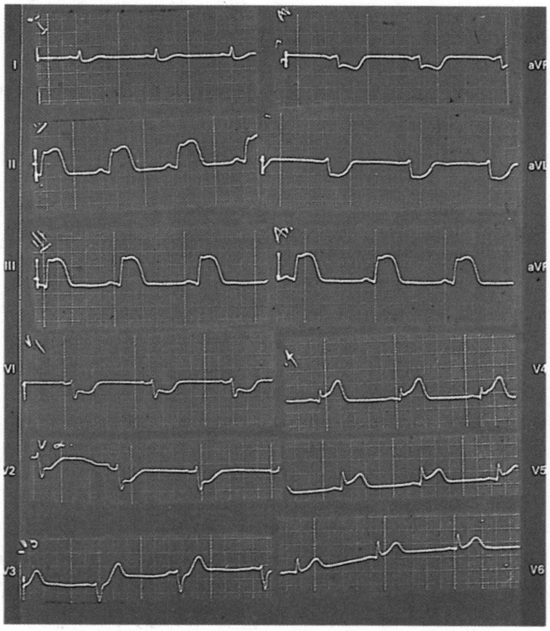

An electrocardiogram (ECG) pattern of a person suffering from a heart attack

The electron gun

Electrons are fired at the screen from the electron 'gun' (Fig. 11). Colour televisions or monitors have three guns, one for each of the primary colours on the display screen. The main components of an electron gun are:

Fig. 11 The electron gun

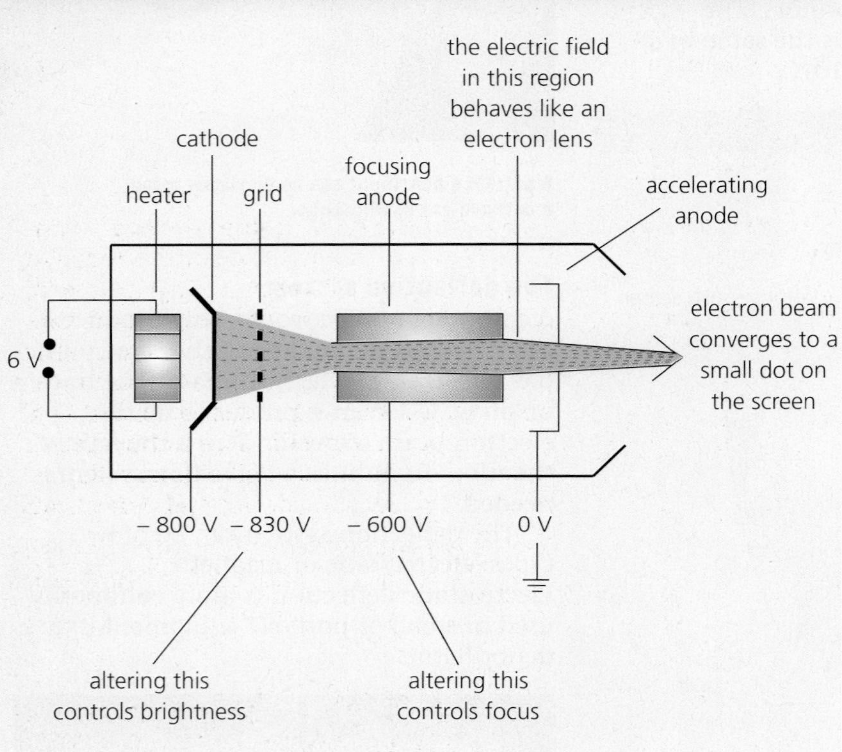

the electric field in this region behaves like an electron lens
cathode
focusing anode
heater
grid
accelerating anode
electron beam converges to a small dot on the screen
6 V
– 800 V
– 830 V
– 600 V
0 V
altering this controls brightness
altering this controls focus

- **Indirectly heated cathode**
  Electrons are released from the cathode by thermionic emission. In a small cathode-ray tube, these electrons are accelerated away from the cathode by a cathode–anode potential difference of about 800 V. Large televisions could use up to 25 000 V.
- **A 'grid' electrode** for brightness control. Brightness can also be controlled by changing the cathode temperature or altering the accelerating voltage, but these two methods affect focusing. The grid is more negative than the cathode, so it repels electrons, thereby reducing the number emitted. Fewer electrons means a dimmer display. The grid is typically between 0 and 50 V more negative than the cathode.
- **Anodes** for focusing and accelerating the electrons. The beam of electrons tends to spread apart because electrons repel each other. The shape of the electric field between the anodes acts as a sort of electron 'lens'. The final accelerating anode is often earthed – at 0 volts – to avoid a further electric field being set up between itself and the screen.

Electrostatic deflection

Charged particles are attracted and repelled by the electric fields produced by other charged particles. We can exploit this by using electric fields to deflect an electron beam. The simplest way to produce a uniform electric field is to use a pair of parallel plates with a p.d. across them. Electrons have a negative charge, so they are attracted to the positive plate (Fig. 12). The pair of plates is able to move the beam horizontally. A second pair of plates at right angles would give vertical deflection.

Fig. 12 Electrostatic deflection

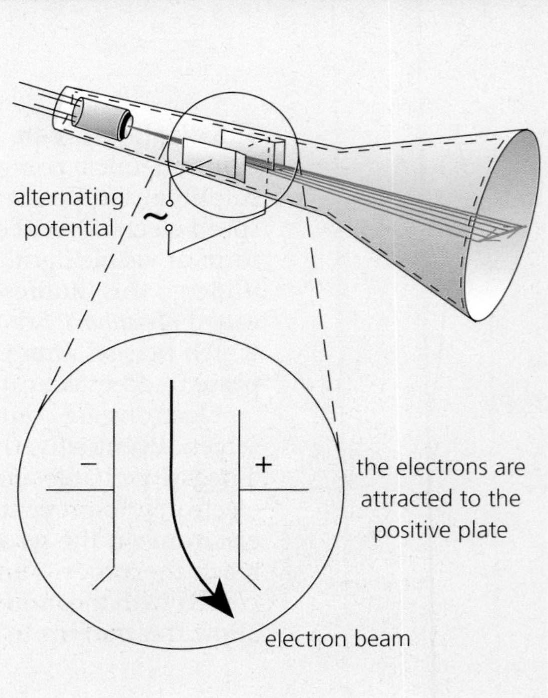

alternating potential
~
–
+
the electrons are attracted to the positive plate
electron beam

Magnetic deflection

Magnetic deflection is commonly used in televisions, as they can accommodate heavy deflecting coils. Moving charged particles are deflected by magnetic fields. A wire carrying a current experiences a force if you put it in a magnetic field. The wire is deflected at right angles to the current and to the magnetic field.

Fleming's left-hand rule is a convenient way of remembering the relative directions of conventional current, magnetic field and resulting force (Fig. 13). Conventional current moves in the direction of the positive charges. You can use Fleming's left-hand rule to find the direction of the force on individual positively charged particles.

Electrons are negatively charged. An electron moving to the right gives a conventional current to the left (Fig. 14). Fleming's left-hand rule only works with conventional current.

Fig. 13 Fleming's left-hand rule

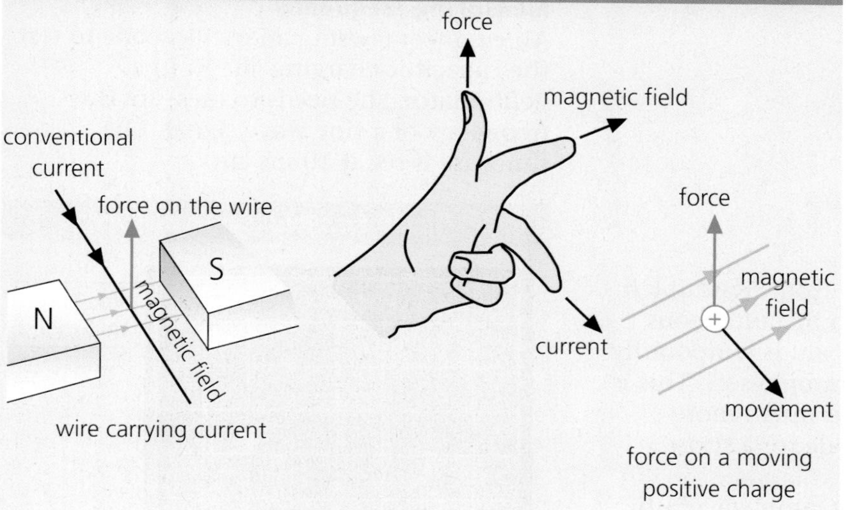
conventional current
force on the wire
S
N
magnetic field
wire carrying current
force
magnetic field
current
force
magnetic field
movement
force on a moving positive charge

Fig. 14 Magnetic deflection

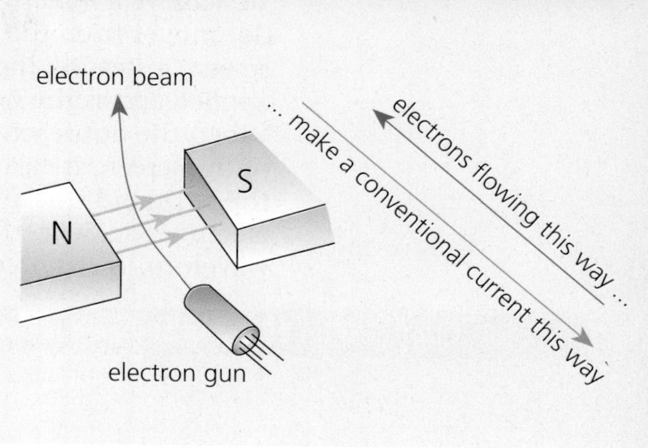
electron beam
S
N
electron gun
electrons flowing this way ...
... make a conventional current this way

The size of the deflection of the beam can be controlled. Varying the current through coils will provide a variable magnetic field (Fig 15). The coils can be mounted outside the tube because the magnetic field passes through glass. Coils placed either side of the glass tube will allow the beam to be deflected. The pair of coils shown is deflecting the beam vertically – a second pair of coils would be needed for horizontal deflections.

Fig. 15 Magnetic coils

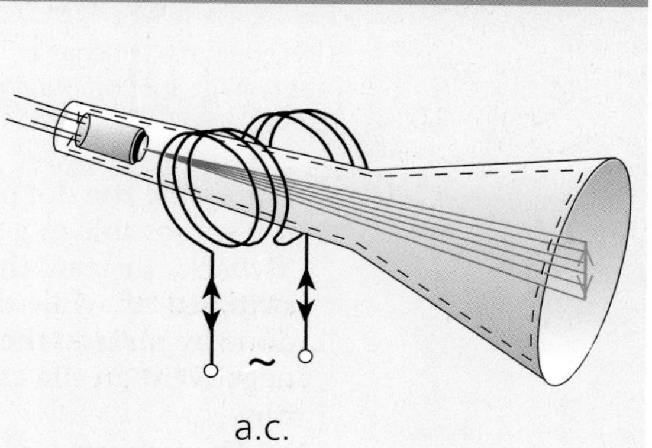
~
a.c.

7.7 Making the picture

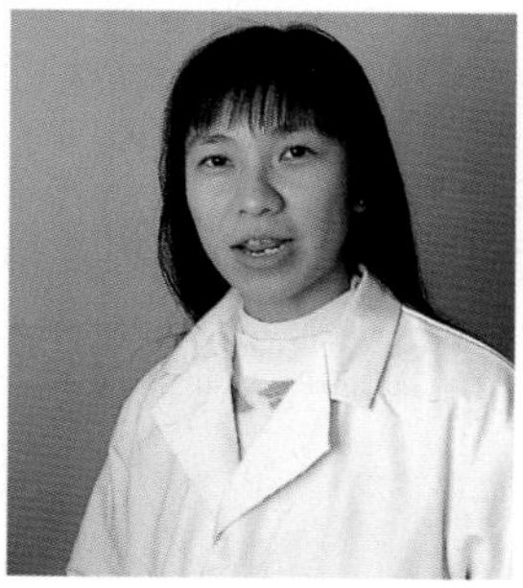

I research the way that nerve cells work together in heart tissue. A lot of my work involves using oscilloscopes to show electrical signals from the nerves. I need to be able to measure voltages and times from the screen.

Heart rate monitors and oscilloscopes need to measure quantities in relation to time. Therefore, we need a deflection system that allows the bright spot to be steered in a regular, repeating pattern across the screen. If the voltages being measured are represented by a vertical deflection, the result is a voltage–time graph on the screen.

Horizontal deflection: the time base

To achieve a linear time scale, in which the dot moves from the left to the right of the screen, a steadily increasing p.d. must be applied across the horizontal X-plates. When the dot reaches the right-hand side of the screen, it clearly needs to go back to the left-hand side and start again. Using electrostatic deflection, a voltage 'ramp' waveform is required (Fig. 16).

Fig. 16 Ramp and grid waveforms

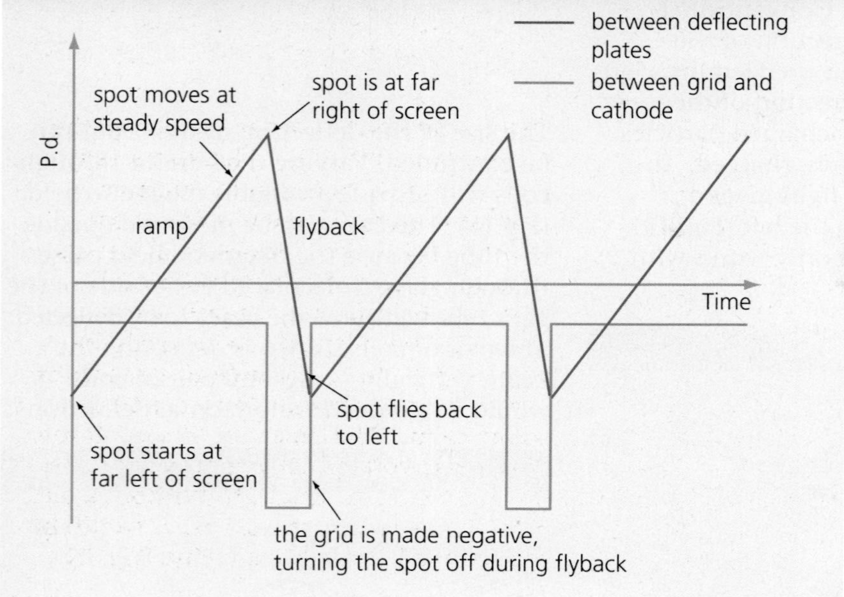
between deflecting plates
between grid and cathode
P.d.
spot moves at steady speed
spot is at far right of screen
ramp
flyback
Time
spot flies back to left
spot starts at far left of screen
the grid is made negative, turning the spot off during flyback

In moving the dot back from right to left, it is impossible to get an instantaneous 'flyback'. Instead, the beam is temporarily switched off while the ramp resets. This is done by making the grid much more negative than the cathode for a short time.

The frequency of the ramp waveform will control the time which the dot takes to sweep across the front of the tube. It is often called the 'time base' or 'sweep' waveform. For oscilloscopes and heart rate monitors, the front of the display tube often has a 1 cm grid drawn across it. The time base is then calibrated in terms of the time taken for the dot to cross 1 cm of the display. Oscilloscope often have settings between 0.5 s cm^{-1} and 0.5 μs cm^{-1}. The horizontal time calibration allows measurement of the period (time between repeating events) and frequency of waves.

Measuring the period

Fig. 17 An ECG display

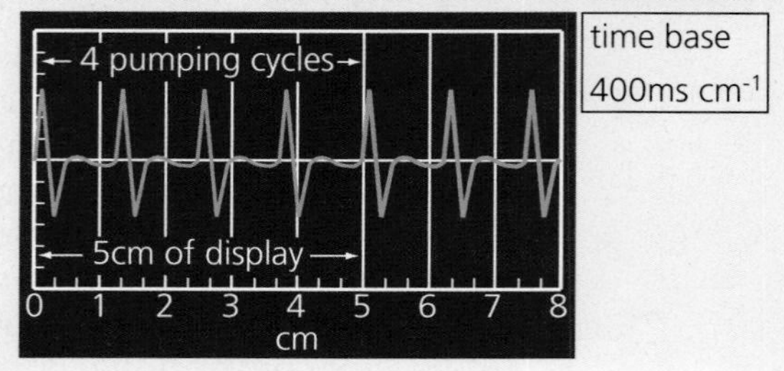
4 pumping cycles
5cm of display
0 1 2 3 4 5 6 7 8
cm
time base
400ms cm-1

In heart rate monitors, the time base is a standard 0.40 s cm^{-1}. The distance between adjacent peaks on the display in Fig. 17 is:

$$\frac{5\text{ cm}}{4\text{ heartbeats}} = 1.25\text{ cm per heartbeat}$$

The time taken for 1 heartbeat is therefore:

$$1.25\text{ cm} \times 0.40\text{ s cm}^{-1} = 500\text{ ms} = 0.5\text{ s}.$$

This heart is beating at a frequency of 2 Hz, or 120 beats per minute.

Measuring frequency

An engineer is using an oscilloscope to test the capacitor-charging circuit in a defibrillator. She needs to measure the frequency of a sine wave signal. The timebase is set at 10 ms cm^{-1}.

Fig. 18 An oscilloscope display

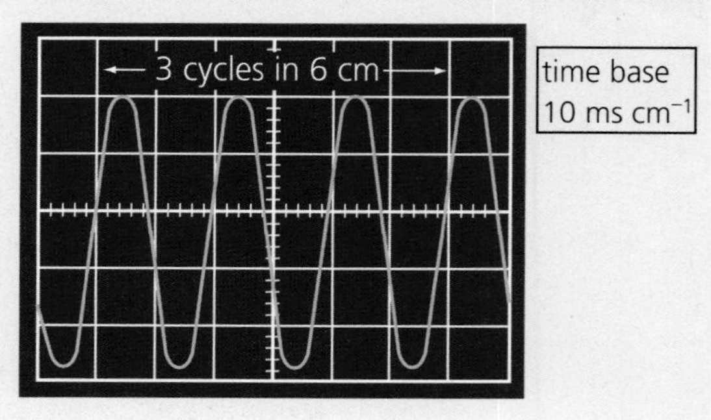
3 cycles in 6 cm
time base
10 ms cm-1

To measure the frequency of the wave, the engineer must first find the period by measuring the width of one cycle. Three cycles of the wave are 6.0 cm wide, so each full cycle of the wave is 2.0 cm wide.

The period of the wave is therefore:

$$T = 2.0\text{ cm} \times 10\text{ ms cm}^{-1} = 20\text{ ms}$$

Frequency = number of cycles per second

$$f = \frac{1}{T} = \frac{1}{20 \times 10^{-3}\text{ s}} = 50\text{ Hz}$$

Comparing phase

Oscilloscopes can also be used to compare the **phase** of two signals. Two signals are 'in phase' if they peak at the same time. They are 'antiphase' if the peak of one coincides with the trough of another.

Phase can be compared directly by using a dual-beam oscilloscope. This has two signal input channels. The display alternates between the two signals, giving two lines on the screen (Fig. 19a).

Fig. 19 Signals in phase and antiphase

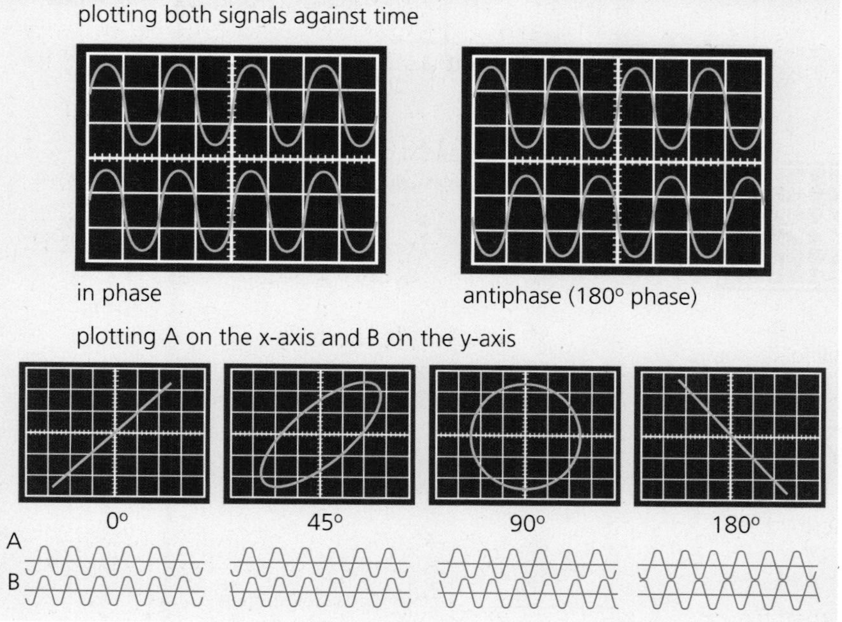

plotting both signals against time
in phase
antiphase (180° phase)
plotting A on the x-axis and B on the y-axis
0°
45°
90°
180°
A
B

Accurate measurements of phase relationships can also be made by using both horizontal (X) and vertical (Y) inputs of a single-beam oscilloscope. If two waves are in phase, then the Y input would always be proportional to the X input: this gives a straight line graph. Other phase relationships give different patterns (Fig. 19b).

Vertical deflection: the signal

The vertical height of a trace on the screen can be used to measure p.d. values. Display screens are calibrated so that each centimetre on the Y-axis of the display screen stands for a known voltage. For example, suppose the Y-amplifier is set to the 2 mV cm^{-1} range (Fig. 20).

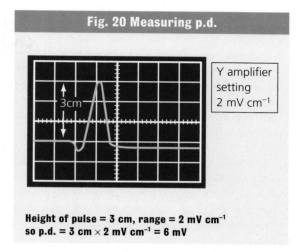

Fig. 20 Measuring p.d.

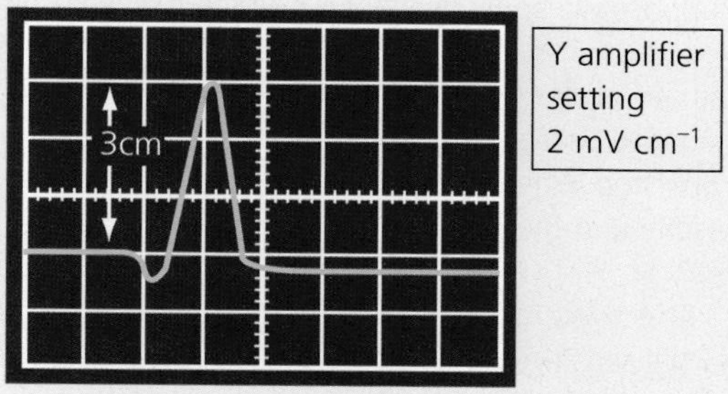

3cm
Y amplifier setting 2 mV cm^{-1}

Height of pulse = 3 cm, range = 2 mV cm^{-1}
so p.d. = 3 cm × 2 mV cm^{-1} = 6 mV

Complications arise where an alternating current (a.c.) signal is added to a steady d.c. voltage. This is common in sensitive electronic amplifier circuits like those which amplify the tiny electrical signals from nerve cells. The amplitude of the alternating signal may be only a few millivolts, while the d.c. level could be several volts. In this situation, a capacitor can be used to separate the a.c. and d.c. components. The capacitor blocks off the steady d.c. voltage, letting only the fluctuating signal through. Without a d.c. blocking capacitor, the a.c. trace would be indiscernable from the d.c. line (Fig. 21).

Fig. 21 Blocking capacitors

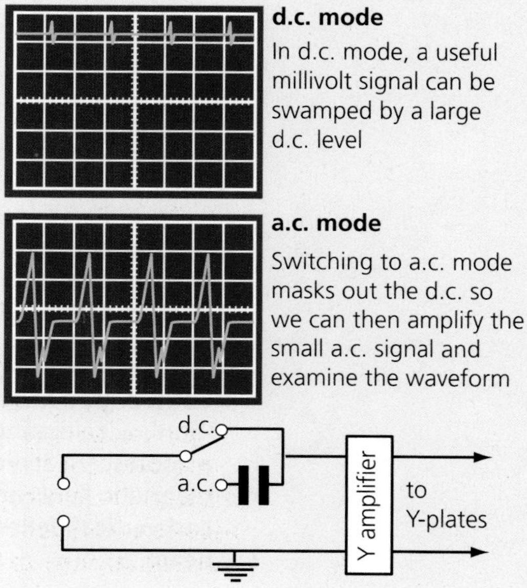

d.c. mode
In d.c. mode, a useful millivolt signal can be swamped by a large d.c. level
a.c. mode
Switching to a.c. mode masks out the d.c. so we can then amplify the small a.c. signal and examine the waveform
d.c.
a.c.
Y amplifier
to Y-plates

Fig. 22 Using a capacitor to block d.c.

Suppose we apply only a d.c. voltage to the circuit shown:

Initially, current will flow through the resistor to allow negative charge to build up on the bottom plate of the capacitor. When the capacitor is 'full', the current stops, resulting in there being no d.c. voltage across the resistor.

Effectively, this has eliminated the d.c. voltage level, so the sensitivity of the amplifier can be increased. A small a.c. signal will cause fluctuations in the amount of charge on the upper plate. A current will flow through the resistor to allow matching fluctuations of the charge on the lower plate. This leads to an a.c. voltage across the resistor which matches the initial a.c. signal. This can be amplified to give a useful display.

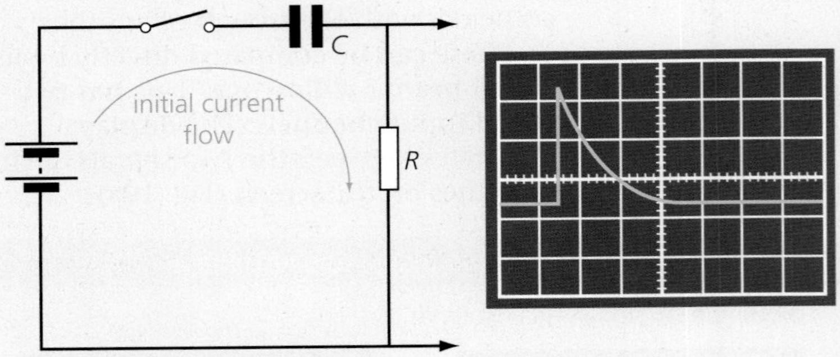

C
initial current
flow
R

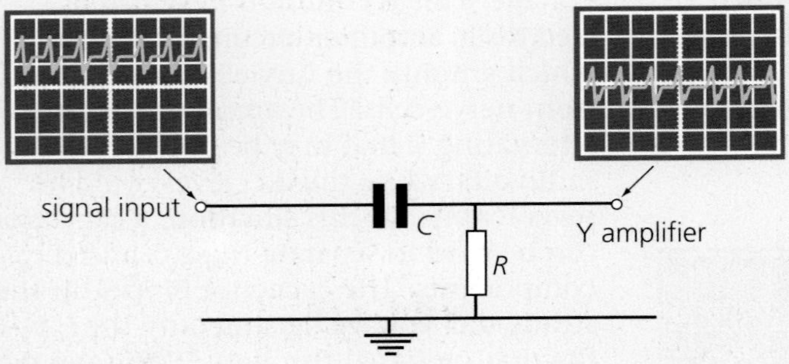

signal input
C
R
Y amplifier

Where both a.c. and d.c. are present, you need to be quite clear about which voltage is being measured.

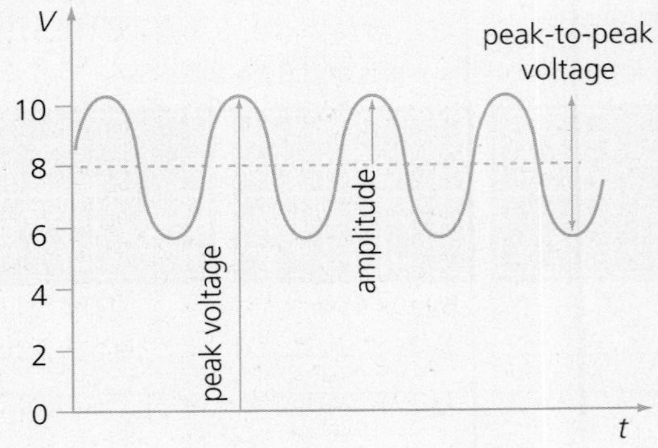

V
10
8
6
4
2
0
t
peak-to-peak
voltage
amplitude
peak voltage

The a.c. signal (shown in the diagram on the right) fluctuates by ± 2 V about a d.c. level of 8 V. The amplitude of this a.c. signal is 2 V.
The peak voltage is the highest voltage reached (10 V).
The peak-to-peak voltage is measured from peak to trough of the a.c. signal (4 V).

Many of the technical problems defibrillator manufacturers originally faced have now been solved. Modern machines are cheaper, more portable and easier to use. Do you think that defibrillators should be made available for use by trained first-aid personnel in workplaces?

Key ideas

- Cathode-ray tubes consist of an electron 'gun', accelerating and focusing anodes and a fluorescent screen. Electrostatic or magnetic fields are used to create horizontal and vertical deflections of the electron beam.
- Ramp waveforms cause linear scanning of the beam across the face of the tube. Oscilloscopes can be used for voltage, time, phase and frequency measurement.

8 Oscillations

Frank works in a company specialising in applications of ultrasonics.

Every year, thousands of tonnes of toxic chemicals – the solvents used in adhesives to join plastics together – end up in the atmosphere. There really is no need for this. We have the technology to join things using sound waves. My company is dedicated to the development of cleaner, safer technologies which use ultrasound.

For hundreds of years, people have used nails, screws and glue to join things together. As plastic goods have become more common, solvent-based adhesives have become one of the main methods of joining components together. Now a new technique is emerging: one that uses the power of sound to melt adjacent faces into each other. These oscillations are well beyond the range of human hearing with frequencies from 20 kHz to 40 kHz. The process is called ultrasonic welding.

High-power ultrasonic technology is not limited to welding. Ultrasonics are also used to melt and cut materials in computer-controlled machining processes for products as diverse as textiles, packaging, carbon fibre and ceramics. Oscillations can be used for cleaning, producing fine sprays, inserting fasteners and even mixing emulsion paints. Ultrasonics have many other uses: sonar systems for boats, scanners in maternity units, motion sensors in burglar alarms and machines to clean laboratory glassware all rely on the properties of high-frequency sound waves.

To use ultrasonics safely and effectively, we need to understand the nature and properties of oscillations.

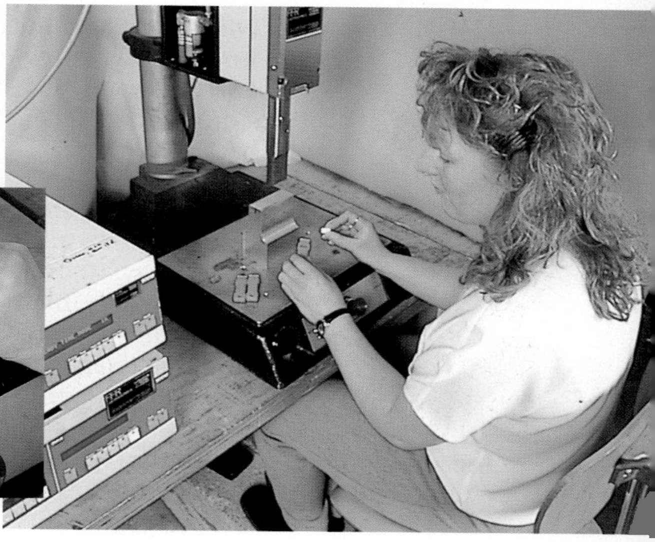

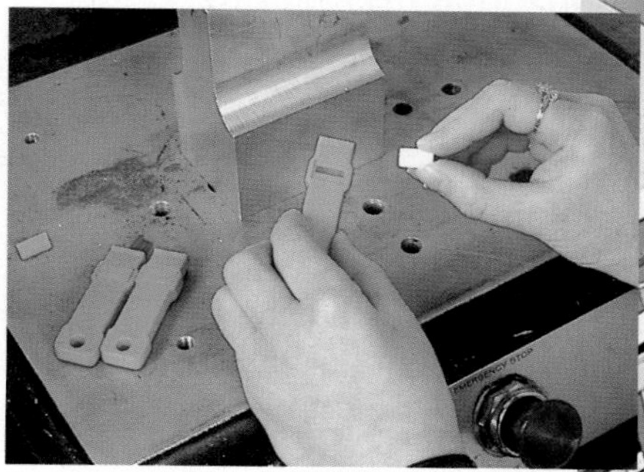

Whistles for life vests need to be completely reliable if they are ever called on in an emergency. Ultrasonic welding is used to manuafacture every whistle perfectly.

8.1 Learning objectives

After working through this chapter, you should be able to:

- **explain** the terms amplitude, frequency, period, simple harmonic motion (SHM);
- **describe** the conditions for SHM;
- **describe** examples of systems which undergo SHM;
- **derive** equations for SHM;
- **explain** what is meant by resonance and give examples of resonant systems;
- **describe** how forced vibration affects both resonant and damped systems.

8.2 Oscillating systems

To join two pieces of plastic, an ultrasonic welder transfers energy from an electrical vibrator (a 'transducer') to the plastic. Although the transducer may be large, the energy is needed in a small region of the working material. The transducer is fitted with a specially shaped 'horn' to concentrate the vibrations in a small space. This boosts the amplitude and energy of vibration, making it large enough for welding or cutting. Both the transducer and horn oscillate naturally at their own frequency. These 'natural frequencies' need to be carefully matched to make sure that the transducer is not damaged.

We need to explore the link between the energy in the oscillations and the size and frequency of the oscillation.

Energy and oscillations

An object will only oscillate if it can store energy when it is disturbed from rest. This stored energy enables the object to move back again.

For example, a horizontal mass–spring system (Fig. 1) stores potential energy through its elastic strain. When it releases this energy, it 'overshoots' its original position. This involves a transfer of potential energy to kinetic energy, back to potential energy and so on. A mass on a spring which oscillates vertically stores energy both as potential energy because of its position in a gravitational field and through its elastic strain.

For a pendulum, moving to the left or to the right has the same effect. The potential energy curve (Fig. 2) is symmetrical, so oscillations are symmetrical. The same is true of a loose spring. Squashing the spring produces the same size forces as stretching it, so the oscillations are symmetrical about the normal resting position.

More energy means bigger oscillations. We can usually link the size of oscillations to the total energy. For example, the elastic strain energy in the spring depends on the amount it is stretched, or displaced, and the spring constant, k. Written as an equation, the energy stored in a spring is $\frac{1}{2}kx^2$, where x is the extension (see Chapter 5). For a given energy of vibration, E, the maximum displacement is given by:

$$E = \tfrac{1}{2}kx^2\text{, so } x = \pm\sqrt{\frac{2E}{k}}$$

The total energy, E, remains constant. Energy is transferred between potential and kinetic forms.

Fig. 2 Energy of oscillation

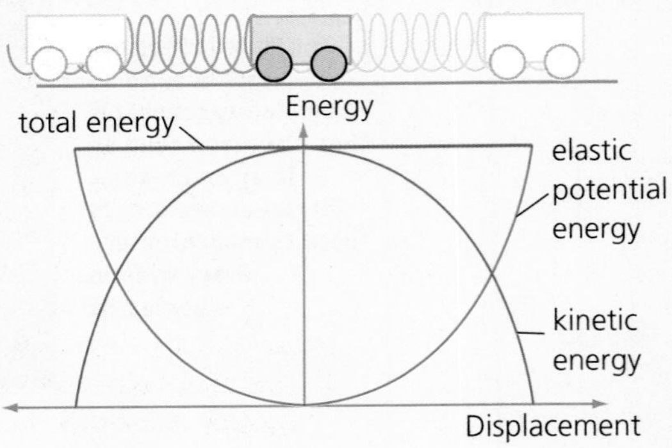

total energy
Energy
elastic potential energy
kinetic energy
Displacement

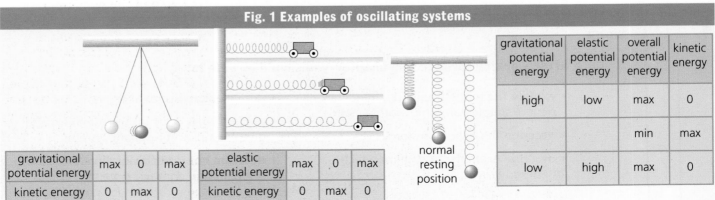

Fig. 1 Examples of oscillating systems

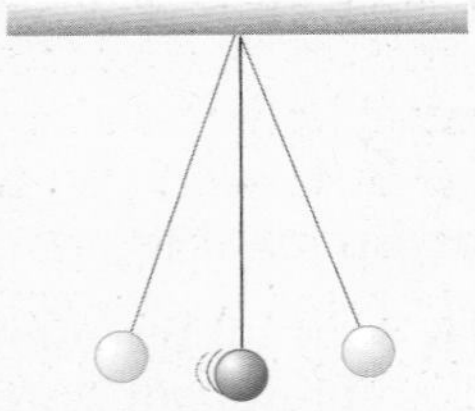

gravitational potential energy	max	0	max
kinetic energy	0	max	0

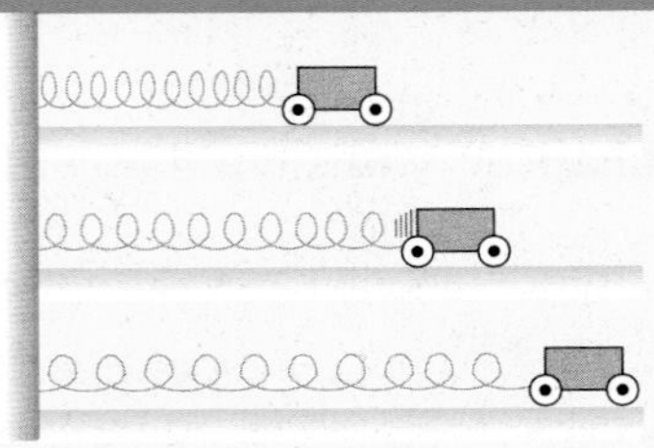

elastic potential energy	max	0	max
kinetic energy	0	max	0

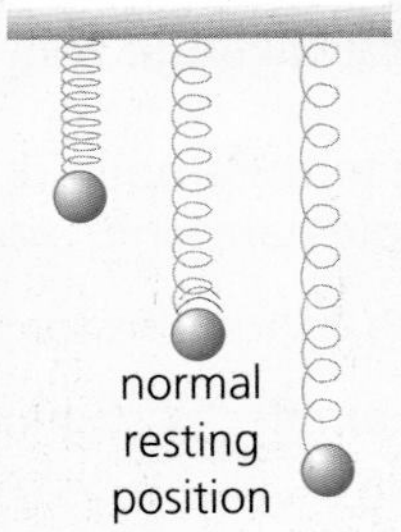

normal resting position

gravitational potential energy	elastic potential energy	overall potential energy	kinetic energy
high	low	max	0
		min	max
low	high	max	0

1 **An ultrasound horn is a solid metal bar which oscillates like a mass–spring system. The mass depends on the mass of the bar and the spring constant is related to the stiffness (Young modulus) of the metal. Using the mass–spring model, predict how the size of oscillations would be affected by:**

a doubling the energy of oscillation?

b using a thicker bar?

c using a less stiff material (lower Young modulus) with the same density?

Fig. 3 Why do materials expand when they are hotter?

Not all oscillations are symmetrical.

On the symmetrical track (see right), the ball spends an equal time to the left and right of *O*. On the other track, it will spend a much longer time on the gentler slope. Its average position is therefore to the right of its resting position.

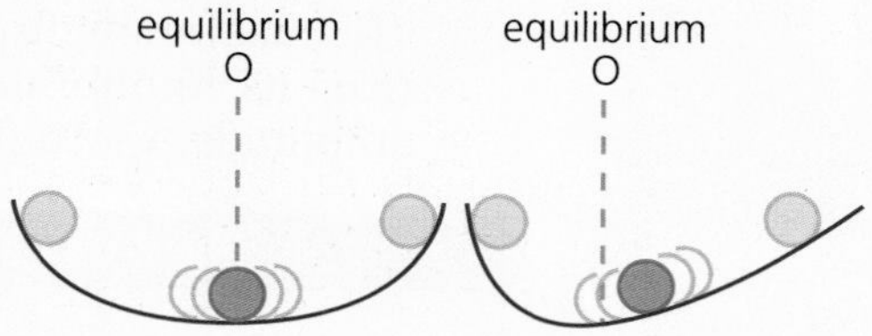

equilibrium
O
equilibrium
O

An atom bonded to another atom acts like a ball bearing on a track rolling back and forth. The asymmetric potential energy curve (pictured below) rises sharply if you try to squash two atoms together because they are not easily compressed. When you separate atoms, the force holding them together gradually gets smaller, so the potential energy rises and levels off at zero (the energy of completely separated atoms).

Given a certain amount of thermal energy, the atoms can oscillate. At energy E_1, the average position during the oscillation is about the same as the normal resting position. At a higher temperature, corresponding to energy E_2, the oscillation is not symmetrical: the atoms will spend more time being further apart. Therefore the material has expanded at the higher temperature.

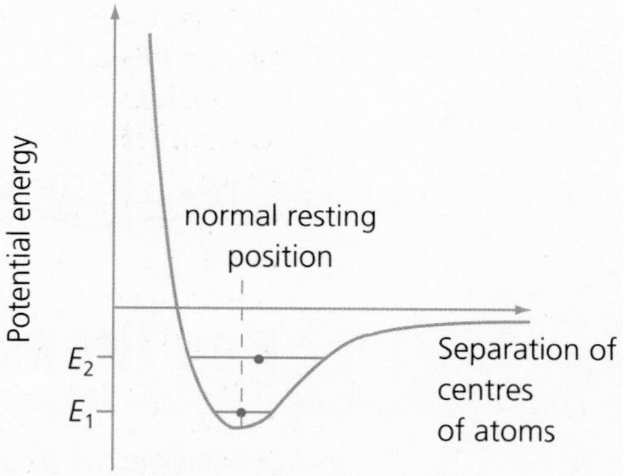

Potential energy
normal resting position
E_2
E_1
Separation of centres of atoms

A large amount of energy can be enough to pull adjacent atoms or molecules apart. This is the basis of ultrasonic cleaning and mixing: the extreme vibrations open up 'cavities' inside liquids by overcoming forces of attraction between molecules.

Fig. 4 Observing a pendulum

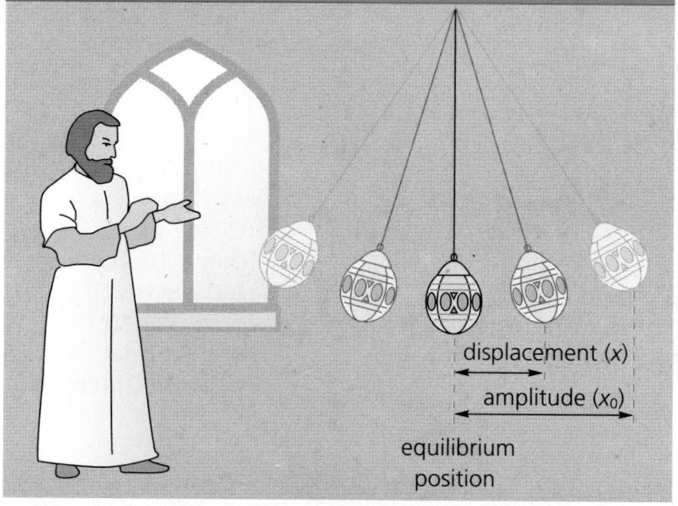

displacement (x)
amplitude (x_0)
equilibrium position

Galileo and the pendulum

Apart from being a scholar in the classics and literature, a musician, a poet and an art critic, Galileo was an inventive and observant young man. One day, so the story goes, he became interested in one of the swinging lamps in the cathedral in Pisa. He noted that the swinging of the lamp gradually died down, but that the time for each swing stayed about the same (Fig. 4).

He checked this by experiment using the most accurate timekeeping device available to him: the pulse in his wrist. This chance observation led to the invention of an accurate timing device – the simple pendulum – which revolutionised the study of motion.

A pendulum oscillates when it is disturbed from its resting place, or **equilibrium position**. At any moment, the object has a certain **displacement**, x, from equilibrium. The maximum displacement of an object from its equilibrium position is called its amplitude, x_0. Amplitude is a scalar quantity.

Fig. 5 One complete cycle

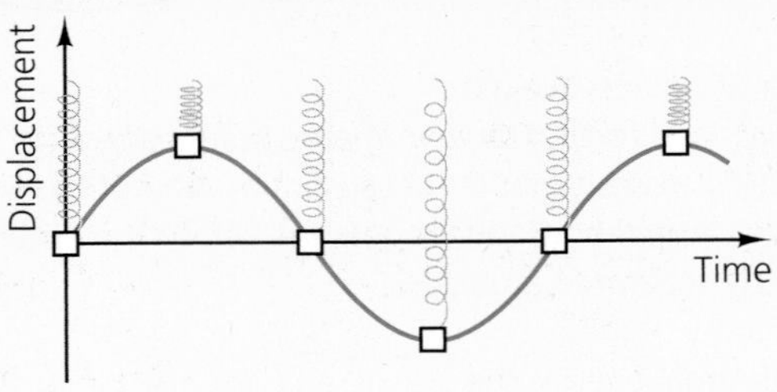

Displacement
Time

t	0	$\frac{1}{4}T$	$\frac{1}{2}T$	$\frac{3}{4}T$	T
ωt	0	$\frac{\pi}{2}$	π	$\frac{3}{2}\pi$	2π
$\sin \omega t$	0	+1	0	−1	0

After one complete **cycle** of an oscillation (Fig. 5), the object returns to the same position, travelling in the same direction. The time for one cycle is called the **period**, T, of the oscillation. Regular oscillations are sometimes called 'periodic motion'.
The frequency, f, of an oscillation is the number of cycles per unit time. Frequency and period are related by the equation $f = 1/T$.

The S.I. unit of frequency is the hertz (Hz), where 1 Hz = 1 oscillation per second.

These terms can be used to describe any oscillation.

Galileo's observation that period does not depend on amplitude seems to go against common sense. You might expect larger amplitude oscillations to take longer, because the pendulum bob has further to travel. However, a larger-amplitude swing means more potential energy and so more kinetic energy. The bob travels faster, so it covers a larger distance in the same time. The period, however, is only constant for fairly small amplitude oscillations. To prove this, we need to use mathematical ideas about oscillating motion.

Key ideas

- Mechanical oscillations involve the interchange of potential and kinetic energies. The total energy in the oscillating system remains constant.
- The amplitude, x_0, of oscillation is the maximum value of displacement, x, from the equilibrium position. The period, T, is the time for one oscillation. Frequency, f, is the number of oscillations per second; $f = 1/T$.

Simple harmonic motion

Ultrasonic processes all rely on very high frequencies at large power. High frequencies are useful because the accelerations and velocities involved are high – high enough to pull molecules apart. To understand this, we need to form a link between the way things oscillate and the acceleration and velocity of the oscillations.

The tension in a pendulum's string always pulls the bob back to the centre. A mass on a stretched or squashed spring always experiences a force towards its normal resting place. Things oscillate if there is a force which always tends to pull them back to their starting positions – a 'restoring' force. When the restoring force is directly proportional to displacement, the oscillation is **simple harmonic motion** (SHM).

Fig. 6 The conditions for SHM

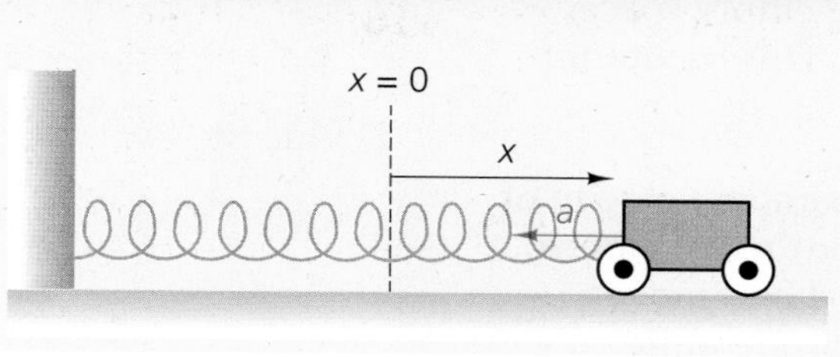

$x = 0$
x
a

If acceleration is a and displacement x, we can write:

$$a \propto -x$$

or $a = -\omega^2 x$ where ω^2 is a constant.

This is the 'simple harmonic motion equation'. A larger value of ω^2 means a larger acceleration, so the object completes its cycle faster. The constant must therefore be related to frequency (Fig. 7).

Fig. 7 Graphing $a = -\omega^2 x$

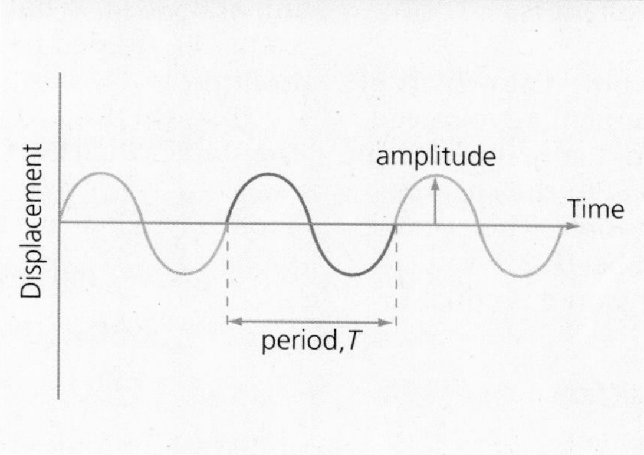

Displacement
amplitude
Time
period, T

Solving the equation

The SHM equation is a differential equation. It can be solved to show how displacement varies with time. The exact solution depends on where the object is when you start timing. We will only consider the simple sine solution, $x = x_0 \sin \omega t$, which assumes that displacement is zero when time is zero.

Many applications of ultrasonics – such as cleaning and mixing – depend on the huge accelerations of molecules as the high-frequency waves pass through the material. We need to be able to relate acceleration to frequency mathematically.

In one complete cycle (Fig. 8), the object will return to its starting position ($x = 0$).

Fig. 8 Stages in one cycle

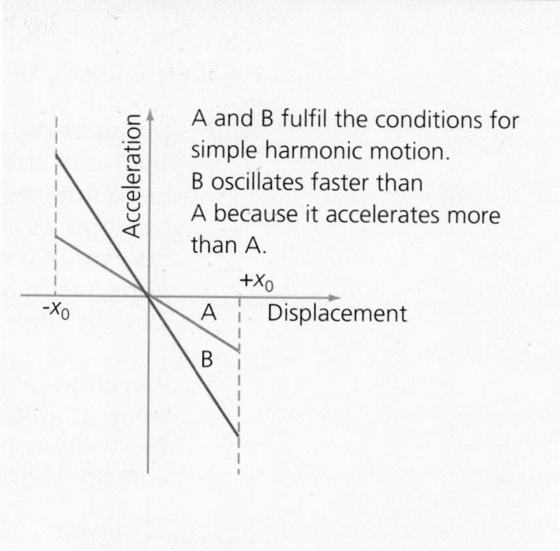

Acceleration
A and B fulfil the conditions for simple harmonic motion.
B oscillates faster than A because it accelerates more than A.
$+x_0$
$-x_0$
A
B
Displacement

This corresponds to the sine function going through a full cycle (2π radians), which takes time $t = T$ seconds, where T is the period of the oscillation. Therefore:

$$\sin \omega t = \sin 2\pi, \text{ or } \omega T = 2\pi.$$

Dividing by T gives $\omega = 2\pi/T$, but we know that $f = 1/T$, so:

$$\omega = 2\pi f \text{ and } T = 2\pi/\omega$$

Sometimes ω is called the angular frequency. The frequency of oscillation depends only on the link between acceleration and displacement (i.e. the term ω). Frequency does not depend on the amplitude of the oscillations.

We can use these equations to show that ultrasonic waves can mix and spray. Consider an ultrasonic paint mixer that uses a horn which vibrates with amplitude 55 μm at a frequency of 20 kHz. What is the maximum acceleration of the horn during its oscillation?

Using $\omega = 2\pi f$

$$= 2\pi \times 20\ 000 \text{ Hz}$$

$$= 1.26 \times 10^5 \text{ s}^{-1}$$

Using $a = -\omega^2 x$, the maximum acceleration is $a = \omega^2 x_0$

$$= (1.26 \times 10^5 \text{ s}^{-1})^2 \times 55 \times 10^{-6} \text{ m}$$

$$= 8.8 \times 10^5 \text{ m s}^{-2}$$

Such a huge acceleration is enough to pull molecules apart, leaving empty spaces ('cavities') in the liquid. This 'cavitation' makes the fluids mix.

2 Estimate the maximum velocity of the tip of the paint mixer's horn, assuming that the end moves through its amplitude uniformly in quarter of a cycle. Will this be an under-estimate or over-estimate? Explain why.

3 A second probe vibrates with the same amplitude at 40 kHz. How will the values of acceleration and velocity change?

Energy of SHM

The use of ultrasonics in industry relies on transferring known quantities of energy.

The acceleration of an object in SHM at displacement x is $a = -\omega^2 x$ so the restoring force of the oscillating system is $F = ma = -m\omega^2 x$.

In order to move the object slowly from equilibrium to a displacement x, you need to exert a force which gradually increases in magnitude from zero to F, in the *opposite direction* to the restoring force. The average force you exerted would be $-F/2$.

The potential energy stored is equal to the work done:

$$E_p = \text{average force} \times \text{distance}$$
$$= \tfrac{1}{2}(0 + m\omega^2 x) \times x$$
$$= \tfrac{1}{2} m\omega^2 x^2$$
$$E_p = \tfrac{1}{2} m\omega^2 x^2$$

When the object is at the extremes of its oscillation ($x = x_0$), it has no kinetic energy. The total energy, E, of the SHM is therefore equal to maximum potential energy (the p.e. when $x = x_0$), so $E = \tfrac{1}{2} m\omega^2 x_0^2$.

At any instant, $E = E_p + E_k$ and $E_k = \tfrac{1}{2} mv^2$, so

$$\tfrac{1}{2} m\omega^2 x_0^2 = \tfrac{1}{2} m\omega^2 x^2 + \tfrac{1}{2} mv^2$$

Divide by $\tfrac{1}{2}m$: $\omega^2 x_0^2 = \omega^2 x^2 + v^2$

$$\text{so, } v^2 = \omega^2 (x_0^2 - x^2)$$
$$\text{or } v = \pm\omega\sqrt{x_0^2 - x^2}$$

This last equation can be used to calculate the velocity and kinetic energy of an object at any position in its SHM.

An ultrasonic stapler can join pieces of recycled plastic together. The energy from the transducer is transferred to the plastic as heat, melting the staple into place. This works better than trying to use adhesives: recycled plastics contain impurities which make it difficult to glue them together.

Suppose the tip of the ultrasonic horn has an effective mass of 12 grams. To have enough energy to melt plastic, the staple needs to oscillate with an amplitude of 80 μm at 35 kHz. What ultrasound power would be needed to drive in 100 staples per minute?

First, we need to work out the energy of the stapler in SHM:

From $E = \tfrac{1}{2} m\omega^2 x_0^2$ and $\omega = 2\pi f$

$$E = \tfrac{1}{2} \times 0.012\ \text{kg} \times (2\pi \times 35\ 000\ \text{s}^{-1})^2 \times (80 \times 10^{-6}\ \text{m})^2$$
$$= 1.86\ \text{J}$$

It takes 1.86 joules to melt each staple. Using power = energy/time, and time = 60/100 = 0.6 seconds:

power = 1.86 J / 0.6 s = 3.1 W

This power is easily achieved by ultrasonic transducers.

Key ideas

- Simple harmonic motion requires acceleration, a, to be proportional and opposite to displacement: $a = -\omega^2 x$ (where angular frequency, $\omega = 2\pi f$).
- For SHM, displacement is related to time, t, by $x = x_0 \sin \omega t$ for an oscillation where $x = 0$ when timing starts. The velocity at any point can be calculated using $v = \pm\omega\sqrt{(x_0^2 - x^2)}$. The total energy of SHM is $E = \tfrac{1}{2} m\omega^2 x_0^2$.

8.3 Predicting the period

An ultrasonic horn has its own 'natural' frequency of vibration. If there is a mismatch between the horn's natural frequency and the frequency of the transducer, the transducer can be badly damaged. To design horns of the right natural frequency, engineers need to be able to predict the period of oscillation from the dimensions and properties of the object. Analysis of simpler systems such as the pendulum and the mass–spring can give a valuable insight into the problem.

Period of a pendulum

Suppose a bob of mass m is fixed to a string of length l (measured to the centre of the bob). The bob is displaced to one side to such a small extent that the vertical movement of the bob is negligible (Fig. 9).

Fig. 9 Restoring force on a pendulum

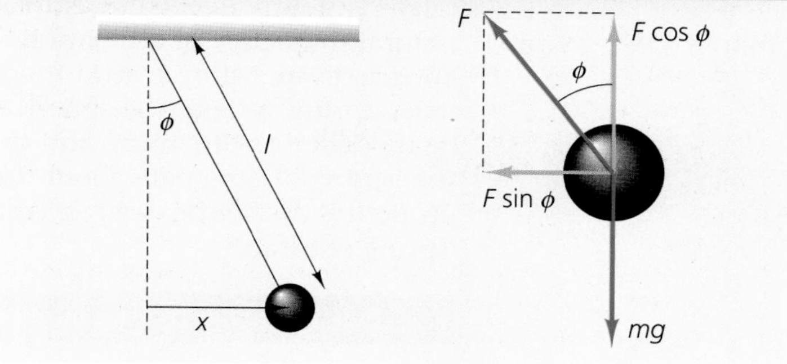

ϕ
l
x
F
F cos ϕ
ϕ
F sin ϕ
mg

The tension in the string has a horizontal component which always acts towards the centre. Because oscillations are small, vertical accelerations are near zero, so the vertical component of tension roughly balances the weight of the bob:

$$F \cos \phi + mg \approx 0$$

For small angles, $\cos \phi \approx 1$. Therefore, for small angles:

$$F \approx -mg$$

The horizontal component of tension causes horizontal acceleration:

$$F \sin \phi = ma$$

Eliminating F from these equations gives:

$$-mg \sin \phi = ma$$

$$\sin \phi = -\frac{a}{g}$$

From the pendulum diagram:

$$\sin \phi = \frac{\text{opposite}}{\text{hypotenuse}} = \frac{x}{l}$$

$$\text{so,} \quad -\frac{g}{a} = \frac{x}{l}$$

$$a = -\frac{g}{l}x$$

Since g and l are constant for a particular pendulum, $a \propto -x$: this is SHM. By comparing with the general equation, we can predict the period of the pendulum.

$$\text{Comparing } a = -\frac{g}{l}x$$

$$\text{with } a = -\omega^2 x$$

$$\text{we find that, } \omega^2 = \frac{g}{l}$$

$$\text{or, } \omega = \sqrt{g/l}$$

We can now get the time period from:

$$T = \frac{2\pi}{\omega} = \frac{2\pi}{\sqrt{g/l}} = 2\pi\sqrt{l/g}$$

For small angles ($\phi < 8°$) the period does not depend on the amplitude. Nor does the period depend on the mass of the bob.

4 A clock pendulum has period of oscillation of 2 seconds. What is its length?

5 What would its period of oscillation be

a on the moon ($g \approx 1.6$ N kg^{-1})?

b on board an orbiting spacecraft?

The period of a horizontal mass–spring system

A car bouncing on its suspension, an ultrasound horn, even atoms vibrating in a solid, are all like mass–spring systems. Suppose you have a spring fixed to a trolley of mass m (Fig. 10). If the mass is displaced, the spring will exert a force which tries to restore it to the resting position. Springs obey Hooke's law: $F = -kx$, where k is the spring constant (in $N\ m^{-1}$).

Fig. 10 Restoring force on a mass and spring

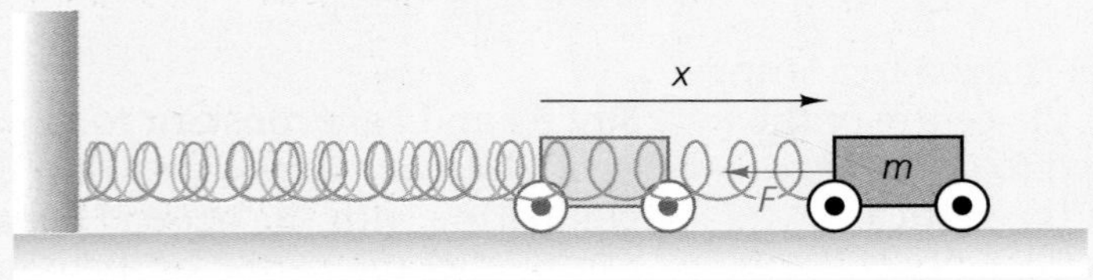

x
F
m

This force causes acceleration $F = ma$, giving:

$$ma = -kx$$

$$\text{so, } a = -\frac{k}{m}x$$

$$\text{From, } a = -\omega^2 x$$

$$\text{we get } \omega = \sqrt{k/m}$$

$$\text{Finally, } T = \frac{2\pi}{\omega} = 2\pi\sqrt{m/k}$$

6 **What factors influence the period of oscillation of a mass on a horizontal spring? Give physical explanations for each effect.**

7 **The same mass on the same spring is now hung vertically. How do you think this will affect the period of oscillation?**

8 **If you doubled the spring constant, how would the following be affected:**
a **frequency;**
b **energy of oscillation;**
c **maximum speed?**

Jenny is developing an ultrasonic horn for emulsifying oil to make mayonnaise. She has found that standard horns don't work well. She thinks that a spherical tip to the horn may be more efficient at transmitting energy uniformly through the viscous fluid.

Jenny's design of ultrasonic horn is a small spherical tip of mass 5 g on the end of a rod of length 4 cm and diameter 5 mm (Fig. 11). Jenny needed to estimate the natural frequency of oscillation of the horn. She tried using simple SHM theory for a mass–spring system; the spherical tip can be modelled as the 'mass' and the rod as the 'spring'. Using data about the elastic properties of the rod, we can work out its 'spring constant'.

Fig. 11 Design for the oil emulsifier

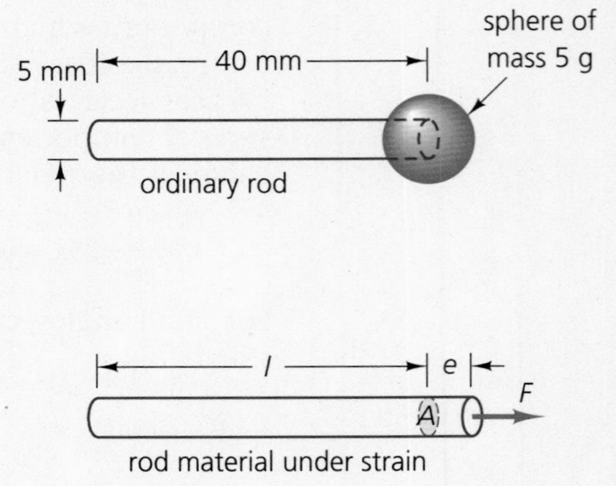

sphere of mass 5 g
5 mm
40 mm
ordinary rod
l
e
A
F
rod material under strain

The spring constant, k, is the force per unit extension: $k = F/e$. The metal rod has a Young modulus, E, of 200 GPa.

$$E = \frac{\text{tensile stress}}{\text{tensile strain}}$$
$$= \frac{F/A}{e/l} = \frac{Fl}{eA} = k\frac{l}{A}$$

or, $k = E\dfrac{A}{l}$

$$A = \pi r^2 = \pi(0.0025 \text{ m})^2$$
$$= 1.96 \times 10^{-5} \text{ m}^2$$
$$l = 0.04 \text{ m}$$
$$E = 200 \times 10^9 \text{ Pa}$$

So, $k = 200 \times 10^9 \text{ Pa} \times \dfrac{1.96 \times 10^{-5} \text{ m}^2}{0.04 \text{ m}}$

$$= 9.8 \times 10^7 \text{ N m}^{-1}$$

We can then use the formula for SHM of a spring to find the period and frequency:

$$T = 2\pi\sqrt{m/k}$$
$$= 2\pi\sqrt{0.005 \text{ kg}/9.8 \times 10^{-7} \text{ N m}^{-1}}$$
$$= 4.5 \times 10^{-5} \text{ s}$$

and $f = \dfrac{1}{T} = \dfrac{1}{4.5 \times 10^{-5} \text{ s}} = 22 \text{ kHz}$

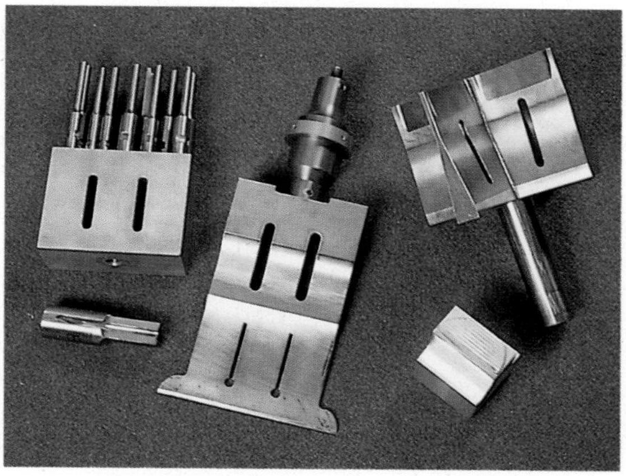

The shape of the horn can focus vibrations for specific uses – from welding the front onto a video recorder to cutting pizzas.

Unfortunately, Jenny's horn would be unsuitable for use in an environment with people. A metal rod of this size would have a significant mass, so the *effective* mass of the probe tip would be greater. This would bring down the natural frequency into the audible range.

9 How could Jenny modify her design to make sure that the horn has a higher natural frequency?

Fig. 12 Period of a vertical mass–spring system

This analysis is similar to that for the horizontal spring.

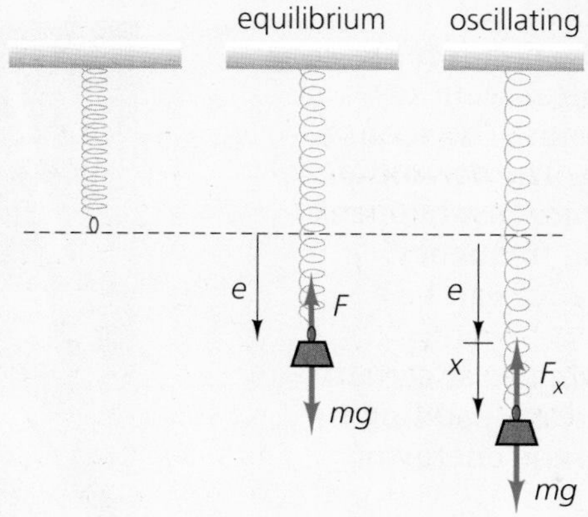

equilibrium
oscillating
e
F
mg
e
x
F_x
mg

The extra forces due to the weight *mg* make no difference to the period of oscillation. The net effect is only to shift the equilibrium position (Fig. 12).

At equilibrium, F must balance mg. From Hooke's Law, $F = ke$, so $ke = mg$.

When oscillating, $F_x = k \times (e + x)$. The *net* force acting in the direction of the displacement is $(mg - F_x)$.

Using $ma = F$

$$ma = mg - F_x$$
$$ma = ke - k(e + x)$$
$$ma = -kx$$
$$\therefore a = -\frac{k}{m}x$$

Comparing with the equation for simple harmonic motion, this gives $T = 2\pi\sqrt{m/k}$

Key ideas

- A mass–spring system performs SHM with period $T = 2\pi\sqrt{m/k}$
- A pendulum performs approximate SHM at small amplitudes with period $T = 2\pi\sqrt{(l/g)}$.

8.4 Resonance and forced vibration

An ultrasonic transducer can be destroyed by attaching the wrong horn. This is because the horn has its own natural frequency of oscillation. If you try to 'drive' it at any other frequency, large and unpredictable forces arise. If the driving frequency is the same as the natural frequency, the horn will continue to accept energy from the transducer, allowing oscillations to increase in amplitude. This build-up of oscillation is an example of **resonance** (Fig. 13).

Fig. 13 Using resonance

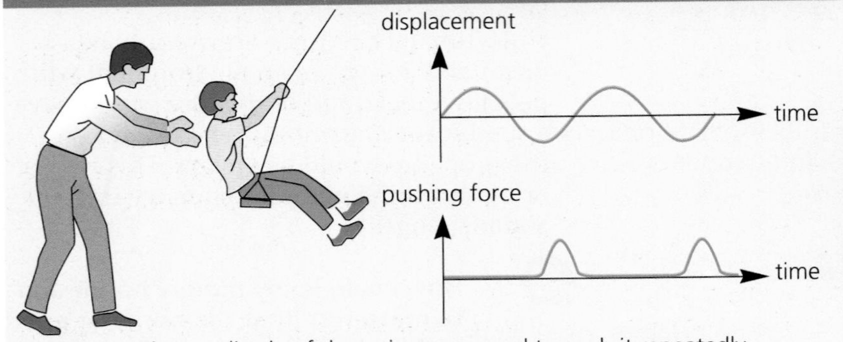
displacement
time
pushing force
time

To increase the amplitude of the swing, you need to push it repeatedly. For effective energy transfer at resonance, the driving oscillation is quarter of a cycle ahead of the driven oscillation. We say that there is a phase difference of a quarter of a cycle – or 90 degrees – between oscillations.

Resonance

The term 'resonance' originates from the study of sound. You probably know of rooms which have odd acoustics: some musical notes or certain voices seem to 'boom' or echo in these rooms. The room is 're-sounding' or resonating. The driving frequency of the note or voice just happens to match the room's natural frequency.

In many systems, resonance can be a nuisance:

- machinery rattles and vibrates at certain operating speeds; e.g. in cars, padding is fixed to panels to absorb the energy of vibration;
- high-frequency and relatively large amplitude vibrations in helicopters cause resonance of the human skull, leading to loss of accurate vision: pilots can fail to see small objects such as overhead power lines;
- structures can be damaged or destroyed by oscillations at the natural frequency. Bridges are particularly vulnerable when swirling air patterns act as a driving oscillation which can cause resonance.

Over 200 French infantrymen died on a bridge in 1850. The regular driving oscillation of their footsteps caused resonance and the bridge tore itself apart and collapsed. Soldiers are now told to break step when crossing a bridge.

The collapse of the Tacoma Narrows Bridge in 1940 was caused by only a mild crosswind. The bridge structure created eddies in the wind of just the right frequencey.

However, resonance has many practical applications:

- many musical wind instruments rely on the resonance of a column of air;

- digital watches and clocks use resonant vibration of a quartz crystal as the basis of their accurate time-keeping;
- radios and televisions are 'tuned' to the right frequency by a resonant electrical (capacitor–inductor) circuit;
- nuclear magnetic resonance (NMR) spectroscopy can help scientists determine the structure of a molecule by analysing patterns of resonant frequencies in a sample;
- in microwave ovens, the frequency of the microwaves matches the natural frequency of vibration of water molecules. Food containing water will absorb energy from the microwaves. Glass and plastic dishes do not contain molecules which vibrate at this frequency, so the microwaves pass through these materials without transferring energy.

Forced vibration

An object resonates when the driving frequency matches the natural frequency. But what happens at other frequencies? What if there is a lot of 'friction'? In the case of ultrasonic welding or cutting systems, the idea is to transfer energy to material as heat, not to make the whole object vibrate!

The effects of forced vibration can be predicted by thinking about a simple mechanical system. Suppose you put a mass on the end of a spring and hold the top of the spring. The mass would naturally oscillate at a frequency f_0. You can provide the driving oscillation by raising and lowering the spring by a small amount at fixed frequency, f.

Consider (or better still, try) three cases:

$f << f_0$:
You raise and lower the spring very slowly. The whole spring–mass system just follows your hand up and down, so $a = a_0$.

$f = f_0$:
Your hand is moving at the natural frequency of oscillation of the mass–spring system. The oscillations build up quickly. This is resonance – soon, the oscillations are destructively large and the mass bounces around uncontrollably. Given the chance, oscillations would become infinitely large: $a \to \infty$.

$f >> f_0$:
Your hand is moving up and down rapidly. The spring cannot exert big enough forces to make the mass accelerate and decelerate that quickly. The mass stays almost still: $a \to 0$.

From this, you can sketch a curve showing how driving frequency affects the amplitude of driven oscillations (Fig. 14).

Fig. 14 Amplitude of forced vibrations

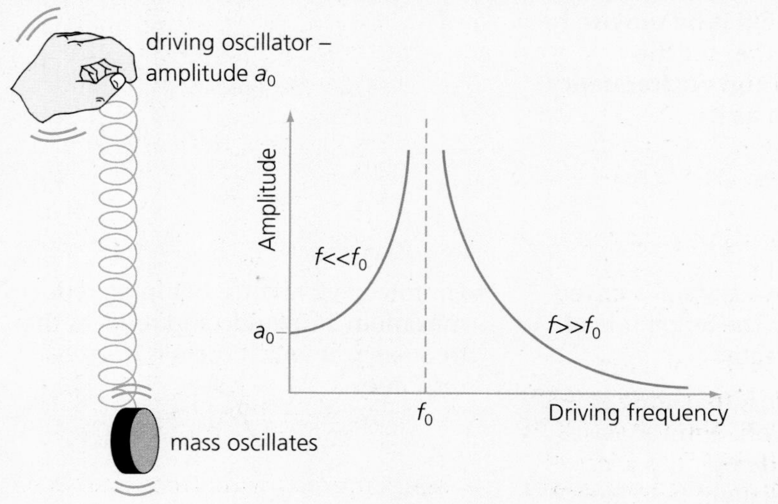

driving oscillator – amplitude a_0
Amplitude
$f<<f_0$
a_0
$f>>f_0$
f_0
Driving frequency
mass oscillates

Damping

In real systems, the amplitude of oscillation cannot rise to infinity. There will always be some resistance to oscillations and this resistance often increases with amplitude. For example, air resistance damps the motion of a pendulum; the effect is greater when the pendulum is moving faster at large amplitudes. Such resistive forces tend to 'damp down' the oscillations. This loss in the energy of vibration is called **damping**.

In ultrasonic mixing and cleaning systems, the liquid's viscosity will cause damping of the horn. This is beneficial; the idea is to transfer vibrational energy to the liquid, not just to make the horn vibrate in ever-increasing oscillations.

Free oscillations die down gradually with light damping. In systems where the resistive force is proportional to velocity, the amplitude dies down exponentially – that is, the amplitude decreases by the same fraction in each cycle (Fig. 15).

Fig. 15 Exponential damping

When the resistive force is proportional to velocity the amplitude drops by the same fraction each time – it dies down exponentially. $\frac{a_1}{a_0} = \frac{a_2}{a_1} = \frac{a_3}{a_2} \ldots$

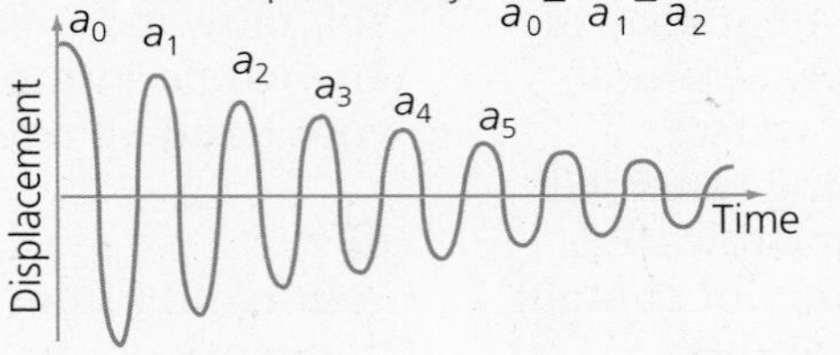

a_0
a_1
a_2
a_3
a_4
a_5
Displacement
Time

Fig. 16 The effects of damping

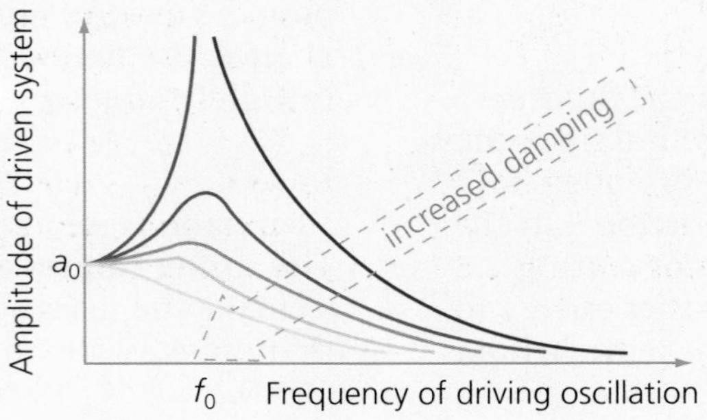

Amplitude of driven system
a_0
increased damping
f_0
Frequency of driving oscillation

10 **An ultrasonic horn is a resonant oscillator. If the horn is for use in liquids, why would it be unwise to 'tune' the horn (i.e. set the oscillator to the correct frequency) with the horn in air?**

Heavy and critical damping

If damping is light, oscillations die away gradually. If resistive forces are very high (heavy damping) the system may not oscillate at all (Fig. 16). Visualise a pendulum swinging in a sea of treacle. Once displaced, the bob would very slowly return to equilibrium without overshooting. Oscillation is prevented.

Heavily damped systems respond slowly to changes. With **critical damping**, the resistive forces are just enough to prevent oscillation. The object returns to equilibrium in the minimum possible time. Critical damping is the ideal state for many mechanical systems:

- fire doors need to close as quickly as possible, but it could be dangerous if they swung past equilibrium;
- moving coil meters need to move swiftly to the new meter reading without oscillating (Fig. 17).

Fig. 17 Damping a moving-coil meter

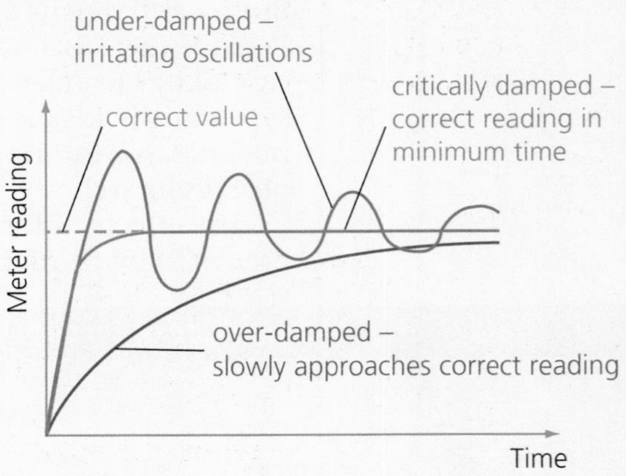

under-damped –
irritating oscillations
critically damped –
correct reading in
minimum time
correct value
Meter reading
over-damped –
slowly approaches correct reading
Time

Key ideas

- Resonance occurs when a system is driven at its natural frequency. The amplitude of oscillations increases greatly.
- Damping is caused by loss of energy of oscillation because of work done against resistive forces. Critical damping is just enough to prevent oscillation, but allows the system to reach equilibrium quickly.
- For forced vibrations, damping reduces the maximum amplitude and reduces the frequency at which there is greatest response.

9 Communicating by waves

Most people in the UK rely on television and radio for news about current affairs. Our team uses electronic communication, such as portable phones and faxes, to help us deliver up-to-date news. Viewers expect high quality sound and pictures, even from outside broadcasts. The technical demands are sometimes daunting.

People communicate using sound and vision. Speech and music rely on sound waves, while visual media use light waves. In these cases, the waves themselves are the message. To communicate over long distances, we use light, radio waves and microwaves – all of which are electromagnetic waves. Information for radios, televisions, fax machines and mobile telephones can be coded – or 'modulated' – onto the wave. Communications satellites have changed the whole nature of news. The ability to manipulate waves now allows stories and events from around the world to reach our screens as they are happening.

9.1 Learning objectives

After working through this chapter, you should be able to:

- **describe** the main features of progressive waves;
- **define** and use the terms amplitude, frequency, wavelength and phase;
- **derive** and use the equation $c = f\lambda$;
- **distinguish** between longitudinal and transverse waves;
- **explain** superposition and coherence;
- **describe** two-source interference;
- **describe** the effects of diffraction;
- **explain** how a diffraction grating works and derive $d \sin \phi = n\lambda$;
- **distinguish** between progressive and standing waves.

9.2 Moving waves

A wave is caused by something which oscillates. For example, sound waves can be created by any object which vibrates. The vibrations are passed on to molecules of the air in a process called **propagation**. As a wave propagates, energy from the oscillator is transferred to different regions of space. **Electromagnetic waves** can be thought of as an oscillation of electric and magnetic fields in space. Unlike sound waves, they do not need a medium: electromagnetic waves can travel through a vacuum.

Longitudinal and transverse waves

Although sound waves and electromagnetic waves have a lot in common, they have one important difference. Electromagnetic waves are **transverse**, whereas sound waves are **longitudinal**. In sound waves, air particles are pushed and pulled by the vibrations along the line of the wave (Fig. 1). The wave spreads as a pressure wave made up of 'compressions' and 'rarefactions' of the air. The air particles vibrate in the same direction that the wave propagates (along the wave). These types of wave are called longitudinal waves.

Fig. 1 Longitudinal waves

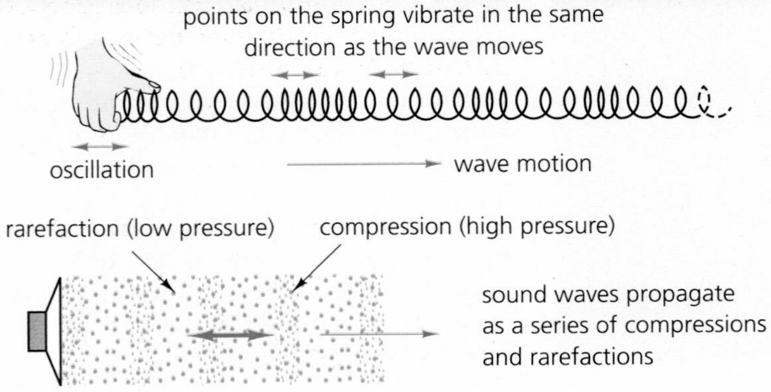
points on the spring vibrate in the same direction as the wave moves
oscillation
wave motion
rarefaction (low pressure)
compression (high pressure)
sound waves propagate as a series of compressions and rarefactions

Examples of longitudinal waves include earthquake 'p-waves' and SONAR, high-frequency pressure waves used for measuring depth and locating objects beneath the sea.

In transverse waves, the vibrations are at right angles to the direction of propagation. This can be demonstrated using a wave travelling along a spring (Fig. 2).

Fig. 2 Transverse waves in a spring

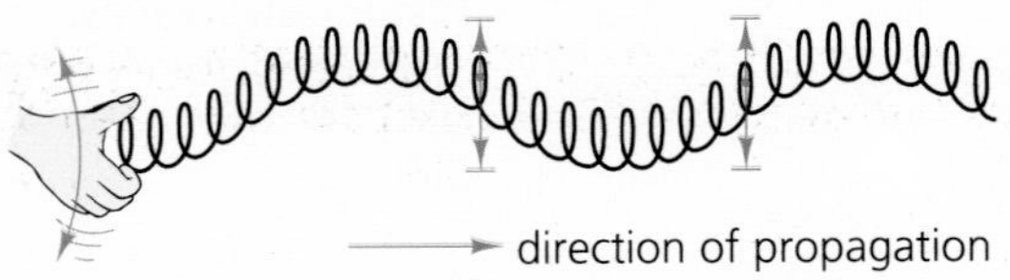
direction of propagation

Points on the spring vibrate at right angles to the direction of propagation.

Electromagnetic waves exchange energy between electric fields and magnetic fields. These fields are perpendicular to each other (Fig. 3). Examples of transverse wave motion include earthquake 's-waves', water ripples and waves on the strings of musical instruments.

Fig. 3 An electromagnetic wave

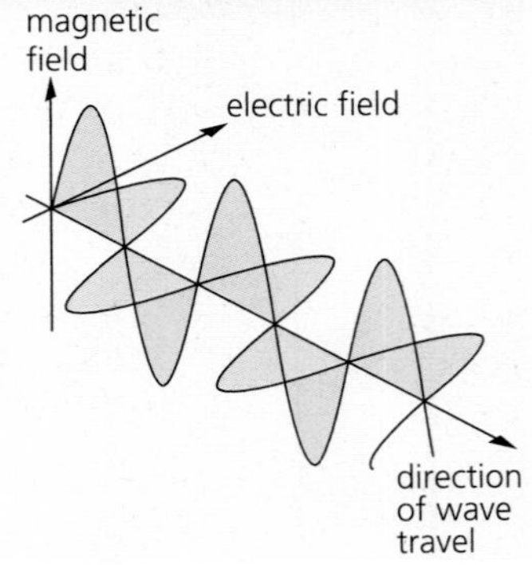
magnetic field
electric field
direction of wave travel

Transverse waves may be **polarised** so that there is only a single direction of oscillation. This is frequently true of waves from aerials (Fig. 4).

Fig. 4 Polarised waves from aerials

The orientation of the aerial affects the polarisation of the wave

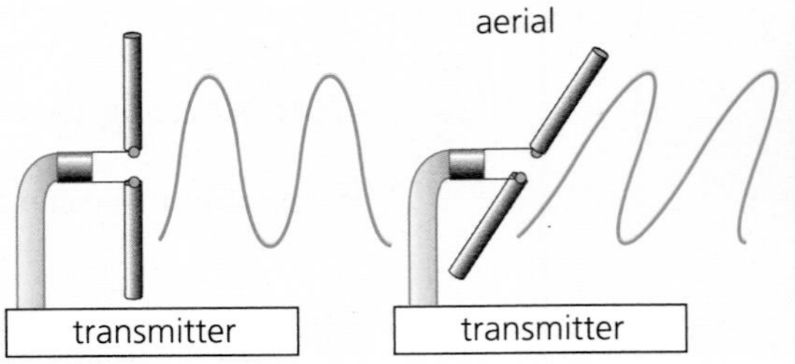
aerial
transmitter
transmitter

Progressive and standing waves

The ability of waves to transfer energy makes them ideal for transmitting information from one place to another. When a news reporter speaks, energy and information from the reporter's voice is carried along waves. Waves that can transfer energy in this way are called '**progressive**'. Electromagnetic waves, such as radio waves from a transmitter, are progressive waves.

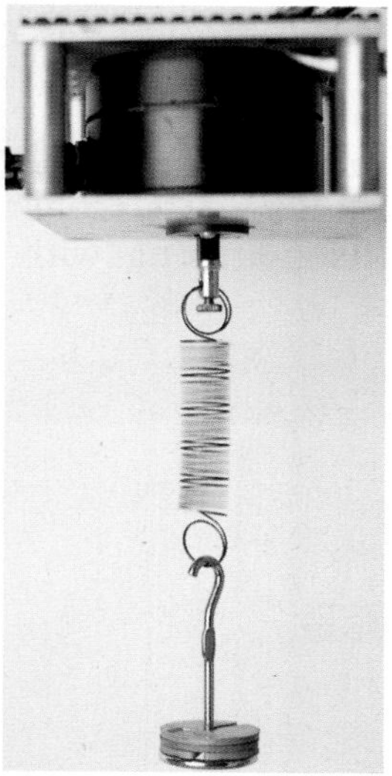

Standing waves can be created in spring systems.

Not all waves are progressive. If a guitar string is plucked at its centre, the disturbance makes the whole string vibrate. This certainly has the appearance of a wave motion, but it is not a progressive wave: there is no transfer of energy from one place on the string to another. Because the wave stands still, we call it a **standing wave** or **stationary wave** (Fig. 5). Standing waves are common in mechanical systems, such as strings and air columns in pipes. Musical instruments often rely on standing waves as the source of vibration to generate sound waves. For waves on strings and waves in pipes, the simplest standing wave (the **fundamental**) occurs when the length of the string or pipe is equal to half a wavelength (Fig. 6).

Fig. 5 Nodes and antinodes on a standing wave

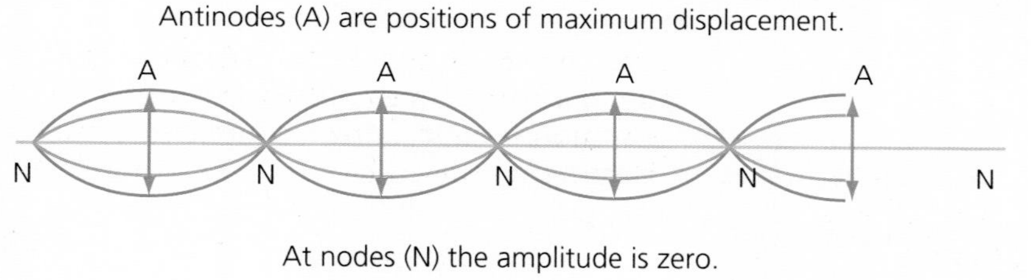
Antinodes (A) are positions of maximum displacement.
A
A
A
A
N
N
N
N
N
At nodes (N) the amplitude is zero.

Fig. 6 The fundamental

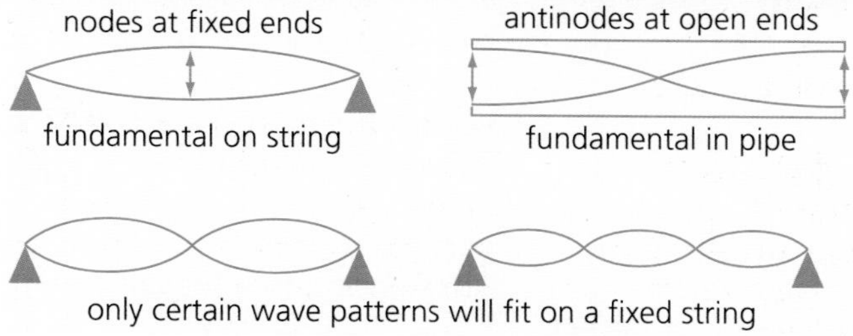
nodes at fixed ends
fundamental on string
antinodes at open ends
fundamental in pipe
only certain wave patterns will fit on a fixed string

There are some important differences between progressive and standing waves (Table 1).

Standing waves in a system can set up progressive waves. For example, a standing wave on a guitar string makes air molecules vibrate, causing a progressive sound wave at the same frequency through the air. The standing wave gradually dies out as its energy transfers to the progressive wave. Mathematically, you can make a standing wave by adding identical waves which are travelling in opposite directions. In practice, a standing wave can be created by allowing two sources of waves to interfere, or by adding a wave and its reflection.

The study of standing waves has become a very topical area in science. The branch of physics called quantum mechanics treats particles as though they are somehow linked with waves (Fig. 7).

Fig. 7 Three-dimensional standing waves

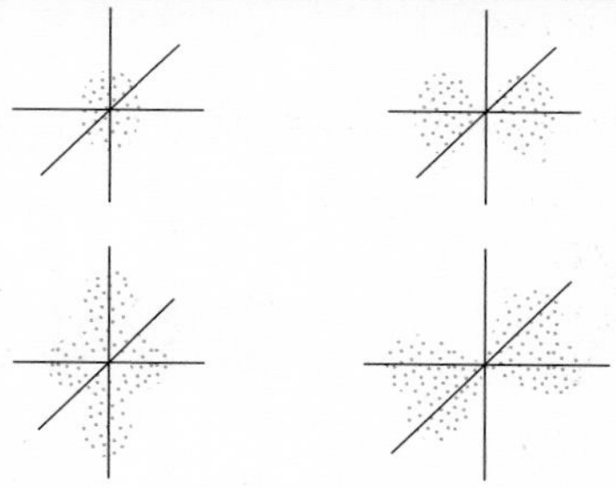

The most probable positions of electrons in atoms are linked with three-dimensional standing wave patterns.

Aerials and wavelengths

Television and radio signals are transmitted and received by aerials. Vibrations from the reporter's speech are transferred via sound waves to the microphone where they are modulated onto a current signal. The electrical variations in the current in turn set up an electrical standing wave in the

Table 1 Comparison of progressive and standing waves

Progressive	Standing
• all points on the wave vibrate • each point has the same amplitude • adjacent points vibrate with different phase • energy is transferred through space	• there are points called nodes which do not vibrate at all • amplitude varies with position • there are only two phases • energy is needed only to maintain the standing wave to compensate for losses

aerial. The standing wave along the aerial gives rise to a progressive radio wave which radiates into space. The frequency of the electrical oscillations needs to match the frequency of the standing wave on the receiving aerial. This is another example of resonance (see Chapter 8). The length of the aerial is therefore very important: it is linked to the frequency (and wavelength) of the radio wave in the air.

The length of one complete wave is called the **wavelength**, λ. For a sinusoidal wave, this is the distance between two adjacent peaks. It takes one **period**, T, of time to complete a wave cycle (Fig. 8). Using:

$$\text{speed} = \frac{\text{distance}}{\text{time}}$$

the speed of the wave, c, is given by:

$$c = \frac{\lambda}{T} = \frac{1}{T} \times \lambda$$

So, for any wave $c = f\lambda$

$c \approx 3.0 \times 10^8 \text{ m s}^{-1}$ for electromagnetic waves

Fig. 8 Wavelength and speed

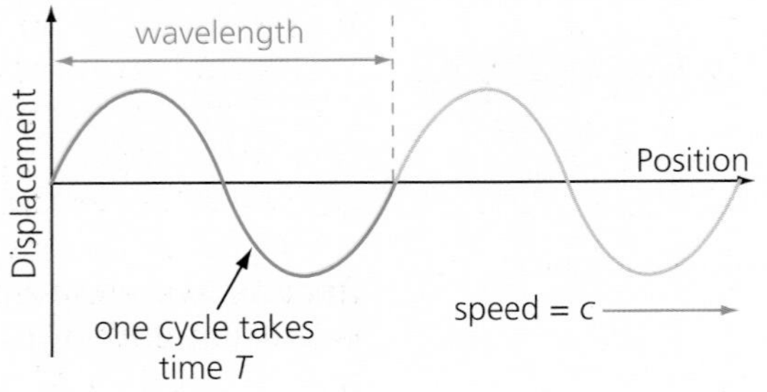

wavelength
Displacement
Position
one cycle takes
time T
speed = c

1 Most young, healthy ears can detect sounds with a frequency between 20 Hz and 20 kHz. What wavelengths are these sounds? (Sound travels at about 340 m s^{-1} in air at room temperature.)

A wide range of frequencies of electromagnetic wave can be used for communication. The low frequency (LF) band (around 200 kHz) gives poor sound quality, but long range. Ground-based TV broadcasts use frequencies around 500 MHz, and satellite broadcasts in the region of 10 GHz. The aerial lengths needed to pick up each of these signals varies enormously. The ideal aerial is a 'half wave dipole' – half a wavelength long, with a central feeder cable (Fig. 9).

Fig. 9 Half wave dipole

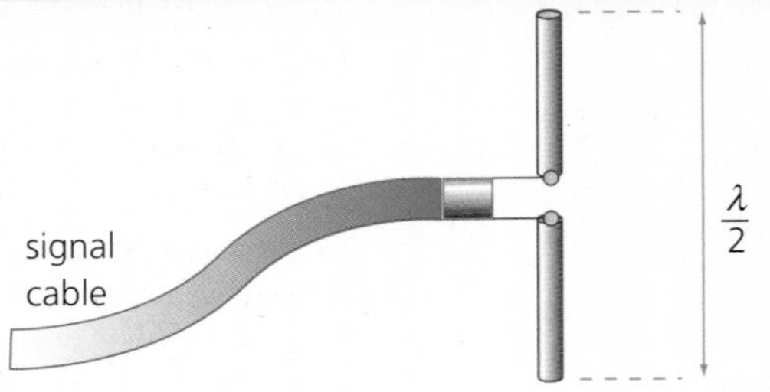

signal
cable
$\frac{\lambda}{2}$

At high frequencies, the wavelength is small. This tends to make the aerial a more practicable length. Signals transmitted at lower frequencies can rarely use a half wave dipole aerial: the aerial would simply be too long. We can calculate the length of aerial required for common broadcasting frequencies by rearranging the equation $c = f\lambda$. For a 200 kHz radio transmission on the LF band:

$$\lambda = \frac{c}{f} = \frac{3.0 \times 10^8 \text{ m s}^{-1}}{200\,000 \text{ Hz}}$$
$$= 1500 \text{ m}$$

so aerial length = $\frac{1}{2}\lambda = 750$ m

Using this method, a 500 MHz ground-based television broadcast would need a 30 cm aerial and a 1.9 GHz cordless phone conversation would require a 16 cm aerial. These two aerial lengths are practicable, but a LF radio receiver with an aerial 750 metres long would not be.

Electromagnetic waves have an electric and a magnetic component. Most receivers of low frequencies pick up the magnetic component of radio waves. If you break open a radio receiver, you will usually be able to see a 'ferrite' rod with coils around it. Ferrite is a magnetic ceramic material which is able to respond to the alternating magnetic field of the radio wave. This induces a current in the coils which can be amplified and decoded.

2 **Yellow light has a wavelength of about 500 nm. What is its frequency?**

3 a **Sketch the standing wave patterns possible on a dipole aerial 10 cm long.**

b **What frequencies could the aerial transmit? (Note: current must be zero at the ends of the aerial and maximum at the central feeder cable.)**

Key ideas

- Longitudinal waves (e.g. sound) oscillate in the direction of propagation. Transverse waves (e.g. electromagnetic) oscillate at right angles to the direction of propagation.
- Waves may be progressive (energy transmitting) or stationary (standing). A standing wave can be viewed as the resultant of the interference of two waves moving in opposite directions.
- Wavelength is the distance the wave propagates in one period of vibration. It is related to wave speed and frequency by the equation $c = f\lambda$

9.3 Adding waves

To transmit TV and radio signals, we need to add information to an electromagnetic **carrier wave**. This process is called modulation. There are two main ways of modulating the carrier wave for broadcasting purposes: AM and FM.

Amplitude modulation

Radio transmissions on the low- and medium-frequency bands (LF and MF) use **amplitude modulation**, or AM (Table 2).

Fig. 10 Amplitude modulation

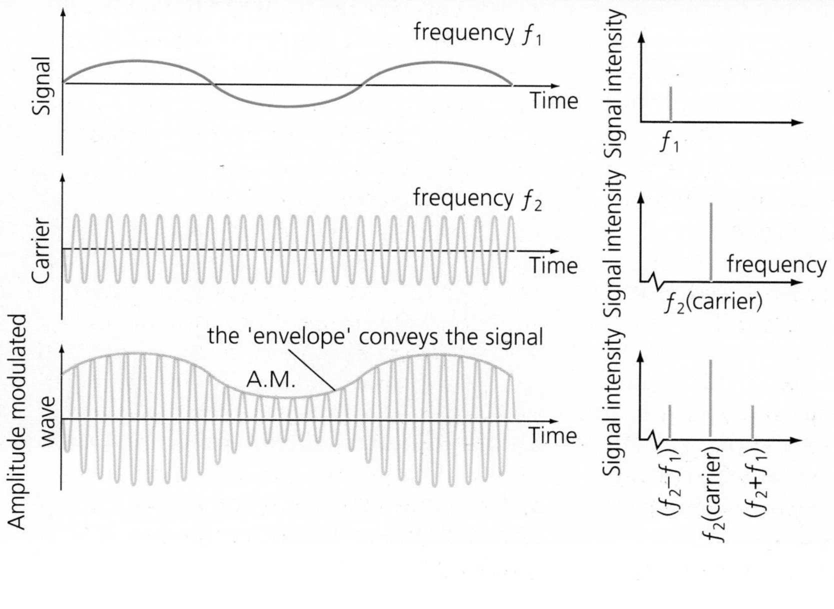

Signal
frequency f_1
Time
Signal intensity
f_1
Carrier
frequency f_2
Time
Signal intensity
frequency
f_2(carrier)
Amplitude modulated wave
the 'envelope' conveys the signal
A.M.
Time
Signal intensity
(f_2-f_1)
f_2(carrier)
(f_2+f_1)

Table 2 AM and FM frequencies

long wave (LW)	BBC Radio 4	198 kHz
medium wave (MW)	BBC Radio 5	909 kHz
	Virgin 1215	1215 kHz
VHF	BBC Radio 1 FM	97.6 – 99.8 MHz
VHF	Classic FM	100 – 102 MHz

In AM, the amplitude of the carrier wave varies with the amplitude of the signal. The AM waveform is no longer a simple sine wave of a single frequency (Fig. 10). It is equivalent to sending the original carrier wave plus two extra frequencies. These 'side frequencies' are equal to the sum and the difference of carrier and signal frequencies, $[f_2 - f_1]$ and $[f_2 + f_1]$. For example, a 10 kHz signal on a 100 kHz carrier would have side frequencies of 90 kHz and 110 kHz.

Real signals are much more complex. High quality audio signals, for example, could contain signal frequencies in the range of human hearing: between 20 Hz and 20 kHz. Every frequency in this 'band' will give rise to two side frequencies in the transmission, so the transmitted signal has two **sidebands** (Fig. 10).

The width of the frequency band is called the **bandwidth**. For a maximum signal frequency F, the transmitted signal contains frequencies from $[f_{carrier} - F]$ to $[f_{carrier} + F]$. The bandwidth is therefore $2F$

for an AM system. To transmit high-quality audio signals up to 20 kHz you would need a bandwidth of 40 kHz. This is too large to fit onto the low-frequency carrier waves in the long and medium wave bands. There would not be a wide enough range of frequencies in the radio spectrum for all the different stations. As a compromise, the highest frequencies are cut out: this is why long and medium wave radio gives low quality sound, lacking 'treble'.

Frequency modulation

Frequency modulation (FM) is used for very high frequency (VHF) radio and for part of TV signals (Table 2). In FM, the *frequency* of the carrier wave varies with the amplitude of the signal (Fig. 11).

Fig. 11 Frequency modulation

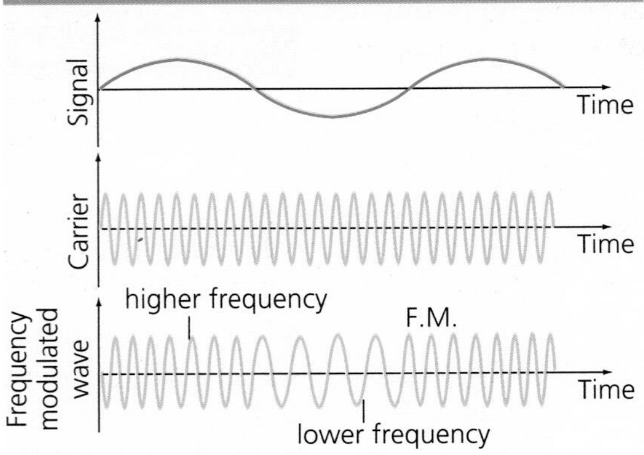
Signal
Time
Carrier
Time
Frequency modulated wave
higher frequency
F.M.
Time
lower frequency

FM signals are far less affected by '**noise**', such as the radio frequency emissions from sparks in motors or car ignition systems. This is because noise affects the amplitude of waves, but has little effect on the frequency of the waves. Therefore, frequency modulation is better than amplitude modulation for mobile transmitters and receivers.

Frequency modulation gives rise to an infinite number of side frequencies. Most of these are at very low amplitude, but FM still always need a bigger bandwidth than AM. This is why FM is only used with high carrier frequencies, typically above 80 MHz. For 'wide band' FM audio transmissions on the VHF band, the bandwidth is 190 kHz, almost five times what you would need for AM. However, the carrier frequency is so high that there is even enough 'space' in the frequency band to send the extra information needed for a stereo signal.

Bandwidth and pictures

Although I do face-to-face interviews, a lot of my investigative work makes use of telephones and faxes. The fax machine has made a huge difference to the way we operate: documents can be with us in minutes rather than days. I'm looking forward to the development of videophones: it will be much easier to get a feel for people's viewpoints if we can see them on the phone!

A bandwidth of up to 20 kHz is needed for the transmission of audio information. However, if you are only interested in transmitting speech, the bandwidth can be reduced. Telephone lines have a bandwidth of about 4 kHz. This gives lower quality sound but allows more telephone calls to be carried within a frequency band. For example, on a microwave satellite link with a carrier frequency of around 10 GHz, you could fit tens of thousands of phone calls. Visual information is harder to send. Television pictures need 25 frames per second, each made up of 625 lines. Each line has several hundred phosphor dots which can change in brightness. Overall, this means a bandwidth of about 5.5 MHz for an ordinary television picture.

Videophones are under development, although the technical problems are challenging. With a telephone line bandwidth of 4 kHz, transmitting even a small moving picture is difficult. 'Data compression' can reduce the amount of information that needs to be transmitted. Rather than sending the complete picture frame-by-frame, the techniques involve only sending information on which parts of the picture are changing.

Fax machines are one of the great technological success stories of recent years. The Japanese language, with over 2000 characters, was the real spur to the development of the fax. International teleprinter codes in the 1970s could only accommodate 56 characters, so researchers worked on a method of transmitting hand-written messages. The digital fax machine works by breaking the image down into tiny black or white squares called pels (Fig. 12). There are about 4 million pels on a sheet of A4 (roughly a resolution of 80 pels per cm). To transmit this on a phone line with a bandwidth of 4 kHz would take about 15 minutes: clearly far too expensive! However, **data compression** techniques can reduce this by a factor of about 20, so that faxing a letter is often cheaper than posting it.

Fig. 12 A fax broken down into pels

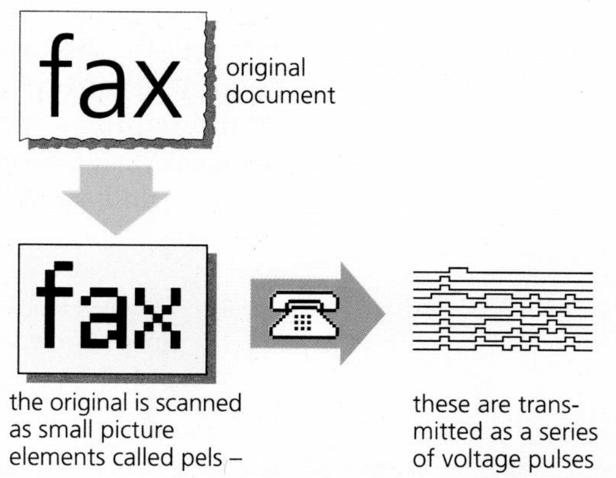
fax
original document
fax
the original is scanned as small picture elements called pels –
these are trans-mitted as a series of voltage pulses

Key ideas

- Modulation is the encoding of a signal onto a carrier wave. The amplitude of the signal alters the carrier amplitude in AM but in FM it alters the carrier frequency. A larger bandwidth is needed for FM transmission but it is less affected by noise.

Phase

I live on a farm which is a long way from the nearest TV transmitter. The signal I receive is very weak. I'm wondering if I can join together several aerials to make a stronger signal...

Fig. 13 Boats on sea

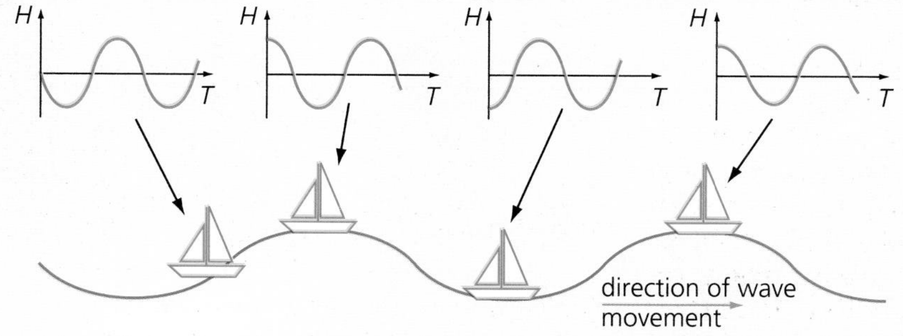
H
T
H
T
H
T
H
T
direction of wave movement

Position affects phase – imagine the movement of the boats as the wave passes.

Arrays of aerials can be used to boost signals in the fields of radar and radio astronomy. However, the exact positioning of the aerials is critical. This can be understood by considering the link between the position of an aerial and the phase of waves.

As a wave moves, each point in its path oscillates. Different points oscillate with different phase (see Chapter 7). This phase difference arises because the vibration takes time to travel from one place to another. Oscillations are in phase if they differ by a whole number of wavelengths. Oscillations are antiphase if there is a half wavelength difference (Fig. 13).

Other phase differences can be calculated by taking a simple ratio. A distance of one wavelength, λ, is equivalent to one complete cycle. One cycle is a phase difference of 2π radians (360 degrees). For points separated by a distance x, the phase difference is therefore:

$$2\pi \times \frac{x}{\lambda}$$

The wavelength of waves used for TV broadcasts is around 0.6 m, so in theory we could put several aerials 0.6 m apart and add the signals. However, exact alignment and spacing of the aerials would require a high degree of accuracy. An electronic amplifier for an existing aerial would be far more practical a solution.

4 Study Fig. 14. Sketch how amplitude varies with time at point D.

Fig. 14 Position and phase

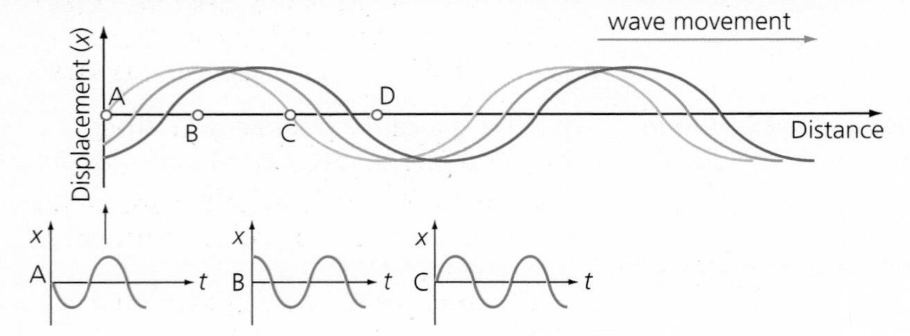

wave movement
Displacement (x)
A
B
C
D
Distance
x
A
t
x
B
t
x
C
t

Interference

When people talk about **interference**, they usually mean unwanted noise on a radio receiver. In physics, the word interference has a much more precise meaning. Interference is the effect produced when two sets of waves are added together.

The fact that two radio stations can be received by a radio set at the same time illustrates an important property of waves. Waves can be added together at any point in space, even though they may have come from different directions.

This is an example of the principle of superposition of waves. The overall displacement is equal to the sum of the displacements from each individual wave (Fig. 15). The principle applies to all electromagnetic waves. It also works for mechanical waves in a medium which obeys Hooke's law. Superposition works even when the waves are of different frequencies.

Suppose that two television transmitters were broadcasting at the same frequency. How would the signal strength vary if the receiver were placed at the at the positions shown in Fig. 16?

Constructive interference occurs when the path difference is a whole number of wavelengths, $n\lambda$. **Destructive interference** occurs when the path difference is $(n + \frac{1}{2})\lambda$, where $n = 0, 1, 2, \ldots$

Fig. 15 Superposition of waves

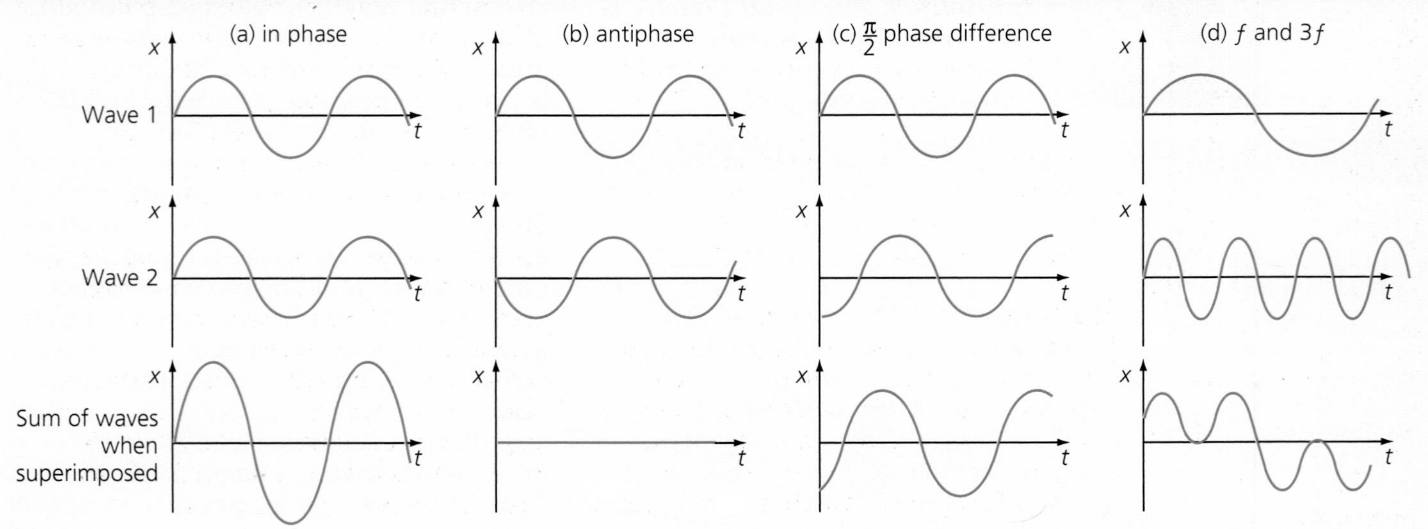

(a) in phase
(b) antiphase
(c) $\frac{\pi}{2}$ phase difference
(d) f and $3f$
Wave 1
Wave 2
Sum of waves when superimposed
x
t

Fig. 16 Good reception

The waves at A have travelled equal distances, AP and AQ, so they *must* be in phase. They will add together, giving twice the signal strength. Waves at B have a path difference of BQ – BP = 1 wavelength. These two waves will be in phase, so the signal will increase in strength. Waves at C don't fit this simple rule. CP is 3.5 wavelengths and CQ is 4 wavelengths. There is a half wavelength difference, so the waves will be antiphase. That means they will cancel out. The antenna at C would receive a very weak signal. A, B and C are three points in space. Performing the same calculations for other points shows that there are lines along which the signal is stronger (constructive interference) and lines of almost complete cancellation (destructive interference).

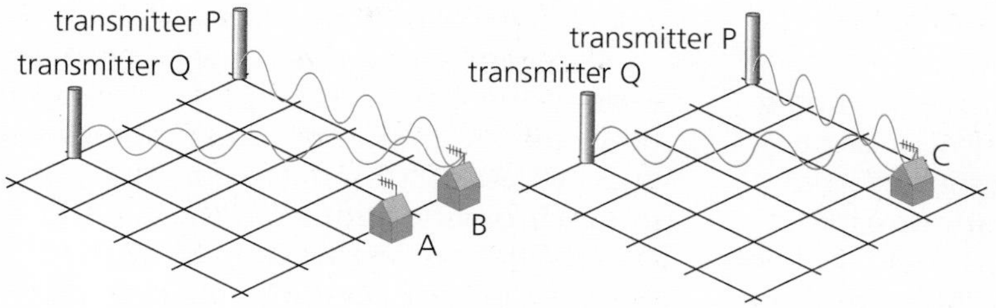
transmitter P
transmitter Q
A
B
transmitter P
transmitter Q
C

Fig. 17 Interference bands

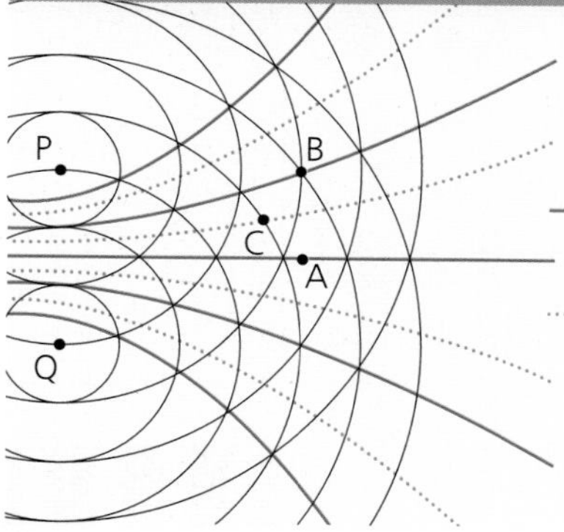
P
B
C
A
Q
constructive interference
destructive interference

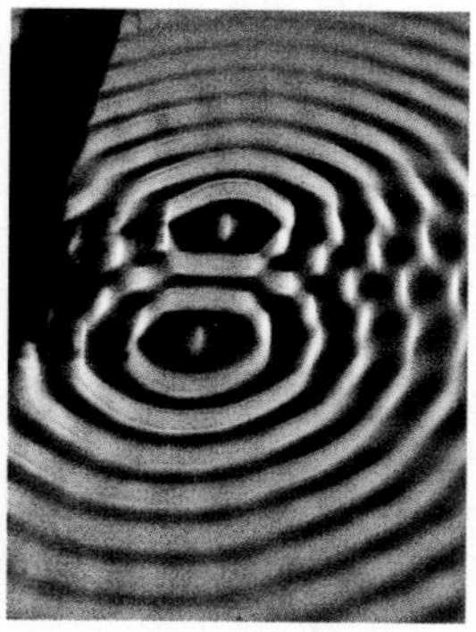

This ripple-tank surface shows two-source interference bands.

It would be a nuisance to have strips of the country where there was very poor TV or radio reception because of destructive interference. Therefore, adjacent transmitters ensure that the waves cannot interfere by using either different frequencies or different polarisations.

Interference and the nature of light

Newton suggested that light was made up of tiny, solid particles which he called corpuscles. His theory was an educated guess, and one which he didn't defend strongly. The case for the wave nature of light was first put convincingly by Thomas Young (1773–1829). He demonstrated that light could show an interference pattern by putting hairs or silk threads in front of an illuminated slit. Supporters of the corpuscle theory could not explain this interference pattern. The Young's slits experiment is still used to demonstrate the wave nature of light. The experiment also allows you to calculate the wavelength of the light.

We now know that neither the particle model nor the wave model is completely correct. Both are models. Models help us to understand something which is not directly observable by comparing it with things we *can* see. Our most recent model of light is that it consists of **photons**. Photons can be thought of as little packets of electromagnetic waves, each lasting about a nanosecond. It is normally very difficult to make white light show interference effects because:

- the wavelength is so small (about 500 nm on average). This means that the interface bands are too close together to be discernible;
- the range of colours in white light hides the interference effects. Destructive interference for one colour is masked by the presence of other colours.
- different photons are not necessarily in phase and have random polarisations.

To show any stable and detectable interference effect, the wave sources need to be **coherent**. They need to be:

- the same frequency;
- in a constant phase relationship;
- polarised in the same plane;
- of roughly the same amplitude.

Coherence can be achieved by selecting monochromatic light (light at a single frequency). The constant phase relationship is achieved by using *diffraction*. Diffraction is where waves spread out after passing through a narrow gap. Young effectively created two slits when he stretched a fibre in front of an illuminated slit (Fig.18, p114).

Fig. 18 Young's double slit

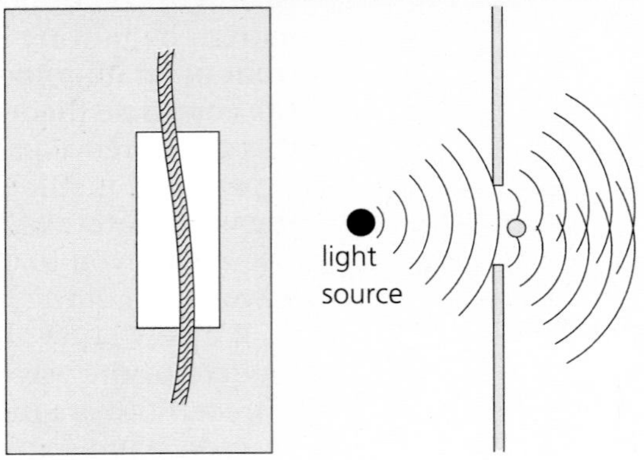
light
source

Each slit acts as a **point source of waves**: the resulting interference system is the same as that for two point sources in a ripple tank of water. You cannot see the ripples in an electromagnetic field, but you can detect the effect when the waves hit a screen. Constructive interference produces a bright area, while destructive interference produces a dark area. These observed patterns are called interference fringes. You can derive a formula to relate wavelength to the fringe spacing:

$$\frac{\text{fringe separation}}{\text{wavelength}} = \frac{\text{distance to screen}}{\text{slit separation}}$$

$$\frac{s}{\lambda} = \frac{D}{w}$$

For example, with the screen at a distance $D = 1$ m, a slit separation of 1 mm would produce two fringes per millimetre for yellow light of 500 nm wavelength.

Coherent sources can now be produced easily using **lasers**. Laser light differs from other sources in that photons are released by a process of 'stimulated emission'. The monochromatic light from the laser is effectively one long wave train, with constant phase over long time periods. Lasers are therefore ideal for showing interference effects with visible light.

Fig. 19 Diffraction and coherence

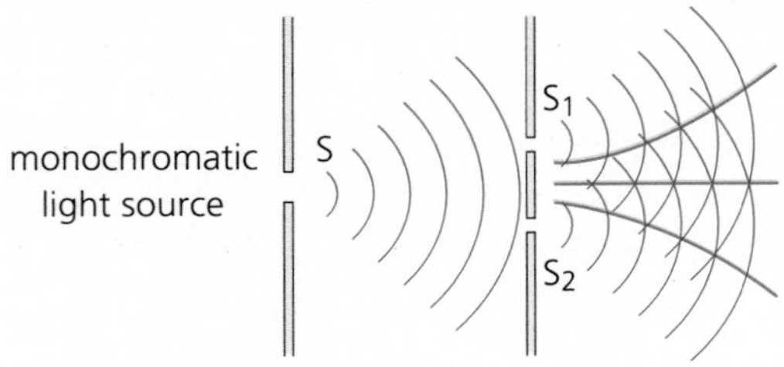
monochromatic
light source
S
S_1
S_2

Waves emerging from S_1 and S_2 are coherent, so produce observable interference.

Fig. 20 Two-source interference fringes

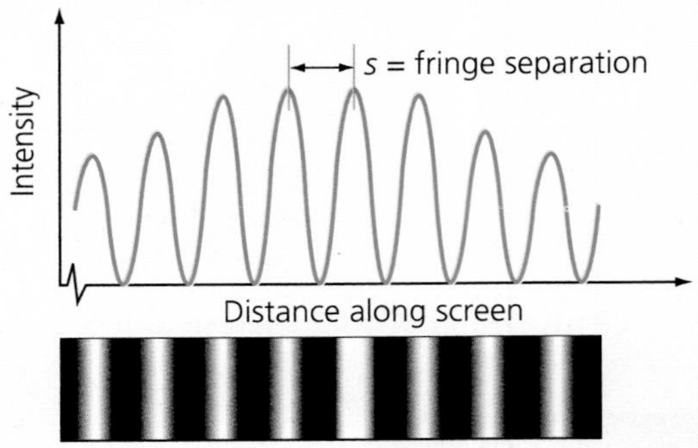
Intensity
s = fringe separation
Distance along screen

5 All electromagnetic waves show the same sort of pattern of two-source interference (Fig. 20), but the spacing of fringes varies enormously. Why?

6 Suggest two ways of increasing fringe separation for the same colour of light.

7 Two radio transmitters are 1 km apart. Both transmit a 3 MHz radio wave. The waves are coherent. If a car moves along a road parallel to the line joining the transmitters, how will the received signal change? If the road is 10 km from the transmitters, how far apart will positions of maximum reception be?

Fig. 21 Deriving the Young's slits equation

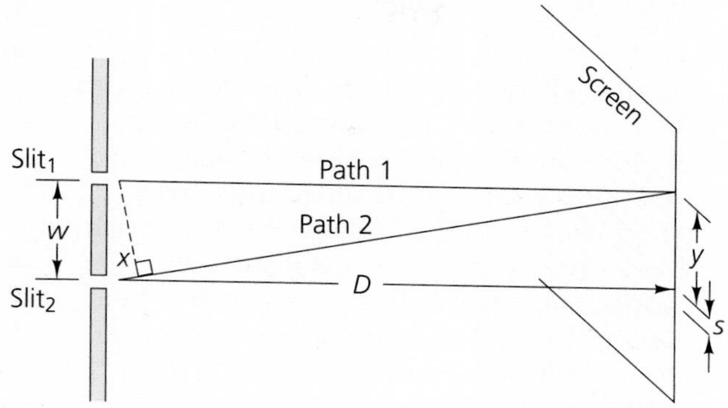

Screen
Slit1
w
Slit2
Path 1
Path 2
x
D
y
s

Paths 1 and 2 differ by a few wavelengths of light in a total distance of around a metre. We can say to within less than a thousandth of a percent error that: path 1 = path 2 = D.

The tiny difference between path 1 and path 2 (shown as x on the diagram) must be a whole number of wavelengths for constructive interference to occur.

There are two similar triangles on the diagram. For similar triangles, the ratio of sides is the same, so:

$$\frac{x}{w} = \frac{y}{\text{path 2}} \approx \frac{y}{D}$$

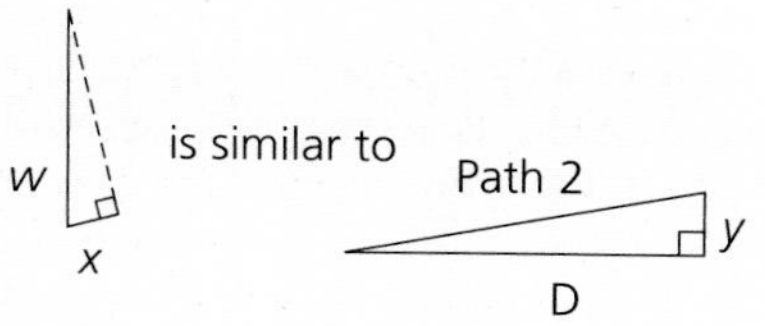

w
x
is similar to
Path 2
y
D

If we now move up to the next bright fringe, x increases by one wavelength, λ, and y increases by the fringe separation, s.

Therefore $\frac{x}{w} = \frac{y}{D}$ gives: $\frac{(x+\lambda)}{w} = \frac{(y+s)}{D}$

and so: $\frac{\lambda}{w} = \frac{s}{D}$ or $\frac{s}{\lambda} = \frac{D}{w}$

The equation is valid whenever there is two-source interference with $D >> \lambda$.

Key ideas

- Superposition is the vector addition of waves. Coherent waves (same frequency, same polarisation, constant phase relationship) can interfere. Two sources with the same phase will interfere constructively if the path difference is a whole number of wavelengths.
- Two source interference (e.g. Young's slits experiment) fits the equation:

$$\frac{\text{fringe separation } (s)}{\text{wavelength } (\lambda)} = \frac{\text{distance to screen } (D)}{\text{slit separation } (w)}$$

Interference and standing waves

Portable televisions often work well in one part of a room, but the signal is much weaker in other places. The signal can change when people walk around the room or cars drive past. These problems occur because of interference between the incoming wave and its reflections, from people or from walls. The problem is much greater when there is a metal surface nearby, such as a car body, which acts as a good reflector. When the incoming wave and the reflected wave travel along the same line, the interference can set up a standing wave (Fig. 22).

Antinodes are positions of constructive interference, separated by a distance $\lambda / 2$. **Nodes** are positions of destructive interference, also separated by $\lambda / 2$. At a reflecting surface, there must always be a displacement node.

For television transmissions, the wavelength is of the order of 0.6 m. Moving a portable television set 15 cm could therefore take it from an antinode to a node. The signal intensity is very weak at a node, so the picture will degenerate.

More distant reflectors can give rise to another television problem: *ghosting*. Ghosting shows on the screen as a faint second image, slightly offset from the first. It arises from the time delay between receiving the wave from the transmitter and the reflected wave. A large building 300 m away would give rise to a time delay of about 2 μs, during which time the dot has moved about a centimetre across a typical screen.

8 Explain why a mobile phone conversation sometimes fades as you walk around the house.

9 Television aerials have a reflector a short distance from their active aerial element (Fig. 23). Suggest two reasons for this.

Fig. 22 Reflections interfering to create a standing wave

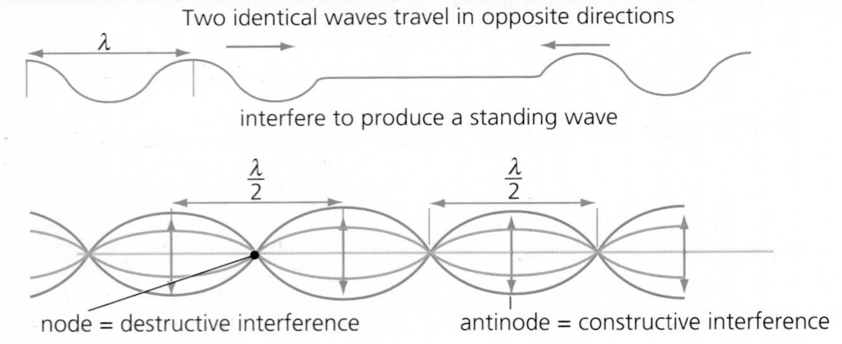
Two identical waves travel in opposite directions
λ
interfere to produce a standing wave
λ/2
λ/2
node = destructive interference
antinode = constructive interference

Fig. 23 Yagi television aerial

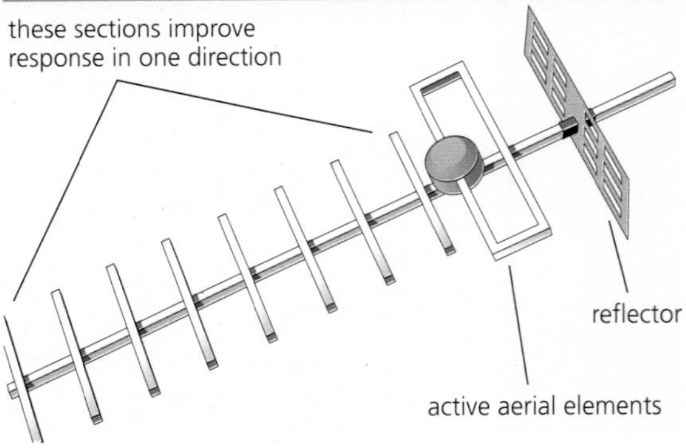
these sections improve response in one direction
reflector
active aerial elements

9.4 Diffraction

People who live in valleys often have poor reception of television and VHF radio, but good reception of long wave and medium wave radio broadcasts. This can be partly explained by the way in which radio waves bounce off the upper layers of the atmosphere. Another reason is the diffraction of waves. **Diffraction** is the name for the way in which waves spread out as they pass an obstacle. As well as spreading out, the waves vary in intensity at different positions (Fig. 24).

Fig. 24 Diffraction at an edge

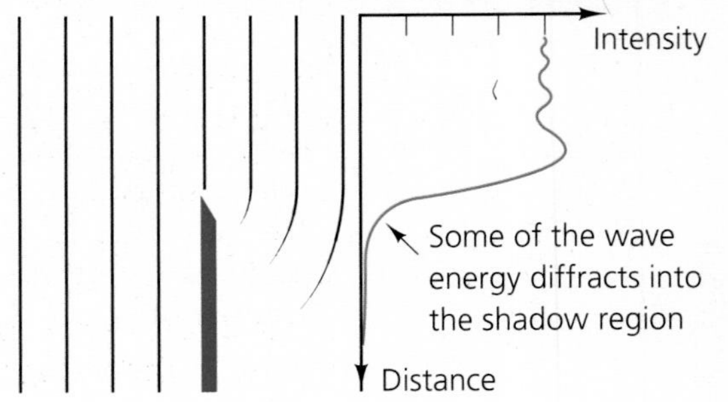
Intensity
Some of the wave energy diffracts into the shadow region
Distance

Waves of different frequencies diffract by different amounts. High-frequency waves, such as visible light, undergo very little diffraction. In everyday life we never notice diffraction of light around corners.

Fig. 25 Different frequencies diffracting

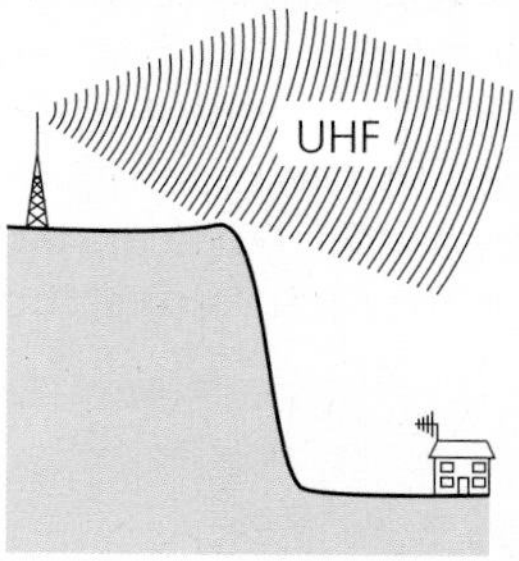
UHF

High frequencies diffract very little so reception of TV is poor in valleys...

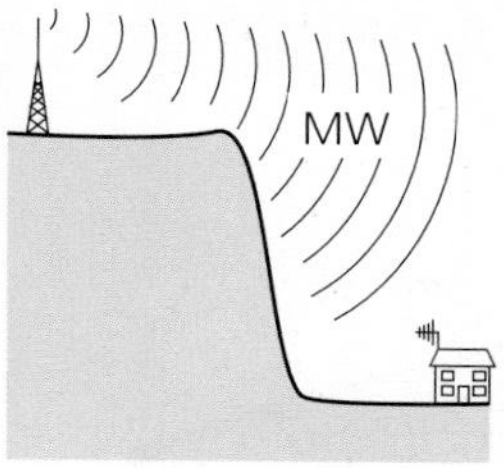
MW

... but longer wavelength radio waves are easier to receive.

Diffraction can be understood by considering the way in which waves spread. When a vibration sets up a wave, it disturbs the medium. Each point on a wavefront is itself a place where the medium is no longer in equilibrium. Therefore, each point can act as a source of disturbance, or **secondary wavelets**. The position of the next wavefront can be found by taking the 'envelope' of these secondary wavelets using Huygens' principle.

Huygens' construction (Fig. 26) can be used to show the position of successive wavefronts. The principle can be extended to show that waves passing through gaps tend to curve at the edges. Very narrow gaps (of width $\approx \lambda$) give almost circular wavefronts: a narrow gap acts as a point source of waves (Fig. 27).

Secondary wavelets are able to interfere with each other. When plane waves pass through a narrow gap, wavelets from the two edges of the gap will be out of phase in some directions. Destructive interference occurs in these directions, and in other positions wavelets reinforce.

Fig. 26 Huygens' construction

The envelope of the 'secondary wavelets' shows the position of the wavefront.

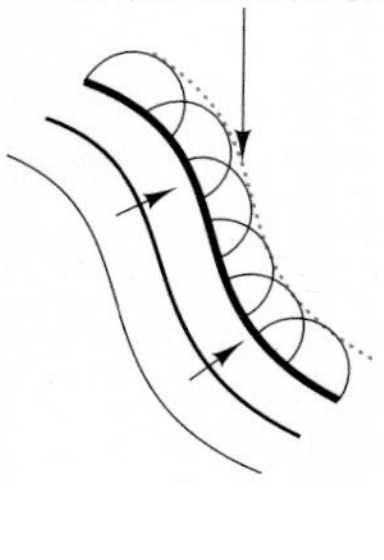

Fig. 27 Diffraction at a gap

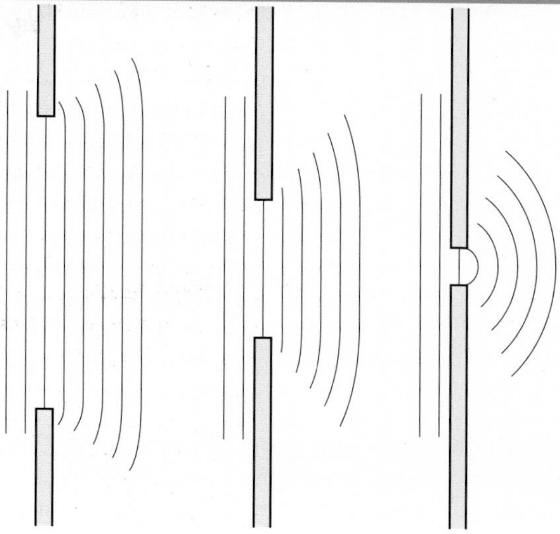

Waves at low frequencies – when obstacle size and wavelength are comparable – will diffract well around the obstacle, but short wavelengths tend to give a geometrical shadow with little diffraction. The intensity distribution curve (Fig. 28) shows that the positions of zero intensity are at angles given by:

$$\sin\phi = \frac{n\lambda}{d} \quad (n = 0, \pm1, \pm2, \pm3\ldots)$$

Fig. 28 Intensity distribution for diffraction at a gap

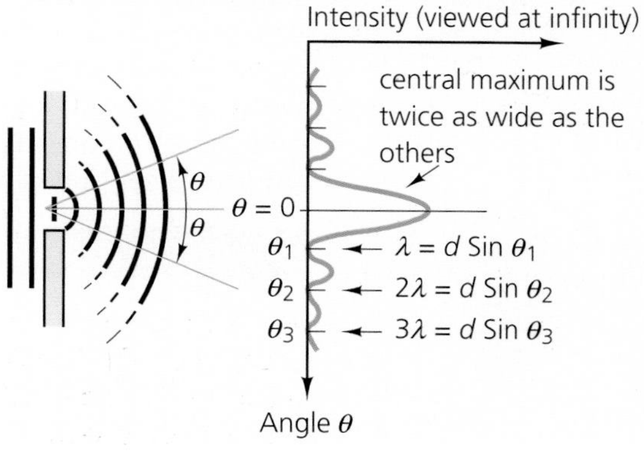
Intensity (viewed at infinity)
central maximum is twice as wide as the others
θ
θ
θ = 0
θ1
θ2
θ3
λ = d Sin θ1
2λ = d Sin θ2
3λ = d Sin θ3
Angle θ

Note that this applies only to plane wavefronts approaching the gap, with the diffraction pattern viewed from a great distance. If the gap is one wavelength wide, the first minimum occurs at $\phi = 90°$: the wave has spread fully into the region of geometrical shadow.

Diffraction gratings

Diffraction gratings give scientists an easy and accurate way to measure wavelengths of light. Different atoms and molecules emit and absorb different frequencies of light. Much of our understanding of the structure of atoms and molecules is based on measurements of frequencies of light. A *spectrometer* is an optical instrument which allows us to measure the angles at which light comes out of the diffraction grating (Fig. 29). From these angle measurements, we can calculate the wavelengths and frequencies.

Fig. 29 Spectrometer

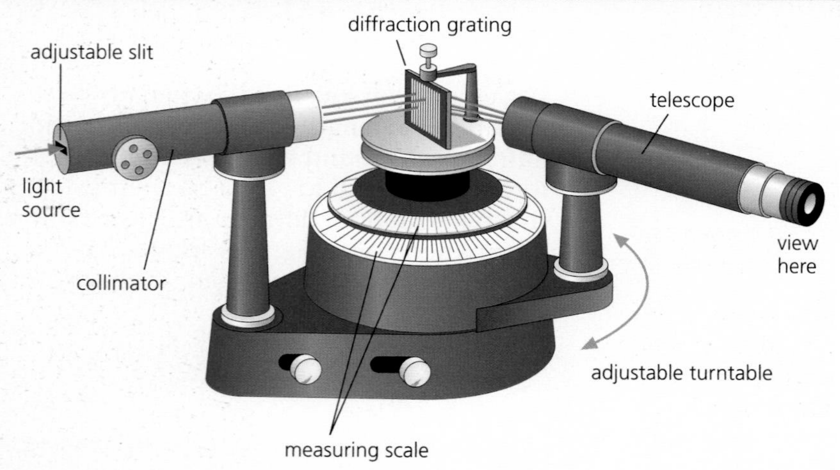
diffraction grating
adjustable slit
telescope
light source
collimator
view here
adjustable turntable
measuring scale

A grating is a set of parallel slits. If waves pass through (or reflect from) such a grating, each slit causes diffraction. The waves from each slit can then interfere to give areas of constructive and destructive interference. Mathematical analysis shows that there is complete destructive interference in most directions. Constructive interference, however, takes place in only a few directions. The different beams are called the 'orders' of diffraction (Fig. 30). The central beam is zero order, the adjacent beams on either side are first order, and subsequent beams are numbered accordingly.

Fig. 30 Orders of diffraction

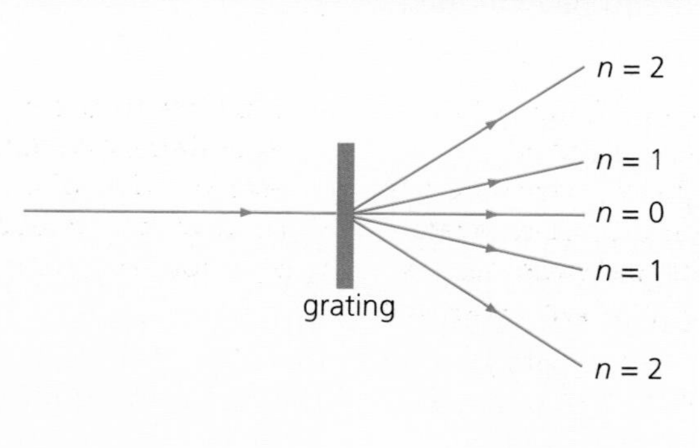
n = 2
n = 1
n = 0
n = 1
n = 2
grating

The direction of the diffracted beams is related to the spacing of the slits and the wavelength. This can be demonstrated using Huygens' construction (Fig. 31).

Fig. 31 Using Huygens' construction to illustrate the occurrence of constructive interference

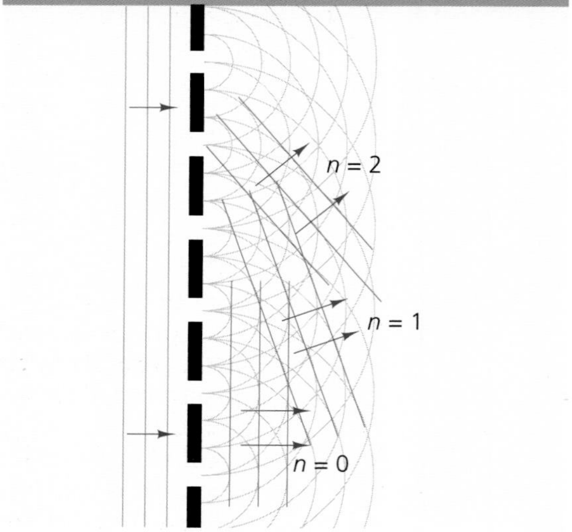
n = 2
n = 1
n = 0

The *n*th order beam is at an angle ϕ to the original wavefront direction. Along this beam, waves from adjacent slits have a path difference of $n\lambda$.

It is possible to relate $n\lambda$ to d and ϕ by using the central triangle of the figure:

$$\text{Using} \quad \sin\phi = \frac{\text{opposite}}{\text{hypotenuse}} = \frac{n\lambda}{d}$$

$$d\sin\phi = n\lambda$$

In optics work, it is usual to be given the number of lines per metre of grating. The grating spacing, d, is then found by dividing:

$$d = \frac{1}{\text{number of lines per metre}}$$

Fig. 32 Relating n, d, λ and ϕ

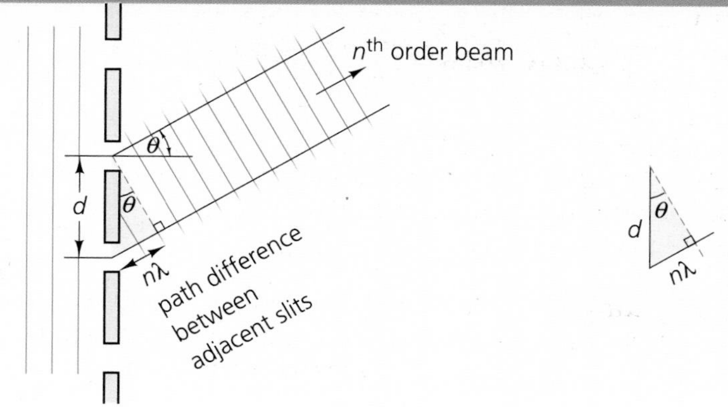
n^{th} order beam
θ
d
nλ
path difference between adjacent slits

For example, with a grating of 400 000 lines per metre, we could use these expressions to calculate the wavelength of light that gives a second order beam at 25°.

Using $n\lambda = d \sin \phi$

$$2\lambda = \frac{1}{400000\ \text{m}^{-1}} \times \sin 25°$$

$$\lambda = 5.28 \times 10^{-7}\ \text{m (528 nm)}$$

From this result, we can calculate how many diffracted beams would be visible. Sin ϕ cannot be bigger than 1, so the maximum value of n is given by $n\lambda = d$:

$$n \leq \frac{d}{\lambda} = \frac{2.5 \times 10^{-6}\ \text{m}}{5.28 \times 10^{-7}\ \text{m}} = 4.73$$

The fourth order beam will be the last possible beam. The total number of visible beams is therefore 4 + 4 + 1 = 9.

Diffraction gratings are used in spectroscopy and astronomy for accurate determination of wavelengths of light.

Beams of X-rays reflecting off planes of atoms in a crystal also behave in the same way as light at a grating: measurements of X-ray diffraction patterns are used to give information about the structure of crystalline materials.

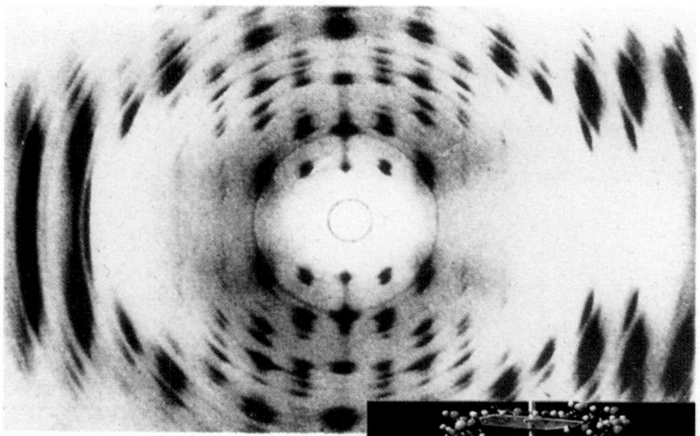

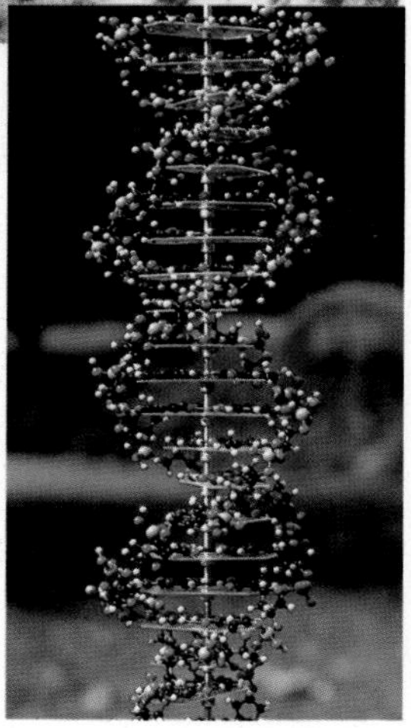

X-ray diffraction pictures gave vital information in the determination of the structure of DNA.

10 If white light passes through a diffraction grating, most of the orders of diffraction split the light into different colours. The central, zero-order beam is always white. Explain why this is so.

Key ideas

- Diffraction is the spreading of waves into the region of 'geometrical shadow'. Diffraction at a gap is greater when the gap is smaller. The diffraction produces several intensity maxima: the central maximum is twice as wide and many times more intense than the others.
- A diffraction grating consists of many slits separated by distance d: it gives rise to several orders of diffraction (n = 0, ±1, ±2, ±3...) which are at angles ϕ given by the equation $n\lambda = d \sin \phi$

9.5 Polarisation

Television and radio aerials must be fixed in the right orientation. This is because radio waves are transverse electromagnetic waves. Transverse waves can be **polarised**. If the direction of the electric field vector of the wave fails to match the aerial direction, the signal received will be weak (Fig. 33).

Fig. 33 Signal strength and wave polarisation

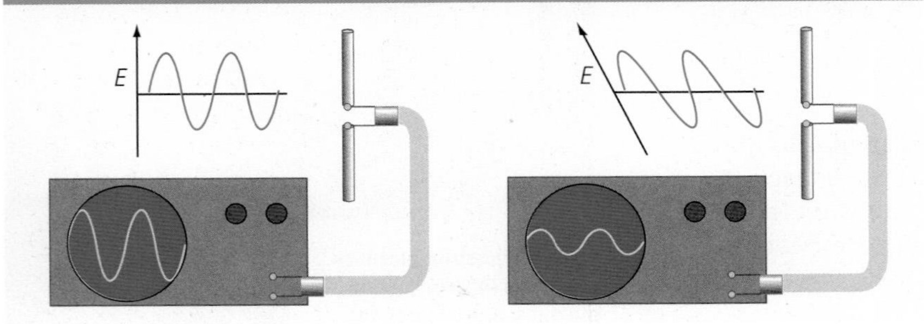

E
E

Alignment of an aerial, however, is not exactly critical. An aerial at an angle to the wave will still pick up a component of the wave's displacement vector (Fig. 34).

Fig. 34 Picking up a component of a wave

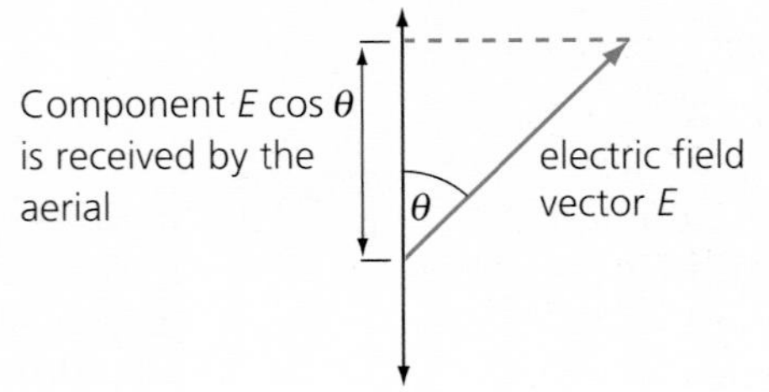

aerial direction
Component E cos θ is received by the aerial
θ
electric field vector E

Polarisation provides the most convincing evidence for the transverse nature of electromagnetic waves. The electric vector of the wave interacts most strongly with matter, because the electric field causes charges to oscillate. Normally, this results in absorption of the wave. This can be demonstrated using a microwave beam with a set of parallel metal bars. If the bars are parallel to the electric field vector, the wave makes a current flow in the bars, which absorbs the energy of the wave. Not much of the wave gets through. With the bars at right angles to the electric field vector, there is little absorption (Fig. 35).

Fig. 35 Microwave polarisation

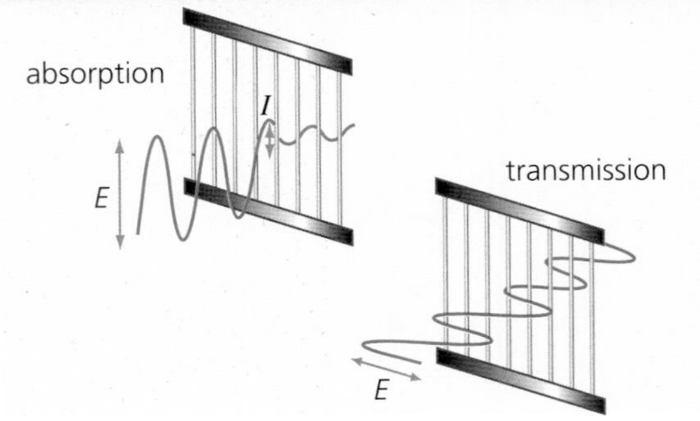

absorption
I
E
transmission
E

Polarisation and light

All electromagnetic waves can be polarised. Ordinary visible light is not polarised because photons are emitted with random orientations. Polarisation can take place when light is reflected from a transparent material. The 'glare' from reflections on glass and water is therefore partly plane polarised and can be greatly reduced by using a polarising filter. 'Polaroid' is the trade name for a filter material consisting of long molecules which work in the same way as the metal bars in the microwave experiment described above.

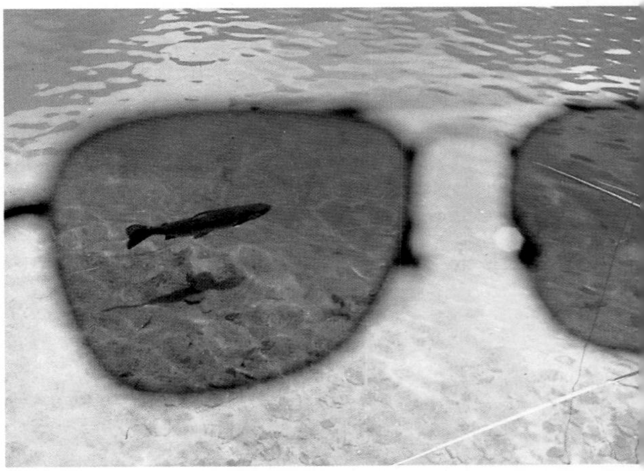

Polaroid lenses reduce the glare from the surface of water by using a polarising filter.

Polaroid sunglasses are not suitable for driving because they pick out strange patterns in windscreens. These patterns arise from stresses which are 'frozen' into the glass. Stressed areas of some materials can cause rotation of the plane of

Polarised light can be used to visualise residual stress in some types of plastic. In this photograph, an engineer is measuring the width of a stress pattern in a thin polymer film.

polarisation. This effect is used by engineers to find concentrations of stress in proposed designs for structures.

Materials which affect the plane of polarisation of light are called 'optically active'. Some sugar molecules, for example, cause rotation of the plane of polarisation. Some materials will rotate the plane of polarisation in the presence of an electric field. This is technologically important: the effect is the basis of 'liquid crystal' displays.

Key ideas

- Transverse waves can be polarised: the direction of the displacement vector is relevant. For electromagnetic waves, the electric field vector is chosen as the direction of the plane of polarisation.

10 Multimedia

My homework assignment was about space research. I got pictures of Jupiter and Saturn off the Internet, straight from NASA's picture library! My e-mail friend in Iceland helped me by searching through data on interplanetary probes.

The Internet is a worldwide computer network. It gives people access to the biggest library of information in the world. Using computers at home, work or college, anyone can get text, music and pictures. The Internet started life as a secure defence system for the US government in the early 1970s, but has since become an open access system. In 1994, there were 34 million people using the Internet and this number was growing at a rate of 20% per month. In the US, the government plans an 'information superhighway', with every home being linked to the Internet using optical fibres.

The marriage of computer and communications technologies is set to change many people's lives. Information is increasingly being transported for entertainment, business or academic uses. Every year, the memory size and processing speed of computers increases. By understanding the physics behind optical fibres, we can see how the wealth of information on the Internet will one day be available to computer users anywhere in the world.

Telesurgery has been a real lifesaver. Expert medical advice was once available only in the big cities. Now we can communicate with the best surgeons and physicians in large hospitals through a videophone link. I have done many unfamiliar operations with the help of a 'tele-mentor'.

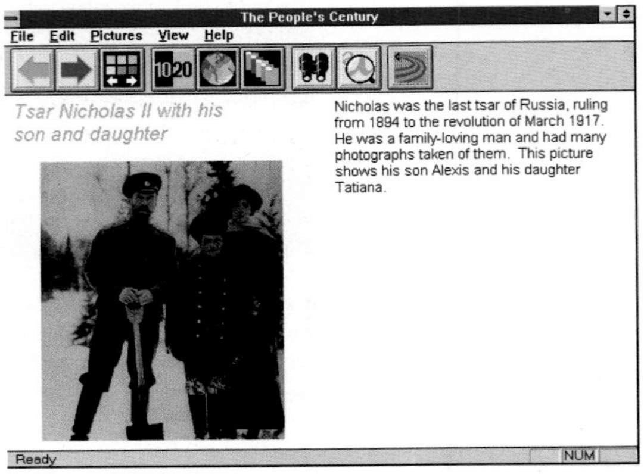

The People's Century
File Edit Pictures View Help
1020
Tsar Nicholas II with his son and daughter
Nicholas was the last tsar of Russia, ruling from 1894 to the revolution of March 1917. He was a family-loving man and had many photographs taken of them. This picture shows his son Alexis and his daughter Tatiana.
Ready
NUM

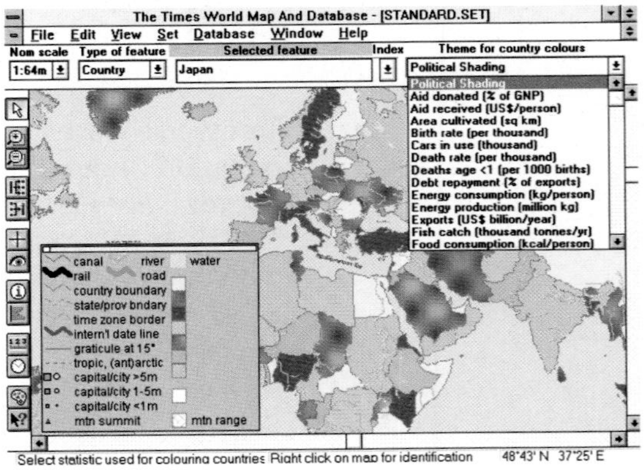

The Times World Map And Database - [STANDARD.SET]
File Edit View Set Database Window Help
Nom scale
Type of feature
Selected feature
Index
Theme for country colours
1:64m
Country
Japan
Political Shading
Political Shading
Aid donated (% of GNP)
Aid received (US$/person)
Area cultivated (sq km)
Birth rate (per thousand)
Cars in use (thousand)
Death rate (per thousand)
Deaths age <1 (per 1000 births)
Debt repayment (% of exports)
Energy consumption (kg/person)
Energy production (million kg)
Exports (US$ billion/year)
Fish catch (thousand tonnes/yr)
Food consumption (kcal/person)
canal
river
water
rail
road
country boundary
state/prov bndary
time zone border
intern'l date line
graticule at 15°
tropic, (ant)arctic
capital/city >5m
capital/city 1-5m
capital/city <1m
mtn summit
mtn range
Select statistic used for colouring countries Right click on map for identification
48°43' N 37°25' E

10.1 Learning objectives

After working through this chapter, you should be able to:

- **explain** how information is converted between digital and analogue forms;
- **describe** how rays of light are reflected and refracted;
- **state** Snell's law of refraction and define refractive index;
- **explain** total internal reflection;
- **relate** critical angle to refractive index;
- **explain** how optical fibres work.

10.2 Digital and analogue

Analogue systems

Humans live in an **analogue** world. We have brains which interpret signals in the outside world in terms of smooth changes. Our eyes respond to many light levels – not just bright or dark. Our ears respond to many different sound pressure levels – not just loud or silent. Human beings are 'analogue systems'. Analogue systems have an infinite number of possible values: they vary continuously. Most computers use very simple electronic components which respond to the world in 'steps'. For information to be stored and used on computers, we need to be able to swap information from our smoothly changing world into the simple steps that computers can process.

Fig. 1 Digital and analogue devices

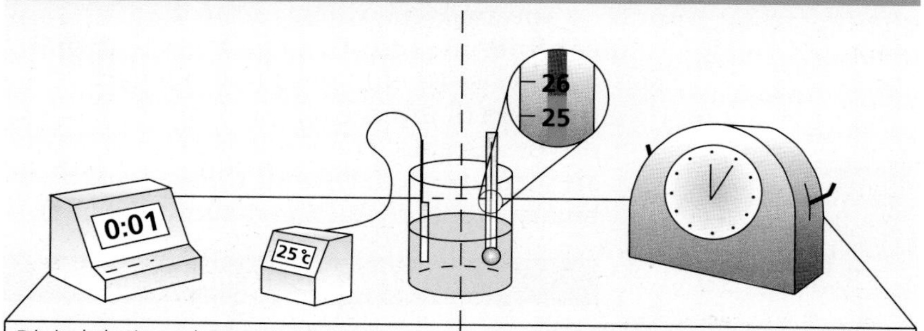
26
25
0:01
25°C

Digital devices change in discrete steps between a finite number of states. | Analogue devices move smoothly between an infinite number of states.

Digital systems

Computers work on a **digital** basis. Because we have ten fingers (digits), our normal number system is base ten, or denary. Counting in whole numbers is a digital system. A digital system uses only a few separate levels.

The current generation of computers uses a two digit system – 0 and 1. Electronic switches can represent these digits by being either off (0) or on (1). The number system which uses only 0 and 1 is called **binary** (Table 1). Binary digits are commonly called **bits**.

Table 1 Denary and binary numbers

Denary number (base 10)	Binary (base 2)
0	0
1	1
2	10
3	11
4	100
5	101

1 Write down the binary conversion for the denary numbers 6, 7 and 8. What is the binary number 100101 in base ten?

Binary numbers can easily be coded to represent letters of the alphabet. The standard system for coding letters of the alphabet is ASCII (American Standard Code for Information Interchange) (Table 2).

Table 2 ASCII letter codes

Letter	Denary number	Binary number
A	65	01000001
B	66	01000010
C	67	01000011

Coding the letters of the alphabet is relatively easy, because the alphabet is already a kind of digital system. Other quantities such as amplitudes of musical sounds or light intensity levels can be represented using more complex coding of binary numbers.

Why digital?

Digital storage and transmission of information now offers such superior quality that it is used almost everywhere, from domestic CD players to the national telephone network. There are three main reasons why.

Digital computers can have a stable memory system in which patterns of binary numbers are stored by digital electronic circuits. Information can be stored permanently if there is a physical on/off change in the storing medium. For example, computer disks use on/off magnetisation of small areas of a magnetic film. CDs use a series of pits in a long spiral track.

It is more reliable to transfer information in digital form (Fig. 2, p124). Resistance of wires and the presence of electrical noise are factors which make analogue electrical signals very difficult to transmit, either within a system or between systems.

Although digital signals also pick up noise and suffer a decrease of amplitude, simple electronic circuits can be used to enhance the signal and make them more readily interpreted (Fig. 3).

With a digital system, you can also make checks for transmission errors. One of the simplest is the **parity check** (Fig. 4). With every group of seven digits (0 or 1), you could send an eighth to clarify whether the transmitter has sent either an odd or even number of 1s. If the receiver does not pick up this odd or even number of 1s, it knows that something is wrong.

Fig. 2 Signal transmission

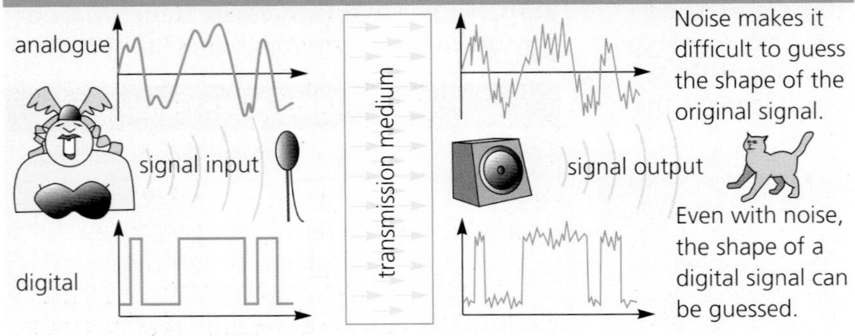

analogue
signal input
digital
transmission medium
Noise makes it difficult to guess the shape of the original signal.
signal output
Even with noise, the shape of a digital signal can be guessed.

Fig. 3 Cleaning signals

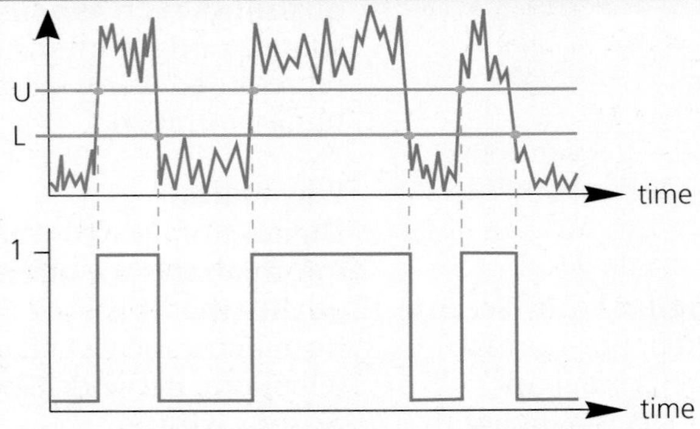

U
L
time
1
time

Simple electronic circuits remove unwanted noise. This relies on switches that trigger when the signal level goes above the upper limit (U) or below the lower limit (L).

Fig. 4 Parity checking

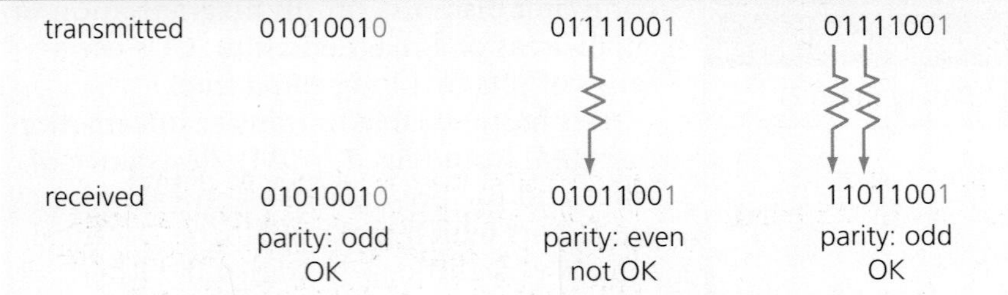

transmitted
01010010
01111001
01111001
received
01010010
parity: odd
OK
01011001
parity: even
not OK
11011001
parity: odd
OK

Conversion from analogue to digital

Our most powerful ways of communicating rely on light and sound. Speech, music, photographs, drawings and video pictures are all types of analogue information. Electronic sensors can convert properties such as light intensity and sound pressure into a varying analogue voltage. For example, scanners convert colour pictures into digital data files by changing light levels into analogue voltages, then changing the analogue voltage into a digital number. The scanner is an **analogue-to-digital converter**. The value of the analogue voltage is measured, or sampled, repeatedly. The measured value is then converted into a binary number, which can be stored and used to re-create the original picture.

The analogue voltage scale is **continuous**. To convert voltages to digital exactly, you would need to use binary numbers of infinite length. This is clearly not practicable. The number of levels that are actually used depends on the length of binary number which you allow (Table 3).

Table 3 Sample levels

four bits give	$2^4 = 16$ levels
eight bits give	$2^8 = 256$ levels
sixteen bits give	$2^{16} = 65\,536$ levels

Fig. 5 Sample quality

The sample rate and number of sampling levels affect how well a digital signal mimics the original analogue signal

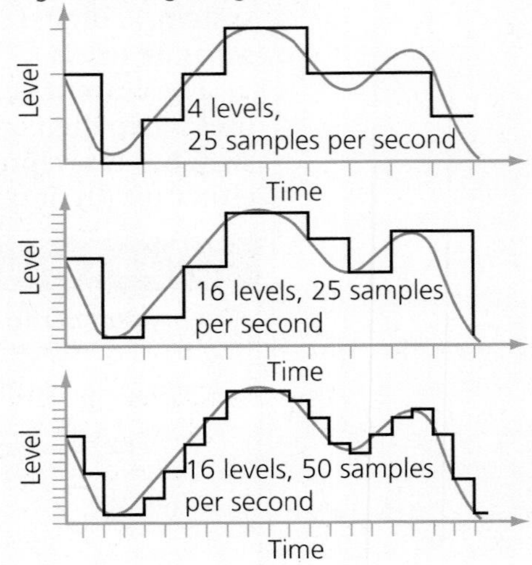

Level
4 levels,
25 samples per second
Time
Level
16 levels, 25 samples
per second
Time
Level
16 levels, 50 samples
per second
Time

The more levels you have, the closer you get to the original analogue signal. However, you have to find a compromise because it takes longer to make, store, process and transmit samples with more bits. The quality also depends on how often you sample the waveform (Fig. 5).

The **sampling frequency** needs to be at least twice the highest frequency in the signal. Otherwise you get '**aliasing**', the generation of unwanted waveforms (Fig. 6).

Fig. 6 Aliasing

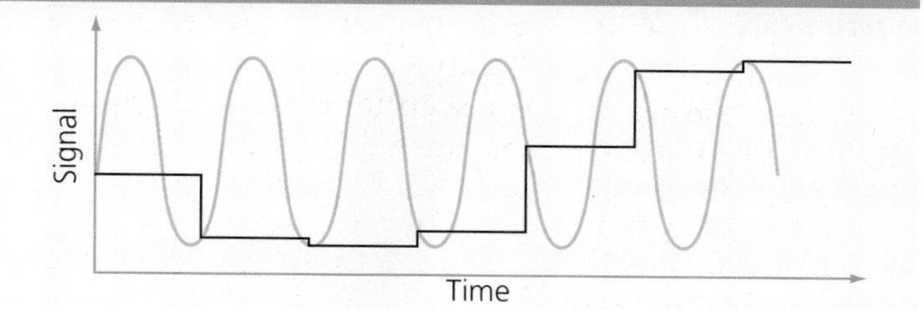

Signal
Time

Audio CDs use 16 bit converters and a sampling frequency of about 42 kHz. People can hear frequencies up to 20 kHz, so the sampling frequency is more than double the maximum signal frequency.

A standard CD can hold a maximum of 74 minutes of music. How many bits of information does it need to store?

The converter produces a 16 bit number 42 000 times per second; data is generated at a rate of $16 \times 42\,000$ (i.e. 672 000) bits s^{-1}. A 74 minute CD therefore stores a minimum of $74 \times 60 \times 672\,000$ (i.e. 3.0×10^9) bits.

This large storage capacity is exploited for CD ROMs and for CD video.

2 European telephone networks digitise conversations at 64 000 bits per second. The voice signals contain frequencies up to 4 kHz. What sampling frequency would you recommend, and how many bits would be used for each sample?

Digital to analogue conversion

Text and picture files can be transmitted as digital pulses over a telephone line. The information then needs to be converted from digital into analogue form (Fig. 7).

Fig. 7 Conversion circuit

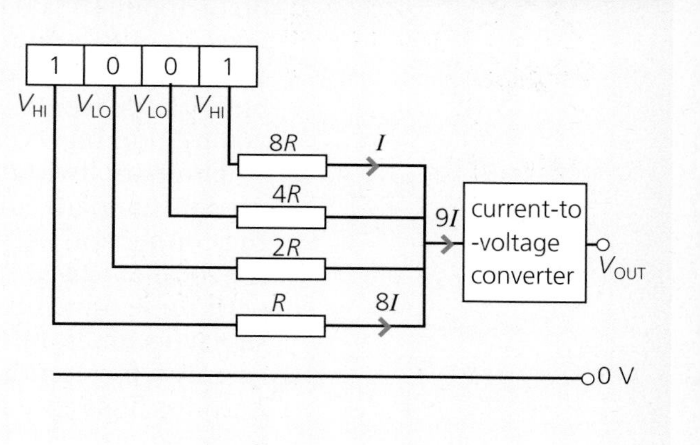

1
0
0
1
V_{HI}
V_{LO}
V_{LO}
V_{HI}
8R
I
4R
2R
R
8I
9I
current-to-voltage converter
V_{OUT}
0 V

The step edges left by the sampling waveform can be filtered out, leaving a good approximation to the original waveform.

Fig. 8 Analogue signal – digital transmission

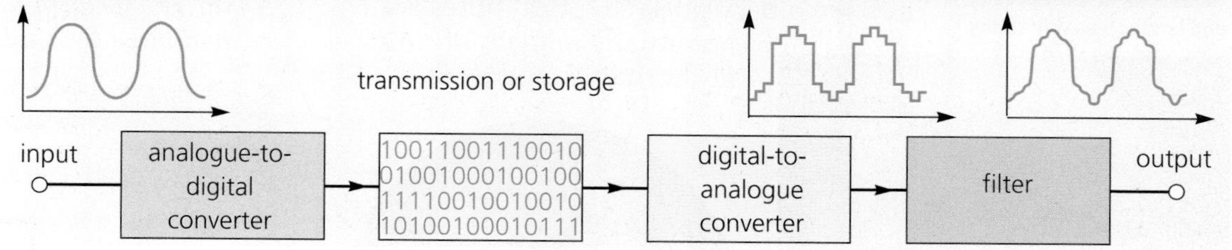

transmission or storage
input
analogue-to-digital converter
10011001110010
01001000100100
11110010010010
10100100010111
digital-to-analogue converter
filter
output

Key ideas

- Analogue systems show continuous variation. Digital systems have only a fixed number of levels.
- Conversion from analogue to digital requires sampling at a frequency at least double the signal frequency. Samples are converted to binary code for storage, processing or transmission.

10.3 Transmitting signals using light

I work on commercial projects for a large telecommunications company. I think the days of the video shop are numbered. People don't always want to collect a video from the shop, then take it back the next day. That's why we're working on ways to transmit video pictures over high speed telephone networks. At our end, there are a few big problems to crack – like storing thousands of videos on a central computer data bank and sending them out on demand. But the potential turnover is enormous.

The demands for rapid, on-line information transfer are increasing. A page of text is made up of about 10 000 bits of information, but takes us only a minute or so to read. Direct conversion from a television camera to binary code would generate over 200 million bits every second!

Ordinary 'twisted pairs' of copper wires, used in standard computer networks and in the connection between telephones and the local exchanges, are not able to cope with these transmission demands. The signal becomes unintelligible over distances of only a few hundred metres. To meet the need for high-speed transmission of information, network designers have developed systems which carry signals by light. Light waves have a frequency of around 10^{14} Hz, far higher than any electronic circuit could use. The capability of **optical fibres** is limited only by the speed at which you can transmit and receive binary pulses. Optical fibres are potentially *millions* of times faster than copper wire.

The fibre-optic cable (left) has a greater signal-carrying capacity than coaxial cable (right). Fibre-optic cable weighs thousands of times less and is much easier to lay.

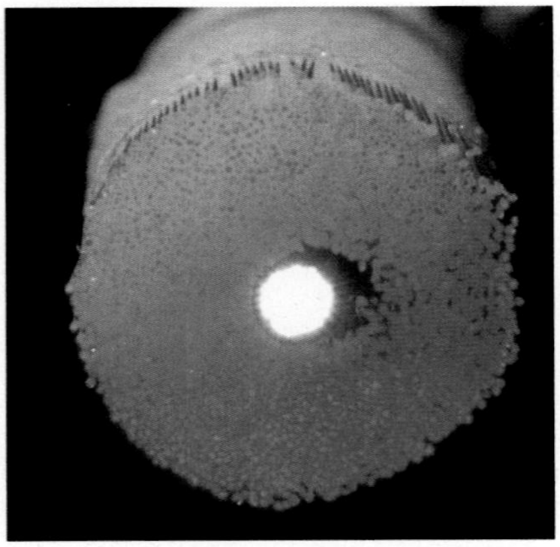

Optical fibres

The laws of reflection and refraction govern the path of light down an optical fibre. We can illustrate this using ray diagrams.

A ray diagram shows the paths taken by light wavefronts. Each ray is drawn perpendicular to the wavefront it represents. Parallel light rays indicate a set of plane wavefronts. Diverging rays can be traced back to a point source of light.

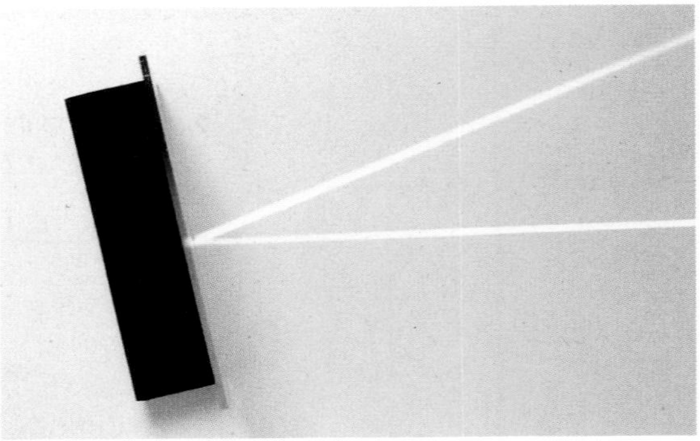

Reflection at a plane mirror

Optical fibres work by repeatedly reflecting the light inside the fibre. The inner walls behave as perfect mirrors. The secondary wavelet theory (see Chapter 9), shows that light reflects from a plane mirror at the same angle it approaches.

In geometrical optics, angles are usually measured from the **normal**, a line at right angles to the surface (Fig. 9). For any reflecting surface:

The angle of incidence and the angle of reflection – measured from the normal – are equal. The incident ray, reflected ray and normal lie in the same plane.

Fig. 9 Curved surfaces

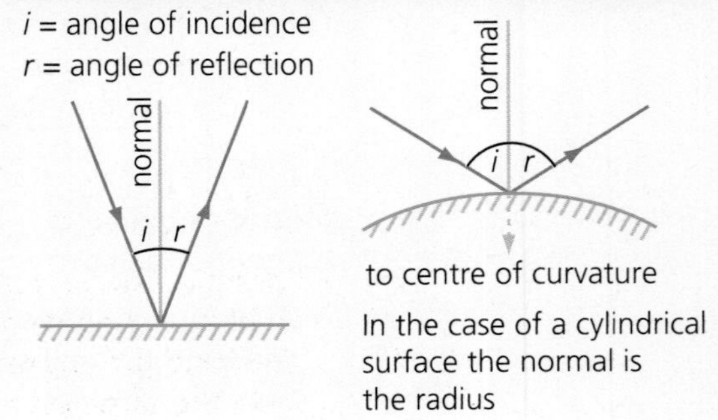

i = angle of incidence
r = angle of reflection
normal
i
r
normal
i
r
to centre of curvature
In the case of a cylindrical surface the normal is the radius

In the case of the plane mirror, we can use the rule with several rays to construct a theoretical ray diagram (Fig. 10). From that, we can predict the type and position of the image.

Fig. 10 Producing a virtual image

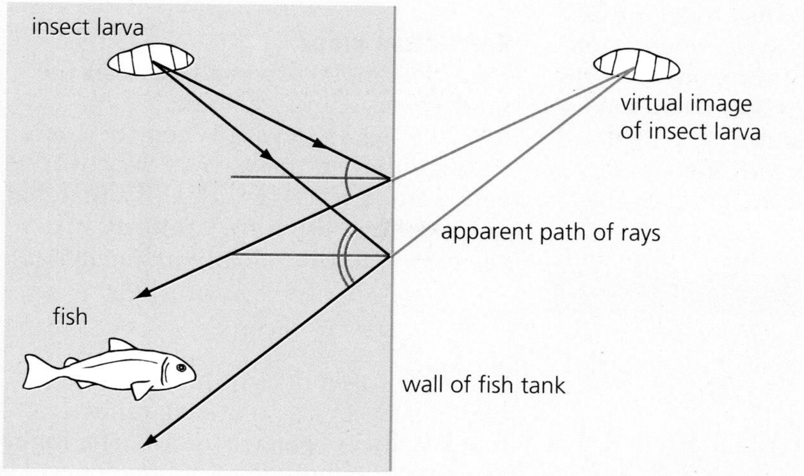

insect larva
virtual image of insect larva
apparent path of rays
fish
wall of fish tank

The reflected rays diverge. The brain interprets the image as a set of rays diverging from a point behind the mirror surface. Images that can be projected onto a screen (e.g. using a slide projector) are called **real images**. No light rays are actually present at the position of the image in a mirror (Fig. 10), so it is called a **virtual image**.

The position of an object's virtual image can be found using the 'no parallax' technique (Fig. 11).

Theoretical ray diagrams successfully predict that the image is erect (upright), laterally inverted (left to right) and the same distance from the reflecting surface as the object.

Fig. 11 Using 'no parallax'

If the pin is correctly positioned at the image point, the image of pin A and the top of pin B will stay together even if you change your viewing position

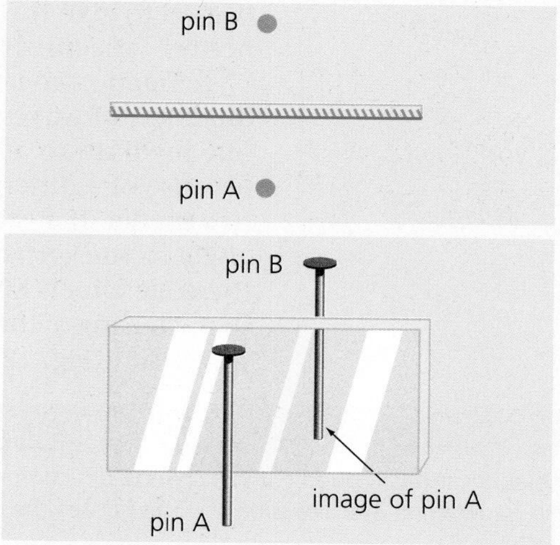

pin B
pin A
pin B
image of pin A
pin A

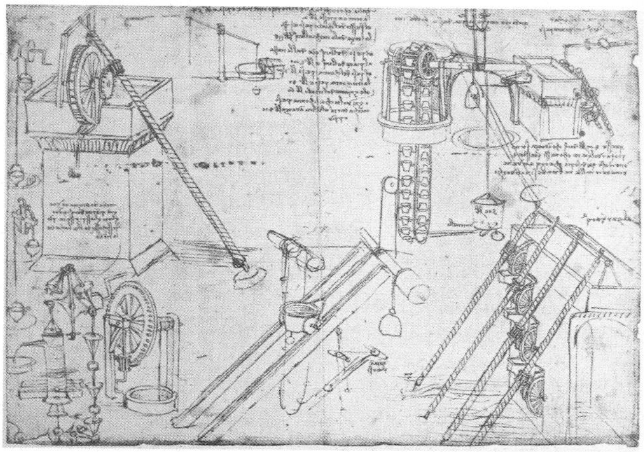

Leonardo da Vinci kept notes on his work secret by using mirror writing.

3 The image in a plane mirror appears laterally inverted (i.e. left and right are swapped). Why isn't the image inverted (i.e. top and bottom swapped)?

Key ideas

- For reflection at a plane mirror, the angle of incidence is equal to the angle of reflection. The incident ray, reflected ray and normal lie in the same plane.
- The image and object are the same distance from the reflecting surface. The image is virtual, erect and laterally inverted.

Refraction at a plane surface

Most optical fibres consist of two layers of glass: an inner core and an outer cladding. The difference between the two types of glass gives rise to **refraction**. This property is used to give the inside of the fibre its perfect reflecting properties.

Refraction means the change of direction of waves when they move from one medium to another. Refraction occurs because of a difference of wave speed in the two media. If a wavefront approaches at an angle to the surface separating the media, the edge which hits first will slow down first, causing a change of direction of the wavefront (Fig. 12).

Fig. 12 A change of speed

When a car hits a puddle it will change direction. This is because wheel A hits the puddle first and slows down. This causes the car to swerve into the puddle

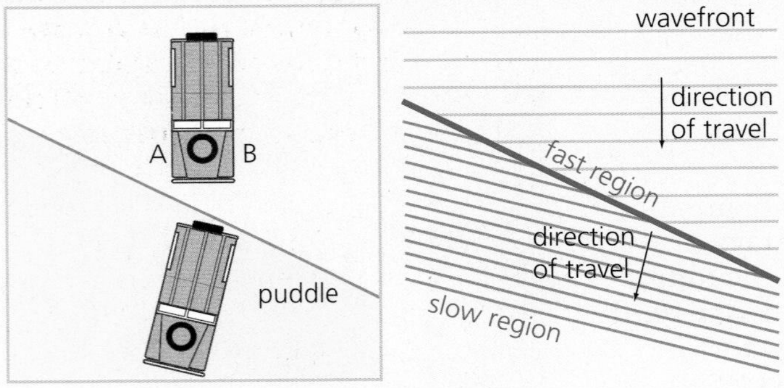
A
B
puddle
wavefront
direction of travel
fast region
direction of travel
slow region

A zig-zag effect takes place as the waves first slow down and then speed up as they re-enter the first medium (see below).

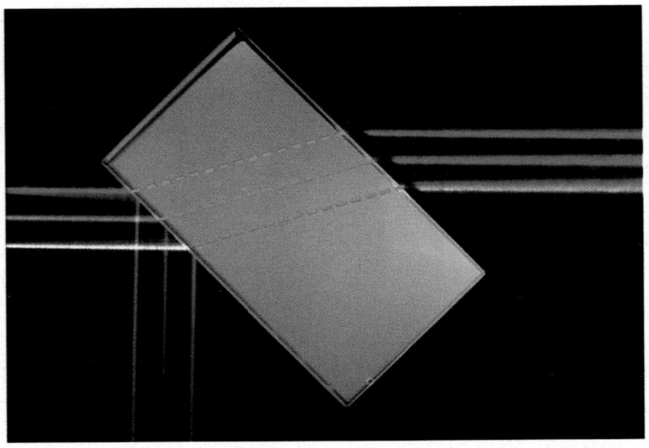

You can work out the angle of refraction by thinking about how the change of speed affects wavefronts. A ray refracts towards the normal when it slows down and away from the normal when it speeds up. The degree of deflection of the light ray depends on the change of speed.

4 Sketch a ray diagram to show why objects under water appear nearer the surface than the true depth of the water.

Refractive index

Electromagnetic waves all travel at the same speed, c, in a vacuum. (c = 299 792 458 m s^{-1}) When they pass through matter, the waves slow down. We define the **refractive index** of a material, n, as the ratio of the wave's velocity in a vacuum, c, to the velocity in a material, v:

$$n = \frac{c}{v}$$

Since the speed of light in a vacuum is higher than in any material, refractive index is always greater than 1. The higher its value, the more the rays are deflected. Air has a refractive index of around 1.0003 (we usually take it as 1).

Table 4 Refractive indexes

diamond	2.42
glass	1.5 to 2.0
perspex	1.50
water	1.33
sea water	1.34
ice	1.31

In general, denser substances have a higher refractive index. Materials with a high refractive index are often referred to as 'optically dense'.

For some materials, the refractive index varies with wavelength. The values quoted in Table 4 are for a standard colour of light: the 589 nm bright orange light which you get from sodium street lamps. For almost all materials, refractive index increases with frequency, so blue light is refracted more than red light. For flint glass, for example, the typical refractive indexes are: red light = 1.640, yellow = 1.646, blue = 1.660. This variation of refractive index is the reason that white light beams are split up into different colours by prisms. The separation of different colours is called **chromatic dispersion**.

Dispersion in a prism

It is important to avoid chromatic dispersion in optical fibres, because a range of wavelengths transmitted as a sharp pulse would spread out as it travelled along the fibre (Fig. 13).

It is difficult to make glass which has no chromatic dispersion. Instead, light with a very narrow wavelength band is used. Lasers make ideal light sources for optical fibres because they are monochromatic – the light is just one colour. Other sources include light-emitting diodes. These are much cheaper but they do transmit light over a wider band of wavelengths. Chromatic dispersion also depends on wavelength; for glass, there is very little chromatic dispersion at wavelengths in the infrared at around 1300 nm. Most telecommunications systems use infrared transmitters.

Fig. 13 Pulse spread

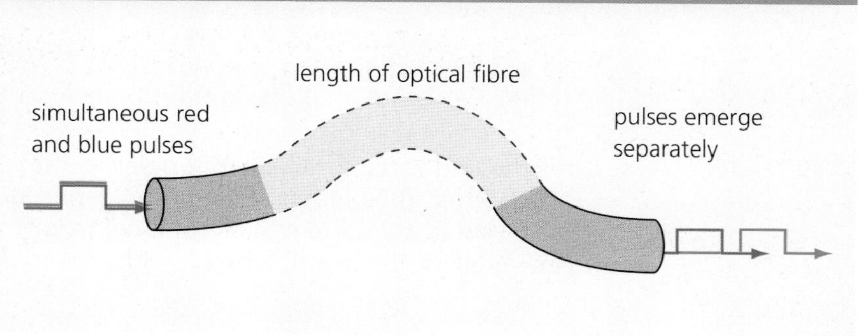
length of optical fibre
simultaneous red and blue pulses
pulses emerge separately

5 **A semiconductor light transmitter has a wavelength range from 750 nm to 790 nm. At these wavelengths, the glass of an optical fibre has refractive index 1.6404 and 1.6400 respectively. The light transmitter is switched on for 100 ns. How long would it take for light at the extremes of the wavelength range to travel 30 km along the optical fibre? What is the time difference (in nanoseconds) between the arrival of the two colours? (Take $c = 3 \times 10^8$ m s^{-1}).**

Most optical fibres are made up of two layers of glass of different refractive index. The signal is transmitted along the inner layer which has a higher refractive index. The boundary between the two layers is important. To work out what happens at such a boundary, it is easier to think in terms of a flat surface between two media.

It is the relative speed in the two media which determines the amount of refraction. We can define the relative refractive index to be:

$${}_1n_2 = \frac{c_1}{c_2}$$

for a ray travelling from medium 1 into medium 2.

Suppose we know that the refractive indexes (measured in air) for the two sorts of glass in an optical fibre are 1.50 and 1.60. How could we find the relative refractive index? Both are related to the speed of waves in a vacuum, c. We need to re-introduce this to the equation:

$$\begin{aligned} {}_1n_2 &= \frac{c_1}{c_2} \\ &= \frac{c}{c_2} \times \frac{c_1}{c} \\ &= n_2 \times \frac{1}{n_1} \end{aligned}$$

$$\text{or, } {}_1n_2 = \frac{n_2}{n_1}$$

Relative refractive index *can* be less than 1; for the ray of light in the central core of the fibre, the glass of the cladding has a refractive index of 1.50/1.60 = 0.938. It is this low refractive index that leads to the perfect reflections inside the optical fibre. The refractive index can be linked to the angles of the rays to predict the way that rays will travel along the fibre.

Snell's law

Refractive index affects the angles of the ray at a boundary (Fig. 14, p 130). The link is surprisingly simple:

$$\text{refractive index} = \frac{\sin\ (\text{angle of incidence})}{\sin\ (\text{angle of refraction})} = \frac{\sin i}{\sin r}$$

This is called **Snell's law** (Fig. 15). Note that you cannot just cancel the sines, although $n = i/r$ is a fair approximation for very small angles.

For light travelling from one medium to another, we can restate the equation more formally as:

$$ {}_1n_2 = \frac{\sin\theta_1}{\sin\theta_2} $$

Fig. 14 Light refracting

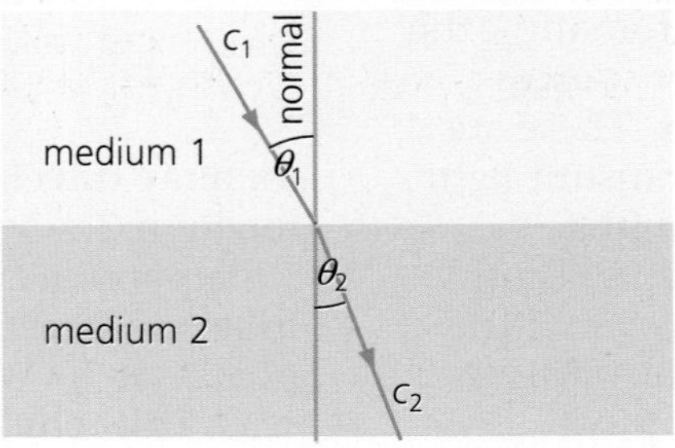

c_1
normal
medium 1
θ_1
θ_2
medium 2
c_2

Fig. 15 Proving Snell's Law

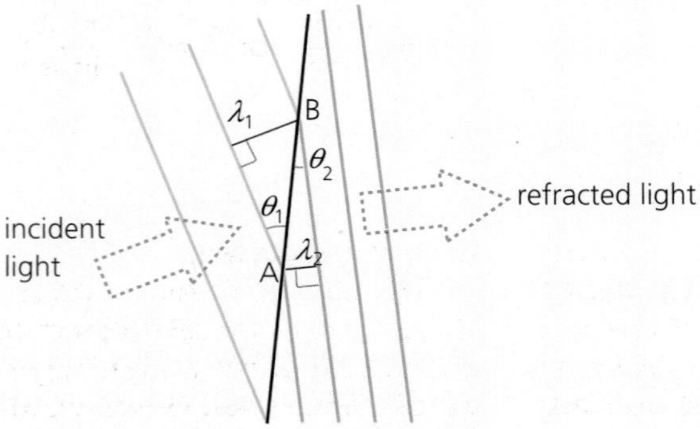

λ_1
B
θ_2
θ_1
refracted light
incident light
λ_2
A

Adjacent wavefronts are separated by one wavelength. As the wave crosses the boundary, its frequency remains constant so the change of speed causes a change of wavelength, from λ_1 to λ_2. By definition $c = f\lambda$ and ${}_1n_2 = \frac{c_1}{c_2}$ so:

$$ {}_1n_2 = \frac{f\lambda_1}{f\lambda_2} = \frac{\lambda_1}{\lambda_2} $$

Using $\lambda_1 = AB\sin\theta_1$ and $\lambda_2 = AB\sin\theta_2$: ${}_1n_2 = \frac{AB\sin\theta_1}{AB\sin\theta_2} = \frac{\sin\theta_1}{\sin\theta_2}$

It is easy to show that θ_1 is equal to i and that θ_2 is equal to r, so:

$$ {}_1n_2 = \frac{\sin i}{\sin r} $$

The angle is always smaller in the more optically dense medium.

We can use Snell's law to work out what happens to rays of light when they enter an optical fibre (Fig. 16). Suppose the rays of light (in air) from a light-emitting diode strike the end of an optical fibre at angles of incidence up to 30 degrees. If the fibre is made of glass of refractive index 1.60, what is the biggest angle of incidence at which rays strike the walls of the fibre?

Fig. 16 Light into an optical fibre

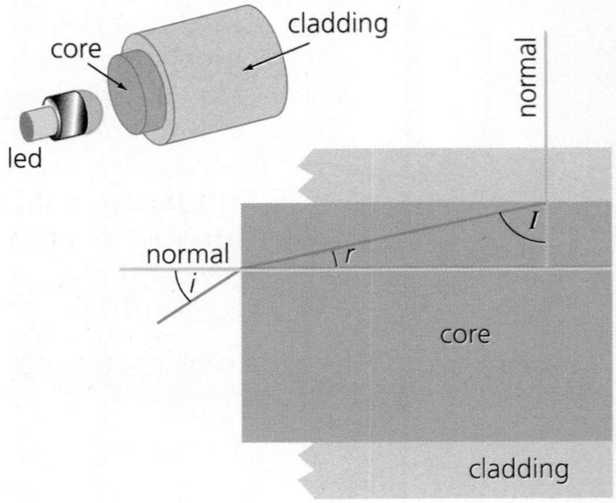

cladding
core
led
normal
I
normal
r
i
core
cladding

If the end is flat and at right angles to the fibre, then the biggest angle of incidence at the wall of the fibre will be for a ray from the edge of the beam, when $i = 30°$.

$$ n = \frac{\sin i}{\sin r} $$

Therefore, $\sin r = \frac{\sin 30°}{1.6} = \frac{0.5}{1.6}$

$$ r = 18.2° $$

From the right-angled triangle:

$$ 90° + I + r = 180° $$
$$ I = 90° - r = 71.8° $$

What will happen to the rays when they meet the interface between the layers? Suppose the outer layer of glass has a refractive index of 1.50.

$$\text{Using } {}_1n_2 = \frac{n_2}{n_1}$$

$$= \frac{1.50}{1.60} = 0.9375$$

$$\text{From } {}_1n_2 = \frac{\sin\theta_1}{\sin\theta_2}$$

$$\sin\theta_2 = \frac{\sin 71.8°}{0.9375} = 1.013$$

If you try to find the inverse sine of 1.013 on your calculator, it will tell you have made an error. This does not mean that the calculation is wrong, only that the mathematics has not kept up with the physics of refraction. Snell's law only works if the ray actually crosses the boundary. At high angles of incidence the rays cannot cross over: they *reflect* instead.

6 To reduce light loss, an LED is stuck onto an optical fibre with a transparent glue. The refractive indexes of glue and fibre are 1.40 and 1.60.

a Calculate the relative refractive index.

b If a ray of light from the LED hits the end of the fibre at 30° to the normal, at what angle will it strike the wall of the fibre?

Key ideas

- Refracted rays deflect towards the normal when they slow down.
- The refractive index is

$$n = \frac{\text{speed of light in a vacuum}}{\text{speed of light in material}}$$

- For a ray travelling from medium 1 into medium 2, relative refractive index is

$${}_1n_2 = \frac{n_2}{n_1} = \frac{c_1}{c_2}$$

- Snell's law says that refractive index

$$n = \frac{\sin i}{\sin r} \quad \text{or} \quad {}_1n_2 = \frac{\sin\theta_1}{\sin\theta_2}$$

10.4 Total internal reflection

Optical fibres work using internal reflection of light rays. This is what allows the light to go around corners when the fibre is bent. The phenomenon occurs when light travels from one medium to another, less optically dense, medium (Fig. 17).

Light refracts as expected at low angles of incidence, but at higher angles reflection increases until the internal surface acts as a perfect mirror. This is called **total internal reflection**, because all of the incident light energy is reflected.

The change to reflection is not sudden; there is always partial reflection inside the block. This effect gets stronger as the angle of incidence rises. However, at one particular angle, the **critical angle**, c, the refracted ray disappears. At this angle, the refracted ray is trying to travel along the boundary between the media ($r = 90°$). Beyond the critical angle ($i > c$) the internal reflection is total.

Fig. 17 Refraction and reflection

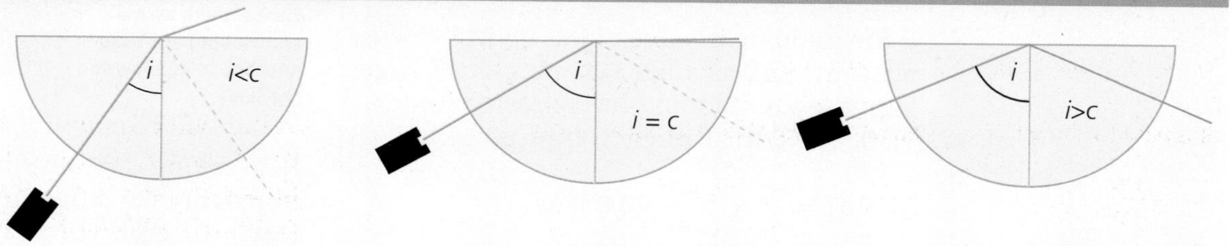

i
i<c
i
i = c
i
i>c

The critical angle depends on the refractive index of the media. At the critical angle, the ray travels at 90° from the normal in the less dense medium 2, so:

$${}_1n_2 = \frac{\sin c}{\sin 90°} = \sin c$$

$${}_1n_2 = \frac{n_2}{n_1}$$

$$\text{so,}\ \sin c = \frac{n_2}{n_1}$$

In the case of rays travelling in a medium of refractive index n where the less dense medium is air, we have $n_2 \approx 1$, so:

$$\sin c = \frac{1}{n}$$

A single pure glass fibre could be used to carry light pulses, but its surface is easily scratched, allowing some light to leak out (Fig. 18). One way to avoid this is to use an outer layer of less pure glass to protect the light-carrying fibre. What effect will this have on total internal reflection?

Fig. 18 Light leakage

Surface scratches lead to light leakage in a single fibre. Scratches in the outer cladding do not matter because it does not carry a light signal

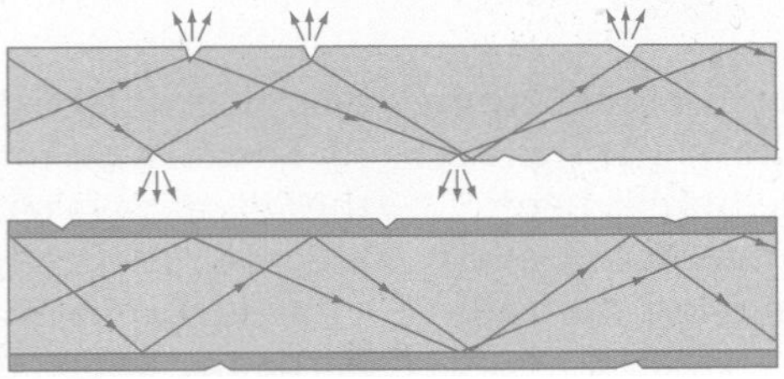

Supposing the core of an optical fibre has a refractive index of 1.60. In air, the critical angle given of the glass is given by

$$\sin c = \frac{1}{n} = \frac{1}{1.60} = 0.625$$

$$c = 39°$$

If the cladding is made of less optically dense glass, the critical angle becomes much larger. Suppose the cladding has refractive index 1.50. The critical angle is now given by:

$$\sin c = \frac{n_2}{n_1} = \frac{1.50}{1.60} = 0.9375$$

$$c = 69.6°$$

The protected fibre only reflects light rays with a very high angle of incidence. This increase of critical angle for the cladded fibre might seem to be a disadvantage, because fewer rays will reflect inside. However, it turns out to be an advantage because the rays that are internally reflected will travel by a more direct route and suffer less relative time delay. When only large angles of incidence are allowed, the zig-zag ray is almost the same length as the direct ray (Fig. 19).

Fig. 19 The longest path

Ray B has the longest possible path with an angle of incidence equal to the critical angle. The ratio of the length of ray B's journey to the length of ray A's journey is PQ/PR=1/sin c = 1/0.9375 = 1.0667. Along 1 km of fibre the maximum path is 1.0667 km.

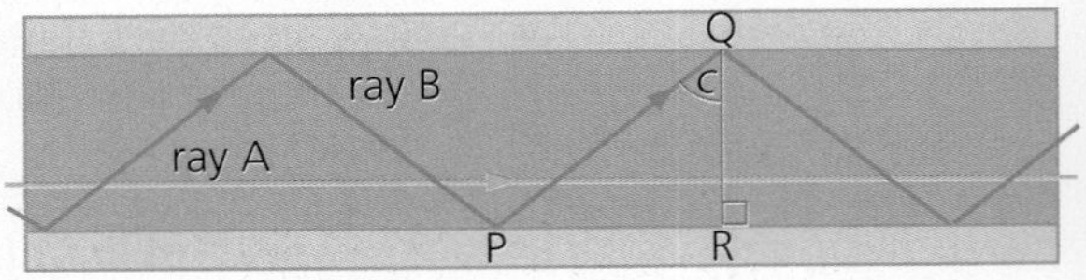
Q
c
ray B
ray A
P
R

The internal reflection properties of optical fibres can be used as a method of force sensing. When a force bends a fibre, more light strikes the sides of the core at less than the critical angle, so light escapes into the cladding. The decrease of detected light intensity can be monitored to measure the size of a force.

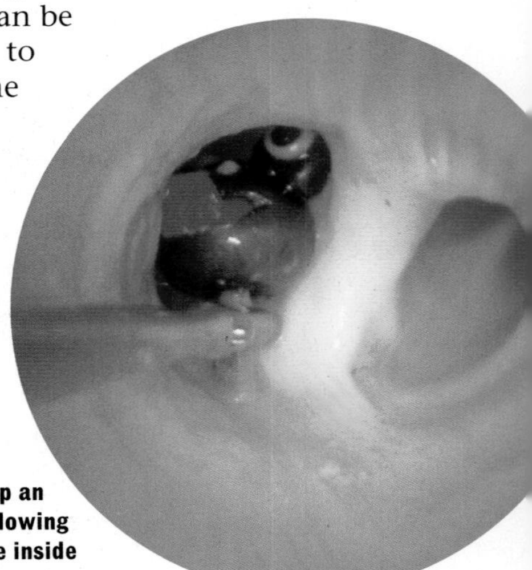

Optical fibres can be used to help perform 'keyhole' surgery. Parallel strands of fibres make up an endoscope, allowing doctors to see inside the body.

Rays taking different paths along an optical fibre will take different amounts of time to reach the end. This is called **multimode dispersion**, because the different modes of travel are dispersed in terms of their time of arrival. It is important to keep multimode dispersion as small as possible. One way of doing this is to use core and cladding of almost identical refractive index. Another way is to keep the core of the fibre so small that only one pattern of electromagnetic wave motion is possible inside the fibre. This is a called monomode fibre. The core of such a fibre is only a few micrometres in diameter – about a hundred times thinner than a human hair!

7 What is the time delay between the straight path and the critical angle path for 1 km of the optical fibre with refractive indexes of 1.50 and 1.60?

8 What would be the maximum frequency of transmission of pulses along 10 km of this cable?

10.5 Optical fibres, CDs and computers

Computers are increasingly turning towards the use of light. We may soon be using integrated circuits that switch light signals instead of electrical voltages. The rate of information transfer around multimedia systems already means that large, fast data networks are linked by optical fibre instead of by wire.

Compact discs are an ideal storage medium for computer information. They cost only a few pence to produce and they are resistant to damage from normal handling.

This scanning electron micrograph of the musical layer of a compact disc shows the depressions that can be read by a laser.

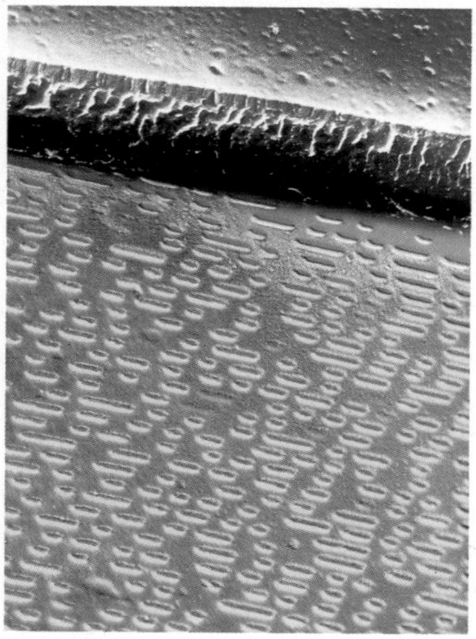

Compact discs are now used as a permanent storage medium. The CD's surface is a reflective sheet onto which is pressed a clockwise spiral of pits. The spiral is 5.7 km long, with a distance of 1.6 mm between tracks. The regular 1.6 mm spacing gives CDs their ability to split light into colours; the surface is effectively a circular reflective diffraction grating.

The surface is read by a laser optical system. The jump from the surface to or from a pit is detected as a logic 1 pulse.

Audio CDs can hold an hour of high-quality music. The same digital storage capacity is equivalent to about 300 ordinary magnetic floppy disks, or about half a million pages of typed text. Software firms now publish encyclopaedias and large dictionaries on CD. The use of optical fibres to link terminals to mainframe computers running large CD libraries is set to transform the way in which we can handle and access information.

Key ideas

- Total internal reflection occurs at angles of incidence greater than the critical angle. For refraction into air, the critical angle is given by:

  $$\sin c = \frac{1}{n}$$

- Optical fibres rely on repeated total internal reflection to transmit light pulses.

11 Messages from space

EDWARD L.ALPERSON
presents
INVADERS FROM MARS
Photographed in COLOR
HELENA CARTER · ARTHUR FRANZ · JIMMY HUNT
WILLIAM CAMERON MENZIES · RICHARD BLAKE · EDWARD L.ALPERSON, JR. · RAOUL KRAUSHAAR

A group in California is convinced that there is life on Mars. What's more they believe that NASA has proof and is hiding it from us. When NASA's Mars Observer mission failed to transmit its pictures to Earth, the Californian Independent Mars Investigation Team alleged that the failure was part of a deliberate cover-up.

Most scientists believe that there is no life elsewhere in our solar system. One school of thought is that the conditions needed for life are so special that they are probably unique: we are alone in the Universe.

The 70-metre Goldstone antenna in California helps NASA to track spacecraft on interplanetary missions.

Others concede that the existence of extraterrestrial life is at least *possible*. Some scientists believe that, given similar planetary conditions, life could begin just as it did on Earth, and evolution would eventually lead to intelligence. Working on the assumption that our galaxy has billions of Earth-like planets orbiting billions of Sun-like stars, NASA began work in 1992 on a Search for Extraterrestrial Intelligence (SETI). They are searching for alien communications. Even if NASA's scientists are right, the exploration is the cosmic equivalent of looking for a needle in a haystack.

11.1 Learning objectives

After working through this chapter, you should be able to:

- **explain** how scattering experiments led to the nuclear model of the atom;
- **describe** emission and absorption spectra;
- **explain** how line spectra and X-ray spectra lead to the idea of allowed energy levels for electrons in the atom;
- **define** the electronvolt;
- **explain** the terms ionisation and excitation;
- **relate** energy changes in atoms to the frequency of radiation emitted;
- **recall** the main regions of the electromagnetic spectrum and discuss how each can be generated and detected.

11.2 The fingerprint of starlight

Our search of the heavens is not new. Since the dawn of civilisation, we have constructed sophisticated observatories such as Stonehenge to survey the skies.

The search for extraterrestrial *intelligence* began more recently. It started with radio astronomy in the 1950s. The first SETI, Project Ozma, began in 1959. Since then, there have been several large-scale projects dedicated to finding evidence of extraterrestrial intelligence. Is this money well spent?

The megalithic monument of Stonehenge is believed to have had astronomical purposes.

Searching for other suns

SETI researchers base their work on the assumption that life can only exist on Earth-like planets. They accept that life-forms may not be humanoid, but they do assume that life elsewhere is based on the chemistry of carbon and relies on the presence of liquid water. The temperature, gravity and atmospheric conditions of a planet must be similar to those found on Earth for life to evolve. Theory suggests that such planets are created naturally when a star like our Sun is formed. The first task is to estimate just how many stars in our galaxy are similar to the Sun.

Our galaxy contains about one hundred billion stars. We can estimate how hot a star is by examining the colour of its light.

All objects emit radiation. This arises from the random vibrations of their molecules and is known as *thermal radiation*. If the temperature of an object increases, its molecules vibrate at a higher frequency, producing radiation with a higher frequency (shorter wavelength). When a piece of metal is heated in a flame, the colour of its surface changes as it gets hotter. The colour is an indication of its temperature.

As the temperature increases, the total energy radiated by a body goes up. The amount of energy emitted also depends on the surface area of the body and the nature of the surface. An object which is at the same temperature as its surroundings is said to be in thermal equilibrium with its environment. It is a dynamic equilibrium; the body emits radiation at the same rate that it absorbs radiation. An object that absorbs all of the radiation that falls on it, and reflects none, is called a **black body**. If it is in thermal equilibrium, the black body must re-radiate all this energy. A black body is therefore a perfect emitter as well as a perfect absorber. A black body emits radiation over a range of wavelengths in a way that just depends on its temperature (Fig. 1). At higher temperatures, a black body emits more of its radiation at shorter wavelengths. The wavelength at which it radiates most energy is inversely proportional to its temperature:

$$\lambda_{max} = \frac{0.003}{T}$$ (where T is the absolute temperature, in K)

In the constellation of Orion, there are two very bright, very different stars. Rigel is a hot, blue star and Betelgeuse is a huge red giant.

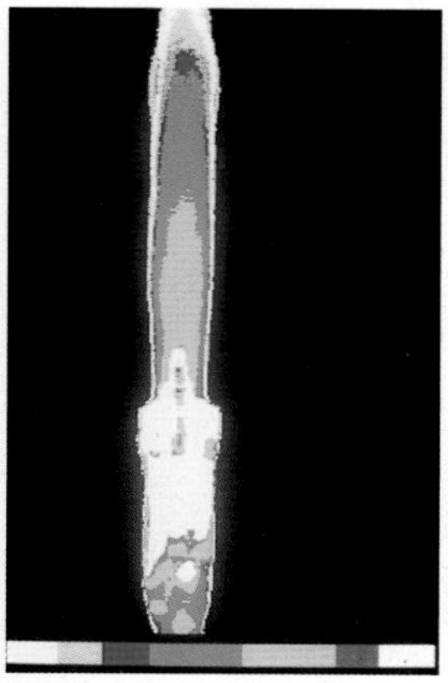

This thermograph shows the variation of temperature in a Bunsen burner flame.

Fig. 1 Radiation curves

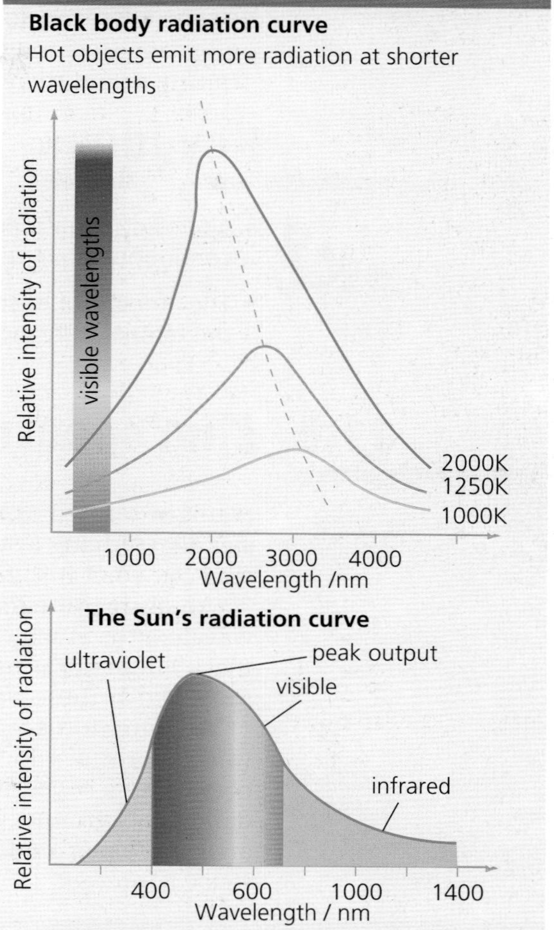

Black body radiation curve
Hot objects emit more radiation at shorter wavelengths
Relative intensity of radiation
visible wavelengths
2000K
1250K
1000K
1000
2000
3000
4000
Wavelength /nm
The Sun's radiation curve
Relative intensity of radiation
ultraviolet
peak output
visible
infrared
400
600
1000
1400
Wavelength / nm

The temperature of the Sun's surface is about 5500 K. It emits most of its radiation in the visible region, though it does radiate in the ultra-violet and infra-red parts of the spectrum.

Below about 750 K, a black body appears black since it doesn't reflect any radiation and does not emit any radiation at visible wavelengths. But a black body can look red, yellow or even blue if it is hot enough. Although it sounds strange, a star is very close to being a black body.

By measuring the amount of energy that a star emits at each wavelength, we can find its surface temperature. Blue-hot stars like Rigel use up their nuclear fuel so quickly that their lives are too brief to allow the evolution of intelligent life. Scientists believe that only stars with a surface temperature in the range 4500 K to 7500 K have the long-term stability to support life. Almost a quarter of the stars in our galaxy fall into this category.

It seems there are about 20 billion stars in our galaxy that could have another Earth orbiting round them.

1 Betelgeuse, the giant star in Orion, appears red. Estimate its surface temperature.

Key ideas

- All objects emit thermal radiation as a continuous spectrum.
- The amount of energy emitted increases as the temperature increases.
- Hotter objects emit more radiation at shorter wavelengths.

11.3 Line spectra

Starlight can tell us about the nature of a star. By studying a star's spectrum we can find out what it is made of.

An **absorption spectrum** shows the wavelengths at which energy is absorbed. Black lines appear on the continuous spectrum at these wavelengths.

An **emission spectrum** shows the wavelengths at which energy is emitted and consists of a series of bright lines against a darker background. Emission spectra can be analysed using a diffraction grating (Fig. 2) (see Chapter 9).

Fig. 2 Diffraction of a cadmium light source

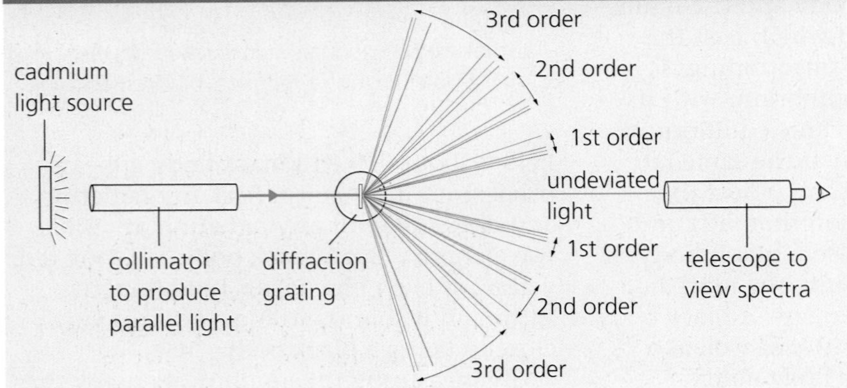
3rd order
2nd order
cadmium light source
1st order
undeviated light
1st order
collimator to produce parallel light
diffraction grating
telescope to view spectra
2nd order
3rd order

The simplest emission spectra come from low pressure monatomic gases such as sodium vapour in a street light (Fig. 3).

Experiments on gases and vapours have shown that each element produces a unique set of sharp lines. If the gas contains molecules of more than one atom, like carbon dioxide for example, the lines in the spectrum are replaced by bands.

Fig. 3 Elemental line spectra

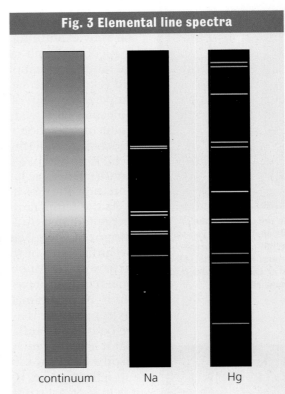
continuum
Na
Hg

Spectra become more complicated if the atoms which produced it are closer together. The spectrum produced by a hot solid or liquid, or a very dense gas, is continuous.

The line spectrum of hydrogen was first observed in 1853. It couldn't be satisfactorily explained until the early 20th century when three scientists made advances critical to our understanding of spectra and atoms. They were Ernest Rutherford, Niels Bohr and Max Planck.

Rutherford's nuclear atom

In 1909, Hans Geiger and Ernest Marsden were working at Manchester University under the supervision of the professor of Physics, Ernest Rutherford. They were investigating the scattering of alpha particles by metal foil (Fig. 4) . To their surprise, they found that about 1 in 8000 alpha particles were 'reflected', scattered back through an angle of more than 90 degrees (Fig. 5).

Until this discovery scientists thought that atoms consisted of a low density positive cloud, with tiny electrons embedded in it – the 'plum-pudding' model of the atom. A comparatively massive alpha particle travelling at 10 000 km s^{-1} should not have bounced off. Rutherford said later, 'It was almost as if you fired a 15-inch shell at a piece of tissue paper and it came back and hit you.'

Rutherford deduced that all the positive charge, and almost all the mass, must be concentrated in the centre of the atom. He called this the nucleus (Fig 6).

We now know that the nucleus is very small, about 10^{-15} m across. An atom is huge by comparison, with a typical radius of 10^{-10} m. If this was scaled up so that the nucleus was the size of a pea, the electrons would be orbiting over 1 km away.

Over 99.9% of the mass of an atom is concentrated into the nucleus. This means that the nucleus is incredibly dense. If you could crush the Earth to the same density, it would fit in St Paul's cathedral.

Fig. 4 The Geiger–Marsden scattering experiment

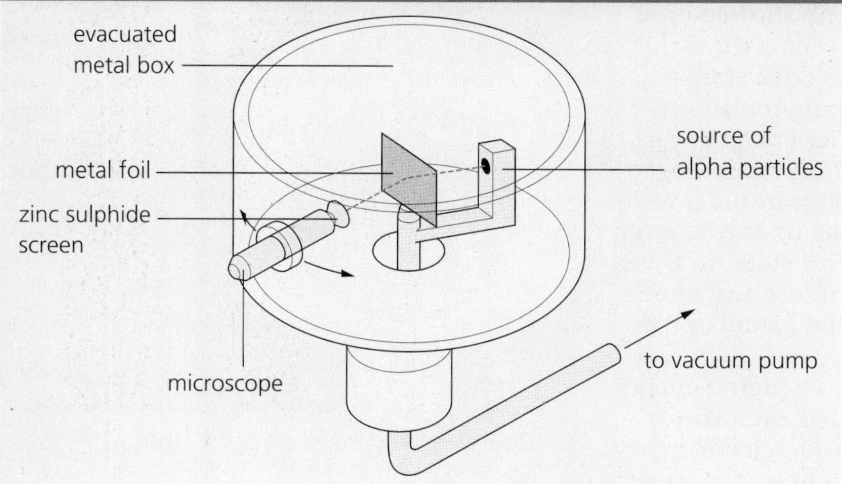
evacuated
metal box
metal foil
zinc sulphide
screen
source of
alpha particles
microscope
to vacuum pump

Fig. 5 Scattering of α-particles

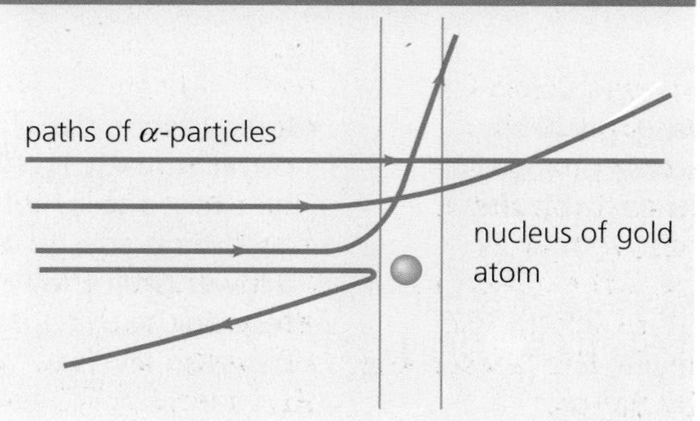
paths of α-particles
nucleus of gold
atom

Bohr's hydrogen atom

In 1911, Niels Bohr attended a lecture given by Rutherford, who described his new vision of the nuclear atom. Bohr was impressed. He wrote: 'If we adopt Rutherford's conception . . . we see that the experiments very strongly suggest that the hydrogen atom contains only one electron outside a positively charged nucleus.'

Fig. 6 Rutherford's atom

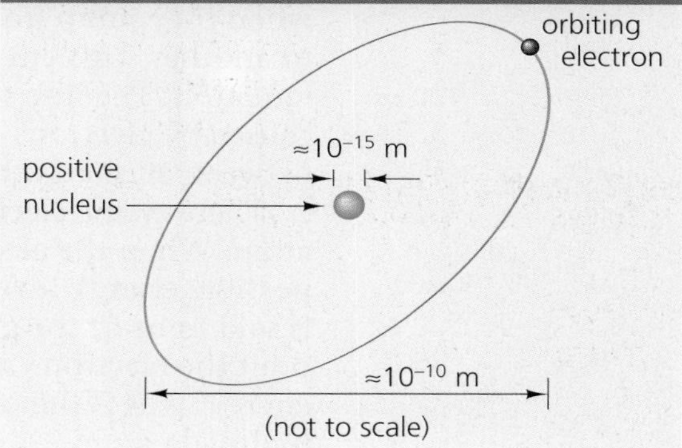
orbiting
electron
positive
nucleus
≈10⁻¹⁵ m
≈10⁻¹⁰ m
(not to scale)

But there was a major problem. All charged particles emit radiation when they accelerate. An electron orbiting a nucleus is accelerating towards the centre of its orbit. According to the laws of classical physics, the electron should be radiating energy. In Rutherford's model of the atom, the electron is rather like a satellite orbiting Earth. If the satellite radiates energy as it travels through the upper atmosphere, it will lose height and eventually crash to the ground. Rutherford's hydrogen atom would be unstable in the same way and as the electron radiated energy it would spiral down onto the nucleus.

Bohr made the bold suggestion that classical physics did not apply to atoms. He argued that only certain electron orbits are allowed. An electron can exist in these allowed orbits without losing energy. He called these orbits 'stationary' states (Fig. 7).

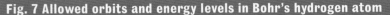

Fig. 7 Allowed orbits and energy levels in Bohr's hydrogen atom

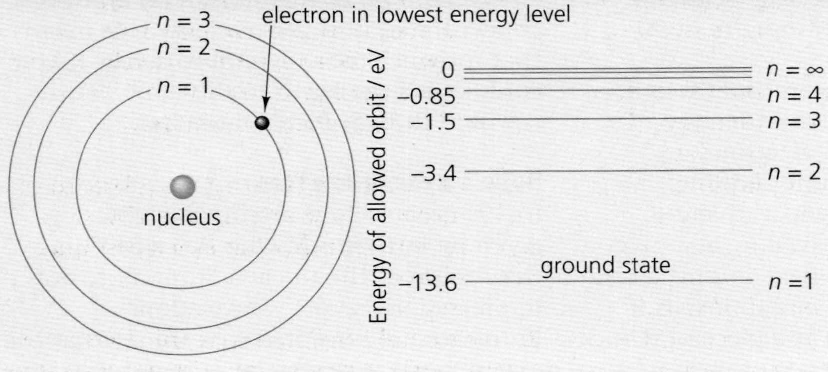

n = 3
n = 2
n = 1
electron in lowest energy level
nucleus
Energy of allowed orbit / eV
0
−0.85
−1.5
−3.4
−13.6
n = ∞
n = 4
n = 3
n = 2
n =1
ground state

The ground state, $n = 1$, is the lowest energy level. An electron in this level needs an energy transfer of 13.6 eV to free it from the atom.

Bohr said that electrons only emit energy when they jump from one allowed orbit to another. This energy is emitted as radiation. The line spectra of a star is caused by electrons making transitions between allowed orbits, or energy levels.

There is one electron in the hydrogen atom. When the electron is in the lowest possible **energy level**, the hydrogen atom is said to be in the **ground state**. In this orbit the electron cannot lose any more energy. This is the preferred state of the hydrogen atom.

Electrons can move to a higher energy level. This process is called **excitation**. Energy can be transferred to electrons when atoms collide with other atoms or

Fig. 8 Electron transitions

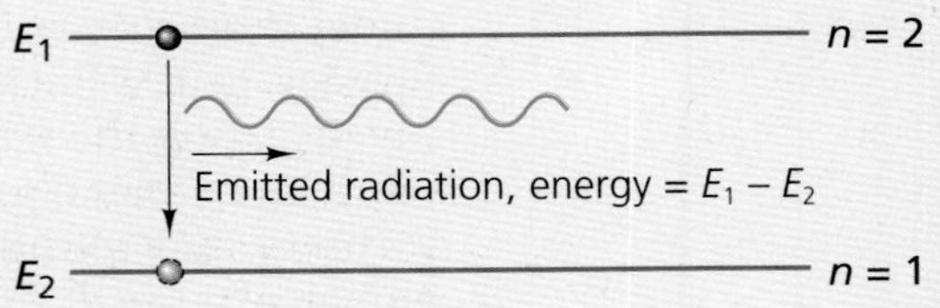

E_1
n = 2
Emitted radiation, energy = $E_1 - E_2$
E_2
n = 1

particles. When the electron is in a higher level, it can drop to a lower level, emitting radiation. The energy of the emitted radiation is equal to that transferred by the electron, i.e. the energy difference between the two states (Fig.8).

The crucial thing about Bohr's model is that an electron can only move from one allowed state to another by gaining or losing exactly the right amount of energy. No intermediate steps are allowed. That is why only certain wavelengths appear in the line spectrum (Fig. 9).

Fig. 9 Atomic shells

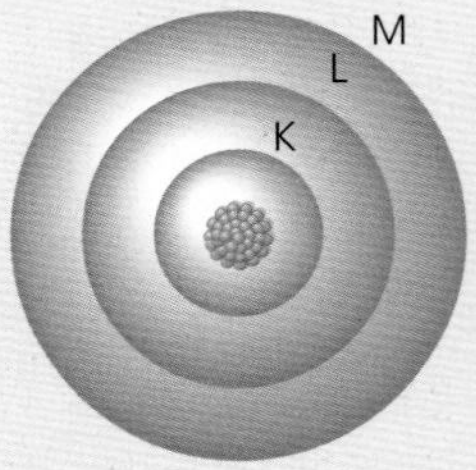

M
L
K

Shell	n	Maximum number of electrons
K	1	2
L	2	8
M	3	18

Bohr's model didn't work well for atoms other than hydrogen. The next model, wave mechanics, kept the idea of allowed energy levels. Each level, or shell has a principal quantum number $n = 1, 2, 3$, etc. The number of electrons that can occupy each shell is given by $2n^2$.

Key ideas

- Atoms have a small, dense, positively charged nucleus. Negatively charged particles known as electrons orbit the nucleus.
- The first evidence for the existence of the nucleus came from Rutherford's scattering experiments.
- In any atom, the electrons can only occupy certain energy levels or orbits. Electrons can be excited to a higher energy orbit by absorbing energy. When electrons move to a lower orbit they emit radiation. Electrons require the exact amount of energy to move between levels.

Planck's photons

As early as 1900, Max Planck was trying to explain the radiation emitted by a black body. Classical physics suggested that black bodies would emit an infinite amount of energy at short wavelengths. This conflict between theory and observation became known as the Ultraviolet Catastrophe. Planck managed to resolve the problem by suggesting that energy, like matter, comes in 'lumps'.

Planck said that radiation could be treated as if it consisted of 'parcels' of energy. The energy of these parcels, ΔE, was related to the frequency, f, of the radiation by:

$$\Delta E = hf$$

where h is a constant known as Planck's constant ($h = 6.626 \times 10^{-34}$ J s).

This idea was the beginning of the **quantum** theory. Quantum theory says that energy, like charge, is quantised; only certain discrete units of energy (quanta) are 'allowed'. By 1926, the quantum of radiation had been named the **photon**.

By combining the ideas of Planck's photons and Bohr's energy levels we can explain the origin of line spectra. Each time an electron falls to a lower energy level a photon of energy ΔE is emitted. So:

$$\Delta E = E_1 - E_2 = hf$$

The energy differences between allowed orbits are small in everyday terms. The joule is too large to be a useful unit, so the electronvolt is used instead.

One electronvolt, eV, is the energy transferred to an electron as it is moved through a potential difference of 1 volt.

The charge carried by an electron is 1.6×10^{-19} C (see Chapter 6). When it moves through a 1 V potential difference, the energy transferred to the electron is:

$$E = 1\text{ V} \times 1.6 \times 10^{-19}\text{ C}$$
$$1\text{ electronvolt} = 1.6 \times 10^{-19}\text{ J}$$

The ground state of the hydrogen atom has an energy of –13.6 eV (see Fig. 7). The negative sign means that the electron is in a bound state, i.e. 13.6 eV needs to be transferred to the electron to pull it free of the atom and cause **ionisation.**

Higher energy levels are less negative; an electron with zero energy is *just* free of the atom.

2 a How many different wavelengths of light could be emitted by an electron moving between the lowest three energy levels in hydrogen (see Fig. 7)?

b Calculate those wavelengths.

3 What is the shortest wavelength of light that can be emitted by an electron transition in a hydrogen atom?

Bohr's model predicted that the energy levels would get closer at higher energies, and this was confirmed by measurements on line spectra.

Fig. 10 Line series in the hydrogen spectrum

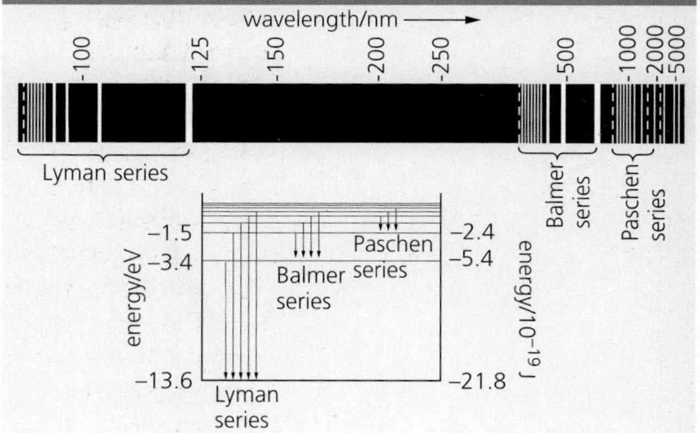

wavelength/nm
100
125
150
200
250
500
1000
2000
5000
Lyman series
Balmer series
Paschen series
energy/eV
–1.5
–3.4
–13.6
–2.4
–5.4
–21.8
energy/10⁻¹⁹ J
Paschen series
Balmer series
Lyman series

In a hydrogen atom, small energy changes cause infrared emission. Larger energy changes emit visible light (the Balmer series, Fig.10). The largest energy changes, where an electron falls back to the ground state, emit ultraviolet radiation.

Hydrogen is the simplest atom. It has only one electron. Although the energy level diagrams for other atoms are more complicated, the same principles apply. The atoms of each element have their own set of allowed energy levels. Each element has a unique line spectrum. The starlight that reaches us on Earth carries a record of the elements that made it.

Absorption spectra

The solar absorption spectrum.

Superimposed on the continuous spectrum from the Sun are a large number of dark lines. This is the absorption spectrum of the Sun.

The lines represent the wavelengths at which photons have been absorbed by cooler gases in the outer regions of the Sun. Only radiation which has exactly the right amount of energy to lift an electron in the cooler gases' atoms from one allowed energy level to another will be absorbed (Fig. 11).

When the cooler gases' atoms return to their ground state, they emit radiation *in all directions*. This reduces the amount of radiation travelling towards Earth, so producing dark lines in the spectra.

4 Explain why absorption lines come from the cooler outer 'atmospheres' of the stars and not the hotter centre.

In 1859, Kirchhoff related the dark lines to particular elements. He observed the Sun's spectrum through a flame into which he sprinkled some kitchen salt (sodium chloride). He found that some of the lines in the Sun's spectrum darkened. Kirchhoff concluded that there must be sodium in the Sun.

Just as in emission, each element has its own, unique absorption spectrum. Helium was discovered on the Sun, using absorption spectra, before it was found on Earth.

5 When Kirchhoff observed the Sun's light through a sodium flame he noticed that, 'If the sunlight is sufficiently damped, then two luminous lines appear at the position of the two dark lines.' Explain why this happens.

Fig. 11 The absorption and transmission of photons

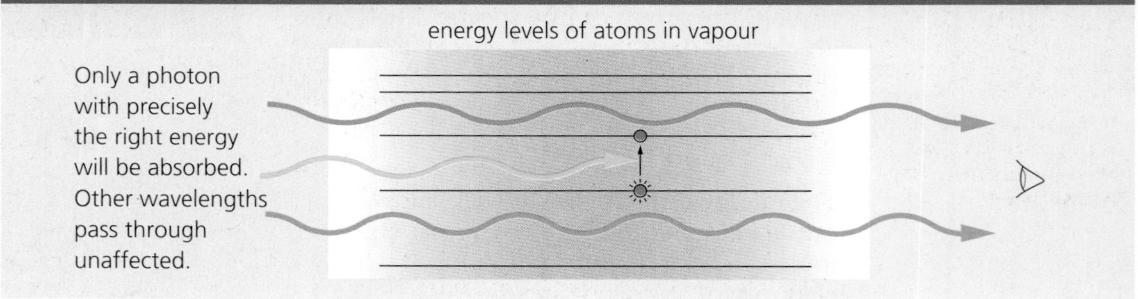

energy levels of atoms in vapour
Only a photon with precisely the right energy will be absorbed. Other wavelengths pass through unaffected.

Key ideas

- Radiation is quantised. It is emitted and absorbed in 'parcels' of energy known as photons.
- A photon is emitted from an atom when an electron drops to a lower energy orbit. The larger the energy gap between orbits, the higher the frequency of radiation emitted. The energy of the photon is given by $\Delta E = E_1 - E_2 = hf$.
- An emission spectrum is a series of bright lines on a darker background. The lines show the wavelength at which energy is emitted.
- An absorption spectrum is a series of dark lines on the background of a continuous spectrum. It is caused by electrons being excited to higher energy levels.
- The positions of the lines in an absorption and emission spectra are characteristic of the element that produced them.

11.4 Across the wavelengths

Little green men?

In 1967, Joscelyn Bell, a research student at Cambridge, was studying the radio waves emitted from stars when she noticed some strange interference. For four minutes each day she detected a series of radio pulses, just over one second apart. At first, Bell regarded these signals as 'scruff', but as she made further observations she realised that the time between pulses was remarkably constant: 1.3373011 seconds. The pulses appeared at a certain time each day. This seemed unnaturally regular.

Human-made interference was the most obvious explanation, but this was dismissed when it became clear that the pulses were not related to Earth-time; they always appeared when a certain part of the sky was overhead. Perhaps this was evidence that intelligent life existed elsewhere in the Universe.

Bell decided to analyse records from a different part of the sky. She found another set of similar pulses.

Soon another source was discovered, and another, all in different parts of the sky. Joscelyn Bell and her colleagues had discovered the first pulsar, a sort of a radio 'lighthouse' created by a rapidly rotating **neutron star**. These stars have the same density as an atomic nucleus; a matchboxful would have a mass of about 1500 million tonnes.

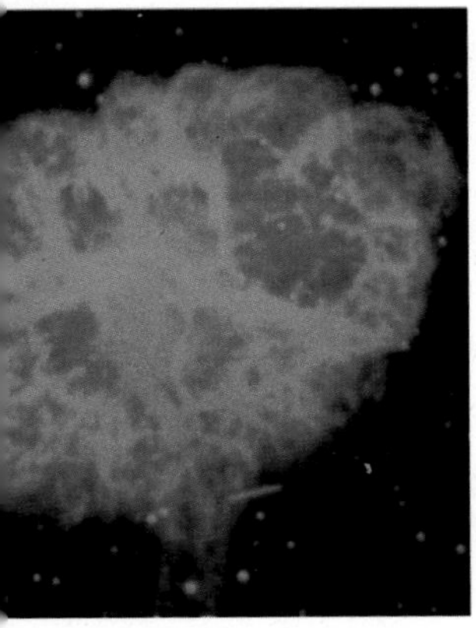

At the centre of the Crab Nebula is a pulsar, the dense remnant of a star that exploded.

The electromagnetic spectrum

If intelligent aliens were trying to contact us they would need to choose something that would stand out from the background of natural phenomena. Communication signals would have to travel quickly and not be absorbed by the atmosphere or by inter-stellar gas clouds.

The choices are limited. Four unmanned spacecraft from Earth have left the solar system but they are unlikely to be detected by extraterrestrials.

Sub-atomic particles, such as neutrinos, travel at or near the speed of light, but they are very difficult to generate and detect.

The only realistic option is to use electromagnetic waves to communicate.

Pioneer 10 crossed Pluto's orbit in 1986 and will make its nearest approach to a star, Ross 248, in the year 34 593.

Electromagnetic waves are transverse waves caused by the oscillation of charged particles (Fig. 12).

Fig. 12 An electromagnetic wave

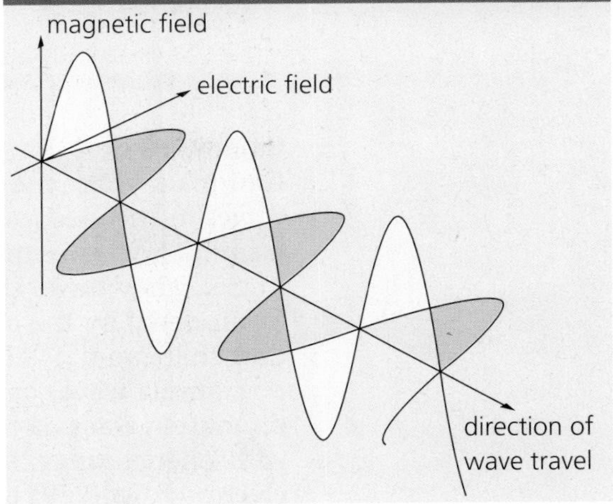
magnetic field
electric field
direction of wave travel

All electromagnetic waves, no matter what frequency they are, travel through a vacuum at the same speed; 3×10^8 m s^{-1}. Because they are waves, all electromagnetic waves can be reflected, refracted and polarised. They show interference and diffraction effects (see Chapter 9). Different frequencies interact with matter in very different ways.

Astronomers no longer rely on just light waves, or even radio signals, to examine the universe. They scan the heavens across the entire electromagnetic spectrum. Radiation from space can arrive as X-rays, ultraviolet and infrared radiation.

These carry information on the history and structure of the universe as well as clues to possible life on other planets.

6 How could you demonstrate that radio signals and light are both waves?

Fig. 13 The electromagnetic spectrum

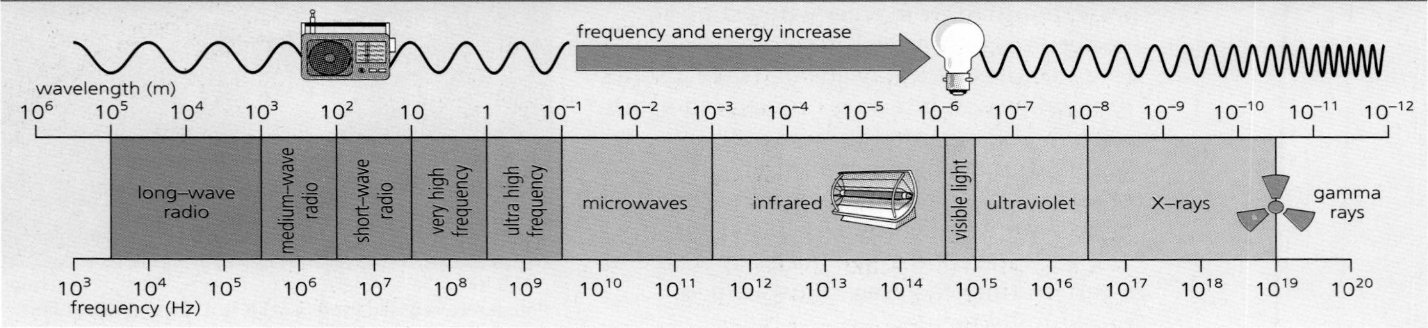

frequency and energy increase
wavelength (m)
10^6 10^5 10^4 10^3 10^2 10 1 10^-1 10^-2 10^-3 10^-4 10^-5 10^-6 10^-7 10^-8 10^-9 10^-10 10^-11 10^-12
long–wave radio
medium–wave radio
short–wave radio
very high frequency
ultra high frequency
microwaves
infrared
visible light
ultraviolet
X–rays
gamma rays
10^3 10^4 10^5 10^6 10^7 10^8 10^9 10^10 10^11 10^12 10^13 10^14 10^15 10^16 10^17 10^18 10^19 10^20
frequency (Hz)

Key ideas

- Electromagnetic waves are electrical and magnetic oscillations which propagate through space without the need for a medium.
- They are transverse waves which travel at $3 \times 10^8 \, m\,s^{-1}$ in a vacuum. All parts of the spectrum demonstrate wave phenomena, but the way they interact with matter depends on their frequency.

Gamma rays

Gamma rays are the highest frequency waves in the electromagnetic spectrum. Gamma rays are emitted from atomic nuclei. They travel through space unhindered by the clouds of interstellar dust that can block light waves.

Gamma waves can have a drastic effect on matter. Gamma ray photons cover a wide energy range, from a few kilo-electronvolts (keV) to over 10 GeV. This is more than enough energy to strip electrons from an atom. This process is called **ionisation**. When ionisation occurs in a gas, charged particles are created and the gas conducts electricity. Gamma rays can therefore be detected using an ionisation chamber or a Geiger counter. Scintillation counters or photographic film can also be used for this purpose.

Gamma radiation can damage living cells by altering the DNA directly or by the chemical changes caused by ionisation.

Fortunately, the Earth's atmosphere is dense enough to absorb (through ionisation of molecules in the air) all but the most energetic gamma rays. This atmospheric absorption has meant that gamma ray astronomy has been impossible until recently.

Scientists first discovered gamma rays in space when satellites designed to look for illicit nuclear weapons tests discovered bursts of gamma rays coming from beyond the solar system. In 1991, NASA launched a satellite, the Compton Gamma Ray Observatory (GRO), to study the universe at these very short wavelengths. Scientists will use the GRO to see what happens in a supernova, the cataclysmic explosion that is the death of a large star. They believe that it is only in these extreme conditions that the heavier elements, essential for life, are created.

X-rays

Just below gamma rays on the energy scale of the electromagnetic spectrum lies the X-ray region. In fact, the regions overlap. The real difference between X-rays and gamma rays lies in their origin.

X-rays are caused by high-energy electrons. These electrons emit X-rays after high-speed collisions or through a high-energy transition in an atom. In space, X-rays come from very hot stars or from charged particles accelerated to enormous speeds, perhaps by the intense gravitational force of a **black hole**. On Earth, X-rays are produced by making high-speed electrons collide with a metal target (Fig. 14).

The position of the peaks in an X-ray spectrum does not change as the tube voltage is increased, but each type of metal has its own set of peaks. These 'characteristic lines' are due to energy changes in the target atoms (Fig.15).

Fig. 14 An X-ray tube

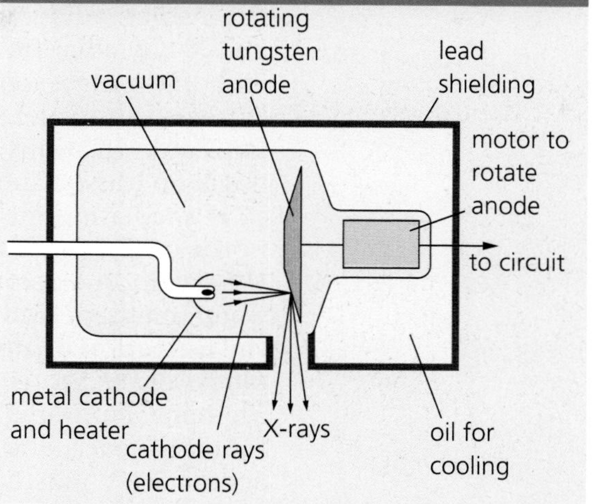
rotating tungsten anode
vacuum
lead shielding
motor to rotate anode
to circuit
metal cathode and heater
cathode rays (electrons)
X-rays
oil for cooling

Fig. 15 X-ray energy levels and spectra

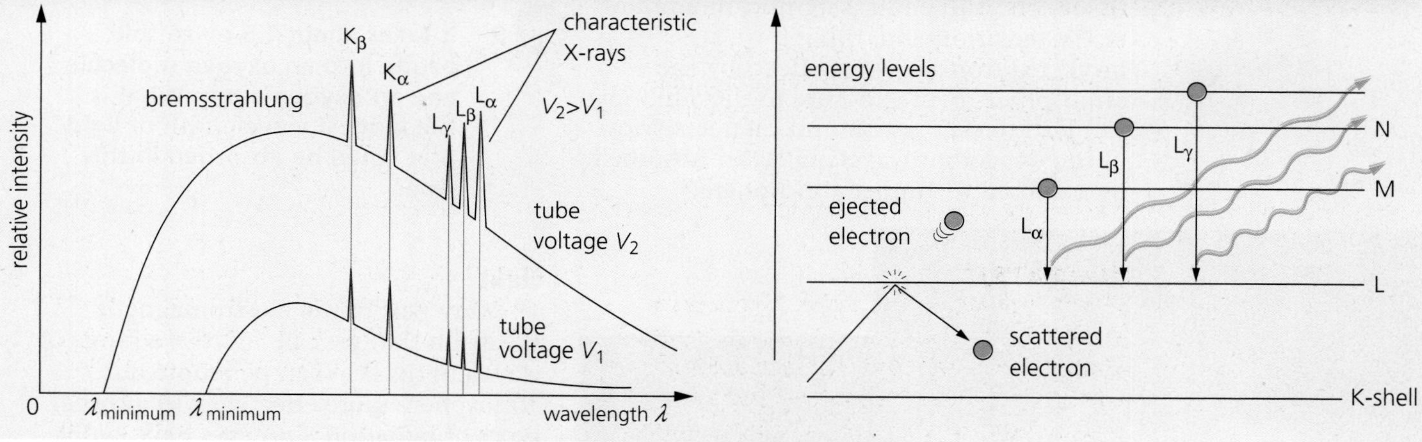
relative intensity
bremsstrahlung
Kβ
Kα
Lγ
Lβ
Lα
characteristic X-rays
V2>V1
tube voltage V2
tube voltage V1
0
λ minimum
λ minimum
wavelength λ
energy levels
N
M
L
K-shell
ejected electron
scattered electron
Lα
Lβ
Lγ

Fig. 16 The minimum wavelength of an X-ray spectrum

An electron gains kinetic energy as it is accelerated across the tube. When it hits the target, the most energetic X-ray (minimun wavelength) is produced if the electron loses all of its energy in just one direct collision with a target atom.

What is this minimum wavelength for a dental X-ray set, with a tube voltage of 60 kV?

For a tube voltage of 60 kV the electron gains an energy of 60 keV. In joules this is:
energy = 1.6×10^{-19} C $\times$ 60×10^{3} V = 9.60×10^{-15} J

Since the energy of a photon is given by $E = hf$, the highest frequency that this X-ray tube can produce is:

$$f = \frac{E}{h} = \frac{9.60 \times 10^{-15}\ \text{J}}{6.63 \times 10^{-34}\ \text{J}} = 1.54 \times 10^{19}\ \text{Hz}$$

So the minimum wavelength is: $\lambda = \frac{c}{f} = \frac{3.00 \times 10^{8}\ \text{m s}^{-1}}{1.54 \times 10^{19}\ \text{Hz}} = 1.95 \times 10^{-11}\ \text{m}$

7 **When the voltage across an X-ray tube is increased, the minimum wavelength at which X-rays are emitted goes down and more characteristic lines may appear in the spectrum. Explain why.**

8 **Suppose an X-ray tube uses a target with a higher atomic number, i.e. the target atoms have more electrons. We find that the minimum wavelength of X-rays stays the same but the characteristic lines move to shorter wavelengths. Why is this?**

Ultraviolet radiation

Ultraviolet radiation lies between visible and X-ray radiation. At the high-energy end of its range, sometimes known as extreme ultraviolet (EUV), it can cause ionisation in atoms and cause molecules to break up (dissociate).

UV radiation may have played a key role in the origin of life on Earth. The action of UV radiation on simple molecules such as water, methane and ammonia can lead to the formation of amino acids, the building blocks of the proteins necessary for life. Methane, ammonia and water have all been found in space, and it is possible that the action of UV radiation could have produced amino acids elsewhere in the universe.

Ultraviolet radiation can damage living tissue. The Sun emits a significant amount of UV radiation and, though we are protected from its worst effects by the atmosphere, over-exposure to the Sun's rays can lead to skin cancer and cataracts. Most of the dangerous wavelengths are absorbed by ozone in the upper atmosphere.

Ultraviolet radiation leads to fluorescence in some materials and can be detected through its ability to darken photographic film. UV can also cause electrons to be emitted from a metal. Photomultiplier tubes use this effect and are capable of detecting a single photon of UV.

In space, photons of ultraviolet radiation are emitted when electrons recombine with positive ions in the hot coronas that surround stars. Stars with a surface temperature of at least 10 000 K also emit a high level of UV radiation. White dwarf stars, the oldest stars in our galaxy, may reach temperatures of 100 000 K before they begin to cool.

Q 9 It takes about 1.5 eV to split ozone into an oxygen molecule and an oxygen atom. What is the longest wavelength of light that could be absorbed in this way?

Light is absorbed by the large dust and gas clouds in space, like the Horsehead Nebula. Even our atmosphere stops some light, so our biggest telescopes are put on top of mountains like the extinct volcano Mauna Kea in Hawaii.

Light

The tiny part of the electromagnetic spectrum that we call 'light' is a range of wavelengths that can penetrate our atmosphere more effectively than other types of radiation. Our eyes have evolved to respond to these wavelengths. Some scientists believe that aliens would have developed similar sense organs.

The surface temperature of the Sun is about 5500 K, and much of its radiation output is in the visible part of the spectrum. Light is produced from electron transitions in other hot objects, such as the tungsten filament in a light bulb. The tungsten, at about 2300 K, is much cooler than the Sun. Only about 5% of its output is visible; the rest is infrared.

Until the start of radio astronomy in the 1950s, all our information about the universe came as light. But there are drawbacks about using it for communications in space. It would take huge amounts of energy to transmit enough light to make it stand out against the galactic background.

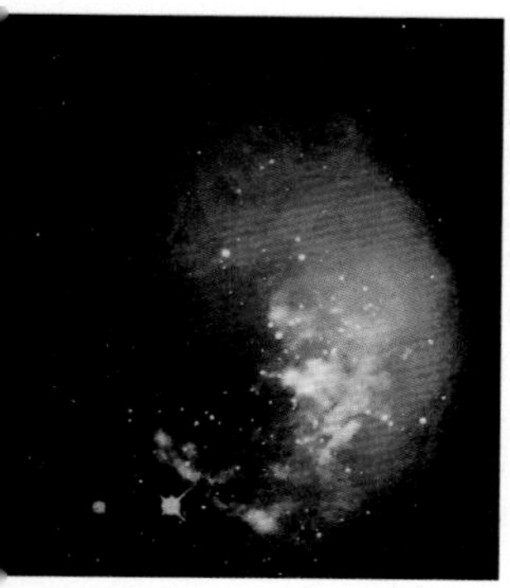

An infrared photograph of the Orion Nebula taken using NASA's Airborne Infrared Observatory.

Infrared

The satellite IRAS made the first map of the sky at infrared wavelengths in 1983. Infrared radiation comes from relatively cool astronomical objects. Some stars, gas clouds and comets fall into this category. Infrared wavelengths are not absorbed by interstellar dust as easily as light and can therefore give us a view of otherwise obscured parts of our galaxy. The Earth's atmosphere, however, does absorb infrared radiation.

IRAS has provided important evidence in the debate about extraterrestrial life. It has revealed a disc of material, from which planets are thought to be formed, around Vega, a star in the constellation of Lyra. Since then, infrared observatories have detected similar discs around other stars. This is the closest we have come to detecting planets outside our own solar system.

10 Why are most infrared observations of the universe carried out using telescopes in balloons or on mountain tops?

When infrared radiation is absorbed by an object, the energy transfer causes an increase in molecular vibration and temperature. Infrared radiation from the Sun makes your skin feel warm. This heating effect can be used to detect infrared radiation. A **thermocouple** provides a way of converting a temperature difference to an electrical signal (Fig. 17).

The low power levels of infrared radiation from space cause a very tiny heating effect so different means of detection must be used.

Photon detectors

When a photon of infrared radiation is absorbed by a semiconductor, such as indium antimonide, the energy can make an electron available for conduction. More photons means a bigger increase in conductivity. The increase in current is amplified and used to generate an image.

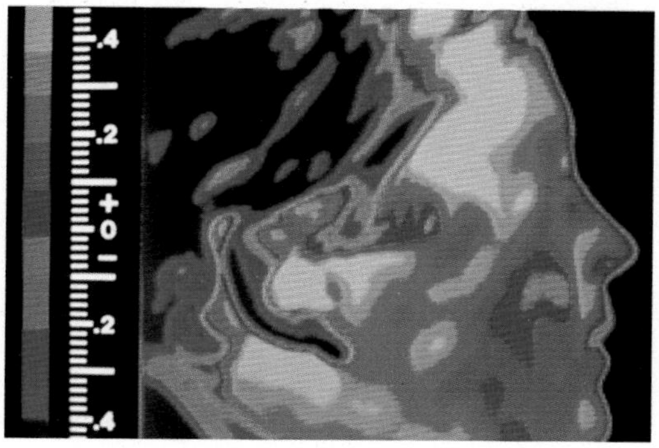

.4
.2
+
0
–
.2
.4

Photon detectors are often used in medical imaging. They can reveal temperature differences of 0.1 K between regions separated by tiny angles.

The pyroelectric effect

Pyroelectric 'vidicon' cameras use a ferromagnetic crystal such as triglycine sulphate. When infrared radiation strikes the crystal it produces an electric charge on its surface, rather like a capacitor. This charge is 'read' by a scanning electron beam to produce an image.

Fig. 17 A thermocouple and thermopile

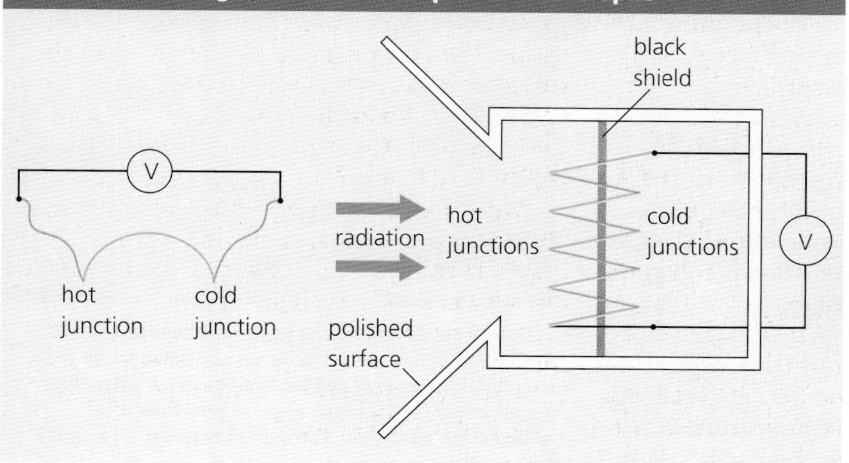

V
hot junction
cold junction
black shield
radiation
hot junctions
cold junctions
V
polished surface

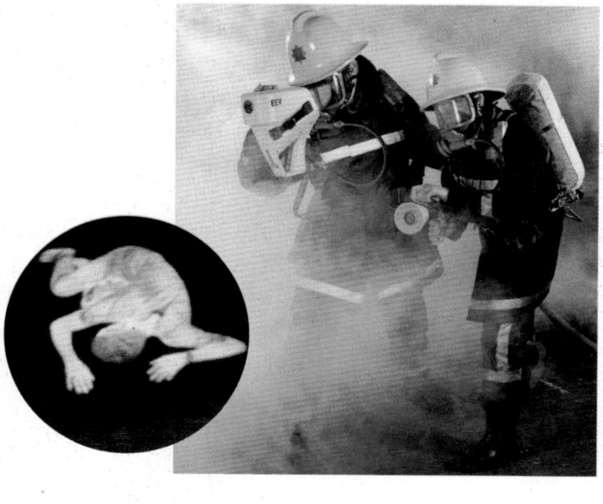

Firemen can use vidicon cameras to 'see' through smoke.

Fig. 18 Infrared absorption spectrum showing O–H and C–H bands

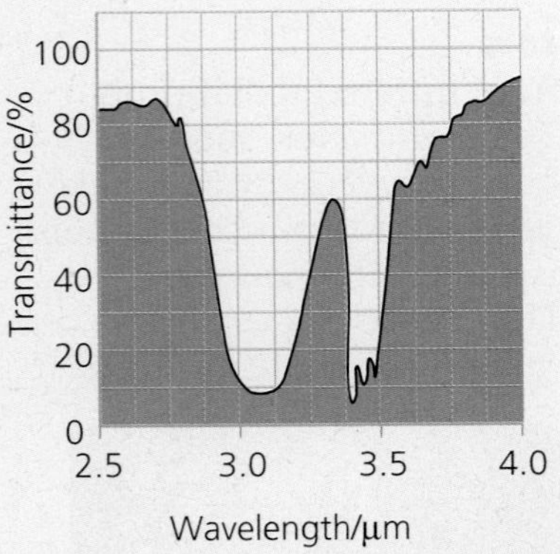
Transmittance/%
100
80
60
40
20
0
2.5
3.0
3.5
4.0
Wavelength/μm

Infrared radiation can cause resonance in molecular bonds. Certain wavelengths are strongly absorbed as molecules increase their vibrational energy. Just like the line spectra caused by electron transitions, these infrared absorption spectra give information about the molecules that are present.

Some infrared wavelengths are strongly absorbed in the atmosphere by gases such as carbon dioxide and methane. This absorption is known as the 'greenhouse effect' and it has serious implications for the chances of life in the universe (Fig. 19).

Fig. 19 The greenhouse effect

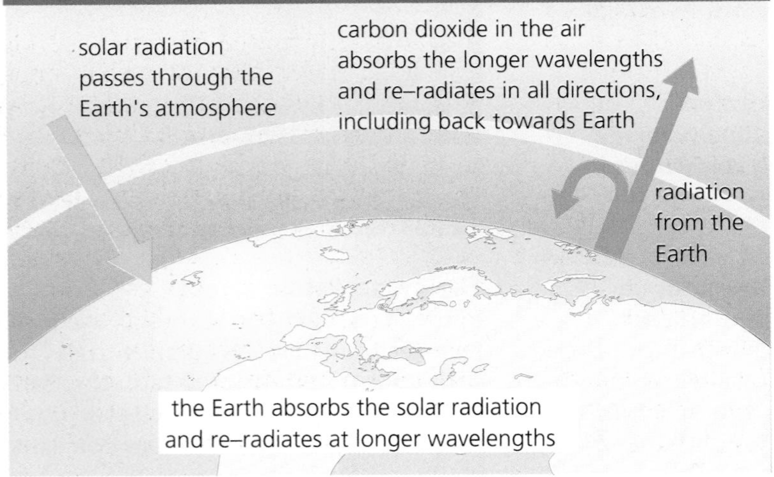
solar radiation passes through the Earth's atmosphere
carbon dioxide in the air absorbs the longer wavelengths and re–radiates in all directions, including back towards Earth
radiation from the Earth
the Earth absorbs the solar radiation and re–radiates at longer wavelengths

Venus suffers from a runaway greenhouse effect. The Venusian atmosphere is about 95% carbon dioxide. Most of the infrared radiation from the planet's surface is absorbed. As a result, the surface temperature of Venus is about 450 °C, hot enough to melt lead. Earth avoided this fate because it is a little further from the Sun and cool enough for water to exist as a liquid. Much of the Earth's carbon dioxide is dissolved in the oceans. Mars is too cold for liquid water, or life, to exist.

Q 11 The moon is about the same distance from the Sun as the Earth, yet its average temperature is much lower than the Earth's. Why?

Microwaves

99% of the Universe's radiation energy is microwave radiation. Microwaves are easy to produce and to detect, and most frequencies are not strongly absorbed by the Earth's atmosphere or by interstellar space.

If aliens were trying to communicate over long distances they would probably concentrate on the use of a specific wavelength. Some scientists believe that the most likely wavelength is the 21 cm line produced when the electron in hydrogen changes its spin axis. Another possibility is the so-called 'cosmic waterhole', the 1.7 GHz wave produced by the hydroxyl radical OH (which combines with hydrogen to make water).

Having tuned in to a frequency, we need to decide where to point the aerial. NASA have invested $100 million in the most recent SETI, a 10-year programme known as the High Resolution Microwave Survey. Two approaches are being used. One is an all-sky survey, looking for strong signals over a wide range of frequencies. The second method is to concentrate on a small range of frequencies, looking for weak signals from the nearest 100 Sun-like stars.

Any contact is unlikely to have immediate practical consequences. If the signals come from just half-way across our galaxy they will be 25 000 years old by the time they reach us! However, if SETI *is* successful we may never see ourselves in quite the same way again.

E.T. will have to hurry if he wants to phone us. Our TV and radio signals are threatening to swamp those from space. All the energy collected since radio astronomy began would light a torch bulb for less than a millisecond, whilst our terrestrial transmitters emit megawatts of power.

12 With radioactivity in mind

> **Extract**
>
> To see a World in a Grain of Sand
> And a Heaven in a Wild Flower,
> Hold Infinity in the palm of your hand
> And Eternity in an hour.
>
> from 'Auguries of Innocence', William Blake

Fig. 1 The functional areas of the brain

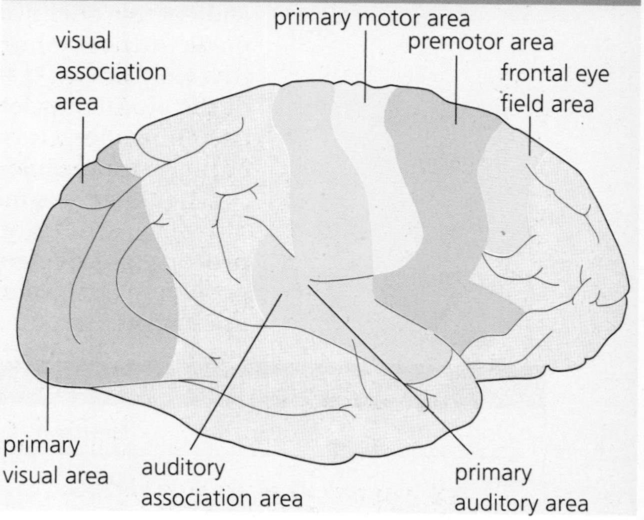
primary motor area
visual association area
premotor area
frontal eye field area
primary visual area
auditory association area
primary auditory area

As you read a piece of poetry, a complex mixture of thought and emotion flows through your mind. Your brain is alive with activity. Some areas are busy with routine functions, like controlling your eye movements, while others are dealing with language and memory. The link between mind and brain lies at the very heart of our efforts to understand what kind of beings we are. Is consciousness merely a set of electrical impulses and chemical reactions, or are we more than just an 'organic computer'?

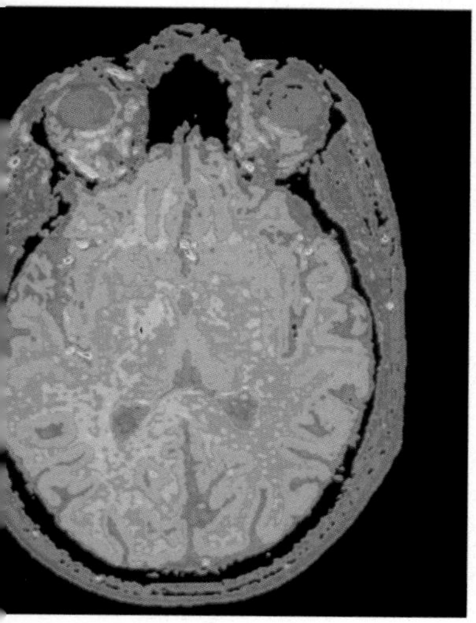

This CT scan shows an axial section through a human head

X-ray computed tomography, or CT scanning, uses beams of X-rays to produce detailed images of the brain, but it can not show the brain working.

Now scientists have found a way of watching a healthy brain in action. Positron Emission Tomography, or PET, was developed during the early 1980s. A radioactive isotope is injected into the body and the radiation emitted from the brain is measured. The data is processed by computer to produce an image, rather like CT scanning, but there is one important difference. PET scans show activity rather than structure. By choosing a suitable radioisotope, it is possible to measure blood flow, oxygen consumption or glucose metabolism. A PET scan can actually 'see' you thinking.

PET scans are being used to investigate conditions such as depression and Alzheimer's disease. One day, PET scans may even help us to understand the link between mind and brain.

12.1 Learning objectives

After working through this chapter, you should be able to:

- **describe** a simple model of the atomic nucleus;
- **explain** what is meant by radioactive decay;
- **recall** the properties of alpha, beta and gamma radiation;
- **use** equations to describe nuclear transformations;
- **use** the exponential decay law to predict how the activity of radioisotopes will change with time;
- **use** the idea of half-life to suggest an appropriate radioisotope for medical use;
- **describe** the photoelectric effect;
- **discuss** the evidence for wave–particle duality.

12.2 Radioisotopes in medicine

Nuclear structure

Radioactive chemicals were first used in medicine over 60 years ago to investigate thyroid disease. At that time, the structure of the atomic nucleus was only just becoming clear. It is the nucleus which is entirely responsible for radioactivity.

The nucleus is made up of two different particles of roughly equal mass; **protons** and **neutrons**. Protons are positively charged and neutrons are uncharged.

Table 1 Proton, neutron and electron data

	Proton	Neutron	Electron
symbol	$^{1}_{1}p$	$^{1}_{0}n$	$^{0}_{-1}e$
charge (C)	$+1.602 \times 10^{-19}$	0	-1.602×10^{-19}
mass (kg)	1.6726×10^{-27}	1.6749×10^{-27}	9.1096×10^{-31}

The number of protons and neutrons in the nucleus varies from element to element. The simplest nucleus is that of hydrogen. It usually has just one proton in its nucleus, though some hydrogen atoms have one or two neutrons as well. These different forms of hydrogen are called **isotopes** (Fig. 2).

Fig. 2 Isotopes of hydrogen

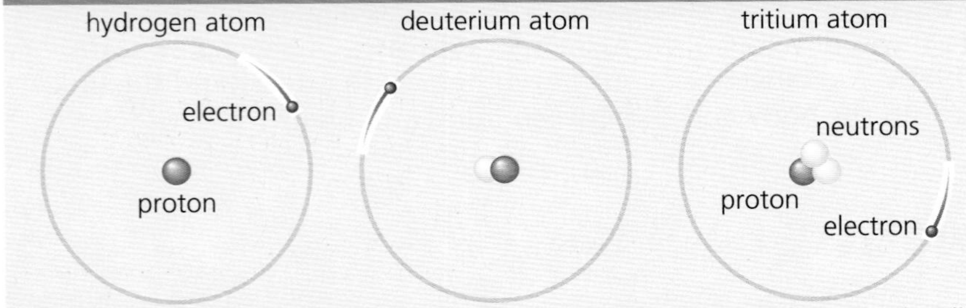
hydrogen atom
deuterium atom
tritium atom
electron
proton
neutrons
proton
electron

The extra neutrons do not affect hydrogen's chemical behaviour; for example, all three isotopes combine with oxygen to make water.

The nuclear composition of an isotope can be described using symbols. The most common isotope of carbon has six protons and six neutrons in its nucleus. It can be written as:

$$^{12}_{6}C$$

The upper figure is the **nucleon number** – the total number of protons and neutrons.

The lower figure is the **atomic number** – the total number of protons.

The nucleon number, sometimes called the mass number, is given the symbol A. In a neutral atom (one that has not been ionised) the atomic number, Z, is equal to the number of electrons in the atom.

Different isotopes of carbon all have the same atomic number. They all have six protons, but they may have more or less than six neutrons. For example, carbon-14 has eight neutrons and is written $^{14}_{6}C$. Although it is chemically identical to carbon-12, a major difference is that carbon-14 is radioactive. It is a **radioisotope**.

Radioisotopes are very useful to doctors. In the body they react just like the stable isotope, but we can trace their movement by the radiation they emit. All we need to do is choose the right radioisotope for each diagnostic test.

The mole

We sometimes need to consider a fixed number of atoms or molecules. The S.I. unit for this is called the mole:

A mole is the amount of a substance that contains the same number of particles as there are atoms in 12 g of the isotope carbon-12 ($^{12}_{6}C$).

There are 6.022×10^{23} atoms in 12 g of carbon-12. This number is called the Avogadro constant, N. The nucleon number of an isotope tells you approximately what the mass of 1 mole will be in grams.

1 Iodine-131 was the first radioisotope used in medicine. It can be written $^{131}_{53}I$. How many protons, neutrons and electrons does an atom of this isotope have?

2 Write down nuclear symbols for the three isotopes of hydrogen (Fig. 2).

Key ideas

- Atomic nuclei consist of positively charged protons and uncharged neutrons.
- A nucleus of element X can be described in symbols as:

$^{A}_{Z}X$

A, the nucleon number, gives the total number of protons and neutrons;

Z, the atomic number, gives the number of protons in the nucleus.

Alpha, beta and gamma rays

Henri Becquerel found that a sample of uranium caused a nearby unused photographic film to blacken, as if it had been placed in strong sunlight. He had discovered radioactivity. The nucleus of uranium is unstable and it decays, changing into a different element. As it does so, it emits invisible radiation that darkens photographic film.

Marie and Pierre Curie discovered other radioactive elements, polonium and radium. They found that the radiation from isotopes of these elements could make gases conduct electricity and some of it could even pass through steel.

Experiments to measure penetration through different materials showed that there were at least three different types of radiation. They were named **alpha, beta** and **gamma** rays.

Table 2 Characteristics of the different types of nuclear radiation

	Alpha	Beta	Gamma
structure	2 protons and 2 neutrons	an electron	very short wavelength electromagnetic wave
symbol	$^{4}_{2}He$ (α)	$^{0}_{-1}e$ (β)	(γ)
range in air	a few cm	a few metres	infinite
ionising ability	very strong	strong	weak
penetration (stopped by)	paper, skin	aluminium, a few cm of flesh/bone	reduced significantly by several m of lead/concrete
charge	+2e	−1e	0
mass (kg)	6.644×10^{-27}	9.109×10^{-31}	zero rest mass

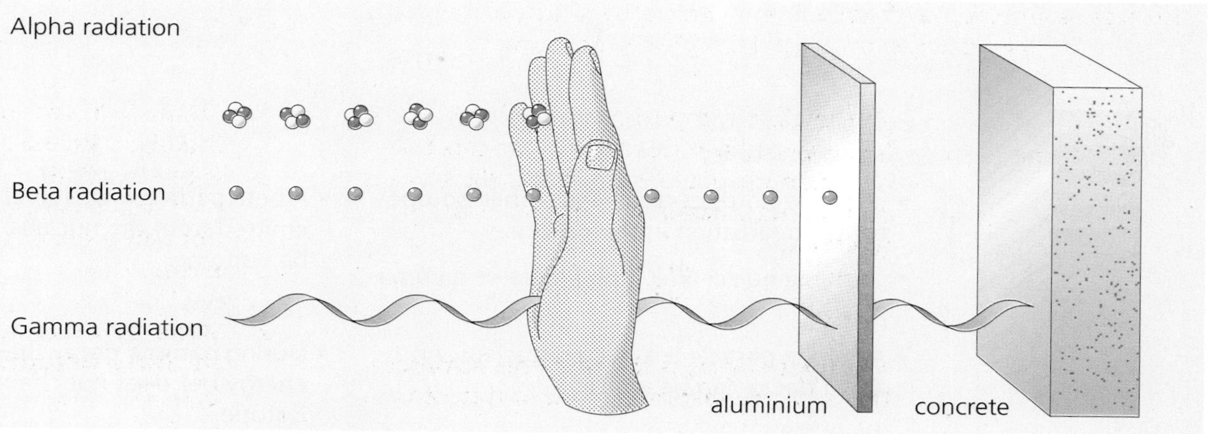
Alpha radiation
Beta radiation
Gamma radiation
aluminium
concrete

Fig. 3 Decay of uranium-238

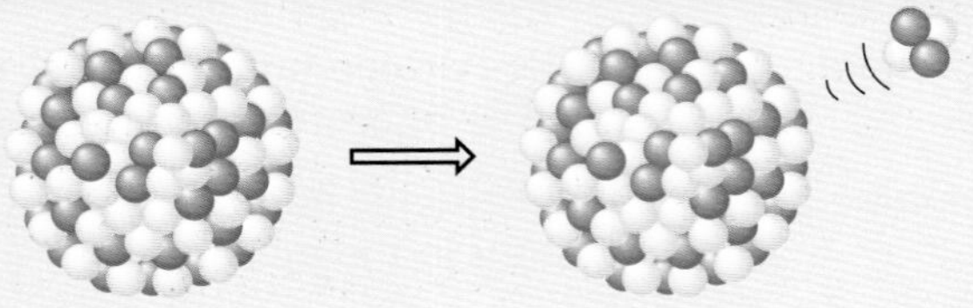

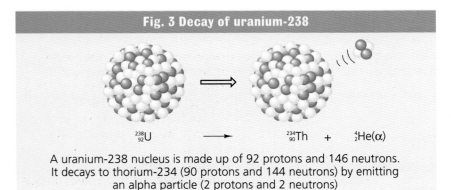

$^{238}_{92}U \longrightarrow {}^{234}_{90}Th + {}^{4}_{2}He(\alpha)$

A uranium-238 nucleus is made up of 92 protons and 146 neutrons. It decays to thorium-234 (90 protons and 144 neutrons) by emitting an alpha particle (2 protons and 2 neutrons)

The total number of nucleons (protons and neutrons) is not changed by a radioactive decay. This means that the nucleon number must balance on each side of the equation. The total charge is also unchanged by a decay, so the sum of the atomic numbers must balance on each side of the equation.

Fig. 4 Effect of electric and magnetic fields on types of radiation

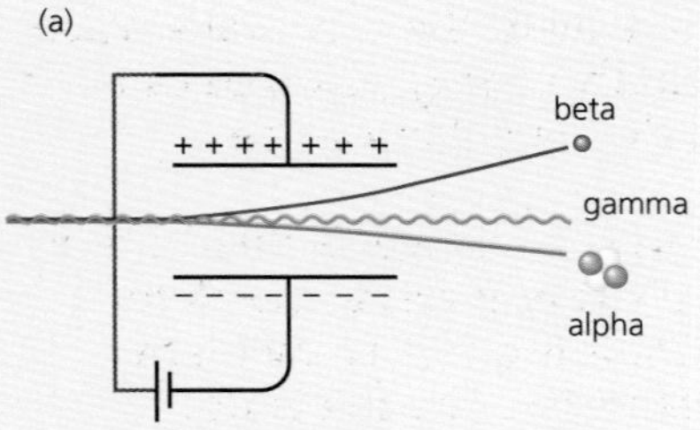

(a)
+ + + + + + +
beta
gamma
- - - - - - -
alpha

In an electric field, α particles are deflected towards the negatively charged plate; β particles are deflected towards the positively charged plate; gamma radiation is undeflected.

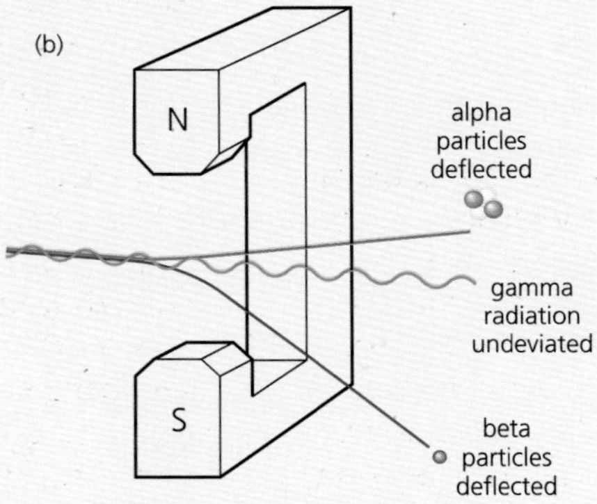

(b)
N
S
alpha particles deflected
gamma radiation undeviated
beta particles deflected

Charged α and β particles are deflected at right angles to the magnetic field; gamma radiation is undeflected.

Alpha decay

An alpha particle is formed from two protons and two neutrons tightly bound together. It is identical to a helium nucleus. Alpha particles are fired out at high speed from some unstable nuclei. Alpha emitters are not used in diagnosis but they can be used to treat cancer in the form of radium needles embedded in tumours. Radium-226 decays into radon, and this decay can be written:

$${}^{226}_{88}Ra \rightarrow {}^{222}_{86}Rn + {}^{4}_{2}He$$

Beta decay

Beta decay occurs when one of the neutrons in an unstable nucleus decays into a proton and an electron. The proton remains in the nucleus but the electron is emitted at very high speed. A beta decay can be written:

$${}^{A}_{Z}X \rightarrow {}^{A}_{Z+1}Y + {}^{0}_{-1}e$$

Gamma decay

Gamma decay arises from an energy change inside the nucleus. A gamma ray is a very short wavelength, electromagnetic wave. The nuclear structure is not changed by gamma decay.

Fig. 5 The ionising effect of radiation

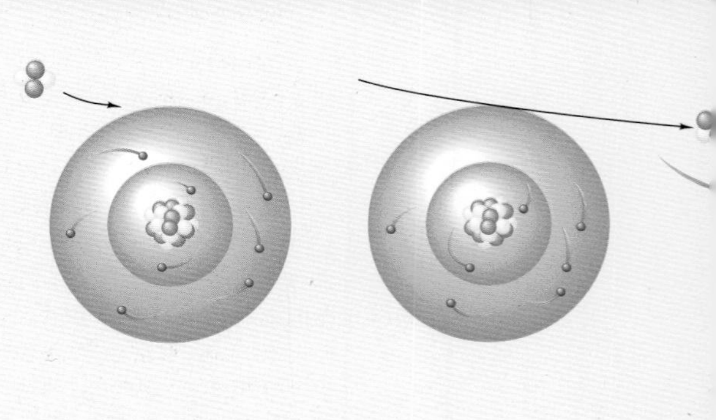

Key ideas

- Unstable isotopes decay into other isotopes, emitting radiation in the process.
- Unstable nuclei emit alpha, beta or gamma rays.
- An alpha particle is a helium nucleus. An alpha decay can be written:

  ${}^{A}_{Z}X \rightarrow {}^{A-4}_{Z-2}Y + {}^{4}_{2}He$

- A beta particle is a high energy electron emitted from the nucleus. A beta decay can be written:

  ${}^{A}_{Z}X \rightarrow {}^{A}_{Z+1}Y + {}^{0}_{-1}e$

- During gamma decay the nucleus loses energy but does not change to a different isotope.

Detecting radiation

One way to monitor radiation is to measure the **ionisation** it causes. The Geiger-Müller (Fig. 6) tube is capable of detecting a single ionisation. Each ionisation leads to a pulse of current which can be counted electronically.

Fig. 6 The Geiger-Müller tube

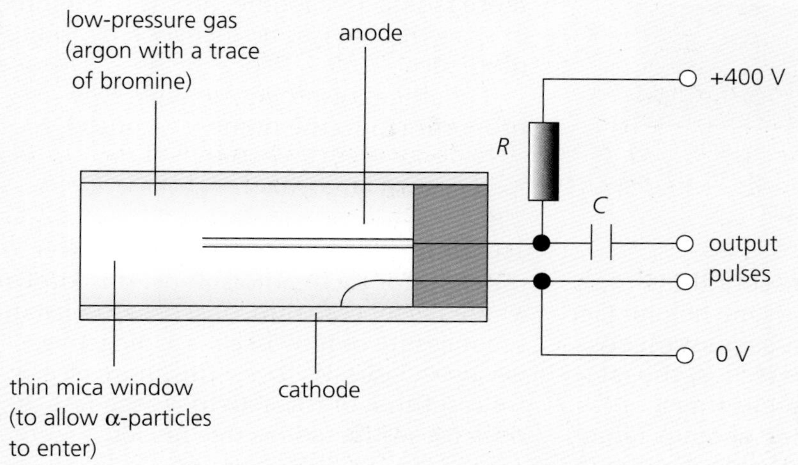

low-pressure gas
(argon with a trace
of bromine)
anode
+400 V
R
C
output
pulses
0 V
thin mica window
(to allow α-particles
to enter)
cathode

A potential difference across the tube of about 400 V creates a very strong electric field, particularly near the central anode.

When an alpha, beta or gamma ray enters the tube it may ionise a gas atom. The free electron produced is attracted towards the central anode. The liberated electron accelerates rapidly and soon has enough energy to ionise more gas atoms. As these free electrons move towards the anode they cause an 'avalanche' of ionisations. As many as 10^8 ionisations may occur in less than a microsecond. When the 'electron shower' reaches the anode it causes a small pulse of current to flow through the tube. The resulting voltage pulse is recorded.

While the electrons are rushing towards the anode, positive ions move slowly towards the cathode. A positive ion will accelerate gradually until it has gained enough energy to cause further ionisation. This could lead to further avalanches of charge. The tube could be discharging continuously, making it impossible to detect any more radiation. This electrical discharge is stopped by using bromine as a 'quenching' agent. If the positive ion collides with bromine molecules, its energy is used to break up the bromine molecule by dissociation rather than ionisation. The dissociated molecules later recombine. The positive ion reaches the cathode in about 100 microseconds without causing any more ionisations.

A Geiger-Müller tube counts the radiation passing through the tube, though it cannot differentiate between alpha, beta or gamma rays. Geiger-Müller tubes are very good at counting beta particles, but are rather poor at detecting alpha or gamma radiation. Most alpha particles are stopped by the tube walls, but the very thin mica window at the end of the tube allows some to be detected.

A Geiger-Müller tube may detect less than 1% of gamma rays because most gamma rays pass straight through the tube without causing any ionisation at all. Gamma rays can sometimes be detected because they eject electrons from atoms in the denser material of the tube walls. These 'secondary' electrons may go on to cause ionisation in the tube that can be recorded.

The main use of a Geiger-Müller tube is to monitor radiation levels to check for contamination. It is not very useful in medicine because the counter is not sensitive enough to γ-rays, nor does it respond quickly enough to produce images of radiation emitted from the body.

Radioactive decay

Radioactive iodine is used to diagnose thyroid disease. The thyroid gland uses iodine to manufacture thyroxin, a hormone that controls metabolism. A patient with a hyperactive thyroid gland will be over-active and will lose weight. A normal gland contains about 25% of the body's iodine, but a hyperactive gland may take up almost all of the available iodine. We can monitor the performance of the thyroid by measuring how quickly it takes up iodine. If a patient drinks a solution of sodium iodide, containing a small amount of radioactive iodine-131, a detector can be used to count the rate of gamma-ray emission from the thyroid over the next few hours. This count-rate can be plotted against time and compared with a curve for a normal thyroid (Fig. 7).

Fig. 7 Iodine-131 uptake

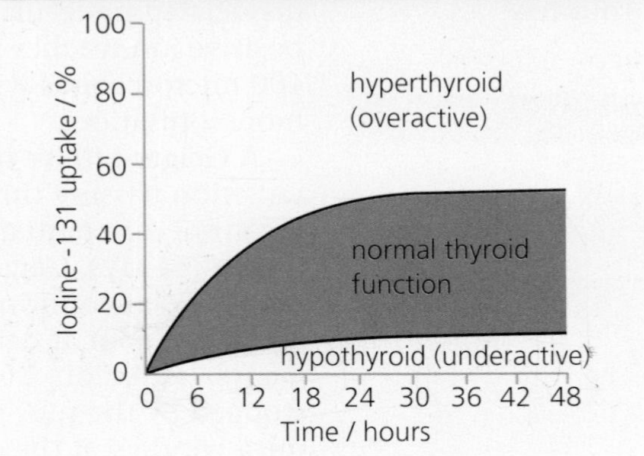

Iodine -131 uptake / %
100
80
60
40
20
0
hyperthyroid (overactive)
normal thyroid function
hypothyroid (underactive)
0 6 12 18 24 30 36 42 48
Time / hours

For a reliable diagnosis the count-rate must be accurate and repeatable. One helpful fact is that radioactive decay is a **spontaneous event**. It is not possible to change the rate of a nucleus of decay by subjecting a radioisotope to high pressure or temperature, or by using strong electric fields. Neither is it affected by chemical change. We can be sure that the count rate from the iodine will not be affected by its surroundings.

Radioactive decay is, however, a random event. There is no way of knowing exactly when a particular nucleus will decay. The most we can say is that the nucleus of a given radioisotope has a certain probability of decay in a given time. Radioactive decay is like playing dice. Although you never know exactly when you will get a six, you know that in every 6000 throws of the dice, roughly 1000 will show a six. In a radioisotope there are millions of nuclei, and though we don't know when individual nuclei will decay, we can still make an accurate prediction of the number of nuclei that will decay in each second.

The number of decays per second is known as the **activity**, measured in becquerel (Bq). One becquerel means one decay per second. The solution of sodium iodide given in thyroid examinations has an initial activity of around 2.0 MBq, 2.0×10^6 decays every second. The activity of the solution can be increased by adding more radioactive iodine, just as the number of sixes thrown can be increased by rolling more dice.

For all radioisotopes, activity, A, is proportional to the number of nuclei, N:

$$A \propto N \text{ or, } A = \lambda N$$

The constant of proportionality, λ, is different for each radioisotope. It is known as the **decay constant**. The decay constant is a measure of how likely a radioactive decay is (Table 3). To see this more clearly we can think of the activity as the rate of decrease of the radioactive nuclei.

$$A = -\frac{\Delta N}{\Delta t}$$

The number of radioactive nuclei always gets less, so ΔN is negative.

Eliminating A from the equation gives:

$$\lambda N = -\frac{\Delta N}{\Delta t}$$

$$\text{so, } \lambda = -\frac{\Delta N / N}{\Delta t}$$

The decay constant is the fraction of nuclei that decay every second. For any particular nucleus, λ is the probability that it will decay in one second.

Table 3 Radioisotope data

Radioisotope	Emission	Half-life	Decay constant (s^{-1})	Comments
^{5}helium	neutron	6×10^{-20} s	1.15×10^{19}	This stuff doesn't hang around!
^{99}technetium	gamma	6 hours	3.2×10^{-5}	Used in over 90% of nuclear medicine tests
^{131}iodine	beta, gamma	8.05 days	9.9×10^{-7}	Used in the diagnosis and treatment of thyroid disease
^{239}plutonium	alpha	24 000 years	9.2×10^{-13}	Nuclear waste product from fission reactors
^{238}uranium	alpha	4.5×10^{9} years	4.4×10^{18}	The most common naturally occurring uranium isotope

We can use this last equation to calculate the mass of radioisotope that needs to be given to a patient undergoing a thyroid examination. What mass of iodine-131 should be used if the patient needs to be given a solution with an initial activity of 2 MBq?

We must first calculate the number of atoms that are needed. The activity $A = 2$ MBq and $\lambda = 9.9 \times 10^{-7}\ s^{-1}$, so from:

$$A = \lambda N$$

$$N = \frac{A}{\lambda}$$

$$N = \frac{2 \times 10^6\ \text{Bq}}{9.9 \times 10^{-7}\ \text{s}^{-1}}$$
$$= 2 \times 10^{12}\ \text{atoms}$$

1 mole (6.022×10^{23} atoms) of iodine-131 has a mass of approximately 131 g.

Therefore, we need

$$\text{mass} = 2 \times 10^{12} \times \frac{131\ \text{g}}{6.02 \times 10^{23}}$$
$$= 4 \times 10^{-10}\ \text{g}$$

3 A 5×10^{-10} g dose of technetium-99 is given to a patient undergoing thyroid tests. Estimate the initial activity using data from Table 3.

Key ideas

- The number of decays per second is called the activity. This is measured in becquerel, Bq.
- Decay is spontaneous and random. The activity is proportional to the number of nuclei, N.
- $A = -\frac{\Delta N}{\Delta t} = \lambda N$, where λ is the decay constant.

Half-life

The use of iodine-131 in diagnosis has rapidly declined in the last few years, although it is still used to *treat* hyperactive thyroid glands. It has been largely replaced by a gamma emitter, technetium-99. One of technetium-99's major advantages is its decay rate. It decays slowly enough to allow sufficient time to carry out the investigation, but quickly enough so that the patient is not radioactive for the rest of the week.

A convenient measure of how quickly a radioisotope decays is its **half-life**. This is the time taken for half of its nuclei to decay. The half-life is also the time taken for the activity to drop to half of its initial value. For a given radioisotope sample, the half-life is the same, regardless of the initial activity of the sample.

The type of constant reduction shown in the graph is an *exponential decrease*. An equation can be used to link the activity, A, at time t, to the initial activity, A_0:

$$A = A_0 e^{-\lambda t}$$

where λ is the decay constant.

Fig. 8 Decay of Tc–99

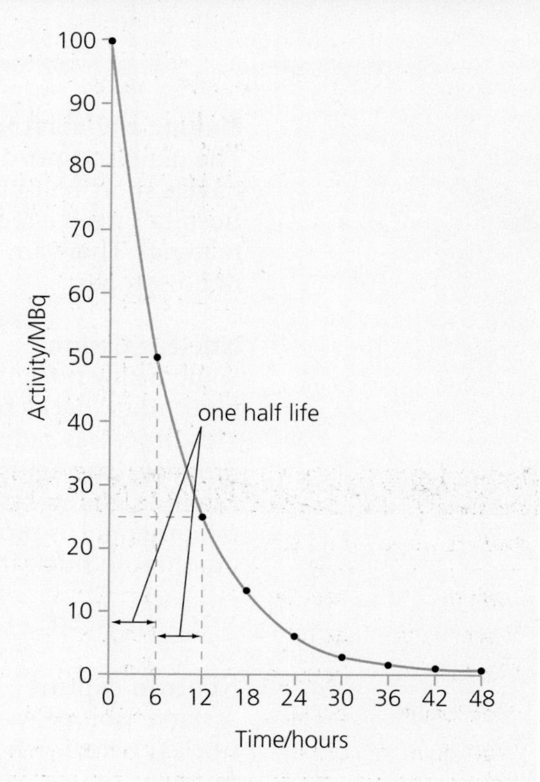

100
90
80
70
60
50
40
30
20
10
0
Activity/MBq
one half life
0
6
12
18
24
30
36
42
48
Time/hours

We can use logarithms to find out how the half-life of an isotope depends on its decay constant.

$$\text{From} \quad A = A_0 e^{-\lambda t}$$

$$\frac{A}{A_0} = e^{-\lambda t}$$

$$\ln\left(\frac{A}{A_0}\right) = \ln\ (e^{-\lambda t})$$

$$\text{As } \ln(e^x) = x, \quad \ln\left(\frac{A}{A_0}\right) = -\lambda t$$

$$\text{So, } t = -\frac{1}{\lambda}\ln\left(\frac{A}{A_0}\right)$$

When the activity drops to half of its original value then $A = 0.5\ A_0$, and $t = T_{1/2}$, the half-life:

$$T_{1/2} = -\frac{1}{\lambda}\ln 0.5$$

$$= \frac{\ln 2}{\lambda}$$

Radioactive isotopes suitable for use in nuclear medicine usually have half-lives of a matter of hours. Iodine-131 has a decay constant of $9.9 \times 10^{-7}\ s^{-1}$. Its half-life is therefore:

$$T_{1/2} = \frac{0.693}{9.9 \times 10^{-7}\ s^{-1}}$$

$$= 7 \times 10^5\ s\ (8.1\ days)$$

In fact, its *effective* half-life in the body is only about 6 days since we excrete some of the isotope. Even so, this is much longer than 99-technetium's half-life of 6 hours.

Key ideas

- The activity and the number of radioactive atoms decrease exponentially with time: $A = A_0 e^{-\lambda t}$ and $N = N_0 e^{-\lambda t}$
- Radioisotopes have a characteristic half-life, $T_{1/2}$, the time taken for the activity to drop to half its original value: $T_{1/2} = \frac{\ln 2}{\lambda}$

Making radioisotopes

The radioisotopes used in medicine usually have a short half-life. This means that hospitals need a regular supply of new material. There are four ways of producing radioisotopes:

Nuclear fission

Some heavy nuclei, like uranium or plutonium, decay by splitting into two. This process is called **fission** and the products may be useful radioisotopes. For example, caesium-137, which is used in radiotherapy, is produced by fission of uranium in nuclear fuel rods.

$${}^{235}_{92}U + {}^{1}_{0}n \rightarrow {}^{236}_{92}U \rightarrow {}^{137}_{55}Cs + {}^{95}_{37}Rb + 4\ {}^{1}_{0}n$$

Neutron capture

A stable isotope can be placed in a nuclear reactor where there are high numbers of free neutrons. The nucleus can capture a neutron and become radioactive. Sodium-24 is made in this way.

$${}^{23}_{11}Na + {}^{1}_{0}n \rightarrow {}^{24}_{11}Na + \gamma$$

Charged particle bombardment

Gallium-67 is a particularly useful radioisotope. Abnormal cells in tumours absorb the gallium-67 and show up on radiation scans. It can be produced in a charged-particle accelerator by bombarding zinc-68 with protons.

$${}^{68}_{30}Zn + {}^{1}_{1}p \rightarrow {}^{67}_{31}Ga + 2\ {}^{1}_{0}n$$

A radionuclide generator

Molybdenum-99 is produced in a nuclear reactor. It decays into technetium-99, which has a half-life of 6 hours and only emits gamma rays of a single energy. This makes it ideal for medical imaging (Fig. 9).

Fig. 9 Producing technetium-99

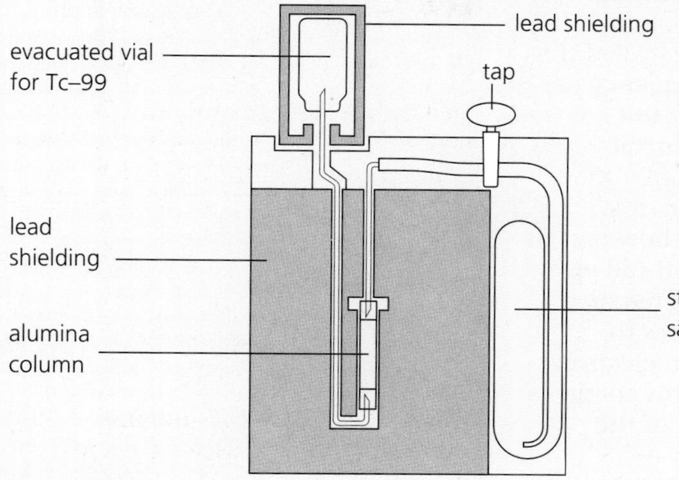
lead shielding
evacuated vial
for Tc–99
tap
lead
shielding
sterile
saline
alumina
column

Using radioisotopes as tracers

Small quantities of radioisotopes can be added to a material to allow us to trace its movements. This can be used to detect leakage, perhaps from underground water pipes. In medicine radioactive chromium is used to detect a small loss of blood into the intestines. Tracers can also be used to measure the amount of a fluid, such as blood or water, in a system. This technique is known as dilution analysis.

We can use dilution analysis to measure the volume of water in a central heating system. A solution labelled with the radioisotope sodium-24, half-life 15 hours, is added to the water in a central heating system. The initial activity of the solution is 1 MBq. The system is left for 10 hours to allow thorough mixing. A 10 cm^3 sample is then drawn off and its activity is measured. From this measurement we can calculate the total volume of water in the system.

Because sodium-24 is constantly decaying, the total activity in the system will have dropped from its initial value of 1 MBq. The new activity can be calculated.

$$T_{1/2} = \frac{\ln 2}{\lambda}$$

$$\lambda = \frac{\ln 2}{T_{1/2}}$$

$$= \frac{0.693}{15 \text{ hr}}$$

$$= 0.046 \text{ hr}^{-1}$$

$$A = A_0 e^{-\lambda t}$$

$$= 1 \times 10^6 \times e^{-0.046 \times 10}$$

$$= 0.63 \text{ MBq}$$

Suppose that the activity of the 10 cm^3 sample is 15 Bq, the total volume of water in the system must be $0.63 \times 10^6 / 15$ greater than the sample. Therefore the total volume of water in the system is 420 litres. A similar technique can be used to find the total amount of red blood cells in a patient.

12.3 Medical imaging

Scintillation detectors

The radioisotopes used in imaging are gamma emitters. Gamma rays interact with matter far less than alpha or beta rays. That means they can pass through materials without much interruption, allowing us to see deep into the body. It also means that they are more difficult to detect. Geiger counters are neither sensitive enough nor quick enough to be used for medical imaging.

Scintillators are substances that emit light when ionising radiation passes through them. The amount of light emitted is proportional to the energy of the ionising radiation. This means that a scintillation detector can count gamma rays and determine their energy, which helps us to construct an image of the radioisotope distribution in the patient.

A large, single crystal of sodium iodide is used as the scintillator in a modern gamma camera.

The photoelectric effect

Detecting emitted gamma rays is only the first stage in building up a radiation picture of the body. The brief flash of light from the scintillation crystal has to be converted to an electrical signal so that it can be recorded. The **photoelectric effect** is used to do this. The photoelectric effect occurs when light knocks electrons out of the surface of a metal.

Not all wavelengths of light give rise to the effect. For electrons to be emitted from a metal surface, the frequency has to be above a certain minimum value, called the **threshold frequency**. If the frequency of the light is below the threshold, the electrons remain bound to the metal surface. Each metal has a different threshold frequency. For sodium, it is 5.5×10^{14} Hz, which is in the yellow part of the spectrum. Blue or violet light can eject electrons from sodium, whereas red or orange light cannot. The light has to provide enough energy to rip an electron free from the metal's surface. This energy is known as the work function, ϕ, of the metal.

The discovery of the photoelectric effect in 1887 seemed to contradict the theory that light was a wave. The energy carried by a wave depends on its amplitude. A more energetic wave has a larger amplitude. This means a brighter light. However, light below the threshold frequency cannot dislodge electrons no matter how bright it is. Several intense red lasers will not prise a single electron from the zinc, whereas a feeble UV glow does so easily.

In 1900, Max Planck suggested that light was not a continuous wave, but instead comes in small 'packets' of light energy called **photons** (see Chapter 11). Planck said that the energy of a photon is proportional to frequency:

$$E = hf$$

where h is Planck's constant (6.63×10^{-34} J s) In 1905, Einstein extended this theory and derived an equation which describes the photoelectric effect. Einstein realised that light is not only *emitted* in discrete chunks or **quanta**, but it is also *absorbed* in them too. When a photon strikes a metal surface either all or none of its energy is absorbed. It is not possible to absorb part of a photon.

Below the threshold frequency, the photon does not have enough energy to free an electron. At the threshold frequency there is just enough energy to free the electron. Above the threshold frequency all of the photon's energy is absorbed. Some of this energy is used to liberate the electron from the surface and any energy left over goes into the kinetic energy of the electron.

Fig. 10 Discharging an electroscope

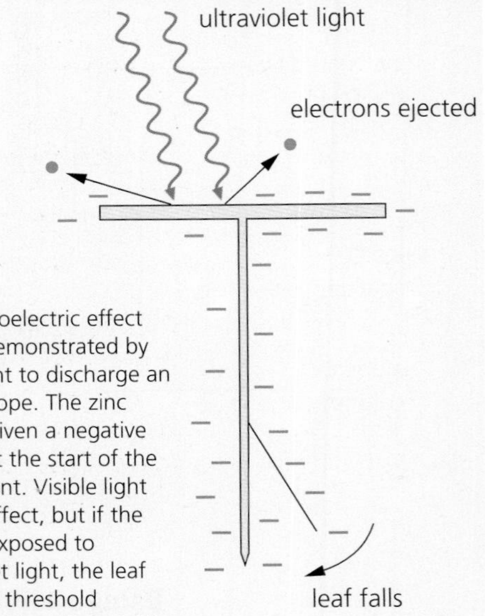
ultraviolet light
electrons ejected
leaf falls

The photoelectric effect can be demonstrated by using light to discharge an electroscope. The zinc plate is given a negative charge at the start of the experiment. Visible light has no effect, but if the plate is exposed to ultraviolet light, the leaf falls. The threshold frequency for zinc must be in the ultraviolet region of the spectrum.

Einstein expressed this in terms of energy conservation:

photon energy in = energy needed to remove the electron (work function) + kinetic energy of emitted electron

$$hf = \phi + E_k$$

The observed kinetic energy of an emitted electron may be less than E_k if it has come from below the surface of the metal.

Q 4 A particular metal surface has a threshold frequency in the blue part of the spectrum. Suppose you can measure the number of electrons emitted. What would you notice when the metal is exposed to;

a Faint red light? Bright red light?

b Faint blue light? Bright blue light? How would the maximum kinetic energy of the electrons alter in each case?

Key ideas

- The energy of a photon of light depends on its frequency, $E = hf$
- The energy needed to cause photoemission is called the work function, ϕ. $\phi = hf_T$ where f_T is the threshold frequency.
- If $E > \phi$, the excess energy goes into the kinetic energy of the electron, E_k. This is represented in Einstein's photoelectric equation: $hf = \phi + E_k$

The stopping voltage

When electrons are emitted from a metal by the photoelectric effect they have a range of kinetic energies up to a maximum value. This value depends on the frequency of light.

Robert Millikan devised an ingenious way of finding the maximum kinetic energy of the electrons. If the collecting electrode of a photocell is made slightly negative with respect to the photocathode it will repel the emitted electrons. Only the most energetic will reach the collecting electrode. The potential difference between the cathode and the collecting electrode can be gradually increased until all the electrons are stopped and the current drops to zero. The value of the p.d. when this happens is called the 'stopping voltage'.

Fig. 11 Millikan's photoelectric experiment

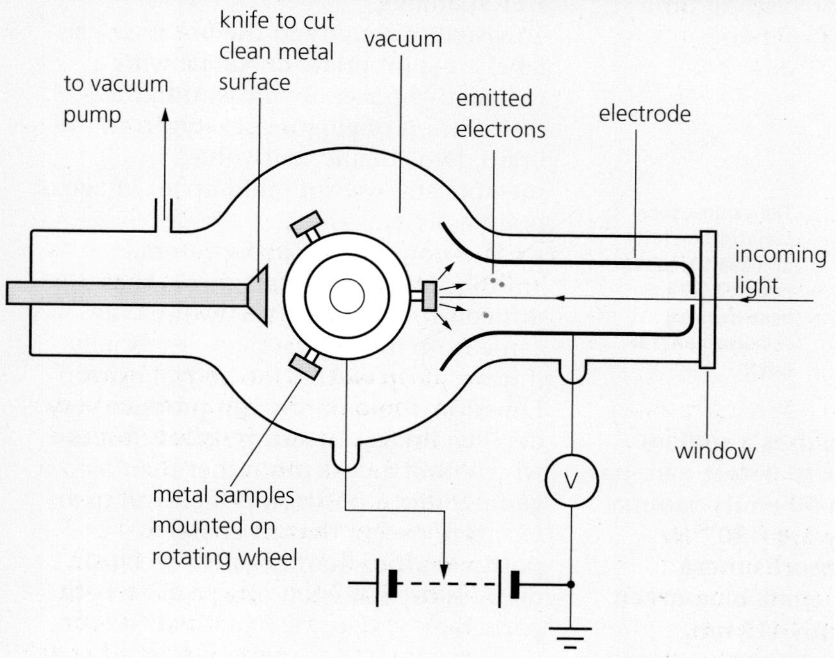

knife to cut clean metal surface
vacuum
to vacuum pump
emitted electrons
electrode
incoming light
window
V
metal samples mounted on rotating wheel

work done = charge × potential difference

The maximum kinetic energy of an electron = electron charge × stopping voltage

$$E = eV_{stop} = E_k$$
$$\text{and } hf = \phi + E_k$$
$$\text{so, } eV_{stop} = hf - \phi$$
$$V_{stop} = \frac{h}{e}f - \frac{\phi}{e}$$

A graph of V_{stop} vs. f is a straight line of gradient h/e with a y-axis intercept of $-\phi/e$ (Fig. 12).

Fig. 12 Stopping voltage

Graph of stopping voltage against frequency of incident light in Millikan's photoelectric experiment.

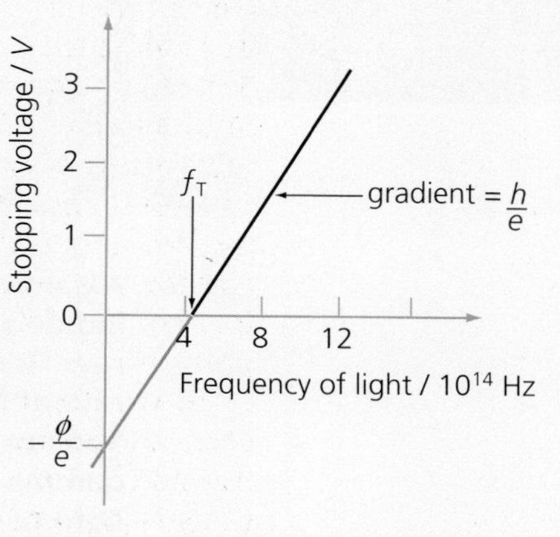

Stopping voltage / V
3
2
1
0
f_T
gradient = $\frac{h}{e}$
4
8
12
Frequency of light / 10^{14} Hz
$-\frac{\phi}{e}$

Fig. 13 Inside the gamma camera

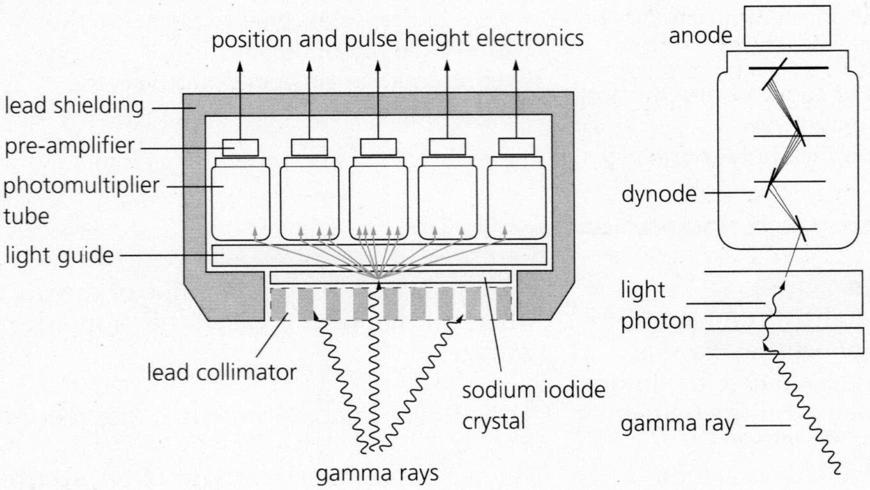
position and pulse height electronics
lead shielding
pre-amplifier
photomultiplier tube
light guide
lead collimator
sodium iodide crystal
gamma rays
anode
dynode
light photon
gamma ray

To produce an image we need to know where the gamma ray came from. The collimator only lets through gamma rays which are travelling at right angles to the crystal. An electron is emitted by the photoelectric effect at the cathode. The electron is accelerated through a potential difference and made to collide with another electrode where it knocks off a shower of secondary electrons. This process is repeated several times, amplifying the current by a factor of about 10^9, until the pulse is large enough to detect.
A single gamma ray has been detected.

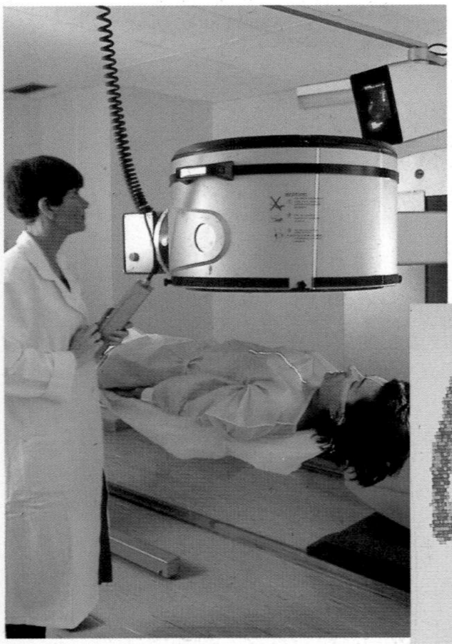

The gamma camera

When a gamma ray passes through the scintillator, a brief flash of light is emitted. The light is detected in photomultiplier tubes (Fig. 13) causing a pulse of electrical current. These pulses are analysed by the computer to reconstruct an image of the radiation coming from the patient.

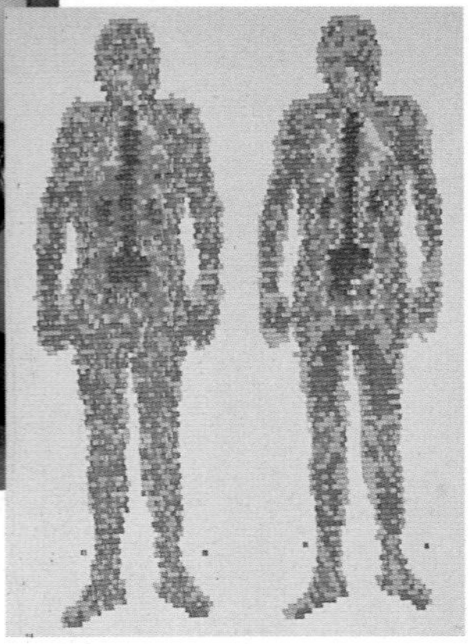

The gamma scan (scintigram, left) of a healthy person injected with a bone-seeking radioisotope (far left).

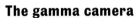

5 A gamma camera uses a sodium iodide scintillator to detect gamma rays. Technetium-99 emits gamma rays of frequency 3.4×10^{19} Hz. Sodium iodide absorbs these gamma rays and emits blue-green light of wavelength 415 nm. Calculate the energy of absorbed and emitted photons.

6 The photocathode in the photomultiplier tubes is made of a bi-alkali material, such as an alloy of caesium and potassium. What is the maximum possible value for the work function of this metal if it is to be used with a sodium iodide scintillator?

PET scanning

To visualise activity in the brain we can label an appropriate chemical with a radioactive tracer. By measuring the distribution of glucose or oxygen in the brain, two chemicals involved in metabolism, we can build up an image of brain activity.

The trouble with using gamma emitters for medical imaging is that it is difficult to tell where the gamma ray came from in the first place, especially if it was deep within the body. Positron Emission Tomography can produce very detailed images by using radioisotopes which emit a positron rather than a gamma ray. A positron is identical to an electron, except that its charge is positive rather than negative. Positron decay is the emission of a positive beta particle.

A positive electron is an example of anti-matter, whose existence was predicted by Paul Dirac in 1931. He thought that a positron would be pulled towards an electron by electrostatic attraction, and that no force existed which could keep them apart. When the anti-matter positron meets its conventional-matter twin, the electron, they are drawn together and annihilate each other. Mass is converted to energy, and two identical gamma rays are emitted in opposite directions.

Fig. 14 Matter and anti-matter

Beta decay

Carbon–14 is a beta emitter; one neutron decays into a proton and an electron:

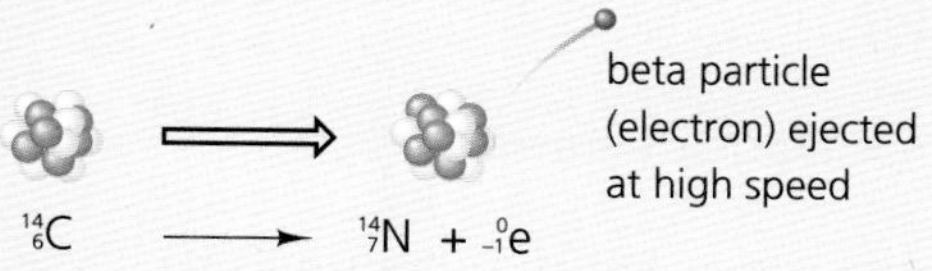

beta particle (electron) ejected at high speed
$^{14}_{6}C \longrightarrow {}^{14}_{7}N + {}^{0}_{-1}e$

Positron decay

Carbon–11 is an artificially produced positron emitter. When it decays a proton is transformed into a neutron and a positron:

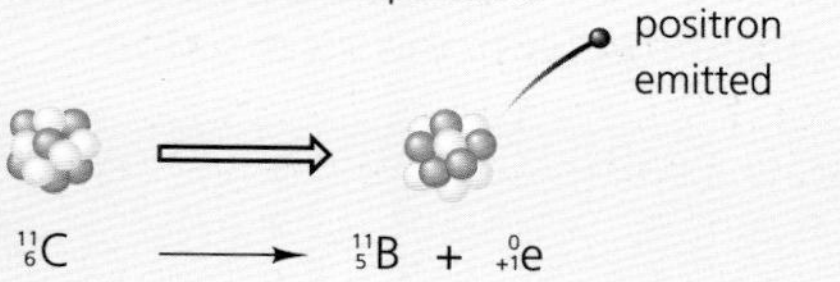

positron emitted
$^{11}_{6}C \longrightarrow {}^{11}_{5}B + {}^{0}_{+1}e$

Positron annihilation

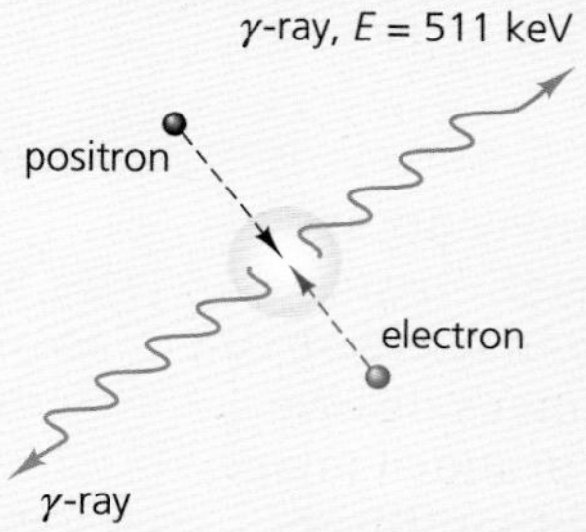

γ-ray, E = 511 keV
positron
electron
γ-ray

When a positron and an electron meet, they annihilate each other. Two identical gamma rays of energy 511 keV are emitted in opposite directions

In the body, a positron only travels about 1 mm before being annihilated. This makes it relatively easy to locate the site of the radioisotope. Scintillation counters placed around the patient are electronically linked to record coincidences, and therefore only detect gamma rays caused by annihilation (Fig. 15).

Carbon-11 is a positron emitter used in brain imaging. It is used to label carbon monoxide gas which the patient inhales. Carbon monoxide molecules attach themselves to the haemoglobin in red blood cells and are transported around the body. When the carbon-11 decays, it reveals areas of high blood flow which correspond to active regions in the brain. PET scans can show which areas are busy when the patient is reading, listening or just sitting with their eyes closed.

Fig. 15 Positron emission tomography

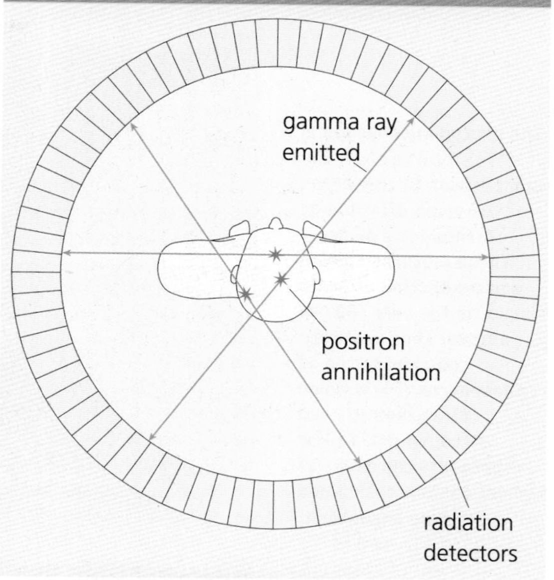

gamma ray emitted
positron annihilation
radiation detectors

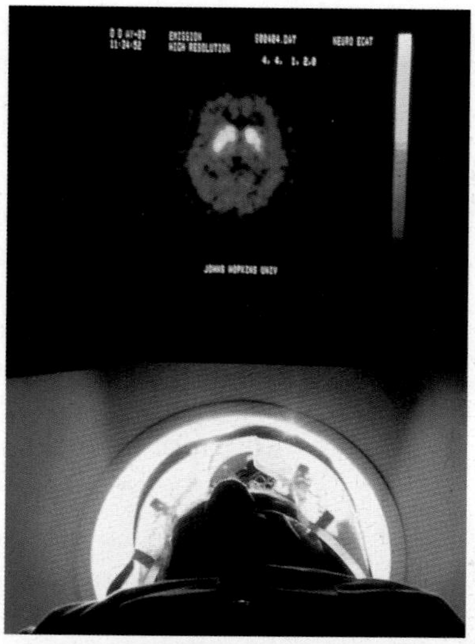

The patient is surrounded by the PET scanner's circular array of detectors. Data from these is processed by computer to produce a cross-sectional image of the brain.

The PET scan – revealing regions of activity in the brain.

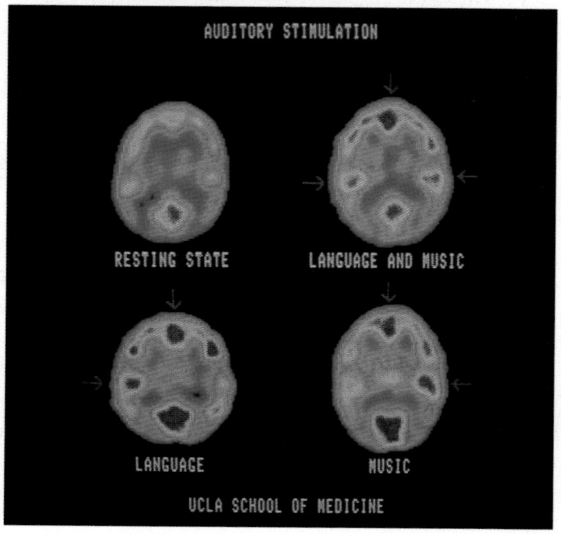

AUDITORY STIMULATION
RESTING STATE
LANGUAGE AND MUSIC
LANGUAGE
MUSIC
UCLA SCHOOL OF MEDICINE

12.4 Seeing with particles

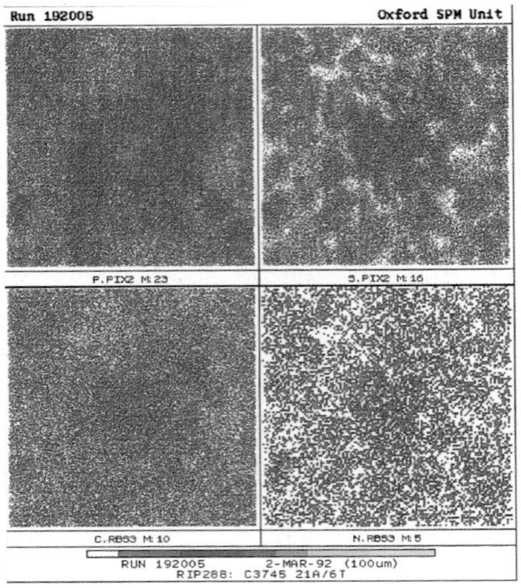

Run 192005
Oxford SPM Unit
P.PIX2 M:23
S.PIX2 M:16
C.RBS3 M:10
N.RBS3 M:5
RUN 192005 2-MAR-92 (100um)
RIP288: C3745 21A/6T

The proton microscope is able to show the composition of tiny areas of the brain affected by Alzheimer's disease. These pictures show a square section of brain tissue that is only 100 μm across. They show the concentration of phosphorus (P), sulphur (S), carbon (C) and nitrogen (N). Yellow represents the areas of highest concentration and blue the lowest.

Wave–particle duality

Some scientists at Oxford University have been looking at samples of brain tissue with a proton microscope to investigate the role of aluminium in Alzheimer's disease. The proton microscope can produce images that are much more detailed than those from an optical microscope.

The electron microscope has been used in medicine for years to allow us to see detailed biological structure, or the viruses and bacteria which cause illness.

In these techniques, electrons and protons behave like waves. In the photoelectric effect, light behaves like a particle. These are examples of **wave–particle duality**.

It is possible to carry out an experiment in which light behaves as a wave in one part of the apparatus, and as a particle in another (Fig. 16).

Fig. 16 Wave–particle duality experiment

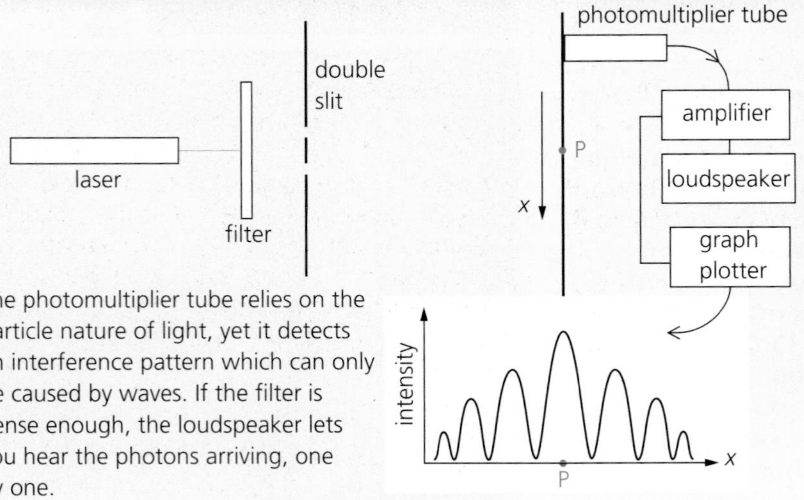

photomultiplier tube
double slit
amplifier
P
loudspeaker
laser
x
filter
graph plotter
intensity
P
x

The photomultiplier tube relies on the particle nature of light, yet it detects an interference pattern which can only be caused by waves. If the filter is dense enough, the loudspeaker lets you hear the photons arriving, one by one.

De Broglie waves

In 1924, the young prince Louis de Broglie wrote in his PhD thesis, 'all material particles have a wave nature.' He predicted that a particle of momentum p would have a wavelength λ given by:

$$\lambda = h/p,$$

where h = Planck's constant

De Broglie suggested that it should be possible to diffract electrons. Davisson and Germer confirmed this theory four years later when they successfully diffracted electrons through a crystal. Today this principle is used in electron microscopes.

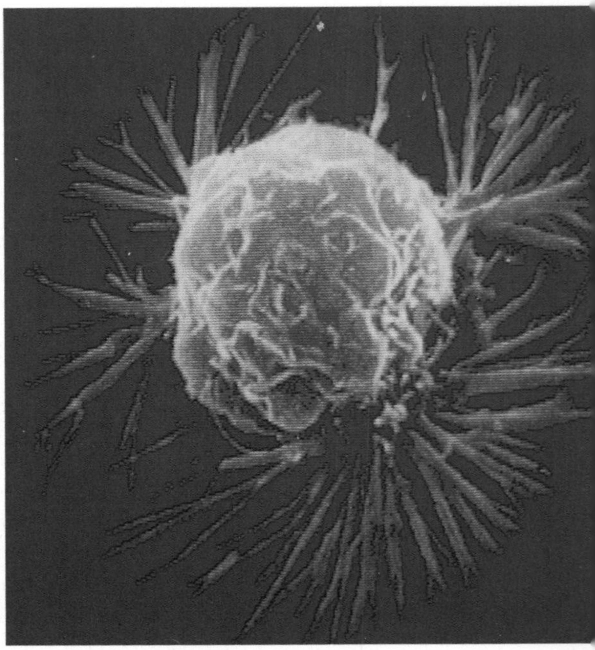

A false-colour electron micrograph of a human cancer cell.

Fig. 17 The electron diffraction tube

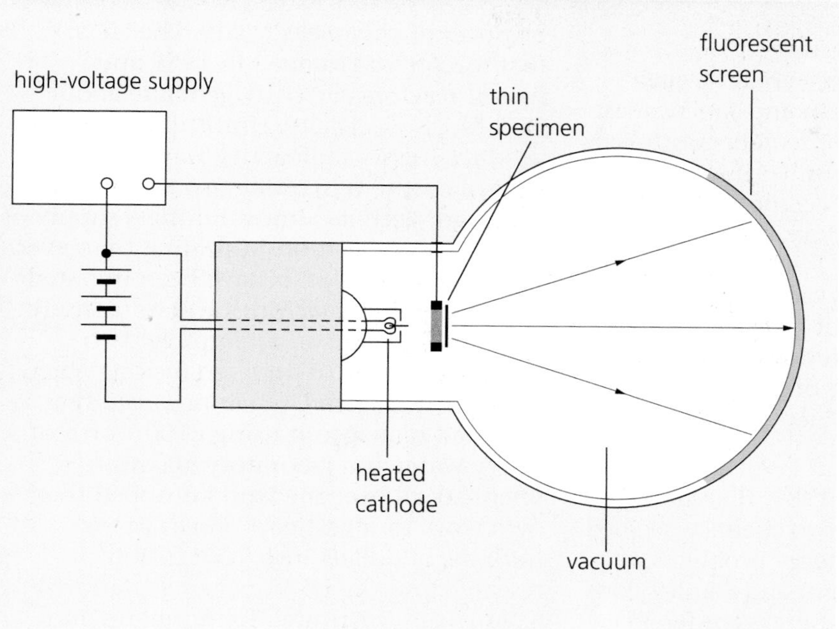

fluorescent screen
high-voltage supply
thin specimen
heated cathode
vacuum

An electron diffraction tube is a primitive form of electron microscope. The tube lacks focusing coils, so it just produces a diffraction pattern on the fluorescent screen (Fig. 17).

If we know the potential difference across the tube (in this case 5 kV), we can work out the de Broglie wavelength of the electrons. The energy gained by the electron:

$$E = q_e V$$
$$= 1.6 \times 10^{-19}\ \text{C} \times 5000\ \text{V}$$
$$= 8 \times 10^{-16}\ \text{J}$$

This is the electron's kinetic energy, so its velocity is approximately:

$$\tfrac{1}{2} m_e v^2 = 8 \times 10^{-16}\ \text{J}$$
$$v^2 = \frac{2 \times 8 \times 10^{-16}\ \text{J}}{9.1 \times 10^{-31}\ \text{kg}}$$
$$v = 4.2 \times 10^{7}\ \text{m s}^{-1}$$

The momentum of the electron is:

$$p = m_e v$$
$$= 9.1 \times 10^{-31}\ \text{kg} \times 4.2 \times 10^{7}\ \text{m s}^{-1}$$
$$= 3.8 \times 10^{-23}\ \text{kg m s}^{-1}$$

So the de Broglie wavelength of the electron is:

$$\lambda = \frac{h}{p}$$
$$= \frac{6.6 \times 10^{-34}\ \text{J s}}{3.8 \times 10^{-23}\ \text{kg m s}^{-1}}$$
$$= 1.7 \times 10^{-11}\ \text{m}$$

The de Broglie wavelength of a particle decreases as its momentum increases. An electron which is accelerated through a potential difference of 60 kV gains a momentum of about 1.3×10^{-22} kg m s^{-1}. This gives it a wavelength of about 0.005 nm, compared with an average value for visible light of about 500 nm. By looking at something with electrons, rather than light, we can improve the detail of the image 100 000 times.

Key ideas

- Interference and diffraction suggest that light is a wave, and the photoelectric effect suggests that light also behaves as a particle.
- Electrons and protons can be diffracted and show interference effects as if they were waves. All particles have a wavelength associated with them; the de Broglie wavelength is given by:

$$\lambda = \frac{h}{p}$$

13 Power from the nucleus

> **Nuclear fusion**
>
> **Scientists claim energy breakthrough**
> Two scientists from Britain and America last night claimed to have carried out controlled nuclear fusion in a test tube. If confirmed, their discovery could become the greatest breakthrough of the century.
>
> Professor Martin Fleischmann, of Southampton University, and Professor Stan Pons, of the University of Utah, released the results of research which could open the door to a limitless source of 'clean' energy.
>
> The Times, 24th March 1989

On Thursday 23 March 1989, the scientific world was shaken when two chemists seemed to have solved global energy problems at a stroke. Martin Fleischmann and Stanley Pons announced at a televised press conference that they had achieved nuclear fusion.

Since World War II, it has been fission, the splitting of the uranium atom, that has offered the nuclear industry's best prospect of cheap electricity. The UK's first reactor was opened in 1956 and fission reactors currently generate about 20% of UK electricity. Unfortunately, they produce highly radioactive waste and have proved costly to maintain, so the prospect of fusion, with its almost limitless supply of 'clean' energy, is more appealing than ever.

Millions of pounds have been invested in giant plasma machines and immensely powerful lasers in an attempt get two hydrogen nuclei to undergo fusion. When the two men from Utah announced that they had managed it using £100 worth of heavy water and laboratory glassware, scientists all over the world dropped their own work to investigate. Japan threw millions of dollars into 'cold fusion' research and the USA opened a 'National Cold Fusion Institute'. Fleischmann and Pons became media stars overnight. To understand why the announcement caused so much excitement we need to look closely at the physics behind nuclear power.

13.1 Learning objectives

After working through this chapter, you should be able to:

- **explain** the processes of nuclear fusion and nuclear fission;
- **use** the equation $E = mc^2$ to calculate the energy transfer in nuclear reactions;
- **describe** the main features of a nuclear reactor;
- **apply** the inverse square law to gamma sources;
- **recall** the main sources of background radiation.

13.2 Splitting the atom

The first public demonstration of the colossal power of the nucleus was the explosion of a uranium bomb over Hiroshima in August 1945. Three years earlier, Enrico Fermi and his team had achieved a controlled release of nuclear power when they built the world's first nuclear reactor at the University of Chicago. Inside this 'reactor', uranium nuclei were allowed to break up into smaller nuclei in a process called nuclear **fission**.

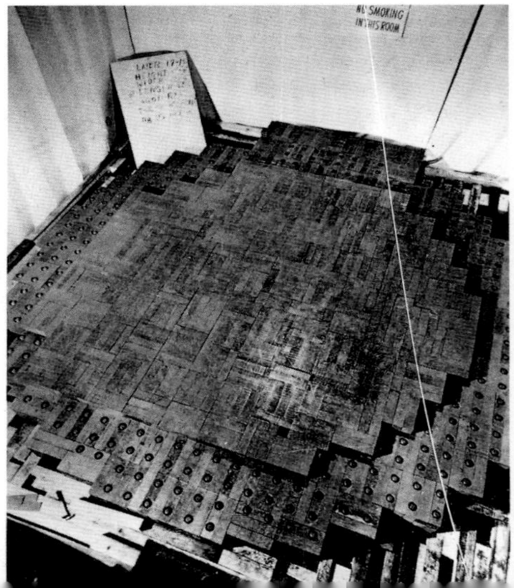
NO SMOKING IN THIS ROOM

Fermi called his reactor a nuclear pile; over 400 tonnes of graphite blocks and uranium rods were stacked together in a squash court.

Fission occurs in large, unstable nuclei which decay by splitting themselves completely in two. Isotopes which decay in this way are said to be fissile. One such isotope is uranium-235, which is used as the fuel in most nuclear reactors.

Uranium-235 (or ^{235}U) atoms can undergo **spontaneous** fission, but this is a relatively rare event. It would take over 700 million years for half of the atoms of a ^{235}U sample to decay. A nuclear reactor increases the fission-rate by bombarding the uranium with neutrons (Fig. 1).

When an atom of ^{235}U absorbs a neutron it changes to ^{236}U. This is a very unstable isotope that splits almost instantly into two fission products and a number of neutrons. It is a matter of chance which isotopes are created, though some are more likely than others.

The fission products and neutrons fly apart at high speed and their kinetic energy is eventually converted to electricity in a nuclear power station (Fig. 2). But where does the kinetic energy of the fission products and neutrons come from in the first place?

Fig. 1 The fission of uranium-235

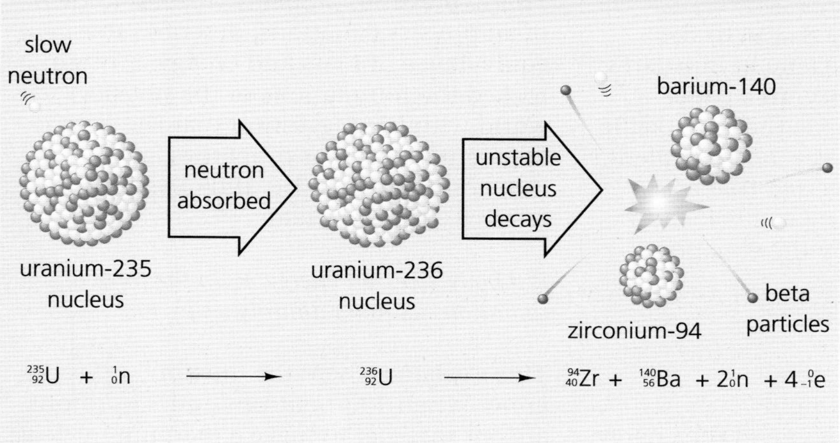
slow neutron
neutron absorbed
unstable nucleus decays
barium-140
uranium-235 nucleus
uranium-236 nucleus
zirconium-94
beta particles
$^{235}_{92}U + ^{1}_{0}n \longrightarrow ^{236}_{92}U \longrightarrow ^{94}_{40}Zr + ^{140}_{56}Ba + 2^{1}_{0}n + 4\,^{0}_{-1}e$

Fig. 2 Energy flow in a nuclear power station

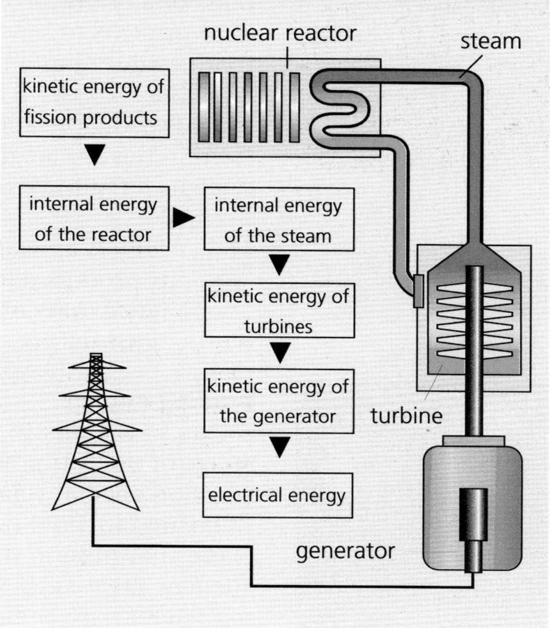
nuclear reactor
steam
kinetic energy of fission products
internal energy of the reactor
internal energy of the steam
kinetic energy of turbines
kinetic energy of the generator
electrical energy
turbine
generator

1 A fission of a uranium-235 nucleus (atomic number, $Z = 92$) can lead to the formation of xenon ($Z = 54$) and strontium ($Z = 38$). Write down an equation which describes this reaction.

Fig. 3 A representation of mass defect

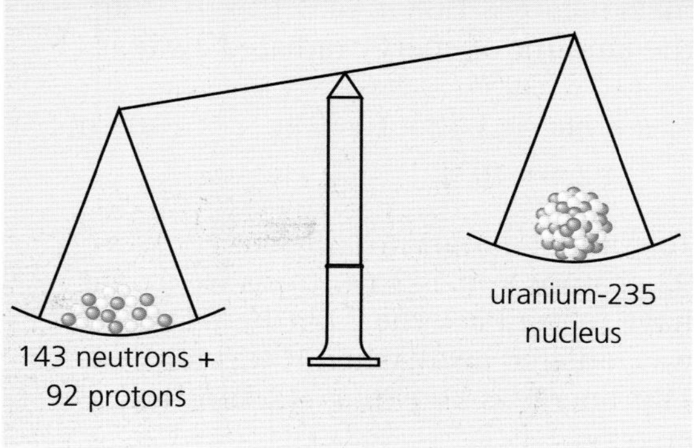
143 neutrons +
92 protons
uranium-235 nucleus

Mass defect

A peculiar kind of arithmetic applies to nuclear physics. If you add up the masses of several neutrons and protons, and then put them together to make a nucleus, you end up with less mass than you started with. A nucleus weighs less than the nuclear particles it is made from (Fig. 3).

The missing mass, or **mass defect**, is a very small quantity. Instead of using kilograms, or even grams, the mass defect is measured using the **atomic (or unified) mass unit**, *u*. One atomic mass unit is defined as being one-twelfth of the mass of a carbon-12 atom:

$$1u = 1.66043 \times 10^{-27}\ \text{kg}$$

A proton has a mass of 1.0073 u and a neutron has a mass of 1.0087 u (to 5 s.f.). Uranium-235 consists of 92 protons and 143 neutrons, so you might expect its total mass to be:

$$92 \times 1.0073\ u + 143 \times 1.0087\ u = 236.92\ u$$

However, accurate measurements give the mass of a uranium-235 nucleus as 235.04 u. Mass appears to have been 'lost'. We say that uranium has a mass defect of 236.92 u – 235.04 u = 1.88 u.

This principle applies to all nuclei. Iron-56 has a mass defect of 0.516 u, a gold nucleus has a mass defect of 1.637 u.

2 $^{239}_{94}$Pu is an isotope of plutonium that is produced in nuclear reactors. It has a mass of 239.052 u. Find its mass defect.

Albert Einstein

Binding energy

A clue to the missing mass, and to the secret of nuclear power, came in Einstein's work on **special relativity**. In a paper published in 1905 he made the remarkable claim that mass and energy are equivalent. His new mechanics suggested that a particle of mass m moving at a velocity v had an energy E given by the equation:

$$E = \frac{mc^2}{\sqrt{1 - v^2/c^2}}$$

where c = the velocity of light.
But Newtonian mechanics gives the energy of a moving mass as:

$$E = \tfrac{1}{2}mv^2$$

The Newtonian expression works very well in most situations. It is only for objects moving close to the speed of light that Einstein's expression for kinetic energy has to be used. At low velocities the two equations should be equivalent.

When the velocity, v, is much less than the speed of light, c, Einstein's equation gives:

$$E = \frac{mc^2}{\sqrt{1 - v^2/c^2}} = mc^2(1 - v^2/c^2)^{-1/2}$$

If $v << c$ we can use the binomial expansion, $(1 + x)^n \approx 1 + nx + \ldots$, to give:

$$E \approx mc^2(1 + \tfrac{1}{2}v^2/c^2) = mc^2 + \tfrac{1}{2}mv^2$$

Compare this with the Newtonian expression:

$$E = \tfrac{1}{2}mv^2$$

Einstein's equation has an extra term, mc^2. This represents a 'rest' energy that depends upon the mass of the object.

When the object is stationary (relative to the observer), $v = 0$, and Einstein's equation becomes:

$$E = mc^2(1 - v^2/c^2)^{-1/2} = mc^2$$

So: $E = mc^2$

This expression, probably the best known of all physics equations, describes the equivalence of mass and energy. Einstein rocked the foundations of the physics world with his suggestion that these two apparently different properties are interconvertible. In his 1905 paper on relativity, Einstein said:

If a body gives off energy, E, in the form of radiation, its mass diminishes by E/c²

This explains where the 'missing' mass has gone. When 143 neutrons and 92 protons are put together to make a uranium nucleus, some of the mass is 'radiated away' as energy. For a nucleus of uranium-235, the mass defect is 1.88 u, or 3.12×10^{-27} kg, so the amount of energy radiated away is:

$$E = mc^2 = 3.12 \times 10^{-27}\ \text{kg} \times (3 \times 10^8\ \text{ms}^{-1}) = 2.8 \times 10^{-10}\ \text{J}$$

To convert a uranium nucleus back to 92 protons and 143 neutrons we would have to put back the 2.8×10^{-10} J that was radiated away when it was formed. This energy is known as the **binding energy**:

$$\text{binding energy} = \text{mass defect} \times c^2$$

Because the amounts of energy are comparatively small, binding energy is usually given in electronvolts, rather than joules. Since one electronvolt = 1.6×10^{-19} J, the binding energy of $^{235}U = 1.749 \times 10^{9}$ eV.

When a uranium nucleus *splits* into two smaller nuclei, the total mass of the fission products is *less* than the original uranium nucleus. The mass difference has been converted to energy. This is the source of the energy released by nuclear fission.
In the fission reaction

$$^{235}_{92}U + ^{1}_{0}n \rightarrow ^{236}_{92}U \rightarrow ^{94}_{40}Zr + ^{140}_{56}Ba + 2\,^{1}_{0}n + 4\,^{0}_{-1}e$$

the total mass was originally

$$235.044\ u\ (^{235}U) + 1.009\ u\ (^{1}_{0}n) = 236.053\ u$$

After the fission the mass is:

$$93.906\ u\ (Zr) + 139.91\ u\ (Ba) + 2 \times 1.009\ u\ (^{1}_{0}n) + 4 \times 0.00055\ u\ (^{0}_{-1}e) = 235.836\ u$$

The mass defect is 0.217 *u*, an energy release of 200 MeV per fission. This is a huge energy output compared with even the most energetic chemical reactions.

3 What is the binding energy of a plutonium-239 nucleus? (give your answer in eV).

4 Calculate the energy released by the fission of ^{239}Pu in the reaction:

$$^{239}_{94}Pu + ^{1}_{0}n \rightarrow ^{240}_{94}Pu \rightarrow ^{87}_{35}Br + ^{150}_{60}Nd + 3\,^{1}_{0}n + ^{0}_{-1}e$$

Nuclear masses: $^{239}Pu = 239.052\ u$, $^{87}Br = 86.922\ u$, $^{150}Nd = 149.920\ u$

5 Einstein's special theory of relativity works both ways. If you put energy *into* an object it will increase its mass. Why don't you notice the gain in mass of a kettle when you are making a cup of tea? (It takes about 400 kJ to boil a kettle of water.)

Nuclear stability

We can not only release energy by splitting a heavy nucleus; it is also possible to release energy by fusing two lighter nuclei. The idea of binding energy can be used to explain this.

The binding energy of a nucleus tells us how much energy is required to pull it to pieces. The more energy that is needed, the more stable the nucleus is likely to be. The average energy needed to pull out each proton and neutron is known as the binding energy per **nucleon**. For uranium, the binding energy per nucleon is:

$$\frac{1800\ \text{MeV}}{235} = 7.6\ \text{MeV}$$

Fig. 4 Relationship between binding energy and mass number

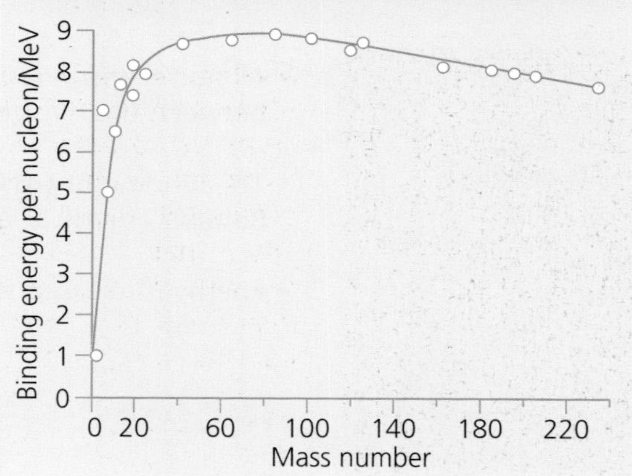

Binding energy per nucleon/MeV
0
1
2
3
4
5
6
7
8
9
0 20
60
100
140
180
220
Mass number

The value of binding energy per nucleon varies with atomic number and has a maximum value at iron-56 (Fig. 4). Iron-56 has the most stable nucleus. A nucleus will increase its stability, and release energy, if a reaction brings it closer to iron-56. There are two ways that this can happen:

(a) Nuclei which are heavier than iron can increase their stability by breaking up into lighter isotopes. This is exactly what happens in nuclear fission.

(b) Nuclei which are lighter than iron can increase their stability by amalgamating with others to form a heavier isotope. This is what happens in nuclear fusion.

6 Why can't we get energy by splitting a carbon nucleus into smaller pieces?

Energy from fusion

Before World War II, scientists had realised that it would be possible to release energy by fusing hydrogen nuclei together to make helium. The energy released by this fusion reaction can be calculated by finding the mass defect.

Helium can be formed by the fusion of two hydrogen isotopes, deuterium ^2_1H, and tritium ^3_1H:

$$^2_1H + ^3_1H \rightarrow ^4_2He + ^1_0n$$

The original mass was:
$2.0141\ u\ (^2_1H) + 3.0160\ u\ (^3_1H) = 5.0301\ u$
After the reaction the mass is:
$4.0026\ u\ (^4_2He) + 1.0087\ u\ (n) = 5.0113\ u$

This is a mass defect of $5.0301\ u - 5.0113\ u$

$= 0.0188\ u$
$= 0.0188 \times 1.6604 \times 10^{-27}$ kg
$= 3.1216 \times 10^{-29}$ kg

The energy released is given by $E = mc^2$

$= 3.1216 \times 10^{-29} \times (2.9979 \times 10^8)^2$
$= 2.81 \times 10^{-12}$ J (about 18 MeV)

Fusion is capable of much greater energy output per kilogram of fuel than fission. One kilogram of deuterium and tritium fuel could produce about 1.2×10^{26} fusion reactions. This would release about 3.4×10^{14} J, enough energy to satisfy the UK's electricity requirements for several hours!

Key ideas

- All nuclei weigh less than the combined mass of their protons and neutrons. The difference between the mass of a nucleus and the mass of its constituents is the mass defect.
- The binding energy is the energy needed to split the nucleus back into its constituents. Binding energy, *E*, and mass defect, *m*, are related by the equation $E = mc^2$.
- Energy is released when heavy nuclei decay by fission or when light nuclei fuse.

13.3 Nuclear fission

Nuclear power and radioactivity

By 1989, when cold fusion hit the headlines, nuclear fission reactors were becoming more and more unpopular. The storage of nuclear waste was proving to be a major problem and the costs of nuclear technology were continuing to rise. The promise of cheap electricity had not been fulfilled. In addition, the tragedy at Chernobyl in 1986 convinced a sceptical public that nuclear power was dangerous as well as expensive.

Russian helicopter pilots flew 1800 missions over the reactor, dropping sand, boron and lead in an attempt to contain the fire and radioactive materials.

During a test, the power output of the Russian reactor surged to a point where the cooling system could not cope and the water boiled out of control. Rather like a huge pan of boiling water, the reactor blew off its lid. The 2500 tonne concrete shield tilted, lifted and fell back into the reactor. This caused a second explosion and fires which destroyed the core of the reactor. The reactor burnt for 10 days, scattering radioactive isotopes into the atmosphere.

A cloud of radioisotopes was blown westwards over Russia, towards Scandinavia and then the UK. Later that week, radioactive rain fell over North Wales and the Lake District.

Eight years later, almost half a million sheep were still subject to radiological controls. In tests, the measured radiation levels are compared with **background radiation**, the radiation that was present before Chernobyl. Background radiation comes from a range of different sources.

Background radiation

Fig. 5 Sources of background radiation

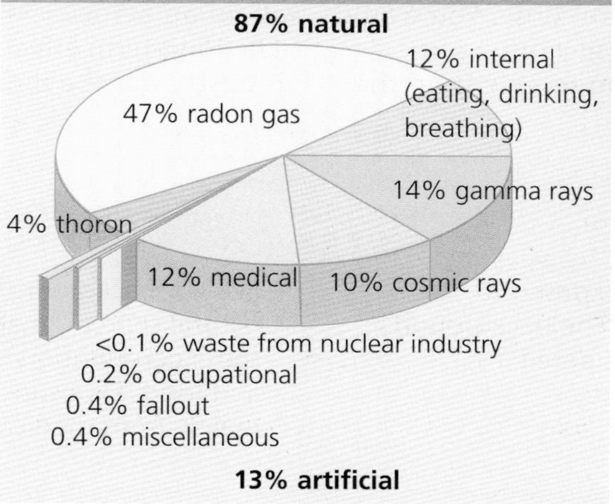

87% natural
12% internal (eating, drinking, breathing)
47% radon gas
14% gamma rays
4% thoron
12% medical
10% cosmic rays
<0.1% waste from nuclear industry
0.2% occupational
0.4% fallout
0.4% miscellaneous
13% artificial

g. 6 The uranium-238 decay series

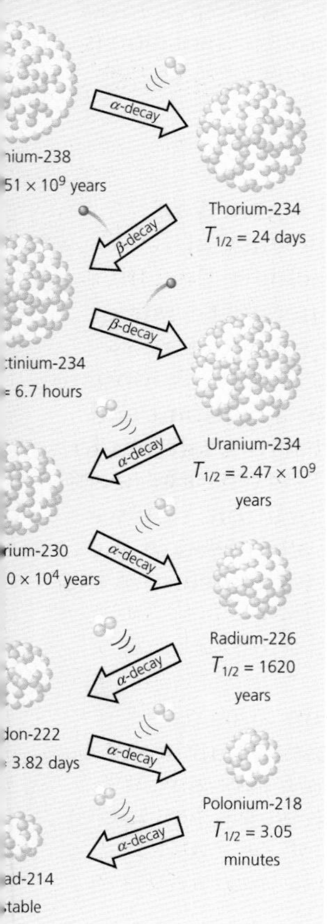

α-decay
ium-238
51 × 10⁹ years
Thorium-234
$T_{1/2}$ = 24 days
β-decay
β-decay
tinium-234
= 6.7 hours
α-decay
Uranium-234
$T_{1/2}$ = 2.47 × 10⁹ years
rium-230
0 × 10⁴ years
α-decay
Radium-226
$T_{1/2}$ = 1620 years
α-decay
don-222
3.82 days
α-decay
Polonium-218
$T_{1/2}$ = 3.05 minutes
α-decay
ad-214
table

The world is naturally radioactive. Every day, we are exposed to radiation from the air, food and the buildings around us. About 87% of the average radiation dose in the UK is due to natural radioactivity (Fig. 5). Most of this comes from radon gas, part of the uranium-238 decay series (Fig. 6).

Exposure to radon is high in areas like Cornwall, where there are large deposits of uranium-bearing rock. In the open air, radon is soon dispersed and poses no threat, but it can seep into houses where the concentration builds up. In modern houses, ventilation tends to be poor, and measures have been taken in high-risk areas to prevent radon from accumulating. Radon's decay products attach themselves to dust particles in the air, which are then inhaled. Some of these radioisotopes have short half-lives and they irradiate the lungs as they decay. Thoron gas is another source of radiation dosage to the lungs.

Cosmic rays are high-energy particles that come from the Sun and from outside the solar system. They are affected by the Earth's magnetic field, so more reach the poles than the equator.

The Aurora Borealis occurs when charged particles from space (cosmic rays) are accelerated by the Earth's magnetic field.

The atmosphere absorbs cosmic rays, so the radiation dose is less at sea-level than at high altitude. You receive an extra radiation dose every time you travel by air, though the effect is small. Concorde flies much higher than subsonic aircraft, so its crew are exposed to more cosmic radiation, approximately doubling their annual dose from all other causes.

Uranium and thorium in rocks and building materials add to our gamma-ray dose. Even food contributes to our radiation dose; coffee and brazil nuts are particularly radioactive.

The most common radioisotope in our bodies is potassium-40. The amount retained varies with the amount of muscle in the body.

Medicine is by far the biggest source of artificial radiation and this is largely due to **X-rays**. Most common X-ray procedures involve low radiation doses. Higher-dose procedures, such as stomach X-rays, still pose only a low risk to health.

Atmospheric testing of nuclear weapons has led to a measurable increase in background radiation. Comparatively small doses of plutonium-239, strontium-90 and caesium-137 have all been distributed by bombs and are now in the food chain.

The contribution made by discharges from the nuclear industry is less than 0.1% of our average total radiation dose. You would get more radiation during a one hour aircraft journey than you receive from the nuclear industry in a whole year. However, in particular places the dose can be much higher.

In Cumbria, near the Sellafield reprocessing plant, caesium-137 discharged into the sea became concentrated in fish. This led to an increased dose to some people in the early 1980s.

The explosion at Chernobyl distributed radioactive iodine and caesium over northern Europe. Because it rained on May 2nd when the radioactive cloud passed over Wales and the Lake District, caesium-137 was deposited on the grass and entered the food chain. The average dose to the UK population as a whole was fairly small – about an extra 2% over the next 50 years. The long-term effect on the nuclear industry may be more dramatic.

Key ideas

- We are all continually exposed to background radiation. The background count needs to be considered in radioactivity experiments.
- 87% of background radiation comes from natural sources, mainly radon gas, with some contribution from cosmic rays, rocks and food. Exposure to artificial radiation is mainly from medical sources.

Nuclear reactors

Advanced Gas-cooled Reactors (AGRs) supply most of Britain's nuclear electricity.

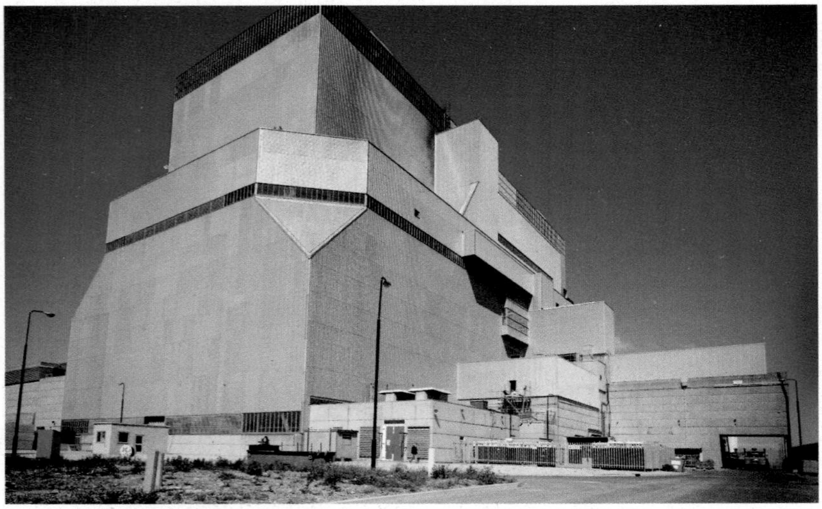

The Advanced Gas-cooled Reactor, Hinkley Point 'B'.

They can generate about 600 MW of electrical power at an efficiency of approximately 35%. To achieve this, the reactor has to produce energy at a rate of around 1700 MW. Since each fission releases about 200 MeV, 5×10^{13} fissions are required each second. For a constant and safe power output this reaction rate has to be carefully controlled. Every fission needs a collision with a 'slow' neutron, so if we can control the number and speed of the neutrons in the reactor, we can control the power output.

The chain reaction

Every time that a uranium nucleus decays by fission it releases a number of free neutrons. If these go on to cause further fissions a chain reaction will be established (Fig. 7).

Fig. 7 A chain reaction

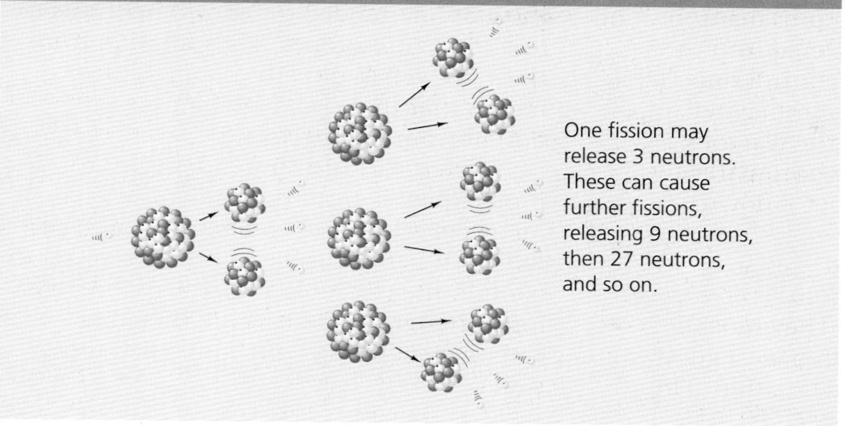
One fission may release 3 neutrons. These can cause further fissions, releasing 9 neutrons, then 27 neutrons, and so on.

In an AGR it takes around 1 ms for a neutron released by one fission reaction to cause another. If each fission released three neutrons, there would be 81 neutrons 4 ms later. If this process went on unchecked there would be a huge release of energy in a very short time.

7 If the chain reaction described above carried on for just $\frac{1}{20}$ of a second how much energy would be released?

The control rods

Not all the neutrons released by a reaction go on to cause another fission. To do that they have to be absorbed by another ^{235}U nucleus. There are a number of other things which can happen to the neutron (Fig. 8).

If the amount of uranium is too small, most of the neutrons will escape from its surface before they have caused any more fissions. There is a minimum mass, called the **critical mass**, which is needed before a chain reaction can take place. This mass depends upon the shape and purity of the uranium. In a reactor, the uranium fuel rods are all *below* the critical mass, but they are arranged so that neutrons from one rod may cause fission in an adjacent one (Fig. 9).

Fig. 8 The fate of fission neutrons

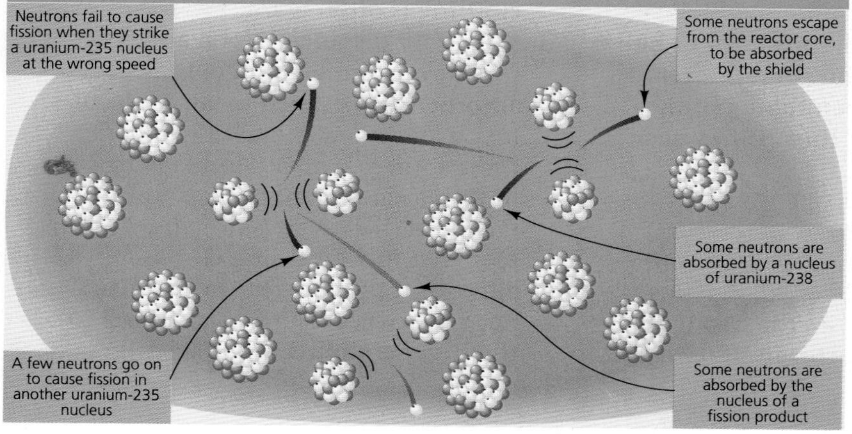
Neutrons fail to cause fission when they strike a uranium-235 nucleus at the wrong speed
Some neutrons escape from the reactor core, to be absorbed by the shield
Some neutrons are absorbed by a nucleus of uranium-238
A few neutrons go on to cause fission in another uranium-235 nucleus
Some neutrons are absorbed by the nucleus of a fission product

Fig. 9 Neutrons in a nuclear reactor

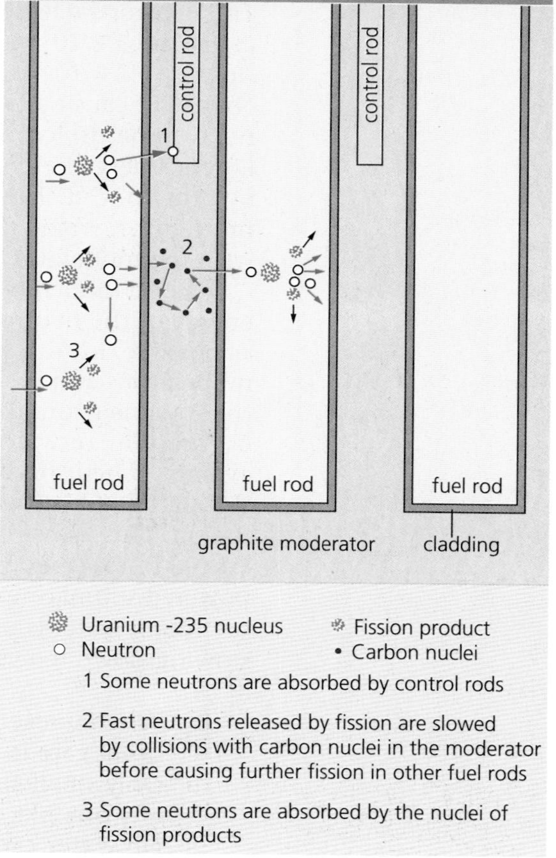
control rod
control rod
1
2
3
fuel rod
fuel rod
fuel rod
graphite moderator
cladding
Uranium -235 nucleus
Fission product
Neutron
Carbon nuclei
1 Some neutrons are absorbed by control rods
2 Fast neutrons released by fission are slowed by collisions with carbon nuclei in the moderator before causing further fission in other fuel rods
3 Some neutrons are absorbed by the nuclei of fission products

It can be quite difficult to sustain the chain reaction. Natural uranium is 1% fissile ^{235}U and 99% non-fissile ^{238}U, so fuel rods are made from enriched uranium which has a higher proportion of ^{235}U atoms. Even so, many neutrons will be absorbed by uranium-238 or by the fission products from previous reactions. These are called 'reactor poisons', as they soak up neutrons and kill off the chain reaction. On average, only one neutron from each fission should cause a further fission. Control rods are used to prevent the number of neutrons from becoming too large, enabling the reactor to run at constant power.

Control rods are usually made from a boron-steel alloy that absorbs neutrons. The rods can be raised or lowered into the reactor. A second set of control rods is held out of the reactor by electromagnets. If a power failure threatens the reactor's cooling system, the rods automatically drop in and shut the reactor down.

Moderation

The neutrons released from fission travel at around 1×10^7 m s^{-1}. They must be slowed to 2×10^3 m s^{-1} to have a good chance of causing another fission. The neutron has to lose 99.99975% of its kinetic energy before it can be absorbed by other nuclei. This is done in the **moderator**, where the neutron collides with the moderator atoms.

A good moderator reduces the kinetic energy of the neutron in as few collisions as possible. Ideally, the mass of the moderator's atoms should be the similar to that of a neutron. In practice, most reactors use graphite or water as a moderator. On average, a neutron will travel 0.191 m through graphite before it can cause a new fission. This 'slowing-down' length is crucial in reactor design. In a nuclear-powered submarine, where space is at a premium, water is used as a moderator. Its slowing-down length is only 0.053 m.

8 When unused uranium fuel is stored, great care is taken to ensure that
i Only small amounts are stored in any one place.
ii No water can enter the storage areas.
Explain why these safety rules help to prevent fission.

9 The uranium fuel rods have to be removed from the reactor after several years, even though only a small fraction of the ^{235}U has been used. Why?

Radiation safety

The high-energy neutrons that are emitted by a nuclear reactor are very dangerous. Neutron irradiation causes the casing and building around the reactor itself to become radioactive. The gas coolant and the graphite moderator absorb neutrons to become radioisotopes. The radiation from these, as well as directly from fission, means that there is a high gamma-ray output from the reactor.

The reactor shielding is designed to protect people from this radiation. Several metres of reinforced concrete are used as a radiation barrier, and as a pressure vessel to contain the gas coolant. Because concrete loses strength as it heats up, there is a carbon-steel lining which is cooled using water.

Workers must wear protective clothing in radioactive environments.

Occasionally it is necessary for people to work in radioactive areas. It is vital that they observe safety rules:

1. Work quickly: This will reduce the total radiation dose.
2. Work cleanly: Disposable protective clothing is often worn.
3. Keep your distance: Alpha and beta rays have a limited range; they get absorbed or scattered by air molecules. If you stay a few metres away from these sources, you are unlikely to receive a significant dose. Gamma radiation, however, is not absorbed or scattered much by air so it has an almost infinite range. The **intensity** decreases with distance according to the **inverse square law** (Fig. 10).

Fig. 10 The inverse square law

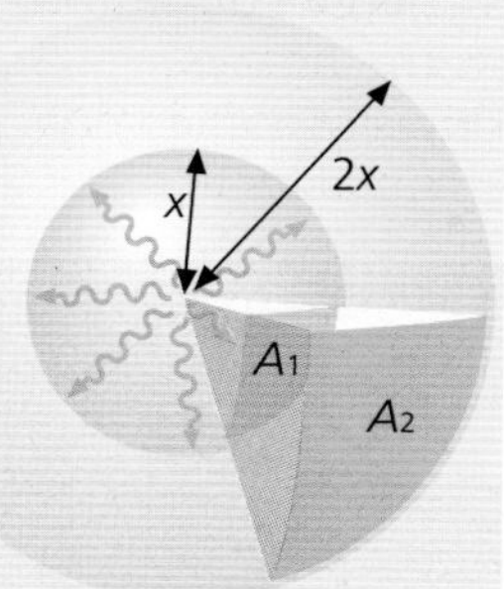
x
2x
A1
A2

The same gamma rays pass through both A_1 and A_2. A_2 is at twice the radius of A_1, so it has four times the area of A_1, so the intensity of gamma rays is a quarter of that at A_1.

Intensity is the energy that flows through a certain area in a second. It is measured in watts per square metre.

$$\text{intensity} = \frac{\text{energy per second}}{\text{area}} \ (\text{W m}^{-2})$$

The gamma rays from a point source spread out to cover the surface of a sphere. Further away from the source, the same energy is distributed over a larger area, so the intensity decreases. The surface area of the sphere is proportional to distance, x, squared. So intensity is inversely proportional to distance squared:

$$I \propto \frac{1}{x^2} \text{ or } I = \frac{kI_o}{x^2}$$

where I_o is the intensity at the source.

In practice, if you move twice as far away from a gamma source, your radiation dose will drop to one-quarter.

10 Why doesn't the inverse square law apply to α- and β-radiation? Could it apply under some conditions?

11 Two metres from a gamma source the radiation intensity is ten times the recommended limit for workers. How far away do they need to move to get to the recommended level?

Nuclear waste

Nuclear fission produces radioactive waste. The quantities are quite small; each power station produces about 100 m^3 per year, of which 95% is low-level waste. The fuel rods are reprocessed and much of the uranium is recovered, but the remaining cladding and fission products are very radioactive.

Storing high-level nuclear waste so that it will remain securely confined is a real challenge. Some of it will be radioactive for thousands of years. In addition to plutonium, radionuclides like strontium and caesium have had to be stored. Strontium-90 is a very dangerous fission product, especially if swallowed. It has a half-life of 28 years and it emits beta particles with a maximum energy of 0.54 MeV.

To find the amount of energy produced by 1 kg of strontium-90 as it decays, we must first calculate the activity. 1 mole of strontium-90 has a mass of about 90 g. 90 g contains 6.022×10^{23} atoms, so 1 kg contains:

$$6.022 \times 10^{23} \times 1000/90 = 6.69 \times 10^{24} \text{ atoms}$$

The activity, A, of a source depends on the number of atoms, N.

$$A = \lambda N$$

where the decay constant $\lambda = \dfrac{\ln 2}{T_{1/2}}$

For strontium-90, $\lambda = 7.85 \times 10^{-10}\ \text{s}^{-1}$

So the activity, $A = 7.85 \times 10^{-10} \times 6.69 \times 10^{24}$
$= 5.25 \times 10^{15}$ Bq

This is the *specific* activity, the activity per kilogram. Since each emitted beta particle carries 0.54 MeV, the energy released per second, i.e. the power, P, by each kilogram of strontium-90 is:

$$P = 0.54 \times 10^{6} \times 1.6 \times 10^{-19} \times 5.25 \times 10^{15}$$
$$= 450 \text{ W}$$

Since the beta particles will be stopped in a very short range, *all* this energy goes into heating the waste. Unless the heat is removed, the waste products become very hot indeed.

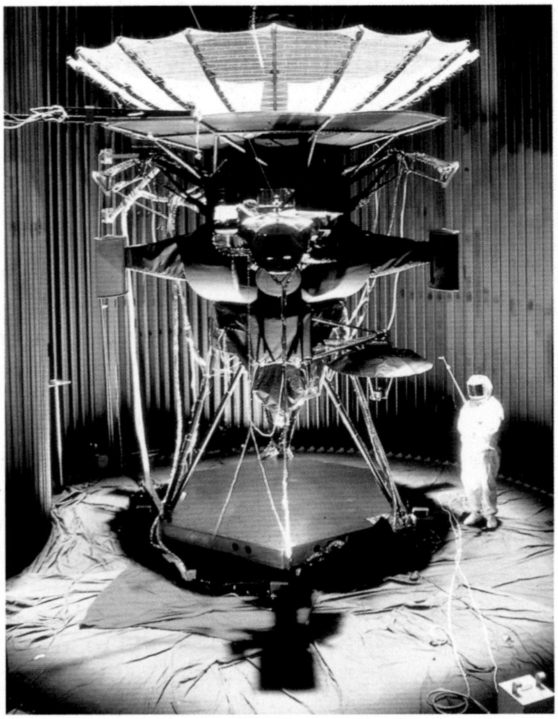

Radioisotope heating can be a useful source of energy; NASA's space probe Galileo, launched in 1989, was powered in this way.

Supporters of nuclear power maintain that radioactivity decays with time, whereas mercury or cadmium dumped by other industries stay toxic for ever. Unlike fossil fuels, nuclear power does not contribute to the air pollution that causes acid rain or the greenhouse effect.

An energy source that would not pollute the air *or* create waste would solve many problems, particularly if its fuel was as abundant as sea-water. Such are the hopes for fusion.

12 Plutonium-239 has a half-life of 24 000 years.

a How long before its activity has dropped to 1% of its original value?

b Why is this an underestimate of the total radioactivity due to plutonium waste?

13 When fuel rods are first removed from a nuclear reactor they are dropped into storage ponds where they are stored for up to a year, before being transported to Sellafield for reprocessing. Give two reasons why the rods need to be kept under water.

13.4 Fusion

In the heart of the Sun, a chain of reactions is gradually turning hydrogen into helium and releasing energy (Fig. 11). The sequence of reactions begins when two protons (^1_1H) collide head-on and fuse to form deuterium:

$$^1_1H + {}^1_1H \rightarrow {}^2_1H + {}^{\ 0}_{+1}e \text{ (a positron)}$$

This reaction is so unlikely to occur that each proton in the Sun travels around for an average of 14 billion years before it reacts with another in this way.

One obstacle is that protons are positively charged. Electrostatic repulsion pushes them apart. Just like trying to compress a spring, the closer you push the

Fig. 11 The fusion process that powers the Sun

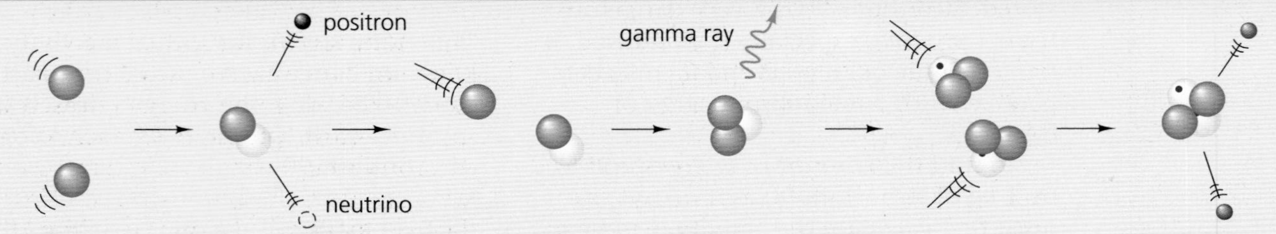

positron
gamma ray
neutrino

Very rarely, two protons collide to form a deuterium nucleus by immediate positron decay. Later, this reacts with another proton to form an isotope of helium, He-3. Two of these He-3 nuclei react to form helium-4 (the common, stable form of helium).

It is hardly surprising that power from fusion has eluded us for so long. After all, we are trying to harness the power which drives the stars.

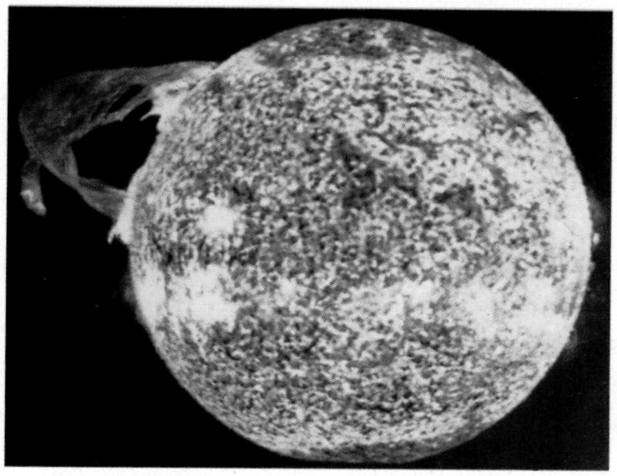

protons together the stronger the force that keeps them apart. At a separation of 10^{-15} m the force of repulsion is about 200 N. This force is enough to push the protons apart with an acceleration of $10^{28}\,g$. To overcome this enormous repulsion the protons have to approach each other at great speed, which demands very high temperatures. If the protons can get to within 10^{-15} m of each other, a force of attraction, called the '**strong nuclear force**', takes over and pulls the protons together.

Fig. 12 The JET fusion reactor

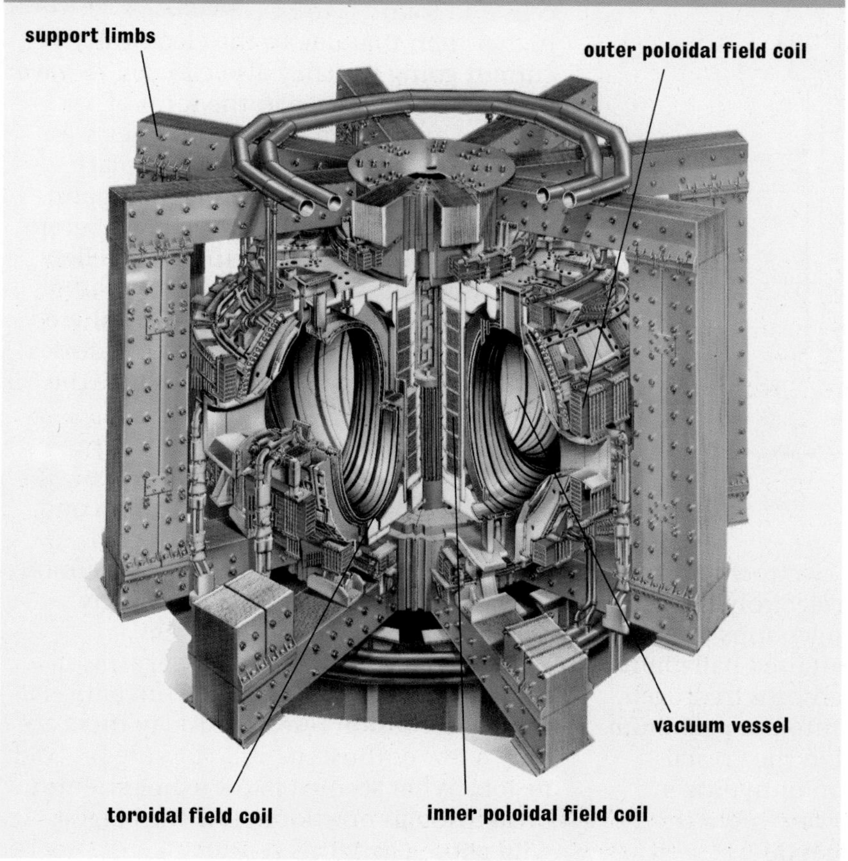

support limbs
outer poloidal field coil
vacuum vessel
toroidal field coil
inner poloidal field coil

In the core of the Sun, the temperature is 15×10^6 K and the density is 12 times that of solid lead. Even here, the reaction proceeds so slowly that it only generates about 20 W m^{-3}. The reaction is not suitable for a fusion reactor.

Fortunately there are more promising fusion reactions which we might be able to use here on Earth. Deuterium and tritium can react to make helium:

$${}^{2}_{1}H + {}^{3}_{1}H \rightarrow {}^{4}_{2}He + {}^{1}_{0}n$$

This reaction releases about 18 MeV of energy and is relatively easy to achieve using a particle accelerator. It has been used in hospitals to provide a beam of neutrons for radiotherapy. Unfortunately, more energy has to be put in than is released by the fusion reaction. For electricity generation you must get more energy out than you have put in, and so far that has not been achieved.

Hot fusion

One way to force deuterium and tritium together is to heat them to a temperature of around 100×10^6 K. At these temperatures – far higher than those in the Sun – deuterium and tritium are completely ionised. The mixture of ions and free electrons is a conducting gas called a plasma.

The Joint European Torus (JET) project at Culham has achieved temperatures of over 300 million degrees Celsius (Fig. 12). For fusion to occur, the plasma must be held together at a density of one thousandth of a gram per cubic metre. Strong magnetic fields are used to confine the plasma long enough for the reaction to become self sustaining (Fig. 13, p 174).

Unfortunately, the hot plasma can become unstable and leak out of the magnetic trap. If it touches the walls of its vacuum containment vessel then it becomes contaminated and cools. It has proved difficult to hold the plasma together long enough for much power to be generated, though fusion reactions have been achieved. In December 1993, an American team achieved a power output of 10 MW which lasted for 0.4 of a second, though they had to provide 33 MW to drive the reaction. The quest for controlled fusion continues.

14 Tritium has a half-life of 12 years and does not exist naturally on Earth. It can be made by allowing lithium-7 to absorb a neutron. Write down an equation for this reaction.

Cold fusion

The cost of hot fusion research is high and there is little prospect of an early return on the investment. So when Fleischmann and Pons announced that they had achieved fusion in a test-tube full of cold water the whole world took notice.

Fig. 14 A cold fusion electrolysis cell

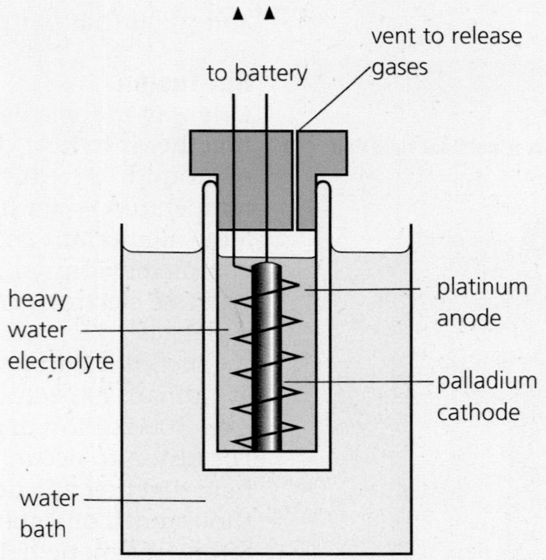
to battery
vent to release gases
heavy water electrolyte
platinum anode
palladium cathode
water bath

Cold fusion is based on electrochemistry (Fig. 14). When water is electrolysed, the positively charged hydrogen ions travel to the cathode. Fleischmann used palladium as the cathode, since it absorbs hydrogen. Hydrogen ions migrate into the palladium and move freely around in the crystal lattice. The concentration of hydrogen within the metal can be very high. If 'heavy' water, deuterium oxide, is used as

Fig. 13 The tokamak

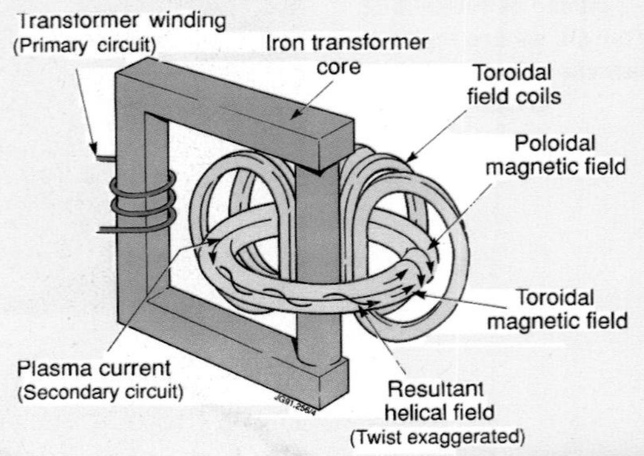
Transformer winding (Primary circuit)
Iron transformer core
Toroidal field coils
Poloidal magnetic field
Toroidal magnetic field
Plasma current (Secondary circuit)
Resultant helical field (Twist exaggerated)

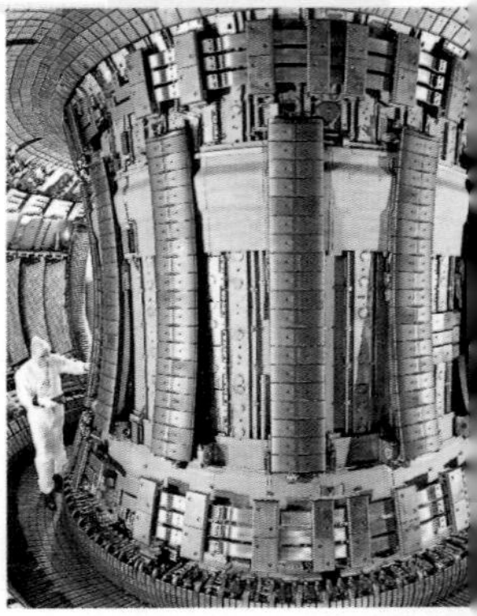

the electrolyte, then collisions and hence fusion between two deuterium nuclei might occur in the palladium.

Fleischmann and Pons measured the temperature rise in their electrochemical cells and found it to be higher than that due to the electrical current going in. They also claimed to have found other evidence in the form of neutron and gamma radiation. They were convinced that fusion was taking place.

Unfortunately, Pons and Fleischmann announced their results to the press before submitting them to the scrutiny of fellow scientists. Accusations were made that critical data had been mysteriously altered and, despite strenuous efforts, laboratories around the world failed to reproduce the results.

Theoretical physicists were openly sceptical. Pons and Fleischmann were claiming thousands of fusions per second, but that would require a mass of cold deuterium bigger than the Sun. Furthermore, the neutron radiation from that many reactions would have killed them!

Within a year of the 'discovery' most nuclear scientists returned to conventional avenues of fusion research. Today there are only a few enthusiasts still working on cold fusion. What seemed like a major scientific breakthrough now looks like the biggest wild goose chase this century.

14

Under the influence of gravity

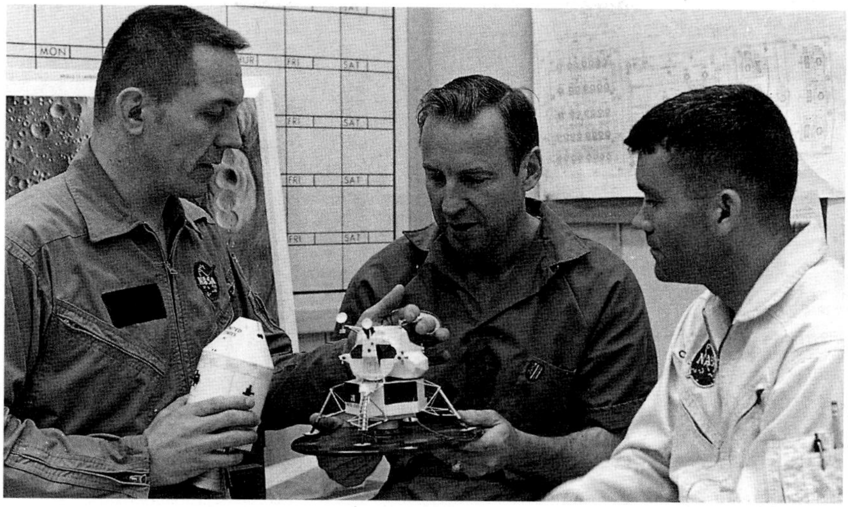

The crew of Apollo 13 examine a model of the lunar module.

Fig. 1 Apollo 13

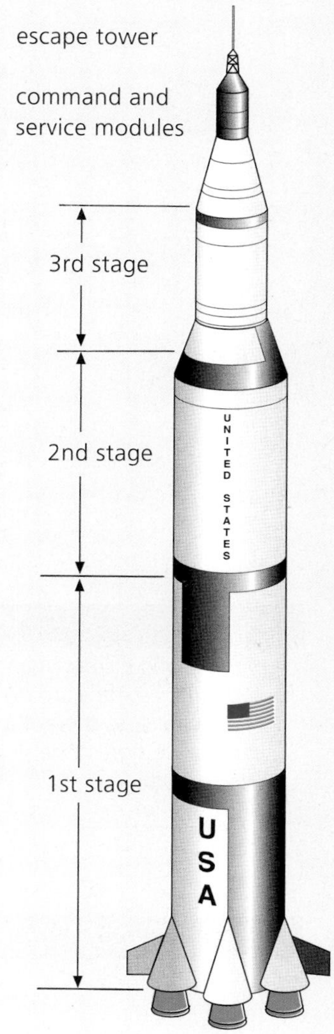

escape tower
command and service modules
3rd stage
2nd stage
1st stage
UNITED STATES
USA

On April 13th 1970, Apollo 13 astronauts Jim Lovell, Jack Swigert and Fred Haise were four-fifths of the way to the Moon when disaster struck. Swigert radioed to NASA mission control in Houston to report, 'We seem to have a problem here.' The problem was serious. The main oxygen supply was leaking into space. Two of the spacecraft's three fuel cells had stopped working and the other one was failing fast.

With only 14 minutes of oxygen left in the main spacecraft, the three astronauts scrambled into the Lunar Excursion Module (LEM). Though originally designed for the last leg of the astronauts' journey to the Moon's surface, the LEM, with its own oxygen supply, would now have to serve as a life-boat.

There were two options open to Mission control. They could fire Apollo's engines to reverse the spacecraft's direction, and bring it back to Earth as rapidly as possible. This was a high risk strategy as there might not be enough fuel left for the final course adjustments needed to get them home safely.

A second option was for the astronauts to continue to the Moon and use its gravity to swing the spacecraft round, like a slingshot, back to Earth. This plan was preferred by the astronauts. At least the spacecraft would definitely return to Earth.

14.1 Learning objectives

After working through this chapter, you should be able to:

- **calculate** the gravitational force between two masses using Newton's law of gravitation;
- **explain** what is meant by a gravitational field;
- **apply** Newton's law of gravitation to satellites in orbit;
- **calculate** the field strength in a radial field;
- **use** the concept of gravitational potential to calculate energy changes.

14.2 Leaving the Earth

Newton's law of gravitation

Pictures of 'floating' astronauts mislead many people into thinking that there is no gravity acting in space. Newton understood gravity to be a universal force of attraction which acts between all objects. He suggested that the force that pulls objects like apples down to the ground, also extends out into space and holds the Moon in its orbit around the Earth. For two objects, the size of the gravitational attraction between them is:

- proportional to the product of their masses, m_1m_2;
- inversely proportional to the square of the distance, r, between them (Fig. 2).

$$F \propto m_1m_2 \quad \text{and} \quad F \propto \frac{1}{r^2}$$

$$\text{or,} \quad F = -\frac{Gm_1m_2}{r^2}$$

The constant G is known as the universal constant of gravitation. In S.I. units, G is measured in N m^2 kg^{-2}.

The period of the Moon's orbit

Newton didn't know the size of the universal constant, G, so he was unable to check his theory by direct measurement. Instead, he tested his hypothesis by using it to predict the orbital period of the Moon (Fig. 3). According to Newton's law, the force of gravity on an object of mass m at the Earth's surface is:

$$F = -\frac{GmM_E}{R^2}$$

where R is the radius of the Earth and M_E is the Earth's mass. This force would lead to an acceleration, a, of:

$$a = \frac{F}{m} = -\frac{GmM_E}{mR^2}$$

$$= -\frac{GM_E}{R^2}$$

In the same way, the acceleration of the Moon in its orbit due to the Earth's gravity is:

$$a = -\frac{GM_E}{r^2}$$

where r is the radius of the Moon's orbit. The ratio of these accelerations is:

$$\frac{a \text{ at Earth's surface}}{a \text{ at Moon's orbit}} = \frac{-\frac{GM_E}{R^2}}{-\frac{GM_E}{r^2}}$$

$$= \frac{r^2}{R^2} \quad \text{or} \quad \left(\frac{r}{R}\right)^2$$

Newton knew that the Moon was about 60 Earth radii away, so he calculated that the acceleration due to the Earth's gravity would be 3600 times greater on the Earth's surface than at the Moon's orbit. At the Earth's surface, the acceleration due to gravity can be measured directly as 9.8 m s^{-2}. Newton calculated that the acceleration of the Moon, due to Earth's gravity, should be:

$$\frac{9.8 \text{ m s}^{-2}}{3600} = 2.72 \times 10^{-3} \text{ m s}^{-2}$$

He used this figure to predict the time taken by the Moon to orbit the Earth. Assuming the Moon is in a circular orbit around the Earth, its acceleration, $a = v^2/r$ (see Chapter 4). This can be rearranged to

Fig. 2 Force of gravity

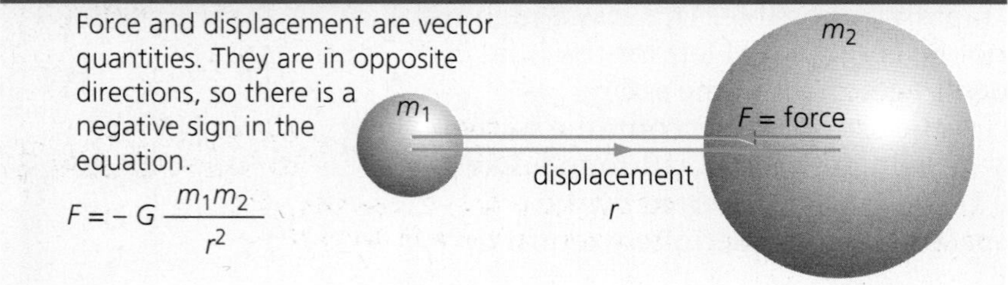

Force and displacement are vector quantities. They are in opposite directions, so there is a negative sign in the equation.
F = – G m1m2 / r2
m1
m2
F = force
displacement
r

Fig. 3 Earth and Moon

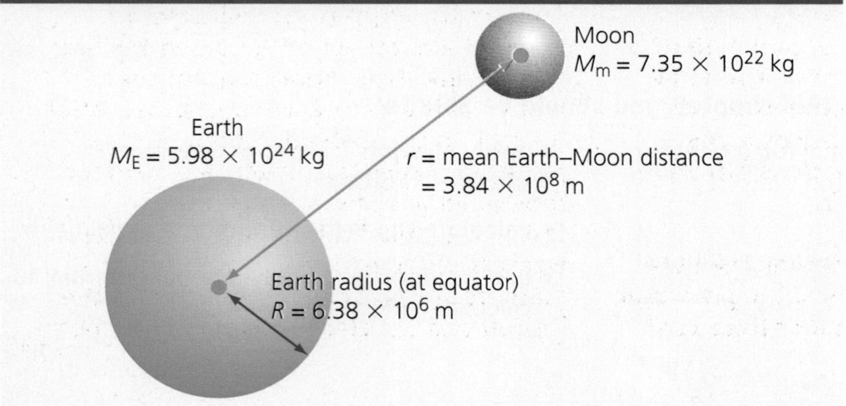

Moon
Mm = 7.35 × 10^22 kg
Earth
ME = 5.98 × 10^24 kg
r = mean Earth–Moon distance
= 3.84 × 10^8 m
Earth radius (at equator)
R = 6.38 × 10^6 m

give $v = \sqrt{ra}$. Since the Moon is, on average, 3.84×10^8 m away from the Earth:

$$v = \sqrt{3.84 \times 10^8 \text{ m} \times 2.72 \times 10^{-3} \text{ m s}^{-2}}$$
$$= 1022 \text{ m s}^{-1}$$

The time taken for one orbit, T, is therefore:

$$T = \frac{2\pi r}{v}$$
$$= 2.36 \times 10^6 \text{ s (27.3 days)}$$

Newton predicted a period of 27.3 days for the Moon's orbit. The time between full moons is actually 29.5 days. This difference is due to the Earth's motion around the Sun. If we measure the Moon's position relative to the distant stars, it has an orbital period of 27.32 days. Newton's theory worked, and though some modifications were made following Einstein's general theory of relativity, Newton's law was still accurate enough to plan ventures to the Moon.

1 A satellite orbiting the Earth at a height of 700 km falls into a lower orbit of 500 km.

a By what factor does the gravitational force increase?

b What effect will this have on the satellite's speed? (Remember to take account of the Earth's radius, $r = 6.4 \times 10^6$ m)

2 Fifty years before Newton, Johannes Kepler published three laws of planetary motion. The third law says that: 'The square of the period of a planet's orbit, T, is proportional to the cube of its mean distance from the sun, r' (i.e. $T^2 \propto r^3$). Use Newton's law of gravitation to derive Kepler's third law. Assume that the planets move in circular orbits and remember that any object moving in a circle has an acceleration of v^2/r.

3 Pluto is 40 times further from the sun than we are. How long is a year on Pluto? (Use Kepler's third law)

The strength of gravity

The Saturn V rocket which carried the Apollo 13 astronauts towards the Moon was 110 metres high and had an initial mass of 3000 tonnes. Three different rocket motors, or stages, were used to send it into Earth orbit. Eight seconds before lift-off, the first stage ignited. At lift-off, the clamps holding the rocket to the launch pad were released. By this time the rocket was burning 15 tonnes of fuel per second and exerting a thrust of 33 million newtons against the Earth's gravitational attraction.

Kennedy Space Centre, April 11th, 1970. The successful launch of Apollo 13.

The gravitational force acting on less massive objects is much smaller. When you jump in the air, you overcome your gravitational attraction to the entire Earth fairly easily. Two people standing one metre apart exert a gravitational attraction on each other of about 0.2 mN. Today, physicists believe that there are just four fundamental ways in which matter interacts (Table 1). Gravity is by far the weakest of these forces. In a hydrogen atom, the electrostatic force between the proton and the electron is about 10^{-7} N.

The gravitational attraction between them is only about 10^{-47} N, a factor of 10^{-40} times smaller. Despite this, it is gravity that keeps the planets in their orbits and holds our galaxy together. Electric charges can be positive or negative. This means that electromagnetic forces can cause either attraction or repulsion. On a larger scale these forces cancel out. However, because particles cannot have negative mass, the force of gravity is always attractive. In space, gravity is the dominant force because the small, attractive forces between particles add together. A consequence of this is that it is not possible to shield against gravity. Unlike electromagnetic forces, the force between two masses is not affected by the material between them.

Table 1 The fundamental forces

	Gravitational	Electromagnetic	Strong nuclear	Weak nuclear
range	infinite	infinite	within the nucleus $< 10^{-12}$ m	within the nucleus $< 10^{-17}$ m
acts between	all masses	all charges	hadrons (nuclear particles like protons and neutrons)	hadrons and leptons (nucleons and electrons)
effect	holds stars together and planets in their orbits	holds atoms together, keeps electrons in their orbits	holds nuclei together	responsible for radioactivity
relative magnitude	10^{-36}	1	100	0.01

The universal constant of gravitation

Rearranging Newton's formula shows the significance of G, the universal constant of gravitation:

$$G = -\frac{Fr^2}{m_1 m_2}$$

Suppose $r = 1$ m and both masses are 1 kg, $m_1 = m_2 = 1$ kg, then $G = -F$. So G is the attractive force between two 1 kilogram masses placed 1 metre apart. This force is extremely small. The first accurate measurement of G was done in 1798 by Henry Cavendish. He used a sensitive torsion balance to measure the turning effect exerted by two masses (Fig. 4).

Fig. 4 Cavendish's apparatus

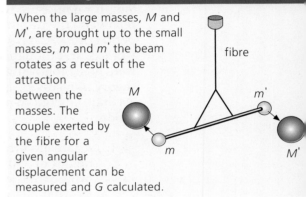

When the large masses, M and M', are brought up to the small masses, m and m' the beam rotates as a result of the attraction between the masses. The couple exerted by the fibre for a given angular displacement can be measured and G calculated.

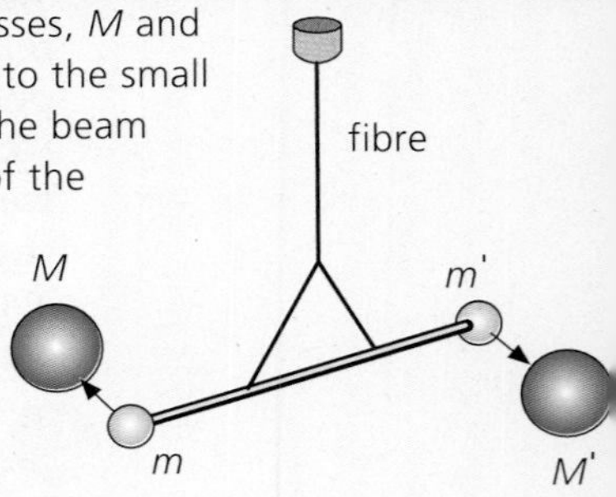
fibre
M
m'
m
M'

Modern measurements of G rely on the same principle. They give a value of 6.673×10^{-11} N m^2 kg^{-2}. Scientists believe that G has the same value throughout the universe.

4 Cavendish's experiment has been called 'weighing the Earth'. Once G was known, the mass of the Earth could be calculated. How?

Key ideas

- Newton's law of gravitation states that the gravitational force of attraction, F, between two masses, m_1 and m_2, a distance r apart is given by:

$$F = -\frac{Gm_1 m_2}{r^2}$$

where G is the universal gravitational constant = 6.673×10^{-11} N m^2 kg^{-2}.

Work done against gravity

Despite the enormous power of the Saturn V rocket, Apollo 13 took more than 10 seconds to clear the launchpad tower. The first and second stages were jettisoned before the third stage carried the astronauts into Earth orbit, just 11 minutes and 25 seconds after lift-off.

To lift the astronauts into orbit, work had to be done against the gravitational force between the spacecraft and the Earth. For a steady force we can calculate the work done using the formula

$$\text{work} = \text{force} \times \text{distance moved}$$

However, the force on the rocket changes as it goes up. This is partly because the mass of the rocket falls as fuel is burnt, but also because the gravitational force decreases as the rocket gets further from the Earth.

In order to simplify things, consider an object with a constant mass, m, at a distance x from the centre of the Earth. We can calculate how much work is done in moving the object a small distance, Δx, further away. If Δx is small enough, the force will not change significantly over that distance, so:

$$\text{work done} = F\Delta x = -\frac{GM_{\mathrm{E}}m\Delta x}{x^2}$$

This is the area of one of the strips marked on Fig. 5.

The total work done, W, is the sum of the areas of all such strips, from the Earth's surface to an infinite distance away. However, it can be found more accurately by integrating the expression $F\,\mathrm{d}x$ between the Earth's radius, R, and infinity:

$$W = \int_R^\infty F\,\mathrm{d}x = -GM_{\mathrm{E}}m\int_R^\infty \frac{1}{x^2}\,\mathrm{d}x$$

$$= -GM_{\mathrm{E}}m\left[-\frac{1}{x}\right]_R^\infty = \frac{GM_{\mathrm{E}}m}{R}$$

This is the work done in taking the mass, m, from the Earth's surface to infinity (i.e. completely out of the influence of Earth's gravity).

Fig. 5 Work done against Earth's gravity

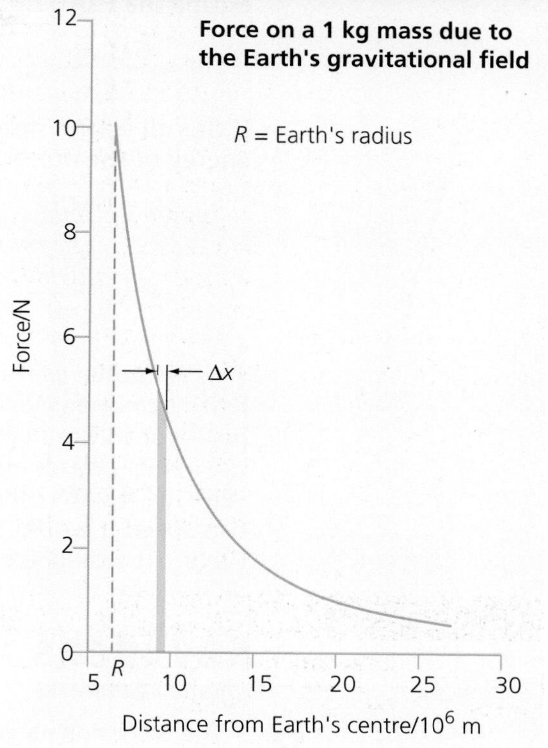

Force on a 1 kg mass due to the Earth's gravitational field
R = Earth's radius
Force/N
Δx
R
Distance from Earth's centre/10⁶ m
0
2
4
6
8
10
12
5
10
15
20
25
30

5 Apollo 13's command, service and lunar modules had a combined mass, *m*, of 44 tonnes. Calculate the work done by the Saturn V rocket in lifting them into orbit at a height, *h*, of 185 km above the Earth (mass = 5.98×10^{24} kg).

6 The ascent stage of the lunar module, mass = 4450 kg, was designed to lift the Apollo astronauts off the surface of the Moon and back into lunar orbit, at a height of about 110 km. How much work does it need to do against the Moon's gravitational field?
(Radius of Moon = 1.74×10^6 m, Mass of Moon = 7.35×10^{22} kg)

Escape velocity

'What goes up must come down' is a saying that reflects our everyday experience of the Earth's gravity. But if you could throw an object fast enough, it might never come down. The energy required by the mass to escape the Earth's pull is:

$$W = \frac{GM_E m}{R}$$

If this all comes from the initial kinetic energy of the object:

$$\tfrac{1}{2}mv^2 = \frac{GM_E m}{R}$$

$$v = \sqrt{\frac{2GM_E}{R}}$$

This is known as the escape velocity. The Earth's escape velocity is 11.2×10^3 m s^{-1}, just over 11 km per second. The mass of the object has no effect on v, the escape velocity. If you could throw a projectile at this speed it would never come down. In theory, it would eventually come to rest an infinite distance from Earth, though it would probably come under the gravitational influence of another object in space. A rocket doesn't have to travel at an initial speed of 11 km s^{-1} to escape from the Earth, but its motors will eventually have to provide an equivalent amount of energy.

7 In 1798, the French mathematician Pierre Laplace predicted the existence of objects so dense, that their escape velocity would be greater than the speed of light ($c = 3 \times 10^8$ m s^{-1}). Two hundred years later, astronomers are looking for these objects, which they call 'black holes'. How small would you have to crush the Earth before it became a black hole?

Key ideas

- The work done against the gravitational attraction of a mass, M, when a mass, m, is moved from a distance R to infinity, is:

  $$W = \frac{GMm}{R}$$

- If all this energy is provided as initial kinetic energy then the escape velocity is:

  $$v = \sqrt{\frac{2GM}{R}}$$

14.3 Orbiting the Earth

Since 1972, when the final Apollo mission went to the Moon, all manned space flights have been confined to orbiting the Earth.

Newton had foreseen the possibility of orbiting the Earth. He thought that if a large enough cannon could be constructed and placed at the top of a very high mountain it could fire a shell that would never fall back to the Earth's surface (Fig. 6).

Fig. 6 Into orbit

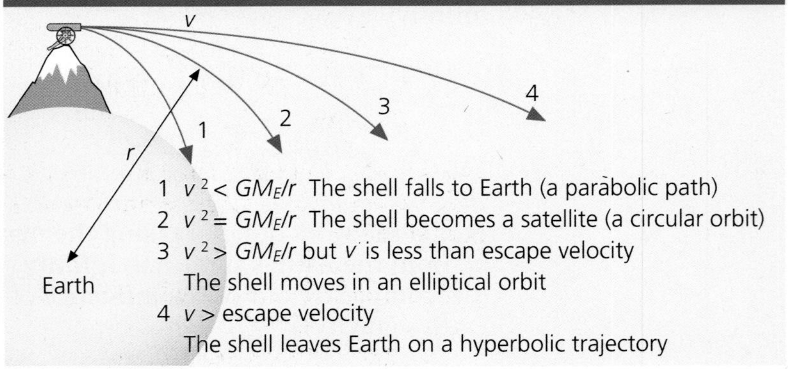

v
1
2
3
4
r
Earth
1 $v^2 < GM_E/r$ The shell falls to Earth (a parabolic path)
2 $v^2 = GM_E/r$ The shell becomes a satellite (a circular orbit)
3 $v^2 > GM_E/r$ but v is less than escape velocity
The shell moves in an elliptical orbit
4 $v >$ escape velocity
The shell leaves Earth on a hyperbolic trajectory

At the right speed, the shell becomes a satellite, falling towards the Earth's surface at exactly the rate that the Earth's surface curves away. If a satellite, of mass m, moves in a circular orbit, of radius r, the gravitational force on the satellite is:

$$F = \frac{GM_E m}{r^2} = ma$$

Since the satellite is moving in a circle, its acceleration is:

$$a = \frac{v^2}{r}$$

$$\text{So,} \quad \frac{GM_E m}{r^2} = \frac{mv^2}{r}$$

$$\text{or,} \quad v^2 = \frac{GM_E}{r}$$

For a satellite orbiting the Earth, GM_E is a constant, so $v^2 \propto 1/r$. This means that there is a unique velocity for each orbit. The lower the satellite, the faster it must travel to stay in orbit.

The trajectory of the Saturn V rocket was calculated to put the astronauts into the correct orbit. The powerful first stage moved the rocket vertically, taking the shortest path through the densest part of the atmosphere. The rocket then climbed at an angle until it reached Earth orbit. During this phase, stage 1 and 2 were jettisoned. A final firing of the rocket motors brought Apollo's speed up to the correct value for that orbit.

The Apollo spacecraft orbited at a height of about 185 km. To find its orbital radius we must add on the radius of the Earth, which is 6.38×10^6 m. Apollo's orbital speed is given by:

$$v = \sqrt{\frac{GM_E}{r}}$$

$$= \sqrt{\frac{6.67 \times 10^{-11}\ \text{N m}^2\,\text{kg}^{-2} \times 5.98 \times 10^{24}\ \text{kg}}{6.56 \times 10^6\ \text{m}}}$$

$$= 7800\ \text{m s}^{-1}$$

We can also calculate the time it took for the spacecraft to complete one orbit. The period, T, is:

$$T = \frac{\text{orbit circumference}}{\text{speed}}$$

$$= \frac{2\pi r}{v} = \frac{2\pi \times 6.56 \times 10^6\ \text{m}}{7800\ \text{m s}^{-1}}$$

$$= 5300 \text{ seconds (about 88 minutes)}$$

Artificial satellites

The space industry now concentrates on putting unmanned satellites into orbit. We use them to send telephone messages and TV pictures around the world and to give us detailed information about the weather. Satellites can also be used for navigation. The Global Positioning System uses a network of 20 satellites to tell users exactly where they are, with an uncertainty of only 15 metres.

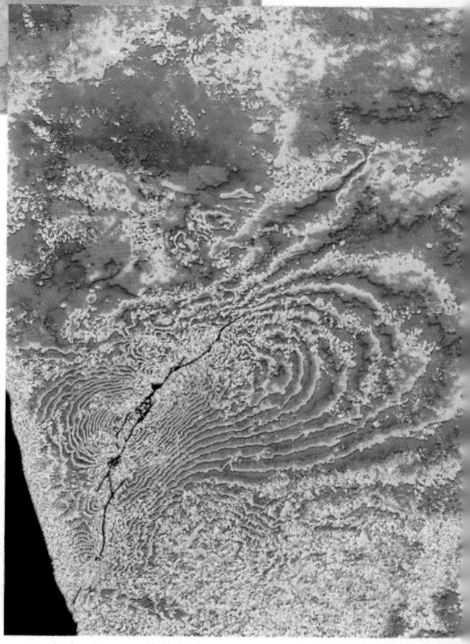

Satellites can give detailed information on a variety of phenomena. The false-colour IR photograph (top) shows the spread of forest fires due to slash and burn farming in Mozambique. Radar imaging from a satellite over California illustrates the ground displacement following an earthquake in June 1992.

Communications satellites such as Astra, which broadcasts TV programmes, are often placed in high orbits. The signals are received by small, fixed dish aerials (Fig. 7). This is only possible if the satellite remains at exactly the same position in the sky relative to the receiver. The satellites must therefore be placed in a **geostationary** orbit, an orbit that has a period of exactly 24 hours. As the Earth rotates, the satellite moves to remain above exactly the same position on the Earth's surface.

Fig. 7 Aligning a dish

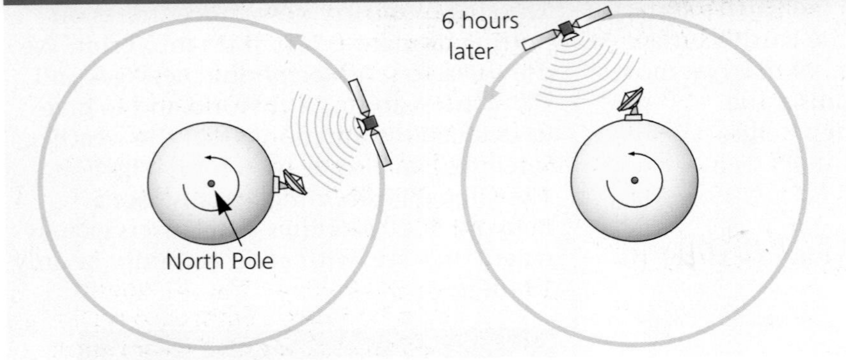
6 hours
later
North Pole

We can relate r and T by combining:

$$T = \frac{2\pi r}{v} \quad \text{and} \quad v = \sqrt{\frac{GM_E}{r}}$$

giving, $$r^3 = T^2 \frac{GM_E}{4\pi^2}$$

If T is 24 hours ($24 \times 60 \times 60 = 86\,400$ seconds), then r must be 42.2×10^6 m. This is a height of about 36 000 km above the Earth's surface. The geostationary satellite also needs to have the same axis of rotation as the Earth.

The work done by a force is given by force × distance moved in the direction of the force. Because a satellite's velocity is always at right angles to the force no work is done against gravity. Once in orbit, a satellite shouldn't need any energy to keep it there. For a geostationary satellite this is practically true. At a height of 36 000 km there is no atmospheric drag acting against the satellite. Satellites in low Earth orbit have a limited lifetime as their energy transfers to molecules in the outer atmosphere as heat. This causes the satellite to slow down and move to a lower orbit.

8 Explain why a geostationary satellite must be in orbit over the equator.

9 If a satellite was in orbit at a height of 700 km above the surface of the Earth, what would its period be?

Key ideas

- For a satellite in a circular orbit, its speed is given by:

  $$v^2 = \frac{GM_E}{r}$$

- A geostationary satellite has the same period and axis of rotation as the Earth.

Weightlessness

Astronauts in orbit around the Earth feel weightless. The Russian cosmonaut, Oleg Atkov, had 8 months of weightlessness in Earth orbit, aboard the Russian space station Salyut 7. He had difficulty sleeping because his head floated from the pillow. The organs of balance in his inner-ear did not work properly in 'weightless' conditions and he felt constantly dizzy. Despite regular, vigorous exercise his muscles wasted and his bones lost calcium. When he returned to Earth he could not support his own weight and had to be carried from his spacecraft on a stretcher.

'Weightlessness' is rather a misleading expression. The force of the Earth's gravity on the astronauts is only slightly less than when they were on Earth. What has changed is the contact force between the astronauts and the spacecraft. When we are standing, it is the contact force of the ground which prevents us from accelerating downwards under gravity. This upwards force acting on our feet makes us aware of our weight. When the ground moves beneath you, in a lift for example, you feel as if your weight is changing (Fig. 8). If the lift accelerates upwards you feel heavier, though gravity has not changed. It is simply that the contact force from the lift floor has increased. When the lift accelerates downwards you feel lighter; the contact force is now less than your weight.

If the lift cable breaks and the lift falls freely under gravity, the contact force between you and the floor disappears altogether, you feel weightless. For an astronaut in Earth orbit, the sensation is the same as being in a freely falling lift. The astronaut, the space-craft and everything in it are falling together, at exactly the same acceleration. This is sometimes called 'weightlessness' or 'zero-gravity', but free-fall is a more accurate term.

The Apollo astronauts did not have to contend with the long-term effects of weightlessness. Several hours after launch, they used the third and final stage of the rocket motors to leave the Earth's orbit and head for the Moon.

Fig. 8 Going up?

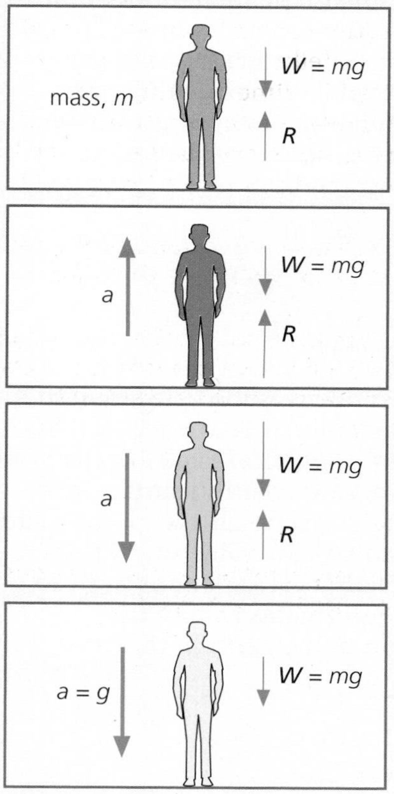
mass, m
$W = mg$
R
a
$W = mg$
R
a
$W = mg$
R
$a = g$
$W = mg$

For a stationary lift, or one moving at constant velocity, the person is in equilibrium, $R = W$.

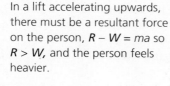

In a lift accelerating upwards, there must be a resultant force on the person, $R - W = ma$ so $R > W$, and the person feels heavier.

As the lift accelerates downwards there is a resultant force downwards on the person, $W - R = ma$ so $R < W$ and the person feels lighter.

If the lift falls freely $a = g$, $W - R = mg$ but $W = mg$, so $R = 0$. There is no constant force between you and the floor. The person feels weightless (for a short time at least).

10 **Suppose one of the astronauts stood on some bathroom scales during their flight. Explain what the scales would show:**

a during the ascent into Earth orbit;

b when the craft was in orbit.

11 **It has been suggested that a space station in Earth orbit could spin to simulate the acceleration due to gravity. The space station could be shaped like a doughnut, rotating about an axis through its centre (Fig. 9). If the radius of the space station was 1 km, how fast would it need to turn? Which surface would the astronauts walk on?**

Fig. 9 Artificial gravity

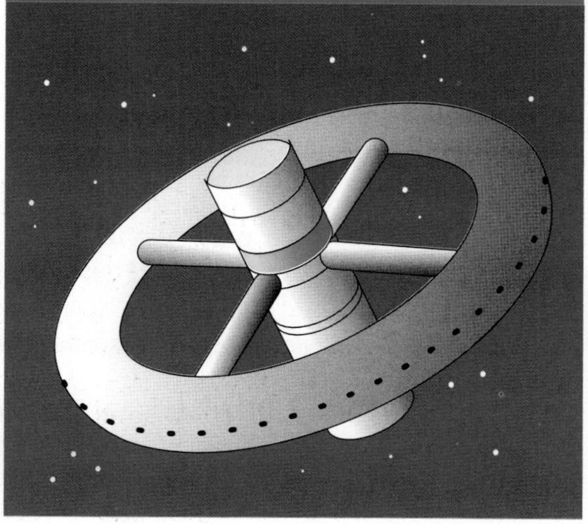

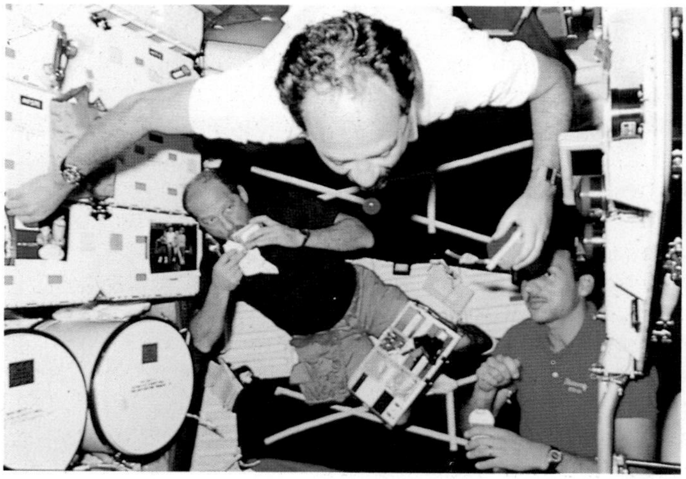

Free-fall or weightlessness? A lunch-time drink is not easy in either case.

14.4 Round the Moon and back

The explosion of oxygen tank number two destroyed an entire panel of the Apollo 13 Service Module. The module was photographed just after it was jettisoned.

Fifty-five hours into the Apollo 13 mission, Commander Jim Lovell heard a bang and discovered that the gauge for number two oxygen tank was reading empty. When he looked out of the window he saw a faint haze issuing from the side of the spacecraft; their oxygen supply was escaping into space. The astronauts climbed into the lunar module. All systems in the main spacecraft were shut down. Its only remaining power supply was the three batteries that would be needed during the re-entry to Earth's atmosphere.

By now Apollo 13 was close to the point where the Moon's gravitational pull takes over from the Earth's. The motors were fired to take the craft back to a free return trajectory. The gravitational field of the Moon would have to turn them round.

Gravitational field strength

Apollo 13 started to accelerate towards the Moon as it entered its **gravitational field.** This is the region of space where a mass is subject to the Moon's gravitational attraction. Every mass produces a gravitational field. The strength of the gravitational field at a point is defined as the force that would be exerted on a unit mass placed at that point:

gravitational field strength = force per unit mass

$$g = \frac{F}{m}$$

In S.I. units, g is measured in N kg^{-1}, though it can also be thought of as the acceleration due to gravity in m s^{-2}.

We can use Newton's law of gravitation to find an expression for g at the surface of the Earth. Since the force of gravity on a mass m on the surface of the Earth (radius r) is given by:

$$F = -\frac{GM_E m}{r^2}$$

$$\text{so,} \quad g = \frac{F}{m} = -\frac{GM_E}{r^2}$$

This expression gives the field strength for a radial gravitational field, such as that produced by a spherical mass like the Moon or the Earth. At the Earth's surface, the gravitational field strength is approximately 10 N kg^{-1}. In fact the value varies from place to place. Local variations in g can give important information about the composition of the Earth in that area.

Key ideas

- The field strength, g, at a point in a gravitational field is the force that is exerted on a unit mass placed at that point.
- For a radial field, such as that produced by a spherical mass M, the field strength is given by $g = -GM / r^2$

Gravitational field lines

We draw gravitational field lines to show the direction of the force acting on a mass. These are similar to the sketches of magnetic field lines that show the direction of the force on the north pole of a magnet (Fig. 10).

Fig. 10 Field lines

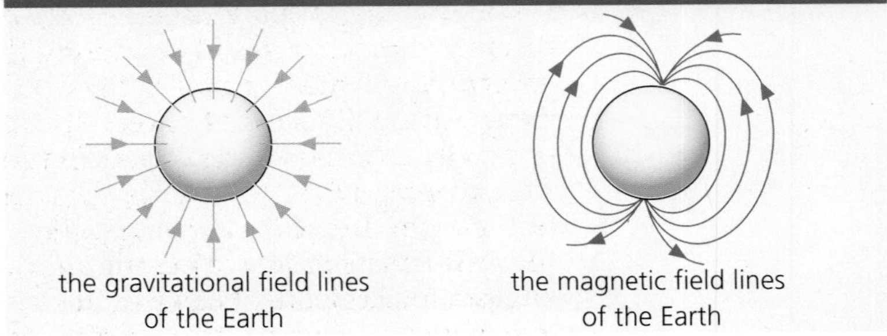

the gravitational field lines of the Earth
the magnetic field lines of the Earth

Fig. 11 Inverse square law

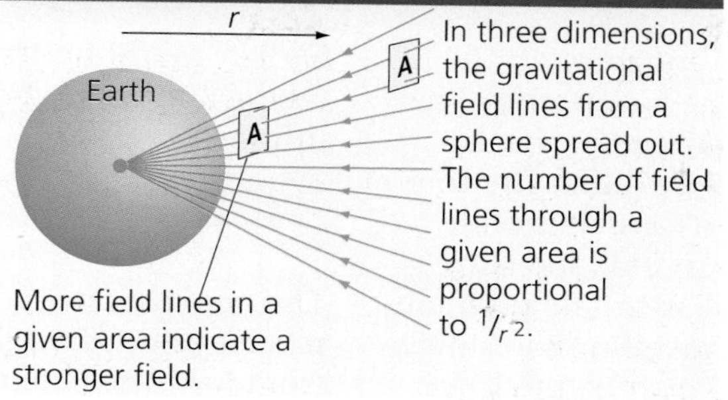

r
Earth
A
A
In three dimensions, the gravitational field lines from a sphere spread out. The number of field lines through a given area is proportional to $^1/_{r^2}$.
More field lines in a given area indicate a stronger field.

For a sphere like the Earth the field lines are radial. The field is stronger where the lines are closer together.

Einstein had another way of looking at gravitational fields, he saw them as distortions in space itself. Try to picture space as a stretched sheet of rubber; it is simpler to imagine this in two-dimensions. Massive objects, like the Earth and the Moon, distort the sheet (Fig. 12). They produce a gravitational 'well', into which objects such as meteorites, or astronauts, may fall. A more massive object will cause a greater distortion in space and have a deeper gravitational well.

Fig. 12 Curved space

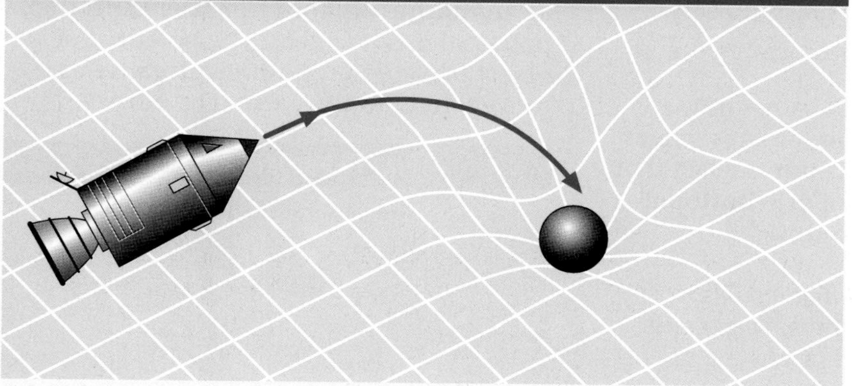

In this picture, gravity is no longer a force; it is a property of space itself. A large mass distorts the space around it, altering the trajectory of a passing object. Einstein said there was no difference between the effects of gravity and the effects of acceleration. An astronaut in a closed space ship could not tell whether she was being pulled towards a mass or just using the ship's engines to accelerate. Both would cause her to experience what we call 'weight'. For most applications it doesn't matter whether you use Einstein's theory or Newton's; they agree in many respects.

The neutral point

Somewhere between the Earth and the Moon there is a point where the gravitational forces from each are equal, but opposite. This is known as a neutral point (Fig. 13). If you could stand exactly at this point, you would experience the same force in each direction and you would be in equilibrium. The equilibrium would be unstable; one slight move in either direction would pull you back to the Earth or on to the Moon.

Fig. 13 The neutral point

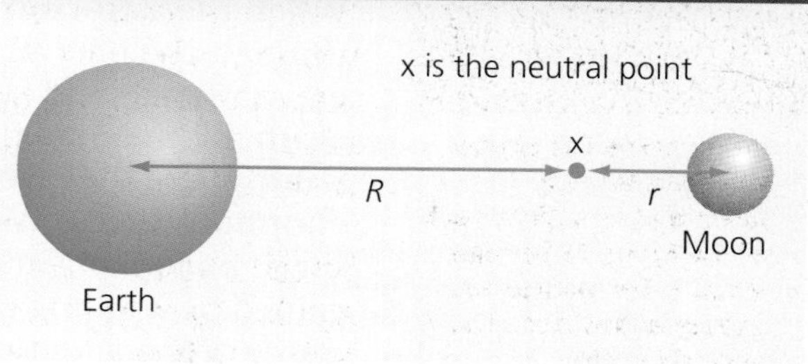

x is the neutral point
x
R
r
Moon
Earth

If the gravitational field strengths are the same at this point:

$$g_{\mathrm{M}} = g_{\mathrm{E}}$$

$$\frac{GM_{\mathrm{M}}}{r^2} = \frac{GM_{\mathrm{E}}}{R^2}$$

$$\text{so,} \quad \frac{R^2}{r^2} = \frac{M_{\mathrm{E}}}{M_{\mathrm{M}}} = 80$$

$$R \approx 9r$$

R is the distance from the Earth, r is the distance from the Moon and the Earth is about 80 times more massive than the Moon.

Apollo 13 was approximately 90 per cent of the way to the Moon (350 000 km from Earth) when it passed through the neutral point.

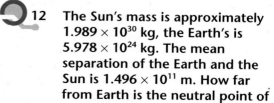

Q12 The Sun's mass is approximately 1.989×10^{30} kg, the Earth's is 5.978×10^{24} kg. The mean separation of the Earth and the Sun is 1.496×10^{11} m. How far from Earth is the neutral point of the Earth–Sun system?

14.5 Returning to Earth

As the Apollo 13 crew went through the neutral point towards the Moon, they knew that they would eventually move back towards Earth. Even if they didn't fire their engines again, the Moon's gravitational pull would swing them round, and sling them back towards the Earth. The problem was speed. Apollo was travelling too slowly to get the crew back to Earth before their oxygen ran out. Therefore, the rocket motors had to be fired as they came out from behind the Moon. A rocket burn of exactly 4 minutes and 28 seconds accelerated them towards home.

Gravitational potential

When the astronauts had passed back through the neutral point, the Earth's gravitational field began to accelerate them again. By the time they reached the Earth's atmosphere they would be travelling at enormous speed. We can calculate this speed by looking at the kinetic energy gained by a falling object. If we ignore air resistance, gravitational potential energy is fully transferred to kinetic energy:

$$mg\Delta h = \tfrac{1}{2}mv^2$$
$$v = \sqrt{2g\Delta h}$$

This works well for small values of the change in height, Δh, but for large values we need to take into account the fact that g varies. We use the idea of **gravitational potential** (Fig. 14) to do this:

The gravitational potential at a point is defined as the work done in moving a unit mass from infinity to that point.

Fig. 14 Gravitational potential

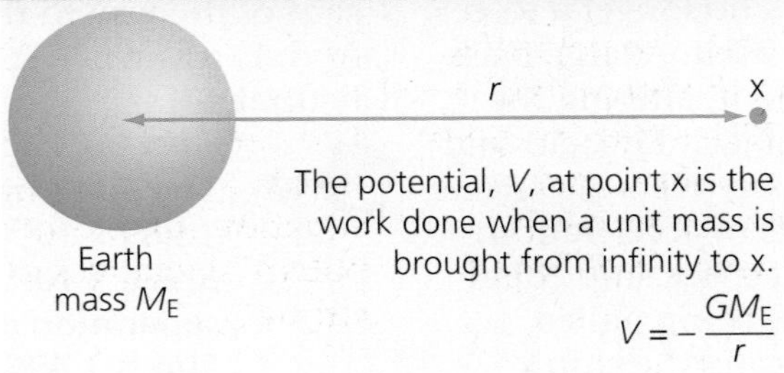

r
x
The potential, V, at point x is the work done when a unit mass is brought from infinity to x.
Earth mass M_E
$V = -\frac{GM_E}{r}$

Earlier, we found that the work done, W, in taking a mass, m, from a distance R to infinity is:

$$W = \frac{GM_E m}{R}$$

The gravitational potential describes the reverse effect, bringing a mass to a point from infinity. Potential is also defined for a unit mass, so the gravitational potential, V, at a distance r from the Earth is given by:

$$V = -\frac{W}{m} = -\frac{GM_E}{r}$$

The gravitational potential is always negative. You would need to do work to take the mass back to infinity. Therefore, the gravitational potential at a point can also be thought of as the potential energy of a unit mass placed there. It is measured in J kg^{-1}. To find the potential energy (E_p) of a real object at a particular point, you need to multiply by its mass:

$$E_p = mV = -\frac{GM_E m}{r}$$

At an infinite distance from the Earth the potential drops to zero. The potential of an object becomes increasingly negative as it moves closer to the Earth (Fig. 15).

Fig. 15 Potential energy

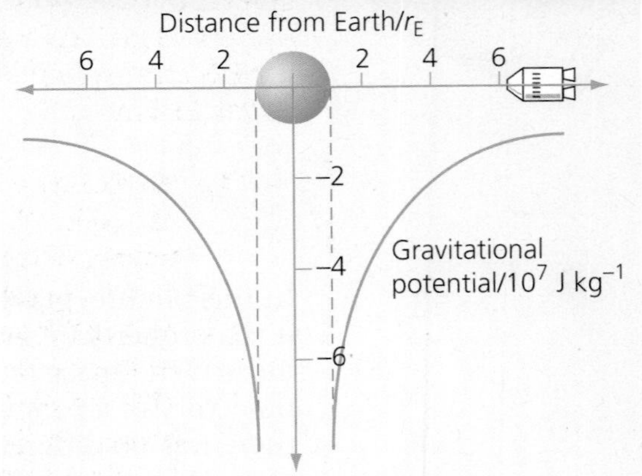

Distance from Earth/r_E
6
4
2
2
4
6
−2
−4
−6
Gravitational potential/10^7 J kg^{-1}

At the Moon, the potential of the Earth's gravitational field is:

$$
\begin{aligned}
V &= -\frac{GM_E}{r} \\
&= -\frac{6.67\times10^{-11}\ \mathrm{N\,m^2\,kg^{-2}}\times6\times10^{24}\ \mathrm{kg}}{3.844\times10^{8}\ \mathrm{m}} \\
&= -1.04\times10^{6}\ \mathrm{J\,kg^{-1}}
\end{aligned}
$$

The potential energy of Apollo 13 (approximate mass = 4.4×10^4 kg) due to the Earth's field was therefore:

$$
\begin{aligned}
E_p &= mV \\
&= 4.4\times10^{4}\ \mathrm{kg}\times-1.04\times10^{6}\ \mathrm{J\,kg^{-1}} \\
&= -4.6\times10^{10}\ \mathrm{J}
\end{aligned}
$$

This potential energy was transferred to kinetic energy as the spacecraft approached Earth.

The total energy of the spacecraft, E_{total}, is the sum of its kinetic and potential energies:

$$E_{total} = E_k + E_p$$

If the total energy is constant, any decrease in potential energy means a corresponding increase in kinetic energy. As the spacecraft's potential energy becomes more negative, its kinetic energy becomes more positive.

Although the Moon's gravity acted to slow the spacecraft, Apollo's rocket motors helped to overcome this effect. By the time Apollo 13 arrived back at the edge of the Earth's atmosphere, it was travelling at about 11 km s^{-1}.

13 a What is the potential at the edge of the Earth's atmosphere, at a height of about 100 km, due to the Earth's gravity?

b At the Moon's orbit, the potential of the Earth's gravitational field is -1.04×10^6 J kg^{-1}. Use this and your answer to (a) to confirm that Apollo 13 would be travelling at about 11 km s^{-1} when it returned to Earth.

Equipotentials and field lines

The potential at a point in a radial gravitational field, such as that produced by a sphere like the Earth, depends on the distance from the centre of the sphere. If all the points at the same potential are joined up, they form a spherical shell (Fig. 16). A surface like this is known as an equipotential surface. It is like a contour line which connects points of equal height on a map.

Fig. 16 Equipotentials and field lines

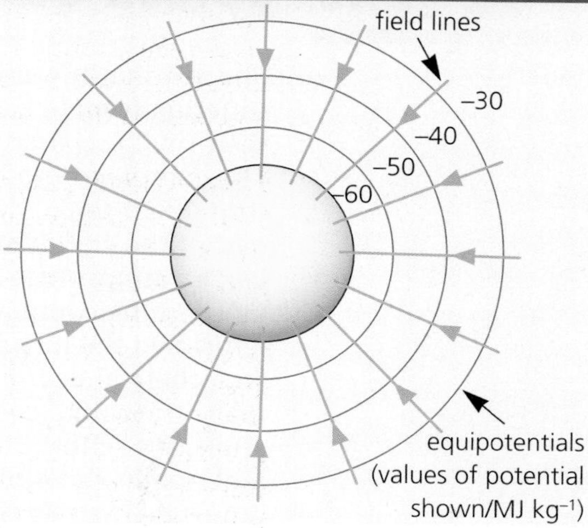

field lines
−30
−40
−50
−60
equipotentials
(values of potential
shown/MJ kg⁻¹)

Suppose a spacecraft of mass m moves a small distance, Δx, away from the Earth. Its potential will increase by ΔV and its potential energy will change by $m\Delta V$.

In order to pull away from the Earth, the spacecraft had to exert a force equal in magnitude, but opposite in direction, to the gravitational attraction, F. So the work done by the spacecraft is:

$$
\begin{aligned}
\text{work done} &= \text{force}\times\text{distance moved} \\
&= -F\times\Delta x = -mg\Delta x \\
\text{so,}\quad -mg\Delta x &= m\Delta V \\
g &= -\frac{\Delta V}{\Delta x}
\end{aligned}
$$

The equation can be read as 'field strength equals the negative potential gradient'. The equation implies that the gravitational potential changes quickly where the field is strong.

Key ideas

- The potential, V, at a point in a gravitational field is the potential energy of a unit mass placed there. The S.I. units of V are J kg^{-1}.
- For a radial field, such as that produced by a spherical body of mass M:

$$V = -\frac{GM}{r}$$

- For any gravitational field:

$$g = -\frac{\Delta V}{\Delta x}$$

14.6 Splash-down

The astronauts were dehydrated, cold and suffering from exhaustion as they made their final preparations to return to Earth. The command module, which had been shut down since the accident, was the only part of the craft which could re-enter the Earth's atmosphere without burning up. Once in the command module, they jettisoned the lunar module which had kept them alive for the last three days and made their final course corrections. The angle of re-entry was critical. Too shallow and Apollo 13 would skim off the atmosphere like a pebble bouncing off the surface of the sea. Too steep and they would burn up in the atmosphere.

Orbital decay

When a satellite enters the atmosphere the drag causes its orbit to decay. The satellite heats up and drops to a lower orbit, where it moves at higher speed. This seems odd as the net effect of drag has been to speed the satellite up. We need to consider the *total* energy of the satellite, the sum of its potential and kinetic energies. If the satellite of mass m is moving at a velocity, v, in a circular orbit of radius r, then:

$$E_{total} = E_k + E_p$$
$$= \tfrac{1}{2}mv^2 - \frac{GM_E m}{r}$$

But, for a circular orbit:

$$\frac{mv^2}{r} = \frac{GM_E m}{r^2}$$

so, $$E_{total} = \tfrac{1}{2}\frac{GM_E m}{r} - \frac{GM_E m}{r}$$
$$= -\tfrac{1}{2}\frac{GM_E m}{r}$$

As a satellite spirals to Earth, r decreases and so the total energy becomes more negative. The decrease in total energy is only half the decrease in potential energy. This difference is due to the increase in kinetic energy.

As the astronauts entered the denser part of the atmosphere, the effects of heating made radio contact impossible. After three minutes of radio silence, the command module appeared through the clouds. It drifted down, slowed by its three parachutes, and dropped in the Pacific Ocean three miles from the US aircraft carrier Iwo Jima. The astronauts were picked up soon afterwards, badly dehydrated and exhausted. They had made it – but only just.

Fig. 17 Energy of different orbits

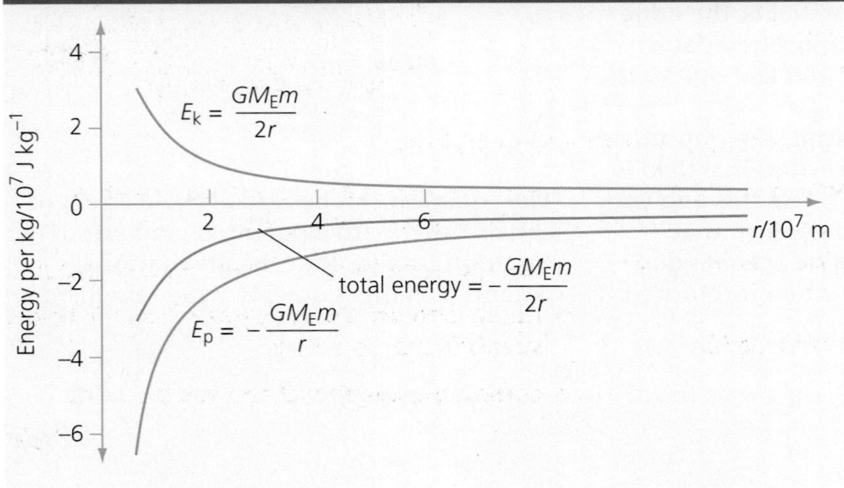

Energy per kg/10^7 J kg^-1
4
2
0
-2
-4
-6
2
4
6
r/10^7 m
E_k = GM_E m / 2r
total energy = – GM_E m / 2r
E_p = – GM_E m / r

15 Atom smashers

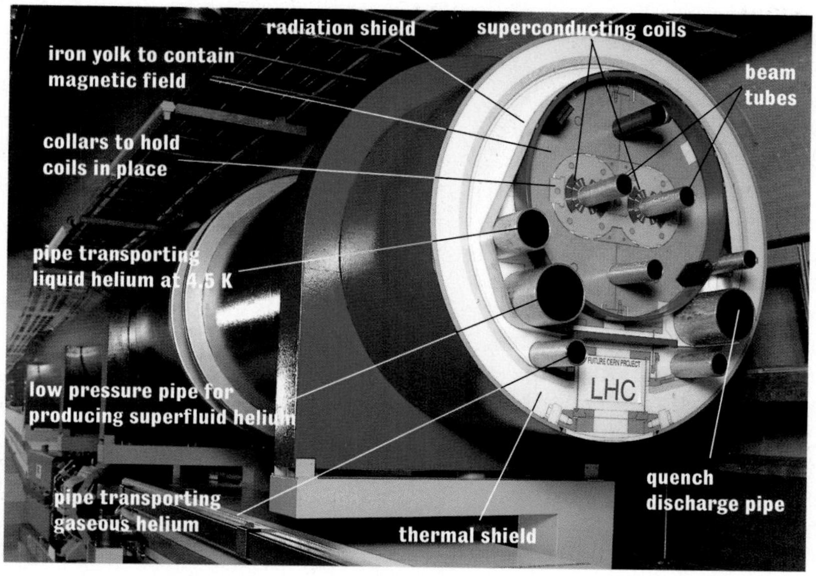

radiation shield
superconducting coils
iron yolk to contain magnetic field
beam tubes
collars to hold coils in place
pipe transporting liquid helium at 4.5 K
low pressure pipe for producing superfluid helium
pipe transporting gaseous helium
thermal shield
quench discharge pipe
LHC

The Large Hadron Collider, currently being built near Geneva, Switzerland, will be used to look for particles at energies of up to 1000 GeV. The collider, which will have a 27 km circumference, is designed to operate at temperatures approaching absolute zero.

The cloud chamber photograph below shows a 'shower' of electrons and positrons produced by a cosmic ray. The electrons and positrons curve in different directions in the chamber's magnetic field. They are able to produce more gamma rays which interact with the sheets of lead (black) to generate new showers.

Physicists have always been interested in matter: what its basic building blocks are; how they fit together; where they come from. The ultimate goal of many theoretical physicists is to produce a theory which explains the origin of all forces, from gravity to the forces which hold nuclei together. To test the accuracy of their theories, physicists need accelerators with enough energy to create the exotic particles that the theories predict. Inside the accelerators, the particles collide – either with each other, or with target atoms – to produce showers of fragments. These fragments are often fundamental particles, with huge energies and short lifetimes.

Physicists have already succeeded in detecting particles such as W and Z bosons in accelerators. These high-energy particles disappeared when the Universe was less than a second old. The hunt is now on for particles with even higher energies.

15.1 Learning objectives

After working through this chapter, you should be able to:

- **explain** the terms magnetic flux and flux density;
- **calculate** the effect of magnetic fields on moving charges;
- **describe** the field patterns caused by electromagnets;
- **explain** how iron cores increase the flux density of electromagnets;
- **calculate** the force between point charges;
- **define** and use the concepts of electric field strength and potential;
- **compare** gravitational and electric fields.

15.2 Cosmic rays

Early experiments on radioactivity used **ionisation chambers** as detectors. Radioactive substances release charged particles which ionise the air (see Chapter 12). Ionised air can carry a tiny electrical current. In 1903, Rutherford and McLennan found that even when their chamber was surrounded by thick lead shielding there was always a slight current. Something other than the radioactive substances must be causing this ionisation of the air. At the time, they put it down to radiation from the earth. However, in 1912, experiments with detectors in high-altitude balloons showed that the ionising current increased as the balloon went higher. This gave rise to the theory of highly penetrating rays from space called cosmic rays.

Photographic film and cloud chambers were used to detect very high energy particles from the stars and galaxies. Photographic emulsion is a thin layer of light-sensitive chemical on the surface of the film. Molecules in the emulsion are easily ionised – even by low-energy photons of visible light. A set of photographic plates inside a dark box will be ionised by any charged particles which enter. Some of these particles will travel along the film, leaving a track. The developed film can reveal the types of particle.

Cloud chambers rely on vapours condensing as tiny droplets. When a liquid evaporates into the air, its molecules mix with air molecules. If the vapour is cooled, the liquid reforms as tiny droplets. This is how clouds are formed. Vapours condense more easily around ions and dust particles so that when an ionising particle passes through the vapour, it leaves an ionisation trail or 'cloud'. The way that a particle is deflected in magnetic fields gives us information about its charge and mass.

Bubble chambers work on the same principle as cloud chambers. Subatomic particles pass through liquid hydrogen in the chamber, leaving a fine trail of bubbles as they momentarily superheat the liquid. Electrons and positrons follow spiral paths due to an intense applied magnetic field.

15.3 Magnetic fields

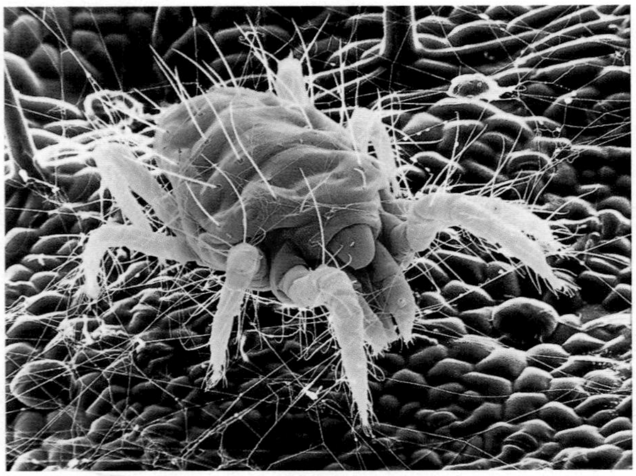

An understanding of how charged particles behave in magnetic fields is used in scanning electron microscopy. This false-colour picture shows a red spider mite climbing over the surface of a leaf.

Flux density

A magnetic field is a region of space where other magnets experience a force. Moving charges also experience a force. The size and direction of the force, and hence the shape of a particle's track, depends on the charge carried by the particle and the nature of the magnetic field. Iron filings can be used to get a picture of the shape and strength of a magnet's field. The filings become tiny **induced** magnets which tend to form a pattern of lines. The idea of field lines (or **flux** lines) is used to describe magnetic fields.

Field lines, shown by the pattern of iron filings, indicate the direction of the force on the North-seeking pole of an imaginary tiny magnet within the field.

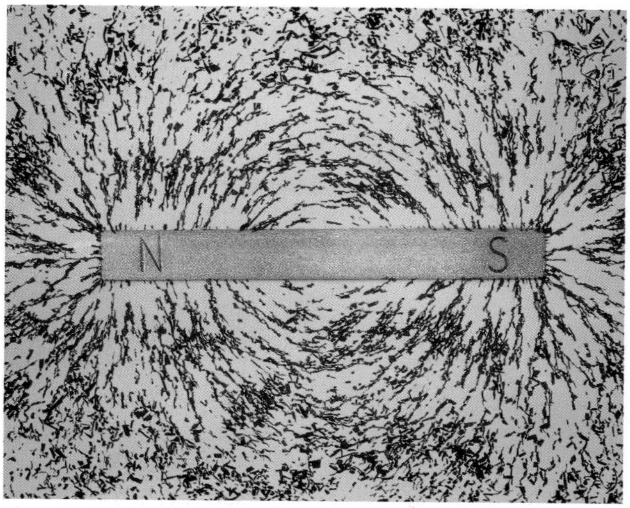

N
S

The flux lines are closer together at the ends of the magnet. This is the region where the magnetic field is strongest.

Fig. 1 Density of flux lines

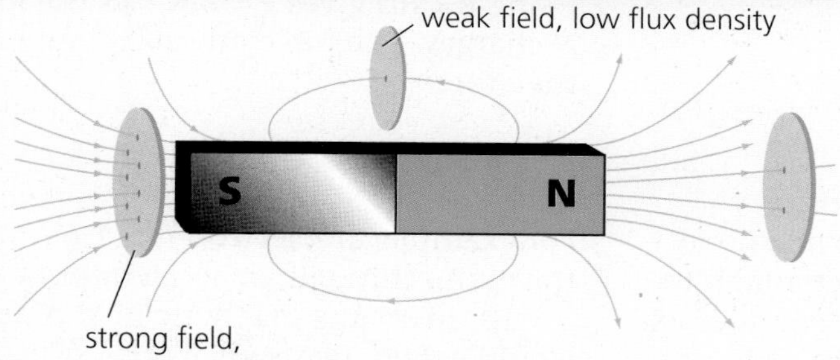

weak field, low flux density
S
N
strong field, high flux density

Picture a small area parallel to the end of the bar magnet; wherever a flux line cuts through, you could imagine a little dot (Fig. 1). Near the magnet, where the field is strong, these imaginary dots would be densely packed over the area. In a weaker field, they would be less dense. The strength of the magnetic field can be described in terms of its **magnetic flux density**, B. This is measured in tesla (T).

If the flux is at right angles to the area, the amount of flux can be expressed as:

flux = flux density × area

$$\Phi = B \times A$$

Flux is measured in **weber** (Wb). 1 Wb = 1 T × 1 m^2. Flux density is a vector quantity, so direction is important (Fig. 2).

Fig. 2 Flux at different angles

The orientation of the area A in the magnetic field is important. The flux passing through A depends on the angle θ.

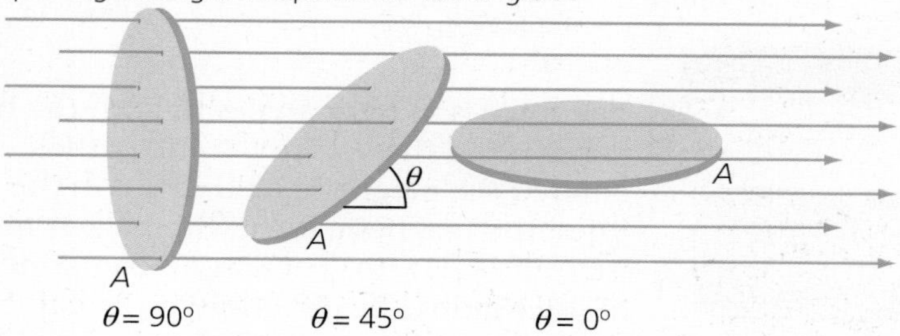

A
θ = 90°
θ
A
θ = 45°
A
θ = 0°

1 How much flux passes through a flat coil of area 2 cm^2 in a field of flux density 0.05 T if the flux density vector is

a at 90° to the plane of the coil?

b parallel to the plane of the coil?

Defining the tesla

In 1819, Oersted discovered a link between electricity and magnetism. He noticed that a small compass was deflected by a nearby electric current. Today, we use this effect to define the unit of magnetic flux density. The magnetic field produced by a wire can be thought of as a set of circles in a plane at right angles to the wire. These are closer together near the wire, because the field is stronger there. The direction of the flux lines is linked to the current by the right-hand grip rule (Fig. 3).

Fig. 3 Right-hand grip rule

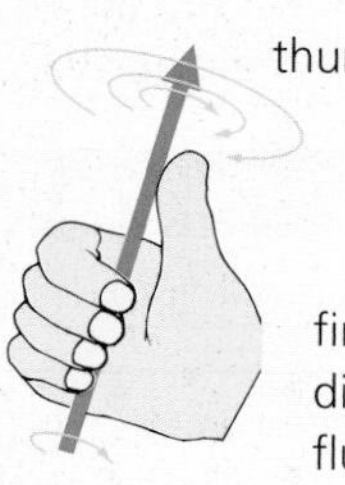

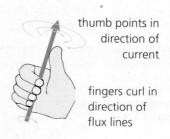

thumb points in direction of current
fingers curl in direction of flux lines

Fig. 4 Fleming's left-hand rule

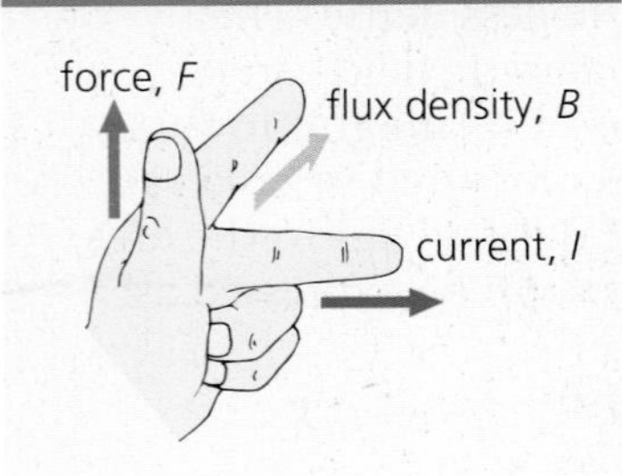
force, F
flux density, B
current, I

If the wire is placed in another magnetic field, it feels a magnetic force. The effect is biggest when the wire is at right angles to the other field. The force is at right angles to both the flux density and the current. Fleming's left-hand rule is useful for remembering directions of force, flux density and current (Fig. 4).

Experimentally, we find that the force on the wire depends on:

- the length of wire, l
- the current, I

We can write this as:

$$F \propto Il$$

A stronger field gives a bigger force. We define the magnetic flux density (B) to be the force per metre of wire per unit current:

$$B = \frac{F}{Il}$$

or $F = BIl$

The **tesla** is the unit of flux density ($1\ \text{T} = 1\ \text{N A}^{-1}\ \text{m}^{-1}$). The Earth's magnetic field is about 50 μT: not strong enough to cause any appreciable force on conductors. Strong permanent magnets have a flux density of around 0.1 T.

Force on a moving charge

A charge moving through a magnetic field experiences a force. The size of this force influences the particle's path through a magnetic field (Fig. 5). Particle accelerators and detectors rely on knowing the relationship between path and flux density. We can link the force on the particle to its velocity.

Fig. 5 A charge in a magnetic field

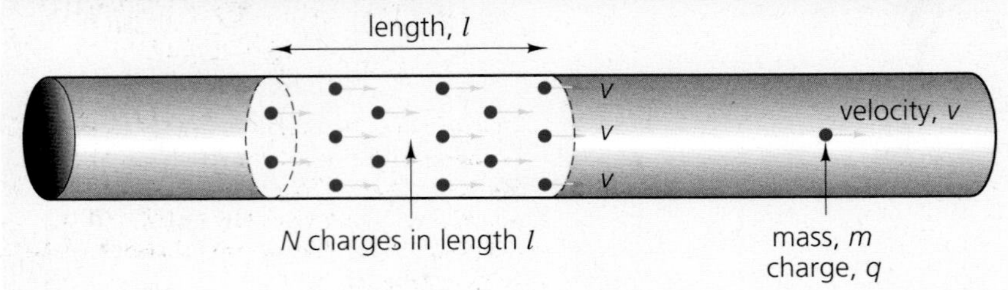
length, l
v
v
v
velocity, v
N charges in length l
mass, m
charge, q

From the definition of flux density, the force on a current-carrying wire is $F = BIl$. This force is due to the moving charges in the wire.

Inside the wire, you can picture the current as a flow of charged particles, each with charge q drifting at average velocity v. If there are N such charges in a length l of wire:

$$\text{current} = \frac{\text{total charge passing a point}}{\text{time to travel length } l}$$

$$I = \frac{Nq}{t}$$

using $t = \frac{l}{v}$

$$I = \frac{Nq}{(l/v)}$$

Rearranging gives $Il = Nqv$

Using $F = BIl$ gives $F = BNqv$ as the force on N charges. The force on each charge is therefore:

$$F = Bqv$$

For example, an electron ($e = 1.6 \times 10^{-19}$ C) travelling through an accelerator at $3 \times 10^6\ \text{m s}^{-1}$ in a magnetic field of 0.02 T would experience a force of:

$$\begin{aligned} F &= Bqv \\ &= 0.02 \times 1.6 \times 10^{-19} \times 3 \times 10^6 \\ &\approx 10^{-14}\ \text{N} \end{aligned}$$

The mass of the electron is only about 10^{-30} kg, so the resulting acceleration of the electron is huge:

$$a = \frac{F}{m}$$

$$\approx 10^{16}\ \text{m s}^{-2}$$

The force is at right angles to both the flux density and the velocity. If the particle entered the magnetic field at 90° to the flux lines, the magnetic force will make it travel in a curve (Fig. 6). There is no component of force along the direction of the curve, so the speed will not alter. This means that the particle experiences a constant force, always at right angles to its direction of motion. The curve will therefore be circular.

Fig. 6 Circular motion in a magnetic field

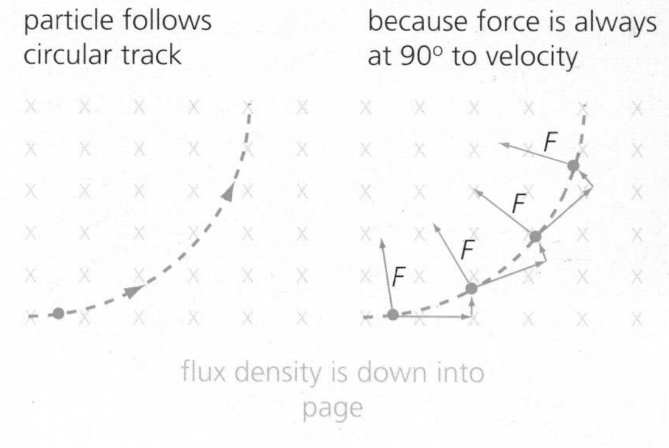
particle follows circular track
because force is always at 90° to velocity
F
F
F
F
flux density is down into page

The acceleration of a body in circular motion at constant speed is $a = v^2/r$. For a particle in the magnetic field, r will be the radius of curvature of its path. This can be measured from photographs of tracks in a cloud chamber. Such measurements gave physicists useful information about particles:

The force on a particle is: $F = Bqv$

Its acceleration is: $a = \frac{F}{m} = \frac{Bqv}{m}$

This is the centripetal acceleration: $a = \frac{v^2}{r}$

So: $\frac{v^2}{r} = \frac{Bqv}{m}$

Rearranging gives: $r = \frac{mv}{Bq} = \left(\frac{v}{B}\right) \times \left(\frac{m}{q}\right)$

For each type of particle, the ratio of charge to mass is constant, so the curvature of the track provides information about the sorts of particles present. Protons are almost 2000 times heavier than electrons and **positrons**. Electron tracks therefore have a much smaller radius than proton tracks.

Fig. 7 Tracks of positive and negative particles

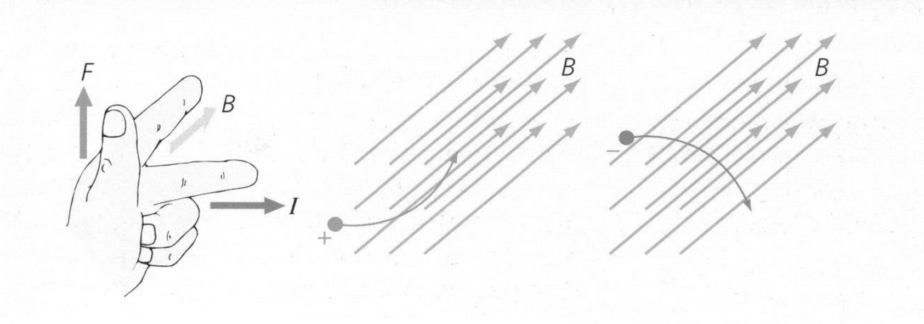
F
B
I
B
+
B
–

This event shows the creation of a pair of oppositely charged particles that spiral away in different directions in the magnetic field.

When a charged particle transfers energy by ionising air molecules, it slows down. The radius of curvature of its track therefore decreases: it makes a spiral track.

The direction of the force is found using Fleming's left-hand rule. For positive particles, the conventional current is the same as the direction of motion. For negative particles it is the opposite – an electron moving to the left represents a conventional current to the right.

2 Study the photograph of a positron passing through a lead plate.
a Identify the direction of the magnetic field.
b Where is the positron travelling faster?

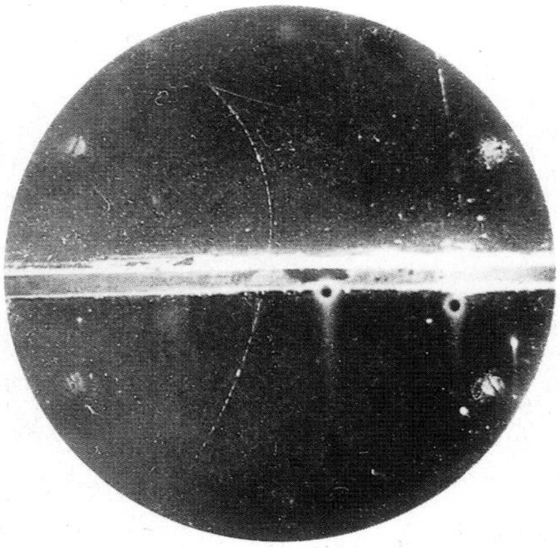

This cloud chamber photograph, taken in 1932, showed for the first time the track of a positron. The particle enters the chamber from below and curves markedly to the left in the magnetic field after passing through a 6 mm thick lead plate.

Mass spectrometry

Chemists sometimes need accurate information on the different elements or isotopes present in a sample. From this information, researchers can start to work out the composition of the material. Distinguishing between isotopes of the same element is impossible using normal chemical techniques. A mass spectrometer uses the principle of magnetic deflection to carry out its analysis (Fig. 8).

A small sample of material is ionised, usually by firing electrons at it. The resulting ions are then accelerated by an electric field. Ions of particular speed are picked out by a **velocity selector**. The ions pass through a uniform magnetic field which deflects them into a semicircular path. The radius of this path depends on the charge-to-mass ratio.

Fig. 8 A simple mass spectrometer

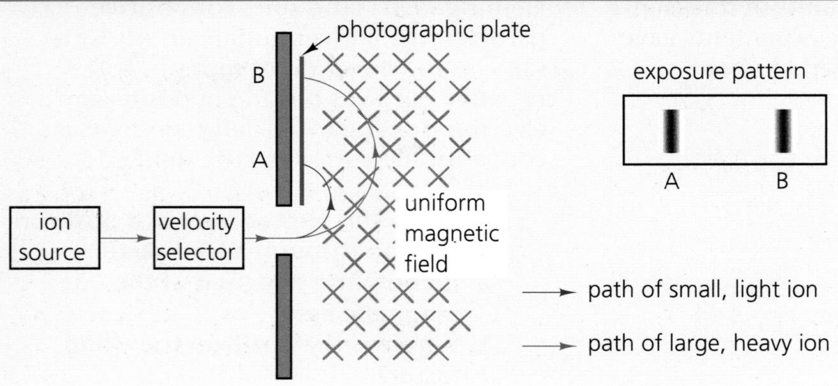

photographic plate
B
A
ion source
velocity selector
uniform magnetic field
exposure pattern
A
B
path of small, light ion
path of large, heavy ion

The position of the lines on the photograph reveals the masses of the ions. The darkness of the lines on the photograph indicates the amount of each ion present in the sample. For singly charged ions, the distance across the plate (i.e. the radius of the circular motion) is proportional to the mass of the ion. The instrument can be calibrated by using standard samples. Doubly charged ions will have only half the radius of path. This can lead to overlap: for example, ${}^{4}_{2}He^{++}$ and ${}^{2}_{1}H^{+}$ would overlap almost exactly.

By replacing the photographic plate with an electronic detector system which measures the ion current as the ions strike at each point on the screen, a computer can very quickly produce a graph of the isotopes present. The output of this sort of mass spectrometer appears as a series of peaks, each representing ions of a particular isotope (Fig. 9).

Fig. 9 A mass spectrograph

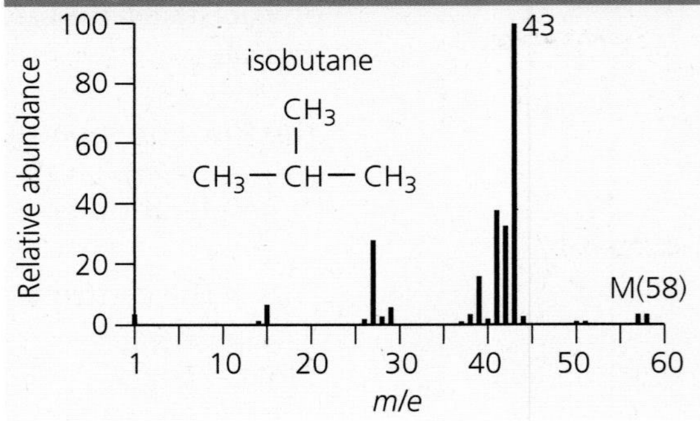

100
80
60
40
20
0
Relative abundance
isobutane
CH3
CH3 — CH — CH3
43
M(58)
1
10
20
30
40
50
60
m/e

Key ideas

- Magnetic flux density (measured in tesla, T) is defined in terms of the force on a current-carrying wire: $F = BIl$ for current at right angles to the field. Directions are given by Fleming's left-hand rule.
- Flux density is a vector field which can be visualised by using iron filings or a small plotting compass. Magnetic flux is defined by $\Phi = BA$ and is measured in weber, Wb.
- A charge q moving with velocity v at right angles to flux density B experiences a force, $F = Bqv$. This force is at 90° to both current and flux density.

15.4 Electromagnets

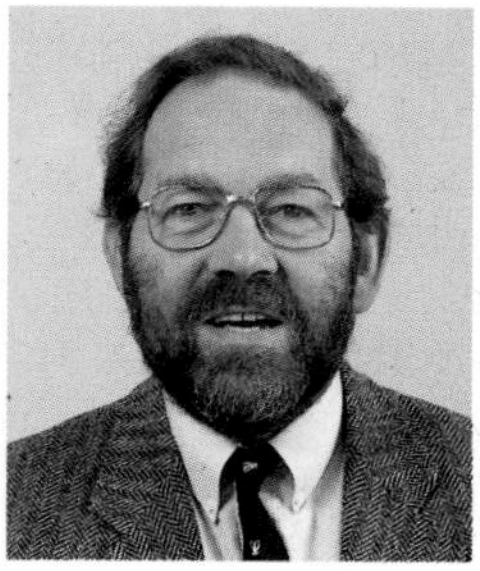

Peter is part of the project team designing superconducting magnets for the new collider at CERN.

People underestimate the strength of these magnets. In our magnet assemblies, the currents are so large, and the wires so close together, that the forces are enough to rip the whole thing apart. We need to know exactly how big these forces can be.

Particle accelerators and particle detectors rely on strong, uniform magnetic fields which can be finely adjusted. You cannot achieve such fields using permanent magnets. Superconducting electromagnets can produce magnetic flux densities which are many times larger and more uniform than any permanent magnet.

A wire carrying a current produces a magnetic field. For an infinitely long wire, flux density is:

- proportional to current;
- inversely proportional to the distance from the wire.

The flux density of the magnetic field near an infinitely long wire (Fig. 10) is:

$$B = \frac{\mu_0 I}{2\pi a}$$

μ_0 is a constant called the '**permeability of free space**'.

Fig. 10 Flux density near a wire

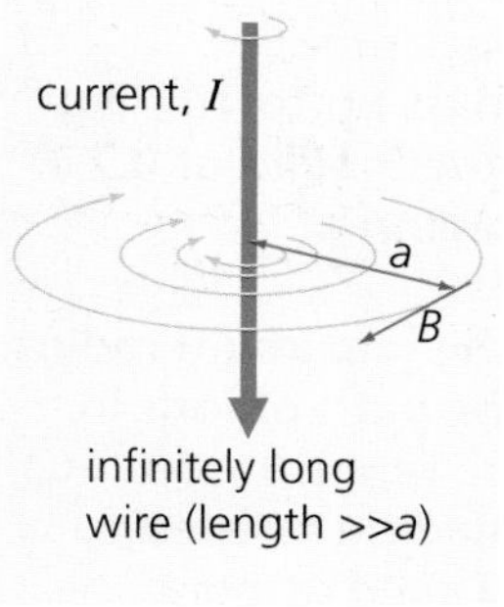

current, I
a
B
infinitely long
wire (length >>a)

Forces on wires

A wire carrying a current produces its own magnetic field. Current-carrying wires will also experience a force in a magnetic field. Therefore, if two current-carrying wires are placed side by side, the magnetic field of one will cause a force on the other, and vice versa (Fig. 11).

We can calculate the size of the force by treating one wire as the source of the field and the other as the wire experiencing the force. Take two long wires at separation x carrying currents I_1 and I_2.

Wire 1 produces a field of flux density:

$$B_1 = \frac{\mu_0 I_1}{2\pi x}$$

Wire 2 experiences force:

$$F = B_1 I_2 l$$

Therefore:

$$F = \frac{\mu_0 I_1 I_2 l}{2\pi x}$$

The force per unit length is therefore:

$$\frac{F}{l} = \frac{\mu_0 I_1 I_2}{2\pi x}$$

The same equation can be used if you take wire 2 as generating the field and wire 1 experiencing the force.

The force on the wires depends only on the current and the distance between them. This link is used to define the ampere:

One ampere is the current flowing in each wire which causes a force of 2×10^{-7} newtons on every metre of two infinitely long parallel wires placed 1 metre apart in a vacuum.

It follows from this that the value of μ_0 must be **exactly** $4\pi \times 10^{-7}$ N A^{-2}.

Fig. 11 Force on parallel wires

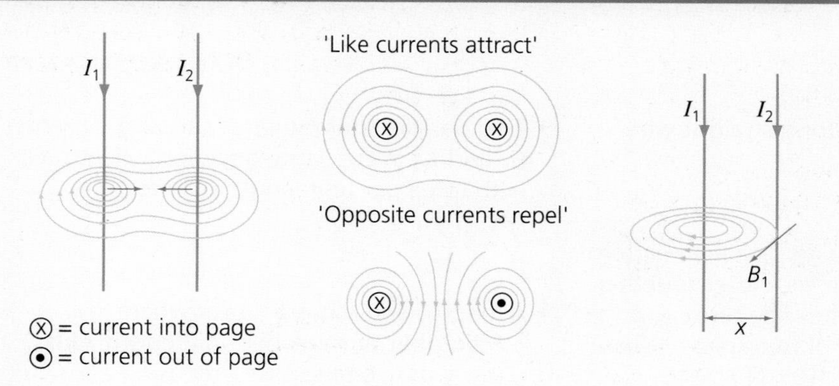

I1
I2
'Like currents attract'
'Opposite currents repel'
I1
I2
B1
x
⊗ = current into page
⊙ = current out of page

Fields of coils

The magnetic field produced by a single wire is not strong enough to be useful. If several wires are placed together by winding the wire into a coil, the flux density contributions from each wire will add together. For a long 'solenoid' coil, the flux density is uniform over the cross section and quite uniform along its length. The flux density of the solenoid depends on the current and the number of turns *per unit length*:

$$B = \mu_0 nI$$

$$\text{where } n = \frac{\text{number of turns}}{\text{length of coil}} = \frac{N}{l}$$

Fig. 12 Field of a solenoid

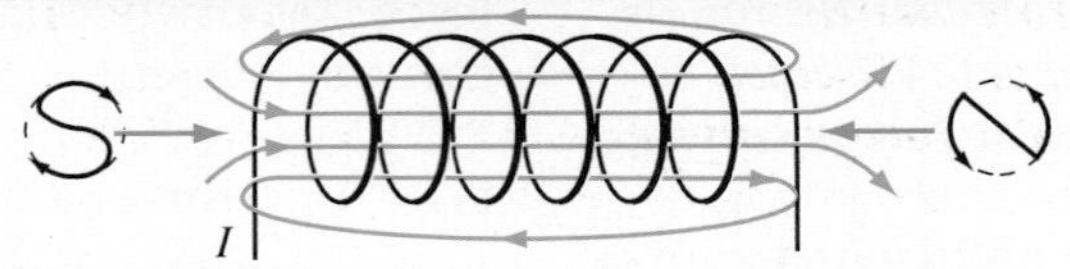
S
N
I

Viewed from this end of the coil, the current appears to go clockwise. It is a south–seeking pole (i.e. field lines into solenoid).

The current appears to go anticlockwise when viewed from this end of the coil. It is north–seeking.

The equation is only strictly correct for an infinitely long solenoid, but it is accurate enough to use when the diameter of the solenoid is small compared to its length. The field is weaker at the ends of the solenoid: only half as much. (Suppose you cut a long solenoid in half; each new end would have provided half of the flux density at the centre of the original coil.)

3 A particle detector uses a solenoid to provide a magnetic field for deflecting particles. A magnetic flux density of 0.2 T is required. If a current of 20 A is available, how many turns per metre would the solenoid need?

A commercial electromagnet could have about 5000 turns per metre with wire carrying a current of 10 A. This would generate a field of flux density less than 0.1 T, still not high enough for many applications. The flux density can be increased by using a ferromagnetic core to the electromagnet (e.g. pure iron, or a purpose-made magnetic alloy). The flux density inside the core can be several thousand times larger than the external field caused by the electromagnet.

Suppose we need a field of around one tesla. Wire with a diameter of about half a millimetre would allow 2000 turns per metre. Using $B = \mu_0 nI$ gives:

$$I = \frac{B}{\mu_0 n} = \frac{1}{(4\pi \times 10^{-7} \times 2000)} = 400 \text{ A}$$

A current this size would melt copper wire of this diameter. To achieve 1 T, the number of turns per metre is increased by winding multiple layers of turns. Unfortunately, this increases the cost and the resistance of the wire, leading to overheating. These problems prompted the development of superconducting magnets. These are made of a superconducting alloy and have to be kept at around –270 °C. The resistance of the wires then drops to zero, so huge currents can be carried by thin wires without any heating effect.

4 A simple mass spectrometer deflects ions of mass up to 10^{-25} kg in a uniform magnetic field of 0.2 T. The ions are travelling at 1.2×10^5 m s^{-1}.

a What would be the maximum radius of curvature of the path of ions in the spectrometer? ($e = 1.6 \times 10^{-19}$ C)

b What current would be needed to produce the 0.2 T field using a solenoid of length 0.5 m consisting of 20 000 turns of wire?

Key ideas

- An electric current in a long straight wire produces flux density
  $$B = \frac{\mu_0 I}{2\pi a}$$
  at distance a from the wire. The field pattern is a set of concentric circles, closer together as you approach the wire. The term μ_0 is called the permeability of free space. It has the assigned value $4\pi \times 10^{-7}$ N A^{-2}.
- Two parallel straight wires carrying currents (I_1 and I_2) in the same direction will attract with force per unit length of wire
  $$\frac{F}{l} = \frac{\mu_0 I_1 I_2}{2\pi a}$$
- A long solenoid has $B = \mu_0 nI$ where n = number of turns per unit length. Flux density may be increased by using a ferromagnetic core.

15.5 Electrostatic force

Geraldine is a consultant radiologist. She uses radioactive substances to trace blood flow.

Isotopes with short half-lives are preferred to avoid long-term exposure of the patient to radioactivity. Half-lives could be as short as 30 minutes – too short to transport the isotopes from a distant manufacturer. The radiology department makes the isotopes in its own particle accelerator.

Magnetic fields can be used to deflect charged particles, but a uniform magnetic field has no effect on the speed of the particles. Electrostatic force is needed to accelerate particles to high enough kinetic energies to make new isotopes.

All charged particles exert a force on each other (Fig. 13). This force can be investigated experimentally. The results of these experiments show that the size of the force:

- is proportional to the size of each charge;
- follows an inverse square law with distance.

Fig. 13 Charge and separation

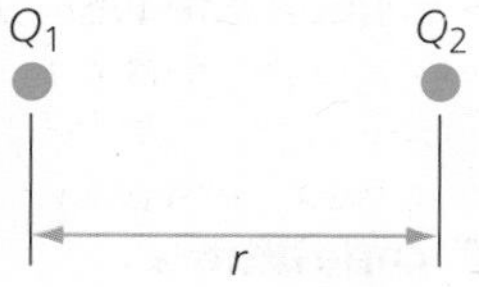
Q1
Q2
r

The experimental results can be summarised by the equation:

$$F \propto \frac{Q_1 Q_2}{r^2}$$

The constant of proportionality is written in an unusual way:

$$F = \left(\frac{1}{4\pi\varepsilon_0}\right) \times \left(\frac{Q_1 Q_2}{r^2}\right)$$

The constant ε_0 is called the **permittivity of free space**; it has a value of 8.854×10^{-12} F m^{-1}.

This expression is called Coulomb's law. It applies only to point charges, but a sphere of charge behaves as though all the charge is concentrated at its centre. Electron scattering experiments show that the force between electrons obeys Coulomb's law at distances as small as 10^{-16} m – about a millionth of the size of an atom.

To make new isotopes, we need to make particles collide with nuclei. The forces and energies involved can be surprisingly large. For example, if we try to make a proton collide with a positively charged carbon nucleus ($Z = 6$), it will experience a repulsive electrostatic force. When they are separated by the diameter of an average nucleus (about 5×10^{-15} m), the force on the proton will be:

$$F = \frac{(1.6 \times 10^{-19}) \times 6 \times (1.6 \times 10^{-19})}{4\pi\varepsilon_0 \times (5 \times 10^{-15})^2}$$

$$= 55 \text{ N}$$

On a particle of mass 10^{-27} kg, this is an astonishing force.

Field strength and potential

To make new radioactive materials, we need to accelerate charged particles to very high speeds. The particles need enough energy to overcome huge electrostatic repulsions from the target nuclei. One way of accelerating particles is to use an electric field. An electric field is any space where a charged particle experiences a force (Fig. 14).

Fig. 14 Parallel plate field pattern

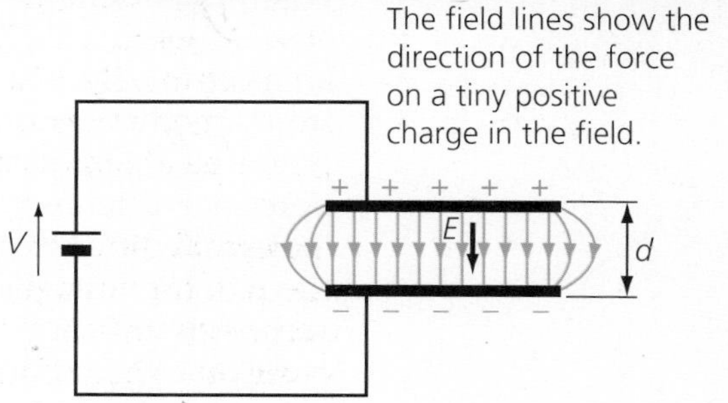
The field lines show the direction of the force on a tiny positive charge in the field.
V
E
d
+
−

The **electric field strength**, *E*, is defined as the force per unit charge on a small charge in an electric field:

$$E = \frac{F}{q}$$

Fig. 15 Electric field strength

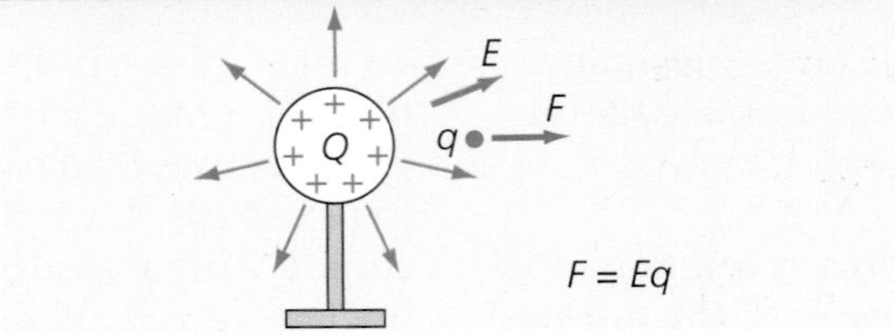
E
F
Q
q
F = Eq

Electric field strength (Fig. 15) is measured in newtons per coulomb ($N\ C^{-1}$), but you may also see it expressed in volts per metre ($V\ m^{-1}$).

As a charged particle moves through an electric field, it experiences a force. Work is therefore done when the particle moves. If a positively charged particle moves to a region of high (positive) electric field, the particle gains electric potential energy. Conversely, the electrostatic force becomes very small at large distances. When the particle is at an infinite distance, the electric potential energy is zero. **Electrical potential** (V) is defined as the electrical potential energy per unit charge. This is the work done per unit charge in bringing a small positive charge from infinity to a point in an electric field:

$$V = \frac{W}{Q}$$

Potential difference is the difference in electrical potential between two points in an electric field. If a charged particle moves from a point at potential V_1 to a point at potential V_2, it has moved through a potential difference of $V = V_2 - V_1$. This 'potential difference' is exactly the same as the p.d. (or voltage) in electrical circuits. Although 'infinity' is the theoretical position of zero potential, for all practical purposes we use the surface of planet Earth as our zero. If we say an object is at a potential of 3000 V, it usually means that the p.d. between the object and the Earth is 3000 V.

The definition of potential can be rearranged to give:

$$W = QV$$

For an electron, $Q = e$, so $W = eV$. Work needs to be done to move a charge (e) through a difference of potential of 1 V. This amount of work is called one **electronvolt**; $1\text{eV} = 1.6 \times 10^{-19}$ J (see Chapter 12).

We can derive equations for the electric field strength and potential in simple arrangements. For parallel plates, a distance d apart (Fig. 14):

$$E = \frac{V}{d}$$

Near a point charge Q (or a sphere of charge), the equations are:

$$E = \frac{Q}{4\pi\varepsilon_0 r^2} \quad \text{and} \quad V = \frac{Q}{4\pi\varepsilon_0 r}$$

These equations apply to charges in a vacuum. In any other medium, the molecules can give rise to an opposing field. This decreases the field strength and the potential. Both are decreased by a factor ε_r – the 'relative permittivity' of the medium.

5 A proton ($q = 1.6 \times 10^{-19}$ C) is given a kinetic energy of 10 MeV by an accelerator. How close could it get to the nucleus of an oxygen atom ($^{16}_{8}O$)?

6 A metal sphere of radius 10 cm is at the centre of a large tank. The sphere is charged to a potential of 20 kV. Calculate the electric field strength at the surface of the sphere if the tank is filled with

a air ($\varepsilon_r \approx 1$)

b ethanol ($\varepsilon_r \approx 26$)

Does gravity hold nuclei together?

Using Coulomb's law, a proton on the edge of a large nucleus (e.g. uranium, diameter = 10^{-14} m) experiences a repulsive force of about 80 N. This is big enough to rip the nucleus apart. Another force must be holding the particles together. Despite the high density of the nucleus, the gravitational force on the protons is only about = 2.5×10^{-29} N. Gravity is evidently an insignificant force on the subatomic scale. Something must hold the protons together inside the nucleus. Scientists are using giant particle accelerators to investigate the nature of a short-ranged **strong nuclear force**.

Gravitational and electrostatic force fields

Electrostatic and gravitational forces share some important features:

- the force is inversely proportional to distance squared;
- the force is proportional to the size of the 'property' (i.e. charge or mass) of each body.

Because they have this common ground, some of the mathematical theory developed for gravitational fields can be applied to electric fields. For example, field strengths are defined as:

force per unit mass for gravitational fields

force per unit charge for electric fields

Table 1 highlights some of the similarities and differences.

Table 1

Electrostatic	Gravitational
force $\propto \frac{1}{r^2}$	force $\propto \frac{1}{r^2}$
force $\propto$ size of charges	force $\propto$ size of masses
potential = work per unit charge	potential = work per unit mass
field strength = force / charge	field strength = force / mass
charges are positive or negative	masses are only positive
force can attract or repel	only attractive forces known
field strength depends on medium	no medium known to affect field strength

An important difference between electrostatic and gravitational fields is that you can have conductors of electricity. Conductors affect electric field and potential:

- you cannot have an electric field inside a conductor. (An electric field exerts a force on charges: charges would redistribute until the field dropped to zero.)
- all points on the surface of a conductor must be at the same potential. (If points had different potential, there would be an electric field between these points which would make charges move as before.)

Fig. 16 E–r and V–r graphs

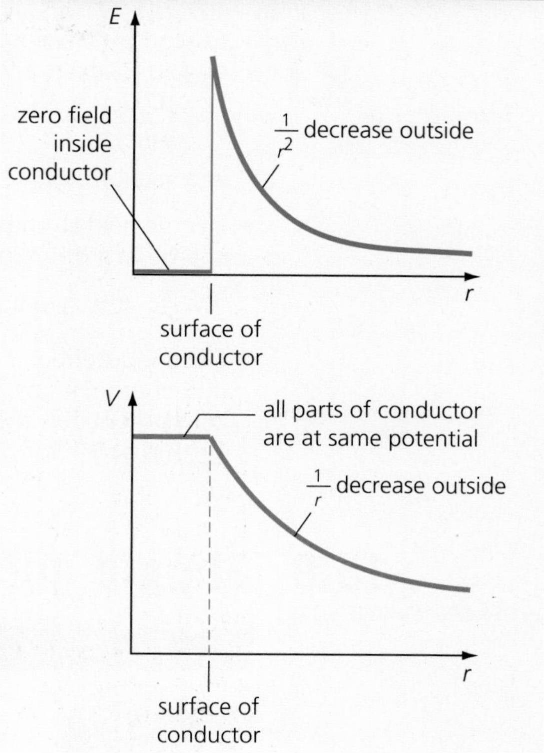

E
zero field inside conductor
$\frac{1}{r^2}$ decrease outside
r
surface of conductor
V
all parts of conductor are at same potential
$\frac{1}{r}$ decrease outside
r
surface of conductor

The field and potential patterns around conducting spheres give the graphs in Fig. 16.

7 A hydrogen atom can be pictured as an electron ($e = -1.6 \times 10^{-19}$ C) orbiting a positive nucleus of charge $+1.6 \times 10^{-19}$ C. The energy needed to remove the electron completely (to infinity) is 2.2×10^{-18} J. Calculate

a the potential at the position of the normal orbit of the electron;

b the radius of the orbit and so state the diameter of the atom;

c the electric field strength at the position of the electron's orbit.

Key ideas

- Coulomb's law shows that charges Q_1 and Q_2 exert a force
  $$F = \frac{Q_1Q_2}{4\pi\varepsilon_0 r^2}$$
  in a vacuum. $\varepsilon_0 = 8.85 \times 10^{-12}$ F m^{-1}.
- Electric field strength is the force per unit charge at a point in the field:
  $E = \frac{F}{Q}$. It is zero inside conductors.
- Electric potential is the potential energy per unit charge at any point. The position of zero potential is theoretically at infinity but Earth is at 0 V for practical purposes.
- Parallel plates at separation d have a uniform field
  $$E = \frac{V}{d}$$
  A point charge in a vacuum has
  $$E = \frac{Q}{4\pi\varepsilon_0 r^2} \text{ and } V = \frac{Q}{4\pi\varepsilon_0 r}$$
  at distance r from the point. These equations also apply to the surface of a uniformly distributed conducting sphere of radius r.
- Electric and gravitational fields are similar in their mathematical form (inverse square law, etc.) but differ in that electrical forces may be attractive or repulsive, while gravitational force is always attractive.

15.9 Simple accelerators

Fig. 17 Van de Graaff generator

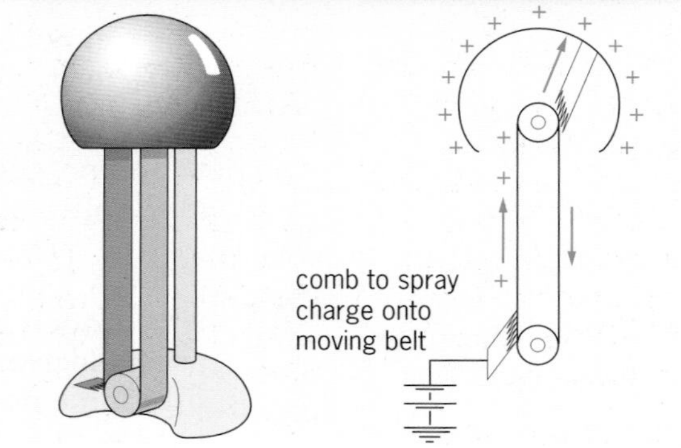
comb to spray
charge onto
moving belt

Van de Graaff generators are one of the simplest early particle accelerators. They are still used in research and as the *injector* – the first stage – for bigger accelerators. Inside a generator, charge is carried on a moving belt onto a metal dome. Suppose the dome is 1.6 m in diameter and that 180 μC of charge accumulates. At the surface of the dome, the electric field strength would be:

$$E = \frac{Q}{4\pi\varepsilon_0 r^2} \approx 2.5 \text{ MV m}^{-1}$$

This is just below the level at which air conducts. Sparks start flying at ≈ 3 MV m^{-1}. The potential of the sphere will be:

$$V = \frac{Q}{4\pi\varepsilon_0 r} \approx 2 \text{ MV}$$

The sphere of the Van de Graaff generator is a capacitor (see Chapter 7). Its capacitance is $C = Q / V \approx 90$ pF. The work done in charging the Van de Graaff sphere is therefore:

$$W = \tfrac{1}{2}CV^2 \approx \tfrac{1}{2} \times 90 \times 10^{-12} \times \left(2 \times 10^6\right)^2$$
$$= 180 \text{ J}$$

This is surprisingly modest: the energy output of a small domestic light bulb for 3 seconds.

Particles of charge e would therefore be accelerated and leave with an energy of 2 MeV. (Van de Graaff generators can produce up to 10 MeV.) Protons with this energy would be travelling quickly.

Using $E_k = \tfrac{1}{2}mv^2$ gives

$$v = \sqrt{\frac{2E_k}{m}} = \sqrt{\frac{2 \times 2 \text{ MeV}}{1.67 \times 10^{-27} \text{ kg}}}$$

$$v = \sqrt{\frac{2 \times 2\,000\,000 \times 1.6 \times 10^{-19} \text{ J}}{1.67 \times 10^{-27} \text{ kg}}}$$

$$v = 2 \times 10^7 \text{ m s}^{-1}$$

about $\frac{1}{15}$th of the speed of light.

Relativity and mass increase

Using $E_k = \frac{1}{2} mv^2$ to calculate speed is acceptable at low energies. If you repeat the calculation for protons at 1 GeV, the proton's velocity would be about 1.5 times the speed of light. Einstein's theory of relativity says that nothing with mass can travel at light speed. Instead, we observe an increase in the mass of particles at high energies. In a 1 GeV machine, a proton would have over three times its rest mass. An electron with 1 GeV of kinetic energy would have more than 2000 times its rest mass. Experiments using electron accelerators provided the first direct evidence that Einstein's theory of mass increase was accurate.

These mass changes are now important in the design of accelerators because the amount of deflection by magnetic fields is dependent on mass. You should be wary of applying Newton's laws to calculations where the speed of particles is more than a fifth of the speed of light.

Creating huge potential differences is not easy; insulation becomes a real problem, with conduction in gases leading to dangerous spark discharges. Instead of trying to accelerate the particles all at once – by one huge electric field – a more successful technique relies on the repeated use of a smaller electric field. The earliest such design was the linear accelerator (linac, Fig. 18).

Fig. 18 A linear accelerator

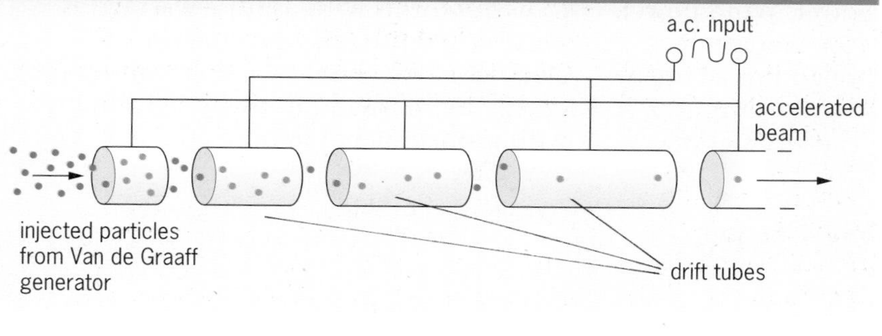
a.c. input
accelerated beam
injected particles from Van de Graaff generator
drift tubes

The fact that the field strength inside a conductor is zero is exploited in linacs. A high-frequency alternating electric field is used to accelerate particles. The particles travel in 'drift tubes' – conductors where the electric field strength inside is zero – when the a.c. voltage would try to make them go backwards. They emerge from the drift tubes in time to be accelerated by the next 'forwards' voltage half–cycle. Drift tubes need to increase in length along the linac because the particles travel faster at each stage.

For a 50 MeV proton the average speed would be around 50 000 km s^{-1}, so to keep the drift tubes small – say 20 cm average length – would need a very high frequency:

$$\text{time inside drift tube} = \frac{\text{distance}}{\text{speed}}$$

$$= \frac{0.2\ \text{m}}{5 \times 10^7\ \text{m s}^{-1}} = 4.10^{-9}\ \text{seconds}$$

This is half a cycle of the a.c. so the period is 8×10^{-9} seconds, giving a frequency in the order of 100 MHz. Electrons travel faster, so even higher frequencies in the microwave region are used.

The longest linac in the world is at the Stanford Linear Accelerator Centre: it is 3 km long and can accelerate electrons to 50 GeV. Working on energy to mass ratio, this is equivalent to giving a human being all the solar energy received by the earth for a month! As theories become more advanced, higher and higher energies are needed to investigate their predictions. The proposed Large Hadron Collider at CERN should be able to accelerate protons to around 7000 GeV: the particle beam would have the energy of several kilograms of high explosive!

Large accelerators often use linacs as the injector stage. Particles are then accelerated in resonant cavities using radio waves or microwaves. The particles are effectively 'surfing' on the electric field vector of the electromagnetic waves. The accelerators are made as giant rings, so that the particles can be accelerated a little more each time they circulate. Magnetic fields are used to make them go around the bending path. The rings need to be very large to keep the centripetal acceleration of the particles low; otherwise, they emit electromagnetic radiation and so slow down. Even with accelerators many kilometres in diameter, the particles emit a lot of radiation – so much so that the intense X-ray emissions from the particle beam are now an important research tool for biochemists and semiconductor technologists.

16 Electricity for ever

Windmills were one of the earliest ways of harnessing energy from the environment. They used the kinetic energy of the wind to drive water-pumps and millstones directly. Now, wind farms can be used to generate pollution-free electricity.

Fossil fuels will not last forever. There is a real need to develop other energy sources and more efficient ways of using energy. One possibility is wind power. Wind power in the UK now generates an average of 30 MW of electricity. Although this is tiny by comparison with the 2000 MW output of a single large fossil fuel or nuclear station, this type of energy is environmentally clean – it produces no waste, no pollution, no radioactivity and no acid rain.

Aerogenerators need to be a safe distance from people, so it is important that we transmit the energy produced efficiently. Electricity is one of the best ways of transferring energy over long distances. It is also important for consumers to transfer this electrical energy to useful forms with as little wastage as possible. Lighting is one vital use of electricity. We could save huge amounts of energy by replacing hot-wire light bulbs with more efficient lamps.

16.1 Learning objectives

After working through this chapter, you should be able to:

- **explain** how a dynamo produces alternating current;
- **explain** how a transformer works;
- **explain** why electricity is transmitted as a high voltage a.c.;
- **relate** peak and r.m.s. values of current and potential difference;
- **define** self-inductance;
- **explain** how capacitors and inductors behave with a.c.

16.2 Aerogenerators

The blades of aerogenerators vary in size from a diameter of around 1 m, suitable for charging the battery on a boat, to the huge generators on 'wind farms', which have diameters of 25 m or more. The large diameters mean that the blades have a large area and can transfer a greater amount of kinetic energy from moving air.

Low wind speeds make the energy transferred per square metre of sail smaller. One of the biggest problems facing wind turbine designers is maximising power output at low wind speeds. The structure also needs to withstand very high wind speeds without breaking. Few designs are able to work well at wind speeds less than 6 m s^{-1}. This means that aerogenerators need to be placed in exposed places with high average wind speeds. Hilltops and coastal areas are favoured locations (Fig. 1).

Fig. 1 Isovent map of the UK

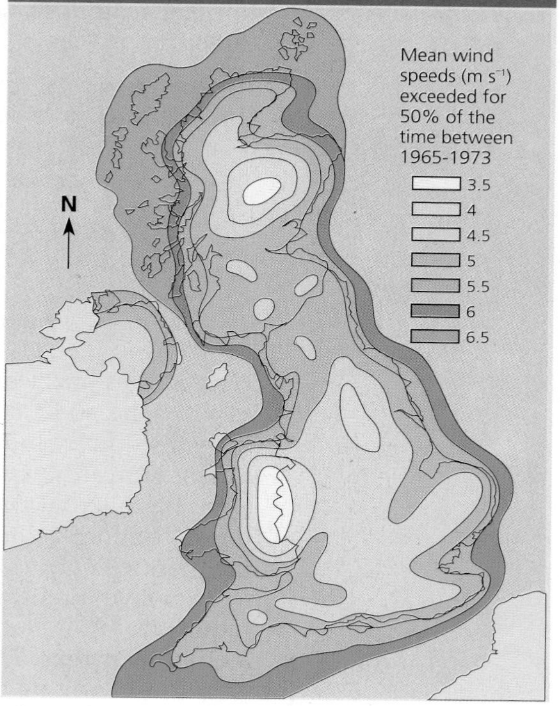
N
Mean wind speeds (m s⁻¹) exceeded for 50% of the time between 1965-1973
3.5
4
4.5
5
5.5
6
6.5

16.3 From wind to electricity

Early windmills used the kinetic energy of wind for applications such as grinding corn. However, it is the potential to generate electricity that now makes wind power attractive. Dynamos are used to convert the movement of the wind into electricity. Dynamos rely on **electromagnetic induction**.

Electromagnetic induction

In 1831, Michael Faraday discovered that electricity is produced in a wire as it moves through a magnetic field. Faraday had already built the first electric motor. This device relied on the magnetic field produced by an electric current. He believed that it should also be possible to make electricity from a magnetic field. Faraday decided to use an electromagnet to provide a magnetic field. Two coils of wire were wound around an iron ring. One coil was connected to a battery. The other coil was connected to a galvanometer, an uncalibrated electrical current detector (Fig. 2). Faraday expected the current from the battery to set up a strong magnetic field in the iron ring. This would then, he thought, 'induce' a steady flow of electrical current through the galvanometer.

Faraday's original transformer

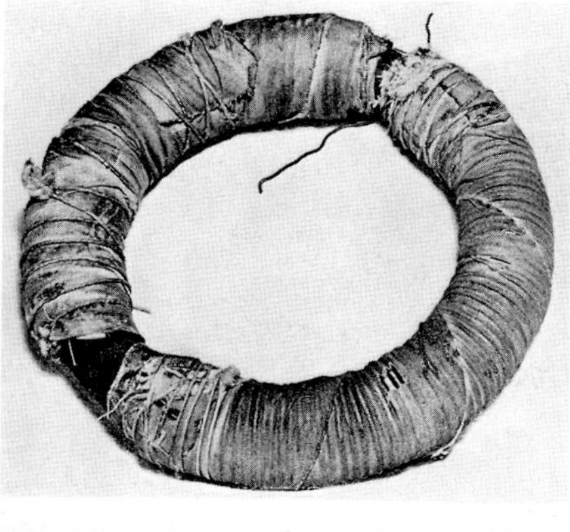

Fig. 2 Faraday's experimental circuit

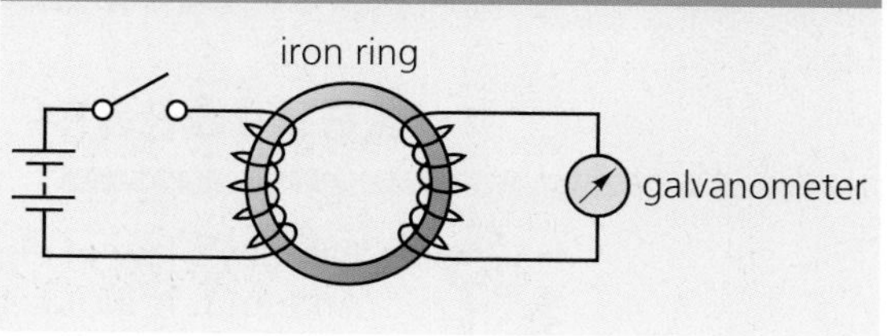
iron ring
galvanometer

The experiment didn't turn out quite as Faraday expected. Instead, he saw the galvanometer needle move quickly to one side when the switch was turned on and then return to zero. Faraday noticed that when the switch was turned off, the needle jumped again, this time in the opposite direction (Fig. 3).

Fig. 3 Galvanometer readings

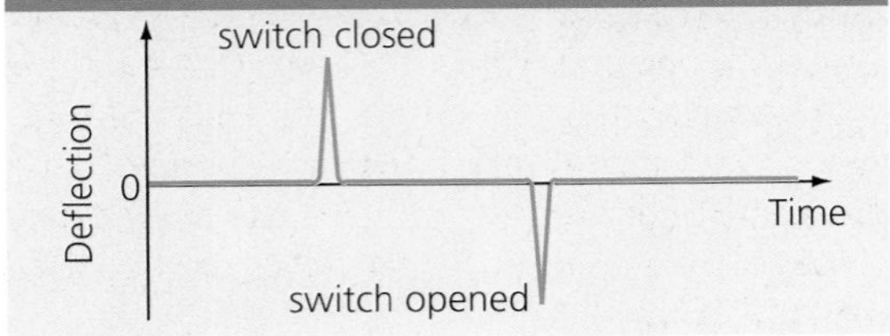
switch closed
Deflection
0
Time
switch opened

Faraday was puzzled by the results of his experiment, so he continued his investigation by moving a permanent magnet towards and away from the coil of wire. He saw that the galvanometer registered current flow *only* when the magnet was *moving* (Fig. 4).

Faraday had discovered the essential requirement for electromagnetic induction: a **change of flux**. This could be achieved either by changing the flux itself or by physically moving a conductor through flux lines. The faster and larger the change of flux, the bigger the **induced e.m.f.** The e.m.f. is proportional to the rate of cutting through flux lines. This law of electromagnetic induction is represented by Faraday's law:

Fig. 4 Electromagnetic induction

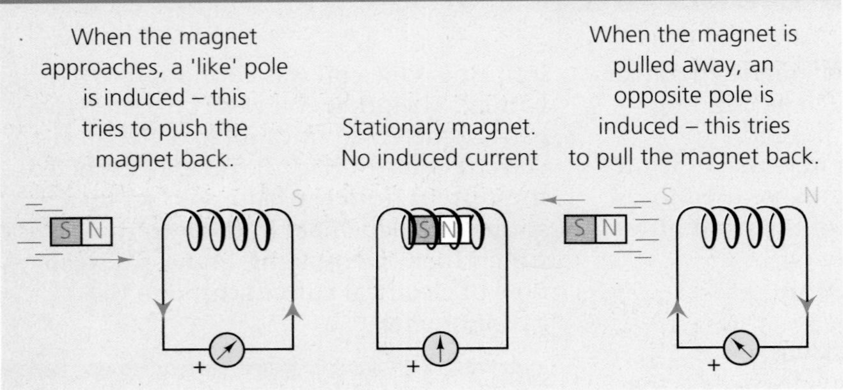
When the magnet approaches, a 'like' pole is induced – this tries to push the magnet back.
Stationary magnet. No induced current
When the magnet is pulled away, an opposite pole is induced – this tries to pull the magnet back.
S
N
S
N
S
N
S
N
+
+
+

The induced e.m.f. in a circuit is equal to the rate at which the circuit cuts flux.

In S.I. units, a flux change of $\Delta\Phi$ in time Δt seconds gives an e.m.f.:

$$\epsilon = \frac{\Delta\Phi}{\Delta t}$$

You can work out the direction of the induced e.m.f. using the principle of conservation of energy. The induced e.m.f. can make a current flow. If this current 'helped' the change of flux, you would be able to make a machine which caused a steadily increasing current without any energy input: a machine in perpetual motion. This is impossible under the law of conservation of energy, so the e.m.f. must try to oppose whatever flux change is causing it. This rule is called Lenz's law.

1 The blade of a wind turbine has a radius of 12 m and turns through a full circle every 6 s. The turbine's axis is aligned North-South, so the blade cuts through the horizontal component of the Earth's magnetic field. This has a horizontal component of flux density of 20 μT. Explain why an e.m.f. is induced along the blade and calculate its magnitude.

Key ideas

- Faraday's law of electromagnetic induction: An e.m.f. is induced when flux changes. The e.m.f. is equal to the rate of change of flux.
- Lenz's law states that the direction of the induced e.m.f. is such that it opposes the change of flux.

Dynamos

Any equipment which contains a conductor cutting through flux lines will work as a **dynamo**. A dynamo is a device for converting mechanical energy into electrical energy. Commercial dynamos consist of a coil spinning inside a magnetic field. We can investigate which factors determine the size of the induced e.m.f. in the coil by analysing a single straight wire of length l moving with speed v through a uniform field of flux density B (Fig. 5).

Fig. 5 Induced e.m.f.

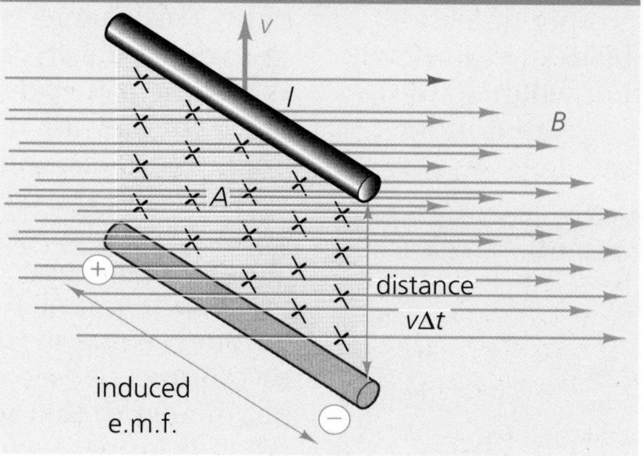
v
l
B
A
+
distance
vΔt
induced
e.m.f.
−

In Δt seconds, the wire moves distance $v\Delta t$ metres, and cuts through an area $A = lv\Delta t$. Therefore, the wire cuts through flux:

$$\Delta\Phi = BA = Blv\Delta t$$

$$\text{so,} \quad \epsilon = \frac{\Delta\Phi}{\Delta t} = \frac{Blv\Delta t}{\Delta t}$$

$$\epsilon = Blv$$

Fig. 6 Fleming's right-hand rule applied to moving wire

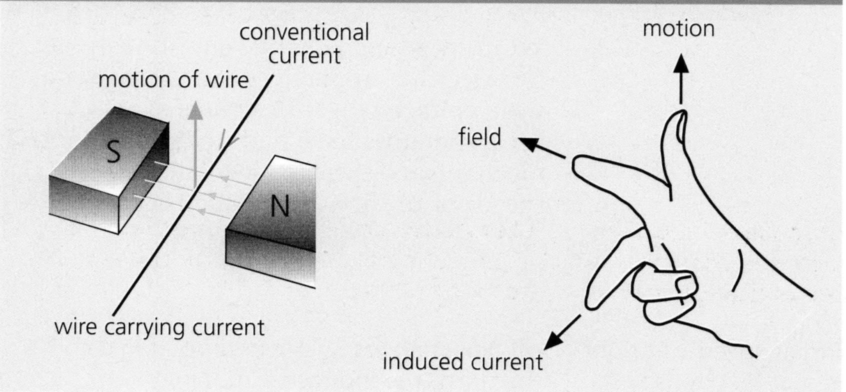
conventional
current
motion of wire
S
I
N
wire carrying current
motion
field
induced current

To work out the direction of the current you could use Lenz's law. Alternatively, Fleming's right-hand dynamo rule can be used. This follows the same principles as the left-hand (motor) rule to give the correct current direction (Fig. 6).

For a rotating coil, each turn of the coil cuts through the magnetic flux lines. For a coil of N turns, each turn would contribute the same amount of e.m.f. All the turns are in series, so the total e.m.f. adds up to:

$$\epsilon = N\frac{\Delta\Phi}{\Delta t}$$

Fig. 7 A dynamo

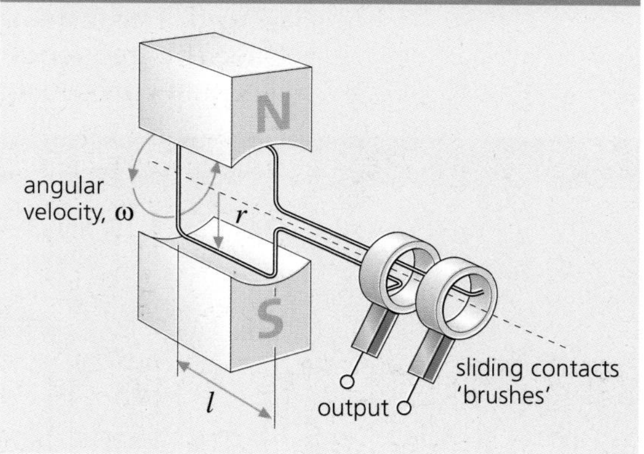
N
angular
velocity, ω
r
S
l
output
sliding contacts
'brushes'

Only the wires on the edge of the coil are cutting through the magnetic flux. We can produce an expression for the maximum magnitude of the e.m.f. The coil has radius r and side length l. It rotates at angular velocity ω. The speed of the edge of the coil is:

$$v = r\omega$$

$$\text{so} \quad \epsilon = Blv = Bl\omega r$$

The coil has width $2r$, so $2rl$ = area A of the coil. For N turns, we have $2N$ coil edges, so the total e.m.f. will be:

$$\epsilon = 2N \times Blr\omega = NB \times 2rl \times \omega = NBA\omega$$

Suppose a large wind turbine rotated once every ten seconds ($\omega = 2\pi/10 = 0.63$ rad s^{-1}). Using strong permanent magnets, we can achieve a magnetic flux density of around 0.1 T. It would be possible to mount a coil of perhaps 0.5 m^2 with 500 turns at the centre of a wind turbine. This would give an e.m.f. of:

$$\begin{aligned} \epsilon &= NBA\omega \\ &= 500 \times 0.1\ \text{T} \times 0.5\ \text{m}^2 \times 0.63\ \text{s}^{-1} \\ &= 16\ \text{V} \end{aligned}$$

To increase the e.m.f. to a useful size, we need to have an arrangement of gears which makes the dynamo spin quickly while the wind turbine blades sweep slowly around. The faster rotation will help to make the frequency of the output more acceptable to consumers.

Fig. 8 Coil alignment and induced e.m.f.

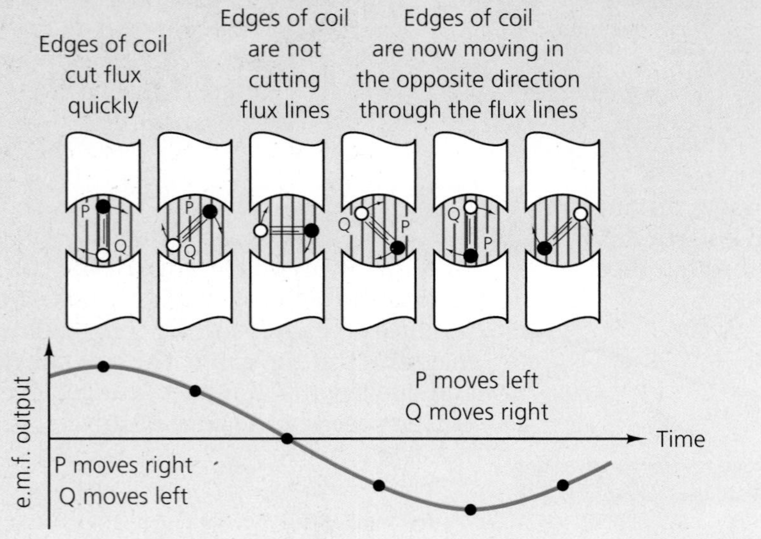

Edges of coil cut flux quickly
Edges of coil are not cutting flux lines
Edges of coil are now moving in the opposite direction through the flux lines
P
Q
e.m.f. output
Time
P moves right
Q moves left
P moves left
Q moves right

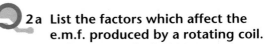

2 a List the factors which affect the e.m.f. produced by a rotating coil.

b A dynamo coil of 5000 turns has length 50 cm and radius 10 cm. It rotates at 3000 r.p.m. in a uniform field of flux density 15 mT. Calculate the magnitude of the maximum e.m.f. output.

Alternating output

We can see why the dynamo produces an alternating output by looking at one side of the coil. Half of the time it is moving left through the field, the other half to the right. This change of direction causes a change of polarity in the induced current. When the coil edges are moving parallel to the field, they are not cutting through flux lines. The e.m.f. will then be zero (Fig. 8).

The faster the coil rotates, the more often it completes a full cycle of the alternating current. For a simple, single coil dynamo the frequency of the dynamo output is equal to the number of revolutions per second. To match the 50 Hz national grid, this generator would need 50 revolutions per second. The speed of rotation also affects the e.m.f. and power output of the generator. For example, doubling the speed of rotation:

- doubles the frequency because twice as many revolutions are completed per second;
- doubles the maximum e.m.f. because the rate of cutting flux has doubled;
- quadruples the power for a particular load, because both current and p.d. are doubled ($P = IV$).

Wind speeds can change enormously, yet few electrical appliances can work over a wide voltage range. Designers of aerogenerators have had to develop control mechanisms, either to regulate allowed speeds or to vary the flux density.

Key ideas

- A wire of length l moving at speed v at right angles to a magnetic field of flux density B will have e.m.f. Blv induced across its ends. The direction of the induced current can be found by using Fleming's right-hand rule.
- If flux changes by $\Delta\Phi$ in time Δt in a coil of N turns, the induced e.m.f. is

$$\epsilon = \frac{N\Delta\Phi}{\Delta t}$$

16.4 Transmitting electricity

The best sites for aerogenerators in the UK are in the exposed, unpopulated areas of north Scotland, and on the western sides of Wales and Cornwall. The electricity generated at these locations needs to be transported to people further afield. If wind farms are to be financially viable, this energy must be transported efficiently.

A group of landowners in the North West Highlands is proposing to build a wind farm capable of generating 100 kW. It will be 30 km from Fort William, the nearest centre of population, so the cost of the cables linking the wind farm to the consumers will be significant. Domestic consumers use a p.d. of 240 V (Fig. 9). Allowing for a 10% energy loss in the supply cables, how thick would these cables need to be?

Fig. 9 Transmission of electricity

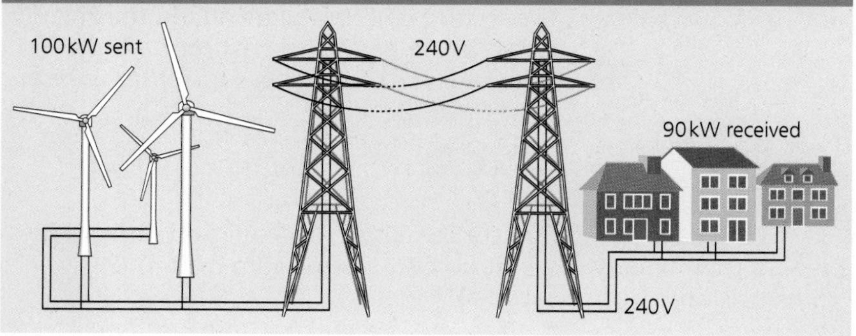
100 kW sent
240 V
90 kW received
240 V

If the consumers receive 90 kW at 240 V, the current will be:

$$I = \frac{P}{V}$$
$$= \frac{90\,000 \text{ W}}{240 \text{ V}} = 375 \text{ A}$$

The cables dissipate 10 kW. Using $P = I^2R$ for the cables:

$$R = \frac{P}{I^2}$$
$$= \frac{10\,000 \text{ W}}{375^2 \text{ A}^2} = 0.0711\ \Omega$$

The cables need to be 60 km long (30 km each way) and are made of copper ($\rho = 1.7 \times 10^{-8}\ \Omega$ m). Using $R = \rho l / A$:

$$A = \frac{\rho l}{R}$$
$$= \frac{1.7 \times 10^{-8}\ \Omega \text{m} \times 60\,000 \text{ m}}{0.0711\ \Omega}$$
$$= 0.0144 \text{ m}^2$$

Assuming circular cross section, the area is πr^2, so $r = 0.068$ m. The wires would need to have a diameter of more than 13 cm! The mass of these cables would be about 7000 tonnes, costing around £20 million. The cost of generating and transporting electricity in this way would be prohibitive.

The solution is to use **transformers** to transport the electricity at very high voltage. The same amount of power can then be transmitted at a low current. For example, the 100 kW from the wind farm could be transmitted as 10 A at 10 000 V, or 2 A at 50 000 V, or even 1 A at 100 000 V.

Heating of the transmission wires causes power loss. The heating effect depends on the square of the current in the wires. For example, reducing the current by a factor of ten would reduce power loss by a factor of 100. Using a higher voltage decreases the

High-voltage transmission needs tall pylons and large insulators to carry the wires at such high potential.

current, so reducing the power loss in the wires. Suppose we transmitted the 100 kW from the wind farm at 11 000 V. We can repeat the calculation of cable diameter (Fig. 10).

Fig. 10 High-voltage transmission

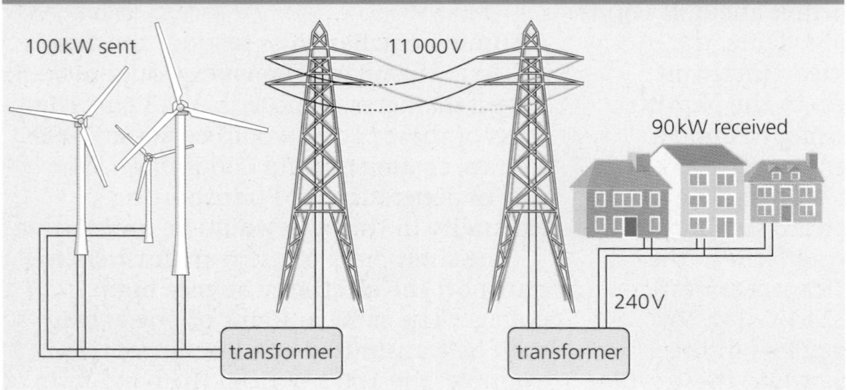

100 kW sent
11 000 V
90 kW received
240 V
transformer
transformer

If the consumer's transformer receives 90 kW at 11 000 V, the current will be 8.18 A. The cables dissipate 10 kW, so using

$P = I^2R$, $R = 149\ \Omega$

Again, using $R = \dfrac{\rho l}{A}$ and $A = \pi r^2$,

$r = 1.9 \times 10^{-3}$ m

The diameter of the wire would then be less than 4 mm, making the transmission of electricity significantly less expensive. Domestic consumers cannot use electricity at very high voltage, so a transformer is used to reduce the voltage for use in the home.

3 A series of wind farms along the western coasts of Scotland could generate 1000 MW. If the resistance of the transmission lines is 10 Ω, calculate the percentage power loss in the cables for transmissions at
a 200 kV
b 400 kV

Transformers

Transformers are used to convert electrical energy from one voltage to another. A transformer consists of two (or more) coils wound around a core of magnetic material (Fig. 11). The structure is remarkably similar to Faraday's original apparatus for the investigation of electromagnetic induction.

Fig. 11 A transformer

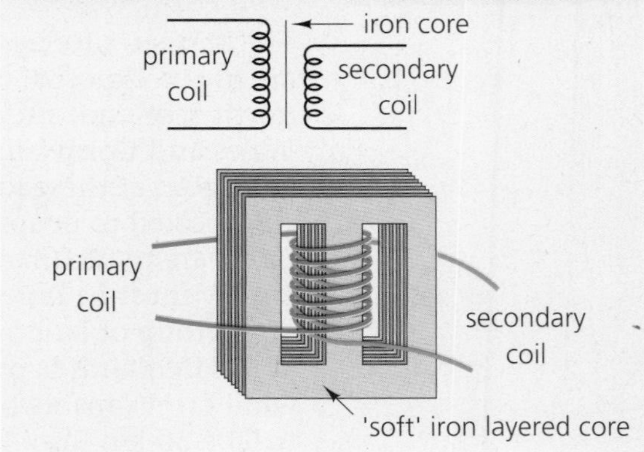

iron core
primary coil
secondary coil
primary coil
secondary coil
'soft' iron layered core

Faraday showed that a direct current (d.c.) does not produce an output voltage in a transformer. This is because there is no change of flux, and so no induced e.m.f. results. Transformers only work with alternating currents. An alternating current creates a continuously changing magnetic flux within the core. This flux cuts through the second coil, inducing an alternating e.m.f. It can be shown that *the ratio of voltages is the same as the ratio of the numbers of turns on the coils*:

$$\frac{V_p}{V_s} = \frac{N_p}{N_s}$$

Strictly speaking, this equation only applies when no current is drawn from the secondary coil.

It is possible make a transformer convert 12 V a.c. into 24 V a.c. by using coils of 200 and 400 turns wrapped around a magnetic core (Fig. 12). If the secondary voltage, V_s,

Fig. 12 Step-up and step-down transformers

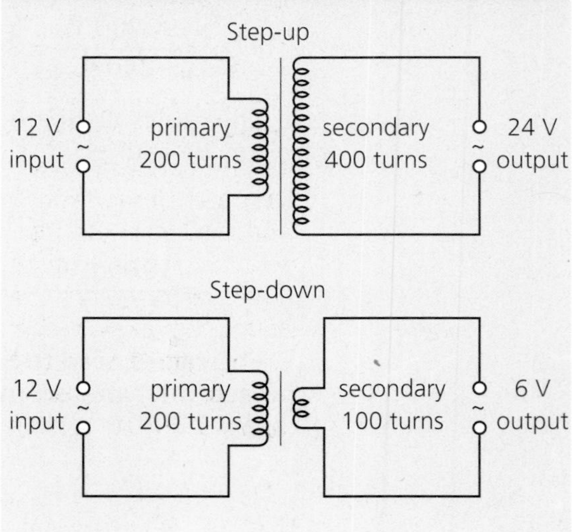

Step-up
12 V input
primary 200 turns
secondary 400 turns
24 V output
Step-down
12 V input
primary 200 turns
secondary 100 turns
6 V output

is bigger than the primary voltage, V_p, the transformer is often called a 'step-up' transformer. Conversely, the primary voltage is bigger than the secondary voltage for a 'step-down' transformer.

An ideal transformer is 100% efficient, so that power input is then equal to power output. Using $P = IV$ gives:

$$I_p V_p = I_s V_s$$

$$\text{so,} \quad \frac{V_p}{V_s} = \frac{I_s}{I_p}$$

$$\text{Therefore:} \quad \frac{V_p}{V_s} = \frac{N_p}{N_s} = \frac{I_s}{I_p}$$

$$\text{voltage ratio} = \text{turns ratio} = \frac{1}{\text{current ratio}}$$

Clearly, a transformer which steps down the voltage will step up the current. This makes it possible for very high current devices (like arc welding machines using 150 A) to operate from a domestic 13 A socket.

4 At a primary current of 350 A, a step-up transformer is 95% efficient. If the primary and secondary voltages are 600 V and 42 kV, calculate the secondary current.

The transformer equation is only approximate. The formula makes the unrealistic assumptions that:

- all flux from the primary cuts through the secondary. However, even with the best core material, you do not get 100% transfer.
- there are no energy losses in the core. However, this is not true because:

a repeatedly magnetising and demagnetising real ferromagnetic materials involves energy loss as heat;

b the core is a conductor inside a changing magnetic field: current will be induced, causing heating.

- there is no resistance in the wires. Real transformers have 'I^2R' (resistive heating) losses in the wires of both primary and secondary coils. Some large transformers are oil cooled to get rid of the heat.

Despite this, it is possible to make transformers for use in electricity distribution which are around 99% efficient.

Eddy currents

Iron cores are often used to increase flux density inside dynamos and transformers. Iron, however, is an electrical conductor. As the core turns inside the field, an e.m.f. is induced in each part of it. Imagine a solid cylinder as a series of wire loops all joined together (Fig. 13). As the cylinder turns, the e.m.f. in each loop makes a current flow. Such currents seem to flow in swirls or eddies: hence the name **eddy currents**.

Fig. 13 Eddy currents in a rotating core

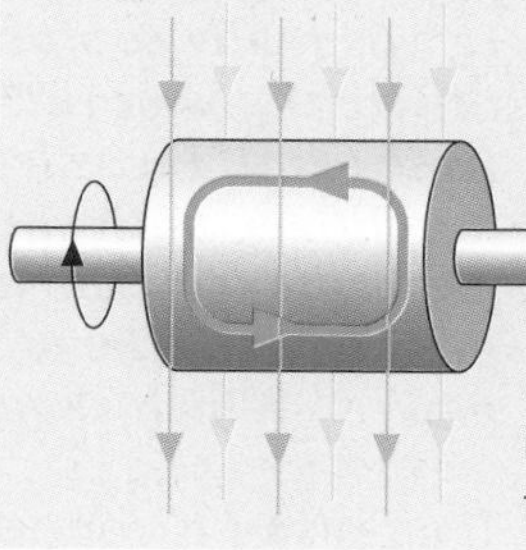
The solid metal core is a moving conductor in a magnetic field...
...so a swirl of current is induced. This opposes the movement of the core.

Lenz's law tells us that the induced current will try to oppose the change which creates it. The current flowing in the iron core will therefore slow the dynamo down. As the core has electrical resistance, the current flow will cause heating. The input kinetic energy is therefore transferred as heat to the surroundings.

In dynamos, motors and transformers, eddy currents can greatly reduce efficiency. The effect is minimised by increasing the resistance of the magnetic material. Several techniques are used:

- bundles of iron wires or even compacted iron dust will both have much higher resistance than a solid metal core.
- ceramic materials called ferrites contain magnetic particles. Ceramics have the mechanical and electrical properties of china – they are hard, brittle and good electrical insulators.
- thin layers (laminations) are bonded together with electrical insulators. This is the most common technique for motors and dynamos.

Key ideas

- Transformers are used for changing voltages. They only work with alternating currents. The ratio of primary to secondary voltages is the same as the turns ratio in ideal transformers. Current ratio is the inverse of voltage ratio if the transformer is 100% efficient.

$$\frac{V_p}{V_s} = \frac{N_p}{N_s} = \frac{I_s}{I_p}$$

- Energy losses in transformers include eddy-current heating of the core; heat output due to repeated cycles of magnetisation; resistive heating of the wires of both coils; and leakage of magnetic flux.
- Power loss due to heating in electricity cables is reduced using high voltage, low current transmission.

16.5 Power and a.c.

I went to buy an new 'amp' for my guitar. It was really confusing: there were lots of different power ratings on the amplifiers. In the end, I was left with a choice of two amplifiers, both similar in cost and performance. One was rated 100 watts peak power', the other '70 watts r.m.s. power'. Which should I choose?

If a resistor is connected to an alternating potential difference, the power fluctuates between zero, when the voltage is zero, and a maximum when the voltage reaches its highest value. The 'peak power' rating of amplifiers and loudspeakers is equal to this maximum value. However, it is rather a misleading value, because the average power is much lower (Fig. 14).

If the peak p.d. output is V_0, the maximum power will be V_0^2/R. By symmetry, you can see that the average power will be only half of this:

$$P = \tfrac{1}{2}\frac{V_0^2}{R}$$

This equation for power in an a.c. circuit can be written as:

$$P = \frac{\left(V_0/\sqrt{2}\right)^2}{R}$$

Comparing this with the d.c. formula:

$$P = \frac{V^2}{R}$$

you can see that a d.c. voltage of $(V_0/\sqrt{2})$ is equivalent to an a.c. with peak voltage V_0.

Fig. 14 Variation of alternating p.d. and power with time

The power delivered to a load of resistance R is $P = V^2/R$, so the power fluctuates continuously for an a.c. generator.

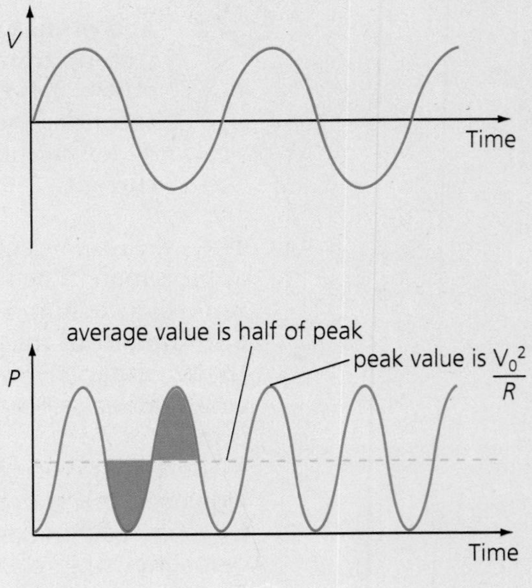
V
Time
average value is half of peak
peak value is V_0^2/R
P
Time

To derive this result, we have in effect taken the mean of the squares of the voltage values (because $P \propto V^2$) and then taken the square root. This is therefore called the **root mean square** (r.m.s.) voltage.

$$V_{\text{r.m.s.}} = \frac{V_0}{\sqrt{2}}$$

You could do the same for current using the d.c. formula $P = I^2R$ giving $I_{r.m.s.} = I_0 / \sqrt{2}$

R.m.s. current and voltage can be used in exactly the same way as d.c. current and voltage in equations such as $R = V/I$ and $P = IV$. Most a.c. electrical meters will give r.m.s. readings. For example, a voltmeter connected to the mains supply in the UK will give a reading of about 240 V. This is the r.m.s. level, so the mains supply reaches a peak voltage of about 340 V. On an oscilloscope, this would show as a wave with peak-to-peak voltage of 680 V.

Fig. 15 Comparison of peak-to-peak and r.m.s. voltage

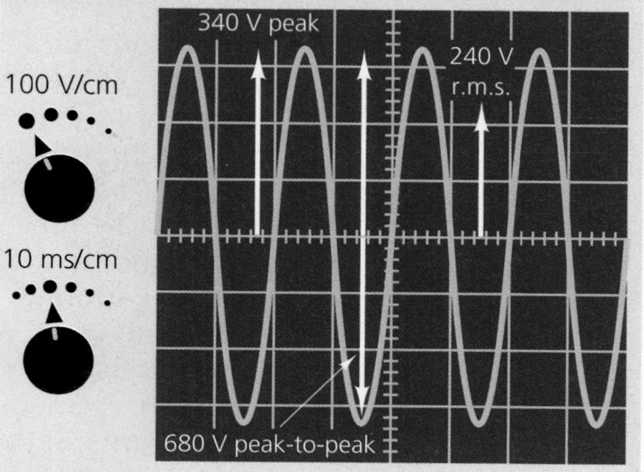
340 V peak
240 V
r.m.s.
100 V/cm
10 ms/cm
680 V peak-to-peak

The mains in the UK is around 240 V r.m.s., but an oscilloscope reveals the much larger p.d. reached.

5 Calculate the peak current through an 8 Ω loudspeaker connected to an amplifier which is generating 72 W r.m.s. from a sine wave a.c.

Key ideas

- The root mean square values of voltage and current can be substituted into the equations $P = IV = I^2R = V^2 / R$. In a pure resistor, a r.m.s. current of I A would cause the same heating effect as a d.c. current I A.
- Peak and r.m.s. values of sine waves are given by:

$$V_{r.m.s.} = \frac{V_0}{\sqrt{2}} \quad \text{and} \quad I_{r.m.s.} = \frac{I_0}{\sqrt{2}}$$

- The r.m.s. power is half of the peak power value of the a.c. sine wave.

16.6 Self-induction

Electricity companies go to great lengths to ensure efficient energy transfer across land, so it seems a shame to waste that energy in inefficient devices. Yet, most of us do just that by using incandescent lamps. These light bulbs rely on glowing wires and convert as little as 5% of the energy into useful light. Other, more efficient forms of lighting are available. Fluorescent lights rely on the conduction of electricity through gases. The atoms of the conducting gas give out electromagnetic radiation – mostly as ultraviolet light. Phosphors on the surface of the tube 'fluoresce', converting the UV energy into visible light. Fluorescent tubes are about six times more efficient than ordinary incandescent lamps, and tubes typically last more than ten times longer.

However, the fluorescent light fitting is much more than a simple electrical connector (Fig. 16).

Fig. 16 A fluorescent light fitting

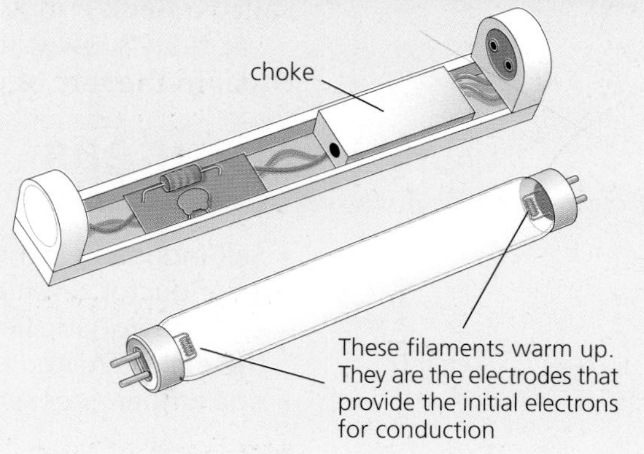
choke
These filaments warm up. They are the electrodes that provide the initial electrons for conduction

To make electricity flow through the gas in a fluorescent tube, you need a very high p.d. and (initially) a source of electrons. The electrons are accelerated by the p.d. They travel fast enough to cause more ionisations by collision. Electrons released in the ionisations could also be accelerated, ultimately leading to an 'avalanche' of electrons. The tube would grow rapidly brighter and blow the fuses in the house. One of the simplest ways to limit the current is to use a 'choke' – a coil of wire that works using an effect called **self-induction**. A coil of wire can act as an electromagnet. If the current in the wire changes, the magnetic flux also changes. This change of flux induces an e.m.f. inside the coil itself. This process is called self-induction (Fig. 17).

Fig. 17 Self-induction

The increasing current causes a change of magnetic flux. This generates an e.m.f.

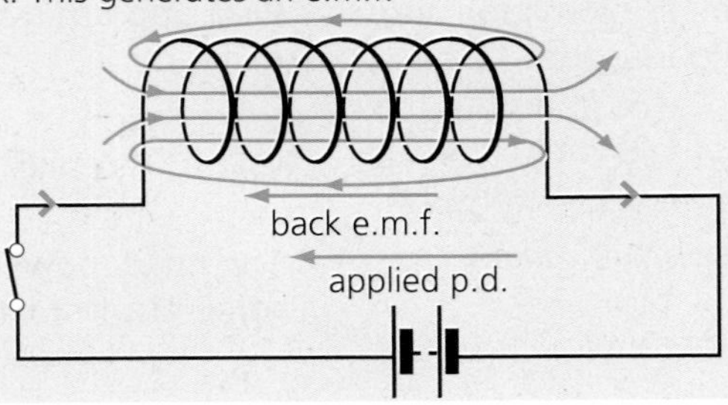
back e.m.f.
applied p.d.

Self-induction has important practical implications: it is impossible for the current inside a coil of wire to change suddenly. Any change of current causes an e.m.f. which opposes the change. Increasing the voltage across the coil gives rise to an e.m.f. in the opposite direction. This is often called a **back e.m.f.**

Faraday's law states that the e.m.f. is equal to the rate of change of flux. The flux for any particular coil or conductor is proportional to the current. Therefore, we can say that the e.m.f., $\in$, is proportional to the rate of change of current:

$$\in \propto \frac{\Delta I}{\Delta t} \quad \text{or} \quad \in = -L\frac{\Delta I}{\Delta t}$$

Fig. 18 Current transition on switching on a coil

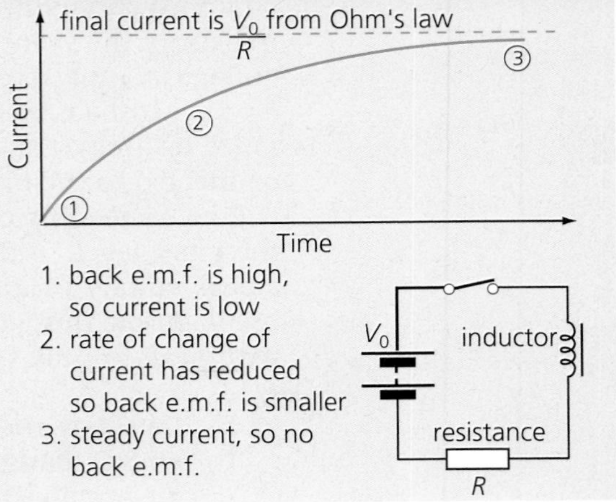
final current is $\frac{V_0}{R}$ from Ohm's law
Current
Time
①
②
③
V_0
inductor
resistance
R

1. back e.m.f. is high, so current is low
2. rate of change of current has reduced so back e.m.f. is smaller
3. steady current, so no back e.m.f.

The minus sign signifies that the e.m.f. is opposing the change, and the constant of proportionality, L, is called the **self-inductance** of the coil. The unit of self-inductance is now called the henry. A self-inductance of one henry (H) will give a back e.m.f. of one volt when the current through it increases at one ampere per second.

6 The electromagnet in an electric buzzer has a self-inductance of 0.30 H and a resistance of 12 Ω.

a What is the maximum current which can flow when the bell is connected to a 6 V battery?

b The maximum back e.m.f. is the same as the battery e.m.f. How quickly can the current rise?

c Could this buzzer vibrate at 100 Hz?

Key ideas

- Self-induction is the creation of a back e.m.f. inside a conductor resulting from a change of its own electromagnetic field. Self-inductance is defined as the e.m.f. created by a rate of change of current at one ampere per second in the conductor.

$$\in = -L\frac{\Delta I}{\Delta t}$$

- The unit of self-inductance is the henry (H). One henry gives a back e.m.f. of one volt when the current rises at one ampere per second.

Self-inductors and a.c.

Induced e.m.f. depends on rate of change of current, which in turn depends on the frequency of the a.c. High frequencies change at a greater rate (Fig. 19).

Fig. 19 Rate of change of current at different frequencies

Higher frequencies have a bigger rate of change of current

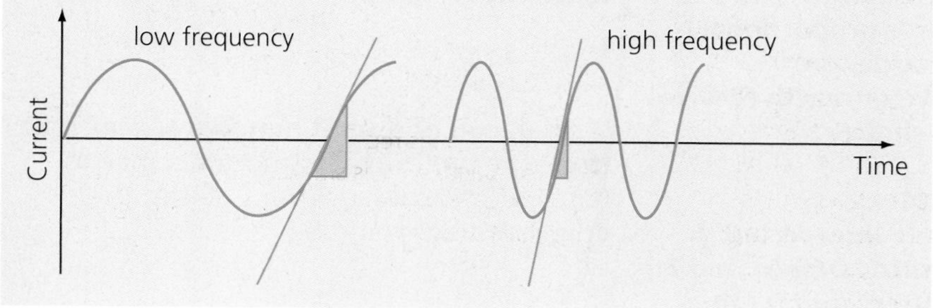

low frequency
high frequency
Current
Time

Higher frequencies therefore produce a larger back e.m.f., so reducing the net current. This effect can be used deliberately to inhibit the flow of a.c. more efficiently than by increasing the resistance. For example, fluorescent light fittings can use an inductor as a **choke** to limit the flow of alternating current to the desired level. The a.c. voltage is constantly changing, giving rise to a back e.m.f. that tends to reduce current flow.

Inductors limit the flow of a.c. by storing and releasing energy using magnetic fields. There is no power loss in an ideal inductor. To distinguish between this effect and electrical *resistance*, which causes a transfer of electrical energy as heat, we refer to the **reactance** of an inductor. Resistance and reactance are similar in most ways. Both are measured in ohms.

Resistance is defined as the ratio of voltage to current at any time. The definition is modified for inductors: we use the *amplitudes* of the a.c. signals.

$$\text{reactance} = \frac{\text{peak voltage}}{\text{peak current}}$$

$$X = \frac{V_0}{I_0}$$

It is possible to show that the reactance X_L of an inductor L is given by:

$$X_L = \omega L = 2\pi f L$$

where ω = angular frequency, f = frequency.

For example, at 50 Hz, a 1.0 H inductor ('choke'), in series with a fluorescent lamp tube, would have the same effect as a resistor of:

$$X_L = \omega L = 2\pi f L$$
$$= 2\pi \times 50\ \text{s}^{-1} \times 1.0\ \text{H} = 314\ \Omega$$

This would safely limit the current from a 240 V supply to a maximum of 0.76 A.

Reactance and power

A self-inductor seems an elaborate way of limiting the current through a fluorescent tube. A simple resistor could be used instead, but power would be transferred as heat when current flows through the resistor. Self-inductors are 'reactive' components: they are able to limit current flow without a loss in power.

The back e.m.f. from an inductor is proportional to the rate of change of current. There is a phase difference (of 90°) between the current and the *rate of change* of current (Fig. 20). For a pure inductor, which has no resistance, the applied p.d. is equal to the back e.m.f. Therefore, current and p.d. are a quarter of a cycle out of phase.

Fig. 20 Variation of current, p.d. and power with time in an inductor

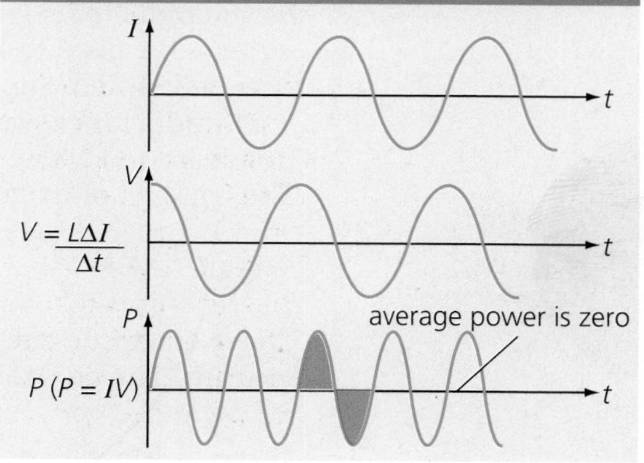

I
t
V
V = LΔI/Δt
t
P
average power is zero
P (P = IV)
t

At any instant, the power 'loss' in a component is p.d. × current: the power loss is sometimes positive, sometimes negative. When power loss is negative, it means that the self-inductor is giving energy back to the circuit. Energy is stored and released by the magnetic fields inside the inductor. The power–time graph is symmetrical about the axis, so the average power is zero.

If resistors were used to limit the current, fluorescent lights would be very inefficient – the current would heat the resistors. Although the inductors are much more expensive to produce, they do not transfer electrical energy as heat.

7 Capacitors store charge. Current is the rate of flow of charge. The p.d. across a capacitor is proportional to the amount of charge. Are capacitors resistive or reactive? Give reasons for your choice.

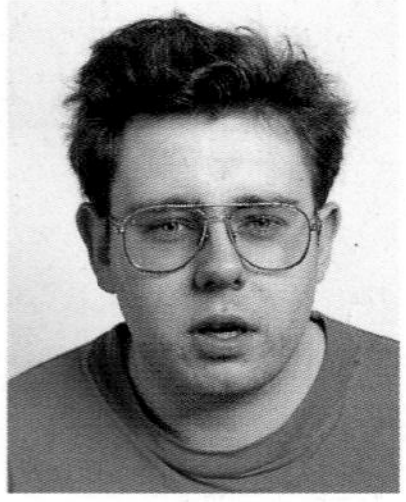

Energy storage in inductors

The shock was completely unexpected. I had disconnected the mains supply, and I was just using a 6 V battery and a lamp to do a continuity test. I held the connectors of the choke straight across the battery by mistake. Nothing happened until I took the wires away ... it was a horrible jolt!

When an inductor is connected to a battery, energy is stored in the magnetic field. If the circuit is suddenly broken, the magnetic field collapses back to zero almost instantly. This gives a huge rate of change of flux and, therefore, a very high p.d. The resulting **back e.m.f. on break** can be many kilovolts. If the energy stored by the inductor is large, the effects can be serious. We need to know how much energy is stored. Suppose the current inside a self-inductance was increased steadily from zero to a value I in time t seconds. The e.m.f. is of magnitude:

$$\epsilon = L\frac{I-0}{t} = \frac{LI}{t}$$

The average current is $I / 2$. It flows for t seconds. The charge that has flowed is current × time = $It / 2$. The work done on the field is then:

$$W = QV = \frac{It}{2} \times \frac{LI}{t} = \tfrac{1}{2}LI^2$$

This work is stored as energy (E) of the magnetic field, so:

$$E = \tfrac{1}{2}LI^2$$

A small coil of several hundred turns on an iron core typically has an inductance of 0.1 H. If it carries a current of 3 A, the energy stored would be:

$$E = \tfrac{1}{2} \times 0.1\ \text{H} \times 3^2\ \text{A}^2 = 0.45\ \text{J}$$

This is enough to make you jump if you happen to be holding onto the connecting leads when the coil is switched off.

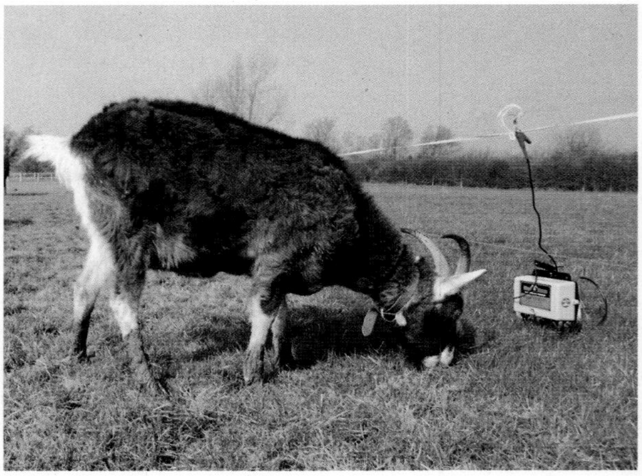

The energy stored in the magnetic field and the high back e.m.f. on break are used in cattle prods and electric fences. The shock energy is carefully set to be safe but irritating.

16.7 Reactance and capacitors

Capacitors are sometimes included in circuits to balance the phase shifts caused by inductors. Capacitors are also reactive components. When an alternating p.d. is applied to a capacitor, energy is stored in the *electric* field on part of the cycle and released later.

Capacitors will not allow a steady direct current to flow. However, if the amount of charge on one plate is altered, an equal and opposite change will affect the other plate. Charge is attracted or repelled from the second plate to keep the capacitor electrically neutral overall. Alternating currents can therefore 'flow through' the capacitor (Fig. 21).

Fig. 21 Alternating currents and capacitors

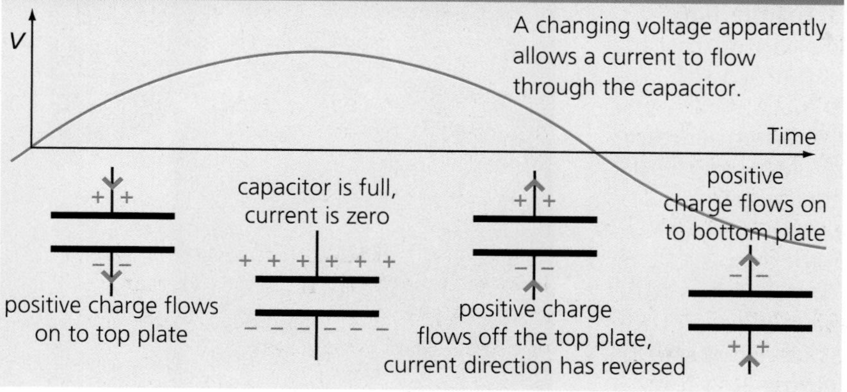
V
A changing voltage apparently allows a current to flow through the capacitor.
Time
positive charge flows on to top plate
capacitor is full, current is zero
positive charge flows off the top plate, current direction has reversed
positive charge flows on to bottom plate

If the alternating potential has a low frequency, only a tiny current needs to flow in order to balance the charge on the second plate. The reactance (= V / I) of the capacitor is then high. At higher frequencies, the same charge flows in a short time. This means that the current is high and so reactance is low.

The reactance of a capacitor is given by:

$$X_C = \frac{1}{\omega C} = \frac{1}{2\pi f C}$$

Capacitors are also used for coupling electronic circuits together, allowing a.c. signals to pass but blocking the d.c. currents. Different circuits can therefore operate on different voltage levels without affecting each other.

Fig. 22 Variation of current, p.d. and power with time in a capacitor

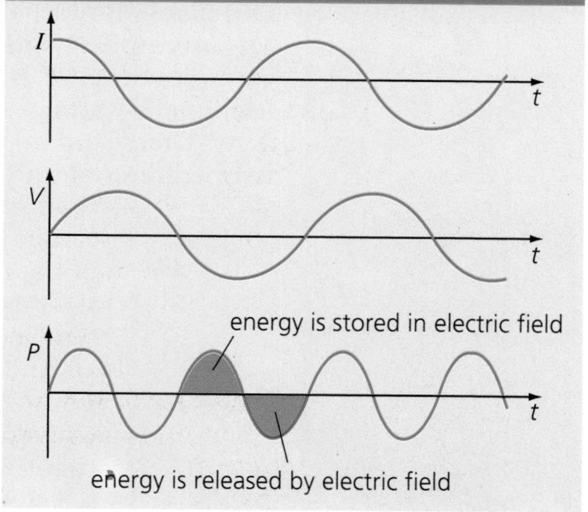
I
t
V
t
P
t
energy is stored in electric field
energy is released by electric field

Capacitors cause a phase difference between current and applied p.d., but in the 'opposite' way to inductors. For inductors, p.d. is proportional to rate of change of current, but for capacitors current is proportional to rate of change of p.d. Again, there is no net power dissipated in a capacitor: capacitors are reactive, not resistive.

8 If a capacitor and an inductor are in series, the same current flows through both. The p.d. across the inductor tends to cancel the p.d. across the capacitor. What size of capacitor would completely cancel the p.d. across a 0.4 H inductor at 50 Hz?

Key ideas

- The energy stored in the magnetic field can give rise to a very high back e.m.f. on break of circuit. The energy stored is:
  $E = \frac{1}{2}LI^2$
- Self-inductors allow a d.c. current to pass, but limit the flow of a.c. with a reactance:
  $X_L = \frac{V_0}{I_0} = \omega L = 2\pi f L$
- Capacitors allow a.c. to pass but block d.c. The reactance of a capacitor is:
  $X_C = \frac{V_0}{I_0} = \frac{1}{\omega C}$
- There is no net power dissipation in a pure reactance. Energy can be stored and released by electric or magnetic fields.

17 The coldest place in the Universe

Our planet is normally a comfortable place. The atmosphere shields us from the harsh extremes of space. It acts as a blanket, keeping us warm. A severe winter frost in arctic Greenland might dip down to temperatures of only –50 °C.

In space, the temperature can be lower. Measurements of the cosmic background radiation give the temperature of deep space as around –270 °C. This is still not the coldest place in the Universe: as far as we know, that title belongs to a few selected places on planet Earth.

We now know that there is a lowest possible temperature called absolute zero. At this temperature, which is about –273 °C, everything would stop: gas molecules would be stationary; no heat radiation would be emitted; nothing would move or vibrate. We also know that absolute zero is unreachable. Many universities have facilities for getting to temperatures approaching absolute zero. When we reach these low temperatures, we open up a mysterious world. The unexpected is commonplace:

Humans can survive in a limited temperature range. Life is tough at –50 °C.

A cylindrical magnet floats freely above a nitrogen-cooled, superconducting ceramic specimen. Liquid nitrogen is needed to keep the ceramic within its superconducting temperature range.

- some electrical conductors lose all their resistance;
- fluids lose their viscosity, flowing freely through tiny gaps;
- oxygen becomes magnetic;
- liquid helium creeps over the walls of containers.

Researchers in this field – cryogenics – strive to reach and sustain low temperatures to investigate the unusual properties of materials. There are many practical problems including inventing new thermometers and avoiding heat transfer. Of course, there is always the temptation to break the current record.

Fig. 1 The journey towards absolute zero

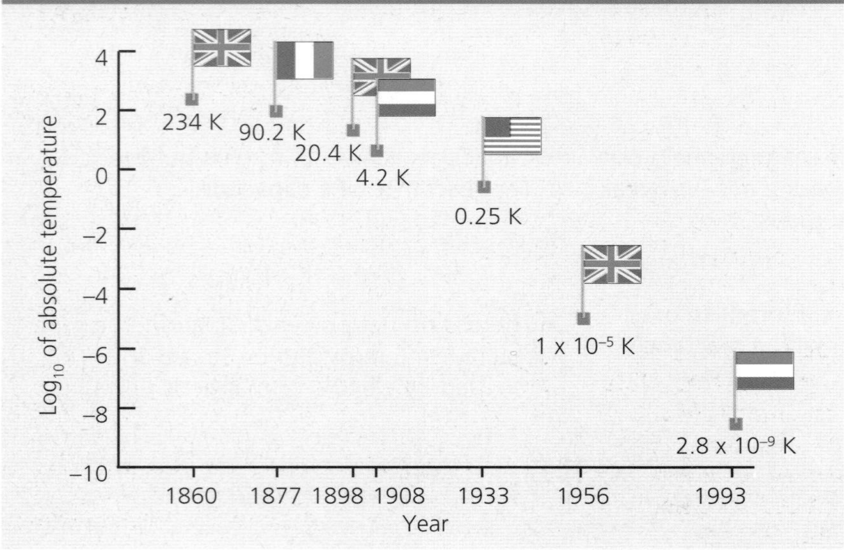

Log10 of absolute temperature
4
2
0
–2
–4
–6
–8
–10
234 K
90.2 K
20.4 K
4.2 K
0.25 K
1 x 10–5 K
2.8 x 10–9 K
1860
1877
1898
1908
1933
1956
1993
Year

As superfluid helium at 1.2 K is heated from above, the increase in its pressure causes the helium to undergo a fountain effect.

17.1 Learning objectives

After working through this chapter, you should be able to:

- **recall** the definition of thermal equilibrium;
- **describe** how internal energy can be changed by heating or by work;
- **recall** the first law of thermodynamics;
- **recall** the definitions of specific heat capacity and specific latent heat;
- **describe** heat transfer mechanisms;
- **recall** the definition of thermal conductivity and calculate heat flows;
- **use** the equation of state from the behaviour of ideal gases;
- **use** the equation $pV = \frac{1}{3}Nm\overline{c^2}$ for an ideal gas;
- **use** the relationship between molecular kinetic energy and temperature.

17.2 Temperature

Our low-temperature research needs accurate ways of measuring temperature. We have real problems here: mercury thermometers are no good because the mercury freezes. Many of our measurements rely on electrical measurements – of resistance, for example. We often need to define our own practical temperature scales when we get really close to absolute zero.

We all have an intuitive idea of temperature based on the messages our brains receive from certain nerve endings in our skin. But our intuitions often let us down.
If two things are at the same temperature then there will be no net flow of energy between them. Both objects will stay in the same state. We say that they are in **thermal equilibrium**. All objects at the same temperature are in thermal equilibrium. This might seem obvious but we are really making an assumption, sometimes called the zeroth law of thermodynamics: 'If two objects are in thermal equilibrium with a third object, they will be in thermal equilibrium with each other.'

Defining a temperature scale

Temperature is a fundamental quantity, like mass or time. The size of the unit and the way we measure it is entirely arbitrary. This has led to a puzzling variety of different scales: Fahrenheit, Centigrade and Celsius are among the more familiar. But all practical temperature scales are based on a change in the property of some substance – a **thermometric property.**

A chosen thermometric property is measured at two definite temperatures – the **fixed points**. Normally the entire scale is worked out by assuming a linear variation between these points (Fig. 2). For example, school science experiments often use mercury-in-glass thermometers which are calibrated on the Celsius scale at fixed points of the melting point of pure ice (0 °C), and the boiling point of pure water (100 °C) at 1 atmosphere pressure. Cryogenics researchers, on the other hand, might choose to use a resistance thermometer calibrated at the boiling points of liquid hydrogen (= –253 °C) and liquid helium (= –269 °C).

Fig. 2 Using a thermometric property

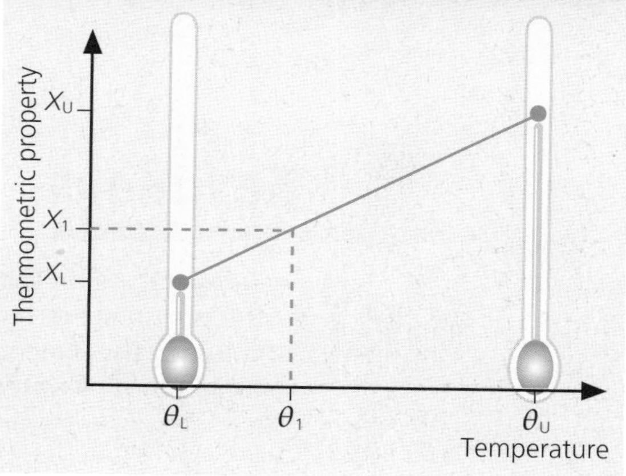

Thermometric property
X_U
X_1
X_L
θ_L
θ_1
θ_U
Temperature

The Kelvin temperature scale

Alcohol and mercury do not expand at exactly the same rate as they warm up. Alcohol thermometers and mercury thermometers often disagree with each other. There are a variety of contradictory practical temperature scales, so a single theoretical scale has been devised: the Kelvin scale. This is based on the behaviour of an 'ideal' gas – a gas where the molecules do not attract one another. Dry gases at low **pressure** show such ideal behaviour. If an ideal gas is kept in a container of fixed volume, the gas pressure drops as the temperature drops.

This graph can be extrapolated back to low temperatures: eventually, the line cuts the *x*-axis (Fig. 3). At this point, the ideal gas is exerting no pressure. Its molecules have stopped moving; they have no kinetic energy left. This is the lowest conceivable temperature: we call it **absolute zero**. The pressure of the ideal gas is used as the thermometric property. This *constant volume ideal gas thermometer* is calibrated with two fixed points:

Fig. 3 Pressure and temperature

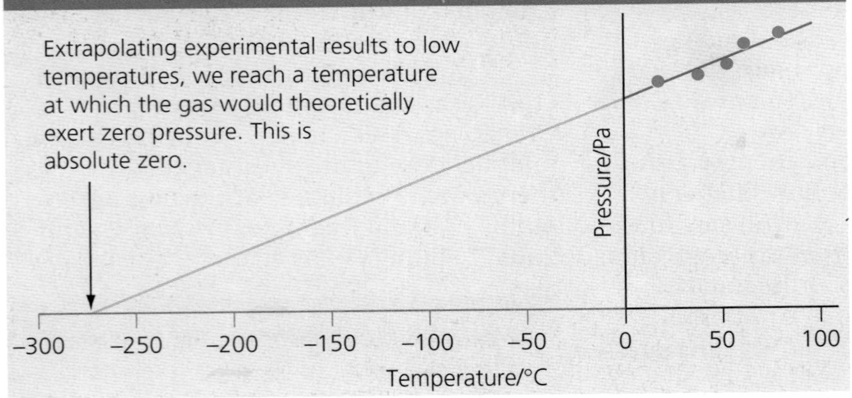
Extrapolating experimental results to low temperatures, we reach a temperature at which the gas would theoretically exert zero pressure. This is absolute zero.
Pressure/Pa
–300
–250
–200
–150
–100
–50
0
50
100
Temperature/°C

- absolute zero – a theoretical fixed point. This is zero on the kelvin scale.
- the triple point of water: the unique condition of pressure and temperature at which all three phases of water (ice, liquid and vapour) can exist in thermal equilibrium. You may not believe it is possible, but it *does* happen when pressure is only 0.6% of normal atmospheric pressure.

The triple point is chosen to be 273.16 on the Kelvin scale. This is done to make 1 kelvin the same size as 1 degree Celsius. On this scale, the ice point works out to be 273.15 K, so converting between Celsius temperatures and Kelvin temperatures means adding or subtracting 273.15. To avoid confusion, it is usual to use θ for Celsius temperatures and T for temperatures on the Kelvin scale.

$$\theta\ (°\mathrm{C}) = T\ (\mathrm{K}) - 273.15$$

All temperatures on the Kelvin scale are then defined by the ratio of pressures in the constant volume ideal gas thermometer:

$$\frac{P}{P_{\mathrm{triple}}} = \frac{T}{T_{\mathrm{triple}}}$$

$$\text{so, } T = 273.16 \times \frac{P}{P_{\mathrm{triple}}}$$

From this standard scale based on a standard instrument, real thermometers can be calibrated. This gives confidence that temperature measurements – while still arbitrary – are at least consistent.

1 **What is the Celsius temperature of the triple point of water?**

Key ideas

- Temperature on the Kelvin scale is defined in terms of the pressure exerted by an ideal gas at constant volume. The fixed points are absolute zero and the triple point of water.

17.3 Warming up

Treating these flowers with liquid nitrogen has the same devastating effect as dipping them in molten solder. In both cases, the temperature change causes a flow of heat that damages living cells.

Heat is energy which flows from one place, or object, to another as a result of a temperature difference. The energy flow results in a change in the internal energy of objects. The **internal energy** of an object is the sum of the kinetic and potential energies of all its particles. When heat flows into an object, its internal energy rises. Changes of internal energy are usually linked with a change in temperature.

When you drop an ice cube into a drink, there is a difference in temperature which causes heat to flow. Energy flows into the ice cube, lowering the internal energy of the drink.

Fig. 4 Linking energy and temperature

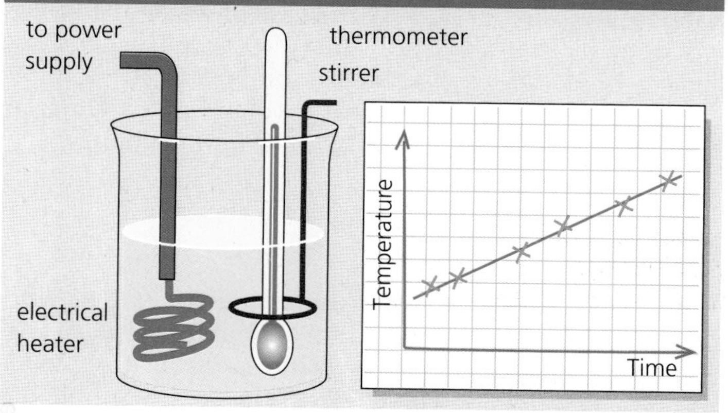

to power supply
thermometer
stirrer
electrical heater
Temperature
Time

Specific heat capacity

You can investigate the link between energy and temperature quite easily in the laboratory. If you put an electric heater into a beaker of water, the temperature will steadily rise (Fig. 4). The results of experiments like this suggest that the amount of heat energy transferred, ΔQ, is proportional to the temperature change, ΔT. The amount of heat needed for any given temperature change is also proportional to the mass, m, of material. These results can be put together:

$$\Delta Q \propto \Delta T \text{ and } \Delta Q \propto m$$

$$\text{so, } \Delta Q \propto m\Delta T$$

$$\Delta Q = cm\Delta T \quad \text{or,} \quad c = \frac{\Delta Q}{m\Delta T}$$

The constant of proportionality, c, is called the **specific heat capacity**. It is equal to the energy needed to raise the mass of one kilogram of a substance by one kelvin. Its units are therefore J kg^{-1} K^{-1} (or J kg^{-1} °C^{-1})

Table 1 Specific heat capacity

Substance	c /J kg^{-1} K^{-1}
hydrogen gas	14 300
water	4200
ethanol	2400
air	993
stainless steel	510
copper	385
mercury	140

Values are quoted at room temperature and standard atmospheric pressure

The range of specific heat capacities is quite large. Some surprising results – like the high specific heat capacity of hydrogen – are of technological use. For example, hydrogen is used as the coolant in large electrical turbines, despite the problems of handling this compressed, highly explosive gas. Measurements of specific heat capacity have also been useful in testing theories on the structure of matter, including the kinetic theory.

The equation $\Delta Q = cm\Delta T$, assumes that no other chemical or physical changes take place. For example, if you tried to measure the specific heat capacity of water between –2 °C and +2 °C, your results would be wrong. You would have included the heat needed to melt the ice: the **latent heat**.

Specific latent heat

The change from one phase (solid, liquid or gas) to another is a change in the distance between molecules and the way in which molecules are arranged. During a change of phase, heat flows into, or out of, the substance, but its temperature stays constant.

As temperature is not changing, heat which flows into the substance is only being used to change the internal structure. When a substance melts or boils, its molecules are pulled further apart and allowed to move more freely. There is an increase in the potential and kinetic energies of the molecules: the internal energy of the material is greater. Energy has therefore flowed into the material, changing the internal energy, but leaving the temperature unaltered. In a sense, this energy is 'hidden' or latent.

The amount of energy needed to change the phase of a kilogram of material is called the **specific latent heat**, *l*.

$$l = \frac{\Delta Q}{m} \quad \text{or,} \quad \Delta Q = ml$$

The specific latent heat of vaporisation for water is more than five times the energy needed to warm water from 0 °C to boiling point (Fig. 5 and Table 2).

Measurements of specific latent heat give us an indication of the strength of the bonds between different sorts of molecules. To make this more accurate, we need to take into account the work done by the material as it expands (Fig. 6).

Fig. 5 Changing phase

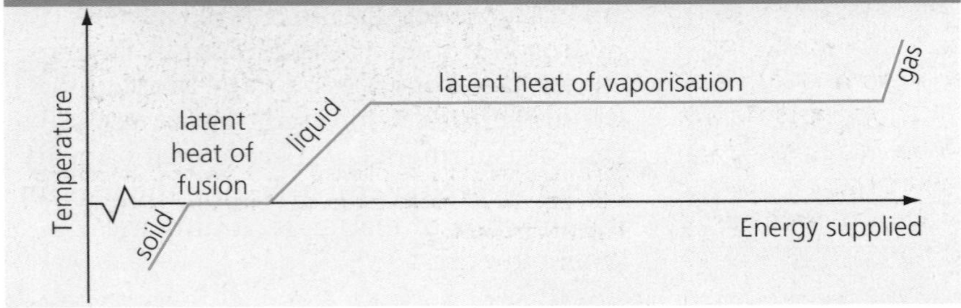
Temperature
latent heat of fusion
latent heat of vaporisation
soild
liquid
gas
Energy supplied

Table 2 Specific latent heat

	Vaporisation/kJ kg^{-1}	Fusion/kJ kg^{-1}
water	2260	334
oxygen	243	14
helium	25	5
mercury	290	11
iron	6339	276
lead	854	25

Fig. 6 Work done by an expanding material

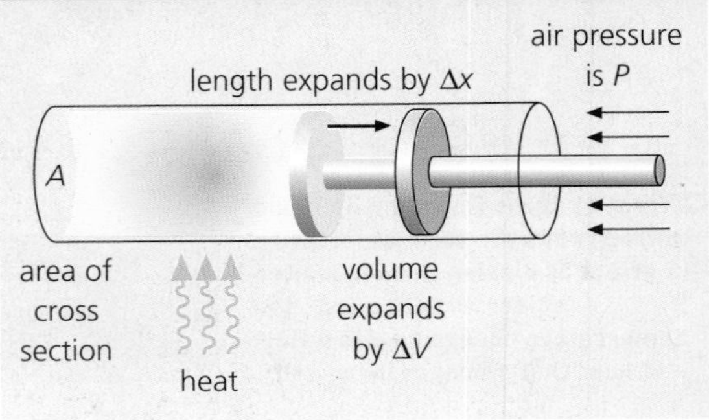
air pressure is P
length expands by Δx
A
area of cross section
heat
volume expands by ΔV

If the material expands by distance Δx, the volume has changed by an amount:

$$\Delta V = A\Delta x$$

The force exerted by the material is:

$$F = PA$$

where P is the external pressure. The work done by the system is therefore:

$$\begin{aligned} W &= F\Delta x \\ &= PA \times \Delta x \\ &= P \times A\Delta x \\ W &= P\Delta V \end{aligned}$$

Take the case of water at 1 atmosphere pressure (= 10^5 Pa). The density of water changes from 958 kg m^{-3} to 0.598 kg m^{-3} as it vaporises at 100 °C. A kilogram of water undergoes a volume change:

$$\begin{aligned} \Delta V &= \frac{1}{0.598} - \frac{1}{958} \\ &= 1.7 \text{ m}^3 \end{aligned}$$

against pressure 10^5 Pa. The work done per kilogram is therefore $W = P\Delta V = 1.7 \times 10^5$ J. The specific latent heat is 2260 kJ kg^{-1}, so over 7% of the energy supplied is used in doing work against atmospheric pressure.

Key ideas

- Heat is energy which flows from one place, or object, to another as a result of a temperature difference.
- Specific heat capacity, c, is the heat needed to raise the temperature of 1 kg of material by 1 K. It is assumed that there is no change of phase.

$$c = \frac{\Delta Q}{m\Delta T}$$

- The internal energy of an object is the sum of the kinetic and potential energies of all its particles.
- The amount of heat needed to change the phase of one kilogram of material is called the specific latent heat, l.

$$l = \frac{\Delta Q}{m}$$

17.4 Cooling down

We make liquid gases and compressed gases for industry and research. Liquid nitrogen is used to shrink metal components to make tightly fitting joins. Liquid argon can be isolated from the air so cheaply that it is also used for welding. Liquid oxygen used in hospitals saves thousands of lives every year. Liquefaction processes often work by making gases expand. Why does this work?

Removing internal energy from something is easy if you have a colder object – heat flows between objects at different temperatures. We could never make liquid nitrogen on Earth this way: the Earth's temperature never drops below nitrogen's boiling point. Instead we can exploit the link between internal energy, heat and work.

The first law of thermodynamics

It was the English brewer James Prescott Joule who first demonstrated convincingly that heat and work were both aspects of the same thing: energy. In a series of experiments in the 1840s, Joule measured mechanical work and temperature rise in all sorts of devices – expanding gases, paddle wheels in drums of water, even in a waterfall while he was on his honeymoon. Joule was able to show that no matter what device did the mechanical work, one unit of work always produced the same heating effect. His work led to one of the fundamental laws of physics: *the principle of conservation of energy.*

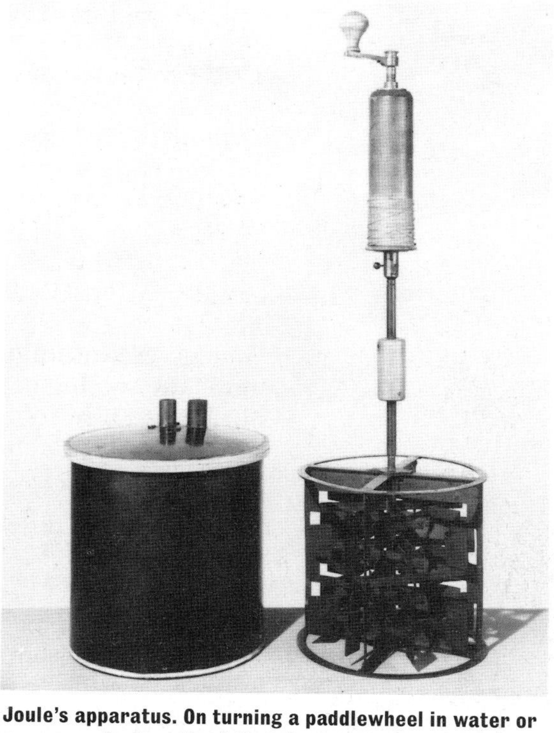

Joule's apparatus. On turning a paddlewheel in water or mercury, Joule noticed that the temperature of the water increased.

When **thermodynamics** was in its early development, the equivalence of work and heat was expressed in a different way: as the **first law of thermodynamics**. If you supply heat to a system, it will increase the internal energy of the system and the system can do mechanical work. Take the case of a cylinder full of air. Heating the cylinder warms up the air, so its internal energy rises. The hot gas expands and lifts the weight, doing mechanical work (Fig. 7).

Fig. 7 Working with hot air

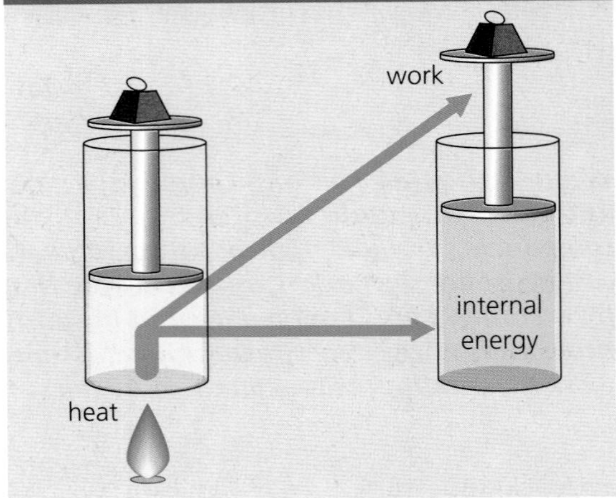
work
internal
energy
heat

Conservation of energy states that:

Heat transferred to a system (ΔQ) is equal to the sum of the increase of internal energy of the system (ΔU) and the work done by the system (ΔW).

$$\Delta Q = \Delta U + \Delta W$$

Sudden expansion of gases can produce dramatic cooling because there is no time for heat to flow into or out of the material ($\Delta Q = 0$). The material does work as it expands and pushes against atmospheric pressure. This work is done at the expense of the internal energy of the gas.

Sudden compression produces high temperatures in the same way. Diesel engines work by compressing the fuel–air mixture so quickly that work done on the gas is nearly all changed into internal energy. The temperature rise is enough to ignite the mixture.

When a fire extinguisher is activated, the sudden decompression causes dramatic cooling of the carbon dioxide which freezes temporarily into a fog of dry ice.

2 Why is there a difference between specific heat capacities measured at constant volume and at constant pressure? (Hint: redraw Fig. 6 with the piston stuck in the same place.)

3 Eighty joules of heat energy is supplied to 0.02 kg of air in a cylinder. The specific heat capacity of air measured at constant volume is 700 J kg^{-1} K^{-1}. The temperature rises by 5 °C. How much work is done by the air as it expands?

Key ideas

- The first law of thermodynamics says that the heat transferred to a system is equal to the sum of the increase of internal energy of the system and the work done by the system:

$$\Delta Q = \Delta U + \Delta W$$

17.5 The theoretical gas

The early drive in cryogenic research was to test ideas about the nature of matter. The first success was the verification that the kinetic theory was a useful model even at low temperatures. Kinetic theory is based on the idea that all matter is made up of atoms or molecules which are in constant movement.

Gases are the easiest system to analyse because the space between molecules is so large. The molecules spend most of their time flying around freely. The simplest possible gas would be made up of particles that:

- are very small so that most of their container is empty space;
- collide quickly and without energy loss, like perfect snooker balls;
- don't exert any intermolecular forces except when they collide;
- are present in large numbers, so that statistics can be used;
- are moving in random directions.

You can calculate the expected behaviour of this theoretical gas by using basic Newtonian mechanics. The process is long (see box on the next page), but the results are surprisingly simple:

pressure = $\frac{1}{3}\times$ density of gas $\times$ average of squared speeds of particles

$$p = \tfrac{1}{3}\rho\overline{c^2}$$

and

pressure $\times$ volume = $\frac{1}{3}\times$ number of particles $\times$ particle mass $\times$ average of squared speeds of particles

$$pV = \tfrac{1}{3}Nm\overline{c^2}$$

We know that at any particular temperature, the total kinetic energy of the particles is constant, and so the mean square speed will be constant. This theoretical gas therefore has the predicted property that:

$$pV = \text{constant}$$

at any particular temperature. The inverse proportionality between pressure and volume is one of the earliest observed properties of real gases, a result published by Robert Boyle in 1662. We call it Boyle's law, but the French call it Mariotte's law. (Mariotte discovered the effect fifteen years later, but to be fair he did make the important qualification that temperature needed to be kept constant.)

We can use the equations for a theoretical gas to calculate how fast air particles travel. Air at room temperature has a density of 1.20 kg m^{-3} at 1 atmosphere pressure (101 000 Pa).

From $p = \frac{1}{3}\rho\overline{c^2}$

$$\overline{c^2} = 3\frac{p}{\rho}$$

$$\sqrt{\overline{c^2}} = \sqrt{\frac{3\times 101000\ \text{Pa}}{1.20\ \text{kg m}^{-3}}}$$

$$= 503\ \text{ms}^{-1}$$

Air molecules are therefore striking you at an average (r.m.s., or **root mean square**) speed of over 1800 km h^{-1}!

4 A cylinder contains dry air at a temperature of 120 K. The volume is reduced to half its initial value and the temperature allowed to return to 120 K. What has happened to:

a the pressure exerted by the gas;

b the density of the gas;

c the r.m.s. speed of the molecules?

5 Follow through the derivations in the box on the next page. Write down where the main assumptions of the kinetic theory are used.

Fig. 8 Applying the kinetic theory

1 Start with a single particle in a box

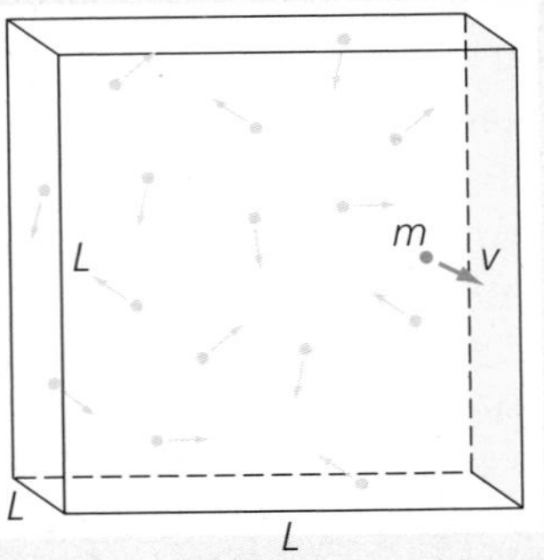

L
m
v
L
L

As the particle bounces inside the box, it hits the sides. On every collision, its momentum changes. The walls of the box exert a force on the particle. The walls of the box experience an equal but opposite force. If you calculate this pressure for one particle, you can estimate the pressure of all the particles in the gas.

2 Find the force from a single collision

In the *x* direction, the momentum before the collision was mv_x. After the perfectly elastic collision, the particle is moving backwards at the same speed, so its momentum is $-mv_x$. The change of momentum is therefore $mv_x - (-mv_x) = 2mv_x$

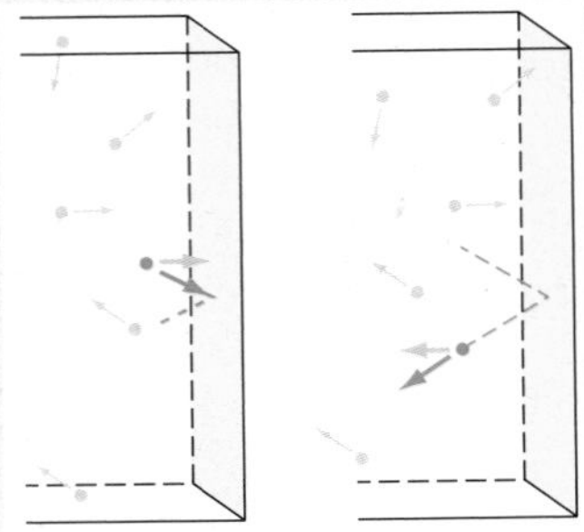

The particle strikes this face again after it has travelled to the other side of the box and back at speed v_x. This takes time $2L / v_x$.

Force is equal to the rate of change of momentum (Newton's 2nd law), so the average force on the particle is:

$$F_1 = \frac{\text{change in momentum}}{\text{time}}$$

$$= \frac{2mv_x}{2L/v_x} \qquad = \frac{mv_x^2}{L}$$

3 Find the pressure for one particle

The wall of the container experiences a force of the same magnitude, so the pressure on it is:

$$\text{pressure} = \frac{\text{force}}{\text{area}}$$

$$p_1 = \frac{mv_x^2/L}{L^2} = \frac{mv_x^2}{L^3} = \frac{mv_x^2}{V}$$

where *V* is the volume of the box.

4 Add in all the other particles.

$$p = p_1 + p_2 + p_3 + \ldots$$

$$= \frac{mv_{x1}^2}{V} + \frac{mv_{x2}^2}{V} + \frac{mv_{x3}^2}{V} + \ldots$$

$$= \frac{m}{V}(v_{x1}^2 + v_{x2}^2 + v_{x3}^2 + \ldots)$$

The quantity in brackets is the total speed squared in the *x* direction. We can rewrite this in terms of the average value.

total = *N* × average

$$p = \frac{Nm\overline{v_x^2}}{V}$$

5 Take into account the other directions

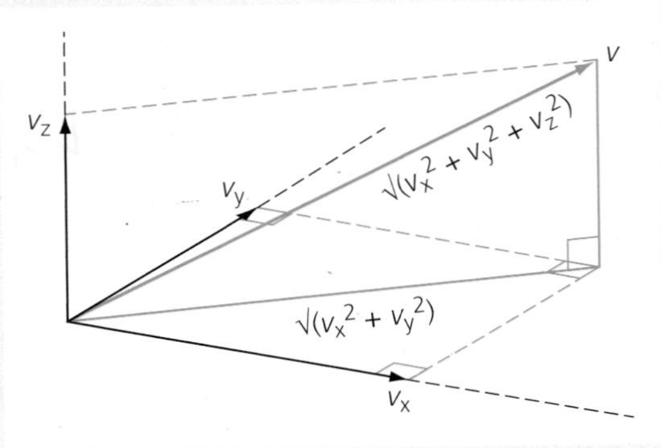

v
vz
vy
vx
√(vx2 + vy2 + vz2)
√(vx2 + vy2)

The particles move in random directions. Some will hit the walls head on but others will only glance off. The speed *c* of the particle can be found by Pythagoras' theorem:

$$c^2 = v_x^2 + v_y^2 + v_z^2$$

The particles are equally likely to be travelling in any direction, so the average values of v_x^2, v_y^2 and v_z^2 will be the same. Then:

$$\overline{c^2} = 3\overline{v_x^2}$$

$$\text{so, } p = \frac{Nm}{V} \times \frac{\overline{c^2}}{3}$$

$$pV = \tfrac{1}{3}Nm\overline{c^2}$$

Nm is the total mass of the gas, so $\frac{Nm}{V} = \frac{\text{mass}}{\text{volume}} = \text{density}$

Then: $p = \frac{1}{3}\rho\overline{c^2}$

Ideal gases

Researchers in the eighteenth century found that most gases behave in similar ways. The similarities become even greater when the gases are hot and at low pressure – when the molecules are a long way apart. In these conditions, you get an 'ideal' behaviour, and the gases were found to obey three simple laws.

Boyle's law

Boyle's law – that pressure was inversely proportional to volume – came from experimental observations on real gases. Most gases give a close approximation to the rule that $p \times V$ is constant at any fixed temperature (Fig. 9).

Boyle's law apparatus shows the relationship between pressure and volume.

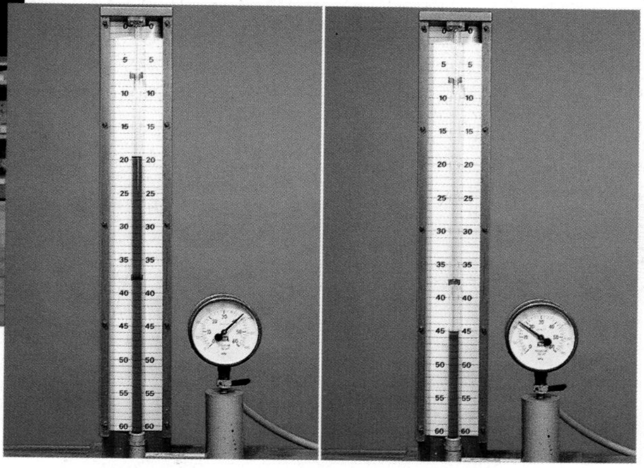

volume = 19.5 cm³
pressure = 280 kPa

volume = 45 cm³
pressure = 120 kPa

Charles' law

In about 1787, the French physicist Jacques Charles discovered that different gases, kept at constant pressure, all expand by the same amount. For every degree they get warmer, they expand by about 1/273 of their volume at 0 °C. Research at low temperatures has confirmed that this rule holds at temperatures close to absolute zero for gases at low pressure. If you measure temperature on the Kelvin scale, Charles' law becomes simply: *volume is proportional to temperature.*

Fig. 10 Charles' law apparatus

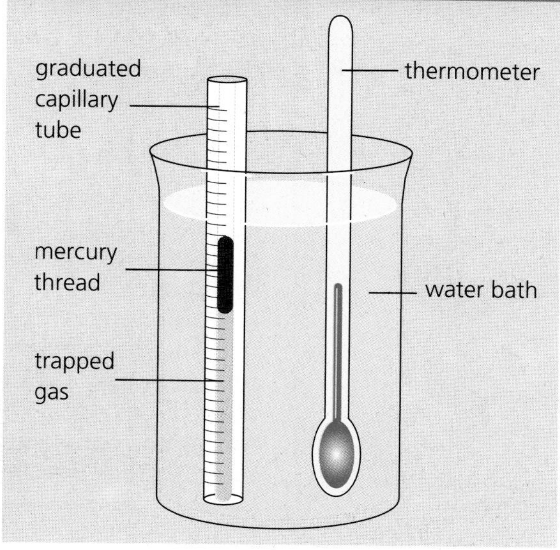
graduated capillary tube
thermometer
mercury thread
water bath
trapped gas

The pressure–temperature law

If a gas is trapped in a container of fixed size, its pressure will go up when temperature rises. This observation forms the basis of the constant volume gas thermometer, which is used to define the kelvin temperature scale. If we measure temperature on the Kelvin scale, pressure is by definition proportional to temperature (for a fixed volume of gas).

The ideal gas equation

An ideal gas is one which obeys these three laws *exactly*. For a fixed mass of dry gas:

$$p \propto \frac{1}{V} \quad \text{constant } T$$

$$p \propto T \quad \text{constant } V$$

$$V \propto T \quad \text{constant } p$$

Fig. 9 An ideal and a real gas

Each of these lines (isotherms) represents the behaviour of a gas at one specific temperature. At low temperatures, real gases can liquefy under pressure.

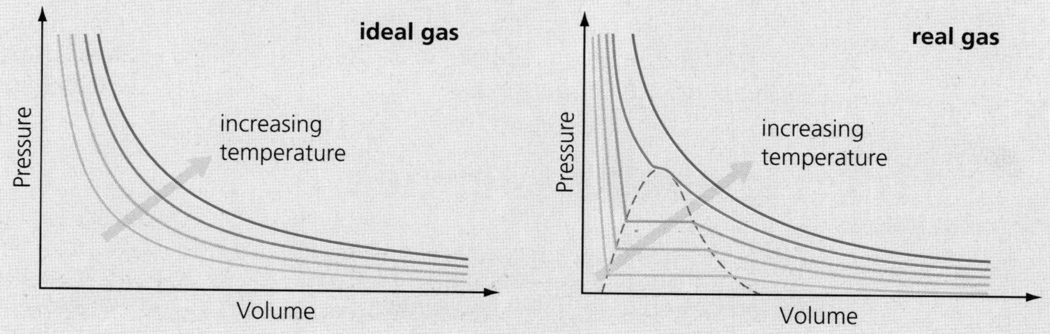
ideal gas
Pressure
increasing temperature
Volume
real gas
Pressure
increasing temperature
Volume

These can all be combined into one equation $pV = RT$ where R is a constant. If any one of the variables is held constant, the appropriate gas law follows.

For a given pressure and temperature, the volume is proportional to the amount of gas present. Early in the investigation into gases, it was discovered that all gases have approximately the same volume for one mole of gas. One mole of material has a mass of M grams, where M is the molecular mass in unified mass units. So, one mole of helium-4 has a mass of 4 g. The constant R for one mole of gas is therefore independent of the type of gas. We call it the **universal molar gas constant**. It has the value 8.314 J mol^{-1} K^{-1}. For n moles of gas:

$$pV = nRT$$

This equation is called the **equation of state** for an ideal gas. Although it works well for real gases at low pressures and high temperatures, the accuracy becomes poor if the gas is close to liquefying (Fig. 11).

Fig. 11 Real gases under pressure

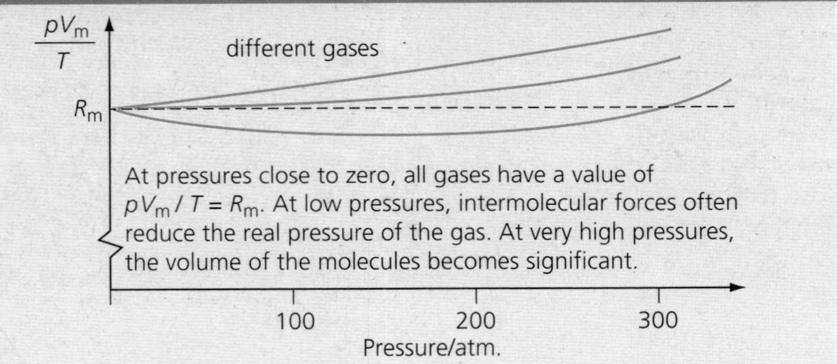
pVm / T
different gases
Rm
At pressures close to zero, all gases have a value of pVm / T = Rm. At low pressures, intermolecular forces often reduce the real pressure of the gas. At very high pressures, the volume of the molecules becomes significant.
100
200
300
Pressure/atm.

The ideal gas equation is often used in problems where an amount of gas moves from one state (p_1, V_1, T_1) to another (p_2, V_2, T_2). In these problems it is often easier to use the equation as:

$$\frac{p_1V_1}{T_1} = \frac{p_2V_2}{T_2}$$

With the equation in this ratio form, non-S.I. units can be used. For example, pressures could be in atmospheres and volumes in litres. Care is needed with temperature, however: proportionality only applies if temperature is measured from absolute zero.

For example, suppose air in a cylinder at 27 °C and 2 atmospheres pressure is cooled to –173 °C and reduced to half its volume (Fig. 12). What would the new pressure be?

Fig. 12 Cooling gas cylinders

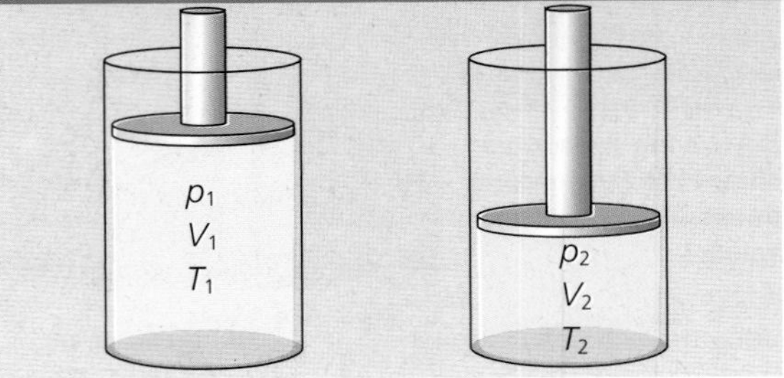
p1
V1
T1
p2
V2
T2

$p_1 = 2$ atm. $V_1 = 2$ units $T_1 = 27\ °C = 300$ K
$p_2 = ?$ $V_2 = 1$ unit $T_2 = -173\ °C = 100$ K

$$\text{Using } \frac{p_1V_1}{T_1} = \frac{p_2V_2}{T_2}$$

$$\frac{2 \text{ atm.} \times 2 \text{ units}}{300 \text{ K}} = \frac{p_2 \times 1 \text{ unit}}{100 \text{ K}}$$

$$p_2 = 1.33 \text{ atm.}$$

6 Use the equation of state to calculate the volume of one mole of ideal gas at standard temperature and pressure (s.t.p. = 273.15 K and 1.013 × 10^5 Pa). Convert your answer to litres. (1 m^3 = 1000 l)

7 Calculate to see if air is an ideal gas. (One mole of dry air has a mass of 28.97 grams and its density at s.t.p. is 1.293 kg m^{-3}.)

17.6 Molecular energies

When substances get cold, most of their properties change. They become stiffer, denser, more brittle, better electrical conductors, and so on. One property which changes surprisingly little is the heat capacity of gases. Can we explain this with the simple theories we have built up so far?

Kinetic theory gives us a formula which links pressure, volume and the speed of molecules. The equation of state links pressure, volume and temperature. The similarity of form of the two equations leads us to the tempting conclusion that the kinetic theory is the right answer – it successfully describes the behaviour of gases. The equations allow us to make testable predictions about energies of the molecules of gases. Consider one mole of gas.

equation of state predicts: $pV_m = RT$

kinetic theory predicts: $pV_m = \frac{1}{3}N_A m\overline{c^2}$

If we assume that the kinetic theory is the correct description of an ideal gas, these two equations should be equivalent. This allows us to find the mean kinetic energy of a gas molecule:

$$RT = \tfrac{1}{3}N_A m\overline{c^2} = \tfrac{2}{3}N_A\,\tfrac{1}{2}m\overline{c^2}$$

$$\text{so, } \tfrac{1}{2}m\overline{c^2} = \frac{3RT}{2N_A} = \tfrac{3}{2}kT \quad \text{where} \quad k = \frac{R}{N_A}$$

(The ratio R/N_A is called the **Boltzmann constant**, k.) This last equation leads to predictions about the heat capacities of different gases. The molar heat capacity is the amount of energy needed to raise the temperature of 1 mole by 1 K:

$$\text{molar heat capacity} = \frac{\text{energy change}}{\text{temperature rise}}$$

$$= \frac{N_A \times \dfrac{3R\Delta T}{2N_A}}{\Delta T} = \tfrac{3}{2}R$$

This gives two surprising predictions:

- that **molar heat capacity** does not depend on temperature;
- that all gases will have the same molar heat capacity.

The first prediction matches observations quite well, at least where gases are behaving ideally. The second observation does not. However, the theory can be made to match observations accurately by taking into account the shapes of molecules – the kinetic theory assumed that the particles concerned were perfect spheres.

The simple particle of an ideal gas has an average energy $\frac{3}{2}kT$. It can only use this energy as kinetic energy along the *x*, *y* and *z* axes – each axis receives $\frac{1}{2}kT$ of energy. Larger molecules are also able to rotate and vibrate. These extra '**degrees of freedom**' also take up $\frac{1}{2}kT$ of energy. When the degrees of freedom are considered, the theoretical predictions are impressively accurate.

Table 3 Degrees of freedom

Gas	Degrees of freedom	Molar heat capacity / J mol^{-1} K^{-1}	
		Predicted	Actual
He	3	20.8	20.96
Ar	3	20.8	20.93
H_2	5	29.1	28.6
O_2	5	29.1	29.2
N_2	5	29.1	29.1

Values measured at s.t.p.

Key ideas

- The kinetic theory model of a gas assumes a large number of perfectly elastic point masses in rapid random motion. Newtonian mechanics and statistics can be used on a particle in a box to predict that:

  $p = \frac{1}{3}\rho\overline{c^2}$ and $pV = \frac{1}{3}Nm\overline{c^2}$

- Ideal gases obey the equation of state $pV = nRT$. Real gases at low pressure and high temperature (well away from liquefying) obey the equation well. The equation is often used in the form:

  $$\frac{p_1V_1}{T_1} = \frac{p_2V_2}{T_2}$$

- The mean kinetic energy of an ideal gas molecule is:

  $\frac{3}{2}kT$ where $k = \frac{R}{N_A}$

  (k is called Boltzmann's constant). Real gas molecules have more energy because of rotation and vibration.

18 If you can't stand the heat ...

Kitchens exhibit extreme temperatures. Gas flames used for cooking can reach several thousand degrees Celsius, whereas freezers store food at temperatures as low as –20 °C. In the kitchen, we often control the flow of energy, making sure that heat is transferred at the right rate to the right places. Cooking involves transferring energy to food to bring about the necessary chemical reactions. Storing food requires sustaining low temperatures, with as little heat transfer as possible from the environment to the fridge or freezer. By selecting appropriate materials and designing efficient devices, we can control heat transfer.

Improvements in the design of kitchen equipment have made appliances more efficient at transferring or storing energy. Many of these improvements come from an understanding of the three heat transfer mechanisms – conduction, convection and radiation.

18.1 Learning objectives

After working through this chapter, you should be able to:

- **describe** heat transfer mechanisms;
- **define** thermal conductivity;
- **calculate** heat flow through single and multiple layers;
- **compare** electrical and thermal conduction processes.

18.2 Convection

Convection is the transfer of energy as heat by moving liquids and gases (fluids). Ovens rely on convective heat transfer. **Natural convection** occurs because of the change of density of fluids. Gases expand when the temperature increases. The same is true for most liquids. Warmer fluid is less dense, so it experiences a 'buoyancy' force. The warm liquid moves upwards, to be replaced by cooler, more dense fluid.

Schlieren photographs reveal the convection currents set up as our bodies lose heat

In an ordinary oven, the air is heated by a gas flame or by electrical heating elements in the base and sides of the oven. This hot air rises, so that the bottom part of the oven is cooler than the top. This uneven distribution of heat is often a nuisance. Foods on different shelves in an oven cook at different rates.

In fridges, air in contact with a cold surface cools down and becomes more dense. This denser air tends to fall, so that the bottom of a fridge is the coldest part. The cooling 'element' of a fridge is placed near the top: warm air rises to the top, is cooled and then falls.

Forced convection involves fanning or pumping a fluid. Fan-assisted ovens use forced convection to transfer energy from the heating element to the air and circulate the heated air around the oven. This allows heat to transfer to the food much faster. As the air heats the food, the layer of air next to the food is cooled down. A forced convection oven constantly replaces this layer of cool air by circulating hot air (Fig. 1). The development of fan-assisted ovens has improved energy efficiency by cutting down both the time and temperature required to cook food. Manufacturers claim that fan-assisted ovens can reduce cooking times by as much as 15%.

Fig. 1 Hot-air flow in an oven

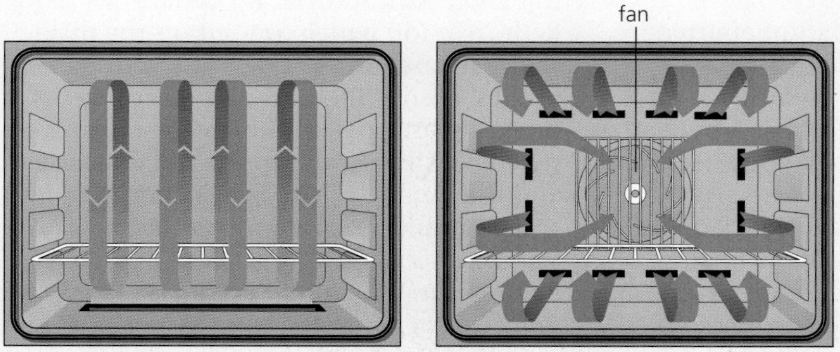
fan

gas ovens rely on natural convection and give uneven temperatures

fan-assisted ovens use forced convection to give faster cooking and even distribution of temperature

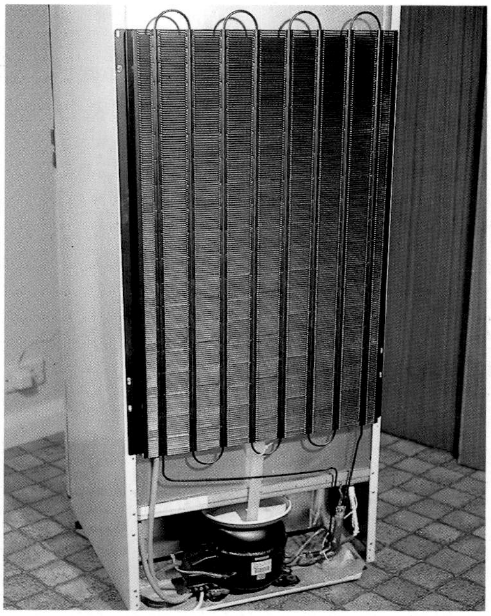

Forced convection is sometimes used in heat exchangers to remove heat energy from the cooling fins of large-scale refrigeration equipment and air conditioning units.

Analysing convection

There are many factors which affect the rate at which energy is transferred by convection. These include:

- the shape and texture of the heating surface;
- whether surfaces are horizontal or vertical;
- the density and viscosity of the fluid;
- how well the fluid conducts heat.

Experiments show that fluid near to the surface of a hot body moves slowly. This

Fig. 2 The boundary layer

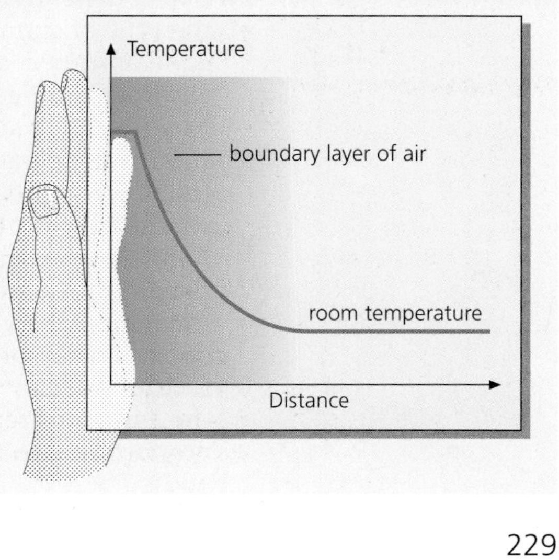
Temperature
boundary layer of air
room temperature
Distance

'boundary layer' of slow-moving fluid heats up. As you move away from the surface of the body, the temperature quickly drops away to the ambient temperature (Fig. 2). The existence of these boundary layers complicates any calculation of heat flow by convection or conduction.

Q 1 Sketch the boundary layer temperature profile which you would expect to find near a very cold object in air at room temperature.

18.3 Radiation

People who cook manipulate radiation. They use grills and toasters to heat food quickly. They also use aluminium foil to reflect radiation back into food to keep it hot, or away to slow down the heating process. Yet few cooks are aware that they are exploiting the properties of electromagnetic waves.

All objects at temperatures above absolute zero emit electromagnetic radiation (see Chapter 11). Hotter objects emit higher frequency radiation. Most objects on Earth emit thermal radiation in the infrared range. Very hot objects emit some visible light. For example, the element in a grill or toaster emits most of its energy as infrared radiation, but a small amount – perhaps 0.1% – is emitted as red light. The hotter something becomes, the greater the proportion of visible light it emits. The frequency of light emitted also moves towards the blue end of the spectrum. At about 1800 °C, things are 'white hot' – they emit colours across the whole visible spectrum.

The *net* amount of radiation emitted by an object depends on:

- the type of surface. Black surfaces are good absorbers and emitters. A perfect absorber is called a 'black body' (see Chapter 11).
- surface temperature. For a black body, the power emitted is proportional to T^4 where T is the absolute temperature (K). A 20% increase in temperature doubles the amount of radiation emitted.
- the temperature of the surroundings. An object will absorb radiation from its surroundings.
- the emitting area. The energy emitted is proportional to the surface area of the body.

The frilled lizard's fan. Its area, compared to the size of the lizard's body, means that it can be used both as a highly visible defence display and as an aid to thermoregulation.

Designers of kitchen equipment often need to reduce heat transfer by radiation. Reflective foil panels are put on the inside of the insulation in cookers. At the back of fridges, absorption of radiation from the heat exchanger is minimised by putting a reflective sheet between the hot exchanger and the outside of the fridge compartment.

Radiation is not a significant heat transfer mechanism until very high temperatures are involved. For example, a saucepan of hot water loses only a few percent of its energy by radiation – conduction and convection are responsible for most of the energy transfer. At higher temperatures, radiation is responsible for a greater proportion of energy transfer. The element of a toaster loses most of its energy by radiation.

18.4 Conduction

Refrigeration accounts for about six per cent of energy consumption in the UK. Fridges use more electricity than any other household device. Fridges and freezers in the UK are amongst the least efficient in Europe. If all European fridges were brought up to the standard of the most efficient, the annual energy saving would be equivalent to the output of several power stations.

Improving the efficiency of refrigerators by controlling convection and radiation would give only tiny energy savings. Most of the heat is transferred by conduction.

Thermal conductivity

Conduction is the flow of heat through a material without the material itself moving. The hotter a material is, the greater the amount of kinetic energy its atoms possess. This energy can be transferred to cooler parts of the material by collisions between higher energy atoms and neighbouring atoms with less energy. Solids are generally better conductors of heat than liquids or gases. In a solid, the kinetic energy of an atom is easily transferred to its neighbouring atoms through vibration. Metals are particularly good at conducting heat because their free electrons are able to transfer internal energy rapidly as they move randomly through the metal. The **thermal conductivity** of a material indicates how well it conducts heat (Table 1).

Q2 **Air-filled mineral fibres are often used for insulating houses. A new alternative consists of air bubbles sandwiched between two thin plastic sheets. The sheets are coated with a thin metallic film. Explain why this material is an effective insulator.**

Thermal conductivity is defined in terms of a steady heat flow through a well-insulated specimen of material. A temperature difference is needed to set up a flow of heat. For the purpose of calculations, it is assumed that the temperature difference has existed for some time, so that temperatures have stabilised. The specimen is then said to be in '**steady state**'. Experimental results show that a linear change of temperature exists in the material. However, this is only true if little heat escapes through the sides (Fig. 3).

The rate of heat flow ($\Delta Q/\Delta t$) through an object in a steady state depends on:

- its cross-sectional area, A;
- the **temperature gradient** (the temperature change per metre). If the surface temperatures are T_1 and T_2, and the length of the object is l, the temperature gradient is:

$$\frac{T_2 - T_1}{l}$$

Table 1 Thermal conductivities

Substance	Thermal conductivity /W m^{-1} K^{-1}
urethane foam (heavy gas filled)	0.015
air	0.024
most other gases	<0.03
air-filled glass fibre	0.04
ice	0.04
hydrogen	0.17
plastics	~0.2
water	0.59
glass	1.0
lead	35
iron	~ 80
copper	385

Fig. 3 The effect of lagging

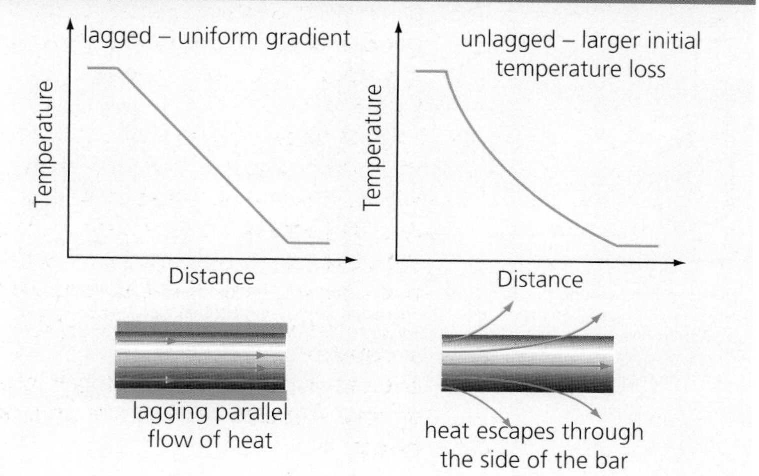

lagged – uniform gradient
Temperature
Distance
unlagged – larger initial temperature loss
Temperature
Distance
lagging parallel flow of heat
heat escapes through the side of the bar

Experiments show that the rate of heat flow is proportional to both area and temperature gradient. We can therefore write:

$$\frac{\Delta Q}{\Delta t} \propto A \times \frac{T_2 - T_1}{l}$$

or,
$$\frac{\Delta Q}{\Delta t} = -kA\frac{T_2 - T_1}{l}$$

The minus sign indicates that heat flows from hot objects to cold, i.e. *down* the temperature gradient. The constant of proportionality, k, is the thermal conductivity. A high value of k indicates a high rate of heat flow, so the material is a good conductor of heat. Thermal conductivity is the rate of flow of heat per square metre through a specimen across which there is a temperature gradient of 1 K per metre. Thermal conductivity has the unit W m^{-1} K^{-1}.

To measure thermal conductivity of a good conductor, a long thin specimen is used (Fig. 4). This allows a measurable flow of heat for a moderate temperature difference. This method is unsuitable for poor conductors, where more heat would escape out of the sides of the specimen than travel along its length. Instead, for poor conductors, a short, wide specimen is used.

Fig. 4 Determining thermal conductivity

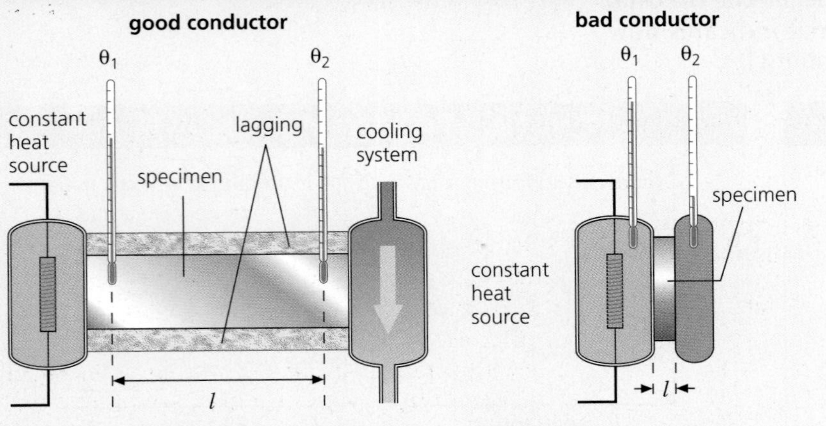
good conductor
bad conductor
θ1
θ2
θ1
θ2
constant heat source
lagging
cooling system
specimen
l
constant heat source
specimen
l

The specimen is a long thin bar. The bar is heated at one end until it reaches steady state. The temperature gradient is measured over a distance of around 10 cm. The rise in temperature of the cooling water can be used to find the rate of heat flow.

The specimen is a thin disc. The temperature gradient is measured over a distance of a few millimetres when steady state has been reached. The rate of heat flow is determined in a separate experiment on the cooling rate of the right hand plate.

Calculating heat conduction

The equation for thermal conductivity is useful for comparing the conduction of materials, but should be used carefully. Suppose you want to calculate the rate of heat flow through a kitchen window. The window might have 1.5 m^2 of glass of thickness 5 mm and thermal conductivity 1 W m^{-1} K^{-1}. In winter, the average temperatures outside is about 2 °C and room temperature is typically 18 °C. Heat flow is therefore:

$$\frac{\Delta Q}{\Delta t} = kA\frac{T_2 - T_1}{l}$$

$$= 1.0 \text{ W m}^{-1}\text{ K}^{-1} \times 1.5 \text{ m}^2 \times \frac{18\ °\text{C} - 2\ °\text{C}}{0.005 \text{ m}}$$

$$= 4800 \text{ W}$$

According to this result, a kitchen with just one small window would need two electric fires running continuously to keep it warm. However, the calculation does not take into account the existence of boundary layers of air either side of the glass (Fig. 5).

Fig. 5 Boundary layers of a window

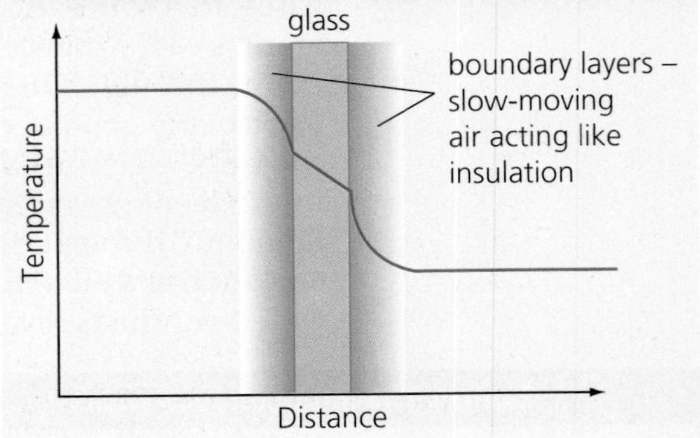
glass
boundary layers – slow-moving air acting like insulation
Temperature
Distance

Air has a thermal conductivity about 40 times lower than glass. A millimetre layer of air has roughly the same resistance to heat flow as eight sheets of glass. Rooms feel much colder in windy weather because the wind continuously replaces the external boundary layer. The insulating property of air is exploited in double glazing: a second layer of glass allows the two panes to maintain a boundary layer.

The existence of boundary layers prevents the exact calculation of heat losses. However, we can still use the general principles of conduction and insulation to estimate the energy efficiency of domestic appliances. If you look at refrigerators in an electrical goods store, it is noticeable that the cheaper models have thinner side walls. Manufacturers often reduce costs by saving on insulating materials. The initial saving in the purchase can quickly be wiped out by the increased energy consumption.

3 A fridge-freezer has fridge and freezer compartments of equal size but the insulation material is 30 mm thick on the fridge and 60 mm on the freezer. Typically, the fridge is maintained at 4 °C and the freezer at –18 °C. If room temperature is 18 °C, which part – the fridge or the freezer – costs more to run?

4 The surface area of a tall domestic freezer is about 5 m^2. Its interior maintains a temperature of –18 °C and the room temperature is 22 °C. The average insulation is 60 mm thick and has thermal conductivity 0.020 W m^{-1} K^{-1}. The energy consumption is rated at '2 kW h / 24 h'. What part does heat conduction play in this?

Heat flow through multiple layers

The walls of a real fridge are more than just a single sheet of insulation. There will be a plastic inner cabinet, thick insulation material and a thin outer shell, probably of rolled steel. To be able to predict the overall heat flow, we need to be able to analyse the flow through each layer of material. A fridge's outer steel case is a good conductor, so it has negligible effect on the overall insulation. We can therefore simplify the problem to an analysis of two layers (Fig. 6).

Fig. 6 Insulation inside a fridge

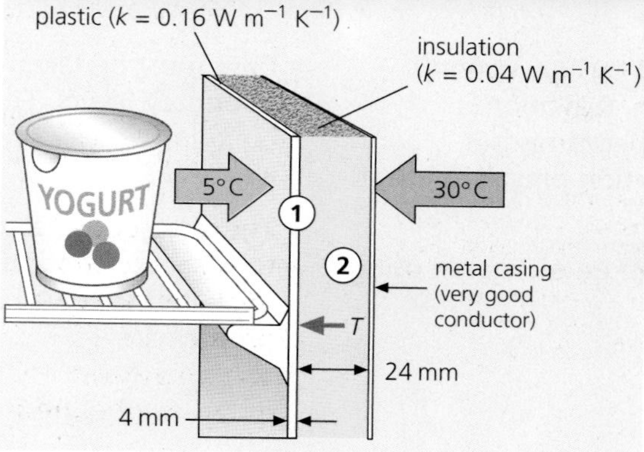

plastic (k = 0.16 W m⁻¹ K⁻¹)
insulation
(k = 0.04 W m⁻¹ K⁻¹)
YOGURT
5°C
30°C
1
2
metal casing
(very good
conductor)
T
24 mm
4 mm

To solve problems like this, you need to assume that the 'interface' between the layers has reached a fixed temperature, T. In steady state, the same heat flows per second through both materials, so you can write:

$$\frac{\Delta Q}{\Delta t} = -k_1 A \frac{T - T_1}{l_1} = -k_2 A \frac{T_2 - T}{l_2}$$

$$\text{or,} \quad k_1 \frac{T - T_1}{l_1} = k_2 \frac{T_2 - T}{l_2}$$

This gives us:

$$0.16 \times \frac{T - 5\ °\text{C}}{0.004} = 0.04 \times \frac{30\ °\text{C} - T}{0.024}$$

$$40 \times (T - 5\ °\text{C}) = 1.67 \times (30\ °\text{C} - T)$$

$$40T - 200\ °\text{C} = 50\ °\text{C} - 1.67T$$

$$41.67T = 250\ °\text{C}$$

$$T = 6.0\ °\text{C}$$

The most marked change in temperature takes place across the 24 mm of insulation. Although the plastic lining takes up 14% of the thickness, it accounts for only 4% of the insulation of the fridge wall.

The rate of heat flow can now be calculated by substituting the value of T back into one of the original equations. For a fridge of area 4 m^2:

$$\frac{\Delta Q}{\Delta t} = -k_2 A \frac{T_2 - T}{l_2}$$

$$= 0.04\ \text{W m}^{-1}\ \text{K}^{-1} \times \frac{30\ °\text{C} - 6\ °\text{C}}{0.024\ \text{m}}$$

$$= 160\ \text{W}$$

To solve problems with more than two layers, you need to assign an unknown temperature to each interface. Solving the problem involves a large set of simultaneous equations. An easier method involves using the link between electrical and thermal conduction instead.

5 If heat is conducting through a series of layers, will the bigger temperature drop occur across a layer of a good conductor or a layer of a poor conductor?

Thermal and electrical conductivities

In an electrical circuit, the current is the rate of flow of charge. Current flows down an electrical potential gradient. The current through a specimen of material depends on the area of cross section. These factors are similar to those affecting thermal conduction, where the rate of flow of heat depends on the area and the temperature gradient. The mathematical form of the equations is identical (Fig. 7).

Fig. 7 Comparing thermal and electrical conduction

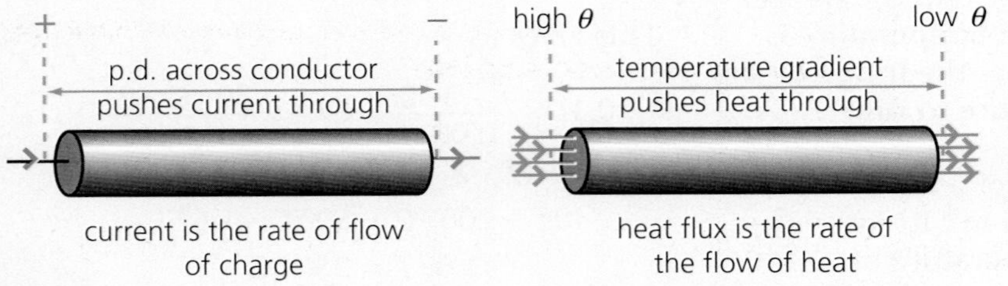

+
−
p.d. across conductor pushes current through
current is the rate of flow of charge
high θ
low θ
temperature gradient pushes heat through
heat flux is the rate of the flow of heat

Current is the rate of flow of charge, so current (I) = charge (ΔQ) / time (Δt). The current through a resistor is:

$$I = \frac{V}{R} \quad \text{or} \quad I = \frac{-\Delta V}{R}$$

where $\Delta V = V_1 - V_2$, the p.d. across the resistor. The minus sign indicates that the current flows from high to low potential. Resistance can be related to the electrical conductivity. Resistivity is calculated using:

$$\rho = R\frac{A}{l}$$

Conductivity, σ, is the inverse of resistivity:

$$\sigma = \frac{1}{\rho} = \frac{l}{AR}$$

$$\text{so,} \quad R = \frac{l}{\sigma A}$$

This gives us:

$$I = \frac{-\Delta V}{R} = \frac{-\Delta V \sigma A}{l}$$

$$\text{or,} \quad \frac{\Delta Q}{\Delta t} = -\sigma A\frac{\Delta V}{l}$$

which is identical in form to:

$$\frac{\Delta Q}{\Delta t} = -kA\frac{\Delta T}{l}$$

This has advantages: simple electric circuit theory can be applied to heat flow. We can define thermal resistances by $R = l/Ak$ (comparable to electrical resistance $R = l/A\sigma$). These thermal resistances will obey the same equations for series and parallel arrangements. Ohm's law can be used to calculate the flow of heat. For example, the problem of calculating the rate of heat flow through fridge walls becomes simple:

For plastic, $R_1 = l/Ak = 0.00625\ \text{K W}^{-1}$

For insulation, $R_2 = 0.15\ \text{K W}^{-1}$

Total thermal resistance = $0.15625\ \text{K W}^{-1}$

So the thermal current is:

$$I = \frac{\Delta V}{R} = \frac{\Delta T}{R}$$

$$= \frac{30\ °\text{C} - 5\ °\text{C}}{0.15625\ \text{K W}^{-1}} = 160\ \text{W}$$

Key ideas

- Heat can be transferred by convection, conduction or radiation. Radiation is significant at high temperatures but conduction and convection prevail at lower temperatures.
- Thermal conduction can be estimated using the equation:

$$\frac{\Delta Q}{\Delta t} = -kA\frac{T_2 - T_1}{l}$$

- Care must be taken to include the effect of boundary layers. The thermal conduction equation applies only to parallel heat flow in a steady state.
- The analogous nature of electrical and thermal conduction processes can be exploited to solve heat conduction problems.

Data section

Units

Physicists usually use the International System of Units (Systèment Internationale, or SI). The base SI units that are most often used in physics are shown in Table 1.

Table 1 Base SI units

Quantity	Unit name	Symbol
length	metre	m
mass	kilogram	kg
time	second	s
electric current	ampere	A
temperature	kelvin	K
amount of substance	mole	mol

For convenience, any of the prefixes in Table 2 may be used with any unit: for example, the kilometre (1 km = 10^3 m) and the milliampere (1 mA = 10^{-3} A) are often useful.

Table 2 Prefixes for units

Prefix	Symbol	Meaning
tera	T	10^{12}
giga	G	10^{9}
mega	M	10^{6}
kilo	k	10^{3}
deci	d	10^{-1}
centi	c	10^{-2}
milli	m	10^{-3}
micro	μ	10^{-6}
nano	n	10^{-9}
pico	p	10^{-12}

Other units can be derived from the base units. For example, energy is normally measured in joules (symbol J), or multiples of joules (kJ, MJ), defined in terms of base units as kg m^2 s^{-2}. Some non-SI units can be converted to SI units as shown in Table 3.

Table 3 Unit conversions

Unit	Symbol	SI equivalent
atomic mass unit	u	1.661×10^{-27} kg
atmosphere	atm	101 325 Pa
degree Celsius	°C	1K
litre	dm^3	$10m^3$

Formulae

Velocity and acceleration

$$v = \frac{\Delta s}{\Delta t}$$

$$a = \frac{\Delta v}{\Delta t}$$

Uniformly accelerated motion

$$v = u + at$$

$$s = \left(\frac{u+v}{2}\right)t$$

$$s = ut + \frac{at^2}{2}$$

$$v^2 = u^2 + 2as$$

Momentum and force

$$p = mv$$

$$F = \frac{\Delta(mv)}{\Delta t}$$

$$F = ma$$

Circular motion

$\omega = \frac{v}{r}$

$\omega = \frac{2\pi}{T}$

$a = \frac{v^2}{r} = r\omega^2$

$F = \frac{mv^2}{r} = mr\omega^2$

Work and energy

$W = Fs\cos\theta$

$\Delta E_p = mg\Delta h$

$E_k = \frac{1}{2}mv^2$

Power and efficiency

$P = \frac{\Delta W}{\Delta t}$

$P = Fv$

$\text{efficiency} = \frac{\text{power output}}{\text{power input}}$

Stress and strain

$\text{tensile stress} = \frac{F}{A}$

$\text{tensile strain} = \frac{e}{l}$

$\text{Young modulus} = \frac{F/A}{e/L}$

$\text{elastic strain energy} = \frac{1}{2}Fe$

Current electricity

$I = \frac{Q}{t}$

$V = \frac{W}{Q}$

$R = \frac{V}{I}$

$E = VIt$

$P = IV = \frac{V^2}{R} = I^2R$

$R_{\text{series}} = R_1 + R_2 + R_3 + \cdots$

$\frac{1}{R_{\text{parallel}}} = \frac{1}{R_1} + \frac{1}{R_2} + \frac{1}{R_3} + \cdots$

$\rho = \frac{RA}{l}$

$\in = \frac{E}{Q}$

$\in = I(R + r)$

Capacitors

$C = \frac{Q}{V}$

$E = \frac{1}{2}CV^2$

$C = \varepsilon_0 \frac{A}{d}$

$\frac{1}{C_{\text{series}}} = \frac{1}{C_1} + \frac{1}{C_2} + \frac{1}{C_3} + \cdots$

$C_{\text{parallel}} = C_1 + C_2 + C_3 + \cdots$

Radioactivity

$I = k\frac{I_0}{x^2}$

$\frac{\Delta N}{\Delta t} = -\lambda N$

$N = N_0 e^{-\lambda t}$

$T_{1/2} = \frac{\ln 2}{\lambda}$

$E = mc^2$

Simple harmonic motion

$$a = -\omega^2 x$$

$$v = \pm\omega\sqrt{{x_0}^2 - x^2}$$

$$T_{\text{pendulum}} = 2\pi\sqrt{\frac{l}{g}}$$

$$T_{\text{spring}} = 2\pi\sqrt{\frac{m}{k}}$$

Waves

$$c = f\lambda$$

$$\lambda = \frac{ws}{D}$$

$$d\sin\theta = n\lambda$$

Refraction

$$n = \frac{c}{v}$$

$${}_1n_2 = \frac{\sin\theta_1}{\sin\theta_2} = \frac{c_1}{c_2} = \frac{n_2}{n_1}$$

$$\sin\theta_c = \frac{1}{n}$$

Photons and duality

$$E = hf$$

$$hf = \phi + E_k$$

$$hf = E_1 - E_2$$

$$\lambda = \frac{h}{p}$$

Magnetism

$$\Phi = BA$$

$$F = BIl$$

$$F = BQv$$

$$B = \mu_0 nI \quad \text{(solenoid)}$$

$$B = \frac{\mu_0 I}{2\pi a} \quad \text{(long straight wire)}$$

Induced current

$$\in = N\frac{\Delta\Phi}{\Delta t}$$

$$\in = -L\frac{\Delta I}{\Delta t}$$

$$E = \tfrac{1}{2}LI^2$$

A.c. and transformers

$$I_{\text{r.m.s.}} = \frac{I_o}{\sqrt{2}}$$

$$V_{\text{r.m.s.}} = \frac{V_o}{\sqrt{2}}$$

$$\frac{V_p}{V_s} \approx \frac{N_p}{N_s} \approx \frac{I_s}{I_p}$$

$$X = \frac{V_0}{I_0}$$

$$X_L = \omega L = 2\pi fL$$

$$X_C = \frac{1}{\omega C} = \frac{1}{2\pi fC}$$

Gravitation

$$F = \frac{-Gm_1m_2}{r^2}$$

$$g = \frac{F}{m}$$

$$g = -\frac{GM}{r^2}$$

$$g = -\frac{\Delta V}{\Delta x}$$

$$V = -\frac{GM}{r} \quad \text{(radial field)}$$

Electrostatics

$$F = \frac{1}{4\pi\varepsilon_0}\frac{Q_1Q_2}{r^2}$$

$$E = \frac{F}{Q}$$

$$E = \frac{V}{d} \quad \text{(uniform field)}$$

$$E = \frac{1}{4\pi\varepsilon_0}\frac{Q}{r^2} \quad \text{(radial field)}$$

$$V = \frac{1}{4\pi\varepsilon_0}\frac{Q}{r} \quad \text{(radial field)}$$

Thermodynamics

$$c = \frac{\Delta Q}{m\Delta T}$$

$$l = \frac{\Delta Q}{m}$$

$$\Delta Q = \Delta U + \Delta W$$

$$\frac{\Delta Q}{\Delta t} = -ka\frac{\Delta T}{\Delta x}$$

Gases

$$pV = nRT$$

$$pV = \tfrac{1}{3}Nm\overline{c^2}$$

$$\tfrac{1}{2}m\overline{c^2} = \tfrac{3}{2}kT = \frac{3RT}{2N_A}$$

Answers to questions

Chapter 1

1 Velocity is a vector quantity. Every time that the athletes change direction they are also changing their velocity. Speed is a scalar quantity. If the athletes are running equal distances in successive equal time intervals their speed stays the same.

2 **a** average speed = total distance / time = 10 000 / 1813.74 = 5.513 m s^{-1}

b average velocity = displacement / time = 0 m s^{-1}

3 The runner with the highest average speed wins. They will cover the distance in the shortest time.

4 It is the instantaneous speed at the moment of take-off which determines the length of the jump; the average speed of the run up is not important.

5 No. An object is only stationary *relative* to an observer. Another observer using a different frame of reference might see the object as moving. For example, you may be stationary relative to this book, but relative to the Sun you are hurtling through space at almost 30 km per second.

6 Horizontally, the Earth is stationary relative to the high jumper. Relative to an observer in space (who is not rotating with the Earth) the high jumper and the Earth are *both* moving with a horizontal velocity of up to 465 m s^{-1}.

7

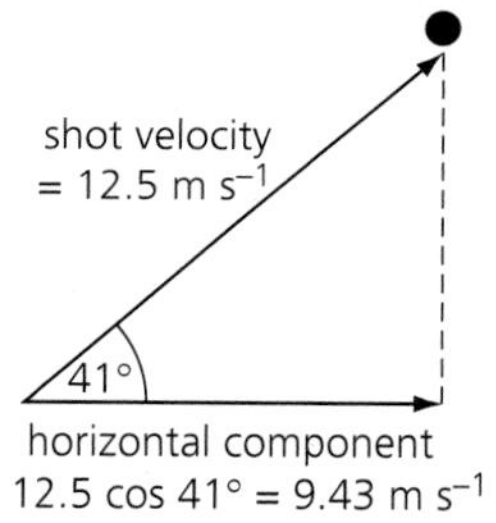
shot velocity
= 12.5 m s−1
41°
horizontal component
= 12.5 cos 41° = 9.43 m s−1

8 Just after the ball is dropped, its velocity and acceleration are downwards. After the ball has bounced, the velocity is upwards but the acceleration is still down.

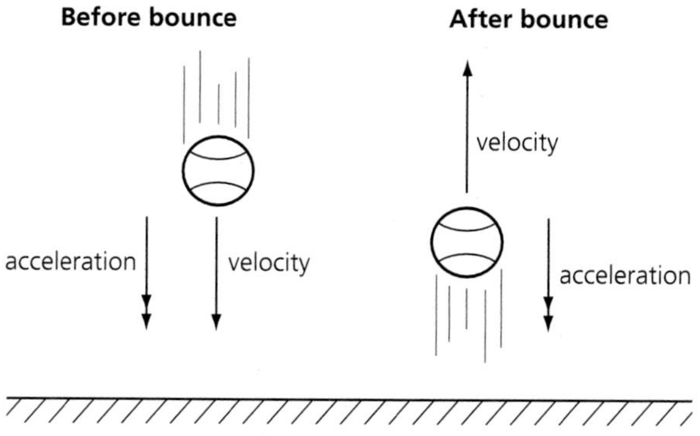
Before bounce
After bounce
acceleration
velocity
velocity
acceleration

9

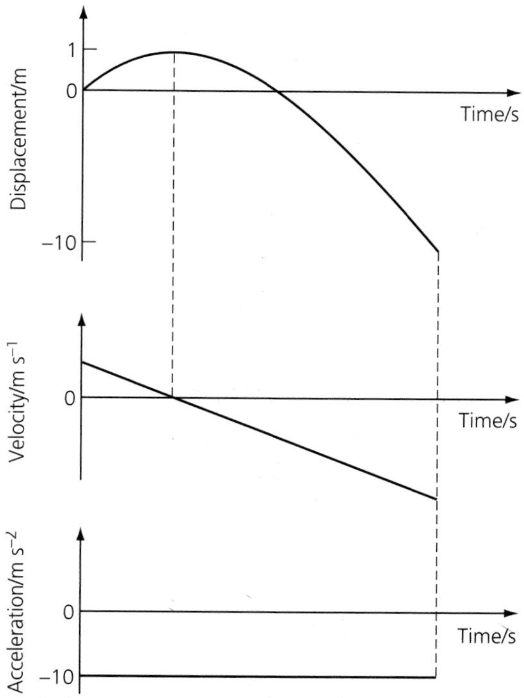
Displacement/m
1
0
−10
Time/s
Velocity/m s−1
0
Time/s
Acceleration/m s−2
0
−10
Time/s

Acceleration is due to gravity only.

10 Use $a = (v - u) / t = (75 - 0) / 0.0005 = 150\ 000$ m s^{-2}. This is 15 000 times the acceleration due to gravity!

11 At the top of the jump $v = 0$ m s^{-1}; $u = 4.8$ m s^{-1}; acceleration is due to gravity and acts down, $a = -9.8$ m s^{-2}. Rearrange $v^2 = u^2 + 2as$ to give:

$$s = \frac{v^2 - u^2}{2a} = \frac{0 - 23.0\ \text{m}^2\,\text{s}^{-2}}{2 \times -9.8\ \text{m}\,\text{s}^{-2}} = 1.18\ \text{m}$$

This is the height *gained* by the centre of mass, so add 0.95 m to give a height of 2.13 m for the centre of mass. (A top class athlete will jump with her centre of mass as close to the bar as possible.)

12 **a** Consider *vertical* motion first, use $s = ut + {}^1/_2\,at^2$ to find the time of flight. Since the jumpers move horizontally at first, $u = 0$ m s^{-1} so:

$$t = \sqrt{\frac{2s}{a}} = \sqrt{\frac{2 \times 26.7\ \text{m}}{9.8\ \text{m}\text{s}^{-2}}} = 2.33\ \text{s}$$

Horizontal distance must be at least 8.22 m so horizontal velocity must be at least, 8.22 m / 2.33 s = 3.52 m s^{-1}

b Horizontal velocity is approximately constant = 3.52 m s^{-1}
Vertical velocity is: $v = u + at = 0 + 9.8 \times 2.33 = 22.8$ m s^{-1}
Use scale drawing (or Pythagoras' theorem) to combine these. Final velocity = 23.1 m s^{-1} at 81.3° to the horizontal.

13 Long jumpers can't manage the 'optimum take-off angle' without dropping their horizontal velocity to match their maximum vertical speed. This would be counter-productive. Some gymnastic events use a springboard which allows the gymnasts to get much closer to 45°.

Chapter 2

1 **a** $80 \times 9.8 = 784$ N
b $128 / 80 = 1.6$ N kg^{-1}

2
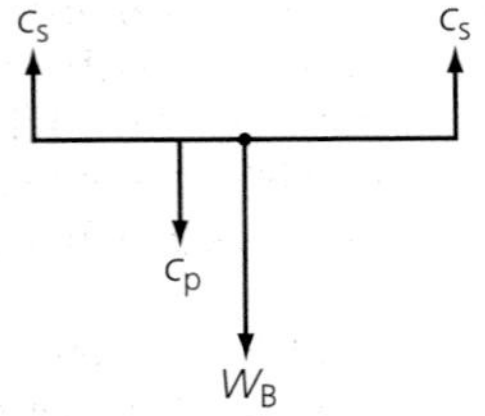

c_s
c_s
c_p
W_B

c_s and c_p are contact forces from the bridge and the person, W_B = weight of the bridge.

3 No. A larger weight means a larger contact force which means more friction, so the car is less likely to skid.

4 Actual contact area could be 0.01% of 4 cm^2, say 4×10^{-8} m^2. Pressure = weight / area and weight = $\rho g V$ $= 8000 \times 10 \times 8 \times 10^{-6} = 0.64$ N
so pressure at points of contact $= 0.64 / 4 \times 10^{-8}$ $= 16 \times 10^6$ Pa = 16 MPa

5 **a** $F = \mu N = 0.02 \times 500 = 10$ N
b Because the normal contact force is now less than the weight. Surfaces are not pressed together as hard.

6 Forces are weight, tension from cables and contact force from ground. Cables are in tension, the mast is in compression.

7
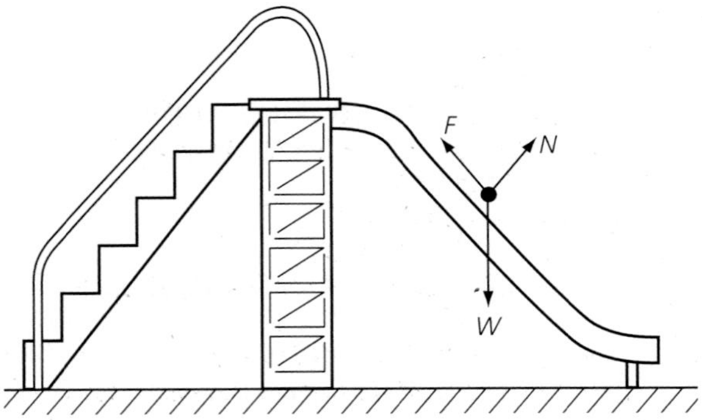

F
N
W

W = child's weight
N = normal contact force
F = friction acting on child

8
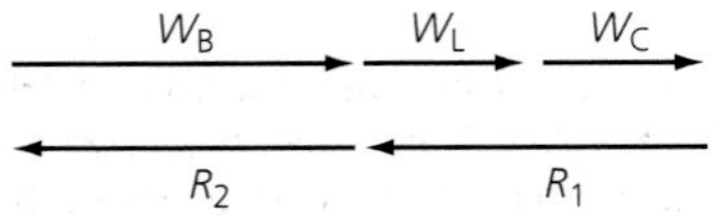

W_B
W_L
W_C
R_2
R_1

9
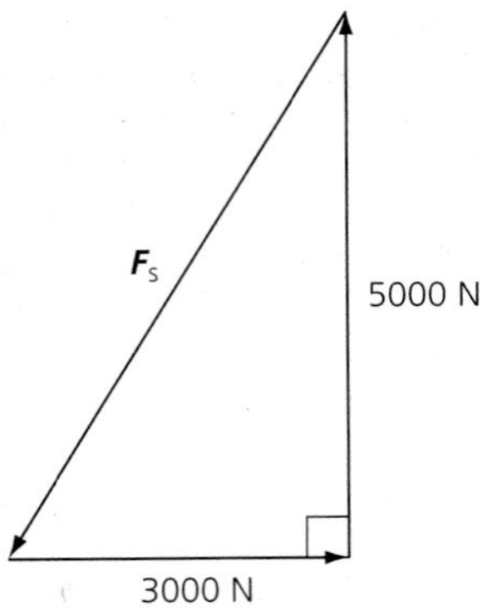

F_s
5000 N
3000 N

By Pythagoras or scale drawing $F_s = 5830$ N

10
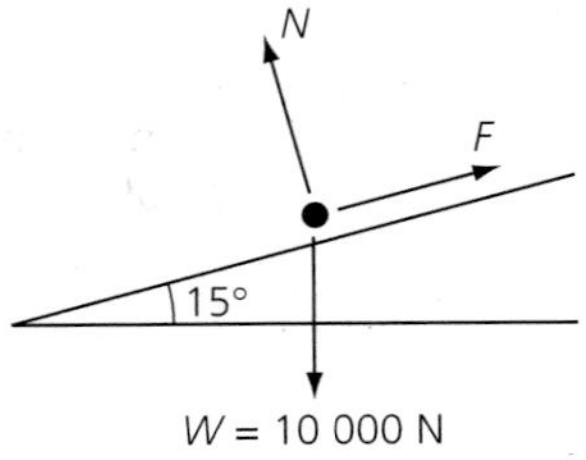

N
F
15°
W = 10 000 N

Resolve the weight.
Perpendicular to the slope,
$10\,000 \times \cos 15° = N = 9660$ N
Parallel to slope,
$10\,000 \times \sin 15° = F = 2600$ N

11 The increased flow over the roof surface leads to a drop in pressure above the roof. The higher pressure below can lift the roof off.

12 As the mast is lifted, the angle increases from 25°. The component of T perpendicular to the mast also increases. The moment of the weight decreases, because the perpendicular distance to X gets smaller.

13
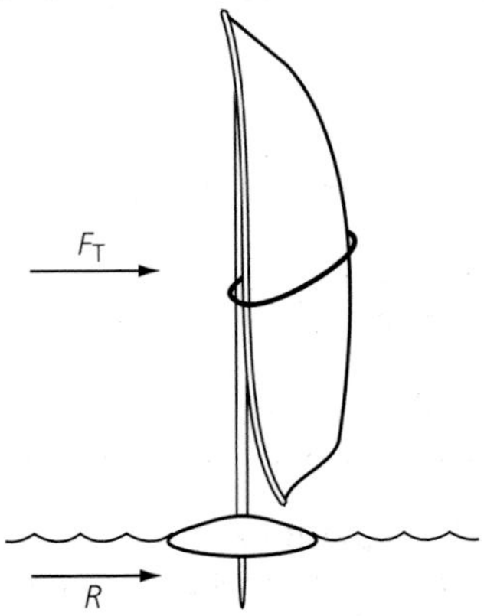

F_T
R

The transverse force caused by the wind would tip the sailboard over. The resistive force of the water on the daggerboard helps to balance this.

Chapter 3

1 In a head-on collision the front of the car is rapidly brought to a halt. Any rear seat passengers will continue at their original velocity until acted upon by a force, in accordance with Newton's first law. It may take a force equal to the weight of an elephant, say 35 000 N, to stop them. Without rear safety belts this force could be provided by the front seat passengers.

2 When a car is hit from behind, it is accelerated forwards. The car seats will accelerate with it, pushing a passenger's body forward. Without an external force to accelerate it, a passenger's head will retain its original velocity, lagging behind the rest of the body until the muscles of the neck pull it forwards. This results in 'whiplash' injuries. A head restraint provides an external force and accelerates the head at the same rate as the body.
Using $F = ma$, $F = 10\text{ kg} \times 200\text{ m s}^{-2} = 2000\text{ N}$. This is close to the force required to beat the world weightlifting record. It would be impossible for an adult to provide this force to restrain a baby in a crash.

4 $s = 23 - 9 = 14$ m, $v = 0\text{ m s}^{-1}$, $u = 48.3 \times 1000 / 3600$ $= 13.4\text{ m s}^{-1}$. Using $v^2 = u^2 + 2as$, $a = (v^2 - u^2) / 2s$ $= -6.4\text{ m s}^{-2}$. Since $F = ma$, $F = 1500 \times 6.4 = 9600$ N.

5 The crash barrier takes time to deform. This extends the duration of the collision. Force = rate of change of momentum (Newton's second law), so if the momentum change takes place over a longer time, the force is reduced.

6 a

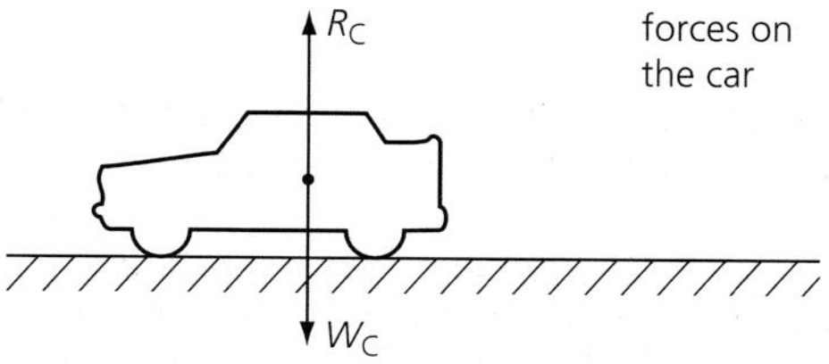

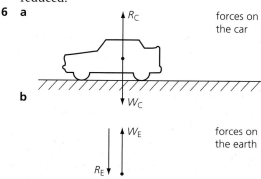

R_C
forces on the car
W_C

b

W_E
forces on the earth
R_E

W_C = gravitational pull of the Earth on the car (the car's weight)
W_E = gravitational pull of the car on the Earth
R_C = contact force of the Earth's surface on the car
R_E = contact force of the car on the Earth's surface

c Because the car and the Earth are in equilibrium, Newton's first law says that there must be no net force, so $R_C = W_C$ and $R_E = W_E$.

d Newton's third law says, $R_C = R_E$ and $W_E = W_C$.

7 A car's wheels are turned by the force provided by the engine. The wheels push the road backwards via the friction between the tyres and the road surface. The road exerts an equal but opposite force on the car (Newton's third law). It is this force which pushes the car forward.

8 a $E_k = {}^1/_2 mv^2 = 500$ kJ

b All the kinetic energy needs to be transferred, so work = 500 kJ

c work = force × distance
force = work / distance
= 500 kJ / 38 = 13 kN

9 Kinetic energy is proportional to speed *squared*. A car travelling at 20 mph has only a quarter of the kinetic energy that it would have at 40 mph. Cutting your speed by half will drastically reduce the effect of a collision.

10 a power = force × velocity, so $F = P / v = 112\,000 / 8.9$ = 12.6 kN at 20 mph and 112 000 / 17.8 = 6.3 kN at 40 mph.

b To find acceleration use $a = F / m$, but F is the resultant force. We need to know the resistive force acting to find the resultant force.

11 Treat the horizontal and vertical components of momentum separately.
Horizontally: As the Volvo accelerates forwards from rest at the top of the building it pushes the Earth backwards (Newton's third law). The gain in the forward momentum of the car is exactly matched by the gain in the Earth's 'backwards' momentum. When the Volvo skids to a halt on the ground below, friction will act equally on the car and the Earth, changing the momentum of the Earth and the car by the same amount.
Vertically: As the car accelerates under gravity it gains momentum in a downwards direction. The car exerts an equal but opposite gravitational pull on the Earth (Newton's third law), so the Earth gains an equal, but opposite, momentum in an upwards direction. During the collision the contact forces act equally, and for the same time, on the Volvo and the Earth. Both bodies lose their vertical momentum. At all time, the *total* vertical momentum is zero.

Chapter 4

1 Earth completes one rotation each day, so $T = 24$ hours = 86 400 s.
$f = 1 / T = 11.6 \times 10^{-6}$ Hz

2 $\omega = 2\pi f$
$f = 10$ rpm = 10 / 60 = 1/6 Hz
$\omega = 2\pi \times 1/6 = 1.05\text{ rad s}^{-1}$

3 $T = 1\text{ year} = 365 \times 24 \times 60 \times 60 = 31.5 \times 10^6$ s
$\omega = 2\pi / T = 2\pi / (31.5 \times 10^6) = 200 \times 10^{-9}\text{ rad s}^{-1}$

4 a $\omega = 2\pi / T = 2.09\text{ rad s}^{-1}$

b $v = r\omega = 5 \times 2.09 = 10.5\text{ m s}^{-1}$

5 $v = r\omega$ and $\omega = 200 \times 10^{-9}$ from Q3
$v = 14.9 \times 10^{10} \times 200 \times 10^{-1} = 29\,800\text{ m s}^{-1}$; almost 30 km s^{-1}

6 $a = v^2 / r = 26^2 / 23 = 29.4\text{ m s}^{-2}$ (about $3g$)

7 a The friction of the road acting on the car's tyres.

b $F = mv^2 / r$
$m \approx 1000$ kg
$r \approx 20$ m
$v \approx 10\text{ m s}^{-1}$
$F \approx 5000$ N

8 The hammer is moving at high speed in a circular path. It is only the tension in the thrower's muscles and the hammer chain that keeps the hammer moving in a circle. When the thrower releases the hammer, it travels in a straight line, at a tangent to the circle from the point of release, in accordance with Newton's first law.

9 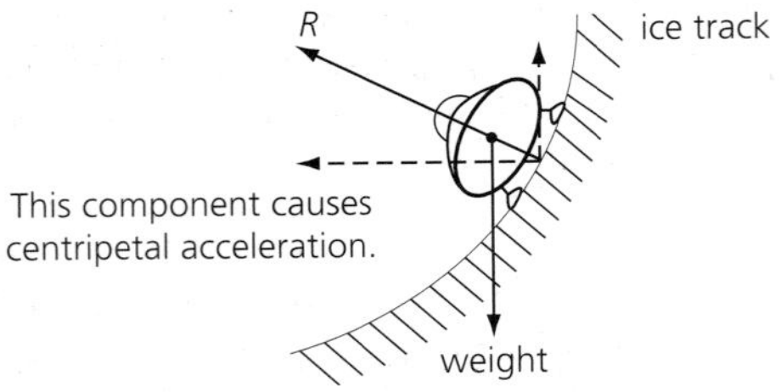
R
ice track
This component causes centripetal acceleration.
weight

The track is banked. The horizontal component of the contact force of the track acting on the bob-sleigh accelerates it round the bend.

10 $\tan \omega = v^2 / gr$
or $v^2 = gr \tan \omega$
$v^2 = 9.8 \times 20 \times \tan 45° = 196$
$v = 14$ m s^{-1}

11 At the top of the circle the balance would read zero. At the bottom of the circle the balance would read 2 kg. (When the weight just doesn't fall on your head,
$v^2 = gr = 10 \times 1 = 10$
so at the bottom of the circle,
tension = $T_B = W + mv^2 / r = 10 + 1 \times 10 / 1 = 20$ N

12 $v = \sqrt{gr} = \sqrt{(10 \times 500)} = \sqrt{5000} = 71$ m s^{-1}

13 $a = v^2 / r = \frac{(100)^2}{500} = 20$ m s^{-2}
- **a** $F = ma = 60 \times 20 = 1200$ N downwards
- **b** $F = ma = 60 \times 20 = 1200$ N upwards
  The *resultant* force is constant around the circle.

14 **a** $v = \sqrt{(gr)} = \sqrt{(10 \times 23)} = 15.2$ m s^{-1}
- **b** E_k comes from change in E_p
  $\Delta E_p = mg\Delta h = {}^1/_2\, mv^2$
  so $\Delta h = {}^1/_2\, v^2 / g = 11.5$ m
  but this is Δh, between initial position and the top of the loop. We need to add the diameter of the loop, initial height = 46 + 11.5 = 57.5 m

Chapter 5

1 **a** $F = A\sigma = \pi \times (1 \times 10^{-3})^2 \times 85 \times 10^6 = 267$ N, approximately 27 kg
- **b** $F = 267 \times 5 = 1335$ N
  $A = F / \sigma = 1335 / (85 \times 10^6) = 15.7 \times 10^{-6}$ m^2, so the radius = 2.24 mm

2 strain = extension / length = $7.5 \times 10^{-2} / 50 = 1.5 \times 10^{-3}$

3 specific strength of Kevlar = 2.15 MPa kg^{-1}
specific stiffness of Kevlar = 86.1 MPa kg^{-1}
Although carbon fibre is stiffer, it is not as strong.

4 **a** B **b** A **c** C **d** C **e** A

5 Because the silk is stiffer, it requires a greater force to stretch it, so the bungee jumper wouldn't fall as far. The silk's lower resilience means that more energy is lost through hysteresis, so the jumper wouldn't rebound as high.

6 More cords would result in a greater force on the jumper for the same extension. The cords wouldn't stretch as far.

7 Increasing the mass of the jumper means that the cords stretch further and more energy is stored as elastic strain energy. When the bag drops, the mass is decreased and so the jumper rebounds much higher, possibly crashing into the platform they left only a brief moment earlier.

8 The glass fibres are very stiff and prevent the fibre glass from deforming very much under stress. The plastic resin prevents cracks propagating through the material and stops brittle fracture.

Chapter 6

1 $E_k = 247$ kJ. This takes 25.5 s.

2 **a** it accelerates faster
- **b** no change of E_k
- **c** higher top speed

3 6.25×10^{18} electrons

4 Overall, 10 C of charge passes in 2 s, giving $I = 5$ A (conventional current to the right)

5 $I = Q / t = 32$ C / 0.2 s = 160 A

6 $W = QV = 2$ C × 160 V = 320 J

7 **a** $Q = It = 15$ C
- **b** $W = QV = 180$ J
- **c** $P = E / t = 36$ W

8 Resistance should be low to avoid wasting power heating the wire.
0.002 Ω → 0.2 V 0.1 Ω → 10 V
Note that headlamps use far less than 100 A.

9 6 V, assuming the heating element obeys Ohm's law.

10 Battery p.d. is 42 V, giving a current of 143 A.
Power loss in the wires is 102 W. Efficiency is 98%.
This p.d. is safer and loss of efficiency is small.

11 P.d. across internal resistance is 6 V
terminal p.d. is 12 V – 6 V = 6 V
efficiency is 6 V /12 V = 0.5 = 50%

12 $E = V + Ir = 168 + (120 \times 0.1) = 180$ V

13 Using $P = I^2R \rightarrow I = 4.0$ A
Using $E = I(R+r) \rightarrow r = 0.5\ \Omega$

14 **a** $R_{lamp} = 3\ \Omega$, $R_{total} = 1.5\ \Omega$, current = 8.0 A
- **b** (12 Ω in parallel with 6 Ω) = 4 Ω → $I = 3.0$ A
- **c** (30 Ω in parallel with 15 Ω) = 10 Ω → $I = 1.2$ A

15 **a** 12 V **b** 11 V **c** 8 V

16 P.d. across 10 Ω resistor ≤ (14 – 9) = 5 V
so power ≤ $V^2/R = 2.5$ W

17 **a** 0.3 A **b** 0.1 A

18 **a** 6 V **b** 50 V **c** 4 V **d** 6 V

19 A moving coil meter could be connected in parallel with a supply lead. The lead becomes the shunt resistor. The p.d. across the lead will be up to 300 A × 0.003 Ω = 0.9 V. You could use any meter where the p.d. across its terminals is around 1 V at full scale deflection e.g. 100 mA, 10 Ω.

20 For resistance of 0.001 Ω you need $A = 6.75 \times 10^{-4}$ m^2. With steel plate 1 mm thick, a width of 0.675 m is needed.

21 The main problems are making batteries which have a high energy storage capacity, low mass, low internal resistance and swift recharge.

Chapter 7

1 Real capacitors gradually discharge as charges move across the imperfect insulating layer.

2 Because human skin has high resistance, a large p.d. is needed, otherwise no significant current would flow.
3 Using $E = \frac{1}{2}CV^2$, $V = \sqrt{(2E / C)} = 2683$ V
4 High voltage is likely to cause insulation to break down, so separation, d, needs to be kept large. But capacitance is inversely proportional to d, so large d gives small capacitance.
5 Using $1 / C = 1 / C_1 + 1 / C_2$
gives $C = 24\ \mu$F
The charge on each plate is $Q = CV = 0.024$ C
Using $V = Q / C$, p.d.s are 400 V and 600 V for the 60 μF and 40 μF capacitors respectively.
6 A chain of three capacitors in series would have a working voltage of 3000 V, but only (50/3) μF capacitance. You would need to link six such chains in parallel.
7 A higher work function means that more energy is needed to free electrons from the surface. You need a higher thermal energy, so higher temperature.
8 The high heater current is for resistive (I^2R) heating. A high anode–cathode p.d. is needed to accelerate the electrons away from the cathode.

Chapter 8

1 a $E = \frac{1}{2}kx^2$, so amplitude increases by a factor of $\sqrt{2}$
b A thicker bar would be heavier and have a higher spring constant. Both factors result in smaller oscillations for a given energy.
c A lower Young modulus gives lower k, so bigger oscillations.
2 Period is 1 / 20 000 = 50 μs, so velocity ≈ 55 μm / (1/4 × 50 μs) = 4.4 m s^{-1}
This is an *underestimate* of maximum speed because it uses the average speed over the quarter cycle.
3 Doubling the frequency means that the same distance is travelled in half the time, so velocity doubles.
Acceleration is quadrupled (×4): doubling f doubles w, and acceleration is proportional to ω^2.
4 Using $T = 2\pi\sqrt{(l / g)} \rightarrow l = gT^2 / 4\pi^2 = 0.994$ m
5 a $T = 2\pi\sqrt{(l / g)} = 4.95$ s
b The pendulum does not oscillate because the bob is in free fall. There is no tension in the string, so the SHM formula is not valid.
6 The factors are:
mass because bigger masses accelerate more slowly
spring constant because stiffer springs give bigger forces, making the mass accelerate faster.
7 Although hanging vertically alters the overall length of the spring, it does not change the effects of mass and spring constant, so the period is unchanged.
8 Doubling k increases ω by $\sqrt{2}$, so:
a $f = \omega / 2\pi$, so f increases by a factor of $\sqrt{2}$
b $E = \frac{1}{2}k\,x^2$, so for the same amplitude, energy doubles
c $v = \omega\sqrt{(x_0^2 - x^2)}$, so speed v increases by a factor of $\sqrt{2}$
9 Frequency is proportional to $\sqrt{(k / m)}$, so Jenny needs to make the horn stiffer (higher k) or lighter (smaller m). She could use a smaller spherical tip, less dense material, material with higher Young modulus or a shorter rod. A wider rod would be stiffer, but it would also be heavier: the net effect is not easy to predict.
10 The liquid will provide much more damping than air. Damping causes the frequency of maximum response to drop. If you tuned the horn in air, it would give a poor performance in the liquid.

Chapter 9

1 Using $c = f\lambda$, wavelengths are between 17 m and 17 mm.
2 Rearranging $c = f\lambda$ gives $f = c / \lambda$, so $f = 0.6 \times 10^{15}$ Hz
3 a

10 cm

Wavelengths are 1, 1/3, 1/5, 1/7, etc of fundamental

b Wavelength could be 20.0 cm, 6.7 cm, 4.0 cm, etc. Using $c = f\lambda$, gives frequencies of 1.50 GHz, 4.50 GHz, 7.50 GHz, etc.
4

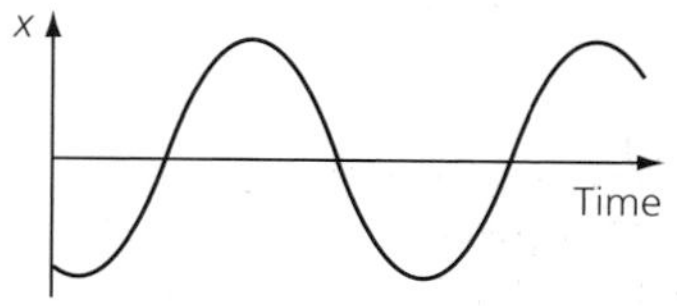
x
Time

5 At longer wavelengths you need a longer path difference for constructive interference. That needs a bigger angle, so the fringe separation is bigger.
6 Fringes get further apart if you move the screen further from the slits or if you move the slits closer together.
7 The car passes through positions of cancellation and positions of strong signal. Using $c = f\lambda$ gives $\lambda = 100$ m. Using $s / \lambda = D / w$ gives $s = 100 \times 10\,000 / 1000 = 1000$, so the car passes through a maximum every 1 km.
8 Mobile phones also use radio waves. Reflections from walls will cause constructive and destructive interference, just as for the TV signal.
9 The reflector increases the signal strength by reflecting back a wave which constructively interferes. The reflecting sheet also stops the aerial picking up waves which have bounced off buildings behind the aerial. This prevents ghosting.
10 Along the zero-order beam, path difference is zero, which is the same for all wavelengths – all colours interfere constructively.

Chapter 10

1 6 = *110*, 7 = *111*, 8 = *1000*
100101 = (*1* × 32) + (*0* × 16) + (*0* × 8) + (*1* × 4) + (*0* × 2) + (*1* × 1) = 37
2 A minimum sampling frequency of 8000 Hz with 8 bit samples could be used, but the sampling frequency is well within the audible range and would need to be filtered out heavily. Or you could sample at 16 000 Hz with 4 bit samples. Both give 64 000 bits per second.
3 Difficult! With lateral inversion, no true inversion has taken place, because each point on the image is actually opposite the corresponding point on the object.

4

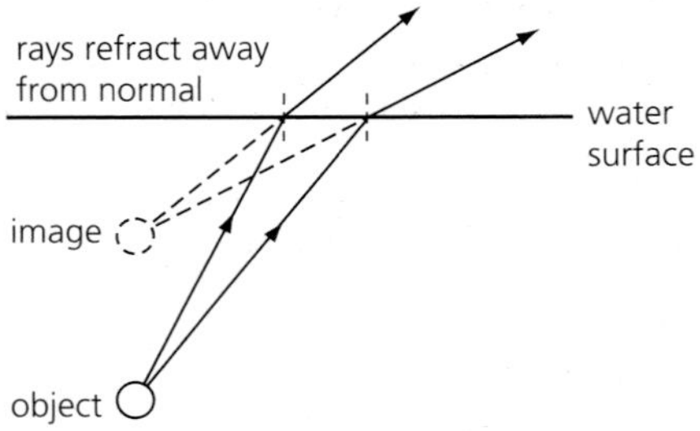
rays refract away
from normal
water
surface
image
object

5 Using $n = c / v$ and time = distance / speed, the times for the two colours are 164.04 and 164.00 µs. The difference of arrival times is therefore 0.04 µs, or 40 ns.

6 The relative refractive index is 1.60 / 1.40 = 1.143
A ray incident at 30° would refract at 25.9°, so strike the wall at (90 – 25.9) = 64.1°

7 The speed of light in the fibre is $c / n = 1.875 \times 10^8$ m s^{-1}, and you can show that for every unit along the fibre, the critical angle path is 1.0667 units; so times are:
straight path $\rightarrow$ 1 km / $v = 5.333 \times 10^{-6}$ s
longest path $\rightarrow$ 1.0667 km / $v = 5.689 \times 10^{-6}$ s
The time delay per kilometre is therefore 0.356 µs.

8 Over a 10 km cable, there would be a time delay of 3.56 µs. You could not transmit waves with a period longer than this. The maximum frequency is therefore $f = 1 / T$ = 284 kHz. (This would be unacceptably low – real fibre optic cables have very close refractive indices for core and cladding to minimise the time delays.)

Chapter 11

1 The star's peak output must be around 700 nm. Using $\lambda_{max} = 0.003 / T$, gives:
$T = 0.003 / (700 \times 10^{-9}) = 4300$ K

2 **a** Three (From 3 to 2, 3 to 1 and 2 to 1)
b 3 to 1: $\Delta E = -1.5 - (-13.6) = 12.1$ eV $= 1.94 \times 10^{-18}$ J
$\lambda = hc / \Delta E = 6.6 \times 10^{-34} \times 3 \times 10^8 / (1.94 \times 10^{-18})$
$\lambda = 102$ nm
Similar calculations give the other wavelengths as 548 nm and 121 nm.

3 The largest possible energy change is 13.6 eV. This gives $\lambda = 91$ nm

4 The cooler atmosphere has many more atoms in their ground state so that absorption can take place. If the gases were as hot as the Sun there would be just as much emission as absorption.

5 The heat of the flame will excite some of the electrons in the sodium atoms to a higher energy level. These emit yellow light as they return to the lower energy level.
With *strong* sunlight shining through the flame, there is more absorption in the sodium vapour; this makes the lines look darker.

6 Radio signals and light can both be reflected and refracted, but the best evidence is that they can both be diffracted. You can shine a laser through a small slit to diffract light. You don't need 'line of sight' to a transmitter to pick up radio waves, because they are diffracted around hills. (You could also use polarisation or interference effects.)

7 Increasing the voltage means that the electrons have more energy. If they lose all that energy in one collision they will emit X-rays with a shorter wavelength. The electrons may now have enough energy to knock out an atomic electron from a lower energy level, leading to more characteristic lines.

8 The minimum wavelength only depends on the energy gained by the electrons as they are accelerated across the tube. This is fixed by the tube voltage. Atoms with higher atomic number have more tightly bound electrons. It takes more energy to knock them out of the lower energy levels and so the X-rays which are emitted have shorter wavelengths.

9 Energy of photon = 1.5 eV = 2.4×10^{-19} J. Using $E = hf$ and $\lambda = c / f$, give:
$\lambda = 8.25 \times 10^{-7}$ m

10 Most wavelengths of infrared are absorbed by the atmosphere.

11 The moon's gravity was too small to hold on to an atmosphere. It has no greenhouse effect to absorb the radiation it emits and so raise its average surface temperature.

Chapter 12

1 53 protons, 53 electrons and 131 – 53 = 78 neutrons

2 Hydrogen $^1_1$H: deuterium $^2_1$H: tritium $^3_1$H

3 5×10^{-10} g is $5 \times 10^{-10} / 99 = 5.05 \times 10^{-12}$ of a mole.
This is $5.05 \times 10^{-12} \times 6.022 \times 10^{23} = 3.04 \times 10^{12}$ nuclei
Activity = $\lambda N = 3.2 \times 10^{-5} \times 3.04 \times 10^{12} = 9.73 \times 10^7$
(97 MBq)

4 **a** No electrons are emitted, no matter how bright the red light is.
b The number of electrons would increase as the blue light got brighter.
The maximum kinetic energy of the electrons is not affected by the brightness of the light. The kinetic energy would increase if higher frequency light, UV for example, was used.

5 energy of ingoing photon = hf
$= 6.6 \times 10^{-34} \times 3.4 \times 10^{19} = 2.24 \times 10^{-14}$ J
energy of outgoing photon = hf
$= (6.6 \times 10^{-34} \times 3 \times 10^8) / (415 \times 10^{-9}) = 4.77 \times 10^{-19}$ J
energy absorbed = $(2.24 \times 10^{-14}\text{ J} - 4.77 \times 10^{-19}\text{ J}) / (2.24 \times 10^{-14}\text{ J})$ = 99.8%

6 $\phi = hf_T = hc / \lambda$
$= (6.6 \times 10^{-34} \times 3 \times 10^8) / (415 \times 10^{-9})$
$= 4.77 \times 10^{-19}$ J = 3 eV

Chapter 13

1 $^{235}_{92}\text{U} + ^{1}_{0}\text{n} \rightarrow ^{236}_{92}\text{U} \rightarrow ^{133}_{54}\text{Xe} + ^{100}_{38}\text{Sr} + 3\,^{1}_{0}\text{n}$
There are a number of possible answers, just make sure that the mass numbers on the right-hand side of the equation add up to 236 and that the atomic numbers add up to 92.

2 mass of 94 protons = 94 × 1.0073 = 94.686 *u*
mass of 145 neutrons = 145 × 1.0087 = 146.262 *u*
total mass of constituents = 240.947 *u*
nuclear mass = 239.052, so mass defect = 1.896 *u*

3 From question 2, the mass defect of Pu-239 = 1.896 u. Convert this to kg:
mass defect = $1.896 \times 1.660 \times 10^{-27} = 3.147 \times 10^{-27}$ kg
binding energy = $3.147 \times 10^{-27} \times (3 \times 10^8)^2$
= 2.833×10^{-10} J or 1.769×10^9 eV

4 Originally the total mass was:
239.052 u (Pu-239) + 1.009 (neutron) = 240.061 u
After the fission the mass is:
86.922 (Br) + 149.920 (Nd) + 3 × 1.009 (neutrons) + 0.000548 (beta particle) = 239.870 u
The mass defect is 0.191 u. This is an energy release of 178 MeV per fission.

5 Mass change = $E / c^2 = 400 \times 10^3 / (3 \times 10^8)^2$
= 4.44×10^{-12} kg (not quite detectable with kitchen scales!)

6 The products of a carbon fission would have less binding energy per nucleon than the original carbon nucleus, so a carbon fission would need more energy to cause it than it could release.

7 $^1/_{20}$ s = 50 ms. This means $3^{50} = 7.2 \times 10^{23}$ fissions. Each fission releases 200 MeV, so $7.2 \times 10^{23} \times 200 \times 10^6 \times 1.6 \times 10^{-19} = 2.3 \times 10^{13}$ J

8 **a** To prevent the critical mass being reached.
b Water could act as a moderator, slow down escaping neutrons and increase the chances of further fission reactions occurring.

9 As time goes on there is a build up of fission products; these absorb neutrons and slow down the chain reaction.

10 Alpha and beta particles are absorbed and scattered much more than gamma rays. An inverse-square law would apply to point sources of alpha and beta radiation in a vacuum, where there would be no absorption or scattering.

11 $I \times (\text{distance})^2$ = constant, so $I_2 \times 4 = I_s \times y^2$
where I_2 = intensity at 2 m and I_s = safety limit for intensity. But $I_2 = 10\, I_s$, $40\, I_s = I_s\, y^2$ so $y^2 = 40$, $y = 6.32$ m

12 **a** Using $A = A_0 \exp(-\lambda t)$ (see Chapter 12)
If $A / A_0 = 0.01$, then:
$\exp(-\lambda t) = 0.01$, $-\lambda t = \ln 0.01 = -4.605$, so $t = 4.605 / \lambda$
Now, $\lambda = \ln 2$ / half-life = $0.693 / 24\,000 = 2.89 \times 10^{-5}$ year^{-1}. So $t = 4.605 / (2.89 \times 10^{-5}) = 159 \times 10^3$ years
b This is an underestimate of the time taken to decay because Pu-239 will decay into a radioisotope which is also radioactive. In fact there will be a decay series of radioactive products.

13 The rods are physically hot, due to the energy released by their own radioactivity. The water helps to dissipate this heat.
The water provides a radiation barrier, to absorb emitted gamma rays, etc.

14 $^7_3\text{Li} + {}^1_0\text{n} \rightarrow {}^3_1\text{H}$ (tritium) + ^4_2He or $^7_3\text{Li} + {}^1_0\text{n} \rightarrow {}^3_1\text{H} + {}^4_2\text{He} + {}^1_0\text{n}$

Chapter 14

1 **a** $F_1 = -GmM_E / (R + h_1)^2$
where M_E = mass of the Earth and
R = radius of the Earth
h_1 = height of initial orbit
$F_2 = -GmM_E / (R + h_2)^2$
where h_2= height of final orbit
$F_2 / F_1 = (R + h_1)^2 / (R + h_2)^2 = (7100)^2 / (6900)^2$
= 1.06 × greater in the lower orbit
b Since F is providing the centripetal force, a = 1.06 times greater than before.
$v^2 = ra$ but r is 1.03 times less than before.
v^2 has increased by a factor of 1.06 / 1.03 = 1.03
v will increase by a factor of 1.015

2 $F = GM_PM_S / r^2 = M_P\, v^2 / r$
combining gives $v^2 = GM_S / r$
but time for one orbit $T = 2\pi r / v$, $v = 2\pi r / T$
which means $4\pi^2 r^2 / T^2 = GM_S / r$
or $r^3 = (GM_S / 4\pi^2)\, T^2$ ($GM_S / 4\pi^2$) is constant
Therefore $r^3 \propto T^2$

3 Since $r^3 \propto T^2$, $T_{\text{Pluto}} = T_{\text{Earth}} \times (40)^{3/2}$ = 253 Earth years

4 The weight of a mass, m, on Earth = $mg = GM_Em / R^2$. So $M_E = R^2g / G$. The radius of the Earth and free-fall acceleration were already known, so measuring G enabled M_E to be calculated.

5 Work done in taking craft from surface of the Earth to infinity = $GM_Em / R = 2.74 \times 10^{12}$ J
Work done in taking craft from 185 km to infinity = 2.67×10^{12} J
Difference = work done in lifting space craft into orbit = 7×10^{10} J

6 work done = $(GmM_{\text{Moon}} / R) - GmM_{\text{Moon}}) / (h + R)$
= 7.46×10^8 J
(where R is the radius of the Moon)

7 $v = \sqrt{(2GM_E / R)}$ which gives $R = 8.9 \times 10^{-3}$ m. If the Earth was crushed to this size, about 1 cm radius, it would be a black hole with a density of 2×10^{30} kg m^{-3}.

8
- If the satellite is to stay above the same place then it must have the same axis of rotation as the Earth.
- The centripetal force on the satellite is due to gravity, so the centre of its orbit must be the centre of the Earth.

The only orbit which meets both conditions is an equatorial one.

9 $T = 2\pi r / v$ and $v = \sqrt{(GM_E / r)}$, $r = 7.1 \times 10^6$ m, and $v = 7.5 \times 10^3$ m s^{-1}
Therefore T = 5930 s

10 a As the rocket accelerated upwards the scales would show an increased reading, since they are supporting the astronaut's weight and are causing an acceleration.
b In orbit both astronaut and scales are falling towards the Earth at the same rate, so the reading is zero.

11 To simulate Earth gravity we need an acceleration of about 10 m s^{-2}.
$a = v^2/ r$ gives v = 100 m s^{-1}.
Such a large space-station would only need to rotate once per minute. The astronauts would walk on the 'inside' of the outer circumference of the doughnut with their heads towards the centre.

12 $R^2 / r^2 = M_E / M_S = 3 \times 10^{-6}$. This gives $R = 1.7 \times 10^{-3}\, r$. The neutral point is 0.998 of the way to the Sun or 1.493×10^{11} m from Earth.

13 $V = -GM_E / r$ so **a** –61 MJ kg^{-1} **b** –1.04 MJ kg^{-1}
$\Delta V = -1.04 - (-63) = 60$ MJ kg^{-1}
Potential is energy per unit mass, so 60 MJ kg$^{-1} \times m = \frac{1}{2} mv^2$
$v = 11.0 \times 10^3$ m s^{-1}

Chapter 15

1 a 10 μT
b zero
2 a flux is down into page
b faster below lead plate
3 Using $B = \mu_0 nI$ gives $n \approx 8000\ m^{-1}$
4 a $r = mv / Bq < 0.375$ m
b $n = 40\ 000\ m^{-1}$, so using $B = \mu_0 nI$ gives $I = 4.0$ A
5 Ignoring movement of the nucleus, the proton can reach a point where $V = 10$ MV. Using $V = Q / (4\pi\varepsilon_0 r)$ gives $r = 1.2 \times 10^{-15}$ m.
6 Using $V = Q / (4\pi\varepsilon_0 r)$ and $E = Q / (4\pi\varepsilon_0 r^2)$ gives $E = V / r$
a $E \approx 200\ 000\ V\ m^{-1}$
b Same answer, although there would be more charge on the sphere.
7 a $V = W / q = W / e = 13.8$ V
b Using $V = Q / (4\pi\varepsilon_0 r)$ gives $r = 1.04 \times 10^{-10}$ m, so diameter of atom $\approx 2 \times 10^{-10}$ m
c Using $E = Q / (4\pi\varepsilon_0 r^2)$ gives $E = 1.33 \times 10^{11}\ V\ m^{-1}$

Chapter 16

1 The blade is a conductor cutting through flux, so an e.m.f. is induced. The blade cuts through an area of 452 m^2 every 6 seconds in a flux density of 20 μT. The flux cut is therefore 452 $m^2 \times 20 \times 10^{-6}$ T = 0.00904 Wb.
Using $E = \Delta F / \Delta t$, the e.m.f. is 0.00904 Wb / 6 s = 0.0015 V
2 Factors are speed of rotation, area of coil, number of turns and flux density.
3000 rpm gives $\omega = 3000 \times 2\pi$ rad / 60 seconds = 314 rad s^{-1}
Using $E = NAB\omega$, $E = 5000 \times (0.50\ m \times 0.10\ m) \times 0.015\ T \times 314 = 1180$ V
3 a At 200 kV, current is $I = P / V = 10^9$ W / 200 000 V = 5000 A, so power loss in cables is $P = I^2R = (5000)^2 \times 10$ = 250 MW, a 25% loss.
b At 400 kV this drops to 6.25%
4 The voltage ratio is 70:1, so the current at 100% efficiency would be 350 / 70 = 5 A
At 95% efficiency, this reduces to 0.95 × 5 A = 4.75 A
5 Using $P = I^2R$, the r.m.s. current is $I = \sqrt{(72\ W / 8\ \Omega)} = 3$ A
The peak current is therefore $\sqrt{(2 \times 3\ A)} = 4.24$ A
6 a $I = V / R = 0.50$ A
b $\epsilon = -L\ \Delta I / \Delta t$ gives $\Delta I / \Delta t = 6\ V / 0.30\ H = 20\ A\ s^{-1}$
c In a hundredth of a second, the current could reach at most 0.01 × 20 = 0.2 A, which is well below the final 0.5 A. The coil is unlikely to be suitable for this frequency.
7 Capacitors also give rise to a phase difference of 90° between a.c. current and voltage, so power will alternately be stored and released. There is no net power dissipated, so the capacitor is reactive, not resistive.
8 We can combine the expressions $V_0 = I_0\omega L$ and $V_0 = I_0 / \omega C$ to give $\omega L = 1 / \omega C$. This rearranges to give $C = 1 / \omega^2 L$. $\omega = 2\pi f = 100\ \pi$ and $L = 0.4$ H. Therefore a capacitance of 25.3 μF would be needed.

Chapter 17

1 Celsius = Kelvin – 273.15 = 273.16 – 273.15 = 0.01 °C
2 At constant volume, no external work is done, so all the heat transfers to internal energy. At constant pressure, the substance expands, so you need to supply extra heat to do the work associated with expansion.
3 Using $Q = mc\Delta T$ gives $Q = 70$ J at constant volume.
80 J was supplied, so 10 J of external work has been done.
4 a Boyle's Law gives that pressure is doubled
b Same mass, half the volume, so the density is doubled.
c Same temperature, so the molecules are travelling at the same speed. (If the gas is ideal, there are no forces between the molecules, so squashing them together doesn't affect speed.)
5

Assumption	In section
molecules small	2, 4
perfectly elastic	1, 2, (4)
collisions are quick	2, (4)
no intermolecular force	4
large numbers	4, (5)
random directions	5
Newton's laws hold	1, 2

6 $V = RT / P = 0.0224\ m^3 = 22.4$ litres
7 Using density = mass / volume, the volume of one mole of air would also be 22.4 litres. It obeys accurately the equation of state of an ideal gas at s.t.p.

Chapter 18

1 There would be a boundary layer of cool air sinking: the temperature would rise as you move though the boundary layer towards the warm room.
2 The air in the bubbles is a very poor conductor. Trapping it in the bubbles minimises convection. The metallic film reflects heat radiation back into the house.
3 The temperature gradients are:
fridge 14 °C / 30 mm = 0.467 °C mm^{-1}
freezer 36 °C / 60 mm = 0.600 °C mm^{-1}
The two compartments are of equal area, so there will be more heat flow into the freezer so it would cost more to run.
4 Using $Q / t = kA\Delta T / l$, with t = 24 hours = 86 400 s; l = 0.06 m; ΔT = 40 °C gives total heat flow Q = 5.76 MJ. The rating of 2 kW h is 2000W × 3600 s = 7.2 MJ. Heat conduction therefore plays a dominant part.
5 The biggest temperature gradient is across the worst conductor because, for the same heat flow, k × temperature gradient will be constant.

Glossary

Absolute zero The lowest possible temperature: all molecular motion stops at absolute zero.

Absorption spectrum Radiation emitted by a source can be selectively absorbed by a material between the source and the observer, e.g. absorption of a star's light by clouds of interstellar gas. This can produce a series of dark lines or bands that are characteristic of the absorber.

Acceleration, *a* The rate of change of velocity (measured in m s^{-2}).

Activity The number of decays (or emissions) per second in a radioactive source (measured in becquerel, Bq).

Air resistance (drag) A force that acts to oppose motion relative to the air. The drag on a moving object increases if its speed relative to the air increases.

Aliasing If the sampling frequency is less than twice the signal frequency, the two will interfere badly.

Alpha particle Strongly ionising, short range radiation emitted by some radioisotopes. An alpha particle is two neutrons and two protons tightly bound together.

Ammeter An instrument of low resistance connected in series with a component to measure the current

Amorphous Materials that have no long range order.

Amplitude modulation, AM The amplitude of the carrier wave is made to vary with the signal amplitude.

Analogue A smoothly changing quantity used to represent information: e.g. angle of hands of a clock represents time.

Analogue-to-digital converter A device which samples an analogue waveform and processes it into a sequence of digital numbers.

Angular frequency, *f* The number of rotations per second (measured in hertz, Hz). Sometimes given as revolutions per minute, rpm, though this is not S.I.

Angular velocity, *ω* The speed of rotation, measured by the angle turned through per second (measured in rad s^{-1}).

Anode Positive electrode or positive terminal.

Antinode The point on a standing wave where a quantity reaches a maximum. Usually refers to maximum displacement.

Atomic mass unit (*u*) A small unit of mass used in nuclear physics. 1 *u* is defined as one-twelfth of the mass of a carbon-12 atom ($1\ u = 1.66043 \times 10^{-27}$ kg).

Atomic number The number of protons in the nucleus of an atom is known as its atomic number. The atomic number is also the number of electrons in the neutral (i.e. not ionised) atom.

Avogadro constant The number of particles in a mole of anything: $N_A = 6.023 \times 10^{23}$ particles per mole.

Back e.m.f. on break A high e.m.f. of opposing polarity to the original p.d., caused by the rapid collapse of a magnetic field when a circuit is broken.

Background radiation The average level of radiation in the environment. It arises from both natural sources, such as radioactive rocks, and artificial sources, such as X-rays used in medicine.

Bandwidth (in modulation) The width of the band of frequencies needed to carry a modulated signal.

Bandwidth (of circuit) The width of the band of frequencies which can be passed by a circuit.

Beta particle A high speed electron emitted from the nucleus of some radioisotopes.

Binary A number system that uses only 1 and 0. In electronics, a switch can either be closed (OFF) or open (ON).

Binding energy In an atomic nucleus this is the energy needed to pull it apart, i.e. to separate the individual neutrons and protons.

Bit An abbreviated word for Binary digIT; eight bits make a byte.

Black body A perfect absorber of (heat) radiation. Black bodies are also the best possible emitters. A black body absorbs all of the radiation that falls upon it and reflects none. The temperature of a black body determines the amount of radiation that it emits at each wavelength.

Black hole An astronomical body that is so dense that its gravitational field is strong enough to prevent even light escaping from it.

Boltzmann constant, *k* The gas constant for a single ideal gas molecule ($k = R / N_A = 1.381 \times 10^{-23}$ J K^{-1}).

Boundary layer A layer of slow-moving fluid next to a surface. It may have significant thermal resistance.

Brittle Describes a material which does not deform plastically before it fractures, e.g. glass.

Capacitance, *C* The charge stored per volt. For parallel plates, the positive charge stored on one plate is used in the calculation.

Capacitor A device which stores electrical charge (and so electrical energy).

Capacity (of battery) The total charge that the battery can supply to the circuit (measured in ampere-hours, A h).

Carrier wave A wave which is encoded with information for transmission: e.g. light waves are the carrier wave in fibre optics.

Cathode Negative electrode or negative terminal.

Centre of gravity The point at which the weight of a body acts.

Centre of mass For some applications, an object can be treated as if all its mass is concentrated at one point. This point is called the centre of mass. If the resultant force acting on a body passes through the centre of mass then the body will accelerate in a straight line. If the resultant force does not pass through the centre of mass the body will also spin.

Centripetal Towards the centre.

Charge A fundamental property of matter; charged objects experience electrostatic forces; charge may be positive, zero or negative.

Choke A device to limit the size of an alternating current by using the reactance of a self-inductor.

Chromatic dispersion The splitting of waves into different wavelengths during refraction: e.g. the coloured spectrum produced by a prism.

Cloud chamber A device which gives a tiny cloud trail along the track of a charged particle.

Coherent Describes waves which are of the same frequency, polarisation and amplitude and in a constant phase relationship.

Component A vector may be replaced by several (usually two) different vectors known as components. Components are usually at right angles to each other, typically horizontally and vertically, and together have exactly the same effect as the original vector.

Conduction (heat) The transfer of heat through a material without any bulk movement of the material.
Conductivity A measure of how well a material conducts electricity (1/resistivity).
Constructive interference Interference which results in an increased amplitude.
Convection The transfer of heat caused by the movement of a hot fluid (liquid or gas) into cooler regions (see also natural convection and forced convection).
Conventional current Consists of positive charge flow. Flows from positive supply terminal, around circuit, to negative.
Critical angle The minimum angle at which total internal reflection occurs; the angle at which the refracted ray travels along the boundary between the media.
Critical damping An amount of damping which is just sufficient to prevent oscillation.
Current, *I* The rate of flow of charge in a circuit (measured in amperes, A).
Damping Any mechanism which absorbs energy of oscillations, causing a reduction of amplitude.
Data compression Technique for reducing the amount of data needing to be sent: e.g. counting blank lines.
Decay constant, λ The probability that a radioactive nucleus will decay in a given time period.
Degrees of freedom Ways of moving which have energy linked with them: e.g. translation, rotation, vibration.
Destructive interference Interference leading to decreased wave amplitude, and ultimately to complete cancellation.
Dielectric An insulator which raises the capacitance of a capacitor.
Diffraction The spreading out of the edges of waves to occupy areas which would otherwise be in 'shadow'.
Diffraction grating A grating of many narrow slits, each causing diffraction. These diffracted waves then interfere.
Digital Digital quantities vary in big steps or jumps. Most systems use on/off switching, i.e. binary (q.v.).
Digital analogue converter A device which takes a series of digital numbers and turns them into an analogue waveform.
Displacement, *s* The distance travelled in a certain direction from a given point. It is a vector quantity (measured in metres, m).
Ductile Describes a material which can withstand large plastic deformation. Copper is easily drawn into wires and is a ductile material.
Dynamic friction The frictional force between two surfaces in relative motion; it acts so as to oppose the sliding.
Dynamo A device which transfers kinetic energy to electrical energy.
E.m.f. Abbreviation for electromotive force (q.v.).
Eddy current A swirl of current inside a solid material caused by movement through a magnetic field or a change of flux density.
Efficiency The ratio of useful energy output to total energy input, or power output to power input.
Elastic A material that stretches under a load and then returns to its original dimensions when the load is removed is said to be elastic.
Elastic collision If the total kinetic energy before and after a collision is the same, the collision is said to be elastic. i.e. kinetic energy is conserved in an elastic collision.
Elastic limit When an object is subjected to a force which is just large enough to cause permanent deformation, it is said to have reached its elastic limit.
Electric field A region of space where charged objects experience a force.
Electric field strength, *E* At any point in an electric field, this is the force per unit charge on a tiny test charge placed at that point.
Electrical potential, *V* The work done per unit charge in bringing a tiny test charge from infinity to a point in an electric field.
Electromagnetic induction The generation of e.m.f. in a conductor when it cuts flux or is in a changing magnetic field.
Electromagnetic waves Waves which propagate by swapping energy between electric and magnetic fields: includes radio waves, microwaves, infrared radiation, visible light, ultraviolet, X-rays and gamma rays.
Electromotive force The energy per coulomb produced by a source of electricity; also the p.d. across a source when no current flows.
Electron Charged particle of charge $\approx 1.6 \times 10^{-19}$ C and mass $\approx 9 \times 10^{-31}$ kg. The main charge carrier in metals.
Electronvolt (eV) A unit of energy used in atomic and nuclear physics. It is the energy gained by an electron when it is accelerated through a potential difference of 1 volt (1 eV = 1.6×10^{-19} J).
Emission spectrum The range of wavelengths emitted by a luminous source is known as its emission spectrum. It may be a line, band or continuous spectrum.
Energy Energy is the stored ability to do work.
Energy level Electrons in an atom can only have specific energy values. These are known as the atom's energy levels.
Equation of state An equation which relates the state of a system (e.g. pressure and volume of a gas) to temperature.
Equilibrium position The usual resting place of a system.
Excitation When an electron absorbs energy and moves to a higher atomic energy level, the atom is said to be in an excited state.
Exponential decay The name given to a mathematical relationship which has a constant reduction period, such as radioactive decay or the discharge of a capacitor.
First law of thermodynamics Heat supplied equals rise of internal energy of the system plus work done by the system ($Q = \Delta U + W$).
Fission The splitting of a large atomic nucleus, usually uranium or plutonium, into two smaller nuclei. The process releases a few free neutrons and a large amount of energy.
Fixed points Measurements made at standard temperatures which are used to calibrate thermometers.
Flux (magnetic) Imaginary lines through space, used to explain magnetic effects. Iron filings give a picture of flux patterns.
Forced convection A rapid heat transfer process involving driving or pumping of hot fluid: e.g. by a fan.
Frequency modulation, FM The frequency of the carrier wave is made to vary with the signal amplitude.
Fundamental The fundamental frequency is the lowest natural frequency of oscillation of a system.

Fusion The joining together of two light nuclei, typically to isotopes of hydrogen, to form a heavier nucleus, such as helium. Energy is released in this process.

Gamma ray Penetrating short wavelength ionising radiation emitted by some radioisotopes.

Geostationary Describes an orbit that keeps a satellite over exactly the same point on the earth.

Gravitational field The region around a mass where another mass would experience a gravitational attraction.

Gravitational field strength, *g* The force exerted on a unit mass by a gravitational field (measured in N kg^{-1}). On Earth, g is approximately equal to 10 N kg^{-1}.

Gravitational potential energy The energy due to the position of a mass, m, in a gravitational field. In a uniform field, such as that close to the surface of the Earth, the change in potential energy due to an increase in height, Δh, is $\Delta E_p = mg\Delta h$, where g is the gravitational field strength.

Gravitational potential, *V* The potential energy of a unit mass in a gravitational field. It is the work done in moving a unit mass from infinity to that point (measured in J kg^{-1}).

Ground state An atom is said to be in its ground state when its electrons all occupy the lowest possible allowed energy levels.

Half-life, $t_{1/2}$ The time taken for the number of radioactive nuclei in a source to drop to half its original value.

Heat Energy transferred from one place to another because the places are at different temperatures.

Induced e.m.f. The e.m.f. induced in a conductor as a result of cutting or changing magnetic flux.

Inelastic collision In an inelastic collision, the total kinetic energy of the system decreases, i.e. kinetic energy is transferred as other forms of energy. Momentum *is* conserved in inelastic collisions.

Instantaneous Values measured over an infinitesimally short period of time, Δt. For example, the instantaneous speed of an object can be calculated from the distance travelled in a very small time interval, Δt.

Intensity The power through a given area (measured in W m^{-2}).

Interference The addition of waves which leads to changes in amplitude.

Internal energy The sum of all kinetic and potential energies of the component parts of a system. In ideal gases, equal to total kinetic energy.

Internal resistance The resistance of the materials inside a source of electricity.

Inverse square law The intensity of gamma radiation from a point gamma source is inversely proportional to the square of the distance from the source. If you double the distance between yourself and the source, you will receive one quarter of the radiation dose. This relationship is known as an inverse square law. It is important in other areas of physics, e.g. the strength of the gravitational field due to a spherical mass or the strength of an electric field due to a point change.

Ion An atom which has gained or lost one or more electrons.

Ionisation The removal of electrons from an atom, or the addition of electrons to an atom.

Ionisation chamber A device relying on charged particles ionising air. The ionisation current is proportional to the number of particles.

Isotope Atoms of an element can exist in different forms. These forms, called isotopes, have the same number of protons and electrons but different numbers of neutrons.

Isotropic The same in all directions.

Kinetic energy The energy stored in a moving mass ($E_K = {}^1/_2 mv^2$).

Kirchhoff's laws 1st law: the sum of currents at a junction is zero. 2nd law: the sum of e.m.f.s is equal to the sum of p.d.s around a closed circuit loop.

Laser A device which produces intense light by stimulated emission from excited molecules (**l**ight **a**mplification by **s**timulated **e**mission of **r**adiation).

Latent heat The heat which you need to supply to a material to change its phase: e.g. heat is needed to convert water into steam.

Limiting friction The maximum frictional force between two surfaces. An applied force greater than this will produce motion.

Longitudinal Describes a wave where oscillations are in the direction of wave travel.

Magnetic flux density, *B* The strength of a magnetic field, measured by the force on a current-carrying wire or moving charge (S.I. unit is the tesla, T).

Mass defect The difference between the mass of a nucleus and the total mass of the nucleons (q.v.) which make up that nucleus.

mmHg The pressure exerted by a column of mercury 1 mm high.

Moderator The material, often graphite or water, used in a nuclear reactor to slow down neutrons.

Molar heat capacity The heat which you need to supply to one mole of a substance to warm it up by 1 °C (or 1 K).

Mole The amount of material containing the same number of particles as 12 g of the isotope carbon-12.

Moment The turning effect of a force around a point. Moment = force × perpendicular distance to the point.

Momentum The linear momentum of a body = mass × velocity. It is a vector quantity, measured in kg m s^{-1}.

Multimode dispersion A sharp pulse of signal is dispersed after going through an optical fibre because rays take different paths.

Multiplier resistor A high resistance which limits current through a moving coil meter, allowing it to function as a voltmeter.

Natural convection The convection caused by density changes of material on heating and cooling.

Natural frequency For a vibrating system this is the frequency at which the system oscillates when disturbed.

Neutron A particle of zero charge found in the nucleus of almost all atoms. A free neutron is unstable and decays to a proton and an electron with a half-life of 11 minutes.

Neutron star The very dense remnant left after the supernova of a star.

Newton The S.I. unit of force. 1 newton is the force that will accelerate a mass of 1 kg at 1 m s^{-2}.

Node (waves) The point on a standing wave where a quantity is zero. Usually refers to zero displacement.

Noise An unwanted signal introduced, for example, by electrical discharges, other signals of similar frequency, etc.

Normal At right angles to a surface.

Nucleon A particle that exists in the nucleus of an atom: i.e. neutrons and protons.

Ohm's law The current through a conductor is proportional to the p.d., if temperature and other physical conditions stay constant.

Optical fibre Thin fibre of very pure glass, normally coated with another layer of glass of lower refractive index. Light passes through the fibre by total internal reflection.

P.d. Abbreviation for potential difference (q.v.).

Parity check A check on whether data was transmitted correctly.

Period Time taken to complete one cycle of oscillation,one complete cycle of vibration, one complete wave or one complete rotation in circular motion.

Permeability In magnetism, this is a term related to the ease with which a magnetic field can go through (permeate) a material.

Permittivity A material with high permittivity will permit large charges to build up with a small electric field strength.

Phase A measurement of the relative timing of two oscillations of the same frequency.

Photoelectric effect The emission of electrons from a metal surface caused by light of sufficiently high frequency.

Photon A quantum of electromagnetic radiation. It carries an amount of energy, E, that depends upon the frequency of the radiation. $E = hf$, where h is Planck's constant.

Plastic A material which does not return to its original dimensions when a deforming force is removed is said to be plastic.

Point source of waves A source which produces circular wavefronts as though they came from a single point in space.

Polarised A transverse wave is polarised when the vibration of the wave is confined to one direction.

Polycrystalline Materials, such as metals, that consist of a large number of small crystals, called grains, at various angles to each other.

Positron A particle of same mass as electron and equal but opposite charge; antielectron.

Potential difference The energy transferred per coulomb when charge moves through a circuit (measured in $J\ C^{-1}$ or V).

Potential divider A pair of resistors which divide input p.d. in the ratio of the resistances.

Potential energy The stored ability to do work. A body may have potential energy due to its position in a field, e.g. a mass raised above the surface of the Earth has **gravitational** potential energy due to its position in the Earth's gravitational field. **Elastic** potential energy is due to work done in changing the shape of an object, e.g. a stretched rubber band has elastic potential energy.

Power, *P* The rate at which work is done. It can also be thought of as the rate at which energy is transferred (measured in watts, W).

Pressure, *P* The normal force per unit area; pressure = force/area (measured in pascals, Pa; 1 Pa = 1 $N\ m^{-2}$). Also measured in bars, atmospheres, mmHg.

Progressive wave A wave which transfers energy from one place to another.

Propagation The process by which a wave spreads itself through space.

Proton A positively charged particle found in the nucleus of all atoms. Thought to be stable.

Quantum theory This theory states that some physical quantities, like the energy of an electron in an atom, can only have certain discrete values. For example, charge is quantised in units of the charge of an electron; it is not possible to have a charge equivalent to 1.5 electrons.

Radian (rad) One radian is the angle subtended at the centre of a circle by an arc whose length is equal to the radius (2π radians = 360°).

Radioisotope A form of a nucleus which is radioactive is known as a radioisotope.

Reactance The ratio of amplitudes of p.d. and current for a device which does not dissipate energy.

Real image An image that can be projected onto a screen.

Refraction The change of direction of waves which results from a change of speed.

Refractive index Light slows down in more dense media. The absolute refractive index of a material is the speed of light in a vacuum divided by the speed in the material.

Relative permittivity The factor by which a dielectric raises the capacitance of a parallel plate capacitor.

Resilient materials can undergo repeated deformations without transferring a significant amount of energy as internal energy.

Resistance, *R* A measure of a component's tendency to oppose electrical current; ratio of p.d. to current ($R = V / I$).

Resistivity A measure of the resistance of materials; resistance of a specimen of unit length and unit cross-sectional area.

Resonance This occurs when a system accepts energy from a driving source at its natural frequency – the amplitude increases greatly.

Resultant It is possible to combine a number of vectors into a single vector which has the same effect. This single vector is called the resultant.

Root mean square, r.m.s. The square root of the average of the squares of the values; a useful average if quantities can be both positive and negative: e.g. r.m.s. of (+3, –4, +6, –5, 0) is 4.14 but arithmetic mean is 0.

S.I. Stands for Système Internationale and refers to the system of units based on the kilogram, metre and second. S.I units are nearly universally used by scientists.

Sampling The process of taking repeated 'snapshots' of the value of a voltage for conversion into a binary number.

Scalar A physical quantity which has magnitude but no direction. Mass, speed, temperature and potential difference are examples of scalar quantities.

Secondary wavelet Every point on a wavefront is a disturbance of the medium, and so acts as a tiny point source of waves called secondary wavelets.

Self-inductance This is equal in magnitude to the self-induced e.m.f. caused by a current changing at 1 ampere per second.

Self-induction The induction of e.m.f. in a conductor as a result of changes in its own magnetic field.

Shunt resistor A low value resistor which increases ammeter range by allowing most of the current to bypass the meter.

Sideband A band of frequencies (near the carrier frequency) which carry energy as a result of modulating the carrier.

Simple harmonic motion Oscillation where acceleration is always towards the equilibrium position and is proportional to the displacement.

Snell's law The refractive index of a material = sin(angle of incidence) / sin(angle of refraction). The angles are measured from the normal. Snell's law relates angles to refractive indices.
Special relativity Einstein's theory of mechanics, published in 1905. The theory gives results which are identical to Newton's laws except when relative velocities approach the speed of light.
Specific This term means 'per unit mass' (in S.I. units, the value per kg).
Specific heat capacity The heat which you need to supply to 1 kg of material to warm it up by 1 °C (or 1 K).
Specific latent heat The latent heat (q.v.) required per kg of material.
Spontaneous A spontaneous event is one that occurs without an external cause. Radioactive decay is a spontaneous event.
Standing wave A state of oscillation of a system which can be regarded as resembling a wave standing still.
Stationary wave Alternative term for standing wave (q.v.).
Steady-state (thermal) If all temperatures have stabilised throughout the specimen/apparatus, it is said to be in steady-state.
Stiffness This is a measure of how difficult it is to stretch a material. Tensile stiffness is measured by the ratio stress/strain (known as the Young modulus).
Strong nuclear force One of the fundamental forces. The strong nuclear force acts between nucleons over a very short range and holds the nuclei of atoms together.
Superconduction At low temperatures, some materials lose all electrical resistance: they become perfect conductors.
Temperature gradient The change of temperature per unit length; temperature difference divided by distance.
Tensile strain Extension per unit length (has no units).
Tensile stress The force per unit cross-sectional area which is tending to elongate an object (measured in Pa).
Tension A force which acts so as to elongate an object, e.g. a tow rope would be in tension.
Terminal p.d. The p.d. across the terminals of a source when current is drawn; energy per coulomb delivered to circuit.
Terminal velocity An object falling through the atmosphere reaches a top speed, known as its terminal velocity. This happens when the opposing forces of weight and air resistance are equal.
Tesla (T) Unit of magnetic flux density.
Thermal conductivity The rate of flow of heat per square metre of cross section for a temperature gradient of 1 °C per metre (measured in W m^{-1} K^{-1}).
Thermal equilibrium If objects are in thermal equilibrium, there is no net flow of heat between them; they are at the same temperature.
Thermionic emission The emission of electrons from a heated cathode.
Thermocouple A thermometer formed by joining two dissimilar metals. A small e.m.f. is produced that depends on the temperature.
Thermodynamics The study of the movement of heat through systems.
Thermometric property Any material property which varies reliably with temperature, and so can be used to make a thermometer.
Threshold frequency The minimum frequency of light which can cause photoelectric emission.
Total internal reflection At high angles of incidence to a less dense medium, all incident radiation is reflected inside the more dense medium.
Transformer A device which uses electromagnetic induction to change the voltage or current of an a.c. supply.
Transverse Describes a wave where vibrations are at right angles to direction of wave travel.
Ultimate tensile stress, UTS The breaking stress of a material.
Ultrasonics The study and use of waves which travel as sound waves, by compression and rarefaction, at inaudible frequencies above 20 kHz.
Universal molar gas constant $R_M = PV / T$ for one mole of gas. It is universal – i.e. the same for all gases when their behaviour is close to ideal (R_M = 8.31 J K^{-1} mol^{-1}).
Upthrust The buoyancy force on an object in a fluid. Upthrust is due to the difference in fluid pressure on the top and bottom surfaces of the object.
Vector A physical quantity which has a direction as well as a magnitude. Force, velocity and electric field strength are examples of vector quantities.
Velocity selector A device using electric and magnetic fields at 90°. Only particles of a particular velocity go straight through.
Velocity, *v* Velocity is the rate of change of displacement measured in m s^{-1}.
Virtual image An image which can be seen through an optical instrument but cannot be formed on a screen.
Voltage An alternative term for potential difference.
Voltmeter An instrument of very high resistance connected in parallel with a component to measure the potential difference.
Wave–particle duality The term used to describe the fact that light can behave as a wave or a particle. Subatomic particles, such as electrons, also show wave and particle properties.
Wavelength, λ The distance travelled by a wave in one period of oscillation; the length in space of one cycle.
Weber (Wb) The unit of magnetic flux, equal to tesla × metre squared.
Weight, *W* Force on a mass, *m*, due to a gravitational field, measured in newtons, N ($W = mg$).
Work Work, *W*, is done by a force, *F*, when it moves its point of application in the direction of the force. If there is an angle θ between the direction of the force and the displacement, *s*, then $W = Fs \cos \theta$. Work is a scalar quantity (measured in joules, J).
Work function The energy needed to remove an electron from a material in thermionic or photoelectric emission processes.
X-rays Very penetrating, ionising radiation from the short wavelength (high frequency) end of the electromagnetic spectrum. An X-ray is produced by rapid deceleration of a charged particle or by a high-energy electron transition in an atom.
Young modulus, *E* A measure of the stiffness of a material, equal to tensile stress divided by tensile strain (measured in pascals).

Index